500 WOK RECIPES

500 WOK RECIPES

SENSATIONAL STIR-FRIES FROM AROUND THE WORLD

Editor: JOY WOTTON

LORENZ BOOKS

This edition is published by Lorenz Books
an imprint of Anness Publishing Ltd
Blaby Road, Wigston, Leicestershire LE18 4SE; info@anness.com

www.lorenzbooks.com; www.annesspublishing.com

If you like the images in this book and would like to investigate using them for publishing, promotions or advertising, please visit our website www.practicalpictures.com for more information.

Publisher: Joanna Lorenz
Editor: Joy Wotton
Jacket Design: Nigel Partridge
Production Controller: Steve Lang

A CIP catalogue record for this book is available from the British Library.

Recipes in this book have previously appeared in other books published by Lorenz Books.

PUBLISHER'S NOTE
Although the advice and information in this book are believed to be accurate and true at the time of going to press, neither the authors nor the publisher can accept any legal responsibility or liability for any errors or omissions that may be made nor for any inaccuracies nor for any harm or injury that comes about from following instructions or advice in this book.

Notes

Bracketed terms are intended for American readers.
For all recipes, quantities are given in both metric and imperial measures and, where appropriate, in standard cups and spoons. Follow one set of measures, but not a mixture, because they are not interchangeable.
Standard spoon and cup measures are level. 1 tsp = 5ml, 1 tbsp = 15ml, 1 cup = 250ml/8fl oz. Australian standard tablespoons are 20ml. Australian readers should use 3 tsp in place of 1 tbsp for measuring small quantities.
American pints are 16fl oz/2 cups. American readers should use 20fl oz/2.5 cups in place of 1 pint when measuring liquids.
Electric oven temperatures in this book are for conventional ovens. When using a fan oven, the temperature will probably need to be reduced by about 10–20°C/20–40°F. Since ovens vary, you should check with your manufacturer's instruction book for guidance.

The nutritional analysis given for each recipe is calculated per portion (i.e. serving or item), unless otherwise stated.
If the recipe gives a range, such as Serves 4–6, then the nutritional analysis will be for the smaller portion size, i.e. 6 servings.
Measurements for sodium do not include salt added to taste.
Medium (US large) eggs are used unless otherwise stated.

Main front cover image shows Chilli Rice with Chinese Sausage – for recipe, see page 192

Contents

Introduction

Stir-frying in a wok is an ancient cooking technique that originated in China. Similar techniques have strong roots throughout South-east Asia and India, using not only woks but also karahis and other deep-sided pans. The wok has now become popular the world over, and this is not surprising: food that has been stir-fried in a wok in the correct way is healthy, delicious and highly convenient.

The unique shape of the wok, with its deep sloping sides, allows ingredients to be cooked speedily at a high temperature in very little fat, thus retaining maximum freshness, taste and nutrients. The shape also makes it suitable for deep-frying, braising and steaming. The wok is therefore ideal for quick, nourishing, everyday one-pot meals as well as for impromptu entertaining.

Many traditional dishes prepared with the wok originated in parts of South-east Asia and the Far East, and have inspired the mouth-watering recipes in this book – from Balti curries to Chinese stir-fries and from spicy Thai vegetables to Indonesian rice. Western cooks have been quick to recognize the ease and speed of wok cookery, and so fusion recipes that marry the best of east and west are featured alongside all the popular wok classics. The fusion recipes bring a new twist to many traditional wok dishes, such as paella and leche frita from Spain, trout and prosciutto risotto rolls from Italy, and spicy chicken Jambalaya and chilli beef with butternut from north America.

There are different types of wok available. First of all there is the carbon-steel, round-bottomed wok that is best suited to a gas hob. Then there is the carbon-steel, flat-bottomed wok, best for use on electric or solid-fuel hobs, as it will give a better distribution of heat. You can also choose woks with either one or two handles – if you have a choice, always select wooden-covered handles. A metal-domed lid is also essential if you are planning to use your wok for steaming or braising.

A well-seasoned wok has a distinctive dark patina. Before using a wok for the first time, wash it in hot soapy water, rinse and dry it, and then heat the wok with 30ml/2 tbsp salt for about 15 minutes, stirring so that the whole surface is coated with the salt. Wipe out the salt, and then wipe the wok round with kitchen paper moistened with a little oil before storing it. After the first use, don't wash your wok with detergent (this will remove the non-stick surface from your wok), simply rinse it in plain hot water and then dry it thoroughly, preferably over a low heat for a few minutes, before you put it away. If you use a non-stick wok, then allow it to cool slightly after use and then wipe out the inside with kitchen paper.

Stir-frying takes very little cooking time: often only minutes, and ensures that ingredients will be cooked evenly, retaining their crispness and texture. For this reason it is important that all the ingredients are

prepared ahead of time and cut to the same shape and size. Many recipes require the vegetables to be cut into matchsticks or thin slices – so use a very sharp knife or cleaver.

Chapters in this book feature soups, appetizers and light bites, poultry dishes, meat and game dishes, fish and shellfish dishes, vegetable dishes, rice and noodle dishes, vegetables and salads, and a final chapter of desserts that can be prepared in a wok.

Once you begin, you will be amazed at the versatility of wok cooking for braising, steaming and deep-frying. Experiment with the wok and adapt risottos, stews, and even steamed puddings to this versatile piece of equipment.

This book offers over 500 recipes that will fill your home with wonderful aromas as you cook. You will be delighted by the delicious dishes that can be cooked in a matter of moments using a wok.

Bean and Beansprout Soup

Any seasonal vegetables can be added or substituted for the beans in this recipe. If preferred, the lemon wedges can be served on the side.

Serves 8

225g/8oz green beans
1.2 litres/2 pints/5 cups lightly salted water
1 garlic clove, roughly chopped
2 macadamia nuts or 4 almonds, finely chopped
1cm/½ in cube shrimp paste
10–15ml/2–3 tsp coriander seeds, dry fried
30ml/2 tbsp vegetable oil
1 onion, finely sliced
400ml/14fl oz can coconut milk
2 bay leaves
225g/8oz/1 cup beansprouts, washed and drained
8 thin lemon wedges
30ml/2 tbsp lemon juice
salt and ground black pepper

1 Trim the beans, then cut them into small pieces. Bring the water to the boil, with a little salt, add the beans and cook for 3–4 minutes. Drain, reserving the cooking water. Set the water and beans aside.

2 Finely grind the chopped garlic, macadamia nuts or almonds, shrimp paste and the coriander seeds to a paste using a pestle and mortar or in a food processor.

3 Heat the oil in a wok, and fry the onion until transparent. Remove with a slotted spoon. Add the nut paste to the wok and fry it for 2 minutes without allowing it to brown.

4 Pour in the reserved vegetable water. Spoon off 45–60ml/3–4 tbsp of the cream from the top of the coconut milk and set it aside. Add the remaining coconut milk to the wok, bring to the boil and add the bay leaves. Cook for 15–20 minutes.

5 Just before serving, reserve a few green beans, fried onions and beansprouts for garnish. Stir the rest into the soup and heat through without boiling

6 Add the lemon wedges, reserved coconut cream, lemon juice and seasoning; stir well. Pour into soup bowls and serve, garnished with the reserved vegetables.

Java Coconut Soup with Pumpkin and Bamboo

This tasty soup is from Java, where it is served on its own with rice or as an accompaniment to a poached or grilled fish dish. In some parts of Java, the dish includes small prawns but, if it is packed with vegetables alone, it makes a satisfying vegetarian meal. Generally, such dishes are accompanied by a chilli sambal, which can be made by pounding chillies with shrimp paste and lime juice.

Serves 4

30ml/2 tbsp palm, groundnut (peanut) or corn oil
150g/5oz pumpkin flesh
115g/4oz snake (yard-long) beans
220g/7½oz can bamboo shoots, drained and rinsed
900ml/1½ pints coconut milk
10–15ml/2–3 tsp palm sugar (jaggery)
130g/4½oz fresh coconut, shredded
salt
cooked rice and chilli sauce, to serve

For the spice paste

4 shallots, chopped
25g/1oz fresh root ginger, chopped
4 red chillies, seeded and chopped
2 garlic cloves, chopped
5ml/1 tsp coriander seeds
4 candlenuts or macadamia nuts, toasted and chopped

1 Make the spice paste. Using a mortar and pestle, grind all the ingredients together to form a smooth paste, or whiz them together in an electric blender or food processor.

2 Heat the oil in a wok or a large, heavy pan, stir in the spice paste and fry for 2–3 minutes until it smells fragrant. Toss the pumpkin, the yard-long beans and the bamboo shoots in the paste and pour in the coconut milk.

3 Add the sugar and bring to the boil. Reduce the heat and cook gently for 5–10 minutes, until the vegetables are tender. Season the soup and stir in half the fresh coconut.

4 Ladle the soup into warmed individual bowls, sprinkle with the remaining coconut and serve with bowls of cooked rice to spoon the soup over, and chilli sauce.

Bean and Beansprout Soup Energy 73kcal/304kJ; Protein 2.3g; Carbohydrate 5.7g, of which sugars 4.2g; Fat 4.8g, of which saturates 0.6g; Cholesterol 0mg; Calcium 40mg; Fibre 1.3g; Sodium 57mg.
Java Coconut Soup Energy 333kcal/1388kJ; Protein 6g; Carbohydrate 26g, of which sugars 23.8g; Fat 23.6g, of which saturates 11.7g; Cholesterol 0mg; Calcium 115mg; Fibre 4.9g; Sodium 258mg.

Spicy Tomato and Egg Drop Soup

Popular in southern Vietnam and Cambodia, this spicy soup with eggs is probably adapted from the traditional Chinese egg drop soup. Served on its own with chunks of crusty bread, or accompanied by jasmine or ginger rice, this is a tasty dish for a light supper.

Serves 4

30ml/2 tbsp groundnut (peanut) or vegetable oil
3 shallots, finely sliced
2 garlic cloves, finely chopped
2 Thai chillies, seeded and finely sliced
25g/1oz galangal, shredded
8 large, ripe tomatoes, skinned, seeded and finely chopped
15ml/1 tbsp sugar
30ml/2 tbsp Thai fish sauce
4 lime leaves
900ml/1½ pints/3¾ cups chicken stock
15ml/1 tbsp wine vinegar
4 eggs
sea salt and ground black pepper

For the garnish

chilli oil, for drizzling
1 small bunch fresh coriander (cilantro), finely chopped
1 small bunch fresh mint leaves, finely chopped

1 Heat the oil in a wok or heavy pan. Stir in the shallots, garlic, chillies and galangal and cook until golden and fragrant. Add the tomatoes with the sugar, Thai fish sauce and lime leaves. Stir until it resembles a sauce. Pour in the stock and bring to the boil. Reduce the heat and simmer for 30 minutes. Season.

2 Just before serving, bring a wide pan of water to the boil. Add the vinegar and half a teaspoon of salt. Break the eggs into individual cups or small bowls.

3 Stir the water rapidly to create a swirl and drop an egg into the centre of the swirl. Follow immediately with the others, or poach two at a time, and keep the water boiling to throw the whites up over the yolks. Turn off the heat, cover the pan and leave to poach until firm enough to lift. Poached eggs are traditional, but you could use lightly fried eggs instead.

4 Using a slotted spoon, lift the eggs out of the water and slip them into the hot soup. Drizzle a little chilli oil over the eggs, sprinkle with the coriander and mint, and serve.

Chicken Broth with Stuffed Cabbage Leaves

The Chinese have a tradition of cooking dumplings or stuffed vegetables in a clear broth.

Serves 4

10 Chinese leaves (Chinese cabbage) halved, main ribs removed
4 spring onions (scallions), green tops left whole, white part finely chopped
5–6 dried cloud ear (wood ear) mushrooms, soaked in hot water for 15 minutes
115g/4oz minced (ground) pork
115g/4oz prawns (shrimp), shelled, deveined and chopped
1 fresh chilli, seeded and chopped
30ml/2 tbsp fish sauce
15ml/1 tbsp soy sauce
4cm/1½in fresh root ginger, peeled and very finely sliced
chopped fresh coriander (cilantro), to garnish

For the stock

1 meaty chicken carcass
2 onions, peeled and quartered
4 garlic cloves, crushed
4cm/1½in fresh root ginger, chopped
30ml/2 tbsp fish sauce
30ml/2 tbsp soy sauce
6 black peppercorns
a few sprigs of fresh thyme
sea salt

1 To make the chicken stock, put the chicken carcass into a wok or deep pan with all the other stock ingredients except the salt. Add 2 litres/3½ pints/8 cups of water. Bring to the boil. Skim, then cover and simmer for 1½–2 hours. Remove the lid and simmer for 30 minutes more. Skim, season, then strain. Measure 1.5 litres/2½ pints/6 cups into a clean pan.

2 Blanch the cabbage leaves in boiling water for 2 minutes, lift out and refresh under cold water. Blanch the spring onion tops and refresh. Tear each piece into 5 strips.

3 Drain the cloud ears, squeeze dry, trim, chop and mix with the pork, prawns, spring onion whites, chilli, fish sauce and soy sauce. Divide the mixture among the cabbage leaves, fold in the bottom edges and sides, roll up and tie with the spring onion green.

4 Heat the stock, stir in the ginger and add the cabbage bundles. Cook very gently for 20 minutes. Garnish with coriander.

Tomato and Egg Soup Energy 181kcal/756kJ; Protein 8g; Carbohydrate 12.3g, of which sugars 11.5g; Fat 11.7g, of which saturates 2.4g; Cholesterol 190mg; Calcium 52mg; Fibre 2.3g; Sodium 280mg.
Chicken Broth Energy 80kcal/334kJ; Protein 12.7g; Carbohydrate 3.9g, of which sugars 3.7g; Fat 1.5g, of which saturates 0.5g; Cholesterol 74mg; Calcium 68mg; Fibre 1.4g; Sodium 891mg.

Spinach and Tofu Soup

If fresh young spinach leaves are not available, watercress or lettuce can be used instead. Sorrel leaves may also be used as a substitute when in season, but they have a distinctively sharp flavour so will change the character of the soup.

Serves 4

200g/7oz tofu
115g/4oz spinach leaves
750ml/1¼ pints/3 cups chicken or vegetable stock
15ml/1 tbsp light soy sauce
salt and ground black pepper

1 Cut the tofu into 12 small pieces, each about 5mm/¼in thick.

2 Wash the spinach leaves thoroughly, drain well and then cut or tear the leaves into small pieces.

3 Put the stock into a wok and bring to a rolling boil. Add the tofu pieces and the soy sauce to the wok, bring back to the boil and simmer for about 2 minutes.

4 Add the spinach and simmer for a further minute. Skim the surface of the soup with a metal spoon to make it clear, then adjust the seasoning and serve immediately.

Variations

- *Use broccoli instead of the spinach – dice the stems and cook with the tofu, then add the broccoli in step 3.*
- *Use chicken instead of the tofu. Dice 1–2 skinless, boneless chicken breast fillets and add to the stock instead of the tofu.*
- *Add the grated rind of 1 lime, a chopped bunch of garlic chives and a handful of small basil leaves with the spring onions (scallions).*

Cook's Tip

Fresh tofu, also known as beancurd, is sold in Chinese food stores. Do not confuse it with fermented tofu, which is much stronger-tasting, quite salty and usually used as a condiment.

Noodle Soup with Tofu

This light and refreshing soup is an excellent pick-me-up. The aromatic, spicy broth is simmered first, and then the tofu, beansprouts and noodles are added.

Serves 4

150g/5oz dried thick rice noodles
1 litre/1¾ pints/4 cups vegetable stock
1 fresh red chilli, seeded and thinly sliced
15ml/1 tbsp light soy sauce
juice of ½ lemon
10ml/2 tsp sugar
5ml/1 tsp finely sliced garlic
5ml/1 tsp finely chopped fresh root ginger
200g/7oz firm tofu
90g/3½oz/scant 1 cup beansprouts
50g/2oz/½ cup peanuts
15ml/1 tbsp chopped fresh coriander (cilantro)
spring onion (scallion) slivers and red chilli slivers, to garnish

1 Spread out the noodles in a shallow dish and pour over boiling water to cover. Soak according to the packet instructions until they are just tender. Drain, rinse and set aside.

2 Meanwhile, place the stock, red chilli, soy sauce, lemon juice, sugar, garlic and ginger in a large wok or heavy pan over high heat. Bring to the boil, cover, reduce to low heat and simmer the mixture gently for 10–12 minutes.

3 Cut the tofu into small pieces, cubes about 5mm/¼in thick. Add it to the pan with the drained noodles and the beansprouts. Cook the mixture gently, without stirring, for 2–3 minutes.

4 Roast the peanuts in a dry non-stick wok, then chop them.

5 Stir the coriander into the soup. Serve in warm bowls with peanuts, spring onions and chilli on top.

Cook's Tip

It is important to use good-quality vegetable stock with plenty of flavour for this simple soup.

Spinach and Tofu Soup Energy 55kcal/231kJ; Protein 7.6g; Carbohydrate 1.4g, of which sugars 1.1g; Fat 2.2g, of which saturates 0.3g; Cholesterol 25mg; Calcium 352mg; Fibre 1.3g; Sodium 300mg.
Noodle Soup with Tofu Energy 261kcal/1092kJ; Protein 10g; Carbohydrate 36.4g, of which sugars 4.3g; Fat 8g, of which saturates 1.4g; Cholesterol 0mg; Calcium 275mg; Fibre 1.2g; Sodium 97mg.

Aromatic Tofu Soup with Shiitake

This clear broth is simply packed with health-giving vegetables. The soup depends on its well-flavoured and aromatic stock.

Serves 4

115g/4oz/scant 2 cups dried shiitake mushrooms, soaked in water for 20 minutes
15ml/1 tbsp vegetable oil
2 shallots, halved and sliced
2 Thai chillies, seeded and sliced
4cm/1½in fresh root ginger, peeled and finely chopped
15ml/1 tbsp fish sauce
350g/12oz tofu, rinsed, drained and cut into bitesize cubes
4 tomatoes, skinned, seeded and cut into thin strips
salt and ground black pepper
1 bunch coriander (cilantro), stems removed, finely chopped, to garnish

For the stock

1 meaty chicken carcass or 500g/1¼lb pork ribs
25g/1oz dried squid or prawns (shrimp), soaked in water for 15 minutes
2 onions, peeled and quartered
2 garlic cloves, crushed
7.5cm/3in fresh ginger, chopped
15ml/1 tbsp nuoc mam (fish sauce)
6 black peppercorns
2 star anise
4 cloves
1 cinnamon stick
sea salt

1 To make the stock, put the chicken carcass or pork ribs in a wok or deep pan. Add the dried squid or prawns, rinsed, with the remaining stock ingredients, except the salt, and pour in 2 litres/3½ pints/8 cups water. Bring to the boil, skim, then reduce the heat and simmer with the lid on for 1½–2 hours.

2 Remove the lid of the pan and simmer for a further 30 minutes to reduce. Skim off any fat, season, then strain and measure out 1.5 litres/2½ pints/6¼ cups.

3 Squeeze dry the shiitake mushrooms, discard the stems and slice the caps into thin strips. Heat the oil in a wok or large pan and stir in the shallots, chillies and ginger. Add the fish sauce and stock.

4 Add the tofu, shiitake mushrooms and tomatoes to the pan, and bring it to the boil. Reduce the heat and simmer for 5–10 minutes. Season to taste and sprinkle the finely chopped fresh coriander over the top. Serve piping hot.

Hot and Sour Tofu Soup

This spicy, warming soup really whets the appetite and is the perfect introduction to a simple Chinese meal.

Serves 4

10g/¼oz dried cloud ear (wood ear) mushrooms
8 fresh shiitake mushrooms
900ml/1½ pints/3¾ cups vegetable stock
75g/3oz firm tofu, cubed
50g/2oz/½ cup canned sliced bamboo shoots
15ml/1 tbsp caster (superfine) sugar
45ml/3 tbsp rice vinegar
15ml/1 tbsp light soy sauce
1.5ml/¼ tsp chilli oil
2.5ml/½ tsp salt
large pinch of ground white pepper
15ml/1 tbsp cornflour (cornstarch)
1 egg white
5ml/1 tsp sesame oil
2 spring onions (scallions), sliced into fine rings
white pepper, to serve

1 Soak the dried cloud ear mushrooms in hot water for 20 minutes or until soft. Drain, trim off and discard the hard base from each cloud ear and then chop the fungus roughly.

2 Wipe the shiitake mushrooms with a damp cloth. Remove and discard the mushroom stems. Cut the caps into thin strips.

3 Place the stock, both types of mushroom, tofu and bamboo shoots in a wok or large pan. Bring the stock to the boil, lower the heat and simmer for about 5 minutes.

4 Stir in the sugar, vinegar, soy sauce, chilli oil, salt and pepper. Mix the cornflour to a paste with a little cold water. Add to the soup, stirring constantly, and bring to the boil, stirring until it thickens slightly.

5 Lightly whisk the egg white with a fork, just enough to break it up, then pour it slowly into the soup in a steady stream, stirring constantly so that it forms threads. Add the sesame oil.

6 Ladle the soup into heated bowls and garnish with spring onion rings. Serve immediately, offering white pepper at the table for anyone who wants a hotter soup.

Aromatic Soup with Shiitake Energy 220kcal/919kJ; Protein 12g; Carbohydrate 26g, of which sugars 4g; Fat 8g, of which saturates 1g; Cholesterol 0mg; Calcium 47.8mg; Fibre 1.1g; Sodium 500mg.
Hot and Sour Soup Energy 102kcal/429kJ; Protein 7.3g; Carbohydrate 7.3g, of which sugars 0.3g; Fat 5.1g, of which saturates 1g; Cholesterol 44mg; Calcium 135mg; Fibre 0.7g; Sodium 208mg.

Hot and Sour Pineapple Prawn Broth

This simple dish is served as an appetite enhancer because of its hot and sour flavour. It is also popular as an accompaniment to plain rice or noodles. In some restaurants, the broth is presented in a hollowed-out pineapple, halved lengthways.

Serves 4

30ml/2 tbsp vegetable oil
15–30ml/1–2 tbsp tamarind paste
15ml/1 tbsp sugar
450g/1lb fresh prawns (shrimp), peeled and deveined
4 thick fresh pineapple slices, cored and cut into bitesize chunks
salt and ground black pepper
fresh coriander (cilantro) and mint leaves, to garnish
steamed rice or plain noodles, to serve

For the spice paste

4 shallots, chopped
4 red chillies, chopped
25g/1oz fresh root ginger, peeled and chopped
1 lemon grass stalk, trimmed and chopped
5ml/1 tsp shrimp paste

1 Using a mortar and pestle or a food processor, grind or process the shallots, chillies, ginger and lemon grass to a paste. Add the shrimp paste and mix well.

2 Heat the oil in a wok or heavy pan. Stir in the spice paste and fry until fragrant. Stir in the tamarind paste and the sugar, then pour in 1.2 litres/2 pints/5 cups water. Mix well and bring to the boil. Reduce the heat and simmer for 10 minutes. Season the broth with salt and pepper.

3 Add the prawns and pineapple to the broth and simmer for 4–5 minutes, or until the prawns are cooked. Using a slotted spoon, lift the prawns and pineapple out of the broth and divide them among four warmed bowls. Ladle over some of the broth and garnish with coriander and mint leaves.

4 The remaining broth can be served separately as a drink, or spooned over plain steamed rice or plain noodles, if they are accompanying this dish.

Noodles in Tangy Prawn Soup

This lovely tangy dish is influenced by the characteristic flavourings of Thailand: the soup has interesting sour notes that come from tamarind and salted soya beans.

Serves 4

vegetable oil, for deep-frying
225g/8oz firm tofu, rinsed, drained and cut into cubes
60ml/4 tbsp dried prawns (shrimp), soaked until rehydrated
5ml/1 tsp shrimp paste
4 garlic cloves, chopped
4–6 dried red chillies, soaked to soften, drained, seeded and the pulp scraped out
90g/3½oz/¾ cup roasted peanuts, ground
50g/2oz salted soya beans
2 lemon grass stalks, trimmed, halved and bruised
30ml/2 tbsp sugar
15–30ml/1–2 tbsp tamarind paste
150g/5oz dried rice vermicelli, soaked in hot water until pliable
a handful of beansprouts, rinsed and drained
4 quails' eggs, hard-boiled, shelled and halved
2 spring onions (scallions), finely sliced
salt and ground black pepper
fresh coriander (cilantro) leaves, finely chopped, to garnish

1 In a wok, heat enough vegetable oil for deep-frying. Drop in the tofu and deep-fry until golden. Drain and set aside.

2 Using a mortar and pestle or food processor, grind the dried prawns, shrimp paste, garlic and chilli pulp together to a paste.

3 Heat 30ml/2 tbsp of vegetable oil in a wok and stir in the paste. Fry for 1 minute until fragrant, then add the peanuts, salted soya beans and lemon grass. Fry for another minute. Stir in the sugar and tamarind paste, followed by 900ml/1½ pints/3¾ cups water. Mix and bring to the boil. Reduce the heat and simmer gently for 10 minutes. Season with salt and pepper.

4 Drain the rice vermicelli and plunge into the broth to heat through. Divide the vermicelli among serving bowls, sprinkle over the beansprouts and add the deep-fried tofu, halved quails' eggs and spring onions. Ladle the spicy broth over the top, garnish with the coriander and serve immediately.

Pineapple Prawn Broth Energy 192kcal/808kJ; Protein 20.4g; Carbohydrate 14.2g, of which sugars 13.9g; Fat 6.4g, of which saturates 0.8g; Cholesterol 219mg; Calcium 111mg; Fibre 1.3g; Sodium 216mg.
Noodles in Prawn Soup Energy 547kcal/2280kJ; Protein 29.5g; Carbohydrate 42.5g, of which sugars 10g; Fat 29g, of which saturates 4.4g; Cholesterol 48mg; Calcium 389mg; Fibre 3.7g; Sodium 203mg.

Sliced Fish and Fresh Coriander Spicy Soup

This delicate clear soup is very simple and quick to make. Its success depends on using perfectly fresh fish and a light, well-flavoured stock. Because the fish is quickly cooked in the soup, it retains its texture.

Serves 4

225g/8oz white fish fillets, such as lemon sole or plaice
5ml/1 tsp cornflour (cornstarch)
15ml/1 tbsp egg white
750ml/1¼ pints/3 cups chicken or vegetable stock
15ml/1 tbsp light soy sauce
about 50g/2oz fresh coriander (cilantro) leaves, chopped
salt and ground black pepper

1 Cut the fish into bitesize square pieces.

2 Make a paste by mixing the cornflour with 5ml/1 tsp water and mix this with the egg white in a bowl. Add the pieces of fish and turn gently in the mixture to coat them evenly.

3 Bring the stock to a rolling boil in a wok and poach the fish pieces for about 1 minute. Add the soy sauce and coriander leaves, adjust the seasoning to taste and serve immediately.

Cook's Tip

It is better not to remove the skin from the fish, as it helps to keep the flesh together when it is poached in the stock. It also adds flavour to the soup, but if you prefer to take the skin off for aesthetic reasons, then do so before you cut it into pieces.

Variation

If you can't get fresh fish, you can defrost frozen white fish or use frozen prawns (shrimp) in place of the fish – simply add them still frozen to the stock, and cook as with the fish.

Crab and Asparagus Soup

Generally, jars of asparagus preserved in brine are used for this recipe, or you can use fresh asparagus steamed until tender.

Serves 4

15ml/1 tbsp vegetable oil
2 shallots, finely chopped
2 garlic cloves, finely chopped
15ml/1 tbsp rice flour or cornflour (cornstarch)
225g/8oz/1⅓ cups cooked crab meat, chopped
450g/1lb preserved asparagus, finely chopped, or 450g/1lb fresh asparagus, trimmed and steamed
salt and ground black pepper
basil and coriander (cilantro) leaves, to garnish
fish sauce, to serve

For the stock

1 meaty chicken carcass
25g/1oz dried shrimp, soaked in water for 30 minutes, rinsed and drained
2 medium onions, peeled and quartered
2 garlic cloves, crushed
15ml/1 tbsp fish sauce
6 black peppercorns
sea salt

1 To make the stock, put the chicken carcass into a wok or large pan. Add all the other stock ingredients, except the salt, and pour in 2 litres/3½ pints/8 cups water. Bring to the boil, boil for a few minutes, skim off any foam, then reduce the heat and simmer with the lid on for 1½–2 hours.

2 Remove the lid of the wok or large pan and simmer for 30 minutes to reduce the stock. Skim off any fat, season, then strain the stock and measure out 1.5 litres/2½ pints/6¼ cups.

3 Heat the oil in a deep pan or wok. Stir in the shallots and garlic, until they begin to colour. Remove from the heat, stir in the flour, and then pour in the stock. Put the pan back over the heat and bring to the boil, stirring constantly, until smooth.

4 Add the crab meat and asparagus to the pan, reduce the heat and leave to simmer for 15–20 minutes. Season the dish to taste with salt and ground black pepper, then ladle the soup into bowls, garnish with fresh basil and coriander leaves, and serve with a splash of fish sauce.

Sliced Fish and Coriander Energy 57kcal/239kJ; Protein 11.1g; Carbohydrate 1.8g, of which sugars 0.6g; Fat 0.6g, of which saturates 0.1g; Cholesterol 26mg; Calcium 31mg; Fibre 0.6g; Sodium 313mg.
Crab and Asparagus Energy 158kcal/652kJ; Protein 9.8g; Carbohydrate 7.6g, of which sugars 4g; Fat 9.9g, of which saturates 5.6g; Cholesterol 38mg; Calcium 87mg; Fibre 3.2g; Sodium 147mg.

Fish Soup with Tamarind and Chillies

Chunky, filling and satisfying, Filipino fish soups are meals in themselves. There are many variations on the theme, but they are usually packed with shellfish, flavoured with sour tamarind combined with hot chilli, and served with coconut vinegar flavoured with garlic.

Serves 4–6

2 litres/3½ pints/8 cups fish stock
250ml/8fl oz/1 cup white wine
15–30ml/1–2 tbsp tamarind paste
30–45ml/2–3 tbsp fish sauce
30ml/2 tbsp palm sugar (jaggery)
2–3 fresh red or green chillies, seeded and finely sliced
50g/2oz fresh root ginger, grated
2 tomatoes, skinned, seeded and cut into wedges
350g/12oz fresh fish, such as trout, sea bass, swordfish or cod, cut into bitesize chunks
12–16 fresh prawns (shrimp), in their shells
bunch of fresh basil, roughly chopped
bunch of fresh flat leaf parsley, roughly chopped
salt and ground black pepper

For serving
60–90ml/4–6 tbsp coconut vinegar
1–2 garlic cloves, finely chopped
1–2 limes, cut into wedges
2 fresh red or green chillies, seeded and quartered lengthways

1 In a wok or large pan, bring the stock and wine to the boil. Stir in the tamarind paste, fish sauce, sugar, chillies and ginger. Reduce the heat and simmer for 15–20 minutes.

2 Add the tomatoes to the broth, stir gently to mix, and season with salt and pepper. Add the fish and prawns and simmer for 5 minutes until the fish is cooked.

3 Meanwhile, mix the coconut vinegar and garlic for serving. Stir half the basil and half the parsley into the broth and ladle into bowls. Garnish with the remaining basil and parsley and serve. Offer the coconut vinegar, lime wedges to squeeze into the soup, and the chillies to chew on for extra heat.

Hot-and-Sour Fish Soup

Chinese hot-and-sour soup is usually meat-based, but this fish version is popular in Cambodia and Vietnam and all over South-east Asia.

Serves 4

1 catfish, sea bass or red snapper, about 1kg/2¼lb, filleted
60ml/4 tbsp fish sauce
2 garlic cloves, finely chopped
15ml/1 tbsp vegetable oil
2 spring onions (scallions), sliced
2 shallots, sliced
4cm/1½in fresh root ginger, peeled and chopped
2–3 lemon grass stalks, cut into strips and crushed
25g/1oz dried squid, soaked in water for 30 minutes
30ml/2 tbsp tamarind paste
2–3 Thai chillies, seeded and sliced
15ml/1 tbsp sugar
225g/8oz fresh pineapple, peeled and diced
3 tomatoes, skinned, seeded and roughly chopped
50g/2oz canned sliced bamboo shoots, drained
small bunch of fresh coriander (cilantro), stalks removed, leaves finely chopped
salt and ground black pepper

For the garnish
115g/4oz/½ cup beansprouts
bunch of dill, fronds roughly chopped
1 lime, cut into quarters

1 Cut the fish into bitesize pieces, mix with 30ml/2 tbsp of the fish sauce and garlic and leave to marinate. Save the head, tail and bones for the stock. Drain and rinse the dried squid.

2 Heat the oil in a wok. Add the spring onions, shallots, ginger, lemon grass and squid. Add the reserved fish trimmings and cook gently for 1–2 minutes. Add 1.2 litres/2 pints/5 cups water. Reduce the heat and simmer for 30 minutes.

3 Strain the stock into another pan and bring to the boil. Stir in the tamarind paste, chillies, sugar and remaining fish sauce. Simmer for 2–3 minutes. Add the pineapple, tomatoes and bamboo shoots and simmer for 2–3 minutes. Stir in the fish and chopped fresh coriander, and cook until the fish turns opaque.

4 Season to taste and ladle the soup into individual hot bowls. Garnish the soup with beansprouts and roughly chopped dill, and serve with the lime quarters to squeeze over.

Soup with Tamarind Energy 137kcal/576kJ; Protein 17.7g; Carbohydrate 8.1g, of which sugars 8g; Fat 1g, of which saturates 0.1g; Cholesterol 92mg; Calcium 76mg; Fibre 1.3g; Sodium 644mg.
Hot-and-Sour Fish Soup Energy 335kcal/1415kJ; Protein 44g; Carbohydrate 24g, of which sugars 19g; Fat 7g, of which saturates 1g; Cholesterol 108mg; Calcium 138mg; Fibre 2.3g; Sodium 1.2g.

Chicken and Tiger Prawn Laksa

Laksa is a spicy noodle soup enriched with coconut milk.

Serves 6

6 dried red chillies, seeded
225g/8oz vermicelli, broken
15ml/1 tbsp shrimp paste
10 shallots, chopped
3 garlic cloves
1 lemon grass stalk, roughly chopped
25g/1oz/¼ cup macadamia nuts
grated rind and juice of 1 lime
60ml/4 tbsp groundnut (peanut) oil
2.5ml/½ tsp ground turmeric
5ml/1 tsp ground coriander
1.5 litres/2½ pints/6¼ cups fish or chicken stock
450g/1lb raw tiger prawns (jumbo shrimp), shelled and deveined
450g/1lb skinless, boneless chicken breast portions, cut into long thin strips
2 x 400g/14oz cans coconut milk
115g/4oz/1 cup beansprouts
½ cucumber, cut into strips
small bunch of spring onions (scallions), shredded, plus extra to garnish
salt and ground black pepper
1 lime, cut into wedges, to serve

1 Soak the chillies in hot water for 45 minutes. Cook the vermicelli according to the packet instructions. Drain; set aside.

2 Drain the chillies and put them in a food processor or blender with the shrimp paste, shallots, garlic, lemon grass, nuts, lime rind and juice. Process to form a thick paste.

3 Heat 45ml/3 tbsp of the oil in a large heavy wok or pan. Add the spice paste and cook for 1–2 minutes, stirring. Add the turmeric and coriander and cook for 2 minutes more. Stir in the stock; simmer for 25 minutes, then strain and set aside.

4 Heat the remaining oil in a clean wok or pan and fry the prawns until pink. Remove and set aside. Add the chicken and fry for 4–5 minutes, until just cooked.

5 Pour in the stock and coconut milk. Reheat gently. Add the vermicelli and prawns, and heat for 2 minutes. Stir in the beansprouts, cucumber and spring onions.

6 Ladle the soup into individual warmed bowls, garnish with spring onions and serve with lime wedges.

Aromatic Chicken and Asparagus Broth

This is a delicate and quite delicious soup. When fresh asparagus is not in season, frozen asparagus is an acceptable substitute. Soy sauce boosts the flavour.

Serves 4

150g/5oz skinless boneless chicken breast
5ml/1 tsp cornflour (cornstarch)
pinch of salt
5ml/1 tsp egg white
115g/4oz asparagus
750ml/1¼ pints/3 cups chicken stock
10ml/2 tsp dark soy sauce
salt and ground black pepper
fresh coriander (cilantro) leaves, to garnish

1 Cut the chicken meat into small, thin slices each about the size of a postage stamp. Mix the cornflour with just a little water to make a smooth paste. Mix with a pinch of salt, then add the egg white and stir to make a smooth, thin paste.

2 Cut off and discard the tough stems of the asparagus (or use for stock, see Cook's Tip below) and diagonally cut the tender ends of the spears into short, even lengths.

3 In a wok, bring the stock to a rolling boil, add the asparagus and soy sauce, and bring back to the boil, cooking for 2 minutes.

4 Add the chicken, stir to separate and bring back to the boil once more. Adjust the seasonings. Serve hot, in warmed bowls, garnished with fresh coriander leaves.

Cook's Tip

Instead of discarding the slightly tough asparagus stems, use them to flavour the stock. Slice them and simmer in the stock for 30 minutes, then strain the stock, pressing all the liquid out of the asparagus. For a cloudy or creamy soup, cook the asparagus trimmings in the stock, then leave to cool for a while before puréeing in a food processor or blender. Press through a sieve (strainer) to remove all the fibrous bits of asparagus.

Chicken and Prawn Energy 414kcal/1734kJ; Protein 36.4g; Carbohydrate 38.9g, of which sugars 8.8g; Fat 12.6g, of which saturates 1.9g; Cholesterol 199mg; Calcium 129mg; Fibre 1.1g; Sodium 352mg.
Chicken and Asparagus Energy 49kcal/208kJ; Protein 9.4g; Carbohydrate 1.7g, of which sugars 0.6g; Fat 0.6g, of which saturates 0.1g; Cholesterol 25mg; Calcium 10mg; Fibre 0.5g; Sodium 24mg.

Corn and Chicken Soup

Using a combination of chicken, creamed corn and whole kernels gives this classic Chinese soup a lovely texture. It tastes delicious, is warming on a cold day and easy to make if you are in a hurry or are planning a quick lunch with friends.

Serves 4–6

1 skinless chicken breast fillet, about 115g/4oz, cubed
10ml/2 tsp light soy sauce
15ml/1 tbsp Chinese rice wine
5ml/1 tsp cornflour (cornstarch)
60ml/4 tbsp cold water
5ml/1 tsp sesame oil
15ml/1 tbsp vegetable oil
5ml/1 tsp grated fresh root ginger
1 litre/1¾ pints/4 cups chicken stock
425g/15oz can creamed corn
225g/8oz can whole kernel corn
2 eggs, beaten
salt and ground black pepper
2–3 spring onions (scallions), green parts only, cut into tiny rounds, to garnish

1 Mince (grind) the chicken breast fillet in a food processor, taking care not to overprocess.

2 Transfer the chicken to a bowl and stir in the soy sauce, rice wine, cornflour, water, sesame oil and seasoning. Cover with clear film (plastic wrap) and leave for about 15 minutes so that the chicken absorbs the flavours.

3 Heat a wok over medium heat. Add the vegetable oil and swirl it around. Add the ginger and stir-fry for a few seconds.

4 Pour in the stock with the creamed corn and corn kernels. Bring to just below boiling point.

5 Spoon about 90ml/6 tbsp of the hot liquid into the chicken mixture until it forms a smooth paste and stir. Return to the wok. Slowly bring to the boil, stirring constantly, then simmer for 2–3 minutes or until the chicken is cooked.

6 Pour the beaten eggs into the soup in a slow, steady stream, using a fork or chopsticks to stir the top of the soup in a figure-of-eight pattern. The egg will set in lacy shreds. Serve immediately with the spring onions on top.

Chicken Soup with Roasted Ham and Prawns

This delicious, simple dish combines chicken, ham and prawns in a high-protein, no-frills Chinese soup.

Serves 4

115g/4oz skinless boneless chicken breast fillet
115g/4oz honey-roast ham
115g/4oz peeled cooked prawns (shrimp)
750ml/1¼ pints/3 cups chicken stock
salt
chopped spring onions (scallions), to garnish

1 Thinly slice the chicken breast fillet and ham into small pieces. If the prawns are large, cut them in half lengthways.

2 In a wok or pan, bring the stock to a rolling boil and add the chicken, ham and prawns. Bring back to the boil, add salt to taste and simmer for 1 minute.

3 Ladle the soup into individual warmed bowls. Serve hot, garnished with chopped spring onions.

Variation

For a mixed meat and vegetable soup, add some shredded Chinese cabbage with the chicken and ham. For a crunchy contrasting texture, try stirring in a few drained and sliced canned water chestnuts. Serve the soup with shredded Chinese pickled ginger and pickled garlic for garnish.

Cook's Tip

This simple, everyday soup is just fine made with economical peeled cooked shellfish even though raw prawns (shrimp) would be superior. The ideal stock would be home-made using chicken and pork (such as a carcass and bones from belly pork or meaty spare ribs) but to be practical simply use good bought stock or a superior bouillon powder or cube.

Corn and Chicken Soup Energy 196kcal/831kJ; Protein 10g; Carbohydrate 29.9g, of which sugars 10.7g; Fat 4.7g, of which saturates 1g; Cholesterol 77mg; Calcium 17mg; Fibre 1.6g; Sodium 447mg.
Chicken with Ham Energy 83kcal/350kJ; Protein 17.4g; Carbohydrate 0.3g, of which sugars 0.3g; Fat 1.5g, of which saturates 0.5g; Cholesterol 93mg; Calcium 27mg; Fibre 0g; Sodium 562mg.

Chicken Soup with Coconut

Coconuts are grown just about everywhere in the Philippines but it is in the southern provinces that production is carried out on a large scale. Coconut milk as a soup base has its early beginnings in India centuries ago, but moved to the Indo-Chinese countries and then to Indonesia, the Philippines and Malaysia.

Serves 4

30ml/2 tbsp vegetable oil
4 garlic cloves, crushed
6 shallots, chopped
25g/1oz young fresh ginger root, grated
350g/12oz boneless chicken, diced
1 litre/1¾ pints/4 cups water
2 lemon grass stalks, 5cm/2in of root end bruised
5ml/1 tsp salt
2.5ml/½ tsp ground black pepper
1 chicken stock cube
1 young coconut, flesh grated and coconut water reserved
holy basil or coriander (cilantro) leaves, to garnish

1 Heat the oil in a large frying pan or wok and fry the garlic until fragrant and golden brown.

2 Add the shallots and ginger to the pan and fry for 2 minutes.

3 Add the chicken to the pan and stir-fry for 5 minutes until the pieces are white all over. Transfer to a larger pan, if necessary, for the next step.

4 Add the water, lemon grass, salt and pepper to the pan and crumble in the stock cube. Stir well.

5 Simmer for 25 minutes until the chicken is very tender. Add the grated coconut flesh and water and simmer for 5 minutes.

6 Serve garnished with fresh basil or coriander leaves.

Cook's Tip
The water inside a coconut is not coconut milk – this comes from grating and squeezing the meat with a little water.

Chicken and Ginger Broth with Papaya

This is a traditional peasant dish that is still cooked every day in rural areas of the Philippines. In some areas, green papaya is added to the broth, which could be regarded as a version of coq au vin. Generally the chicken and broth are served with steamed rice, but the broth is also sipped during the meal to cleanse and stimulate the palate.

Serves 4 to 6

15–30ml/1–2 tbsp palm or groundnut (peanut) oil
2 garlic cloves, finely chopped
1 large onion, sliced
40g/1½oz fresh root ginger, finely grated
2 whole dried chillies
1 chicken, left whole or jointed, trimmed of fat
30ml/2 tbsp fish sauce
600ml/1 pint/2½ cups chicken stock
1.2 litres/2 pints/5 cups water
1 small green papaya, cut into fine slices or strips
1 bunch fresh young chilli or basil leaves, plus extra to garnish
salt and ground black pepper
cooked rice, to serve

1 Heat the oil in a wok or a large pan that has a lid. Stir in the garlic, onion and ginger and fry gently for 2–3 minutes until they begin to colour. Stir in the chillies, add the chicken and fry until the skin is lightly browned all over.

2 Pour in the fish sauce, stock and water, adding more water if necessary so that the chicken is completely covered. Bring the pan to the boil, reduce the heat, and then cover and simmer gently for about 1½ hours, until the chicken is very tender when pierced with a sharp knife.

3 Season the stock to taste with salt and pepper and add the papaya. Continue to simmer for a further 10–15 minutes, then stir in the chilli or basil leaves.

4 Serve the chicken and broth in warmed individual bowls, with the same number of bowls of steamed rice. Alternatively, combine the chicken and broth in bowls, garnishing with basil or chilli leaves.

Chicken with Coconut Energy 87kcal/371kJ; Protein 13.1g; Carbohydrate 6.8g, of which sugars 6.7g; Fat 1.1g, of which saturates 0.4g; Cholesterol 35mg; Calcium 42mg; Fibre 0.3g; Sodium 620mg.
Chicken and Ginger Broth Energy 290kcal/1219kJ; Protein 46.4g; Carbohydrate 9.8g, of which sugars 8.7g; Fat 7.5g, of which saturates 1.5g; Cholesterol 169mg; Calcium 40mg; Fibre 2.2g; Sodium 150mg.

Aromatic Five-spice Duck Broth

This soup has a lively, spicy flavour, for those who love fiery food. Fresh or marinated chillies may be served with it as a side dish.

Serves 4

15ml/1 tbsp vegetable oil
2 shallots, thinly sliced
4cm/1½in fresh root ginger, peeled and sliced
15ml/1 tbsp soy sauce
5ml/1 tsp five-spice powder
10ml/2 tsp sugar
175g/6oz pak choi (bok choy)
450g/1lb fresh egg noodles
350g/12oz roast duck, sliced
sea salt

For the stock

1 chicken or duck carcass
2 carrots, peeled and quartered
2 onions, peeled and quartered
4cm/1½in fresh root ginger, peeled and cut into chunks
2 lemon grass stalks, chopped
30ml/2 tbsp fish sauce
15ml/1 tbsp soy sauce
6 black peppercorns

For the garnish

4 spring onions (scallions), sliced
1–2 red Serrano chillies, seeded and finely sliced
1 bunch each coriander (cilantro) and basil, stalks removed, leaves chopped

1 To make the stock, put the chicken or duck carcass into a deep pan or wok. Add all the other stock ingredients and 2.5 litres/4¼ pints/10¼ cups water. Bring to the boil, and boil for a few minutes, skim off any foam, then reduce the heat and simmer gently with the lid on for 2–3 hours. Remove the lid and continue to simmer for a further 30 minutes to reduce the stock. Skim off any fat, season with salt, then strain the stock. Measure out 2 litres/3½ pints/8 cups.

2 Heat the oil in a deep pan or wok and stir in the shallots and ginger. Add the soy sauce, five-spice powder, sugar and stock and bring to the boil. Reduce the heat and simmer for 15 minutes.

3 Meanwhile, cut the pak choi into wide strips and blanch in boiling water. Drain and refresh. Bring a large pan of water to the boil, then add the noodles. Cook for 5 minutes, then drain.

4 Divide the noodles among four bowls, lay the pak choi and sliced duck over them, and then ladle over the hot broth. Garnish with the spring onions, chillies and herbs, and serve.

Fruity Duck Soup

This rich soup originates in the Chiu Chow region of southern China. This recipe can be made with chicken stock and leftover duck meat from a roasted duck, or by roasting a duck, and slicing off the breast portion and thigh meat for use in the soup.

Serves 4–6

1 lean duck, about 1.5kg/3lb 5oz
2 preserved limes (see Cook's Tip)
25g/1oz fresh root ginger, thinly sliced
sea salt and ground black pepper

For the garnish

vegetable oil, for frying
25g/1oz fresh root ginger, thinly sliced into strips
2 garlic cloves, thinly sliced into strips
2 spring onions (scallions), finely sliced
thin segments of lime

1 Place the duck in a wok or large pan with enough cold water to cover. Season with salt and pepper and bring the water to the boil. Reduce the heat, cover the pot, and simmer for 1½ hours, checking from time to time so that the dish does not boil dry.

2 Add the preserved limes and ginger to the pan. Continue to simmer for another hour, skimming off the fat from time to time until the liquid has reduced a little and the duck is so tender that it almost falls off the bone.

3 Meanwhile heat some vegetable oil in a wok. Stir in the ginger and garlic strips and fry until gold and crispy. Drain them well on kitchen paper and set aside for garnishing.

4 Remove the duck and shred the meat into individual bowls. Check the broth for seasoning, then ladle it over the duck. Sprinkle the spring onions, the fried ginger and the garlic over the top, add a lime segment for garnish and serve.

Cook's Tip

Preserved limes have a distinct bitter flavour. Look for them in Asian markets or specialist delicatessens.

Aromatic Duck Broth Energy 673kcal/2836kJ; Protein 37g; Carbohydrate 86g, of which sugars 22g; Fat 6g, of which saturates 1g; Cholesterol 81mg; Calcium 4mg; Fibre 0.7g; Sodium 700mg
Fruity Duck Soup Energy 124kcal/520kJ; Protein 19.8g; Carbohydrate 0.3g, of which sugars 0.3g; Fat 6.5g, of which saturates 1.3g; Cholesterol 110mg; Calcium 19mg; Fibre 0g; Sodium 110mg.

Duck, Nut and Date Soup

This rich soup is delicious, and is packed with nuts and sweetened with jujubes (dried Chinese red dates). Whether served on its own or with rice and pickles, it is a meal in itself.

Serves 4

30–45ml/2–3 tbsp vegetable oil
4 duck legs, split into thighs and drumsticks
water from 1 coconut
60ml/4 tbsp fish sauce
4 lemon grass stalks, bruised
12 chestnuts, peeled
90g/3½oz unsalted cashew nuts, roasted
90g/3½oz unsalted almonds, roasted
90g/3½oz unsalted peanuts, roasted
12 jujubes (see Variation)
sea salt and freshly ground black pepper

1 Heat the oil in a wok or heavy pan. Brown the duck legs in the oil and drain on kitchen paper.

2 Bring 2 litres/3½ pints/8 cups water to the boil in a wok or large pan. Reduce the heat and add the coconut water, fish sauce, lemon grass and duck legs. Cover the pan and simmer over a gentle heat for 2–3 hours. Skim off any fat.

3 Add the nuts and jujubes and cook for 40 minutes until the chestnuts are soft and the duck is very tender. Skim off any fat, and season to taste.

Variation

Jujubes are also known as Chinese red dates and are sold in Chinese supermarkets. However it is also worth looking in healthfood or wholefood shops for small dried red dates that can be used instead. Otherwise use ordinary dried dates.

Cook's Tip

To extract the water from a coconut, pierce the eyes on top and turn the coconut upside down over a bowl.

Duck Consommé

This soup is a good example of the influence that the Vietnamese community in France has had on modern French cooking.

Serves 4

1 duck carcass (raw or cooked), plus 2 legs or any giblets, trimmed of fat
1 large onion, unpeeled, root off
2 carrots, cut into chunks
1 parsnip, cut into chunks
1 leek, cut into chunks
2–4 garlic cloves, crushed
2.5cm/1in piece fresh root ginger, peeled and sliced
15ml/1 tbsp black peppercorns
4–6 sprigs of fresh thyme
small bunch of coriander (cilantro), leaves and stems separated

For the garnish

1 small carrot
1 small leek, halved lengthways
4–6 shiitake mushrooms, sliced
soy sauce
2 spring onions, sliced
watercress, rocket (arugula) or finely shredded Chinese leaves
ground black pepper

1 Put the duck carcass and legs or giblets, onion, carrots, parsnip, leek and garlic in a large, heavy wok or pan or flameproof casserole. Add the ginger, peppercorns, thyme and coriander stems, cover with cold water and bring to the boil, skimming off any foam that rises to the surface.

2 Reduce the heat and simmer gently for 1½–2 hours, then strain through a muslin-lined (cheesecloth) sieve (strainer) into a bowl, discarding the bones and vegetables.

3 Cool the stock and chill for several hours or overnight. Skim off congealed fat and blot with kitchen paper.

4 For the garnish, cut the carrot and leek into 5cm/2in pieces and slice into thin strips. Place in a pan with the mushrooms.

5 Pour in the stock and add a few dashes of soy sauce and some pepper. Bring to the boil, skimming off any foam. Taste and adjust the seasoning. Stir in the spring onions and watercress, rocket or Chinese leaves. Ladle the consommé into warmed bowls and sprinkle with the coriander leaves before serving.

Duck, Nut and Date Energy 604kcal/2512kJ; Protein 43.8g; Carbohydrate 8.9g, of which sugars 3.6g; Fat 44g, of which saturates 9.2g; Cholesterol 165mg; Calcium 49mg; Fibre 3.1g; Sodium 231mg.
Duck Consommé Energy 12kcal/51kJ; Protein 1.4g; Carbohydrate 1.9g, of which sugars 1.6g; Fat 0.6g, of which saturates 0.2g; Cholesterol 0mg; Calcium 13mg; Fibre 1g; Sodium 550mg.

Pork Broth with Winter Melon

Winter melon is excellent for absorbing the rich flavours of this recipe. Traditionally the soup is served in China in a scooped-out winter-melon shell for a dramatic effect.

Serves 4

350g/12oz winter melon
25g/1oz light golden tiger lilies, soaked in hot water for 20 minutes
salt and ground black pepper
1 small bunch coriander (cilantro) and mint, stalks removed, leaves chopped, to garnish

For the stock

25g/1oz dried shrimp, soaked in water for 15 minutes
500g/1¼lb pork ribs
1 onion, peeled and quartered
175g/6oz carrots, peeled and cut into chunks
15ml/1 tbsp fish sauce
15ml/1 tbsp soy sauce
4 black peppercorns

1 To make the stock, drain and rinse the dried shrimp. Put the pork ribs in a large pan or wok and cover with 2 litres/3½ pints /8 cups water. Bring the water to the boil, skim off any fat, and add the dried shrimp and the remaining stock ingredients. Cover and simmer for 1½ hours, then skim again. Continue simmering, uncovered, for a further 30 minutes. Strain and check the seasoning. You should have about 1.5 litres/2½ pints/6¼ cups.

2 Halve the winter melon lengthways and remove the seeds and inner membrane. Finely slice the flesh into half-moons. Squeeze the soaked tiger lilies dry and tie them in a knot.

3 Bring the stock to the boil in a deep pan or wok. Reduce the heat and add the winter melon and tiger lilies.

4 Simmer for 15–20 minutes, or until the melon is tender. Season to taste, and serve in bowls with the herbs on the top.

Variation

Winter melon or musk melon has porous white flesh and a scent reminiscent of courgettes (zucchini). Use butternut squash or any other squash for an excellent variation.

Pork and Egg Ramen-style Soup

This is a famous Japanese soup.

Serves 4

250g/9oz dried ramen noodles

For the stock

4 spring onions (scallions)
7.5cm/3in fresh root ginger, sliced
2 raw chicken carcasses
1 large onion, quartered
4 garlic cloves
1 large carrot, roughly chopped
1 egg shell
120ml/4fl oz/½ cup sake
60ml/4 tbsp shoyu or soy sauce
2.5ml/½ tsp salt

For the pot-roast pork

500g/1¼lb pork shoulder, boned
30ml/2 tbsp vegetable oil
2 spring onions (scallions), chopped
2.5cm/1in fresh root ginger, peeled and sliced
15ml/1 tbsp sake
45ml/3 tbsp shoyu or soy sauce
15ml/1 tbsp sugar

For the toppings

2 hard-boiled eggs
150g/5oz pickled bamboo shoots, soaked for 30 minutes and drained
½ nori sheet, broken into pieces
2 spring onions (scallions), chopped
ground white pepper
sesame oil or chilli oil

1 To make the stock, bruise the spring onions and ginger. Boil 1.5 litres/2½ pints/6¼ cups water in a wok. Add the chicken bones and boil for 5 minutes. Drain and rinse the bones. Bring another 2 litres/3½ pints/8 cups water to the boil. Add the bones and other stock ingredients, except the shoyu and salt. Simmer gently for up to 2 hours, until reduced by half. Strain.

2 For the pork, roll the meat up tightly and tie. Heat the oil, stir in the spring onions and ginger. Add the meat, and brown it.

3 Sprinkle with sake and add 400ml/14fl oz/1⅔ cups water, the shoyu and sugar. Boil, then cover and cook for 25–30 minutes, turning every 5 minutes. Remove from the heat. Slice the pork.

4 Boil 1 litre/1¾ pints/4 cups soup stock. Add the shoyu and salt. Cook the noodles according to the packet instructions. Drain. Divide among four bowls. Cover with soup. Add the boiled eggs, pork, pickled bamboo shoots, and nori. Sprinkle with spring onions. Serve with pepper and sesame or chilli oil.

Pork Broth with Melon Energy 25kcal/103kJ; Protein 1.6g; Carbohydrate 2.6g, of which sugars 1.9g; Fat 0.9g, of which saturates 0.1g; Cholesterol 0mg; Calcium 55mg; Fibre 1.5g; Sodium 616mg.
Pork and Egg Energy 521kcal/2193kJ; Protein 38.9g; Carbohydrate 55.6g, of which sugars 8.7g; Fat 17.5g, of which saturates 3.2g; Cholesterol 174mg; Calcium 57mg; Fibre 3g; Sodium 843mg.

Wonton Soup

In China, wonton soup is generally served as a snack or dim sum rather than as a soup course during a large meal. You need to use a good-quality stock.

Serves 4

175g/6oz pork, not too lean, roughly chopped
50g/2oz prawns (shrimp), chopped
5ml/1 tsp light brown sugar
15ml/1 tbsp Chinese rice wine or dry sherry
15ml/1 tbsp light soy sauce
5ml/1 tsp finely chopped spring onions (scallions)
5ml/1 tsp finely chopped root ginger
24 ready-made wonton wrappers
about 750ml/1¼ pints/3 cups chicken or vegetable stock

To serve

15ml/1 tbsp light soy sauce
finely chopped spring onions (scallions), to garnish

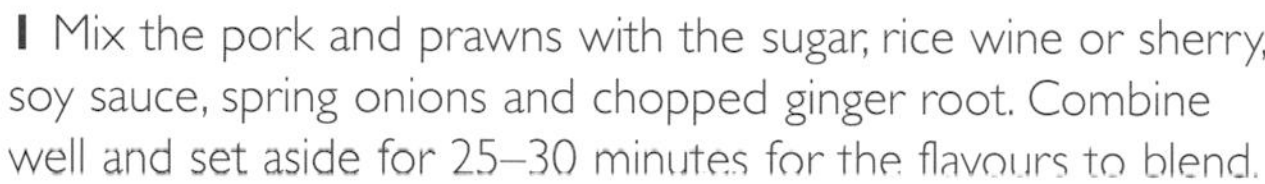

1 Mix the pork and prawns with the sugar, rice wine or sherry, soy sauce, spring onions and chopped ginger root. Combine well and set aside for 25–30 minutes for the flavours to blend.

2 Place about 5ml/1 tsp of the pork and prawn filling at the centre of each wonton wrapper.

3 Holding the wonton in the palm of your hand, wet the edges of the wrapper with a little water and press them together with your fingers to seal, then fold over. Fill all the wrappers.

4 Bring the stock to a rolling boil in a wok or large heavy pan, add the wontons and cook for 4–5 minutes.

5 Season with the soy sauce, sprinkle with finely chopped spring onions, and serve in warmed individual bowls.

Variation

If you feel like treating yourself, these wontons can be made with lobster meat rather than prawns. It will increase the cost of the dish, but the resulting taste will be a special treat.

Tamarind Pork and Vegetable Soup

Sour soups, usually flavoured with tamarind or lime, are very popular in South-east Asia. They can be made with any combination of meat or fish and vegetables. Tamarind pods or kamias, a sour fruit similar in shape to star fruit, are used as souring agents in Filipino recipes.

Serves 4–6

2 litres/3½ pints/8 cups pork or chicken stock, or a mixture of stock and water
15–30ml/1–2 tbsp tamarind paste (see Cook's Tip)
30ml/2 tbsp fish sauce
25g/1oz fresh root ginger, finely grated
1 yam or sweet potato, cut into bitesize chunks
8–10 snake (yard-long beans) or 225g/8oz green beans, topped and tailed
225g/8oz water spinach or ordinary spinach, well rinsed
350g/12oz pork tenderloin, sliced widthways
2–3 spring onions (scallions), white parts only, finely sliced, to garnish
salt and freshly ground black pepper

1 Bring the stock to the boil in a wok or deep pan. Stir in the tamarind paste, fish sauce and ginger, reduce the heat and simmer for about 20 minutes. Season with salt and lots of pepper.

2 Add the yam and snake beans to the pan and bring back to the boil, then immediately reduce the heat and cook gently for 3–4 minutes, until the yam is tender.

3 Stir in the spinach and the sliced pork and simmer gently for 2–3 minutes, until the pork is just cooked and turns opaque.

4 Ladle the soup into individual warmed bowls and sprinkle the sliced spring onions over the top.

Cook's Tip

Tamarind is a sour-sweet fruit, which becomes extremely sour when dried. Fresh tamarind pods, packaged tamarind pulp and pots of tamarind paste are all available in Middle-Eastern, Indian, African and South-east Asian food shops.

Wonton Soup Energy 134kcal/568kJ; Protein 13.6g; Carbohydrate 16.3g, of which sugars 1.9g; Fat 2.1g, of which saturates 0.7g; Cholesterol 52mg; Calcium 42mg; Fibre 0.6g; Sodium 589mg.
Pork and Vegetable Energy 126kcal/532kJ; Protein 14g; Carbohydrate 12.3g, of which sugars 4.1g; Fat 2.7g, of which saturates 0.9g; Cholesterol 37mg; Calcium 31mg; Fibre 2g; Sodium 417mg.

Thick Pork and Vegetable Soup

This delicious stew of tender pork loin is vibrantly coloured with red chilli and has a fiery taste to match. The succulent pork is cooked with an array of vegetables in an aromatic, thick soup with an uplifting kick of ginger.

Serves 4

250g/9oz pork loin
30ml/2 tbsp vegetable oil
1 garlic clove, crushed
30ml/2 tbsp gochujang chilli paste
5ml/1 tsp Korean chilli powder
90g/3½oz potato, cubed
20g/¾oz fresh root ginger, peeled
1 green chilli, sliced
½ leek, sliced
1 courgette (zucchini), sliced
5ml/1 tsp sesame oil
50g/2oz watercress or rocket (arugula), roughly chopped
5ml/1 tsp sesame seeds, to garnish

1 Trim any excess fat from the pork loin, and roughly cut the meat into bitesize cubes.

2 Place a heavy pan or wok over a high heat and add the vegetable oil. Add the garlic and pork and stir until the meat is lightly browned on all sides. Then add the gochujang chilli paste and chilli powder and briefly sauté the ingredients, evenly coating the meat with the spices.

3 Add the potato, fresh root ginger and chilli and then pour in enough water to cover all the ingredients. Bring the pan to the boil and add the leek, courgette and sesame oil. Stir the mixture well and cover the pan. Cook over a high heat for 3 minutes, then reduce the heat and simmer for a further 5 minutes. Skim off any excess fat from the surface as the dish stews.

4 Remove from the heat and stir in the watercress or rocket. Discard the root ginger and ladle the stew into bowls. Garnish with the sesame seeds before serving.

Cook's Tip

To make this dish spicier, increase the quantity of gochujang chilli paste, but be careful as a little makes a big difference.

Rice Soup with Pork and Roasted Garlic

This warming and sustaining rice soup combines the the Filipino rice culture with the Spanish colonial culinary techniques of browning and sautéing. Chicken breast fillet may be used instead of pork.

Serves 4–6

15–30ml/1–2 tbsp palm or groundnut (peanut) oil
1 large onion, finely chopped.
2 garlic cloves, finely chopped
25g/1oz fresh root ginger, finely chopped
350g/12oz lean boneless pork, cut into bitesize slices
5–6 black peppercorns
115g/4oz/1 cup plus 15ml/1 tbsp short grain rice
2 litres/3½ pints/8 cups pork or chicken stock
30ml/2 tbsp fish sauce
salt

To serve

2 garlic cloves, finely chopped
2 spring onions (scallions), white parts only, finely sliced
2–3 fresh green or red chillies, seeded and quartered lengthways

1 Heat the oil in a wok or deep, heavy pan that has a lid. Stir in the onion, garlic and ginger and fry until fragrant and beginning to colour. Add the pork and fry, stirring frequently, for 5–6 minutes, until lightly browned. Stir in the peppercorns.

2 Meanwhile, put the rice in a sieve (strainer), rinse under cold running water until the water runs clear, then drain. Toss the rice into the pan, making sure that it is coated in the mixture. Pour in the stock, add the fish sauce and bring to the boil. Reduce the heat and partially cover.

3 Simmer for about 40 minutes, stirring the dish occasionally to make sure that the rice does not stick to the bottom of the pan. Season with salt to taste.

4 Just before serving, dry-fry the garlic in a small, heavy pan, until golden brown, then stir it into the soup. Ladle the soup into individual warmed bowls and sprinkle the spring onions over the top. Serve the chillies separately, to chew on.

Pork and Vegetable Energy 220kcal/918kJ; Protein 17.2g; Carbohydrate 15.2g, of which sugars 2.2g; Fat 10.6g, of which saturates 2g; Cholesterol 39mg; Calcium 45mg; Fibre 1.6g; Sodium 55mg.
Rice with Pork Energy 195kcal/813kJ; Protein 14.8g; Carbohydrate 19.9g, of which sugars 3.4g; Fat 6.2g, of which saturates 1.3g; Cholesterol 37mg; Calcium 24mg; Fibre 0.8g; Sodium 399mg.

Lamb and Cucumber Soup with Sesame Oil

This is a very simple soup to prepare, and the creative mixture of flavours make it quite delicious.

Serves 4

225g/8oz lamb steak
2.5ml/½ tsp sesame oil
15ml/1 tbsp light soy sauce
10ml/2 tsp Chinese rice wine or dry sherry
7.5cm/3in piece cucumber
750ml/1¼ pints/3 cups chicken or vegetable stock
15ml/1 tbsp rice vinegar
salt and ground white pepper

1 Trim off any excess fat from the lamb. Thinly slice the lamb into small pieces and place in a bowl. Add the sesame oil, the soy sauce, and the wine or sherry. Mix well. then cover and set aside to marinate for 25–30 minutes. Discard the marinade.

2 Halve the cucumber lengthways (do not peel), then cut it into thin slices diagonally.

3 In a wok or saucepan, bring the stock to a rolling boil, add the lamb and stir. Simmer for 5 minutes until the lamb is cooked.

4 Bring the soup back to the boil, then add the cucumber slices, vinegar and seasoning. Bring back to the boil, remove from the heat and serve at once in warmed bowls.

Variations

- *Use fine-cut, lean boneless pork instead of lamb.*
- *Add a little chopped fresh root ginger to spice up the soup.*
- *For a sweet-sour soup, stir in honey to taste – it is delicious with both lamb and pork*
- *For a really punchy flavour, thinly slice a mild to medium fresh green chilli and add it to the soup with a handful of chopped fresh mint leaves.*
- *For additional crunch, cut some celery and spring onions (scallions) into fine shreds and soak them in iced water until they curl. Drain, dry and use as a garnish.*

Spicy Tripe Soup with Citrus

This popular Indonesian soup is packed with spices, lemon grass and lime. Locally, tripe is served chewy in this spicy soup, with its sambal on the side. Supermarkets and butchers usually sell tripe boiled, so step 1 may not be needed. Look for tripe with a pale off-white colour.

Serves 4

900g/2lb beef tripe, cleaned
250ml/8fl oz/1 cup rice wine vinegar
2 litres/3½ pints/8 cups beef stock or water
2–3 garlic cloves, crushed whole
2 lemon grass stalks
25g/1oz fresh root ginger, finely grated
3–4 kaffir lime leaves
225g/8oz white radish or turnip, finely sliced
15ml/1 tbsp palm, groundnut (peanut) or vegetable oil
4 shallots, finely sliced
salt and ground black pepper

For the sambal

2 garlic cloves, crushed
2–3 hot red chillies, seeded and finely chopped
15ml/1 tbsp palm, groundnut (peanut) or vegetable oil
15ml/1 tbsp chilli and shrimp paste
25ml/1½ tbsp tomato purée (paste)

1 Simmer the tripe in a large pan of salted water with the vinegar added. Allow 1 hour for a chewy result or 4–5 hours for tender tripe, topping up the water as necessary. Drain and cut into squares.

2 For the sambal, fry the garlic and chillies in the oil. Stir in the chilli, shrimp and tomato pastes until thoroughly mixed. Tip the paste into a small dish and put aside.

3 Bring the stock or water to the boil in a large wok. Reduce the heat and add the tripe, garlic, lemon grass, ginger, lime leaves and radish or turnip and seasoning. Cook gently for 20 minutes.

4 Heat the oil in a small frying pan. Add the shallots and fry for about 5 minutes until golden brown. Drain on kitchen paper.

5 Serve the soup topped with shallots with the spicy sambal, which can be added in a dollop and stirred in as required.

Lamb and Cucumber Energy 105kcal/438kJ; Protein 11.2g; Carbohydrate 0.4g, of which sugars 0.3g; Fat 6.6g, of which saturates 3g; Cholesterol 43mg; Calcium 6mg; Fibre 0g; Sodium 316mg.
Spicy Tripe Soup Energy 160kcal/668kJ; Protein 19.2g; Carbohydrate 5.5g, of which sugars 4.8g; Fat 7g, of which saturates 1.1g; Cholesterol 163mg; Calcium 198mg; Fibre 1.9g; Sodium 299mg.

Beef and Aubergine Soup

A wonderful Khmer dish, this soup is sweet and spicy.

Serves 6

4 dried New Mexico chillies
15ml/1 tbsp vegetable oil
75ml/5 tbsp curry paste
2–3 fresh red chillies
75ml/5 tbsp tamarind extract
15–30ml/1–2 tbsp fish sauce
30ml/2 tbsp palm sugar (jaggery)
1 bunch watercress or rocket (arugula), trimmed and chopped
12 aubergines (eggplants), cut into bitesize chunks
1 handful fresh curry leaves
sea salt and ground black pepper

For the stock

1kg/2¼lb beef shanks or brisket
2 large onions, quartered
2–3 carrots, cut into chunks
90g/3½oz fresh root ginger, sliced
2 cinnamon sticks
4 star anise
5ml/1 tsp black peppercorns
30ml/2 tbsp soy sauce
45–60ml/3–4 tbsp fish sauce

1 To make the stock, mix all the ingredients apart from the soy sauce and fish sauce in a wok or large pan. Cover the ingredients with 3 litres/5 pints/12 cups water and bring to the boil. Simmer, covered, for 2–3 hours.

2 Meanwhile, soak the New Mexico chillies in water for 30 minutes. Split them open, remove the seeds and scrape out the pulp. Stir the sauces into the stock and simmer, uncovered, until it has reduced to about 2 litres/3½ pints/8 cups.

3 Skim the sauce, strain into a bowl and set aside. Tear the meat into thin strips and put half of it aside for the soup. Save the rest of the meat for another dish.

4 Heat the oil in a wok. Stir in the curry paste and pulp with the whole chillies. Stir until the mixture sizzles. Add the tamarind extract, fish sauce, sugar and reserved stock. Stir well and bring to the boil. Add the reserved beef, watercress or rocket and aubergines. Continue cooking for 20 minutes.

5 Dry-fry the curry leaves until they begin to crackle. Season the soup, stir in half the curry leaves and serve in heated bowls, with the remaining leaves on top.

Indonesian Beef Soup with Lime

This is a delicious soupy stew from Indonesia. Serve the soup with a bowl of rice and a chilli sambal, bearing in mind that the quantity of rice should be great, as the role of the soup is to moisten and flavour it.

Serves 4

30ml/2 tbsp palm, groundnut (peanut) or corn oil
150g/5oz lean beef, cut into thin strips
500ml/17fl oz/generous 2 cups coconut milk
10ml/2 tsp sugar
1 large aubergine (eggplant), cut into wedges
3–4 kaffir lime leaves
juice of 1 lime
salt

For the spice paste

4 shallots, chopped
4 fresh red Thai chillies, seeded and chopped
25g/1oz fresh root ginger, chopped
2.5ml/½ tsp ground turmeric
2 garlic cloves, chopped
5ml/1 tsp coriander seeds
2.5ml/½ tsp cumin seeds
2–3 candlenuts or macadamia nuts

To serve

cooked rice
1 lime, quartered
chilli sambal

1 To make the spice paste, use a mortar and pestle to grind all the ingredients together to form a textured paste, or whiz them together in a food processor or blender.

2 Heat the oil in a wok or deep pan, stir in the spice paste and fry for 2–3 minutes until fragrant.

3 Add the beef to the wok, stirring to coat it well in the spice paste, then add the coconut milk and sugar. Bring to the boil, then reduce the heat and simmer gently for 10 minutes.

4 Add the aubergine wedges and kaffir lime leaves to the pan and cook gently for a further 5–10 minutes, until tender but not mushy. Stir in the lime juice and season with salt to taste.

5 Ladle the soup into individual warmed bowls and serve with bowls of cooked rice to spoon the soup over, wedges of lime to squeeze on the top and a chilli sambal.

Beef and Aubergine Energy 303kcal/1276kJ; Protein 36.7g; Carbohydrate 16.5g, of which sugars 14.5g; Fat 10.6g, of which saturates 4.2g; Cholesterol 90mg; Calcium 35mg; Fibre 2.4g; Sodium 303mg.
Indonesian Beef Soup Energy 224kcal/938kJ; Protein 12.1g; Carbohydrate 14.6g, of which sugars 12.6g; Fat 13.6g, of which saturates 3.2g; Cholesterol 22mg; Calcium 79mg; Fibre 3g; Sodium 181mg.

Beef Noodle Soup

A steaming bowl of beef noodle soup is both nutritious and filling, and makes an intensely satisfying meal at any time of day.

Serves 6

500g/1¼lb dried noodles, soaked in water for 20 minutes
1 onion, halved and finely sliced
6–8 spring onions (scallions), cut into long pieces
2–3 fresh red chillies, seeded and finely sliced
115g/4oz/½ cup beansprouts
1 large bunch each fresh coriander (cilantro) and mint, stalks removed, leaves chopped, to garnish
2 limes, cut in wedges, and hoisin sauce and fish sauce, to serve

For the stock
1.5kg/3lb 5oz oxtail, trimmed of fat and cut into thick pieces
1kg/2¼lb beef shank or brisket
2 large onions
2 carrots
7.5cm/3in fresh root ginger, cut into chunks
6 cloves
2 cinnamon sticks
6 star anise
5ml/1 tsp black peppercorns
30ml/2 tbsp soy sauce
45–60ml/3–4 tbsp fish sauce
salt

1 To make the stock, put the oxtail into a large, deep wok or pan and cover with water. Bring it to the boil and cook for 10 minutes. Drain the oxtail, rinsing off any scum, and return it to the clean pan with the other stock ingredients, apart from the fish sauce. Cover with 3 litres/5¼ pints/12 cups water. Boil, then simmer for 2–3 hours with the lid on, and 1 hour without it. Skim, then strain 2 litres/3½ pints/8 cups stock into a wok.

2 Cut the cooked meat into thin pieces; discard the bones. Bring the stock to the boil, stir in the fish sauce, season to taste, and keep simmering until ready to use.

3 Cook the noodles in boiling water until tender, then drain and divide among six wide soup bowls. Top each serving with beef, onion, spring onions, chillies and beansprouts.

4 Ladle the hot stock over the top of the beef and noodles, sprinkle the soup with fresh herbs and serve with the lime wedges to squeeze over and the sauces to pass around.

Chinese Leaf Soup with Meatballs

This wonderfully fragrant combination makes for a hearty, warming soup for a chilly winter evening.

Serves 4

10 dried shiitake mushrooms
90g/3½oz bean thread noodles
30ml/2 tbsp sunflower oil
1.5 litres/2½ pints/6¼ cups beef or chicken stock
50ml/3½ tbsp light soy sauce
5ml/1 tsp sugar
150g/5oz enokitake mushrooms or tiny button (white) mushrooms, trimmed
200g/7oz Chinese leaves (Chinese cabbage), very thinly sliced
salt and ground black pepper

For the meatballs
675g/1½lb minced (ground) beef or pork
10ml/2 tsp finely grated garlic
10ml/2 tsp finely grated fresh root ginger
1 fresh red chilli, seeded and chopped
6 spring onions (scallions), sliced
1 egg white
15ml/1 tbsp cornflour (cornstarch)
15ml/1 tbsp Chinese rice wine

1 Place the dried mushrooms in a medium bowl and pour over 250ml/8fl oz/1 cup boiling water. Leave to soak for 30 minutes and then squeeze dry, reserving the liquid. Remove and discard the mushroom stems; thickly slice the caps and set aside.

2 Put the noodles in a large bowl and pour over boiling water to cover. Soak for 3–4 minutes, then drain, rinse and set aside.

3 For the meatballs, place all the ingredients with seasoning in a food processor. Process to combine well. Divide the mixture into 30 portions, then shape each into a ball. Heat the stock.

4 Heat a wok or large heavy pan and add the sunflower oil. Fry the meatballs, in batches, for 2–3 minutes on each side. Remove with a slotted spoon and drain on kitchen paper.

5 Add the meatballs to the simmering beef stock with the soy sauce, sugar, shiitake mushrooms and reserved soaking liquid. Cook gently for 20–25 minutes.

6 Add the noodles, enokitake mushrooms and cabbage and cook gently for 4–5 minutes. Serve in wide bowls.

Beef Noodle Soup Energy 180kcal/748kJ; Protein 10.8g; Carbohydrate 4.8g, of which sugars 4.1g; Fat 4.2g, of which saturates 1.6g; Cholesterol 24mg; Calcium 35mg; Fibre 1g; Sodium 219mg.
Chinese Leaf with Meatballs Energy 102kcal/424kJ; Protein 5.4g; Carbohydrate 5.8g, of which sugars 3g; Fat 6.5g, of which saturates 1.9g; Cholesterol 13mg; Calcium 39mg; Fibre 0.9g; Sodium 308mg.

Tung Tong

Popularly called 'gold bags', these crisp pastry purses from Thailand have a coriander-flavoured filling that is based on water chestnuts and corn. Tung tong are the perfect vegetarian snack, and they look very impressive.

Makes 18

18 spring roll wrappers, about 8cm/3in square, thawed if frozen
oil, for deep-frying
plum sauce, to serve

For the filling

4 baby corn cobs
130g/4½oz can water chestnuts, drained and chopped
1 shallot, coarsely chopped
1 egg, separated
30ml/2 tbsp cornflour (cornstarch)
small bunch fresh coriander (cilantro), chopped
salt and ground black pepper

1 Make the filling. Place the baby corn cobs, chopped water chestnuts, coarsely chopped shallot and egg yolk in a food processor or blender. Process to a coarse paste. Place the egg white in a cup and whisk it lightly with a fork.

2 Put the cornflour in a small pan and stir in 60ml/4 tbsp water until smooth. Add the corn mixture and chopped coriander and season with salt and pepper to taste. Cook over a low heat, stirring constantly, until it has thickened.

3 Leave the filling to cool slightly, then place 5ml/1 tsp in the centre of a spring roll wrapper. Brush the edges with the beaten egg white, then gather up the points and press them firmly together to make a pouch or bag.

4 Repeat with the remaining spring roll wrappers and filling, keeping the finished bags and the wrappers covered until needed so they do not dry out.

5 Heat the oil in a deep-fryer or wok until a cube of bread added to the oil browns in about 45 seconds. Fry the bags in batches for about 5 minutes, until golden brown.

6 Drain on kitchen paper and serve hot, with the plum sauce.

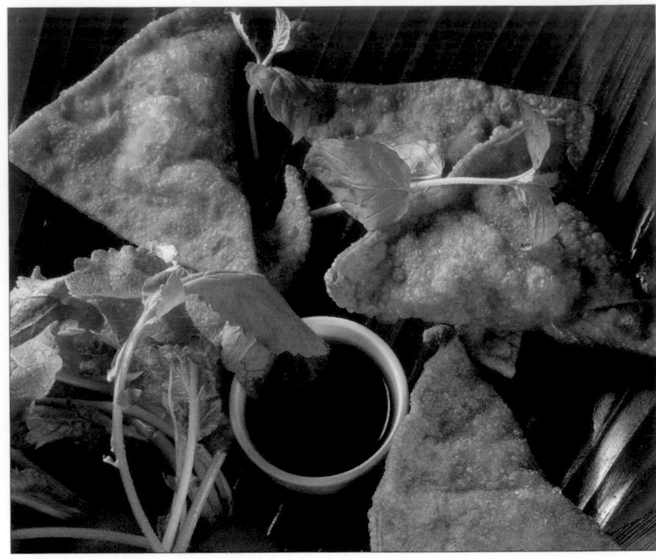

Fried Wontons

These delicious vegetarian wontons are filled with a mixture of tofu, spring onions, garlic and ginger.

Makes 30

30 wonton wrappers
1 egg, beaten
oil, for deep-frying

For the filling

10ml/2 tsp vegetable oil
15ml/1 tbsp grated fresh root ginger
2 garlic cloves, finely chopped
225g/8oz firm tofu
6 spring onions (scallions), chopped
10ml/2 tsp sesame oil
15ml/1 tbsp soy sauce
salt and ground black pepper

For the dipping sauce

30ml/2 tbsp soy sauce
15ml/1 tbsp sesame oil
15ml/1 tbsp rice vinegar
2.5ml/½ tsp chilli oil
2.5ml/½ tsp honey
30ml/2 tbsp water

1 Prepare a large baking sheet or tray to hold the completed wontons by lining it with baking parchment or sprinkling it lightly with flour, then set it aside.

2 To make the filling, heat the oil in a wok or large frying pan. Add the ginger and garlic and fry for 30 seconds. Crumble in the tofu and stir-fry for a few minutes. Add the spring onions, sesame oil and soy sauce to the pan. Stir well and taste for seasoning. Remove from the heat and set aside to cool.

3 Meanwhile, make the dipping sauce by combining all the ingredients in a bowl and mixing well.

4 Place a wonton wrapper on a board in a diamond position. Brush the edges lightly with beaten egg. Spoon 5ml/1 tsp of the filling into the centre of the wonton wrapper. Pull the top corner down to the bottom corner to make a triangle. Press the edges firmly to seal. Place on the prepared baking sheet. Repeat with the rest of the wonton wrappers.

5 Pour enough oil to deep-fry the wontons into a wok and heat. Carefully add the wontons, a few at a time, and cook for a few minutes until golden brown. Drain on kitchen paper, then serve at once with the dipping sauce.

Tung Tong Energy 55kcal/229kJ; Protein 1.2g; Carbohydrate 6.3g, of which sugars 0.4g; Fat 2.9g, of which saturates 0.4g; Cholesterol 12mg; Calcium 19mg; Fibre 0.5g; Sodium 42mg.
Fried Wontons Energy 68kcal/284kJ; Protein 1.6g; Carbohydrate 8.1g, of which sugars 0.4g; Fat 3.5g, of which saturates 0.4g; Cholesterol 0mg; Calcium 53mg; Fibre 0.3g; Sodium 108mg.

Potato and Shallot Samosas

Most samosas are deep-fried, but these are baked, with the filling made in a wok. They are perfect for parties, since the pastries need no last-minute attention.

Makes 25

1 large potato, about 250g/9oz, diced
15ml/1 tbsp groundnut (peanut) oil
2 shallots, finely chopped
1 garlic clove, finely chopped
60ml/4 tbsp coconut milk
5ml/1 tsp Thai red or green curry paste
75g/3oz/¾ cup peas
juice of ½ lime
25 samosa wrappers or 10 x 5cm/4 x 2in strips of filo pastry
salt and ground black pepper
oil, for brushing

1 Preheat the oven to 220°C/425°F/Gas 7. Bring a small pan of water to the boil, add the diced potato, cover and cook for 10–15 minutes, until tender. Drain and set aside.

2 Meanwhile, heat the groundnut oil in a wok and cook the shallots and garlic over a medium heat, stirring occasionally, for 4–5 minutes, until softened and golden.

3 Add the drained diced potato, coconut milk, red or green curry paste, peas and lime juice to the wok. Mash together coarsely with a wooden spoon.

4 Season to taste with salt and pepper and cook over a low heat for 2–3 minutes, then remove the pan from the heat and set aside until the mixture has cooled a little.

5 Lay a samosa wrapper or filo strip flat on the work surface. Brush with a little oil, then place a generous teaspoonful of the mixture in the middle of one end. Turn one corner diagonally over the filling to meet the long edge.

6 Continue folding over the filling, keeping the triangular shape as you work down the strip. Brush with a little more oil if necessary and place on a baking sheet. Repeat with the other samosas.

7 Bake the samosas for 15 minutes, or until the pastry is golden and crisp. Leave to cool slightly before serving.

Rice Paper Parcels

Translucent rice paper makes a crisp wrapping for the lightly spiced filling in these parcels.

Serves 4

90ml/6 tbsp plain (all-purpose) flour
12 medium rice paper wrappers
sunflower oil, for deep-frying
500g/1¼lb choi sum or Chinese greens, roughly sliced
egg fried rice, to serve

For the filling

30ml/2 tbsp sunflower oil
90g/3½oz shiitake mushrooms, stalks discarded, and finely chopped
30ml/2 tbsp chopped garlic
90g/3½oz water chestnuts, finely chopped
90g/3½oz firm tofu, finely chopped
2 spring onions (scallions), finely chopped
½ red (bell) pepper, seeded and finely chopped
50g/2oz mangetouts (snow peas), finely chopped
15ml/1 tbsp light soy sauce
15ml/1 tbsp sweet chilli sauce
45ml/3 tbsp chopped fresh coriander (cilantro)
30ml/2 tbsp chopped fresh mint leaves

1 Heat the oil in a large wok, add the mushrooms and stir-fry for 3–4 minutes. Add the garlic, water chestnuts, tofu, spring onions, red pepper and mangetout, and stir-fry for 2–3 minutes. Add the soy and chilli sauces to the wok. Remove from the heat, stir in the coriander and mint, and leave to cool completely.

2 Place the flour in a bowl and stir in 105ml/7 tbsp of cold water to make a thick, smooth paste. Fill a bowl with warm water and dip a rice wrapper in it for a few minutes until softened. Remove and drain on a dish towel.

3 Spoon a portion of the filling on each wrapper. Fold in each side and roll up tightly. Seal the ends with a little flour paste.

4 Fill a wok one-third full with the oil and heat to 180°C/350°F. Working in batches of 2–3, deep-fry the parcels for 3 minutes until crisp. Drain on kitchen paper and keep warm.

5 Pour off most of the oil, reserving 30ml/2 tbsp. Heat the wok, add the choi sum and stir-fry for 3–4 minutes. Divide among four bowls and top with the parcels. Serve with egg fried rice.

Potato and Shallot Samosas Energy 42Kcal/178kJ; Protein 1.2g; Carbohydrate 8.5g, of which sugars 0.6g; Fat 0.6g, of which saturates 0.1g; Cholesterol 0mg; Calcium 14mg; Fibre 0.5g; Sodium 4mg.
Rice Paper Parcels Energy 252Kcal/1051kJ; Protein 10.2g; Carbohydrate 34.6g, of which sugars 6.6g; Fat 8.5g, of which saturates 1g; Cholesterol 0mg; Calcium 448mg; Fibre 6.8g; Sodium 313mg.

Peanut Crackers

These tasty, nutty crackers are ideal to enjoy as a appetizer to take the edge off your hunger while you wait for your meal.

Serves 4–5

225g/8oz/1¼ cups rice flour
5ml/1 tsp baking powder
5ml/1 tsp ground turmeric
5ml/1 tsp ground coriander
300ml/½ pint/1¼ cups coconut milk
115g/4oz/¾ cup unsalted peanuts, coarsely chopped or crushed
2–3 candlenuts or macadamia nuts, crushed
2–3 garlic cloves, peeled and crushed
corn or groundnut (peanut) oil, for shallow frying
salt and ground black pepper
chilli sambal, for dipping (optional)

To season

5ml/1 tsp paprika or fine chilli flakes
salt

1 Put the rice flour, baking powder, ground turmeric and ground coriander into a bowl. Make a well in the centre, pour in the coconut milk and stir to mix well, drawing in the flour from the sides. Beat well to make a smooth batter.

2 Add the peanuts, candlenuts or macadamia nuts and garlic and mix well. Season with salt and pepper, and put aside for 30 minutes.

3 Meanwhile, in a small bowl, prepare the seasoning by mixing the paprika or fine chilli flakes with a little salt.

4 Heat a thin layer of oil in a wok or large frying pan and drop in a spoonful of batter for each cracker – the size of spoon doesn't matter as the crackers are supposed to vary in size.

5 Work in batches, flipping the crackers over when the lacy edges become crispy and golden brown. Drain on kitchen paper and toss them into a basket.

6 Sprinkle the paprika and salt over the crackers and toss them lightly for an even dusting of seasoning.

7 Serve the peanut crackers immediately with chilli sambal.

Vegetable Tempura

Serves 4

2 medium courgettes (zucchini)
½ medium aubergine (eggplant)
1 large carrot
½ small Spanish (Bermuda) onion
1 egg
120ml/4fl oz/½ cup iced water
115g/4oz/1 cup plain (all-purpose) flour
salt and ground black pepper
vegetable oil, for deep-frying
salt, lemon and soy sauce, to serve

1 Cut the courgettes, aubergine and carrot into strips about 7.5–10cm/3–4in long and 3mm/⅛in wide. Thinly slice the onion from top to base, discarding the plump pieces in the middle. Mix the vegetables together and season with salt and pepper.

2 Mix the egg and iced water in a bowl, sift in the flour and mix briefly with a fork. Add the vegetables and mix to combine.

3 Half-fill a wok with oil and heat to 180°C/350°F. Lower one tablespoon of the mixture at a time into the oil. Deep-fry in batches for approximately 3 minutes, until crisp. Drain the tempura on kitchen paper. Serve with salt, lemon and soy sauce.

Spiced Yam Slices

Serves 8

1kg/2¼lb yam
1 tsp salt or to taste
1 tsp ground turmeric
5–7.5ml1–1½ tsp chilli powder
½ tsp aniseed seeds
25g/1oz/¼ cup gram flour, sifted
15g/½oz/1 tbsp ground rice
oil for deep-frying
relish, to serve

1 Peel the yam and cut into 5mm/¼in thick slices. Put the salt, turmeric, chilli powder, aniseed, flour and rice in a bowl and mix well. Add the yam slices and mix until they are fully coated.

2 Heat the oil for deep-frying in a wok. Fry the yam slices in batches in a single layer for 3–4 minutes.

3 Drain the yam slices on kitchen paper. Serve with a relish, such as mango chutney, a spicy pickle or cucumber raita.

Peanut Crackers Energy 403kcal/1679kJ; Protein 9.7g; Carbohydrate 42.2g, of which sugars 4.6g; Fat 21.3g, of which saturates 3.4g; Cholesterol 0mg; Calcium 44mg; Fibre 2.5g; Sodium 69mg.
Vegetable Tempura Energy 313kcal/1305kJ; Protein 7.1g; Carbohydrate 30.6g, of which sugars 7.3g; Fat 18.9g, of which saturates 2.5g; Cholesterol 48mg; Calcium 94mg; Fibre 3.6g; Sodium 28mg.
Spiced Yam Slices Energy 335kcal/1415kJ; Protein 3.5g; Carbohydrate 53.1g, of which sugars 1.3g; Fat 13.7g, of which saturates 1.6g; Cholesterol 0mg; Calcium 39mg; Fibre 2.4g; Sodium 4mg.

Curry-spiced Pakoras

These delicious bites make a wonderful snack drizzled with the fragrant chutney.

Makes 25

115g/4oz/1 cup gram flour
25g/1oz/¼ cup self-raising (self-rising) flour
40g/1½oz/⅓ cup rice flour
large pinch of turmeric
10ml/2 tsp crushed coriander seeds
350ml/12fl oz/1½ cups water
vegetable oil, for frying
salt and ground black pepper

For the filling

15ml/1 tbsp sunflower oil
20ml/4 tsp cumin seeds
5ml/1 tsp black mustard seeds
1 small onion, finely chopped
10ml/2 tsp grated fresh root ginger
2 green chillies, seeded and chopped
600g/1lb 6oz potatoes, cooked
200g/7oz fresh peas
juice of 1 lemon
90ml/6 tbsp chopped fresh coriander (cilantro) leaves

For the chutney

105ml/7 tbsp coconut cream
200ml/7fl oz/scant 1 cup natural (plain) yogurt
50g/2oz mint leaves, finely chopped
5ml/1 tsp golden caster (superfine) sugar
juice of 1 lime

1 To make the filling, heat a wok over a medium heat and add the oil. When hot, fry the cumin and mustard seeds for 1–2 minutes. Add the onion, ginger and chillies to the wok and cook for 3–4 minutes. Add the cooked potatoes and peas and stir-fry for 5–6 minutes. Season, then stir in the lemon juice and coriander.

2 Leave the mixture to cool slightly, then divide into 25 portions. Shape each portion into a ball and chill.

3 To make the chutney, place all the ingredients in a blender and process until smooth. Season, then chill. To make the batter, put the gram flour, self-raising flour and rice flour in a bowl. Season and add the turmeric and coriander seeds. Gradually whisk in the water to make a smooth batter.

4 Fill a wok one-third full of oil and heat to 180°C/350°F. Working in batches, dip the chilled balls in the batter, then drop into the oil and deep-fry for 1–2 minutes, or until golden. Drain on kitchen paper, and serve immediately with the chutney.

Sweet Potato Cakes

These sweet potato balls from Cambodia are delicious dipped in a fiery sauce, such as nuoc cham. Simple to make, they are ideal for serving as nibbles with drinks.

Serves 4

450g/1lb sweet potatoes or taro root, boiled or baked, and peeled
30ml/2 tbsp sugar
15ml/1 tbsp Indian curry powder
25g/1oz fresh root ginger, peeled and grated
150g/5oz/1¼ cups glutinous rice flour or plain (all-purpose) flour
salt
sesame seeds or poppy seeds
vegetable oil, for deep-frying
nuoc cham, to serve

1 In a bowl, mash the cooked sweet potatoes or taro root. Beat in the sugar, curry powder, and ginger.

2 Add the rice flour or plain flour and salt, and work into a stiff dough – adding more flour if necessary.

3 Pull off lumps of the dough and mould them into small balls using your hands – you should be able to make roughly 24 balls. Roll the balls on a bed of sesame seeds or poppy seeds until they are completely coated.

4 Heat enough oil for deep-frying in a wok. Fry the sweet potato balls in batches, until golden. Drain on kitchen paper. Serve the balls with wooden skewers to make it easier to dip them into the nuoc cham.

Cook's Tips

- *Taro root is a staple in South-east Asia. It is used in similar ways to the potato, but has a pronounced nutty taste. The peel can irritate the skin, so it is wise to wear gloves when handling the raw vegetable.*
- *Nuoc cham is a piquant Vietnamese dipping sauce made with chillies, garlic, vinegar and nuoc mam, or Vietnamese fish sauce.*

Curry-spiced Pakoras Energy 126kcal/525kJ; Protein 4.1g; Carbohydrate 8.3g, of which sugars 2.6g; Fat 8.8g, of which saturates 5.2g; Cholesterol 0mg; Calcium 35mg; Fibre 1.3g; Sodium 16mg.
Sweet Potato Cakes Energy 354kcal/1495kJ; Protein 5g; Carbohydrate 61g, of which sugars 14.8g; Fat 11.8g, of which saturates 1.5g; Cholesterol 0mg; Calcium 84mg; Fibre 3.9g; Sodium 50mg.

Crystal Dumplings

A much-loved street food, these South Chinese dumplings are especially delicious with a sweet soy sauce and chilli dip.

Serves 6–8

200g/7oz/1¾ cups sweet potato flour
400ml/14fl oz/1⅔ cups water
75ml/5 tbsp vegetable oil
3 garlic cloves, crushed
400g/14oz can bamboo shoots, rinsed, drained and shredded
30ml/2 tbsp dark soy sauce
30ml/2 tbsp oyster sauce
5ml/1 tsp ground black pepper
200ml/7fl oz/scant 1 cup water
115g/4oz/1 cup tapioca flour

For the dip

45ml/3 tbsp dark soy sauce
15ml/1 tbsp ginger purée
15ml/1 tbsp rice vinegar
15ml/1 tbsp sesame oil
5ml/1 tsp sugar
5ml/1 tsp chilli bean paste

1 Put the sweet potato flour, water and 30ml/2tbsp vegetable oil in a non-stick pan. Cook over low heat, stirring occasionally, until thick. Remove from the heat and leave to cool for 15 minutes.

2 Heat the remaining vegetable oil in a wok and fry the garlic over low heat for 40 seconds. Add the bamboo shoots, soy sauce, oyster sauce, pepper and water. Cook over medium heat for 10 minutes. Remove from the heat and leave to cool.

3 Stir the tapioca flour into the cool sweet potato flour mixture. Mix well, then transfer to a floured board. Knead for 5 minutes, punching the dough as you roll and fold. Shape the dough into a long roll, about 5cm/2in in diameter. Slice off pieces 9mm/⅜in thick and flatten each with a rolling pin to form very thin circles.

4 Place about 30ml/2 tbsp bamboo shoots on each dough circle, fold over and seal the edges. Fold and pinch until you get a serrated edge on each dumpling.

5 Place the dumplings on a lightly oiled plate and steam over a wok of rapidly boiling water for 30 minutes.

6 Mix together all the ingredients for the dip in a small bowl. Serve the dumplings warm with the dip.

Aubergine and Pepper Tempura with Sweet Chilli Dip

These crunchy vegetables in a beautifully light batter are quick to make and taste very good with the piquant dip.

Serves 4

2 aubergines (eggplants)
2 red (bell) peppers
vegetable oil, for deep-frying

For the tempura batter

250g/9oz/generous 2 cups plain (all-purpose) flour
2 egg yolks
500ml/17fl oz/generous 2 cups iced water
5ml/1 tsp salt

For the dip

150ml/¼ pint/⅔ cup water
10ml/2 tsp granulated sugar
1 fresh red chilli, seeded and finely chopped
1 garlic clove, crushed
juice of ½ lime
5ml/1 tsp rice vinegar
35ml/2½ tbsp fish sauce
½ small carrot, finely grated

1 Slice the aubergines into thin batons. Halve and seed the peppers and slice them thinly.

2 Mix together the dip ingredients in a bowl and stir until the sugar has dissolved. Cover with clear film (plastic wrap) and set aside.

3 Set aside 30ml/2 tbsp of the flour for the tempura batter. Put the egg yolks in a bowl and beat in the iced water using a fork. Add the rest of the flour with the salt and stir briefly together – the mixture should be lumpy and not properly mixed. If it is too thick, add a little more iced water.

4 Use the batter immediately. Heat the oil in a wok or deep-fryer to a temperature of 190°C/375°F, or until a cube of bread dropped in the oil browns in about 45 seconds.

5 Dust a few aubergine batons and pepper slices with the reserved flour, then dip into the batter and drop into the hot oil, taking care as the oil will froth up. Make two or three more fritters. Cook for 3–4 minutes, until golden and crisp, then lift out with a slotted spoon. Drain on kitchen paper. Repeat with the remaining vegetables. Serve with the dip.

Crystal Dumplings Energy 244kcal/1022kJ; Protein 3.6g; Carbohydrate 38.2g, of which sugars 5.2g; Fat 8.7g, of which saturates 1.1g; Cholesterol 0mg; Calcium 21mg; Fibre 1.3g; Sodium 1134mg.
Tempura Energy 404kcal/1699kJ; Protein 9.4g; Carbohydrate 61g, of which sugars 12.5g; Fat 15.4g, of which saturates 2.4g; Cholesterol 101mg; Calcium 124mg; Fibre 5.8g; Sodium 15mg.

Tempeh Cakes with Dipping Sauce

These tasty little rissoles go very well with the light dipping sauce that accompanies them. Serve with a green salad for a quick and easy lunch.

Makes 8

1 lemon grass stalk, outer leaves removed and inside finely chopped
2 garlic cloves, chopped
2 spring onions (scallions), finely chopped
2 shallots, finely chopped
2 fresh red chillies, seeded and finely chopped
2.5cm/1in piece fresh root ginger, finely chopped
60ml/4 tbsp chopped fresh coriander (cilantro), plus extra to garnish
250g/9oz/generous 2 cups tempeh, thawed if frozen, sliced
15ml/1 tbsp fresh lime juice
5ml/1 tsp sugar
45ml/3 tbsp plain (all-purpose) flour
1 large (US extra large) egg, lightly beaten
salt and ground black pepper
vegetable oil, for frying

For the dipping sauce

45ml/3 tbsp mirin (sweet rice wine)
45ml/3 tbsp white wine vinegar
2 spring onions (scallions), thinly sliced
15ml/1 tbsp sugar
2 fresh red chillies, seeded and finely chopped
30ml/2 tbsp chopped fresh coriander (cilantro)
large pinch of salt

1 Make the dipping sauce. Mix the ingredients in a small bowl. Cover with clear film (plastic wrap) and set aside.

2 Place the lemon grass, garlic, spring onions, shallots, red chillies, ginger and fresh coriander in a food processor or blender, then process to a coarse paste.

3 Add the tempeh, fresh lime juice and sugar and process until it is all combined. Add the flour and egg, with salt and pepper to taste. Process to a coarse, sticky paste.

4 Scrape the paste into a bowl. Take one-eighth of the mixture at a time and form it into rounds with your hands.

5 Fry the cakes in a wok for 5–6 minutes, turning once, until golden. Drain, garnish with coriander and serve with the sauce.

Crispy Fried Tempeh with Chilli Spices

Often cooked at street stalls, this crispy fried tempeh can be served as a snack or as part of a selection of Indonesian dishes. For a substantial meal, try serving it with stir-fried noodles or rice and pickled vegetables.

Serves 3 to 4

45–60ml/3–4 tbsp coconut or groundnut (peanut) oil
500g/1¼lb tempeh, cut into bitesize strips
4 shallots, finely chopped
4 garlic cloves, finely chopped
25g/1oz fresh galangal or fresh root ginger, finely chopped
3–4 red chillies, seeded and finely chopped
150ml/¼ pint/⅔ cup sweet soy sauce
30–45ml/2–3 tbsp unsalted peanuts, crushed
1 small bunch fresh coriander (cilantro) leaves, roughly chopped
noodles or rice, to serve

1 Heat 30–45ml/2–3 tbsp of the oil in a wok or large, heavy frying pan. Add the tempeh and stir-fry until golden brown all over. Using a slotted spoon, transfer the tempeh to kitchen paper to drain, then set aside.

2 Wipe the wok or frying pan clean with kitchen paper. Heat the remaining 15ml/1 tbsp oil in the wok or pan, stir in the shallots, garlic, galangal and chillies and fry for 2–3 minutes until fragrant and beginning to colour. Stir in the sweet soy sauce and add the fried tempeh. Stir-fry until the sauce has reduced and is clinging to the tempeh.

3 Transfer the crispy fried tempeh to a serving dish and sprinkle with the peanuts and coriander leaves. Serve immediately with stir-fried noodles or cooked rice.

Variation

Tempeh, which is fermented tofu, can be bought from Chinese and South-east Asian supermarkets. If you are unable to purchase it, then tofu can be used as an alternative.

Tempeh Cakes Energy 79kcal/332kJ; Protein 4.5g; Carbohydrate 9.1g, of which sugars 4.3g; Fat 2.3g, of which saturates 0.4g; Cholesterol 26mg; Calcium 192mg; Fibre 0.8g; Sodium 15mg.
Crispy Fried Tempeh Energy 258kcal/1071kJ; Protein 14.8g; Carbohydrate 7.7g, of which sugars 5.5g; Fat 18.9g, of which saturates 2.6g; Cholesterol 0mg; Calcium 682mg; Fibre 1.7g; Sodium 2680mg.

Fresh Corn Fritters with Chilli Sauce

Sometimes the simplest dishes taste the best. These fritters, packed with crunchy corn, are easy to prepare and will prove popular.

Makes 12

3 corn cobs, total weight about 250g/9oz
1 garlic clove, crushed
small bunch fresh coriander (cilantro), chopped, plus extra to garnish
1 small fresh red or green chilli, seeded and finely chopped
1 spring onion (scallion), finely chopped
15ml/1 tbsp soy sauce
75g/3oz/⅔ cup rice flour or plain (all-purpose) flour
2 eggs, lightly beaten
60ml/4 tbsp water
sunflower oil, for shallow frying
salt and ground black pepper
sweet chilli sauce, to serve

1 Using a sharp knife, slice the kernels from the corn cobs and place them in a large bowl.

2 Add the garlic, chopped coriander, red or green chilli, spring onion, soy sauce, flour, beaten eggs and water to the bowl and mix together until well combined.

3 Season the mixture with salt and pepper to taste and mix together again. The mixture should be just firm enough to hold its shape, but not too stiff.

4 Heat the sunflower oil in a wok or large frying pan. Add spoonfuls of the corn mixture, gently spreading each one out with the back of the spoon to make a roundish fritter. Cook for 1–2 minutes on each side until lightly browned.

5 Drain the cooked fritters on kitchen paper and keep them hot while frying more fritters in the same way. Serve with sweet chilli sauce for dipping and coriander to garnish.

Cook's Tip
Sweet chilli sauce is a common condiment in many South-east Asian cuisines. It is ideal as a dipping sauce for these fritters.

Pan-fried Kimchi Fritters

A classic appetizer and popular snack, these fritters have a crisp golden coating. The contrast of the crunchy exterior and smooth filling makes for a delicious juxtaposition of textures and the dish is served with a zesty soy dip to help bring out the flavours.

Serves 2

90g/3½oz cabbage kimchi
1 potato, peeled and cut into pieces
a little milk (optional)
50g/2oz firm tofu, squeezed to remove excess water
25g/1oz/¼ cup plain (all-purpose) flour
1 egg, beaten
5ml/1 tsp crushed garlic
15ml/1 tbsp vegetable oil
salt and ground black pepper

For the dip

45ml/3 tbsp light soy sauce
2.5ml/½ tsp sesame oil
5ml/1 tsp lemon juice

1 Gently squeeze the kimchi to remove any excess liquid. Boil the potato and mash it, adding a little milk if required.

2 Crumble the tofu into a bowl. Add the kimchi, mashed potato, flour, egg, garlic and seasoning. Mix well and form spoonfuls of mixture into small round patties.

3 Coat a frying pan or wok with the oil and place over a medium heat. Add the patties and fry until golden brown on both sides. Drain on kitchen paper.

4 For the dip, mix the soy sauce, sesame oil and lemon juice, and then serve with the fritters.

Cook's Tip
Kimchi is a popular Korean condiment served at almost every meal. It is made from vegetables such as cabbage or turnips, which are seasoned, sealed in an airtight container and left to ferment. It is spicy, hot and extraordinarily pungent. Commercial kimchi can be purchased in Asian stores. Once opened, it will keep indefinitely in the refrigerator.

Fresh Corn Fritters Energy 76kcal/315kJ; Protein 2.1g; Carbohydrate 7.6g, of which sugars 0.5g; Fat 4.1g, of which saturates 0.6g; Cholesterol 32mg; Calcium 12mg; Fibre 0.5g; Sodium 102mg.
Kimchi Fritters Energy 206kcal/863kJ; Protein 8.4g; Carbohydrate 20.9g, of which sugars 3.8g; Fat 10.5g, of which saturates 1.8g; Cholesterol 105mg; Calcium 188mg; Fibre 1.9g; Sodium 583mg.

Vegetable Fritters

These light and crunchy vegetable fritters are equally good as an appetizer or a quick snack on the go.

Serves 4

1 potato, thinly sliced
1 small carrot, thinly sliced
½ small white onion, sliced
½ courgette (zucchini), thinly sliced
1 red chilli, seeded and sliced
salt and ground black pepper
vegetable oil, for cooking

For the batter

115g/4oz/1 cup plain (all-purpose) flour
45ml/3 tbsp cornflour (cornstarch)
1 egg, beaten
5ml/1 tsp salt

For the dip

30ml/2 tbsp dark soy sauce
15ml/1 tbsp fish stock
15ml/1 tbsp Chinese white radish, grated
5ml/1 tsp vinegar
5ml/1 tsp sesame seeds

1 To make the batter, sift the flour and cornflour into a bowl. Make a well in the middle and add the beaten egg and salt with 250ml/8fl oz/1 cup water. Using a wire whisk, gradually work in the flour mixture until it combines in a smooth batter.

2 Place the potato, carrot, onion, courgette and chilli in a bowl. Mix them together well, then pour in the batter and mix it into the vegetables, adding a small amount of seasoning.

3 For the dip, mix the soy sauce, stock, white radish, vinegar and sesame seeds. Set aside to allow the flavours to mingle.

4 Heat a little vegetable oil in a frying pan or wok over a medium heat. Ladle three or four small portions of the fritter mixture into the pan (depending on the size of pan) and cook until they are set and golden brown underneath. Turn and cook the fritters on the second side until they are golden.

5 Drain the cooked fritters on kitchen paper and keep warm. Cook the remaining mixture in the same way.

6 Divide the dipping sauce among four small individual dishes. Serve the hot fritters on individual warmed platters with the little dishes of the dipping sauce.

Spicy Corn and Coconut Patties

Serve these spicy treats with fresh lime wedges and a dollop of chilli sambal to give that extra fiery kick.

Serves 4

2 fresh corn on the cob
3 shallots, chopped
2 garlic cloves, chopped
25g/1oz galangal or fresh root ginger, chopped
1–2 chillies, seeded and chopped
2–3 candlenuts or macadamia nuts, ground
5ml/1 tsp ground coriander
5ml/1 tsp ground cumin
15ml/1 tbsp coconut oil
3 eggs
45–60ml/3–4 tbsp grated fresh coconut or desiccated (dry unsweetened shredded) coconut
2–3 spring onions (scallions), white parts only, finely sliced
corn or groundnut (peanut) oil, for shallow frying
1 small bunch fresh coriander (cilantro) leaves, chopped, plus extra for garnish
salt and ground black pepper
1 lime, quartered, for serving
chilli sambal, for dipping

1 Put the corn on the cob into a large pan of water, bring to the boil and boil for about 8 minutes, until cooked but still firm. Drain the cobs and refresh under running cold water. Using a sharp knife, scrape all the corn off the cob and set aside.

2 Using a mortar and pestle, grind the shallots, garlic, galangal and chillies until they form a paste. Add the candlenuts, ground coriander and cumin and beat well together.

3 Heat the coconut oil in a small wok or heavy pan, stir in the spice paste and stir-fry until the paste becomes fragrant and begins to colour. Transfer on to a plate and leave to cool.

4 Beat the eggs in a large bowl. Add the coconut and spring onions and beat in the corn and the paste. Season the mixture.

5 Heat a thin layer of corn oil in a heavy frying pan. Working in batches, drop spoonfuls of the corn mixture into the oil and fry the patties for 2–3 minutes, until golden brown on both sides.

6 Drain the patties and arrange on a dish on the coriander. Serve hot or at room temperature with lime wedges and a sambal.

Vegetable Fritters Energy 317kcal/1330kJ; Protein 6.7g; Carbohydrate 45.5g, of which sugars 5.3g; Fat 13.3g, of which saturates 1.9g; Cholesterol 48mg; Calcium 77mg; Fibre 2.7g; Sodium 1063mg.
Spicy Corn Patties Energy 368kcal/1531kJ; Protein 10.8g; Carbohydrate 18.1g, of which sugars 8.2g; Fat 28.7g, of which saturates 9.7g; Cholesterol 143mg; Calcium 68mg; Fibre 4.1g; Sodium 196mg.

Golden Corn Cakes with Aioli

East meets West in these crisp cakes that bring creamy goat's cheese and tangy Mediterranean peppers together in the Asian wok.

Serves 4

300g/11oz/scant 2 cups fresh corn kernels
200g/7oz/scant 1 cup ricotta cheese
200g/7oz/scant 1 cup goat's cheese, crumbled
30ml/2 tbsp thyme leaves
50g/2oz/½ cup plain (all-purpose) flour
1 large (US extra large) egg, lightly beaten
150g/5oz natural dried breadcrumbs
vegetable oil, for deep-frying
salt and ground black pepper

For the aioli

2 red (bell) peppers, halved and seeded
2 garlic cloves, crushed
250ml/8fl oz/1 cup mayonnaise

1 Make the aioli. Preheat the grill (broiler) to medium-high and cook the peppers, skin-side up, for 8–10 minutes, until the skins blister. Place the peppers in a plastic bag for 10 minutes and then peel away the skin. Place the flesh in a food processor with the garlic and mayonnaise and blend until fairly smooth. Transfer to a bowl and chill.

2 In a bowl, combine the corn, cheeses and thyme, then stir in the flour and egg and season well.

3 Place the breadcrumbs on a plate. Roll 15ml/1 tbsp of the corn mixture into a ball, flatten slightly and coat in the breadcrumbs. Place on baking parchment and chill for 30 minutes.

4 Fill a wok one-third full of vegetable oil and heat the oil to 180°C/350°F (or until a cube of bread, dropped into the oil, browns in 45 seconds). Working in batches, deep-fry the corn cakes for 1–2 minutes, until golden. Drain the corn cakes well on kitchen paper and serve with the aioli.

Cook's Tip
If you're short on time, make the aioli with bottled peppers.

Deep-fried Eggs with Red Chilli

Another name for this Chinese dish is mother-in-law eggs, which comes from a story about a prospective bridegroom who very much wanted to impress his future mother-in-law and devised a new recipe based on the only dish he knew how to make – boiled eggs.

Serves 4 to 6

30ml/2 tbsp vegetable oil
6 shallots, thinly sliced
6 garlic cloves, thinly sliced
6 fresh red chillies, sliced
oil, for deep-frying
6 hard-boiled eggs, shelled
salad leaves, to serve
sprigs of fresh coriander (cilantro), to garnish

For the sauce

75g/3oz/6 tbsp palm sugar (jaggery) or light muscovado (brown) sugar
75ml/5 tbsp Thai fish sauce
90ml/6 tbsp tamarind juice

1 Make the sauce. Put the sugar, fish sauce and tamarind juice in a pan. Bring to the boil, stirring until the sugar dissolves, lower the heat and simmer for 5 minutes. Taste and add more sugar, fish sauce or tamarind juice, if needed. Transfer to a bowl.

2 Heat the vegetable oil in a frying pan and cook the shallots, garlic and chillies for 5 minutes. Transfer to a bowl and set aside.

3 Heat the oil in a deep-fryer or wok to 190°C/375°F or until a cube of bread added to the oil, browns in about 45 seconds. Deep-fry the eggs in the hot oil for about 3–5 minutes, or until they turn a golden brown colour. Remove from the oil and drain well on kitchen paper.

4 Cut the eggs into quarters and arrange them on a bed of salad leaves. Drizzle the dish with the prepared sauce, and sprinkle over the shallot mixture. Garnish with the coriander sprigs and serve immediately.

Cook's Tip
The level of heat varies, depending on which type of chillies are used and whether or not you include the seeds.

Golden Corn Cakes Energy 1048Kcal/4363kJ; Protein 26.1g; Carbohydrate 68.2g, of which sugars 17.3g; Fat 76.5g, of which saturates 22g; Cholesterol 162mg; Calcium 156mg; Fibre 3.9g; Sodium 1091mg.
Deep-fried Eggs Energy 215kcal/894kJ; Protein 14.2g; Carbohydrate 2.4g, of which sugars 2.2g; Fat 16.9g, of which saturates 4.2g; Cholesterol 381mg; Calcium 112mg; Fibre 0.8g; Sodium 1223mg.

Boiled and Fried Eggs with Sambal

The two-step cooking method employed here results in a mouth-watering dish that is often eaten socially. When you are making the sambal, it is wise to make a large batch, as it is a sauce that goes with many salads, stir-fries and grilled foods.

Serves 4

15ml/1 tbsp vegetable oil
4 hard-boiled eggs, shelled
sliced cucumber, to serve (optional)

For the sambal

2 large onions, finely chopped
6 garlic cloves, finely chopped
45g/3 tbsp shrimp paste
10 dried chillies, soaked in warm water until soft, then finely chopped
6 candlenuts
30g/2 tbsp tomato purée (paste)
1.5ml/½ tsp salt
5ml/1 tsp sugar
30ml/2 tbsp tamarind concentrate
45ml/3 tbsp vegetable oil

1 For the sambal, grind the onions, garlic, shrimp paste, chillies and candlenuts using a mortar and pestle until very fine.

2 Add the remaining sambal ingredients, except for the oil, and continue to pound until a rough paste is formed.

3 Fry the mixture in the oil over a low heat until it is fragrant and separates, so that the oil seeps out.

4 In a clean wok, heat 1 tbsp of oil and fry the eggs all over until a crisp, brown skin forms. Remove and halve.

5 To serve, spoon the sambal over the halved eggs, with sliced cucumber on the side, if you like.

Cook's Tips

- *Even if you omit the frying step for the hard-boiled eggs, you will still get a lovely spicy egg dish.*
- *If you cannot find candlenuts in your local store, use about eight macadamia nuts instead.*

Hard-boiled Eggs in Red Sauce

A perennially popular snack, this spicy egg dish originates from Indonesia. Served as a street food wrapped in a banana leaf, the Malays often eat it with plain steamed rice, sliced chillies, onion and coriander – it is ideal for a quick, tasty snack or a light lunch.

Serves 4

vegetable oil, for deep-frying
8 eggs, hard-boiled and shelled
1 lemon grass stalk, trimmed, quartered and crushed
2 large tomatoes, skinned, seeded and chopped to a pulp
5–10ml/1–2 tsp sugar
30ml/2 tbsp dark soy sauce
juice of 1 lime
fresh coriander (cilantro) and mint leaves, coarsely chopped, to garnish

For the rempah

4–6 fresh red chillies, seeded and chopped
4 shallots, chopped
2 garlic cloves, chopped
2.5ml/½ tsp shrimp paste

1 Using a mortar and pestle or food processor, grind the ingredients for the rempah to form a smooth purée. Set aside.

2 Heat enough oil for deep-frying in a wok or large heavy pan and deep-fry the whole boiled eggs until golden brown. Lift them out and drain on kitchen paper.

3 Reserve 15ml/1 tbsp of the oil and discard the rest. Heat the oil in the wok or heavy pan and stir in the rempah until it becomes fragrant. Add the lemon grass, followed by the tomatoes and sugar. Cook for 2–3 minutes, until it forms a thick paste. Reduce the heat and stir in the soy sauce and lime juice.

4 Add 30ml/2 tbsp water to thin the sauce. Toss in the eggs, making sure they are thoroughly coated, and serve hot, garnished with chopped coriander and mint leaves.

Variation

For a fusion twist, serve these hard-boiled eggs with a refreshing cucumber raita.

Boiled and Fried Eggs Energy 230kcal/956kJ; Protein 14.4g; Carbohydrate 12g, of which sugars 9.1g; Fat 14.3g, of which saturates 2.6g; Cholesterol 247mg; Calcium 198mg; Fibre 2g; Sodium 1070mg.
Eggs in Red Sauce Energy 266kcal/1104kJ; Protein 15.6g; Carbohydrate 7.1g, of which sugars 6.7g; Fat 19.9g, of which saturates 4.2g; Cholesterol 387mg; Calcium 99mg; Fibre 1g; Sodium 739mg.

Firecrackers

It's easy to see how these snacks got their name. They whiz round the wok like rockets, and when you take a bite, they explode with flavour.

Makes 16

16 large, raw king prawns (jumbo shrimp), heads and shells removed but tails left on
5ml/1 tsp red curry paste
15ml/1 tbsp fish sauce
16 small wonton wrappers, about 8cm/3¼in square, thawed if frozen
16 fine egg noodles, soaked in water until soft
oil, for deep-frying
lime wedges, to serve

1 Place the prawns on their sides and cut two slits through the underbelly of each, one about 1cm/½in from the head end and the other about 1cm/½in from the first cut, cutting across the prawn. This will prevent the prawns from curling when cooked.

2 Mix the curry paste with the fish sauce in a shallow dish. Add the prawns and turn them in the mixture until they are well coated. Cover and leave to marinate for 10 minutes.

3 Place a wonton wrapper on the work surface at an angle so that it forms a diamond shape, then fold the top corner over so that the point is in the centre.

4 Place a prawn, slits down, on the wrapper, with the tail projecting from the folded end, then fold the bottom corner over the other end of the prawn.

5 Fold each side of the wrapper over in turn to make a tightly folded roll. Tie a noodle in a bow around the roll and set it aside. Repeat with the remaining prawns and wrappers.

6 Heat the oil in a wok to 190°C/375°F or until a cube of bread added to the oil browns in 40 seconds. Fry the prawns, a few at a time, for 5–8 minutes, until golden brown and cooked through. Drain well on kitchen paper and keep hot while you cook the remaining batches. Serve with lime wedges.

Radish Cake

This recipe makes use of the large white radish that is also known as mooli or daikon. White radishes are much larger than the more common red ones. Choose those that are pearly white and firm, as old ones become fibrous. White radish is fairly bland, although it is useful for making soup stock. Process it to a paste and mix it with rice flour, however, and it is magically transformed.

Serves 6–8

50g/2oz dried shrimp
1kg/2¼lb white radish, (also called mooli or daikon)
300g/11oz/2 cups rice flour
115g/4oz/1 cup tapioca flour or 115g/4oz/1 cup cornflour (cornstarch)
750ml/1¼ pints/3 cups water
5ml/1 tsp salt
30ml/2 tbsp vegetable oil
30ml/2 tbsp light soy sauce
30ml/2 tbsp sesame oil
2.5ml/½ tsp ground black pepper
dipping sauce, optional, to serve

1 Put the dried shrimp in a bowl and pour over enough water to cover. Soak for 1 hour, until soft.

2 Meanwhile, peel the radish and chop it roughly. Process it in batches in a blender or food processor to a soft white purée. Scrape into a strainer and press down with a spoon to extract as much liquid as possible. Tip the radish purée into a bowl and stir in the rice flour and the tapioca or cornflour. Add the water and salt. Mix well.

3 Drain the soaked shrimp and chop them roughly. Spoon the radish purée into a non-stick pan and cook over low heat, stirring frequently, for 5 minutes.

4 Heat the vegetable oil in a frying pan or wok. Add the chopped shrimp and fry for 2 minutes, then add the radish purée. Stir well, then add the soy sauce, sesame oil and black pepper. Mix thoroughly to combine.

5 Press the mixture into a lightly oiled steaming tray. Steam over a pan of rapidly boiling water for 20 minutes. Set aside. When cold, slice into bite-size pieces and serve plain or with a dipping sauce of your choice.

Firecrackers Energy 71kcal/298kJ; Protein 3.2g; Carbohydrate 7.1g, of which sugars 0.2g; Fat 3.5g, of which saturates 0.5g; Cholesterol 25mg; Calcium 20mg; Fibre 0.3g; Sodium 30mg.
Radish Cake Energy 263kcal/1099kJ; Protein 7g; Carbohydrate 44.2g, of which sugars 2.7g; Fat 6.3g, of which saturates 0.9g; Cholesterol 32mg; Calcium 11mg; Fibre 1.9g; Sodium 560mg.

Deep-fried Sweet Potato Rosti

This dish is a speciality of Hanoi in Vietnam, where the street sellers are well known for their delicious recipes. Traditionally, the patties are served with herbs and lettuce leaves for wrapping.

Serves 4

50g/2oz/½ cup plain (all-purpose) flour
50g/2oz/½ cup rice flour
4ml/scant 1 tsp baking powder
10ml/2 tsp sugar
2.5cm/1in fresh root ginger, peeled and grated
2 spring onions (scallions), finely sliced
1 slim sweet potato, about 225g/8oz, peeled and cut into fine matchsticks
vegetable oil, for deep-frying
salt and ground black pepper
chopped fresh coriander (cilantro), to garnish
lettuce leaves and nuoc cham or other dipping sauce, to serve

1 Sift the plain and rice flour and baking powder into a medium bowl. Add the sugar and about 2.5ml/½ tsp each of salt and pepper. Gradually stir 250ml/8fl oz/1 cup water into the mixture, until thoroughly combined.

2 Add the grated ginger and sliced spring onions to the batter and leave to stand for 30 minutes for the flavours to develop. Add extra ginger if you like a strong flavour.

3 Add the sweet potato matchsticks to the batter and fold them in, making sure they are well coated.

4 Heat enough oil for deep-frying in a wok. Lower a heaped tablespoon of the sweet potato mixture into the oil, pushing it off the spoon so that it floats in the oil. Fry for 2–3 minutes, turning it over so that it is evenly browned and crisp all over. Drain on kitchen paper. Continue preparing the rostis with the rest of the batter.

5 Arrange each rosti on a lettuce leaf on small individual serving plates, garnish each one with coriander, and then serve immediately with nuoc cham or another dipping sauce of your choice.

Sweet Potato and Prawn Cakes

Grated sweet potato and pumpkin contribute both texture and flavour to these delicious fried cakes, and the sweetness of the ingredients is a perfect foil for lively oriental flavourings. Serve the cakes warm with a fish sauce or dark soy sauce.

Serves 4-6

200g/7oz strong white bread flour
2.5ml/½ tsp salt
2.5ml/½ tsp dried yeast
175ml/6fl oz/¾ cup hand-hot water
1 egg, beaten
150g/5oz sweet potato
225g/8oz pumpkin, seeded
2 spring onions (scallions)
50g/2oz water chestnuts
200g/7oz fresh king prawn (jumbo shrimp) tails, peeled
2.5ml/½ tsp chilli sauce
1 clove garlic, crushed
juice of ½ lime
30–45ml/2–3 tbsp vegetable oil
spring onions (scallions), to garnish

1 Sift the flour and salt into a large mixing bowl and make a well in the centre. Dissolve the yeast in the water, then pour it into the well. Pour in the egg and leave for a few minutes until bubbles appear. Mix vigorously to a batter.

2 Peel and grate the sweet potato and pumpkin. Chop the spring onions and slice and chop the water chestnuts.

3 Place the peeled prawns in a saucepan and cover with water. Bring to the boil and simmer for 10–12 minutes. Drain, refresh in cold water and drain again. Chop the prawns and set aside.

4 Stir the grated sweet potato and pumpkin into the batter, then add the chopped spring onions, water chestnuts, chilli sauce, crushed garlic and lime juice. Mix together well, then stir in the chopped prawns.

5 Pour a little oil into a wok or a large frying pan. Heat the oil then spoon in the batter in small heaps and fry, a few at a time, until golden. Add more oil to the pan as required.

6 Drain the cakes on kitchen paper and serve on a warmed serving platter garnished with spring onions.

Sweet Potato Rosti Energy 276kcal/1159kJ; Protein 11g; Carbohydrate 35g, of which sugars 6g; Fat 11g, of which saturates 1g; Cholesterol 85mg; Calcium 83mg; Fibre 81g; Sodium 200mg.
Sweet Potato Cakes Energy 212kcal/898kJ; Protein 12.1g; Carbohydrate 38.4g, of which sugars 6.1g; Fat 2.1g, of which saturates 0.6g; Cholesterol 97mg; Calcium 144mg; Fibre 4g; Sodium 256mg.

Mung Bean Pancakes with Chilli

These spicy mung bean pancakes are deliciously light.

Serves 3 to 4

375g/13oz/2 cups mung beans, soaked overnight in cold water
15ml/1 tbsp pine nuts
30ml/2 tbsp rice flour
75g/3oz beef flank, sliced
200g/7oz prawns (shrimp), peeled and finely chopped
15ml/1 tbsp vegetable oil, plus extra for shallow-frying
1 button (white) mushroom, sliced
½ onion, thinly sliced
½ cucumber, seeded and sliced
½ cup cabbage kimchi, thinly sliced
3 spring onions (scallions), sliced
1 red chilli, shredded
salt and ground black pepper

For the marinade

5ml/1 tsp rice wine
2.5ml/½ tsp grated fresh root ginger
5ml/1 tsp dark soy sauce
1 garlic clove, crushed
2.5ml/½ tsp sesame seeds
5ml/1 tsp sesame oil
ground black pepper

For the dipping sauce

60ml/4 tbsp dark soy sauce
10ml/2 tsp rice vinegar
1 spring onion (scallion), finely chopped

1 Drain the beans and roll them between your hands to remove the skins. Rinse well, and place in a processor with the pine nuts and 120ml/4fl oz/½ cup water. Blend to a milky paste. Transfer to a bowl and add the rice flour and 5ml/1 tsp salt. Mix well.

2 Put the beef into a bowl. Pour over the rice wine for the marinade. Add the other marinade ingredients and mix well. Leave for 20 minutes. Season the prawns. Combine all the dipping sauce ingredients in a serving bowl.

3 Coat a wok with oil. Stir-fry the marinaded beef, sliced mushrooms and onion until the meat has browned. Add the cucumber, cabbage kimchi and spring onions. Mix well and then remove the mixture from the heat.

4 Heat the oil in a frying pan. Add a spoonful of the bean paste and flatten slightly to form a pancake. Spoon some beef mixture on to the pancake, with some chilli and prawns. Press flat and fry until golden on each side. Serve immediately with the soy dipping sauce.

Parchment-wrapped Prawns

These succulent pink prawns coated in a fragrant spice paste make the perfect dish for informal entertaining. Serve the prawns in their paper parcels and allow your guests to unwrap them at the table and enjoy the aroma of exotic spices as the parcel is opened and the contents are revealed.

Serves 4

2 lemon grass stalks, very finely chopped
5ml/1 tsp galangal, very finely chopped
4 garlic cloves, finely chopped
finely grated rind and juice of 1 lime
4 spring onions (scallions), chopped
10ml/2 tsp palm sugar (jaggery)
15ml/1 tbsp soy sauce
5ml/1 tsp fish sauce
5ml/1 tsp chilli oil
45ml/3 tbsp chopped fresh coriander (cilantro) leaves
30ml/2 tbsp chopped fresh Thai basil leaves
1kg/2¼lb raw tiger prawns (jumbo shrimp), heads and shells removed; tails left on
basil leaves and lime wedges, to garnish

1 Place the lemon grass, galangal, garlic, lime rind and juice and spring onions in a food processor or blender. Blend in short bursts until the mixture forms a coarse paste.

2 Transfer the paste to a large bowl and stir in the palm sugar, soy sauce, fish sauce, chilli oil and chopped herbs. Add the prawns to the paste and toss to coat evenly. Cover and marinate in the refrigerator for 30 minutes to 1 hour.

3 Cut out eight 20cm/8in squares of baking parchment. Place one-eighth of the spicy prawn mixture in the centre of each square, then fold over the edges and twist them together to make a neat sealed parcel.

4 Place the parcels in a large steamer, cover and steam them over a wok of simmering water for 10 minutes.

5 Serve the prawn parcels immediately, garnished with scattered basil leaves and lime wedges.

Mung Bean Pancakes Energy 492kcal/2070kJ; Protein 38.2g; Carbohydrate 55.4g, of which sugars 6.9g; Fat 14.2g, of which saturates 2.2g; Cholesterol 108mg; Calcium 175mg; Fibre 11.7g; Sodium 1867mg.
Wrapped Prawns Energy 169kcal/713kJ; Protein 35.4g; Carbohydrate 2.4g, of which sugars 2.4g; Fat 2g, of which saturates 0.3g; Cholesterol 390mg; Calcium 163mg; Fibre 0.2g; Sodium 381mg.

Prawn Rissoles

This is a Portuguese-influenced dish from Goa, where seafood is caught fresh and cooked each day. Small frozen prawns are ideal for this recipe, since they will be chopped and blended with a selection of pungent spices.

Makes 12

2 slices of white bread, a day or two old
400g/14oz cooked peeled prawns (shrimp)
3 tbsp sunflower oil or olive oil
1 tsp fennel seeds
1 large onion, finely chopped
2 green chillies, finely chopped (seeded if preferred)
2 tsp ginger purée
½ tsp garam masala
2 tbsp chopped coriander (cilantro) leaves
salt to taste
25g/1oz/¼ cup plain (all-purpose) flour
1 egg, beaten
75g/3oz/1½ cups golden breadcrumbs
oil for deep-frying
salad and lemon wedges, to garnish

1 Soak the bread in cold water and drain. Place it in a food processor and blend until it is smooth. Add the prawns and, using the pulse action, chop them coarsely. Remove and place the mixture into a medium-sized mixing bowl.

2 Heat the oil in a small pan over a medium heat and add fennel seeds. Stir-fry for 30 seconds. Add the onion, chilli and ginger. Continue stir-frying until the mixture begins to brown, then add the garam masala.

3 Add this mixture to the prawns, then add the chopped coriander and salt to taste. Mix the ingredients thoroughly, cover the bowl and chill for 30–40 minutes.

4 Divide the prawn mixture into 12 rissoles. Dust each rissole in the flour, dip in the egg and roll in the breadcrumbs.

5 Heat the oil in a wok and deep-fry the rissoles over a medium to high heat in small batches until they are crisp and golden brown. Drain well on kitchen paper and serve them with a salad garnish and lemon wedges.

Seaweed-wrapped Prawn Rolls

Japanese nori seaweed is used to enclose the fragrant filling of prawns, water chestnuts, and fresh herbs and spices in these pretty steamed rolls. Ideal for entertaining, the rolls can be prepared in advance and stored in the refrigerator until ready to steam.

Serves 4

675g/1½lb raw tiger prawns (jumbo shrimp), peeled and deveined
5ml/1 tsp finely chopped kaffir lime leaves
1 red chilli, seeded and chopped
5ml/1 tsp finely grated garlic clove
5ml/1 tsp finely grated root ginger
5ml/1 tsp finely grated lime rind
60ml/4 tbsp very finely chopped fresh coriander (cilantro)
1 egg white, lightly beaten
30ml/2 tbsp chopped water chestnuts
4 sheets of nori
salt and ground black pepper
sweet soy sauce, to serve

1 Place the prawns in a food processor with the lime leaves, red chilli, garlic, ginger, lime rind and coriander. Process the mixture until smooth.

2 Add the egg white and water chestnuts to the food processor, season and process again until combined. Transfer the mixture to a bowl, cover and chill for 3–4 hours.

3 Lay the nori sheets on a clean, dry surface and spread the prawn mixture over each sheet, leaving a 2cm/¾in border at one end. Roll up to form tight rolls, wrap in clear film (plastic wrap) and chill for 2–3 hours.

4 Unwrap the rolls and place on a board. Cut each roll into 2cm/¾in lengths. Place the slices in a baking parchment-lined bamboo steamer, cover and place over a wok of simmering water (making sure the water does not touch the steamer).

5 Steam the rolls for 6–8 minutes, or until cooked through. Serve warm or at room temperature with a dish of sweet soy sauce for dipping.

Prawn Rissoles Energy 165kcal/688kJ; Protein 8.1g; Carbohydrate 11.2g, of which sugars 2.2g; Fat 10.1g, of which saturates 1.2g; Cholesterol 81mg; Calcium 53mg; Fibre 0.7g; Sodium 139mg.
Seaweed Rolls Energy 136Kcal/574kJ; Protein 30.8g; Carbohydrate 0.4g, of which sugars 0.4g; Fat 1.2g, of which saturates 0.2g; Cholesterol 329mg; Calcium 162mg; Fibre 0.7g; Sodium 345mg.

Prawn Toasts with Sesame Seeds

Choose very fresh prawns for this recipe to achieve maximum flavour. This is a healthy version of an ever-popular appetizer, but it has lost none of its classic crunch and taste. Serve the toasts as a snack, too. They are great for getting a party off to a good start.

Serves 4–6

6 slices medium-cut white bread, crusts removed
15ml/1 tbsp sesame seeds
225g/8oz raw tiger prawns (jumbo shrimp), peeled and deveined
50g/2oz/⅓ cup drained, canned water chestnuts
1 egg white
5ml/1 tsp sesame oil
2.5ml/½ tsp salt
2 spring onions (scallions), finely chopped
10ml/2 tsp dry sherry
shredded spring onion (scallion), to garnish

1 Preheat the oven to 120°C/250°F/Gas ½. Cut each slice of bread into four triangles. Spread out on a baking sheet and bake for 25 minutes or until crisp.

2 Toast the sesame seeds by putting them in a dry wok over medium heat until the seeds change colour. Shake the wok constantly so that the seeds brown evenly and do not burn.

3 Meanwhile, put the prawns in a food processor with the water chestnuts, egg white, oil and salt. Process the mixture, using the pulse facility, until a coarse purée is formed.

4 Scrape the mixture into a bowl, stir in the chopped spring onions and sherry, and set aside for 10 minutes at room temperature to allow the flavours to blend.

5 Remove the toast from the oven and raise the temperature to 200°C/400°F/Gas 6. Spread the prawn mixture on the toast, sprinkle with the sesame seeds and bake for 12 minutes.

6 Garnish the crisp prawn toasts with shredded spring onion and serve hot or warm on a warmed serving platter.

Butterflied Prawns in Chocolate Sauce

There is a tradition in Spain, which originates in Mexico, of cooking savoury food, and this includes shellfish, with chocolate. Known as *langostinos en chocolate* in Spanish, this is just the kind of culinary adventure that Basque chefs love.

Serves 4

8 large raw prawns (shrimp), in the shell
15ml/1 tbsp seasoned plain (all-purpose) flour
15ml/1 tbsp pale dry sherry
juice of 1 large orange
15g/½oz dark (bittersweet) chocolate, chopped
30ml/2 tbsp olive oil
2 garlic cloves, finely chopped
2.5cm/1in piece fresh root ginger, finely chopped
1 small dried chilli, seeded and chopped
salt and ground black pepper

1 Peel the prawns, leaving just the tail sections intact. Make a shallow cut down the back of each one and carefully pull out and discard the dark intestinal tract. Turn the prawns over so that the undersides are uppermost, and then carefully slit them open from tail to top, using a small sharp knife, cutting them almost, but not quite, through to the central back line.

2 Press the prawns down firmly to flatten them out. Coat with the seasoned flour and set aside.

3 Gently heat the sherry and orange juice in a small pan. When warm, remove from the heat and stir in the chopped chocolate until melted.

4 Heat the oil in a frying pan. Add the garlic, ginger and chilli and cook for 2 minutes until golden. Remove with a slotted spoon and reserve. Add the prawns, cut side down and cook for 2–3 minutes until golden brown with pink edges. Turn the prawns and cook for a further 2 minutes.

5 Return the garlic mixture to the pan and pour the chocolate sauce over. Cook for 1 minute, turning the prawns to coat them in the glossy sauce. Season to taste and serve hot.

Prawn Toasts Energy 392kcal/1635kJ; Protein 19.1g; Carbohydrate 21.1g, of which sugars 1.2g; Fat 25.9g, of which saturates 3.4g; Cholesterol 110mg; Calcium 270mg; Fibre 2.7g; Sodium 558mg.
Prawns in Chocolate Energy 125kcal/520kJ; Protein 8.5g; Carbohydrate 6.5g, of which sugars 3.6g; Fat 6.9g, of which saturates 1.5g; Cholesterol 88mg; Calcium 44mg; Fibre 0.2g; Sodium 88mg.

Deep-fried Prawn Sandwiches

In the busy street markets of Phnom Penh, the capital city of Cambodia, there is always something interesting being cooked. Next to the stall selling deep-fried furry black spiders, you might come across the less alarming snack of deep-fried prawn sandwiches.

Serves 4

3–4 shallots, roughly chopped
4 garlic cloves, roughly chopped
25g/1oz fresh root ginger, peeled and chopped
1 lemon grass stalk, trimmed and chopped
1 Thai chilli, seeded and chopped
10ml/2 tsp sugar
225g/8oz fresh prawns (shrimp), shelled and deveined
30ml/2 tbsp fish sauce
1 egg, beaten
12 thin slices of day-old baguette
vegetable oil, for deep-frying
ground black pepper
chilli oil, for drizzling

1 Using a large mortar and pestle, pound the chopped shallots, garlic, ginger, lemon grass, chilli and sugar. Add the shelled prawns and pound them to make a paste.

2 Mix well and bind all the ingredients with the fish sauce and beaten egg. Season with ground black pepper.

3 Spread the mixture on each piece of bread, patting it down firmly. In a wok, heat enough oil for deep-frying. Using a slotted spoon, lower the sandwiches, prawn side down, into the oil.

4 Cook in batches, flipping them over so they turn golden. Drain on kitchen paper and serve hot drizzled with chilli oil.

Cook's Tip
If you deep-fry regularly, then you will soon learn to judge when the oil has reached optimum temperature. If you need reassurance, buy a deep-fat thermometer. The safest and most reliable are those thermometers that can be clipped to the side of the wok before the oil is hot.

Deep-fried Small Prawns and Corn

Inspired by the Japanese dish tempura, this simple snack food is a good way of using up small quantities of vegetables. This is easy to cook in a wok.

Serves 4

200g/7oz small cooked, peeled prawns (shrimp)
4–5 button (white) mushrooms
4 spring onions (scallions)
75g/3oz/½ cup canned, drained or frozen sweetcorn, thawed
30ml/2 tbsp frozen peas, thawed
vegetable oil, for deep-frying
chives, to garnish

For the tempura batter
300ml/½ pint/1¼ cups ice-cold water
2 eggs, beaten
150g/5oz/1¼ cups plain (all-purpose) flour
1.5ml/¼ tsp baking powder

For the dipping sauce
400ml/14fl oz/1⅔ cups second dashi stock, made with instant dashi powder and water
100ml/3fl oz/scant ½ cup soy sauce
100ml/3fl oz/scant ½ cup sweet rice wine
15ml/1 tbsp chopped chives

1 Roughly chop half the prawns. Cube the mushrooms. Slice the white part from the spring onions and chop this roughly.

2 To make the tempura batter, mix the ice-cold water and eggs in a medium mixing bowl to a smooth batter using a fork.

3 Add the flour and baking powder to the ice-cold water and eggs, and roughly fold in with a pair of chopsticks or a fork. Do not beat the mixture since the batter should be quite lumpy.

4 Heat plenty of oil in a wok to 170°C/338°F.

5 Mix the prawns and vegetables into the batter. Pour a quarter of the batter into a small bowl, then drop gently into the oil. Using wooden spoons, carefully gather the batter to form a fist-size ball. Deep-fry until golden. Drain on kitchen paper.

6 In a small pan, mix all the liquid dipping-sauce ingredients together and bring to the boil, then immediately turn off the heat. Sprinkle with chives. Garnish the fritters with chives, and serve with the dipping sauce.

Prawn Sandwiches Energy 489Kcal/2065kJ; Protein 22.5g; Carbohydrate 70.6g, of which sugars 6.3g; Fat 15g, of which saturates 2g; Cholesterol 157mg; Calcium 202mg; Fibre 3.1g; Sodium 860mg.
Small Prawns and Corn Energy 246Kcal/1039kJ; Protein 17.6g; Carbohydrate 37.4g, of which sugars 4.7g; Fat 4g, of which saturates 1g; Cholesterol 193mg; Calcium 117mg; Fibre 2g; Sodium 1963mg.

Crisp-fried Japanese Panko Prawns

When butterflied and battered tiger prawns are deep-fried in the wok, they curl up beautifully, and look gorgeous on green seaweed topped with white rice.

Serves 4

20 large raw tiger or king prawns (jumbo shrimp), heads removed
30ml/2 tbsp cornflour (cornstarch)
3 large (US extra large) eggs, lightly beaten
150g/5oz panko (Japanese-style breadcrumbs)
sunflower oil, for frying
4 sheets of nori
400g/14oz cooked sushi rice
wasabi, soy sauce, sweet chilli sauce and pickled ginger, to serve

1 Peel and devein the prawns, leaving the tails on. Cut down the back of each prawn, without cutting all the way through, and press the prawns out flat to butterfly them.

2 Place the cornflour, beaten eggs and panko in 3 separate bowls. Dip each prawn first into the cornflour, next into the egg and then into the panko, to coat it evenly.

3 Fill a wok one-third full of sunflower oil and heat to 180°C/350°F (or until a cube of bread added to the oil browns in 45 seconds).

4 Working in batches, deep-fry the prawns for 1 minute, or until lightly golden and crisp. Remove from the wok with a slotted spoon and drain the prawns on kitchen paper.

5 Carefully cut each nori sheet into a 10cm/4in square. Place each square on a serving plate and divide the sushi rice among them, then spread out the rice using the back of a spoon. Top each serving with 5 deep-fried prawns and serve with wasabi, soy sauce, sweet chilli sauce and pickled ginger.

Cook's Tip
Panko are Japanese-style breadcrumbs, which give a fabulously crunchy result when deep-fried. They make the perfect coating for these tender, juicy prawns. If you can't find panko, use coarse, dried breadcrumbs instead.

Chilli Satay Prawns

This delicious dish, inspired by Indonesian satay, combines mild peanuts, aromatic spices, fiery chilli, coconut milk and lemon juice in the spicy dip.

Serves 4 to 6

450g/1lb king prawns (jumbo shrimp), peeled and deveined
25ml/1½ tbsp vegetable oil

For the peanut sauce
25ml/1½ tbsp vegetable oil
15ml/1 tbsp chopped garlic
1 small onion, chopped
3–4 red chillies, seeded and chopped
3 kaffir lime leaves, torn
1 lemon grass stalk, bruised and chopped
5ml/1 tsp medium curry paste
250ml/8fl oz/1 cup coconut milk
1cm/½in piece cinnamon stick
75g/3oz/⅓ cup crunchy peanut butter
45ml/3 tbsp tamarind juice, made by mixing tamarind paste with warm water
30ml/2 tbsp Thai fish sauce
30ml/2 tbsp palm sugar (jaggery) or muscovado (brown) sugar
juice of ½ lemon

For the garnish
½ bunch fresh coriander (cilantro) leaves (optional)
4 fresh red chillies, finely sliced (optional)
spring onions (scallions), sliced

1 Make the peanut sauce. Heat half the oil in a wok or heavy frying pan. Add the garlic and onion and cook, stirring, for 3–4 minutes, until the mixture has softened but not browned.

2 Add the chillies, kaffir lime leaves, lemon grass and curry paste. Cook for 2–3 minutes, then stir in the coconut milk, cinnamon stick, peanut butter, tamarind juice, fish sauce, sugar and lemon juice. Bring to the boil, then reduce the heat to low and simmer gently for 15–20 minutes, until the sauce thickens.

3 Thread the prawns on to skewers and brush with a little oil. Cook under a preheated grill (broiler) for 2 minutes on each side until they turn pink and are firm to the touch. Alternatively, pan-fry the prawns, then thread on to skewers.

4 Remove the cinnamon from the sauce and discard. Arrange the prawns on a warmed platter, garnish with spring onions, and coriander and red chillies, if liked, and serve with the sauce.

Panko Prawns Energy 472Kcal/1989kJ; Protein 20.2g; Carbohydrate 63g, of which sugars 1g; Fat 17.4g, of which saturates 2.8g; Cholesterol 240mg; Calcium 127mg; Fibre 0.9g; Sodium 437mg.
Satay Prawns Energy 321kcal/1340kJ; Protein 24.6g; Carbohydrate 13.5g, of which sugars 8.2g; Fat 13.3g, of which saturates 3.6g; Cholesterol 219mg; Calcium 52mg; Fibre 1.2g; Sodium 794mg.

Spicy Shrimp and Scallop Satay

One of the tastiest satay dishes, this is succulent, spicy and extremely moreish. Serve with rice and a fruity salad or pickled vegetables and lime.

Serves 4

250g/9oz shelled shrimp or prawns, deveined and chopped
250g/9oz shelled scallops, chopped
30ml/2 tbsp potato, tapioca or rice flour
5ml/1 tsp baking powder
12–16 wooden or metal lemon grass or sugar cane skewers
1 lime, quartered, to serve

For the spice paste
2 shallots, chopped
2 garlic cloves, chopped
2–3 red chillies, seeded and chopped
25g/1oz galangal or fresh root ginger, chopped
15g/½oz fresh turmeric, chopped or 2.5ml/½ tsp ground turmeric
2–3 lemon grass stalks, chopped
15–30ml/1–2 tbsp palm or groundnut (peanut) oil
5ml/1 tsp shrimp paste
15ml/1 tbsp tamarind paste
5ml/1 tsp palm sugar (jaggery)

1 Make the paste. In a mortar and pestle, pound the shallots, garlic, chillies, galangal, turmeric and lemon grass to form a paste.

2 Heat the oil in a wok or heavy frying pan, stir in the paste. Fry until fragrant. Add the shrimp paste, tamarind and sugar and cook, stirring, until the mixture darkens. Set aside to cool.

3 In a bowl, pound the shrimps and scallops together to form a paste, or whiz them in an electric blender or food processor. Beat in the spice paste, then the flour and baking powder, and beat until blended. Chill in the refrigerator for 1 hour. If using wooden skewers, soak them in water for about 30 minutes.

4 Meanwhile, prepare the barbecue, or, if you are using the grill (broiler), preheat 5 minutes before you start cooking. Using your fingers, scoop up lumps of the shellfish paste and wrap it around the skewers.

5 Place each skewer on the barbecue or under the grill and cook for 3 minutes on each side, until golden brown. Serve with the lime wedges to squeeze over them.

Shiitake and Scallop Bundles

A wok does double duty for making these delicate mushroom and seafood treats, first for steaming and then for deep frying.

Serves 4

4 scallops
8 large fresh shiitake mushrooms
225g/8oz long yam, unpeeled
20ml/4 tsp miso
50g/2oz/1 cup fresh breadcrumbs
cornflour (cornstarch), for dusting
2 eggs, beaten
vegetable oil, for deep-frying
salt
4 lemon wedges, to serve

1 Slice the scallops in two horizontally, then sprinkle with salt. Remove the stalks from the shiitake and discard them. Cut shallow slits on the top of the shiitake to form a 'hash' symbol. Sprinkle with a little salt.

2 Heat a steamer over a wok of gently simmering water and steam the long yam for 10–15 minutes, or until soft. Test with a skewer. Leave to cool, then remove the skin. Mash the flesh in a bowl, add the miso and mix well. Take the breadcrumbs into your hands and break them down finely. Mix half into the mashed long yam, keeping the rest on a small plate.

3 Fill the underneath of the shiitake caps with a scoop of mashed long yam. Smooth down with the flat edge of a knife and dust the mash with cornflour. Add a little mash to a slice of scallop and place on top.

4 Spread another 5ml/1 tsp mashed long yam on to the scallop and shape to completely cover. Make sure all the ingredients are clinging together. Repeat to make eight little mounds.

5 Place the beaten eggs in a shallow container. Dust the shiitake and scallop mounds with cornflour, then dip into the egg. Handle with care as the mash and scallop are quite soft. Coat well with the remaining breadcrumbs.

6 Deep-fry the bundles in hot oil until they are golden and cooked through. Drain well on kitchen paper. Serve hot on individual plates with a wedge of lemon.

Spicy Shrimp Satay Energy 220kcal/922kJ; Protein 27.1g; Carbohydrate 11.5g, of which sugars 1g; Fat 7.3g, of which saturates 1g; Cholesterol 151mg; Calcium 99mg; Fibre 1.5g; Sodium 249mg.
Shiitake Bundles Energy 812kcal/3396kJ; Protein 45.8g; Carbohydrate 54g, of which sugars 12.6g; Fat 47.8g, of which saturates 7.5g; Cholesterol 428mg; Calcium 279mg; Fibre 7g; Sodium 741mg.

Sweet and Sour Deep-fried Squid

This is an example of a dish where the Western influence comes into play – with tomato ketchup and Worcestershire sauce used alongside more traditional ingredients.

Serves 4
900g/2lb fresh young, tender squid
vegetable oil, for deep-frying

For the marinade
60ml/4 tbsp light soy sauce
15ml/1 tbsp sugar

For the dipping sauce
30ml/2 tbsp tomato ketchup
15ml/1 tbsp Worcestershire sauce
15ml/1 tbsp light soy sauce
15ml/1 tbsp vegetable or sesame oil
sugar or honey, to sweeten
chilli oil, to taste

1 First prepare the squid. Hold the body in one hand and pull off the head with the other. Sever the tentacles and discard the rest. Remove the backbone and clean the body sac inside and out. Pat dry using kitchen paper and cut into rings.

2 In a bowl, mix the soy sauce with the sugar until it dissolves. Toss in the squid rings and tentacles and marinate for 1 hour.

3 Meanwhile prepare the sweet-and-sour sauce. Mix together the tomato ketchup, Worcestershire sauce, soy sauce and oil. Sweeten the sauce with sugar or honey to taste and a little chilli oil to give the sauce a bit of bite. Set aside.

4 Heat enough oil for deep-frying in a wok or heavy pan. Thoroughly drain the squid of any marinade and pat with kitchen paper to avoid spitting

5 Fry the squid in small batches until golden and crispy. Pat dry on kitchen paper and serve immediately with the dipping sauce.

Cook's Tip
To avoid the spitting fat, lightly coat the squid in flour before deep-frying. Alternatively, fry in a deep-fat fryer with a lid or use a splatterproof cover on the wok or pan.

Crispy Salt and Pepper Squid

Serves 4
750g/1lb 10oz fresh squid, cleaned
juice of 4–5 lemons
15ml/1 tbsp ground black pepper
15ml/1 tbsp sea salt
10ml/2 tsp caster (superfine) sugar
115g/4oz/1 cup cornflour (cornstarch)
3 egg whites, lightly beaten
vegetable oil, for deep-frying
chilli sauce, for dipping
skewers or toothpicks, to serve

1 Cut the squid into bitesize pieces. Trim the tentacles. Marinate in a bowl with the lemon juice for 15 minutes. Drain and pat dry.

2 Mix the pepper, salt, sugar and cornflour. Dip the squid in the egg whites and toss lightly in the seasoned flour.

3 Fill a wok one-third full of oil and heat to 180°C/350°F. Deep-fry the squid in small batches for 1 minute. Drain the crispy pieces on kitchen paper and serve immediately, threaded on to skewers, with chilli sauce for dipping.

Black Pepper Fried Squid

Serves 4
450g/1lb baby squid, cleaned
30ml/2 tbsp coarse salt
15ml/1 tbsp ground black pepper
50g/2oz/½ cup rice flour or cornflour (cornstarch)
vegetable oil, for deep-frying
2 limes, cut into wedges

1 Using a sharp knife, slice the squid into rings and pat them dry with kitchen paper. Put them in a dish with the tentacles.

2 Combine the salt and pepper with the rice flour or cornflour, add it to the squid and toss well to coat evenly.

3 Heat the oil for deep-frying in a wok or heavy pan. Cook the squid in batches, until the rings turn crisp and golden.

4 Drain on kitchen paper and serve with lime wedges to squeeze over. This dish can also be served with noodles, or with chunks of baguette and fresh chillies.

Sweet and Sour Squid Energy 315kcal/1320kJ; Protein 35.2g; Carbohydrate 4.5g, of which sugars 1.7g; Fat 17.6g, of which saturates 2.5g; Cholesterol 506mg; Calcium 39mg; Fibre 0g; Sodium 1361mg.
Salt and Pepper Squid Energy 346kcal/1462kJ; Protein 31.2g; Carbohydrate 31.3g, of which sugars 2.6g; Fat 11.6g, of which saturates 1.8g; Cholesterol 422mg; Calcium 32mg; Fibre 0g; Sodium 1741mg.
Black Pepper Fried Squid Energy 339kcal/1405kJ; Protein 14g; Carbohydrate 5g, of which sugars 0g; Fat 29g, of which saturates 4g; Cholesterol 146mg; Calcium 70mg; Fibre 0g; Sodium 140mg.

Lemon Chilli Razor Clams

Razor clams have beautiful striped gold and brown tubular shells and make a wonderful and unusual appetizer. Here they are lightly steamed and tossed in a fragrant Italian-style dressing of chilli, lemon, garlic and parsley. Serve with plenty of crusty bread for mopping up the delicious pan juices.

Serves 4
12 razor clams
90–120ml/6–8 tbsp olive oil
finely grated rind and juice of 1 small lemon
2 garlic cloves, very finely grated
1 red chilli, seeded and chopped
60ml/4 tbsp chopped flat leaf parsley
salt and ground black pepper
mixed salad leaves and crusty bread, to serve

1 Wash the razor clams well in plenty of cold running water. Drain and arrange half the clams in a steamer, placing them side by side, with the hinge side down.

2 Pour 5cm/2in water into a wok and bring to the boil. Balance the steamer over the water and cover tightly. Steam for 3–4 minutes until the clams have opened. Discard any clams that remain closed. Remove the clams from the wok and keep warm while you steam the remaining clams in the same way.

3 Pour the olive oil into a small bowl. Add the grated lemon rind and juice, stir well, then add the garlic, red chilli and flat leaf parsley. Mix thoroughly.

4 Season the dressing well with salt and pepper. Spoon the steamed razor clams on to plates and spoon the dressing over. Serve immediately with mixed-leaf salad and crusty bread.

Cook's Tip
To avoid the risk of food poisoning, it is essential that the clams are live before cooking. Tap any open clams with the back of a knife. Any that do not close are dead and so must be discarded; and any that remain closed after cooking should also be thrown away immediately.

Stir-fried Clams with Orange

Serves 4
1kg/2¼lb fresh clams
15ml/1 tbsp sunflower oil
30ml/2 tbsp finely chopped garlic
4 shallots, finely chopped
105ml/7 tbsp fish stock
grated rind and juice of 1 orange
a large handful of roughly chopped flat leaf parsley
salt and ground black pepper

1 Scrub the clams under cold running water. Discard any that are open and do not close when tapped lightly with a knife.

2 Heat the oil in a wok. Add the garlic, shallots and clams and stir-fry for 4–5 minutes. Add the stock and orange and season well. Cover and cook for 3–4 minutes, or until the clams have opened. (Discard any unopened clams.)

3 Stir the parsley into the clams, then serve immediately.

Steamed Oysters with Zesty Tomato and Cucumber Salsa

Serves 4
30ml/2 tbsp sunflower oil
1 garlic clove, crushed
15ml/1 tbsp light soy sauce
12–16 oysters, opened

For the salsa
1 plum tomato, seeded and diced
½ small cucumber, diced
¼ small red onion, diced
15ml/1 tbsp very finely chopped coriander (cilantro)
1 small red chilli, seeded and very finely chopped
juice of 1–2 limes
salt and ground black pepper

1 Place the salsa ingredients in a bowl and season to taste. Set aside (at room temperature) for 15–20 minutes.

2 In a separate bowl, mix together the oil, garlic and soy sauce. Arrange the oysters in their half shells in a steamer and spoon over the sauce. Cover the steamer and place over a wok of simmering water. Steam for 2–3 minutes. Place the oysters in a dish, top with a little salsa and serve.

Razor Clams Energy 188Kcal/775kJ; Protein 6.1g; Carbohydrate 2.9g, of which sugars 0.5g; Fat 16.9g, of which saturates 2.4g; Cholesterol 20mg; Calcium 47mg; Fibre 1.1g; Sodium 364mg.
Clams with Orange Energy 142kcal/596kJ; Protein 21.4g; Carbohydrate 5.9g, of which sugars 1.6g; Fat 3.8g, of which saturates 0.6g; Cholesterol 84mg; Calcium 121mg; Fibre 1.2g; Sodium 1506mg.
Steamed Oysters Energy 82Kcal/339kJ; Protein 4.5g; Carbohydrate 2.4g, of which sugars 1.3g; Fat 6.1g, of which saturates 0.8g; Cholesterol 21mg; Calcium 60mg; Fibre 0.4g; Sodium 461mg.

Crab Dim Sum with Chinese Chives

These delectable Chinese-style dumplings have a wonderfully sticky texture and make a perfect appetizer. You can make these in advance, storing them in the refrigerator until ready to cook. Steam them just before serving, then enjoy the sensation as your teeth sink through the soft wrapper into the savoury crab filling.

Serves 4

150g/5oz fresh white crab meat
115g/4oz minced (ground) pork
30ml/2 tbsp chopped Chinese chives
15ml/1 tbsp finely chopped red (bell) pepper
30ml/2 tbsp sweet chilli sauce
30ml/2 tbsp hoisin sauce
24 fresh dumpling wrappers (available from Asian stores)
Chinese chives, to garnish
chilli oil and soy sauce, to serve

1 Place the crab meat, pork and chopped chives in a bowl. Add the finely chopped red pepper and mix together well using a metal spoon, then pour in the sweet chilli and hoisin sauces. Stir until thoroughly combined.

2 Working with 2–3 wrappers at a time, put a spoonful of the mixture on to each wrapper. Brush the edges of a wrapper with water and fold over to form a half-moon shape. Press and pleat the edges to seal, and flatten. Cover with a clean, damp dish towel and make the rest.

3 Arrange the dumplings on three lightly oiled plates and fit inside three tiers of a bamboo steamer. Alternatively, use a stainless steel steamer or an electric steamer.

4 Cover the bamboo steamer and place over a wok of simmering water (making sure the water does not touch the steamer). Steam for 8–10 minutes, or until the dumplings are cooked through and become slightly translucent. If using an electric steamer follow the manufacturer's instructions.

5 Divide the dumplings among four plates. Garnish with Chinese chives and serve immediately with chilli oil and soy sauce for dipping.

Eel Wrapped in Bacon with Lemon Grass and Ginger

Rich in flavour, eel is delicious grilled or stir-fried. Serve this spicy dish with a dipping sauce, a crunchy salad and jasmine rice.

Serves 4–6

2 lemon grass stalks, trimmed and chopped
25g/1oz fresh root ginger, peeled and chopped
2 garlic cloves, chopped
2 shallots, chopped
15ml/1 tbsp palm sugar (jaggery)
15ml/1 tbsp vegetable or groundnut (peanut) oil, plus extra if frying
30ml/2 tbsp nuoc mam
1.2kg/2½lb fresh eel, skinned and cut into 2.5cm/1in pieces
12 rashers (slices) streaky (fatty) bacon
ground black pepper
a small bunch of fresh coriander (cilantro) leaves, to garnish
nuoc cham, for dipping

1 Using a mortar and pestle, pound the lemon grass, ginger, garlic, shallots and sugar to a paste. Mix in the oil and nuoc mam, and season with pepper. Put the eel in a dish and smear with the paste. Cover and place in the refrigerator for 2–3 hours to marinate.

2 Wrap each piece of marinated eel in a strip of bacon, gathering up as much of the marinade as possible.

3 To cook the eel parcels, you can use a wok or grill (broiler). Heat a little oil in a wok. Fry the eel parcels until browned and crispy, roughly 2–3 minutes on each side.

4 Alternatively, place the eel parcels in a grill or griddle pan. Cook the parcels until they are browned and crispy, roughly 2–3 minutes on each side.

5 Serve with fresh coriander leaves and nuoc cham for dipping.

Cook's Tip
When buying fresh eel, ask the fishmonger to gut it, cut off the head, bone it, skin it and slice it for you.

Crab Dim Sum Energy 166kcal/700kJ; Protein 14.7g; Carbohydrate 20.5g, of which sugars 1.4g; Fat 3.3g, of which saturates 1.1g; Cholesterol 46mg; Calcium 83mg; Fibre 0.8g; Sodium 287mg.
Eel Wrapped in Bacon Energy 460kcal/1911kJ; Protein 39.3g; Carbohydrate 0.8g, of which sugars 0.6g; Fat 33.3g, of which saturates 9g; Cholesterol 324mg; Calcium 43mg; Fibre 0.1g; Sodium 650mg.

Tempura Seafood with Squid and Whiting

This Japanese dish actually has its origins in the West, as tempura was introduced to Japan by Portuguese traders in the 17th century.

Serves 4

130g/4½oz squid body, cleaned, skinned and cut open
115g/4oz whiting fillets
⅛ nori sheet, 5 x 4cm/2½ x 1in
20g/¾oz dried harusame noodles
8 okra
4 fresh shiitake mushrooms, stalks removed
8 large raw prawns (shrimp), heads and shells removed, tails intact, and deveined
vegetable oil and sesame oil, for deep-frying
plain (all-purpose) flour, for dusting
salt

For the dipping sauce
400ml/14fl oz/1⅔ cups water
15ml/1 tsp second dashi stock
200ml/7fl oz/scant 1 cup shoyu
200ml/7fl oz/scant 1 cup mirin

For the condiment
4cm/1½in fresh root ginger, peeled and finely grated
450g/1lb mooli (daikon), peeled and finely grated

For the tempura batter
ice-cold water
1 large (US extra large) egg, beaten
200g/7oz/1¾ cups plain flour
2–3 ice cubes

1 Cut the squid and whiting into 2.5 x 6cm/1 x 2½in strips. Cut the nori into four long strips. Tie each nori strip round the middle of a bunch of harusame noodles. Wet the end to fix it.

2 For the condiment, lay clear film (plastic wrap) over an egg cup and press 2.5ml/½ tsp grated ginger into the bottom. Add 30ml/2 tbsp grated daikon. Press and invert on to a small plate. Make three more ginger and daikon moulds in the same way.

3 Half-fill a wok with 3 parts vegetable oil to 1 part sesame oil. Bring to 175°C/347°F over a medium heat.

4 Make the tempura batter. Add enough ice-cold water to the egg to make 150ml/¼ pint/⅔ cup, then pour into a bowl. Add the flour and mix roughly with chopsticks. Do not beat; leave the batter lumpy. Add some ice cubes to keep the temperature cool.

5 Dip the okra into the batter and deep-fry until golden. Drain. Batter the underside of the shiitake, and deep-fry. Then fry the harusame by dipping them into the oil for a few seconds. Drain on kitchen paper and sprinkle with salt.

6 Hold the tail of a prawn, dust with flour, then dip into the batter. Deep-fry one to two prawns at a time until crisp. Dust the whiting strips, dip into the batter, then deep-fry until golden. Wipe the squid strips well with kitchen paper, dust with flour, then dip in batter. Deep-fry until the batter is crisp.

7 Drain excess oil from the tempura on a wire rack for a few minutes, then arrange them on individual plates. Set the condiment alongside the tempura.

8 Bring the dipping sauce ingredients to the boil in a pan, then pour into four small bowls. Serve immediately, mixing the condiment into the dipping sauce and dunking the tempura as you eat.

Salmon and Ginger Fish Cakes

These light fish cakes are scented with the exotic flavours of sesame, lime and ginger. They make a tempting appetizer served simply with a wedge of lime for squeezing over, but are also perfect for a light lunch or supper, served with a refreshing salad. The fish cakes need to be chilled before they are cooked, so make them about two hours before you wish to cook them.

Makes 25

500g/1¼lb salmon fillet, skinned and boned
45ml/3 tbsp dried breadcrumbs
30ml/2 tbsp mayonnaise
30ml/2 tbsp sesame seeds
30ml/2 tbsp light soy sauce
finely grated rind of 2 limes
10ml/2 tsp fresh root ginger, grated
4 spring onions (scallions), sliced
vegetable oil, for frying
salt and ground black pepper
spring onions (scallions), to garnish
lime wedges, to serve

1 Finely chop the salmon and place in a bowl. Add the dried breadcrumbs, mayonnaise, sesame seeds, soy sauce, finely grated lime rind, grated ginger and sliced spring onions and use your fingers to mix well.

2 With wet hands, divide the mixture into 25 portions and shape each into a small round cake. Place the cakes on a baking sheet lined with baking parchment, cover and chill for at least two hours. They can be left overnight.

3 When you are ready to cook the fish cakes, heat about 5cm/2in vegetable oil in a wok and fry the fish cakes in batches, over a medium heat, for 2–3 minutes on each side.

4 Drain the fish cakes well on kitchen paper and serve warm or at room temperature, garnished with spring onion slivers and plenty of lime wedges for squeezing over.

Cook's Tip
When chopping the salmon, look out for stray bones and pick these out with tweezers.

Tempura Seafood Energy 401Kcal/1683kJ; Protein 27.3g; Carbohydrate 42.8g, of which sugars 4.1g; Fat 14.5g, of which saturates 2.2g; Cholesterol 231mg; Calcium 167mg; Fibre 3.2g; Sodium 1080mg.
Salmon Fish Cakes Energy 83Kcal/343kJ; Protein 4.6g; Carbohydrate 1.6g, of which sugars 0.2g; Fat 6.5g, of which saturates 0.9g; Cholesterol 11mg; Calcium 16mg; Fibre 0.2g; Sodium 117mg.

Fish Balls with Chinese Greens

These tasty fish balls are steamed over a wok and served with a selection of green vegetables.

Serves 4

For the fish balls

450g/1lb white fish fillets, skinned, boned and cubed
3 spring onions (scallions), chopped
1 lean bacon rasher (strip), rinded and chopped
15ml/1 tbsp Chinese rice wine
30ml/2 tbsp light soy sauce
1 egg white

For the vegetables

1 small head pak choi (bok choy)
30ml/2 tbsp groundnut oil
2 garlic cloves, sliced
2.5cm/1in fresh root ginger, cut into thin shreds
75g/3oz green beans
175g/6oz mangetouts (snow peas)
3 spring onions (scallions), sliced diagonally into 5–7.5cm/2–3in lengths
5ml/1 tsp cornflour (cornstarch)
15ml/1 tbsp light soy sauce
150ml/¼ pint/⅔ cup fish stock
salt and ground black pepper

1 Put the fish, spring onions, bacon, rice wine, soy sauce and egg white in a food processor and process until smooth. With wetted hands, form the mixture into about 24 small balls.

2 Steam the fish balls in batches in a lightly greased bamboo steamer in a wok for 5–10 minutes until cooked through and firm. Remove from the steamer and keep warm.

3 Meanwhile trim the pak choi, removing any damaged leaves or stems, then tear into manageable pieces.

4 Heat a wok until hot, add the oil and swirl it around. Add the garlic and ginger and stir-fry for 2–3 minutes. Add the beans and stir-fry for 2–3 minutes.

5 Add the mangetouts, the spring onions and the pak choi to the wok. Stir-fry for 2–3 minutes.

6 Blend the cornflour, soy sauce and stock and add to the wok.

7 Cook, stirring, until the sauce thickens. Taste and season if necessary. Serve with the fish balls.

Thai Fish Cakes with Cucumber Relish

These wonderful little nibbles are a very familiar and popular appetizer.

Serves 4

300g/11oz white fish fillet, such as cod, cut into chunks
30ml/2 tbsp Thai red curry paste
1 egg
30ml/2 tbsp Thai fish sauce
5ml/1 tsp granulated (white) sugar
30ml/2 tbsp cornflour (cornstarch)
3 kaffir lime leaves, shredded
15ml/1 tbsp chopped fresh coriander (cilantro)
50g/2oz green beans, thinly sliced
vegetable oil, for frying
Chinese mustard cress, to garnish

For the cucumber relish

60ml/4 tbsp rice vinegar
60ml/4 tbsp water
50g/2oz/¼ cup sugar
1 whole bulb pickled garlic
1 cucumber, quartered and sliced
4 shallots, thinly sliced
15ml/1 tbsp chopped fresh root ginger

1 To make the cucumber relish, bring the vinegar, water and sugar to the boil. Stir until the sugar dissolves, then remove from the heat and leave to cool.

2 Combine the rest of the relish ingredients together in a bowl and pour the vinegar mixture over.

3 Combine the fish, curry paste and egg in a food processor and process until combined. Transfer the mixture to a bowl, add the Thai fish sauce, sugar, cornflour, lime leaves, coriander and green beans and mix well.

4 Mould and shape the mixture into patties about 5cm/2in in diameter and 5mm/¼in thick.

5 Heat the oil in a wok or deep-fryer. Add the fish cakes, in small batches, and deep-fry for about 4–5 minutes, or until golden brown. Remove and drain well on kitchen paper. Keep the cooked fish cakes warm in a low oven while you cook the remainder. Garnish with Chinese mustard cress and serve immediately with a little cucumber relish spooned on the side.

Fish Balls with Greens Energy 194kcal/812kJ; Protein 24.9g; Carbohydrate 8.7g, of which sugars 6.8g; Fat 6.7g, of which saturates 0.8g; Cholesterol 52mg; Calcium 81mg; Fibre 3.2g; Sodium 892mg.
Thai Fish Cakes Energy 86kcal/361kJ; Protein 6.2g; Carbohydrate 8.1g, of which sugars 5.4g; Fat 3.4g, of which saturates 0.5g; Cholesterol 27mg; Calcium 16mg; Fibre 0.2g; Sodium 2040mg.

Ginger and Chilli Steamed Fish Custards

These pretty little custards make an unusual and exotic appetizer for a dinner party. The pandanus leaves impart a distinctive flavour – but don't be tempted to eat them once the custards are cooked: they are inedible.

Serves 4

2 eggs
200ml/7fl oz/scant 1 cup coconut cream
60ml/4 tbsp chopped fresh coriander (cilantro)
1 red chilli, seeded and sliced
15ml/1 tbsp finely chopped lemon grass
2 kaffir lime leaves, finely shredded
30ml/2 tbsp red Thai curry paste
1 garlic clove, crushed
5ml/1 tsp finely grated fresh root ginger
2 spring onions (scallions), finely sliced
300g/11oz mixed firm white fish fillets (cod, halibut or haddock), skinned
200g/7oz raw tiger prawns (shrimp), peeled and deveined
4–6 pandanus (screwpine) leaves
salt and ground black pepper
shredded cucumber, steamed rice and soy sauce, to serve

1 Beat the eggs in a bowl, then stir in the coconut cream, coriander, chilli, lemon grass, lime leaves, curry paste, garlic, ginger and spring onions. Finely chop the fish and roughly chop the prawns and add to the egg mixture. Stir well and season.

2 Grease four ramekins and line them with the pandanus leaves. Divide the fish mixture between them, then arrange in a bamboo steamer.

3 Pour 5cm/2in water into a wok and bring to the boil. Suspend the steamer over the water, cover, reduce the heat to low and steam for 25–30 minutes, or until cooked through. Serve with shredded cucumber, steamed rice and soy sauce.

Cook's Tip
Pandanus leaves are available from Asian markets.

Steamed Sole Lettuce Wraps

Lettuce has a delicate texture and subtle flavour that makes it ideal for light fish mixtures such as this.

Serves 4

2 large sole or flounder fillets, skinned
15ml/1 tbsp sesame seeds
15ml/1 tbsp sunflower oil
10ml/2 tsp sesame oil
2.5cm/1in piece of fresh root ginger, peeled and grated
3 garlic cloves, peeled and finely chopped
15ml/1 tbsp soy sauce or fish sauce, plus extra, to serve
juice of 1 lemon
1 spring onion (scallion), thinly sliced
8 large soft lettuce leaves
12 large fresh mussels, scrubbed and bearded
salt and freshly ground black pepper

1 Cut the sole or flounder fillets in half lengthways. Season well and set aside. Prepare a steamer. Heat a heavy frying pan and lightly toast the sesame seeds. Transfer into a bowl and set aside.

2 Heat both oils in the frying pan over medium heat. Add the ginger and garlic and cook until lightly coloured, then stir in the soy sauce or fish sauce with the lemon juice and spring onion. Remove from the heat, add the sesame seeds and stir well.

3 Lay a piece of fish, skin side up, on a board or square of baking parchment. Spread evenly with the ginger mixture, then roll up, starting at the tail end. Repeat with the remaining fish and filling.

4 Plunge the lettuce leaves into the boiling water in the wok below the steamer. Immediately lift them out, using tongs or a slotted spoon. Pat dry with kitchen paper. Wrap each fish roll in two lettuce leaves, making sure that the filling is well covered.

5 Arrange the parcels in the steamer basket, cover and steam for 8 minutes. Add the mussels and steam for 2–4 minutes, until they have opened. Discard any that remain closed.

6 Halve each parcel and arrange two halves on each plate. Drizzle soy sauce or fish sauce around, and place three mussels on each plate.

Ginger Fish Custards Energy 150kcal/632kJ; Protein 26.2g; Carbohydrate 2.8g, of which sugars 2.7g; Fat 3.9g, of which saturates 1g; Cholesterol 227mg; Calcium 100mg; Fibre 0.6g; Sodium 234mg.
Steamed Sole Energy 118kcal/492kJ; Protein 15.3g; Carbohydrate 0.9g, of which sugars 0.9g; Fat 5.9g, of which saturates 0.7g; Cholesterol 41mg; Calcium 46mg; Fibre 0.3g; Sodium 359mg.

Fiery Tuna Spring Rolls

This modern take on the classic spring roll is substantial enough to serve as a main meal.

Serves 4

1 large chunk of very fresh thick tuna steak , approximately 12 x 20cm/4½ x 8in
45ml/3 tbsp light soy sauce
30ml/2 tbsp wasabi
16 mangetouts (snow peas), trimmed
8 spring roll wrappers
sunflower oil, for deep-frying
soft noodles and stir-fried Asian greens, to serve
soy sauce and sweet chilli sauce, for dipping

1 Place the tuna on a board. Using a sharp knife cut it into eight slices, each measuring about 12 x 2.5cm/4½ x 1in.

2 Place the tuna in a large, non-metallic dish in a single layer. Mix together the soy sauce and the wasabi and spoon evenly over the fish. Cover and marinate for 10–15 minutes.

3 Meanwhile, blanch the mangetouts in boiling water for about 1 minute, drain and refresh under cold water. Drain and pat dry with kitchen paper.

4 Place a spring roll wrapper on a clean work surface and place a piece of tuna on top, in the centre. Top the tuna with two mangetouts and fold over the sides and roll up. Brush the edges of the wrappers to seal.

5 Repeat with the remaining tuna, mangetouts and wrappers.

6 Fill a large wok or heavy pan one-third full with oil and heat to 180°C/350°F or until a cube of bread browns in 45 seconds. Working in batches, deep-fry the spring rolls for 1–2 minutes, until they are crisp and golden.

7 Drain the rolls on kitchen paper and serve immediately with soft noodles and Asian greens.

8 Serve the spring rolls with side dishes of soy sauce and sweet chilli sauce for dipping.

Crisp Chicken Rolls with Chilli

These Indonesian spring rolls are packed with vegetables and strips of chicken.

Serves 3 to 4

15–30ml/1–2 tbsp palm or corn oil
2–3 garlic cloves, finely chopped
225g/8oz chicken breast fillets, cut into fine strips
225g/8oz fresh shrimp, shelled
2 leeks, cut into matchsticks
2 carrots, cut into matchsticks
½ green cabbage, finely shredded
175g/6oz fresh beansprouts
30ml/2 tbsp patis (Filipino fish sauce)
30ml/2 tbsp kecap manis (sweet soy sauce)
1 egg, lightly beaten
corn or vegetable oil, for deep-frying
4 red or green Thai chillies, seeded and finely sliced, to serve

For the spring roll wrappers
115g/4oz/1 cup rice flour
30ml/2 tbsp cornflour (cornstarch)
2 eggs, beaten
15ml/1 tbsp palm or coconut oil
400ml/14fl oz/1⅔ cups water
corn or vegetable oil, for frying
salt

For the dipping sauce
200ml/7fl oz kecap manis (sweet soy sauce)
1 red chilli, seeded and chopped

1 Sift the flours for wrappers into a bowl. Add the eggs and oil, and beat in the water until a smooth batter forms. Set aside. Mix together the ingredients for the sauce into a serving bowl.

2 Heat a little oil in a frying pan. Ladle in a little batter and cook on one side until lightly browned. Lift the wrapper on to a plate. Repeat with the remaining batter.

3 Heat 15ml/1 tbsp oil in a wok. Fry the garlic, chicken and shrimp until cooked. Set aside. Heat the remaining oil and stir-fry the leeks, carrots and cabbage for 3 minutes. Stir-fry the beansprouts for 1–2 minutes. Add the chicken, shrimp, patis and kecap manis. Tip on to a plate and leave to cool.

4 Fill the wrappers by adding a spoonful of the filling on to one side. Spread to form a log, then roll the wrapper over, tuck in the sides and continue rolling. Seal the end with beaten egg.

5 Heat the oil in a wok. Fry two rolls at a time for 4 minutes, until golden. Remove, drain and serve with sauce and chillies.

Fiery Tuna Spring Rolls Energy 171kcal/717kJ; Protein 14.1g; Carbohydrate 11.4g, of which sugars 1.7g; Fat 8g, of which saturates 1.3g; Cholesterol 14mg; Calcium 36mg; Fibre 0.8g; Sodium 825mg.
Crisp Chicken Rolls Energy 585kcal/2446kJ; Protein 35.4g; Carbohydrate 43.5g, of which sugars 7.2g; Fat 31.2g, of which saturates 4.5g; Cholesterol 292mg; Calcium 170mg; Fibre 5.1g; Sodium 744mg.

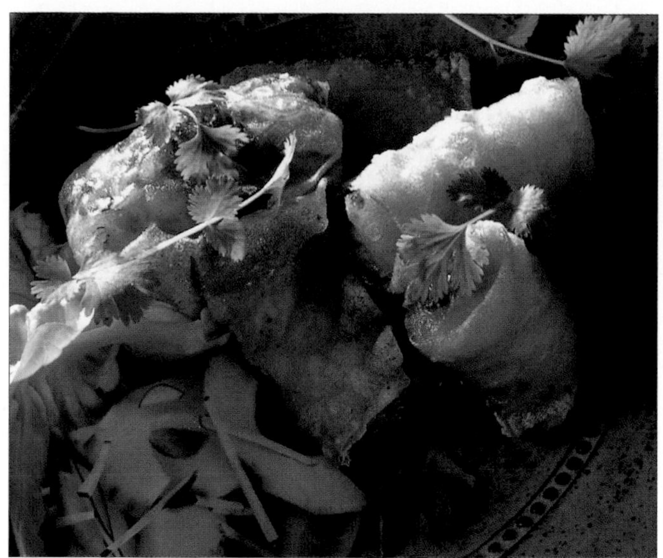

Rice Paper Rolls with a Spicy Dip

Vietnamese nuoc cham is a the perfect dipping sauce for these rice paper rolls.

Makes 25

6 dried Chinese mushrooms, soaked in hot water for 30 minutes
225g/8oz lean ground pork
115g/4oz uncooked prawns (shrimp), peeled, deveined and chopped
115g/4oz white crabmeat
1 carrot, shredded
50g/2oz cellophane (bean thread) noodles, soaked in water, drained and cut into short lengths
4 spring onions (scallions), sliced
2 garlic cloves, finely chopped
30ml/2 tbsp fish sauce
juice of 1 lime
freshly ground black pepper
25 x 10cm/10 x 4in Vietnamese rice sheets
oil, for deep-frying
lettuce leaves, cucumber slices and coriander leaves, to garnish

For the nuoc cham

2 garlic cloves, finely chopped
30ml/2 tbsp white wine vinegar
juice of 1 lime
30ml/2 tbsp sugar
120ml/4fl oz/½ cup fish sauce
120ml/4fl oz/½ cup water
2 red chillies, seeded and chopped

1 Drain the mushrooms, squeezing out the excess moisture. Remove the stems and thinly slice the caps into a bowl. Add the pork, prawns, crabmeat, carrot, noodles, spring onions and garlic. Season with the fish sauce, lime juice and pepper. Set aside for about 30 minutes to allow the flavours to blend.

2 Make the nuoc cham by mixing the garlic, vinegar, lime juice, sugar, fish sauce, water and chillies in bowl. Cover and set aside.

3 Assemble the spring rolls. Place a rice sheet on a flat surface and brush with warm water until it is pliable. Place 10ml/2 tsp of the filling near the edge of the rice sheet. Fold the sides over the filling, fold in the ends, then roll up, sealing the ends with a little water. Make more rolls until the filling is used up.

4 Add the oil for deep-frying to a wok and heat to 180°C/350°F. Fry the spring rolls, a few at a time, until crisp. Drain on kitchen paper. Serve hot, garnished with lettuce leaves, cucumber and coriander, and accompanied by the nuoc cham dipping sauce.

Thai Spring Rolls

Crunchy spring rolls are as popular in Thailand as in China. Everyone loves them.

Makes 24

4–6 Chinese dried mushrooms, soaked for 30 minutes
50g/2oz cellophane noodles
30ml/2 tbsp vegetable oil
2 garlic cloves, chopped
2 fresh red chillies, seeded and chopped
225g/8oz minced (ground) pork
50g/2oz cooked prawns (shrimp)
30ml/2 tbsp Thai fish sauce
5ml/1 tsp sugar
ground black pepper
1 carrot, grated
50g/2oz drained canned bamboo shoots, chopped
50g/2oz/1 cup beansprouts
2 spring onions (scallions), finely chopped
15ml/1 tbsp chopped fresh coriander (cilantro)
24 x 15cm/6in square spring roll wrappers
flour and water paste, for sealing rolls
vegetable oil, for deep-frying
Thai sweet chilli dipping sauce, to serve (optional)

1 Drain the soaked dried Chinese mushrooms, discard the stems and chop the caps finely.

2 Soak the noodles in boiling water for 10 minutes. Drain the noodles and chop them into 5cm/2in lengths.

3 Heat the oil in a wok, add the garlic and chillies and stir-fry for 30 seconds. Transfer to a plate. Add the pork to the wok and stir-fry until browned. Add the noodles, mushrooms and prawns. Stir in the fish sauce and sugar; season with pepper.

4 Tip the noodle mixture into a bowl and stir in the carrot, bamboo shoots, beansprouts, spring onions and chopped coriander together with the reserved chilli mixture.

5 Unwrap the spring roll wrappers. Place a spoonful of filling in the centre of each wrapper, turn up the bottom edge, fold in the sides, then roll up and seal with flour and water paste.

6 Heat the oil and fry the spring rolls until crisp and golden brown. Drain on kitchen paper and keep hot while cooking successive batches. Serve hot, with a chilli sauce, if you like.

Rice Paper Rolls Energy 55kcal/232kJ; Protein 4.5g; Carbohydrate 7g, of which sugars 0.3g; Fat 0.9g, of which saturates 0.3g; Cholesterol 31mg; Calcium 10mg; Fibre 0.1g; Sodium 24mg.
Thai Spring Rolls Energy 74kcal/310kJ; Protein 3.1g; Carbohydrate 7.2g, of which sugars 0.7g; Fat 3.8g, of which saturates 0.7g; Cholesterol 10mg; Calcium 13mg; Fibre 0.4g; Sodium 12mg.

Chicken and Bean Curd Parcels

Serves 4
4 dried Chinese black mushrooms
300g/11oz chicken breast fillet
30ml/2 tbsp vegetable oil
30ml/2 tbsp black bean sauce
2.5ml/½ tsp ground black pepper
2.5ml/½ tsp sugar
30ml/2 tbsp sesame oil
100ml/3½fl oz/scant ½ cup water
1–2 sheets of beancurd skins

1 Soak the mushrooms in a bowl of boiling water for 20 minutes. Drain and slice into thin strips, discarding the stems. Slice the chicken into 1cm/½in thick strips.

2 Heat the oil in a wok. Add the chicken and mushroom and stir-fry for 3 minutes. Add the black bean sauce, pepper, sugar and sesame oil and stir-fry for 2 minutes. Pour in the water. Cook over high heat until the mixture is almost dry. Leave to cool.

3 Cut the beancurd into pieces about 10cm/4in wide. Top with the chicken and mushroom, tuck in the edges and roll up to make parcels about 6cm/2½in long. Place the parcels on a plate and steam over a wok of boiling water for 10 minutes. Serve hot.

Chicken and Banana Rolls

Serves 4
2 boneless chicken breast fillets, skinned
2 ripe bananas
1 egg, lightly beaten
150g/5oz/1¼ cups cornflour (cornstarch)
vegetable oil for deep-frying

1 Slice the chicken breasts diagonally into 3–4 thin escalopes. Put these between pieces of clear film (plastic wrap) and pound lightly with a meat mallet to tenderize.

2 Slice each banana into 3–4 lengths. Dip each piece in a little egg and place on an escalope. Roll up and coat with cornflour.

3 Heat the oil in a wok to 190°C/375°F. Fry the rolls, in batches, for 3–4 minutes, until crisp. Drain on kitchen paper, then slice each roll diagonally, pile the pieces on a plate and serve.

Chicken Lettuce Parcels

Known as sang choy in Hong Kong, this is a popular assemble-it-yourself treat. The filling is served with crisp lettuce leaves, which are used as wrappers.

Serves 6
2 chicken breast fillets, total weight about 350g/12oz
4 dried Chinese mushrooms, soaked for 30 minutes in warm water to cover
30ml/2 tbsp vegetable oil
2 garlic cloves, crushed
6 drained canned water chestnuts, thinly sliced
30ml/2 tbsp light soy sauce
5ml/1 tsp Szechuan peppercorns, dry-fried and crushed
4 spring onions (scallions), finely chopped
5ml/1 tsp sesame oil
vegetable oil, for deep-frying
50g/2oz cellophane noodles
salt and ground black pepper (optional)
1 crisp lettuce, divided into leaves, and 60ml/4 tbsp hoisin sauce, to serve

1 Remove the skin from the chicken breast fillets, pat dry and set aside. Chop the chicken into thin strips.

2 Drain the soaked mushrooms. Cut off and discard the mushroom stems; slice the caps finely and set aside.

3 Heat the oil in a wok or large frying pan. Add the garlic, then add the chicken. Stir-fry until the pieces are cooked through. Add the sliced mushrooms, water chestnuts, soy sauce and peppercorns. Toss for 2–3 minutes, then season. Stir in half the spring onions, then the sesame oil. Set aside.

4 Cut the chicken skin into strips, deep fry in hot oil until very crisp and drain on kitchen paper.

5 Deep fry the noodles until crisp. Drain on kitchen paper.

6 Crush the noodles and put in a serving dish. Top with the chicken skin, chicken mixture and the remaining spring onions. Arrange the lettuce leaves on a platter. Toss the chicken and noodles to mix. Invite guests to take a lettuce leaf, spread the inside with hoisin sauce and add a spoonful of filling, turning in the sides of the leaf and rolling it into a parcel before eating it.

Chicken and Bean Curd Energy 188kcal/785kJ; Protein 18.6g; Carbohydrate 1.9g, of which sugars 0.6g; Fat 11.9g, of which saturates 1.7g; Cholesterol 53mg; Calcium 7mg; Fibre 0.2g; Sodium 46mg.
Chicken and Banana Energy 402kcal/1689kJ; Protein 20.4g; Carbohydrate 46.1g, of which sugars 10.5g; Fat 16.4g, of which saturates 2.3g; Cholesterol 100mg; Calcium 20mg; Fibre 0.6g; Sodium 83mg.
Lettuce Parcels Energy 237kcal/984kJ; Protein 15.3g; Carbohydrate 7.6g, of which sugars 1.1g; Fat 16.1g, of which saturates 2g; Cholesterol 41mg; Calcium 24mg; Fibre 0.6g; Sodium 41mg.

Scented Chicken Wraps

Serves 4
45ml/3 tbsp soy sauce
30ml/2 tbsp finely grated garlic
15ml/1 tbsp cumin
15ml/1 tbsp ground coriander
15ml/1 tbsp golden caster (superfine) sugar
5ml/1 tsp finely grated fresh root ginger
1 fresh bird's eye chilli
30ml/2 tbsp oyster sauce
15ml/1 tbsp fish sauce
400g/14oz skinless chicken thighs, boned, cut into bitesize pieces
1 bunch of pandanus (screwpine) leaves, to wrap
vegetable oil, for deep-frying
sweet chilli sauce, to serve

1 Place the soy sauce, garlic, cumin, coriander, sugar, ginger, chilli, oyster sauce and fish sauce in a blender and process. Pour over the chicken and marinate in the refrigerator for 6–8 hours.

2 When ready to cook, drain the chicken from the marinade and wrap each piece in a pandanus leaf (you will need to cut the leaves to size) and secure with a cocktail stick (toothpick).

3 Fill a wok one-third full of oil and heat to 180°C/350°F or until a cube of bread dropped into the oil browns in 45 seconds. Carefully add the chicken parcels, 3–4 at a time, and deep-fry for 3–4 minutes, or until cooked through.

4 Drain on kitchen paper and serve with the chilli sauce. (Do not eat the leaves!)

Lemon Grass Snails

Serves 4
24 fresh snails in their shells
225g/8oz lean minced (ground) pork, passed through the mincer (grinder) twice
3 lemon grass stalks, trimmed and finely chopped or ground (reserve the outer leaves)
2 spring onions (scallions), chopped
25g/1oz fresh root ginger, peeled and finely grated
1 fresh red chilli, seeded and finely chopped
10ml/2 tsp sesame oil
sea salt and ground black pepper
chilli sauce or other sauce, for dipping

1 Pull the snails out of their shells. Rinse thoroughly in cold water and pat dry with kitchen paper. Rinse the shells and leave to drain.

2 Chop the snails finely and put in a bowl. Add the minced pork, lemon grass, spring onions, ginger, chilli and oil. Season well.

3 Tear the best lemon grass leaves into thin ribbons, roughly 7.5cm/3in long. Bend each ribbon in half and put it inside a snail shell, so that the ends are poking out to help diners gently prize the steamed morsel out of its shell.

4 Stuff each shell with the snail and pork mixture, pushing it to the back of the shell so that it fills the shell completely.

5 Fill a wok a third of the way up with water and bring it to the boil. Arrange the snail shells, open side up, in a steamer that fits the wok. Cover and steam for about 10 minutes, until the mixture is cooked. Serve hot with chilli sauce.

Lotus Leaf Parcels with Chicken

The lotus leaves impart a delicious smoky flavour to the sticky jasmine rice in this dish.

Serves 4
2 large lotus leaves
300g/11oz/1½ cups Thai jasmine rice
400ml/14fl oz/1⅔ cups vegetable or chicken stock
8 dried shiitake mushrooms
15ml/1 tbsp sunflower oil
200g/7oz chicken thigh fillets, cut into small cubes
50g/2oz pancetta, cubed
3 garlic cloves, finely sliced
10ml/2 tsp finely grated fresh root ginger
50g/2oz carrots, cut into thin batons
50g/2oz mangetout (snow peas), halved lengthways
60ml/4 tbsp light soy sauce
15ml/1 tbsp Chinese rice wine
5ml/1 tsp cornflour (cornstarch)

1 Place the lotus leaves in a bowl and cover with hot water. Leave to soak for 1½ hours. Drain and cut in half, then set aside.

2 Place the rice in a wok with the stock. Bring to the boil, cook gently for 10 minutes, remove from the heat and leave to stand.

3 Soak the mushrooms in boiling water for 15 minutes, then drain, reserving the soaking liquid. Squeeze the mushrooms dry, discard the stems and thinly slice the caps. Set aside.

4 Add the oil to a clean wok and heat. Add the chicken and pancetta and stir-fry for 2–3 minutes. Add the garlic, ginger, carrots, mangetout and mushrooms and stir-fry for 30 seconds.

5 Add half the soy sauce, the rice wine and 60ml/4 tbsp of the reserved mushroom liquid to the wok. Mix the cornflour with 15ml/1 tbsp cold water, add to the wok and cook until the mixture thickens. Add the rice and remaining soy sauce and mix well.

6 Place the lotus leaves brown-side down and divide the chicken mixture among them. Fold in the sides, then roll up and place the parcels in a baking parchment-lined bamboo steamer. Cover the steamer and place over a wok of simmering water for about 20 minutes (replenishing the water in the wok if necessary). Serve immediately and unwrap at the table.

Chicken Wraps Energy 159kcal/669kJ; Protein 24.5g; Carbohydrate 6.8g, of which sugars 6.6g; Fat 3.9g, of which saturates 0.6g; Cholesterol 70mg; Calcium 10mg; Fibre 0.1g; Sodium 1055mg.
Lemon Grass Snails Energy 136kcal/573kJ; Protein 24.2g; Carbohydrate 0.2g, of which sugars 0.2g; Fat 4.3g, of which saturates 1.1g; Cholesterol 70mg; Calcium 9mg; Fibre 0.1g; Sodium 70mg.
Lotus Leaf Parcels Energy 377kcal/1581kJ; Protein 20.7g; Carbohydrate 63.7g, of which sugars 2.4g; Fat 4g, of which saturates 1.2g; Cholesterol 43mg; Calcium 31mg; Fibre 0.8g; Sodium 1082mg.

Pork Stuffed Omelettes

A chilli filling makes an interesting contrast to the delicate flavour of the egg in this delicious light lunch or supper dish.

Serves 4

30ml/2 tbsp groundnut (peanut) oil
2 garlic cloves, finely chopped
1 small onion, finely chopped
225g/8oz minced (ground) pork
30ml/2 tbsp fish sauce
5ml/1 tsp sugar
2 tomatoes, peeled and chopped
15ml/1 tbsp chopped fresh coriander (cilantro)
ground black pepper
fresh coriander (cilantro) sprigs and sliced fresh red chillies, to garnish

For the omelettes

5 eggs
15ml/1 tbsp fish sauce
30ml/2 tbsp groundnut (peanut) oil

1 Heat the oil in a wok and fry the chopped garlic and onion for 3–4 minutes, until they are soft.

2 Add the pork and cook for about 8 minutes, stirring frequently, until lightly browned.

3 Stir in the fish sauce, sugar and tomatoes, season to taste with pepper and simmer until slightly thickened. Mix in the fresh coriander. Remove from the heat and cover to keep warm while you make the omelettes.

4 Beat the eggs and fish sauce together lightly with a fork. Heat 15ml/1 tbsp of the oil in an omelette pan over a medium heat. When the oil is hot, but not smoking, add half the egg mixture and immediately tilt the pan to spread the egg into a thin, even layer. Cook over a medium heat until the omelette is just set and the underside is golden.

5 Spoon half the filling into the centre of the omelette. Fold into a neat square parcel by bringing the opposite sides of the omelette towards each other. Slide the parcel on to a serving dish, folded side down. Make another omelette parcel in the same way. Garnish with the coriander sprigs and chillies. Cut each omelette in half to serve.

Spicy Pork Spareribs

These make a great appetizer, albeit a slightly messy one, for an informal meal.

Serves 4

675–900g/1½–2lb meaty pork spareribs
5ml/1 tsp Szechuan peppercorns
30ml/2 tbsp coarse sea salt
2.5ml/½ tsp Chinese five-spice powder
25ml/1½ tbsp cornflour (cornstarch)
groundnut (peanut) oil, for deep-frying
coriander (cilantro) sprigs, to garnish

For the marinade

30ml/2 tbsp light soy sauce
5ml/1 tsp caster (superfine) sugar
15ml/1 tbsp dry sherry
ground black pepper

1 Using a sharp, heavy cleaver, chop the spareribs into pieces about 5cm/2in long. Place them in a shallow dish and set aside.

2 Heat a wok to medium heat. Add the Szechuan peppercorns and salt and dry-fry for about 3 minutes, stirring until the mixture colours slightly. Remove from the heat and stir in the five-spice powder. Cool, then grind to a fine powder.

3 Sprinkle 5ml/1 tsp of the spice powder over the spareribs and rub in well with your hands. Add all the marinade ingredients and toss the ribs to coat thoroughly. Cover with clear film (plastic wrap) and leave in the refrigerator to marinate for about 2 hours.

4 Pour off any excess marinade from the spareribs. Sprinkle the ribs with the cornflour and mix to coat evenly.

5 Deep fry the spareribs in batches for 3 minutes until golden. Remove and set aside. When all the batches of spareribs have been cooked, reheat the oil and deep-fry the ribs for a second time for 1–2 minutes, until crisp and thoroughly cooked. Drain on kitchen paper.

6 Transfer the ribs to a warm serving platter and sprinkle over 5–7.5ml/1–1½ tsp of the remaining spice powder. Garnish with coriander sprigs and serve immediately.

Stuffed Omelettes Energy 305kcal/1267kJ; Protein 19.2g; Carbohydrate 4.8g, of which sugars 4.5g; Fat 23.6g, of which saturates 5.7g; Cholesterol 275mg; Calcium 48mg; Fibre 0.7g; Sodium 130mg.
Spicy Pork Spareribs Energy 424kcal/1763kJ; Protein 32.2g; Carbohydrate 2.6g, of which sugars 1.3g; Fat 31.4g, of which saturates 9.8g; Cholesterol 111mg; Calcium 33mg; Fibre 0g; Sodium 345mg.

Steamed Pork Buns

These soft textured buns have a spiced meat filling, and are a popular street snack in China.

Serves 4

30ml/2 tbsp golden caster (superfine) sugar
10ml/2 tsp dried yeast
300g/11oz/2¾ cups plain (all-purpose) flour
30ml/2 tbsp sunflower oil
10ml/2 tsp baking powder

For the filling

250g/9oz pork sausage meat
15ml/1 tbsp barbecue sauce
30ml/2 tbsp oyster sauce
15ml/1 tbsp sweet chilli sauce
15ml/1 tbsp Chinese rice wine
15ml/1 tbsp hoisin sauce
5ml/1 tsp chilli oil

1 To make the dough pour 250ml/8fl oz/1 cup warm water into a mixing bowl. Add the sugar and stir to dissolve. Stir in the yeast, cover and leave in a warm place for 15 minutes.

2 Sift the flour into a large bowl. Add the sugar and yeast mixture to it with the sunflower oil. Stir the mixture together using your fingers and turn out on to a lightly floured surface.

3 Knead the dough for 8–10 minutes until smooth and elastic. Place in a lightly oiled bowl, cover with a dish towel and leave to rise in a warm place for 3–4 hours.

4 When risen, place the dough on a floured surface and shape into a circle. Sprinkle over the baking powder, bring the edges towards the centre and knead for 6–8 minutes. Divide the dough into 12 balls, cover with a clean, damp dish towel and set aside.

5 Mix the sausage meat, barbecue sauce, oyster sauce, sweet chilli sauce, rice wine, hoisin sauce and chilli oil in a large bowl.

6 Press each dough ball to form a 12cm/4½in round. Place a spoonful of pork in the centre of each round, bring the edges up, press together to seal and form a bun shape.

7 Arrange the buns on several layers of a bamboo steamer, cover and steam over a wok of simmering water for 20–25 minutes until cooked through. Serve immediately.

Pork and Nut Dumplings

These dainty little bites have an unusual filling, with succulent pork, crunchy nuts and aromatics. This dim sum dish is from Shantou. located on the eastern coast of Guangdong.

Serves 6–8

150g/5oz/1¼ cups wheat starch
200ml/7fl oz/scant 1 cup water
15ml/1 tbsp vegetable oil
50g/2oz/½ cup tapioca flour
pinch of salt

For the filling

30ml/2 tbsp vegetable oil
200g/7oz/scant 1 cup minced (ground) pork
50g/2oz/½ cup peanuts, chopped
30ml/2 tbsp light soy sauce
15ml/1 tbsp sesame oil, plus extra for brushing
2.5ml/½ tsp black pepper

For the dip

5ml/1 tbsp fresh root ginger
45ml/3 tbsp balsamic vinegar
small pinch of salt

1 Put the wheat starch in a non-stick pan. Add the water and oil and cook over low heat, stirring occasionally, until very thick. Remove from the heat and leave to cool for 15 minutes.

2 Meanwhile, make the filling. Heat the oil in a pan and fry the pork for 2 minutes. Add 90ml/6 tbsp water, peanuts, soy sauce, sesame oil and pepper. Stir for 3 minutes until the pork is cooked through and there is the barest hint of sauce. Set aside to cool.

3 Stir the tapioca flour and salt into the cool wheat starch mixture. Mix well, then transfer to a floured board. Knead for at least 5 minutes. Divide into 12 portions. Flatten each piece of dough and roll them into 7.5cm/3in circles.

4 Place 1 heaped tablespoon of the filling on each dough circle and fold to make half-moon shapes. Seal the edges with a little water. Brush each dumpling with a little sesame oil to prevent them from sticking together when being steamed.

5 Place the dumplings on a large plate and steam over a wok of rapidly boiling water for 10 minutes.

6 For the dip, shred the ginger and mix with the vinegar and salt in a bowl. Serve the dumplings hot, with the dipping sauce.

Steamed Pork Buns Energy 588Kcal/2468kJ; Protein 14g; Carbohydrate 76.4g, of which sugars 14g; Fat 27.3g, of which saturates 8.5g; Cholesterol 29mg; Calcium 137mg; Fibre 2.8g; Sodium 722mg.
Pork Dumplings Energy 216kcal/906kJ; Protein 6.7g; Carbohydrate 24.3g, of which sugars 0.7g; Fat 10.9g, of which saturates 2.1g; Cholesterol 17mg; Calcium 10mg; Fibre 0.4g; Sodium 294mg.

Deep-fried Wontons

Crisp on the outside and with a tender filling, wontons are ever popular so why not make double the quantity for a party?

Serves 4

300g/11oz/1½ cups minced (ground) pork
15ml/1 tbsp light soy sauce
15ml/1 tbsp sesame oil
2.5ml/½ tsp ground black pepper
15ml/1 tbsp cornflour (cornstarch)
16 wonton wrappers
vegetable oil for deep-frying
chilli dipping sauce or plum sauce, to serve

1 Put the minced pork in a bowl. Add the light soy sauce, sesame oil, ground black pepper and cornflour. Mix well.

2 Place about 5ml/1 tsp of the mixture in the centre of a wonton wrapper, bring the corners together so that they meet at the top, and pinch the neck to seal. Fill the remaining wontons in the same way.

3 Heat the oil in a wok or deep-fryer. Carefully add the filled wontons, about four or five at a time, and deep-fry for a few minutes until they are golden brown.

4 When cooked through, carefully lift the wontons out of the pan using a slotted spoon, drain them on kitchen paper and keep them hot while frying successive batches. Serve the wontons hot with chilli dipping sauce or plum sauce.

Variations

For seafood wontons, use finely chopped crab, scallops or prawns (shrimp) in place of the pork.

Cook's Tips

- *If the wonton skins are brittle, wipe them with a damp towel or they will be difficult to shape without cracking.*
- *Filled wontons take very little time to cook. Make sure your oil is not too hot as they scorch very quickly.*

Filipino Black Pudding

Flavoured with garlic and ginger, this Filipino dish – called batchoy locally – is served hot with noodles or rice as a popular street snack throughout the day. In this recipe, however, rather than boiling the offal until it becomes soft, the pig's meat is sautéed Spanish-style and served straight from the pan with toasted bread.

Serves 4

30ml/2 tbsp groundnut (peanut) or vegetable oil
1 onion, finely chopped
2 garlic cloves, finely chopped
25g/1oz fresh root ginger, finely chopped or grated
50g/2oz pig's fat, finely chopped
225g/8oz pig's liver, chopped
115g/4oz pig's kidney, finely chopped
115g/4oz pig's heart, chopped
15–30ml/1–2 tbsp patis (Filipino fish sauce)
a handful of fresh chilli leaves or flat leaf parsley, finely chopped, plus extra to garnish
about 8 slices French bread or any crusty rustic loaf
salt and ground black pepper
2 red or green chillies, seeded and quartered lengthways, to serve

1 Heat the oil in a wok or large, heavy frying pan, stir in the onion, garlic and ginger and fry until fragrant and lightly browned. Add the chopped fat and offal and sauté until lightly browned. Stir in the patis and chopped chilli leaves or parsley and season with salt and lots of black pepper.

2 Lightly toast the slices of bread.

3 Spoon the sautéed offal on top of the bread and garnish with chilli leaves or parsley. Serve as a quick and easy snack or a light lunch, with the chillies to chew on.

Cook's Tip

Prepared entirely with pig offal, batchoy is traditionally cooked to a smooth mixture in a pan rather than rolled into a neat sausage like black pudding. It is also served as part of a noodle soup made with a mixture of pork offal with prawns, chicken, beef, vegetables and round noodles.

Deep-fried Wontons Energy 326kcal/1357kJ; Protein 16.3g; Carbohydrate 18.3g, of which sugars 0.6g; Fat 21.3g, of which saturates 4.4g; Cholesterol 50mg; Calcium 33mg; Fibre 0.6g; Sodium 319mg.
Filipino Black Pudding Energy 518kcal/2175kJ; Protein 26g; Carbohydrate 56.7g, of which sugars 7g; Fat 22.6g, of which saturates 6.9g; Cholesterol 181mg; Calcium 133mg; Fibre 3.2g; Sodium 893mg.

Dry-cooked Pork Strips

This very simple dish is quick and light on a hot day. Pork, chicken, prawns and squid can all be cooked this way. With the lettuce and herbs, the pork strips make a very flavoursome snack, but you can also serve them with a dipping sauce.

Serves 2–4

15ml/1 tbsp groundnut (peanut) oil
30ml/2 tbsp fish sauce
30ml/2 tbsp soy sauce
5ml/1 tsp sugar
225g/8oz pork fillet (tenderloin), cut into thin, bitesize strips
8 lettuce leaves
shreds of spring onion (scallion)
chilli oil, for drizzling
a handful of fresh coriander (cilantro) leaves
a handful of fresh mint leaves

1 In a wok or large heavy pan, heat the oil, fish sauce and soy sauce with the sugar until they are combined.

2 Add the pork strips and stir-fry them over a medium heat, until all the liquid has evaporated. Cook the pork until it turns brown, almost caramelized, but not burnt.

3 For a light snack, serve the dry-cooked pork strips with a few salad leaves and add a few shreds of spring onion (scallion).

4 For wraps, drop a few strips of dry-cooked pork on to eight large lettuce leaves, drizzle a little chilli oil over the top, add a few coriander and mint leaves, wrap them up and serve immediately. These make good finger food.

Cook's Tip
'Dry-cooking' usually refers to the large-scale reduction of the liquid content during cooking, rather than an absence of liquid.

Variation
Try serving the pork strips on basil leaves or flat leaf parsley, sprinkled with sliced red onion.

Crispy Fried Pork Belly

This dish is a great Filipino treat. Delicious and moreish, the crispy belly pork can be sliced and eaten as a snack with salad and pickles, or it can be added to salads, soups and vegetable dishes, making it highly versatile. It can be stored in the refrigerator for up to 5 days to use in soups and stews.

Serves 4

3 garlic cloves, chopped
40g/1½oz fresh root ginger, chopped
500g/1¼lb pork belly with the rind, cut into thick slabs
3–4 bay leaves
corn, groundnut (peanut) or vegetable oil, for deep-frying
salt and ground black pepper

1 Using a mortar and pestle, grind the garlic and ginger with a little salt and pepper to a fairly smooth paste.

2 Thoroughly rub the garlic and ginger paste all over each of the pork slabs. Place in a glass dish, cover the pork with clear film (plastic wrap) and chill for at least 1 hour or overnight.

3 Fill a large wok or heavy pan with water and bring to the boil. Add the bay leaves, reduce the heat and slip in the marinated pork slabs. Cook the pork gently for about an hour, until the meat is tender but still firm.

4 Put the slabs of pork in a colander to drain and leave them there for 30–40 minutes to dry out.

5 Heat enough oil in a wok or pan for deep-frying. Fry the pork pieces for 5 minutes, until they are golden brown. Using a slotted spoon, lift them out and drain on kitchen paper. If eating straight away, slice thinly and serve with rice and pickled vegetables, if you like.

Variation
The patties are delicious served in a baguette, halved lengthways, layered with lettuce leaves, coriander, mint, yogurt and a hot chutney or a chilli sauce.

Dry-cooked Pork Strips Energy 104kcal/435kJ; Protein 12.5g; Carbohydrate 2.1g, of which sugars 2g; Fat 5.1g, of which saturates 1.2g; Cholesterol 35mg; Calcium 13mg; Fibre 0.2g; Sodium 574mg.
Crispy Pork Belly Energy 576kcal/2377kJ; Protein 19.2g; Carbohydrate 0.1g, of which sugars 0.1g; Fat 55.4g, of which saturates 17.7g; Cholesterol 90mg; Calcium 14mg; Fibre 0.1g; Sodium 97mg.

Spicy Lentil and Meat Patties

Although of Indian origin, these lentil and lamb patties of Malaysia and Singapore, where they are called shami kebabs, have been adapted to suit the local tastes. They are often served with rice and a sambal, or between chunks of bread with tomato ketchup like a burger.

Serves 4

150g/5oz/generous ½ cup red, brown or green lentils, rinsed
30ml/2 tbsp vegetable oil
2 onions, finely chopped
2 garlic cloves, finely chopped
1 green chilli, seeded and chopped
25g/1oz fresh root ginger, finely chopped
250g/9oz lean minced (ground) lamb
10ml/2 tsp Indian curry powder
5ml/1 tsp turmeric powder
4 eggs
vegetable oil, for shallow frying
salt and ground black pepper
fresh coriander (cilantro) leaves, roughly chopped, to garnish
1 lemon, quartered, to serve

1 Put the lentils in a pan and cover with plenty of water. Bring to a gentle boil and cook until they have softened but still have a bite to them – this can take 20–40 minutes. Drain well.

2 Heat the oil in a wok or heavy pan and stir in the onions, garlic, chilli and ginger. Fry until they begin to colour, then add the lentils and minced lamb. Cook for a few minutes, then add the curry powder and turmeric. Season with salt and pepper and cook the mixture over a high heat until the moisture has evaporated. The mixture needs to be dry for the patties.

3 Leave the meat mixture aside until it is cool enough to handle. Beat one of the eggs in a bowl and mix it into the meat. Using your fingers, take small portions of the mixture and roll them into balls about the size of a plum or apricot. Press each ball in the palm of your hand to form thick, flat patties – if the mixture is sticky, wet your palms with a little water.

4 Beat the remaining eggs in a bowl. Heat enough oil in a wok or heavy pan for shallow frying. Dip each patty in the beaten egg and place them all into the oil. Fry for about 3–4 minutes each side until golden. Garnish with fresh coriander and serve with lemon wedges to squeeze over.

Beef Fondue

The stock for this dish is flavoured with onion, soy sauce and warm spices.

Serves 4–6

30ml/2 tbsp sesame oil
1 garlic clove, crushed
2 shallots, finely chopped
2.5cm/1in fresh root ginger, peeled and finely sliced
1 lemon grass stalk, cut into several pieces and bruised
30ml/2 tbsp sugar
250ml/8fl oz/1 cup white rice vinegar
300ml/½ pint/1¼ cups beef stock
700g/1lb 10oz beef fillet (tenderloin), thinly sliced into rectangular strips
salt and ground black pepper
salad vegetables, herbs and rice wrappers, to serve

For the dipping sauce

15ml/1 tbsp white rice vinegar
juice of 1 lime
5ml/1 tsp sugar
1 garlic clove, peeled and chopped
2 fresh red chillies, seeded and chopped
12 canned anchovy fillets, drained
2 slices of pineapple, cored and chopped

1 To make the dipping sauce, in a small mixing bowl, mix the white rice vinegar and lime juice with the sugar, until the sugar dissolves. Using a mortar and pestle, pound the garlic, chillies and anchovy fillets to a paste, then add the pineapple slices and pound it all to a pulp. Stir in the vinegar and lime juice mixture, and set aside.

2 When ready to eat, heat 15ml/1 tbsp of the sesame oil in a heavy pan, wok or fondue pot.

3 Quickly stir-fry the garlic, shallots, ginger and lemon grass until fragrant and golden, then add the sugar, vinegar, beef stock and the remaining sesame oil. Bring to the boil, stirring and season with salt and pepper.

4 Transfer the pan or fondue pot to a lighted burner at the table. Lay the beef strips on a large serving dish.

5 Using chopsticks or fondue forks, each person cooks their own meat in the broth and dips it into the sauce. Serve with salad vegetables, chopped herbs and rice wrappers.

Spicy Lentil Patties Energy 488Kcal/2033kJ; Protein 28g; Carbohydrate 25.7g, of which sugars 3.7g; Fat 31.2g, of which saturates 7.4g; Cholesterol 238mg; Calcium 87mg; Fibre 3.1g; Sodium 140mg.
Beef Fondue Energy 293kcal/1225kJ; Protein 28.9g; Carbohydrate 10.4g, of which sugars 10.1g; Fat 15.4g, of which saturates 5.1g; Cholesterol 72mg; Calcium 42mg; Fibre 0.5g; Sodium 333mg.

Spicy Meat-filled Parcels

In Indonesia these snacks, called martabak, are made with the finest gossamer dough. You can achieve equally good results if you decide to use filo pastry or spring roll wrappers.

Makes 16

450g/1lb lean minced (ground) beef
2 small onions, finely chopped
2 small leeks, very finely chopped
2 garlic cloves, crushed
10ml/2 tsp coriander seeds, dry-fried and ground
5ml/1 tsp cumin seeds, dry-fried and ground
5–10ml/1–2 tsp mild curry powder
2 eggs, beaten
400g/14oz pack filo pastry
45–60ml/3–4 tbsp sunflower oil
salt and freshly ground black pepper
light soy sauce, to serve

1 To make the filling, mix the meat with the onions, leeks, garlic, coriander, cumin, curry powder and seasoning. Cook the mixture in a heated wok, without oil, stirring all the time, until the meat has changed colour and looks cooked, about 5 minutes.

2 Turn the spicy cooked meat into a mixing bowl and allow to cool, then mix in enough beaten egg to bind to a soft consistency. (Any remaining egg can be used to seal the edges of the dough parcels; otherwise, use milk.)

3 Brush a sheet of filo with oil and lay another sheet on top. Cut the sheets in half. Place a large spoonful of the filling on each double piece of filo. Fold the sides to the middle so that the edges just overlap. Brush these edges with beaten egg or milk and fold the other two sides to the middle to make a square, flat parcel. Repeat with the remaining fifteen parcels and place on a floured tray in the refrigerator.

4 Heat the remaining oil in a shallow pan and cook several parcels at a time, depending on the size of the pan. Cook for 3 minutes on the first side and then turn them over and cook for a further 2 minutes, or until the pastry is browned and crisp and the filling is heated through. Remove from the pan and keep warm. Cook the remaining parcels in the same way and serve hot, sprinkled with light soy sauce.

Golden Beef and Potato Puffs

These crisp, golden pillows of pastry filled with spiced beef and potatoes are delicious served straight from the wok. The light pastry puffs up in the hot oil and contrasts enticingly with the fragrant spiced beef.

Serves 4

15ml/1 tbsp sunflower oil
½ small onion, finely chopped
3 garlic cloves, crushed
5ml/1 tsp fresh root ginger, grated
1 red chilli, seeded and chopped
30ml/2 tbsp hot curry powder
75g/3oz minced (ground) beef
115g/4oz mashed potato
60ml/4 tbsp chopped fresh coriander (cilantro)
2 sheets ready-rolled, fresh puff pastry
1 egg, lightly beaten
vegetable oil, for frying
salt and ground black pepper
fresh coriander (cilantro) leaves, to garnish
tomato ketchup, to serve

1 Heat the oil in a wok, then add the onion, garlic, ginger and chilli. Stir-fry over a medium heat for 2–3 minutes. Add the curry powder and beef and stir-fry over a high heat for a further 4–5 minutes, or until the beef is browned and just cooked through, then remove from the heat.

2 Transfer the beef mixture to a large bowl and add the mashed potato and chopped fresh coriander. Stir well, then season well and set the mixture aside.

3 Lay the pastry sheets on a clean, dry surface and cut out eight rounds, using a 7.5cm/3in pastry (cookie) cutter. Place a large spoonful of the beef mixture in the centre of each pastry round. Brush the edges of the pastry with the beaten egg and fold each round in half to enclose the filling. Press and crimp the edges with the tines of a fork to seal.

4 Fill a wok one-third full of oil and heat to 180°C/350°F (or until a cube of bread dropped into the oil browns in 15 seconds).

5 Deep-fry the puffs, in small batches, for about 2–3 minutes until they turn a golden brown colour. Drain on kitchen paper and serve garnished with fresh coriander leaves. Offer tomato ketchup to diners for dipping.

Meat-filled Parcels Energy 164kcal/685kJ; Protein 8.5g; Carbohydrate 16.1g, of which sugars 1.4g; Fat 7.7g, of which saturates 2.5g; Cholesterol 41mg; Calcium 40mg; Fibre 1.2g; Sodium 33mg.
Beef and Potato Puffs Energy 408kcal/1695kJ; Protein 9g; Carbohydrate 24.2g, of which sugars 1.8g; Fat 31.8g, of which saturates 4.2g; Cholesterol 67mg; Calcium 46mg; Fibre 0.5g; Sodium 202mg.

Sesame Chicken with Noodles and Crisp Shredded Vegetables

This beautiful salad offers the appetizing contrasts of crisp shredded vegetables, soft noodles, spicy chicken and crunchy sesame seeds. Serve while the chicken is still warm.

Serves 4–6

400g/14oz fresh thin egg noodles
1 carrot, cut into long fine strips
50g/2oz mangetouts (snow peas), cut into fine strips and blanched
115g/4oz beansprouts, blanched
30ml/2 tbsp olive oil
225g/8oz skinless, boneless chicken breasts, finely sliced
30ml/2 tbsp sesame seeds, toasted
2 spring onions (scallions), finely sliced diagonally
coriander (cilantro) leaves, to garnish

For the dressing

45ml/3 tbsp sherry vinegar
75ml/5 tbsp soy sauce
60ml/4 tbsp sesame oil
90ml/6 tbsp light olive oil
1 garlic clove, finely chopped
5ml/1 tsp grated fresh root ginger
salt and ground black pepper

1 To make the dressing, combine all the ingredients in a small bowl with a pinch of salt and mix together well using a whisk.

2 Cook the noodles in a large pan of boiling water. Stir them occasionally to keep them separate. They will take only a few minutes to cook: be careful not to overcook them. Drain, rinse under cold running water and drain well. Place in a large bowl.

3 Add the vegetables to the noodles. Pour in half the dressing, then toss the mixture well and adjust the seasoning to taste.

4 Heat the oil in a wok or large frying pan. Add the chicken and stir-fry for 3 minutes, or until all the pieces are cooked and golden. Remove from the heat. Add the sesame seeds and drizzle in some of the remaining dressing.

5 Arrange the noodles and vegetables on individual serving plates, making a nest shape on each plate. Spoon the chicken on top. Sprinkle with spring onions and coriander leaves and serve any remaining dressing separately.

Tangy Chicken Salad

This fresh and lively dish typifies the character of Thai cuisine. It is ideal for a light lunch on a hot and lazy summer's day.

Serves 4–6

4 skinned chicken breast fillets
2 garlic cloves, crushed
30ml/2 tbsp soy sauce
30ml/2 tbsp vegetable oil
115g/4oz/½ cup water chestnuts, sliced
50g/2oz/½ cup cashew nuts, roasted and coarsely chopped
4 shallots, thinly sliced
4 kaffir lime leaves, thinly sliced
1 lemon grass stalk, thinly sliced
5ml/1 tsp chopped fresh galangal
1 large fresh red chilli, seeded and finely chopped
2 spring onions (scallions), thinly sliced
10–12 fresh mint leaves, torn
1 lettuce, separated into leaves, to serve
2 fresh red chillies, seeded and sliced, to garnish

For the coconut cream

120ml/4fl oz/½ cup coconut cream
30ml/2 tbsp Thai fish sauce
juice of 1 lime
30ml/2 tbsp palm sugar or light muscovado (brown) sugar

1 Place the chicken breast fillets in a large dish. Rub the fillets with the garlic, soy sauce and 15ml/1 tbsp of the vegetable oil. Cover and leave them to marinate for 1–2 hours.

2 Heat the remaining vegetable oil in a large wok or frying pan and stir-fry the chicken for 3–4 minutes on each side, or until cooked. Remove and set aside to cool.

3 To make the coconut dressing, heat the coconut cream, fish sauce, lime juice and sugar in a pan. Stir until the sugar has dissolved; set aside.

4 Tear the cooked chicken into strips and put it in a large mixing bowl. Add the sliced water chestnuts, roasted and chopped cashew nuts, shallots, lime leaves, lemon grass, galangal, red chilli, spring onions and mint leaves.

5 Pour the coconut dressing over the mixture and toss well. Serve the chicken salad on top of a bed of lettuce leaves on a large serving platter and garnish with sliced red chillies.

Sesame Chicken Energy 546kcal/2286kJ; Protein 19.3g; Carbohydrate 50.9g, of which sugars 3.8g; Fat 30.9g, of which saturates 5.3g; Cholesterol 46mg; Calcium 69mg; Fibre 3.2g; Sodium 860mg.
Tangy Chicken Salad Energy 404kcal/1691kJ; Protein 40.4g; Carbohydrate 11.3g, of which sugars 9g; Fat 22.3g, of which saturates 9.8g; Cholesterol 105mg; Calcium 25mg; Fibre 0.8g; Sodium 666mg.

Fragrant Chicken with Fresh Tarragon and Pickled Lemons

Chicken thighs have a particularly good flavour and stand up well to the robust ingredients used in this dish. Few people think of using a wok for braising, but it works extremely well, provided you have a lid that fits snugly.

Serves 4

3 heads of garlic, cloves separated but still in their skins
2 onions, peeled and quartered
8 chicken thighs
90ml/6 tbsp chopped fresh tarragon leaves
8 small pickled lemons,
30–45ml/2–3 tbsp olive oil
750ml/1 ¼ pints/3 cups dessert wine
250ml/8fl oz/1 cup chicken stock
sea salt and ground black pepper
sautéed potatoes and steamed yellow or green beans, to serve

1 Arrange the garlic cloves and the peeled and quartered onions in the base of a large wok and lay the chicken thighs over the top of the garlic and onions in a single layer.

2 Sprinkle the tarragon over the top of the chicken, season well with salt and ground black pepper and drizzle over the olive oil.

3 Chop the pickled lemons and add them to the wok.

4 Pour the wine and chicken stock over and bring the wok to the boil. Cover the wok tightly, reduce the heat to low and simmer the dish gently for 1½ hours. Remove from the heat, and leave to stand, covered, for 10 minutes.

5 Serve with sautéed potatoes and steamed beans.

Cook's Tip

Pickled lemons are a popular addition to stews and sauces in Indian. North African and Moroccan cooking. Quartered, halved or whole lemons are pickled in a brine of water, lemon juice and salt and left to ferment for weeks or months.

Stir-fried Chicken with Ginger

Serves 4

30ml/2 tbsp sunflower oil
3 garlic cloves, finely sliced
50g/2oz fresh young root ginger, finely sliced in strips
2 chillies, seeded and finely sliced
4 chicken breasts, skinned and cut into bitesize chunks
30ml/2 tbsp tuk prahoc (Cambodian fish sauce)
10ml/2 tsp sugar
1 small bunch coriander (cilantro) stalks removed, roughly chopped
ground black pepper
jasmine rice and crunchy salad or baguette, to serve

1 Heat a wok or heavy pan and add the oil. Add the garlic, ginger and chillies, and stir-fry until fragrant and golden. Add the chicken and toss it around the wok for 1–2 minutes.

2 Stir in the tuk prahoc and sugar, and stir-fry for a further 4–5 minutes until cooked. Season with pepper and add some of the fresh coriander.

3 Transfer the chicken to a serving dish and garnish with the remaining coriander. Serve hot with jasmine rice and a crunchy salad with fresh herbs, or with chunks of freshly baked baguette.

Larp of Chiang Mai

Serves 4-6

450g/1lb minced (ground) chicken
1 stalk lemon grass, finely chopped
3 kaffir lime leaves, finely chopped
4 red chillies, seeded and chopped
60ml/4 tbsp lime juice
30ml/2 tbsp fish sauce
15ml/1 tbsp roasted ground rice
2 spring onions (scallions), chopped
30ml/2 tbsp coriander (cilantro) leaves
mixed salad leaves, de-seeded cucumber and tomato, to serve
a few sprigs of mint, to garnish

1 Heat a wok and add the chicken and a little water. Stir for 10 minutes until the meat is cooked. Transfer the chicken to a large bowl and mix in the rest of the ingredients.

2 Serve on a bed of mixed salad leaves, cucumber and tomato slices and garnish with sprigs of mint.

Fragrant Chicken Energy 390Kcal/1630kJ; Protein 24g; Carbohydrate 21.8g, of which sugars 17.2g; Fat 8.8g, of which saturates 1.6g; Cholesterol 105mg; Calcium 86mg; Fibre 2.7g; Sodium 122mg.
Chicken with Ginger Energy 222Kcal/935kJ; Protein 36.4g; Carbohydrate 3g, of which sugars 2.9g; Fat 7.3g, of which saturates 1.1g; Cholesterol 105mg; Calcium 32mg; Fibre 0.6g; Sodium 100mg.
Larp of Chiang Mai Energy 93kcal/395kJ; Protein 18.7g; Carbohydrate 2.3g, of which sugars 0.3g; Fat 1g, of which saturates 0.2g; Cholesterol 53mg; Calcium 24mg; Fibre 0.5g; Sodium 49mg.

Lemon and Sesame Chicken

These delicate strips of chicken are at their best if you leave them to marinate overnight.

Serves 4

4 large chicken breast fillets, skinned and cut into strips
15ml/1 tbsp light soy sauce
15ml/1 tbsp Chinese rice wine
2 garlic cloves, crushed
10ml/2 tsp finely grated fresh root ginger
1 egg, lightly beaten
150g/5oz cornflour (cornstarch)
sunflower oil, for deep-frying
toasted sesame seeds, to sprinkle
rice or noodles, to serve

For the sauce

15ml/1 tbsp sunflower oil
2 spring onions (scallions), finely sliced
1 garlic clove, crushed
10ml/2 tsp cornflour (cornstarch)
90ml/6 tbsp chicken stock
10ml/2 tsp finely grated lemon rind
30ml/2 tbsp lemon juice
10ml/2 tsp sugar
2.5ml/½ tsp sesame oil
salt

1 Mix the chicken strips with the soy sauce, rice wine, garlic and ginger in a bowl. Toss together to combine, then cover and marinate in the refrigerator for 8–10 hours.

2 When ready to cook, add the beaten egg to the chicken and mix well, then drain off any excess liquid.

3 Put the cornflour in a plastic bag and add the chicken strips. Seal the bag and shake it to coat the chicken strips.

4 Heat the sunflower oil in a wok. Deep-fry the chicken strips for 3–4 minutes for each batch. As each batch cooks, lift it out and drain on kitchen paper. Reheat the oil and deep-fry all the chicken in batches for a second time, for 2–3 minutes. Remove and drain well.

5 To make the sauce, add the oil to a hot wok and stir-fry the spring onions and garlic for 1–2 minutes. Add the remaining ingredients and cook for 2–3 minutes until thickened.

6 Return the chicken to the wok, toss lightly to coat with sauce, and sprinkle over the sesame seeds. Serve with rice or noodles.

Chicken Pot

This nourishing main-course soup is one of many brought to the Philippines by the Spanish in the sixteenth century. The recipe and method are based on Potajes, a stew still enjoyed throughout much of Spain.

Serves 4–6

175g/6oz dried haricot (navy) beans
3 chicken legs
15ml/1 tbsp vegetable oil
350g/12oz lean pork, diced
1 chorizo (optional), sliced
1 small carrot, peeled and roughly chopped
1 medium onion, roughly chopped
1.75 litres/3 pints/7½ cups water
1 garlic clove, crushed
30ml/2 tbsp tomato purée (paste)
1 bay leaf
2 chicken stock (bouillon) cubes
350g/12oz sweet potatoes, peeled
10ml/2 tsp chilli sauce
30ml/2 tbsp white wine vinegar
3 firm tomatoes, skinned, seeded and chopped
225g/8oz Chinese leaves (Chinese cabbage)
salt and ground black pepper
3 spring onions (scallions), shredded, to garnish
boiled rice, to serve

1 Soak the beans in plenty of cold water for 8 hours. Drain.

2 Divide the chicken drumsticks from the thighs. Chop off the narrow end of each drumstick and discard.

3 Heat the vegetable oil in a wok or large pan, add the chicken, pork, chorizo (if using), carrot and onion, then brown evenly.

4 Drain the beans and add them to the pan with the water, garlic, tomato purée and bay leaf. Bring to the boil and simmer for 2 hours, until the beans are almost tender.

5 Crumble in the chicken stock cubes, then add the sweet or new potatoes and the chilli sauce, then simmer for 15–20 minutes, until the potatoes are cooked.

6 Add the vinegar, tomatoes and Chinese leaves, then simmer for 1–2 minutes. Season to taste. The dish is intended to provide enough liquid to be served as a first-course broth. This is followed by a main course of the meat and vegetables garnished with the shredded spring onions. Serve with rice.

Lemon Chicken Energy 450kcal/1892kJ; Protein 38.2g; Carbohydrate 37.1g, of which sugars 2.5g; Fat 17.6g, of which saturates 2.6g; Cholesterol 157mg; Calcium 25mg; Fibre 0.1g; Sodium 397mg.
Chicken Pot Energy 309kcal/1304kJ; Protein 33.2g; Carbohydrate 30.7g, of which sugars 9.2g; Fat 6.7g, of which saturates 1.7g; Cholesterol 98mg; Calcium 79mg; Fibre 7.7g; Sodium 143mg.

Soy-braised Chicken

As the chicken is braised, the spicy ginger sauce releases its flavour into the meat to create a succulent dish. Enjoy it hot or cold.

Serves 6

1 chicken, about 1.5kg/3–3½lb
15ml/1 tbsp ground Szechuan peppercorns
30ml/2 tbsp crushed fresh root ginger
45ml/3 tbsp light soy sauce
30ml/2 tbsp dark soy sauce
45ml/3 tbsp Chinese rice wine or dry sherry
15ml/1 tbsp soft light brown sugar
vegetable oil, for deep-frying
about 600ml/1 pint/2½ cups stock or water
10ml/2 tsp salt
25g/1oz crystal sugar
lettuce leaves, to serve

1 Rub the chicken both inside and out with the ground Szechuan pepper and fresh ginger.

2 Mix together the soy sauces, rice wine or sherry and sugar and spoon the mixture over the chicken in a large bowl. Leave to marinate for at least 3 hours, turning the chicken several times, so that the flavours penetrate the flesh.

3 Heat the oil in a wok, remove the chicken from the marinade and deep-fry for 5–6 minutes, or until brown all over. Remove and drain. Pour off the excess oil, add the marinade with the stock or water, salt and crystal sugar and bring to the boil.

4 Cover and braise the chicken in the sauce for 35–40 minutes, turning once or twice. Remove the chicken from the wok and let it cool down a little before chopping it into approximately 30 bite-sized pieces using a cleaver or sharp knife.

5 Arrange in a serving dish on a bed of lettuce leaves, then pour some of the sauce over the chicken and serve.

Cook's Tip
Szechuan peppercorns have a mouth-numbing quality, and should preferably not be replaced with other types of peppercorn.

Chicken with Shrimp Paste

This dish is an innovation that draws on Singaporean cooking elements in its use of shrimp paste, ground coriander and turmeric. These ingredients are generally unknown in southern Chinese cooking but have been adopted with enthusiasm in recent years as they add an extra savoury note to a simple dish.

Serves 4

450g/1lb boneless chicken thighs
20g/¾oz shrimp paste
30ml/2 tbsp water
30ml/2 tbsp ground coriander
5ml/1 tsp ground turmeric
5ml/1 tsp ground black pepper
10ml/2 tsp sugar
115g/4oz/1 cup cornflour (cornstarch)
vegetable oil for deep-frying
thin slices of red chilli, to garnish
chilli dipping sauce, to serve

1 Rinse the chicken thighs under cold running water then pat dry with kitchen paper. Cut each chicken thigh into 2–3 pieces.

2 Put the shrimp paste in a small bowl and add the water. Mash well to mix, then add the ground coriander and turmeric with the pepper and sugar. Mix to a smooth paste. Spread out the cornflour in a shallow bowl.

3 Rub the spicy shrimp paste all over the chicken, pressing it in well, then transfer the chicken pieces to the bowl of cornflour and turn to coat them on all sides.

4 Heat the vegetable oil in a wok or deep-fryer to 190°C/375°F. Carefully add the coated chicken pieces and deep-fry, in batches for 3–4 minutes, until golden brown and cooked through.

5 Lift out the pieces using a slotted spoon and keep them hot while you cook the remaining pieces in the same way. Drain on kitchen paper to absorb any excess oil and serve immediately, garnished with red chillies, and with a chilli dipping sauce.

Variation
To give this dish extra fire, add 2.5ml/½ tsp chilli powder to the seasoning.

Soy-braised Chicken Energy 404 kcal /1678kJ; protein 31.5g; carbohydrate 5.9g, of which sugars 4.9g; fat 42.5g, of which saturates 6.9g; cholesterol 165mg; calcium 18.1mg; fibre 0g; sodium 707mg.
Chicken with Shrimp Paste Energy 411kcal/1721kJ; Protein 31.5g; Carbohydrate 30g, of which sugars 0g; Fat 19.4g, of which saturates 2.5g; Cholesterol 104mg; Calcium 88mg; Fibre 0g; Sodium 302mg.

Exotic Fried Chicken

In this spicy Indonesian dish the chicken is cooked in spice paste to ensure a wonderful depth of flavour and then it is deep-fried to form a crisp, golden skin.

Serves 4

12 chicken thighs or drumsticks, or 12 legs, separated into thighs and drumsticks
30ml/2 tbsp kecap manis (sweet soy sauce)
150ml/¼ pint/⅔ cup water
vegetable oil, for deep-frying
salt and ground black pepper
sambal or pickle, to serve

For the spice paste
2 shallots, chopped
4 garlic cloves, chopped
50g/2oz fresh root ginger, chopped
25g/1oz fresh turmeric, chopped
2 lemon grass stalks, chopped

1 Grind the spice paste ingredients to a coarse paste using a pestle and mortar or an electric food processor or blender.

2 Put the chicken pieces in a large, flameproof casserole or heavy pan and smear the spice paste over them.

3 Add the kecap manis and the measured water to the pan and bring to the boil, stirring to mix, then reduce the heat and simmer, uncovered, for about 25 minutes.

4 Turn the chicken occasionally, until all the liquid has evaporated. The chicken must be dry before you deep-fry it, but the spices should be sticking to it. Season with salt and pepper.

5 Heat enough vegetable oil for deep-frying in a wok. Add the chicken pieces, in batches, and fry for 6–8 minutes until golden brown and crisp. Remove from the wok with a slotted spoon, drain on kitchen paper and serve hot.

Cook's Tip
Kecap manis is soy sauce sweetened with palm sugar (jaggery). If you cannot find it replace it with the same quantity of dark soy sauce and 15ml/1 tbsp sugar.

Spicy Fried Chicken

Although the chicken cooks quickly, it does benefit from being marinated first. This only takes a moment and ensures that there is no last-minute work to do when guests arrive.

Serves 4

4 skinless chicken breast fillets
2 whole star anise
45ml/3 tbsp olive oil
30ml/2 tbsp soy sauce
15ml/1 tbsp sunflower oil
ground black pepper

1 Put the chicken breast fillets in a shallow, non-metallic dish and add the star anise.

2 In a small bowl, whisk together the olive oil and soy sauce and season with ground black pepper to make a marinade. Extra salt will not be necessary as the soy sauce is salty.

3 Pour the marinade over the chicken and stir to coat each breast fillet all over. Cover the dish with clear film (plastic wrap) and set aside for as much time as you have. If you are able to make it ahead, leave the chicken in the marinade for around 6–8 hours as the flavour will constantly improve. Place the covered dish in the refrigerator. When ready to cook, allow the fillets to come to room temperature.

4 Heat a wok and add the sunflower oil to the wok. When hot, swirl the oil around the wok and add the chicken. Fry for about 5–7 minutes on each side depending on the thickness until cooked through. Place each piece on a warmed plate and serve.

Variation
If you prefer, cook on a barbecue. When the coals are dusted with ash, spread them out evenly. Remove the chicken breasts from the marinade and cook for 8 minutes on each side, spooning over the marinade from time to time until the chicken is cooked through. The chicken can also be cooked on the top of the stove on a ridged griddle (grill) pan. Get the pan very hot first, add the chicken and turn the pieces after a few minutes so that they are branded in a criss-cross fashion.

Exotic Fried Chicken Energy 410kcal/1719kJ; Protein 60.8g; Carbohydrate 4.6g, of which sugars 3.4g; Fat 16.6g, of which saturates 2.4g; Cholesterol 175mg; Calcium 26mg; Fibre 0.7g; Sodium 686mg.
Spicy Fried Chicken Energy 237kcal/992kJ; Protein 36.2g; Carbohydrate 0.6g, of which sugars 0.6g; Fat 9.9g, of which saturates 1.6g; Cholesterol 105mg; Calcium 9mg; Fibre 0g; Sodium 624mg.

Chicken and Pumpkin Casserole

In Cambodian homes a big pot of this casserole is made daily and placed in the middle of the table for everyone to help themselves. The flavourings include kroeung (a blend of lemon grass and galangal with fish sauce) and tuk prahoc, or fermented fish paste. It is good served with jasmine rice.

Serves 4–6

30ml/2 tbsp groundnut (peanut) oil
4 garlic cloves, halved and crushed
25g/1oz galangal, peeled and finely sliced
2 chillies
30ml/2 tbsp kroeung
15ml/1 tbsp palm sugar (jaggery)
12 chicken thighs
30ml/2 tbsp tuk prahoc
a handful kaffir lime leaves
600ml/1 pint/2½ cups coconut milk
350g/12oz pumpkin flesh, seeded and cut into bitesize chunks
1 long aubergine (eggplant), quartered lengthways, each quarter cut into three
115g/4oz long beans, trimmed and cut into 5cm/2in lengths
3 tomatoes, skinned, quartered, and seeded
1 handful spinach leaves, washed and trimmed
a small bunch basil leaves
sea salt and ground black pepper
1 small bunch each fresh coriander (cilantro) and mint, stalks removed, coarsely chopped, to garnish

1 Heat the groundnut oil in a large wok or heavy pan. Add the garlic, galangal and whole chillies and stir-fry until they are fragrant and golden. Add the kroeung and the palm sugar to the pan, stirring until they have dissolved.

2 Add the chicken thighs to the pan, tossing them well, and stir in the tuk prahoc, the lime leaves and the coconut milk. Reduce the heat and simmer for 10 minutes. Add the pumpkin, aubergine and beans to the pan.

3 Simmer the casserole for a further 10 minutes, until tender. If you need to add more liquid, stir in a little water. Add the tomatoes and spinach, and the basil leaves.

4 Cook for a further 2 minutes, then season the dish to taste. Garnish with coriander and mint and serve.

Richly Spiced Chicken Curry

There are many recipes for Cambodian chicken or seafood curries, but the one thing they all have in common is the use of Indian curry powder and coconut milk in their sauces.

Serves 4

45ml/3 tbsp Indian curry powder or garam masala
15ml/1 tbsp ground turmeric
500g/1¼lb skinless chicken thighs or chicken portions
25ml/1½ tbsp raw cane sugar
30ml/2 tbsp sesame oil
2 shallots, chopped
2 garlic cloves, chopped
4cm/1½in galangal, peeled and chopped
2 lemon grass stalks, chopped
10ml/2 tsp chilli paste or dried chilli flakes
2 medium sweet potatoes, peeled and cubed
45ml/3 tbsp nuoc mam (Vietnamese fish sauce)
600ml/1 pint/2½ cups coconut milk
1 small bunch each fresh basil and coriander (cilantro), stalks removed
salt and ground black pepper

1 In a small bowl, mix together the curry powder or garam masala and the turmeric. Put the chicken in a bowl and coat it with half of the spice. Cover the chicken and set aside.

2 To make the caramel sauce, heat the sugar in a small pan with 7.5ml/1½ tsp water, until the sugar dissolves and the syrup turns golden. Remove from the heat and set aside.

3 Heat a wok or heavy pan and add the oil. Stir-fry the shallots, garlic, galangal and lemon grass. Stir in the rest of the turmeric and curry powder with the chilli paste or flakes, followed by the chicken, and stir-fry for 2–3 minutes.

4 Add the sweet potatoes, then stir in the nuoc mam, the caramel sauce, coconut milk and 150ml/¼ pint/⅔ cup water, mixing thoroughly to combine the flavours.

5 Bring the mixture in the wok to the boil, reduce the heat and cook for about 15 minutes until the chicken is cooked through.

6 Season and stir in half the basil and coriander. Garnish with the remaining herbs and serve immediately.

Chicken Pumpkin Casserole Energy 418Kcal/1747kJ; Protein 31g; Carbohydrate 15g, of which sugars 14.3g; Fat 26.4g, of which saturates 6.7g; Cholesterol 160mg; Calcium 127mg; Fibre 3g; Sodium 350mg.
Richly Spiced Chicken Curry Energy 387Kcal/1632kJ; Protein 31g; Carbohydrate 38g, of which sugars 19g; Fat 14g, of which saturates 3g; Cholesterol 131mg; Calcium 1.8mg; Fibre 1g; Sodium 1000mg.

Hot Chilli Chicken with Lemon Grass and Ginger

This tantalizing mixture of lemon grass and ginger provides the flavourings for a superb chicken feast, which is gently simmered in a wok and then topped with crunchy peanuts.

Serves 4-6

3 whole chicken legs, separated into thighs and drumsticks
15ml/1 tbsp vegetable oil
2cm/¾in fresh root ginger, peeled and finely chopped
1 clove garlic, crushed
1 small red chilli, seeded and finely chopped
5cm/2in lemon grass stalk, shredded
150ml/¼ pint/⅔ cup chicken stock
15ml/1 tbsp fish sauce (optional)
10ml/2 tsp sugar
2.5ml/½ tsp salt
juice of ½ lemon
50g/2oz raw peanuts
2 spring onions (scallions), shredded
rind of 1 satsuma, shredded
30ml/2 tbsp fresh mint, to garnish
rice or rice noodles, to serve

1 With the heel of the knife, chop through the narrow end of the drumsticks. Cut through the joints to divide the legs into drumsticks and thighs, then remove the skin.

2 Heat the oil in a large preheated wok. Add the chicken, ginger, garlic, chilli and lemon grass and cook for 3–4 minutes. Add the chicken stock, fish sauce, if using, sugar, salt and lemon juice. Lower the heat, cover and simmer for 30–35 minutes.

3 To prepare the peanuts for the topping, grill (broil) or roast them under a steady heat for about 2–3 minutes until they are evenly brown. Turn the nuts out on to a dish towel and rub briskly to loosen the skins.

4 Shred the rind of the mandarin orange into fine strips. Discard the mint stalks and chop the leaves.

5 Serve the chicken scattered with roasted peanuts, shredded spring onions and the rind of the mandarin orange or satsuma. Garnish with mint and serve with rice or rice noodles.

Chicken with Basil and Chilli

This easy chicken dish is an excellent introduction to Thai cuisine. Thai basil, which is sometimes known as holy basil, has a unique, pungent flavour that is both spicy and sharp. Deep-frying the leaves adds another dimension to this dish.

Serves 4 to 6

45ml/3 tbsp vegetable oil
4 garlic cloves, thinly sliced
2–4 fresh red chillies, seeded and finely chopped
450g/1lb skinless boneless chicken breast portions, cut into bitesize pieces
45ml/3 tbsp Thai fish sauce
10ml/2 tsp dark soy sauce
5ml/1 tsp sugar
10–12 fresh Thai basil leaves
2 fresh red chillies, seeded and finely chopped, and about 20 deep-fried Thai basil leaves, to garnish

1 Heat the oil in a wok or large frying pan. Add the garlic and chillies and stir-fry for 1–2 minutes until the garlic is golden. Take care not to let the garlic burn, otherwise it will taste bitter.

2 Add the pieces of chicken to the wok or pan, in batches if necessary, and stir-fry until the chicken changes colour.

3 Stir in the fish sauce, soy sauce and sugar. Stir-fry the mixture for 3–4 minutes, or until the chicken is cooked and golden brown.

4 Stir in the fresh Thai basil leaves. Spoon the mixture on to a warm platter. Garnish with the chopped chillies and deep-fried Thai basil and serve the dish immediately.

Cook's Tip

To deep-fry Thai basil leaves, first make sure that the leaves are completely dry or they will splutter when added to the oil. Heat vegetable or groundnut (peanut) oil in a wok or deep-fryer to 190°C/375°F or until a cube of bread added to the oil browns in about 45 seconds. Add the leaves and deep-fry them briefly until they are crisp and translucent – this will take only about 30–40 seconds. Lift out the leaves using a slotted spoon or wire basket and leave them to drain on kitchen paper before using.

Hot Chilli Chicken Energy 171kcal/715kJ; Protein 19.6g; Carbohydrate 4.6g, of which sugars 3.3g; Fat 8.4g, of which saturates 1.6g; Cholesterol 85mg; Calcium 81mg; Fibre 2.1g; Sodium 197mg.
Chicken with Basil Energy 214kcal/899kJ; Protein 28g; Carbohydrate 4g, of which sugars 10g; Fat 10g, of which saturates 1g; Cholesterol 79mg; Calcium 14mg; Fibre 0.1g; Sodium 700mg.

Stir-fried Chicken with Chillies

This chicken dish is good home cooking at its best – simple spicy food that you can enjoy as an everyday meal. There are variations of this dish using pork or seafood throughout South-east Asia so this is a good place to start. The essential elements of this dish, as with many dishes from the area, are the fragrant lemon grass and the fire of the chillies, so add as much as you like. Serve with a table salad, rice wrappers and a dipping sauce.

Serves 4

15ml/1 tbsp sugar
30ml/2 tbsp sesame or groundnut (peanut) oil
2 garlic cloves, finely chopped
2–3 green or red Thai chillies, seeded and finely chopped
2 lemon grass stalks, finely sliced
1 onion, finely sliced
350g/12oz skinless chicken breast fillets, cut into bitesize strips
30ml/2 tbsp soy sauce
15ml/1 tbsp Thai fish sauce
1 bunch fresh coriander (cilantro), stalks removed, leaves chopped
salt and ground black pepper
nuoc cham (chilli sauce), to serve

1 To make a caramel sauce, put the sugar into a small pan with a few splashes of water, but not enough to soak it. Heat it gently until the sugar has dissolved and turned golden. Set aside.

2 Heat a wok or heavy pan and add the oil. Stir in the garlic, chillies and lemon grass, and cook until they become fragrant. Add the onion and stir-fry for 1 minute, then add the chicken.

3 When the chicken begins to brown a little, add the soy sauce, fish sauce and caramel sauce. Keep the chicken moving around the wok for a minute or two, then season with a little salt and pepper. Toss the fresh coriander into the chicken and serve immediately with nuoc cham drizzled over it.

Cook's Tip

Nuoc cham is a chilli sauce popular in Vietnam and it can be found in Asian food stores. It is used as a condiment and dipping sauce and is usually made from dried red chillies, garlic and sugar, processed with water, fish sauce and lime juice.

Chicken and Vegetables in Spicy Chilli Sauce

With a medley of crunchy vegetables for texture and rice cake to help diffuse some of the spiciness, this recipe is always a popular favourite at family gatherings in Korea. The dish is very piquant, so don't offer it to the fainthearted.

Serves 4

500g/1¼lb chicken breast fillet
115g/4oz rice cake, sliced
150g/5oz sweet potato, finely diced
½ white onion, thinly sliced
1 carrot, thinly sliced
4 cabbage leaves, thinly sliced
50g/2oz perilla or shiso leaves, thinly sliced
1 leek, finely sliced
2 green chillies, seeded and sliced
vegetable oil, for cooking

For the marinade

45ml/3 tbsp gochujang chilli paste
22.5ml/4½ tsp Korean chilli powder
30ml/2 tbsp soy sauce
30ml/2 tbsp maple syrup
22.5ml/4½ tsp sugar
30ml/2 tbsp sake or mirin (sweet rice wine)
3 garlic cloves, crushed
22.5ml/4½ tsp grated fresh root ginger
15ml/1 tbsp sesame oil
15ml/1 tbsp sesame seeds
7.5ml/1½ tsp Korean or Japanese curry powder

1 Prepare the marinade in a large bowl. Thoroughly mix the chilli paste and powder, soy sauce, maple syrup, sugar, sake or mirin, garlic, ginger, sesame oil and seeds, and curry powder.

2 Slice the chicken into bitesize pieces with a sharp knife and add them to the marinade. Coat the pieces thoroughly with the mixture and leave to stand for 1 hour.

3 Heat a little vegetable oil in a wok or large heavy pan, add the rice cake and sweet potato and stir-fry.

4 Add the marinated chicken to the pan and stir-fry for a further 6 minutes, stirring to make sure the chicken is cooked through.

5 Stir in the onion, carrot and cabbage and stir-fry for a further 3 minutes, then remove from the heat. Add the perilla or shiso, leek and chillies. Toss the ingredients together and serve.

Stir-fried Chicken Energy 202kcal/847kJ; Protein 22g; Carbohydrate 9g, of which sugars 7g; Fat 9g, of which saturates 1g; Cholesterol 61mg; Calcium 32mg; Fibre 0.6g; Sodium 800mg.
Chicken and Vegetables Energy 368kcal/1545kJ; Protein 32.8g; Carbohydrate 37.5g, of which sugars 19g; Fat 10.2g, of which saturates 1.6g; Cholesterol 88mg; Calcium 47mg; Fibre 3.3g; Sodium 1033mg.

Stir-fried Chicken and Cashews

Although it is not native to South-east Asia, the cashew tree is highly prized in Thailand and the classic partnership of these slightly sweet nuts with chicken is immensely popular both in Thailand and abroad.

Serves 4 to 6

450g/1lb boneless chicken breast portions
1 red (bell) pepper
2 garlic cloves
4 dried red chillies
30ml/2 tbsp vegetable oil
30ml/2 tbsp oyster sauce
15ml/1 tbsp soy sauce
pinch of sugar
1 bunch spring onions (scallions), cut into 5cm/2in lengths
175g/6oz/1½ cups cashew nuts, roasted

1 Remove and discard the skin from the chicken breast portions and trim off any excess fat. Using a sharp knife, cut the chicken into bitesize pieces and set aside.

2 Cut the red pepper in half, scrape out and discard the pepper seeds and the paler membranes. Then cut the flesh of the pepper into 2cm/¾in dice.

3 Peel and thinly slice the garlic, and finely chop the red chillies.

4 Preheat a wok or large heavy pan and then heat the oil. The best way to do this is to drizzle the oil around the inner rim, so that it runs down and coats the entire wok.

5 Add the garlic and dried chillies to the pan and then stir-fry them over a medium heat until golden. Be careful not to let the garlic burn, since this will make it will taste bitter.

6 Add the chicken pieces to the pan and stir-fry until the chicken is cooked through, then add the red pepper. If the mixture is very dry, then add a little water.

7 Stir in the oyster sauce, soy sauce and sugar. Add the spring onions and cashew nuts. Stir-fry for 1–2 minutes more until heated through. Spoon the mixture into a warm dish and serve immediately.

Chicken with Bamboo Shoots

This popular Chinese dish is quick and easy to make and it can be enjoyed to the full by using good-quality organic products that are full of flavour.

Serves 4

350g/12oz skinless chicken breast fillets
pinch of ground white pepper
15ml/1 tbsp dry sherry
300ml/½ pint/1¼ cups chicken stock
15ml/1 tbsp sunflower oil
1 garlic clove, finely chopped
1 small carrot, cut into cubes
½ cucumber, about 75g/3oz, cut into 1cm/½in cubes
50g/2oz/½ cup drained canned bamboo shoots, cut into 1cm/½in cubes (optional)
5ml/1 tsp cornflour (cornstarch)
15ml/1 tbsp soy sauce
25g/1oz/¼ cup dry-roasted cashew nuts
2.5ml/½ tsp sesame oil
noodles, to serve

1 Cut the chicken into 2cm/¾in cubes. Place the cubes in a bowl, stir in the white pepper and sherry, cover with clear film (plastic wrap) and marinate for 10 minutes.

2 Bring the stock to the boil in a wok or large heavy pan. Add the chicken and cook, stirring, for 3 minutes.

3 Drain the pan, reserving 90ml/6 tbsp of the stock, and set the chicken aside on a plate.

4 Heat the sunflower oil in a large non-stick wok or frying pan until it is very hot, and then add the finely chopped garlic and stir-fry for a few seconds.

5 Add the cubed carrot and cucumber to the frying pan with the bamboo shoots, if using, and continue to stir-fry the vegetables over a medium heat for 2 minutes.

6 Stir in the chicken and reserved stock. Put the cornflour in a cup or small bowl and stir in the soy sauce. Add the mixture to the pan. Cook, stirring, until the sauce thickens slightly.

7 Finally, add the cashew nuts and sesame oil. Toss to mix thoroughly, then serve with noodles.

Stir-fried Chicken Energy 458kcal/1909kJ; Protein 37.1g; Carbohydrate 17.7g, of which sugars 17.6g; Fat 7.1g, of which saturates 1.2g; Cholesterol 79mg; Calcium 26mg; Fibre 0g; Sodium 447mg.
Chicken with Bamboo Shoots Energy 153kcal/645kJ; Protein 22.9g; Carbohydrate 5.1g, of which sugars 2.8g; Fat 4.3g, of which saturates 0.9g; Cholesterol 61mg; Calcium 14mg; Fibre 0.7g; Sodium 342mg.

Fu-Yung Chicken

Because the chicken is mixed with egg whites and milk and deep-fried for this dish, some imaginative cooks have been prompted to refer to it as "Deep Fried Milk". In fact it is an omelette-like mixture with a delicate flavour and colour.

Serves 4

175g/6oz chicken breast fillet, skinned
5ml/1 tsp cornflour (cornstarch)
5ml/1 tsp salt
4 egg whites, lightly beaten
30ml/2 tbsp milk
vegetable oil, for deep-frying
1 lettuce heart, separated into leaves
about 120ml/4fl oz/½ cup chicken or vegetable stock
15ml/1 tbsp Chinese rice wine or dry sherry
15ml/1 tbsp green peas
few drops sesame oil
5ml/1 tsp minced (ground) ham, to garnish

1 Finely mince (grind) the chicken and put into a large bowl.

2 In a small bowl, blend the cornflour to a smooth paste with 15ml/1 tbsp water and mix into the chicken together with a pinch of the salt, the beaten egg whites and the milk. Blend the mixture well until it is smooth.

3 Heat the vegetable oil over a medium heat in a wok, and gently spoon the chicken and egg white mixture into the oil in batches. Be careful not to stir the mixture, since this will make it scatter. Stir the oil from the bottom of the wok so that the egg whites rise to the surface.

4 Remove the chicken and egg white mixture from the wok as soon as the colour turns bright white. Drain it on kitchen paper to remove any excess oil.

5 Pour off the excess oil, leaving about 15ml/1 tbsp. Stir-fry the separated lettuce leaves with the remaining salt for 1 minute, add the stock and bring to the boil.

6 Add the chicken to the wok with the Chinese rice wine or sherry and peas, and blend well. Sprinkle with sesame oil, garnish with ham and serve the fu-yung dish immediately.

Japanese-style Seaweed Chicken

The taste of hijiki – a type of seaweed – is somewhere between rice and vegetable. It goes well with meat or tofu products, especially when stir-fried in the wok first with a little oil.

Serves 2

90g/3½oz dried hijiki seaweed
150g/5oz chicken breast fillet
½ small carrot, about 5cm/2in
15ml/1 tbsp vegetable oil
100ml/3½fl oz/scant ½ cup instant dashi powder plus 1.5ml/¼ tsp dashi-no-moto
30ml/2 tbsp sake
30ml/2 tbsp caster (superfine) sugar
45ml/3 tbsp shoyu
a pinch of cayenne pepper

1 Soak the hijiki seaweed in cold water for about 30 minutes. It is ready to cook when it can be easily crushed between the fingers. Pour it into a sieve (strainer) and wash under running water. Drain.

2 Peel the skin from the chicken and par-boil the skin in rapidly boiling water for 1 minute, then drain. Using a sharp knife, shave off all the yellow fat from the skin. Discard the clear membrane between the fat and the skin as well. Cut the skin into thin strips about 5mm/¼in wide and 2.5cm/1in long. Cut the meat into small, bitesize chunks.

3 Peel and chop the carrot into long, narrow matchsticks.

4 Heat the oil in a wok or frying pan and stir-fry the strips of chicken skin for 5 minutes, or until golden and curled up. Add the chicken meat and keep stirring until the colour changes.

5 Add the hijiki and carrot, then stir-fry for a further minute. Add the remaining ingredients. Lower the heat and toss over the heat for 5 minutes more. Remove the wok from the heat and stand for 10 minutes. Season and serve in individual bowls.

Cook's Tip

Hijiki, dashi, sake, shoyu and other Japanese ingredients can be found in specialist food stores and online.

Fu-Yung Chicken Energy 202kcal /842kJ; protein 13.7g; carbohydrate 1.9g, of which sugars 0.5g; fat 15.2g, of which saturates 1.9g; cholesterol 31mg; calcium 14mg; fibre 0.2g; sodium 578mg.
Japanese-style Chicken Energy 154kcal/644kJ; Protein 10g; Carbohydrate 10.4g, of which sugars 10.2g; Fat 8.4g, of which saturates 2g; Cholesterol 39mg; Calcium 76mg; Fibre 1.1g; Sodium 884mg.

Chicken with Soy Sauce, Garlic and Galangal

The local name for this Cantonese classic is see yau gai, and it has as many variations as a chicken has feathers. Caramelizing the chicken gives it a delicious bittersweet flavour.

Serves 4–6

30ml/2 tbsp vegetable oil
15ml/1 tbsp sugar
1 chicken, about 1.6kg/3½lb
150ml/¼ pint/⅔ cup dark soy sauce
8 garlic cloves, peeled and bruised
1 large knob of galangal, bruised
1.5 litres/2½ pints/6¼ cups water
30ml/2 tbsp cornflour (cornstarch) mixed with 30ml/2 tbsp water
sliced cucumber, to garnish
chilli sauce, to serve (optional)

1 Heat the oil in a wok large enough to hold the chicken. Sprinkle in the sugar and cook over medium to high heat until the mixture froths and caramelizes. When it is pale brown, add the chicken and turn it several times to coat the skin.

2 Add the soy sauce to the wok. Using two spatulas or large forks, turn the chicken several times to coat it thoroughly all over and allow it to steep in the sauce.

3 Add the garlic, galangal and water. Bring to the boil, reduce the heat, cover and simmer for 50 minutes. Turn off the heat, leaving the wok covered with the lid, and leave for a further 10 minutes, during which time the chicken will continue to cook.

4 Check that the chicken is fully cooked, then transfer it to a board. Cover with foil and leave to stand. Strain the cooking liquid into a pan. Discard the solids in the strainer.

5 Bring the liquid in the pan to the boil, add the cornflour mixture and stir until the sauce is thick and glossy.

6 Carve the chicken and arrange the slices on a platter. Garnish with the cucumber. Serve the thick, slightly reduced sauce on the side with a side dip of chilli sauce, if you like.

Plum Sauce Chicken

The fruity sweetness of plum sauce is the perfect foil for meat and poultry, either on its own or used as an ingredient in a sweet and sour sauce. In this recipe, plum sauce partners tender chicken that is coated with cracker crumbs and deep-fried quickly to give a flavoursome and crisp crust.

Serves 4

2 boneless chicken breast fillets, skinned
1 egg, beaten
6 crackers, finely crushed (about ⅔ cup cracker crumbs)
vegetable oil for deep-frying
45ml/3 tbsp plum sauce
15ml/1 tbsp hoisin sauce
100ml/3½fl oz/scant ½ cup water
cucumber sticks, to garnish

1 Cut each chicken breast fillet into four even pieces. Put the beaten egg in one shallow bowl and the cracker crumbs in another. Heat the oil in a wok or deep-fryer.

2 Dip each piece of the chicken breast in the beaten egg and then in cracker crumbs, patting the crumbs on firmly to coat the chicken. Discard any excess crumbs.

3 Deep-fry the coated chicken, in several batches if necessary, for 3–4 minutes, until golden brown and cooked through. Using a slotted spoon, transfer to a board.

4 Put the plum sauce and hoisin sauce in a pan and stir in the water. Heat until bubbling. Meanwhile cut the chicken into bitesize pieces and pile on a serving platter.

5 Pour the rich plum and hoisin sauce over the chicken, garnish with the cucumber sticks and serve on warmed dishes.

Cook's Tip
Plum sauce is also known as duck sauce. It is dark red in colour, and it is often made with plums, apricots, sugar and seasonings, including ginger and chillies, and is generally served with duck, pork or spare ribs.

Chicken with Soy Sauce Energy 445kcal/1846kJ; Protein 33g; Carbohydrate 8.2g, of which sugars 3.5g; Fat 31.2g, of which saturates 8.4g; Cholesterol 171mg; Calcium 18mg; Fibre 0g; Sodium 1026mg.
Plum Sauce Chicken Energy 270kcal/1132kJ; Protein 20.4g; Carbohydrate 16g, of which sugars 8.8g; Fat 14.3g, of which saturates 2.4g; Cholesterol 91mg; Calcium 23mg; Fibre 0.3g; Sodium 188mg.

Caramelized Chicken Wings with Fresh Ginger

Cooked in a wok or in the oven, these caramelized wings are drizzled with chilli oil and eaten with the fingers, so that every bit of tender meat can be gnawed off the bone. Variations of this recipe can be found throughout Vietnam and Cambodia, often served with rice and pickles.

Serves 2–4
75ml/5 tbsp sugar
30ml/2 tbsp groundnut (peanut) oil
25g/1oz fresh root ginger, peeled and finely shredded or grated
12 chicken wings, split in two
chilli oil, for drizzling
mixed pickled vegetables, to serve

1 To make the caramel sauce, gently heat the sugar with 60ml/4 tbsp water in a small, heavy pan until it turns golden. Do not stir but allow the sugar to dissolve slowly. Set aside.

2 Heat the oil in a wok or heavy pan. Add the shredded ginger and stir-fry for 1–2 minutes until fragrant. Add the chicken wings and toss them around the wok to brown.

3 Pour in the caramel sauce and make sure that the chicken wings are thoroughly coated in it. Reduce the heat, cover the wok or pan, and cook for about 30 minutes, until the chicken is tender and the sauce has caramelized.

4 Drizzle chilli oil over the chicken wings and serve from the wok or pan with mixed pickled vegetables.

Cook's Tip
For the pickled vegetables, cut a large carrot and a piece of mooli (daikon) of about the same size into matchsticks. Sprinkle with salt and leave for 30 minutes. Heat 50ml/3½ tbsp rice vinegar with 100ml/3½fl oz/scant ½ cup water and 15ml/1 tbsp sugar until dissolved and leave to cool. Mix in the rinsed vegetables and marinate for up to 24 hours.

Stir-fried Orange Chicken

Oranges and almonds are favourite ingredients in southern Spain, especially around Seville where the orange and almond trees, laden with blossom and fruit, are a familiar and uplifting sight.

Serves 4
1 orange
8 chicken thighs
plain flour, seasoned with salt and pepper
45ml/3 tbsp olive oil
1 large Spanish onion, roughly chopped
2 garlic cloves, crushed
1 red (bell) pepper, sliced
1 yellow (bell) pepper, sliced
115g/4oz chorizo, sliced
50g/2oz/½ cup flaked almonds
225g/8oz/generous 1 cup brown basmati rice
about 600ml/1 pint/2½ cups chicken stock
400g/14oz can chopped tomatoes
175ml/6fl oz/¾ cup white wine
generous pinch of dried thyme
salt and ground black pepper
fresh thyme sprigs, to garnish

1 Pare a thin strip of peel from the orange and set it aside. Peel the orange, then cut it into segments, working over a bowl to catch the juice. Dust the chicken thighs with seasoned flour.

2 Heat the oil in a wok or large frying pan and fry the chicken pieces on both sides until nicely brown. Transfer to a plate. Add the onion and garlic to the pan and fry for 4–5 minutes until the onion begins to brown. Add the red and yellow peppers and fry, stirring occasionally, until slightly softened.

3 Add the chorizo, stir-fry for a few minutes, then sprinkle over the almonds and rice. Cook, stirring, for 1–2 minutes.

4 Pour in the chicken stock, tomatoes and wine and add the orange strip and thyme. Season well. Bring to simmering point, stirring, then return the chicken pieces to the pan.

5 Cover tightly and cook over a very low heat for 1–1¼ hours until the rice and chicken are tender. Just before serving, add the orange segments and allow to cook briefly to heat through. Garnish with fresh thyme and serve.

Caramelized Chicken Energy 393kcal/1641kJ; Protein 30.5g; Carbohydrate 14.4g, of which sugars 14.4g; Fat 24g, of which saturates 6.3g; Cholesterol 134mg; Calcium 16mg; Fibre 0g; Sodium 100mg.
Orange Chicken Energy 861kcal/3598kJ; Protein 65.3g; Carbohydrate 67.1g, of which sugars 17.1g; Fat 34g, of which saturates 5.6g; Cholesterol 155mg; Calcium 172mg; Fibre 6.3g; Sodium 453mg.

Crispy Five-spice Chicken

Strips of chicken fillet, with a spiced rice flour coating, become deliciously crisp and golden when fried.

Serves 4

200g/7oz thin egg noodles
30ml/2 tbsp sunflower oil
2 garlic cloves, very thinly sliced
1 fresh red chilli, seeded and sliced
½ red (bell) pepper, very thinly sliced
2 carrots, peeled and cut into strips
300g/11oz Chinese broccoli or Chinese greens, roughly sliced
45ml/3 tbsp hoisin sauce
45ml/3 tbsp soy sauce
5ml/1 tsp caster (superfine) sugar
4 skinless chicken breast fillets, cut into strips
2 egg whites, lightly beaten
115g/4oz/1 cup rice flour
15ml/1 tbsp five-spice powder
salt and ground black pepper
vegetable oil, for frying

1 Cook the noodles in a pan of salted boiling water according to the packet instructions, drain and set aside.

2 Heat the oil in a wok, then add the garlic, chilli, red pepper, carrots and broccoli or greens and stir-fry over a high heat for 2–3 minutes. Add the sauces and sugar to the wok and cook for a further 2–3 minutes. Add the drained noodles, toss to combine, then remove from the heat, cover and keep warm.

3 Dip the chicken strips into the egg white. Combine the rice flour and five-spice powder in a shallow dish and season. Add the chicken strips to the flour mixture and toss to coat.

4 Heat about 2.5cm/1in oil in a clean wok. When hot, shallow-fry the chicken for 3–4 minutes until crisp and golden.

5 To serve, divide the noodle mixture between warmed plates or bowls and top each serving with the chicken.

Cook's Tip

Five-spice powder is used extensively in Chinese cooking. It usually consists of equal portions of cinnamon, cloves, fennel seed, star anise and Szechuan peppercorns.

Chicken Rendang

Rendang is a spicy dish that originated in Indonesia. It is a great dish for a buffet. Serve it with prawn crackers.

Serves 4

1 chicken, about 1.3kg/3lb
5ml/1 tsp sugar
75g/3oz/1 cup desiccated (dry unsweetened) coconut
4 small onions, chopped
2 garlic cloves, chopped
2.5cm/1in piece fresh root ginger, peeled and sliced
1–2 lemon grass stalks, root trimmed
2.5cm/1in piece fresh galangal, peeled and sliced
75ml/5 tbsp vegetable oil
10–15ml/2–3 tsp chilli powder
400ml/14fl oz can coconut milk
10ml/2 tsp salt
fresh chives and deep-fried anchovies, to garnish

1 Joint the chicken into eight pieces and remove the skin, sprinkle with the sugar and leave to stand for 1 hour.

2 Meanwhile, dry-roast the coconut in a wok or heavy pan, turning all the time until it is crisp and golden. Tip into a food processor and process to an oily paste. Set aside.

3 Add the onions, garlic and ginger to the processor. Cut off the lower 5cm/2in of the lemon grass, chop and add to the processor with the galangal. Process to a fine paste.

4 Heat the oil in a wok or large pan and fry the onion mixture for a few minutes. Reduce the heat, stir in the chilli powder and cook for 2–3 minutes, stirring constantly. Spoon in 120ml/4fl oz/½ cup of the coconut milk and add salt to taste.

5 As soon as the mixture bubbles, add the chicken pieces to the pan, turning them until they are well coated with the spices. Pour in the coconut milk, stirring constantly to prevent curdling. Bruise the top of the lemon grass stalks and add to the wok or pan. Cover and cook for 45 minutes until the chicken is cooked through and very tender.

6 Just before serving stir in the coconut paste. Bring to just below boiling point, then simmer for 5 minutes. Garnish with fresh chives and deep-fried anchovies and serve.

Five-spice Chicken Energy 574kcal/2419kJ; Protein 49.6g; Carbohydrate 68g, of which sugars 9.4g; Fat 12.3g, of which saturates 2.5g; Cholesterol 120mg; Calcium 83mg; Fibre 5.1g; Sodium 1210mg.
Chicken Rendang Energy 501kcal/2098kJ; Protein 55.4g; Carbohydrate 7.2g, of which sugars 7.2g; Fat 28.1g, of which saturates 12.5g; Cholesterol 158mg; Calcium 45mg; Fibre 2.6g; Sodium 1233mg.

Stir-fried Sweet and Sour Chicken

This stir-fry with a South-east Asian influence makes a quick and easy dish, as all the ingredients go into the wok together and you can serve it straight from the pan.

Serves 4

275g/10oz medium egg noodles
30ml/2 tbsp vegetable oil
3 spring onions (scallions), chopped
1 garlic clove, crushed
2.5cm/1in fresh root ginger, peeled and grated
5ml/1 tsp hot paprika
5ml/1 tsp ground coriander
3 chicken breast fillets, sliced
115g/4oz sugar snap peas, topped and tailed
115g/4oz baby corn, halved
225g/8oz fresh beansprouts
15ml/1 tbsp cornflour (cornstarch)
45ml/3 tbsp soy sauce
45ml/3 tbsp lemon juice
15ml/1 tbsp sugar
salt
45ml/3 tbsp chopped fresh coriander (cilantro) or spring onions (scallions), to garnish

1 Cook the noodles in a large pan of boiling water, stirring occasionally to separate. Drain thoroughly, cover and keep warm.

2 Heat the oil in a wok. Add the spring onions and cook over a gentle heat, making sure they do not brown. Add the garlic, ginger, paprika, coriander and chicken. Stir-fry for 3–4 minutes.

3 Add the peas, baby corn and beansprouts, cover and cook briefly. Add the noodles.

4 Combine the cornflour, soy sauce, lemon juice and sugar in a small bowl. Add this mixture to the wok, toss all the ingredients together and simmer briefly until the sauce thickens and coats the noodles. Serve immediately, garnished with chopped coriander leaves or spring onion tops, if you like.

Cook's Tip

Follow the instructions on the packet when cooking dried Chinese noodles and time them carefully so that you do not overcook them. Fresh noodles do not need soaking and can be stir-fried straight from the packet.

Kung Po Chicken

This recipe, which hails from the Szechuan region of western China, has become one of the classic recipes in the Chinese repertoire. The combination of yellow salted beans and hoisin, spiked with chilli and softened with cashews, makes for a very tasty and spicy sauce.

Serves 3

1 egg white
10ml/2 tsp cornflour (cornstarch)
2.5ml/½ tsp salt
2–3 skinless chicken breast fillets, cut into neat pieces
45ml/3 tbsp sunflower oil
2–3 dried chillies, broken into small pieces
115g/4oz/1 cup roasted cashew nuts
fresh coriander (cilantro) leaves, to garnish

For the bean sauce

30ml/2 tbsp yellow salted beans
15ml/1 tbsp hoisin sauce
5ml/1 tsp soft light brown sugar
15ml/1 tbsp dry sherry or Chinese rice wine
15ml/1 tbsp wine vinegar
4 garlic cloves, crushed
150ml/¼ pint/⅔ cup chicken stock

1 Lightly whisk the egg white in a dish, whisk in the cornflour and salt, then add the chicken and stir until coated.

2 For the bean sauce, mash the yellow salted beans with a spoon in a separate bowl. Stir in the hoisin sauce, brown sugar, dry sherry, vinegar, garlic and chicken stock.

3 Heat a wok, add the oil and then stir-fry the chicken, turning constantly, for about 2 minutes until tender. Either drain the chicken over a bowl to collect excess oil, or lift out each piece with a slotted spoon, leaving the oil in the wok.

4 Heat the reserved oil and fry the chilli pieces for 1 minute.

5 Return the chicken to the wok and pour in the bean sauce mixture. Bring to the boil and stir in the cashew nuts.

6 Spoon the chicken into a heated serving dish, garnish with coriander leaves and serve immediately.

Sweet and Sour Chicken Energy 501kcal/2116kJ; Protein 37.3g; Carbohydrate 63g, of which sugars 9.8g; Fat 12.8g, of which saturates 2.6g; Cholesterol 91mg; Calcium 70mg; Fibre 4.7g; Sodium 1319mg.
Kung Po Chicken Energy 490kcal/2040kJ; Protein 37.7g; Carbohydrate 12.4g, of which sugars 2.6g; Fat 31.9g, of which saturates 5.6g; Cholesterol 82mg; Calcium 24mg; Fibre 1.9g; Sodium 204mg.

Orange Glazed Poussins

Succulent poussins coated in a spiced citrus glaze make a great alternative to a traditional roast.

Serves 4

4 poussins, 300–350g/11–12oz each
juice and finely grated rind of 2 oranges
2 garlic cloves, peeled and crushed
15ml/1 tbsp grated fresh root ginger
90ml/6 tbsp soy sauce
75ml/5 tbsp clear honey
2–3 star anise
30ml/2 tbsp Chinese rice wine
about 20 kaffir lime leaves
a large bunch of spring onions (scallions), shredded
60ml/4 tbsp butter
1 large orange, segmented, to garnish

1 Rinse the poussins inside and out and pat them dry with kitchen paper. Place them in a deep, non-metallic dish.

2 Combine the orange rind and juice, garlic, ginger, half the soy sauce and honey, star anise and rice wine, then coat the poussins with the mixture. Marinate in the refrigerator for at least 6 hours.

3 Line a large, heatproof plate with the lime leaves and spring onions. Lift the poussins out of the marinade and place on the leaves. Reserve the marinade.

4 Place a trivet or steamer rack in the base of a large wok and pour in 5cm/2in water. Bring the water to the boil and carefully lower the plate of poussins on to the trivet. Cover, reduce the heat to low and steam for 45 minutes–1 hour, or until the poussins are cooked through and tender. (Check the water level regularly and add more as needed.)

5 Remove the poussins from the wok and keep hot while you make the glaze. Wipe out the wok and pour in the reserved marinade, butter and the remaining soy sauce and honey.

6 Bring the glaze to the boil, then reduce the heat and cook gently for 10–15 minutes, or until thick, stirring from time to time. Spoon the glaze over the poussins and serve immediately, garnished with the orange segments, if liked.

Hot Chicken with Spices and Soy

This spicy dish is an Indonesian favourite, known as ayam kecap. Any leftovers taste equally good when reheated the following day.

Serves 4

1.6kg/3½lb chicken, jointed and cut into 16 pieces
3 onions, sliced
3 garlic cloves, crushed
3–4 red chillies, seeded and sliced, or 15ml/1 tbsp chilli powder
45–60ml/3–4 tbsp vegetable or sunflower oil
2.5ml/½ tsp ground nutmeg
6 whole cloves
5ml/1 tsp tamarind pulp, soaked in 45ml/3 tbsp warm water
30–45ml/2–3 tbsp dark or light soy sauce
salt
fresh red chilli shreds, to garnish
boiled rice, to serve

1 Prepare the chicken and place the pieces in a large pan with one of the onions. Pour over enough water to just cover. Bring to the boil and then simmer gently for 20 minutes.

2 Meanwhile, grind the remaining onions with the garlic and chillies to a fine paste in a food processor or with a mortar and pestle. Heat a little of the oil in a wok or frying pan and cook the paste to bring out the flavour, but do not allow to brown.

3 Lift the chicken out of the stock in the pan using a slotted spoon and put it straight into the spicy mixture. Toss everything together over a fairly high heat so that the spices permeate the chicken pieces. Reserve 300ml/½ pint/1¼ cups of the chicken stock to add to the pan later.

4 Stir in the nutmeg and cloves. Strain the tamarind and add the tamarind juice and the soy sauce to the chicken. Cook for a further 2–3 minutes, then add the reserved stock.

5 Taste and adjust the seasoning and cook, uncovered, for a further 25–35 minutes, until the chicken pieces are tender.

6 Serve the chicken in warmed individual bowls, garnished with the shredded chilli, and eat with boiled rice.

Glazed Poussins Energy 544kcal/2264kJ; Protein 36.2g; Carbohydrate 5.8g, of which sugars 5.8g; Fat 42.1g, of which saturates 14.5g; Cholesterol 215mg; Calcium 16mg; Fibre 0g; Sodium 207mg.
Hot Chicken with Spices Energy 630kcal/2615kJ; Protein 48.8g; Carbohydrate 13.8g, of which sugars 10.7g; Fat 42.5g, of which saturates 10.6g; Cholesterol 248mg; Calcium 52mg; Fibre 2.6g; Sodium 798mg.

Bali Fried Poussins

Serves 4
4 poussins
150g/5oz Thai spice paste
450ml/14fl oz/1⅔ cups coconut milk
3 lemon grass stalks, 5cm/2in of root end bruised
5ml/1 tsp salt
5ml/1 tsp black peppercorns, crushed
105ml/7 tbsp vegetable oil
juice of 1 lime
4 limes, halved, to garnish
chilli dipping sauce, to serve

1 Spatchcock each poussin by cutting down the backbone and spreading out the bird so that the breast is one broad piece and the bird lies flat on the work surface.

2 Whisk together the spice paste and coconut milk, and bring them to the boil with the lemon grass, salt and peppercorns. Simmer the poussins in this blend for 8 minutes. If your pot is too crowded, cook in two batches.

3 Remove the poussins and drain. Heat the oil in a large wok or frying pan and fry the poussins, two at a time, until the skin is golden brown. Turn once or twice to cook through thoroughly.

4 Drizzle the lime juice over the poussins and serve warm with a chilli dipping sauce and lime halves to squeeze over.

Chicken with Green Papaya

This Filipino dish uses the green papaya that is plentiful on the islands. The Filipino fish sauce (patis) used here is a strong condiment, but you can replace the patis with light soy sauce if you prefer a milder taste.

Serves 4
1 whole green papaya
30ml/2 tbsp vegetable oil
4 garlic cloves, crushed
1 small onion, sliced
5ml/1 tsp black peppercorns, crushed
4 skinless, boneless chicken breast fillets, cubed
30ml/2 tbsp patis (Filipino fish sauce)
2.5ml/½ tsp sugar
5ml/1 tsp salt
500ml/17fl oz/generous 2 cups water
juice of 1 lime
4 fresh green chillies, seeded and sliced
boiled rice, to serve

1 Peel the papaya with a vegetable peeler and remove any seeds or pith. Slice it into thin pieces about 5cm/2in square and 5mm/¼in thick. Wash and drain.

2 Heat the vegetable oil in a wok or heavy frying pan and fry the garlic until golden. Add the onion and fry until soft, and then add the peppercorns and fry for 1 minute.

3 Add the chicken, patis, sugar and salt to the pan and stir it over a high heat for about 5 minutes until the chicken is sealed and has gone white. Add the water.

4 Bring to the boil, then reduce the heat and simmer for 20 minutes. Add the lime juice, chillies and papaya, cook for 5 minutes until soft, then serve with rice.

Indonesian-style Satay Chicken

Satay forms part of an Indonesian rice table – a vast feast of up to 40 dishes. For the less ambitious, a creamy coconut and peanut sauce makes this chicken mouth-watering at any time.

Serves 4
50g/2oz raw peanuts
45ml/3 tbsp vegetable oil
1 small onion, finely chopped
2.5cm/1in fresh root ginger, peeled and finely chopped
1 clove garlic, crushed
675g/1½lb chicken thighs, skinned and cut into cubes
90g/3½oz creamed coconut, roughly chopped
15ml/1 tbsp chilli sauce
60ml/4 tbsp crunchy peanut butter
5ml/1 tsp soft dark brown sugar
150ml/¼ pint/⅔ cup milk
1.5ml/¼ tsp salt

1 Shell the peanuts and remove the skins by rubbing them between the palms of the hands. Put them in a small bowl, add just enough water to cover and soak for 1 minute. Drain the nuts and cut them into slivers.

2 Heat the wok and add 5ml/1 tsp oil. When the oil is hot, stir-fry the peanuts for 1 minute until crisp and golden. Remove with a slotted spoon and drain on kitchen paper.

3 Add the remaining oil to the wok. When the oil is hot, add the onion, ginger and garlic and stir-fry for 2–3 minutes until softened but not browned. Drain on kitchen paper.

4 Add the chicken to the wok and stir-fry for 3–4 minutes until crisp and golden. Thread them on to skewers and keep warm.

5 Add the coconut to the wok and stir-fry until melted. Add the chilli sauce, peanut butter and ginger mixture and simmer for 2 minutes. Stir in the sugar, milk and salt, and simmer for a further 3 minutes. Serve with the skewered chicken.

Cook's Tip
If you can't find creamed coconut, which is sold in blocks, use 200ml/7fl oz/scant 1 cup coconut milk instead.

Bali Fried Poussins Energy 288kcal/1200kJ; Protein 24.3g; Carbohydrate 3.5g, of which sugars 2.9g; Fat 20.6g, of which saturates 4.9g; Cholesterol 123mg; Calcium 47mg; Fibre 0.5g; Sodium 183mg.
Chicken with Papaya Energy 291kcal/1226kJ; Protein 37.6g; Carbohydrate 19.5g, of which sugars 19.2g; Fat 7.5g, of which saturates 1.1g; Cholesterol 105mg; Calcium 61mg; Fibre 4.6g; Sodium 101mg.
Satay Chicken Energy 600kcal /2500kJ; protein 44.7g; carbohydrate 10.1g, of which sugars 8.1g; fat 42g, of which saturates 19g; cholesterol 179mg; calcium 79mg; fibre 1.8g; sodium 289mg.

Chicken in White Coconut Milk Sauce

This mild, creamy Indonesian stew makes a good introduction to curries for those not accustomed to the fire of chilli-based curries. It is delicious served with chunks of crusty baguette or with plain boiled rice.

Serves 4

30ml/2 tbsp vegetable oil
8 shallots, sliced
7 garlic cloves, sliced
15ml/1 tbsp ground coriander
5ml/1 tsp chopped fresh root ginger
1 chicken, about 600g/1lb 6oz, cut into 5cm/2in pieces on the bone
2 lemon grass stalks, 5cm/2in of root end bruised
4 salam leaves (Indonesian bay leaves) or curry leaves
450ml/¾ pint/scant 2 cups coconut milk
5ml/1 tsp salt
lime slices, to garnish
boiled rice, to serve

1 Heat the oil in a wok and fry the shallots and garlic until light golden. Remove three-quarters of the shallots and half the garlic from the pan and set aside to use as a garnish. Add the ground coriander and chopped ginger and fry for 2 minutes.

2 Add the chicken pieces and lemon grass to the pan and continue to fry for 5 minutes, stirring frequently.

3 Transfer to a heavy pan and add the salam leaves or curry leaves, coconut milk and salt. Bring to the boil, then reduce the heat and simmer, covered, for 35 minutes.

4 Serve the dish in warmed bowls, garnished with the reserved fried garlic and shallots, with rice and lime slices.

Cook's Tip
If you want to add a little fire, slit 2 or 3 green chillies lengthways but not all the way through. Seed them and add during the last 10 minutes of cooking.

Aromatic Chicken from Madura

This dish is best cooked ahead so that the flavours have time to permeate the chicken flesh, making it even more delicious. A cool cucumber salad is a good accompaniment.

Serves 4

1.5kg/3–3½lb chicken, cut in quarters, or 4 chicken quarters
5ml/1 tsp sugar
30ml/2 tbsp coriander seeds
10ml/2 tsp cumin seeds
6 whole cloves
2.5ml/½ tsp ground nutmeg
2.5ml/½ tsp ground turmeric
1 small onion
2.5cm/1in fresh root ginger, peeled and sliced
300ml/½ pint/1¼ cups chicken stock or water
salt and freshly ground black pepper
boiled rice and deep-fried onion rings, to serve

1 Cut each chicken quarter in half and place in a wok, sprinkle with sugar and salt and toss together. Use any remaining bones to make chicken stock for use later in the recipe if you like.

2 Dry-fry the coriander, cumin and whole cloves until the spices give off a good aroma. Add the nutmeg and turmeric and heat briefly. Grind in a food processor or a pestle and mortar.

3 If using a processor, process the onion and ginger until finely chopped. Otherwise, finely chop the onion and ginger and pound to a paste with a pestle and mortar. Add the spices and stock or water and mix well.

4 Pour the spice mixture over the chicken in the wok. Cover with a lid and cook over a gentle heat until the chicken is really tender and the sauce is reduced, about 45–50 minutes.

5 Serve portions of the chicken, with the sauce, on a bed of boiled rice, scattered with crisp deep-fried onion rings.

Cook's Tip
Add a large piece of bruised ginger and a small onion when making the chicken stock to ensure a good flavour.

Chicken in Coconut Energy 311kcal/1294kJ; Protein 19.8g; Carbohydrate 9.3g, of which sugars 6.9g; Fat 22g, of which saturates 5.5g; Cholesterol 96mg; Calcium 56mg; Fibre 0.4g; Sodium 202mg.
Aromatic Chicken Energy 604kcal/2514kJ; Protein 55.7g; Carbohydrate 4.1g, of which sugars 2.2g; Fat 40.6g, of which saturates 10.8g; Cholesterol 330mg; Calcium 66mg; Fibre 1.7g; Sodium 269mg.

Spiced Coconut Chicken with Cardamom, Chilli and Ginger

You need to marinate the chicken legs overnight in an aromatic blend of yogurt and spices before gently simmering with hot green chillies in creamy coconut milk. Serve with rice or Indian breads.

Serves 4

1.6kg/3½lb large chicken drumsticks
30ml/2 tbsp sunflower oil
400ml/14fl oz/1⅔ cups coconut milk
4–6 large green chillies, halved
45ml/3 tbsp finely chopped coriander (cilantro)
salt and ground black pepper
natural (plain) yogurt, to drizzle

For the marinade

15ml/1 tbsp crushed cardamom seeds
15ml/1 tbsp grated fresh root ginger
10ml/2 tsp finely grated garlic
105ml/7 tbsp natural (plain) yogurt
2 green chillies, seeded and chopped
5ml/1 tsp ground cumin
5ml/1 tsp ground coriander
5ml/1 tsp turmeric
finely grated zest and juice of 1 lime

1 Make the marinade. Place the cardamom, ginger, garlic, half the yogurt, green chillies, cumin, coriander, turmeric and lime zest and juice in a blender. Process the marinade until it is smooth, then season and pour into a large glass bowl.

2 Add the chicken to the marinade and toss to coat evenly. Cover the bowl and marinate in the refrigerator overnight.

3 Heat the oil in a large, non-stick wok or heavy pan over a low heat. Remove the chicken from the marinade, reserving the marinade. Add the chicken to the wok and brown all over, then add the coconut milk, remaining yogurt, reserved marinade and green chillies and bring to a boil.

4 Reduce the heat and simmer gently, uncovered, for 30–35 minutes. Check the seasoning, adding more if needed. Stir in the coriander, ladle into warmed bowls and serve immediately. Drizzle with yogurt if liked.

Devil's Chicken Curry

Every Eurasian household in Malaysia has its own version of this devilishly hot and delicious chicken and vegetable hotpot. Served as a meal on its own with bread to mop up the sauce, it is often eaten at family celebration meals.

Serves 6

4–6 skinless chicken breast fillets or 12 boned chicken thighs, cut into chunks
60ml/4 tbsp vegetable oil
1 onion, halved and sliced
25g/1oz fresh root ginger, peeled and cut into julienne strips
4 garlic cloves, cut into strips
30–45ml/2–3 tbsp vinegar
10ml/2 tsp sugar
3 medium potatoes, cut into bitesize pieces
2 courgettes (zucchini), halved lengthways, seeded and sliced
8 Chinese leaves (Chinese cabbage), cut into squares
10ml/2 tsp brown mustard seeds, ground and mixed to a paste with a little water
salt
fresh crusty bread, to serve

For the spice paste

10 dried chillies, soaked in warm water, seeded and patted dry
6 fresh red chillies, seeded and chopped
8 shallots, chopped
6 garlic cloves, chopped
25g/1oz fresh root ginger, peeled and chopped
6 candlenuts or macadamia nuts
10ml/2 tsp ground turmeric

For the marinade

15ml/1 tbsp light soy sauce
15ml/1 tbsp dark soy sauce
10ml/2 tsp rice wine vinegar
10ml/2 tsp caster (superfine) sugar

1 Mix together the ingredients for the marinade and rub it into the chicken pieces. Leave to marinate for 30 minutes. Using a mortar and pestle or food processor, grind the chillies, shallots, garlic, ginger and nuts to a paste. Stir in the turmeric.

2 Heat the oil in a wok or heavy pan. Stir in the onion, ginger and garlic and fry until golden. Add the spice paste, stir, toss in the chicken and stir until it browns. Pour in water to cover.

3 Bring to the boil and add the vinegar, sugar and potatoes. Reduce the heat and cook until the potatoes are tender. Add the courgettes and cabbage and cook for 2 minutes. Stir in the mustard paste and season with salt. Serve hot with bread.

Coconut Chicken Energy 706kcal/2935kJ; Protein 48.1g; Carbohydrate 15.8g, of which sugars 15.6g; Fat 50.4g, of which saturates 12.8g; Cholesterol 240mg; Calcium 91mg; Fibre 1.5g; Sodium 305mg.
Devil's Chicken Energy 270Kcal/1136kJ; Protein 32.5g; Carbohydrate 15.4g, of which sugars 4.6g; Fat 9.1g, of which saturates 1.3g; Cholesterol 88mg; Calcium 36mg; Fibre 1.8g; Sodium 441mg.

Curry with Coconut Chilli Relish

Fresh and roasted coconut gives this lovely chicken curry its distinctive flavour. This classic combination of fresh coriander, lime and coconut characterises many South-east Asian recipes.

Serves 4

15–30ml/1–2 tbsp tamarind pulp
1 fresh coconut, grated (shredded)
30–45ml/2–3 tbsp vegetable oil
1–2 cinnamon sticks
12 chicken thighs, boned and cut into bitesize strips lengthways
600ml/1 pint/2½ cups coconut milk
15ml/1 tbsp brown sugar
1 fresh green and 1 red chilli, seeded and sliced
fresh coriander (cilantro) leaves, finely chopped (reserve a few leaves for garnishing)
2 limes
salt and ground black pepper
steamed rice, to serve

For the rempah spice paste

6–8 dried red chillies, soaked in warm water until soft, seeded and squeezed dry
6–8 shallots, chopped
4–6 garlic cloves, chopped
25g/1oz fresh root ginger, chopped
5ml/1 tsp shrimp paste
10ml/2 tsp ground turmeric
10ml/2 tsp five-spice powder

1 First make the rempah. Using a mortar and pestle or food processor, grind the chillies, shallots, garlic and ginger to a paste. Beat in the shrimp paste and stir in the dried spices.

2 Soak the tamarind pulp in 150ml/¼ pint/⅔ cup warm water until soft. Squeeze to extract the juice, then strain. In a heavy pan, roast half the grated coconut until brown, then grind it in a food processor until it resembles sugar grains.

3 Heat the oil in a wok or heavy pan and stir in the rempah and cinnamon sticks until fragrant. Add the chicken, coconut milk, tamarind water and sugar. Cook gently for 10 minutes. Thicken by stirring in half the ground roasted coconut, and season.

4 Make a relish by mixing the remaining grated coconut with the chillies, coriander and juice of 1 lime. Cut the other lime into wedges. Spoon the curry into a serving dish and garnish with coriander. Serve with the rice, relish and lime wedges.

Yellow Chicken Curry

The pairing of slightly sweet coconut milk and fruit with savoury chicken and spices is at once a comforting and exotic combination.

Serves 4

300ml/½ pint/1¼ cups chicken stock
30ml/2 tbsp tamarind paste mixed with a little warm water
15ml/1 tbsp sugar
200ml/7fl oz/scant 1 cup coconut milk
1 green papaya, peeled, seeded and thinly sliced
250g/9oz skinless chicken breast fillets, diced
juice of 1 lime
lime slices, to garnish

For the curry paste

1 fresh red chilli, seeded and coarsely chopped
4 garlic cloves, coarsely chopped
3 shallots, coarsely chopped
2 lemon grass stalks, sliced
5cm/2in piece fresh turmeric, coarsely chopped, or 5ml/1 tsp ground turmeric
5ml/1 tsp shrimp paste
5ml/1 tsp salt

1 Make the yellow curry paste. Put the red chilli, garlic, shallots, lemon grass, turmeric, shrimp paste and salt in a food processor. Process to a paste, adding a little water if needed.

2 Pour the stock into a wok or medium pan and bring it to the boil. Stir in the curry paste to mix.

3 Bring the pan back to the boil and add the tamarind juice, sugar and coconut milk. Stir well to mix.

4 Add the papaya and chicken and cook over a medium heat for about 15 minutes, stirring frequently, until the chicken is cooked.

5 Stir in the lime juice, transfer to a warm dish and serve immediately, garnished with lime slices.

Cook's Tip
Fresh turmeric resembles root ginger in appearance and is a member of the same family. When preparing turmeric, wear rubber gloves to protect your hands from staining.

Curry with Coconut Energy 706kcal/2935kJ; Protein 48.1g; Carbohydrate 15.8g, of which sugars 15.6g; Fat 50.4g, of which saturates 12.8g; Cholesterol 240mg; Calcium 91mg; Fibre 1.5g; Sodium 305mg.
Yellow Chicken Curry Energy 149kcal/633kJ; Protein 17.2g; Carbohydrate 18.9g, of which sugars 17.2g; Fat 1.1g, of which saturates 0.3g; Cholesterol 50mg; Calcium 70mg; Fibre 2.8g; Sodium 153mg.

Chicken and Lemon Grass Curry

Quick-cook curries work well in a wok, especially if you use an electric one. The chicken is wonderfully spicy, so a bowl of rice and a fresh green salad are the best accompaniments to the dish.

Serves 4

45ml/3 tbsp vegetable oil
2 garlic cloves, crushed
500g/1¼lb skinless chicken thighs, boned and chopped into small pieces
45ml/3 tbsp Thai fish sauce
120ml/4fl oz/½ cup chicken or vegetable stock
5ml/1 tsp granulated (white) sugar
1 lemon grass stalk, chopped into 4 sticks and lightly crushed
5 kaffir lime leaves, rolled into cylinders and thinly sliced across, plus extra to garnish
chopped roasted peanuts and chopped fresh coriander (cilantro), to garnish

For the curry paste

1 lemon grass stalk, chopped
2.5cm/1in piece fresh galangal, peeled and coarsely chopped
2 kaffir lime leaves, chopped
3 shallots, coarsely chopped
6 coriander (cilantro) roots, coarsely chopped
2 garlic cloves
2 fresh green chillies, seeded and coarsely chopped
5ml/1 tsp shrimp paste
5ml/1 tsp ground turmeric

1 Make the curry paste. Place all the ingredients in a large mortar, or food processor. Pound or process to a paste.

2 Heat the vegetable oil in a wok or large, heavy frying pan, add the garlic and cook over a low heat, stirring frequently, until it is golden brown. Add the curry paste and stir-fry with the garlic for about 30 seconds more.

3 Add the chicken pieces to the pan and stir until thoroughly coated with the curry paste. Stir in the Thai fish sauce and chicken stock with the sugar, and cook for 2 minutes more.

4 Add the lemon grass and lime leaves to the pan, reduce the heat and simmer for 10 minutes. If the mixture begins to dry out, add a little more stock or water.

5 Spoon the curry into four dishes, garnish with the lime leaves, peanuts and coriander and serve immediately.

Chicken and Coconut Milk Curry

This mild coconut curry flavoured with turmeric, coriander and cumin seeds demonstrates the influence of Malaysian cooking on Asian cuisine. Serve with plain boiled rice or steamed noodles.

Serves 4

60ml/4 tbsp vegetable oil
1 large garlic clove, crushed
1 chicken, weighing about 1.5kg/3–3½lb, chopped into 12 large pieces
400ml/14fl oz/1⅔ cups coconut cream
250ml/8fl oz/1 cup chicken stock
30ml/2 tbsp fish sauce
30ml/2 tbsp sugar
juice of 2 limes

For the curry paste

5ml/1 tsp dried chilli flakes
2.5ml/½ tsp salt
5cm/2in piece fresh turmeric or 5ml/1 tsp ground turmeric
2.5ml/½ tsp coriander seeds
2.5ml/½ tsp cumin seeds
5ml/1 tsp dried shrimp paste

To garnish

2 small fresh red chillies, seeded and finely chopped
1 bunch spring onions (scallions), thinly sliced

1 First make the curry paste. Put the chilli flakes, salt, turmeric, coriander seeds, cumin seeds and dried shrimp paste in a mortar, food processor or spice grinder and pound, process or grind the mixture to a smooth paste.

2 Heat the oil in a large wok or frying pan and cook the garlic for 2–3 minutes or until golden. Add the chicken and brown on all sides. Remove the chicken and set aside.

3 Reheat the oil and add the curry paste and then half the coconut cream. Cook for a few minutes until fragrant.

4 Return the chicken to the wok or pan, add the chicken stock, mixing well, then add the remaining coconut cream, the fish sauce, sugar and lime juice. Stir well and bring to the boil, then lower the heat and simmer for 15 minutes until the chicken is completely cooked through.

5 Spoon the curry into four warm serving bowls, garnish with the chillies and spring onions and serve immediately.

Chicken and Lemon Grass Energy 229Kcal/959kJ; Protein 31.3g; Carbohydrate 4.3g, of which sugars 3.4g; Fat 9.7g, of which saturates 1.4g; Cholesterol 94mg; Calcium 32mg; Fibre 0.5g; Sodium 397mg.
Chicken and Coconut Energy 706kcal/2935kJ; Protein 48.1g; Carbohydrate 15.8g, of which sugars 15.6g; Fat 50.4g, of which saturates 12.8g; Cholesterol 240mg; Calcium 91mg; Fibre 1.5g; Sodium 305mg.

Fragrant Thai Chicken Curry

This dish is perfect for a party as the chicken and sauce can be prepared in advance and combined and heated at the last minute.

Serves 4

45ml/3 tbsp oil
1 onion, coarsely chopped
2 garlic cloves, crushed
15ml/1 tbsp Thai red curry paste
115g/4oz creamed coconut dissolved in 900ml/1½ pints/3¾ cups boiling water, or 1 litre/1¾ pints/4 cups coconut milk
2 lemon grass stalks, coarsely chopped
6 kaffir lime leaves, chopped
150ml/¼ pint/⅔ cup strained natural (plain) yogurt
30ml/2 tbsp apricot jam
1 cooked chicken, about 1.5kg/3–3½lb
30ml/2 tbsp chopped fresh coriander (cilantro)
salt and ground black pepper
kaffir lime leaves, toasted coconut shreds and fresh coriander (cilantro), to garnish
boiled rice, to serve

1 Heat the oil in a wok or large pan. Add the onion and garlic and cook over a low heat for 5–10 minutes until soft. Stir in the red curry paste. Cook, stirring constantly, for 2–3 minutes.

2 Stir in the diluted creamed coconut or coconut milk, then add the lemon grass, lime leaves, yogurt and apricot jam. Stir well. Cover and simmer for 30 minutes.

3 Remove the wok or pan from the heat and leave to cool slightly. Transfer the sauce to a food processor or blender and process to a smooth purée, then strain it back into the rinsed-out pan, pressing as much of the puréed mixture as possible through the sieve (strainer) with the back of a wooden spoon. Set aside while you prepare the chicken.

4 Remove the skin from the chicken, slice the meat off the bones and cut it into bitesize pieces. Add to the sauce.

5 Bring the sauce back to simmering point and reheat the chicken thoroughly. Stir in the fresh coriander and season to taste with salt and pepper. Garnish with extra lime leaves, shredded coconut and coriander. Serve with rice.

Kashmiri Chicken Curry

Surrounded by the snow-capped Himalayas, Kashmir is popularly known as the "Switzerland of the East". The state is also renowned for its rich culinary heritage, and this aromatic dish is one of the simplest among the region's repertoire.

Serves 4–6

20ml/4 tsp Kashmiri masala paste
60ml/4 tbsp tomato ketchup
5ml/1 tsp Worcestershire sauce
5ml/1 tsp five-spice powder
5ml/1 tsp granulated sugar
8 chicken joints, skinned
5cm/2in piece fresh root ginger
45ml/3 tbsp vegetable oil
4 garlic cloves, crushed
juice of 1 lemon
15ml/1 tbsp coriander (cilantro) leaves, finely chopped
salt
plain boiled rice, to serve

1 To make the marinade, mix the masala paste, tomato ketchup, Worcestershire sauce and five-spice powder with the sugar and a little salt. Cover the mixture and leave the marinade to rest in a warm place until the sugar has dissolved.

2 Rub the chicken pieces with the marinade, cover with clear film (plastic wrap) and set aside in a cool place for at least 2 hours, or preferably in the refrigerator overnight. Bring the chicken to room temperature before cooking.

3 Thinly peel the fresh root ginger, using a sharp knife or vegetable peeler. Grate the peeled root finely.

4 Heat the oil in a karahi, wok or large pan and fry half the ginger and all the garlic until golden.

5 Add the chicken to the pan and fry it until both sides are sealed. Cover and cook until the chicken is cooked through and tender, and the oil has separated from the sauce.

6 Sprinkle the chicken with the lemon juice, the remaining grated ginger and chopped coriander leaves, and mix in well.

7 Serve the chicken piping hot on warmed individual dishes. Plain boiled rice makes a good accompaniment.

Fragrant Thai Chicken Energy 237kcal/991kJ; Protein 33.8g; Carbohydrate 7.2g, of which sugars 5.9g; Fat 8.3g, of which saturates 1.6g; Cholesterol 165mg; Calcium 149mg; Fibre 3.1g; Sodium 253mg.
Kashmiri Chicken Energy 256kcal/1066kJ; Protein 16.9g; Carbohydrate 12.3g, of which sugars 10.2g; Fat 15.8g, of which saturates 3.5g; Cholesterol 75mg; Calcium 93mg; Fibre 2.4g; Sodium 411mg.

Spicy Chicken Jalfrezi

A jalfrezi curry is a stir-fried dish cooked with onions, ginger and garlic in a rich pepper sauce.

Serves 4

675g/1½lb skinless chicken breast fillets
30ml/2 tbsp vegetable oil
5ml/1 tsp cumin seeds
1 onion, finely chopped
1 green (bell) pepper, finely chopped
1 red (bell) pepper, finely chopped
1 garlic clove, crushed
2cm/¾in piece fresh root ginger, finely chopped
15ml/1 tbsp curry paste
1.5ml/¼ tsp chilli powder
5ml/1 tsp ground coriander
5ml/1 tsp ground cumin
2.5ml/½ tsp salt
400g/14oz can chopped tomatoes
30ml/2 tbsp chopped fresh coriander (cilantro), plus leaves, to garnish
plain boiled rice, to serve

1 Remove any visible fat from the chicken with a sharp knife and discard. Cut the chicken meat into 2.5cm/1in pieces.

2 Heat the oil in a wok or large frying pan and fry the cumin seeds for 2–3 minutes until they begin to splutter.

3 Add the onion, green and red peppers, garlic and ginger to the pan and fry for 6–8 minutes.

4 Add the curry paste to the pan and fry for about 2 minutes, stirring constantly, until it releases its fragrant aromas.

5 Stir the chilli powder, ground coriander, cumin and salt into the pan and stir in about 15ml/1 tbsp cold water. Cook, stirring constantly, for a further 2–4 minutes.

6 Add the chicken to the pan and cook for about 5 minutes, stirring occasionally. Add the chopped tomatoes and the fresh coriander and stir well.

7 Cover the pan with a lid and simmer over low heat for about 15–20 minutes, or until the chicken is cooked through and tender. Garnish with the coriander and serve immediately with plain boiled rice, if you like.

Chicken Curry Anglo-Indian Style

This recipe uses plenty of curry powder to give it a real bite. When made with pieces of chicken on the bone, it becomes a beautifully classic 'Anglo-Indian' curry, best served with plain boiled rice to moderate the spicy flavours.

Serves 4

675g/1½lb chicken leg or breast joint pieces on the bone
½ tsp ground turmeric
1 tbsp plain (all-purpose) flour
1 tsp salt, or to taste
1 large onion, roughly chopped
2.5cm/1in piece of fresh root ginger, roughly chopped
4–5 garlic cloves, roughly chopped
4 tbsp sunflower oil or olive oil
1½ tbsp curry powder
½ tsp chilli powder (optional)
175g/6oz fresh tomatoes, chopped
2 tbsp chopped fresh coriander (cilantro)
plain boiled rice, to serve

1 Skin the chicken and separate the legs from the thighs using a sharp knife. If you are using breast meat, cut each one into three pieces. Mix the turmeric, flour and salt together and rub this mixture into the chicken. Set the chicken aside to rest while you prepare the other flavourings.

2 Put the onion, ginger and garlic in a food processor to make a purée; alternatively, you can pound them together into a paste using a mortar and pestle.

3 Heat the sunflower oil in a wok or medium-sized pan and add the puréed ingredients. Cook over a medium heat, stirring regularly, for 8–10 minutes.

4 Add the curry powder and chilli powder to the pan, if using, and cook for 2–3 minutes. Add around 2 tbsp water and continue to cook for a further 2–3 minutes.

5 Add the chicken, increase the heat to medium-high and stir until the chicken begins to brown. Add 425ml/15fl oz/1¾ cups warm water, bring it to the boil, cover and reduce the heat to low. Cook for another 35–40 minutes and add the tomatoes. Cook for 2–3 minutes longer, stir in the chopped coriander and remove from the heat. Serve with plain boiled rice.

Spicy Jalfrezi Energy 338kcal/1422kJ; Protein 44.8g; Carbohydrate 20.1g, of which sugars 14g; Fat 9.5g, of which saturates 1.5g; Cholesterol 118mg; Calcium 66mg; Fibre 3.8g; Sodium 120mg.
Chicken Curry Anglo-Indian Energy 392kcal/1632kJ; Protein 24.3g; Carbohydrate 12.5g, of which sugars 7.3g; Fat 27.6g, of which saturates 5.8g; Cholesterol 135mg; Calcium 67mg; Fibre 2.6g; Sodium 108mg.

Balti Chicken in a Lentil Sauce

Traditionally this dish is made with lamb, but it is equally delicious made with chicken breast.

Serves 4

30ml/2 tbsp chana dhal or yellow split peas
50g/2oz/¼ cup masoor dhal or red split peas
15ml/1 tbsp oil
2 medium onions, chopped
5ml/1 tsp crushed garlic
5ml/1 tsp grated fresh root ginger
2.5ml/½ tsp ground turmeric
7.5ml/1½ tsp chilli powder
5ml/1 tsp garam masala
2.5ml/½ tsp ground coriander
7.5ml/1½ tsp salt
175g/6oz skinned chicken breast fillets, cubed
45ml/3 tbsp fresh coriander (cilantro) leaves
1 or 2 fresh green chillies, seeded and chopped
30–45ml/2–3 tbsp lemon juice
300ml/½ pint/1¼ cups water
2 tomatoes, peeled and halved

For the tarka
5ml/1 tsp oil
2.5ml/½ tsp cumin seeds
2 garlic cloves
2 dried red chillies
4 curry leaves

1 Put the pulses in a pan with water and bring to the boil. Cook for 30–45 minutes until soft and mushy. Drain and set aside.

2 Heat the oil in a karahi, wok or heavy frying pan and fry the onions until soft and golden brown. Stir in the garlic, ginger, turmeric, chilli powder, garam masala, ground coriander and salt.

3 Next, add the chicken pieces to the pan and fry for 5–7 minutes, stirring constantly over a medium heat to seal in the juices and lightly brown the meat.

4 Add half the fresh coriander, the green chillies, lemon juice and water and cook for 3–5 minutes. Stir in the cooked pulses, then add the tomatoes. Sprinkle over the remaining coriander leaves. Take the pan off the heat and set aside.

5 To make the tarka, heat the oil and add the other ingredients. Heat for about 30 seconds then pour the tarka over the top of the chicken and lentils. Serve the dish immediately.

Balti Chicken with Paneer and Peas

This Balti dish has a rather unusual combination of ingredients, but it really works well. Serve with plain boiled rice.

Serves 4

1 small chicken, about 675g/1½lb
30ml/2 tbsp tomato purée (paste)
45ml/3 tbsp natural (plain) low-fat yogurt
7.5ml/1½ tsp garam masala
5ml/1 tsp crushed garlic
5ml/1 tsp grated fresh root ginger
pinch of ground cardamom
15ml/1 tbsp chilli powder
1.5ml/¼ tsp ground turmeric
5ml/1 tsp salt
5ml/1 tsp granulated sugar
10ml/2 tsp oil
2.5cm/1in cinnamon stick
2 black peppercorns
300ml/½ pint/1¼ cups water
115g/4oz paneer, cubed
30ml/2 tbsp fresh coriander (cilantro) leaves
2 fresh green chillies, seeded and chopped
50g/2oz/¼ cup low-fat fromage frais or ricotta cheese
75g/3oz/¾ cup frozen peas, thawed

1 Skin the chicken and cut it into six to eight equal pieces.

2 Mix the tomato purée, yogurt, garam masala, garlic, ginger, cardamom, chilli powder, turmeric, salt and sugar in a bowl.

3 Heat the oil with the whole spices in a karahi, wok or heavy pan, then pour the yogurt mixture into the oil. Lower the heat and cook gently for about 3 minutes, then pour in the water and bring the sauce to a simmer.

4 Add the chicken pieces to the pan. Stir-fry for 2 minutes, then cover the pan and cook over medium heat for about 10 minutes, stirring from time to time.

5 Add the paneer cubes to the pan, followed by half the coriander leaves and half the green chillies. Mix well and cook for a further 5–7 minutes.

6 Stir in the fromage frais or ricotta and peas, heat through and serve with the reserved coriander and chillies.

Chicken in a Lentil Sauce Energy 196kcal/823kJ; Protein 20.3g; Carbohydrate 9.8g, of which sugars 2.6g; Fat 8.7g, of which saturates 1.2g; Cholesterol 47mg; Calcium 41mg; Fibre 2.5g; Sodium 51mg.
Balti Chicken Energy 313kcal/1303kJ; Protein 27.7g; Carbohydrate 7.3g, of which sugars 5.6g; Fat 19.3g, of which saturates 5.9g; Cholesterol 117mg; Calcium 87mg; Fibre 1.3g; Sodium 75mg.

Balti Chicken with Dhal and Leeks

Slightly sour mango powder gives this Balti dish a deliciously tangy flavour.

Serves 4–6

2 medium leeks
75g/3oz/⅓ cup chana dhal or yellow split peas
60ml/4 tbsp corn oil
6 large dried red chillies
4 curry leaves
5ml/1 tsp mustard seeds
10ml/2 tsp mango powder (amchur)
2 medium tomatoes, chopped
2.5ml/½ tsp chilli powder
5ml/1 tsp ground coriander
5ml/1 tsp salt
450g/1lb skinless, boneless chicken, cubed
15ml/1 tbsp chopped fresh coriander (cilantro), to garnish

1 Using a sharp knife, slice the leeks thinly into rounds. Separate the slices, rinse them in a colander under cold water to wash away any grit, then drain well.

2 Wash the chana dhal or split peas carefully and remove any stones or sticks. Put the pulses into a pan with enough water to cover, and boil for about 10 minutes until they are soft but not mushy. Drain and set to one side in a bowl.

3 Heat the oil in a karahi, wok or deep pan. Lower the heat slightly and add the leeks, dried red chillies, curry leaves and mustard seeds. Stir-fry gently for a few minutes.

4 Add the mango powder, tomatoes, chilli powder, ground coriander, salt and chicken, and stir-fry for 7–10 minutes.

5 Mix in the chana dhal or split peas and fry for a further 2 minutes, or until you are sure the chicken is cooked through.

6 Garnish the dish with fresh coriander and serve immediately, from the pan, into individual warmed bowls.

Cook's Tip
Use flat breads as an accompaniment to the dish to scoop up all the delicious juices in the sauce.

Khara Masala Balti Chicken

Whole spices (khara) are used in this recipe, giving it a wonderful, rich flavour.

Serves 4

3 curry leaves
1.5ml/¼ tsp mustard seeds
1.5ml/¼ tsp fennel seeds
1.5ml/¼ tsp onion seeds
2.5ml/½ tsp crushed dried red chillies
2.5ml/½ tsp white cumin seeds
2.5ml/½ tsp crushed pomegranate seeds
1.5ml/¼ tsp fenugreek seeds
5ml/1 tsp salt
5ml/1 tsp shredded fresh root ginger
3 garlic cloves, sliced
60ml/4 tbsp corn oil
4 fresh green chillies, slit
1 large onion, sliced
1 medium tomato, sliced
675g/1½lb skinless, boneless chicken, cubed
15ml/1 tbsp chopped fresh coriander (cilantro)

1 Mix together the curry leaves, mustard seeds, fennel seeds, onion seeds, crushed red chillies, cumin seeds, crushed pomegranate seeds, fenugreek seeds and salt in a large bowl. Add the shredded ginger and garlic cloves to the spice mixture in the bowl and stir well.

2 Heat the oil in a medium karahi, wok or deep pan. Add the spice mixture, then tip in the green chillies. Spoon the sliced onion into the pan and fry over a medium heat for 5–7 minutes, stirring constantly to flavour the onion with the spices.

3 Finally add the sliced tomato and the chicken pieces, and cook over a medium heat for about 7 minutes. The chicken should be cooked through and the sauce reduced.

4 Stir everything together over the heat for a further 3–5 minutes. Serve from the pan, into individual warmed dishes, garnished with chopped fresh coriander.

Cook's Tip
This is a dry dish, so it is best served with a cucumber and yogurt raita and paratha or flat breads.

Balti Chicken with Dhal and Leeks Energy 309kcal/1295kJ; Protein 29.2g; Carbohydrate 20.8g, of which sugars 3.7g; Fat 17.2g, of which saturates 1.9g; Cholesterol 65mg; Fibre 2.8g; Sodium 508mg.
Khara Masala Energy 299kcal/1254kJ; Protein 41.5g; Carbohydrate 3.4g, of which sugars 1.7g; Fat 13.5g, of which saturates 1.9g; Cholesterol 118mg; Calcium 28mg; Fibre 0.6g; Sodium 106mg.

Baby Chicken in a Chilli Tamarind Sauce

The tamarind in this recipe gives the dish a tasty sweet-and-sour flavour. This is also quite a hot balti.

Serves 4 - 6

60ml/4 tbsp tomato ketchup
15ml/1 tbsp tamarind paste
60ml/4 tbsp water
7.5ml/1½ tsp chilli powder
7.5ml/1½ tsp salt
15ml/1 tbsp sugar
7.5ml/1½ tsp crushed ginger
7.5ml/1½ tsp crushed garlic
30ml/2 tbsp desiccated (dry unsweetened shredded) coconut
30ml/2 tbsp sesame seeds
5ml/1 tsp poppy seeds
5ml/1 tsp ground cumin
7.5ml/1½ tsp ground coriander
2 x 450g/1lb baby chickens, skinned and cut into 6–8 pieces each
75ml/5 tbsp corn oil
about 20 curry leaves
2.5ml/½ tsp onion seeds
3 large dried red chillies
2.5ml/½ tsp fenugreek seeds
10–12 cherry tomatoes
45ml/3 tbsp chopped fresh coriander (cilantro)
2 fresh green chillies, chopped

1 Put the tomato ketchup, tamarind paste and water into a large mixing bowl and use a fork to blend everything together.

2 Add the chilli powder, salt, sugar, ginger, garlic, coconut, sesame and poppy seeds, ground cumin and ground coriander to the mixture, and stir well to mix.

3 Add the chicken pieces to the bowl and stir until they are well coated with the spice mixture. Set to one side.

4 Heat the oil in a deep wok, frying pan or a large karahi. Add the curry leaves, onion seeds, dried red chillies and fenugreek seeds and fry for about 1 minute.

5 Add the chicken pieces to the pan, along with their spice paste, mixing as you go. Simmer gently for about 12–15 minutes, or until the chicken is thoroughly cooked.

6 Add the tomatoes, fresh coriander and green chillies, and serve immediately in warmed individual bowls.

Jungle Spiced Curry of Guinea Fowl

This is a traditional spicy curry from Thailand.

Serves 4

1 guinea fowl or similar game bird
15ml/1 tbsp vegetable oil
10ml/2 tsp green curry paste
15ml/1 tbsp Thai fish sauce
2.5cm/1in piece fresh galangal, peeled and finely chopped
15ml/1 tbsp fresh green peppercorns
3 kaffir lime leaves, torn
15ml/1 tbsp whisky, preferably Mekhong
300ml/½ pint/1¼ cups chicken stock
50g/2oz snake (yard-long) beans, cut into 2.5cm/1in lengths (about ½ cup)
225g/8oz/3¼ cups chestnut mushrooms, sliced
1 piece drained canned bamboo shoot, about 50g/2oz, shredded
5ml/1 tsp dried chilli flakes, to garnish (optional)

1 Cut up the guinea fowl, remove the skin, then strip the meat off the bones. Chop into bitesize pieces and set aside.

2 Heat the oil in a wok or frying pan and add the paste. Stir-fry over a medium heat for 30 seconds, until it gives off its aroma.

3 Add the fish sauce and the guinea fowl meat and stir-fry until the meat is browned all over. Add the galangal, peppercorns, lime leaves and whisky, then pour in the stock.

4 Bring to the boil. Add the vegetables, return to a simmer and cook gently for 2–3 minutes, until they are just cooked. Spoon into a dish, sprinkle with chilli flakes, if you like, and serve.

Cook's Tips

- *Guinea fowl originated in West Africa and was regarded as a game bird, but has been domesticated in Europe for over 500 years. Their average size is about 1.2kg/2½lb. American readers could substitute two or three Cornish hens, depending on size.*
- *Fresh green peppercorns are simply unripe berries. They are sold on the stem. Look for them at Thai and Asian supermarkets. If unavailable, substitute bottled green peppercorns, but rinse well and drain them first.*

Baby Chicken Energy 268kcal/1120kJ; Protein 26g; Carbohydrate 4.1g, of which sugars 4g; Fat 16.6g, of which saturates 4.5g; Cholesterol 70mg; Calcium 60mg; Fibre 2.2g; Sodium 152mg.
Jungle Spiced Curry Energy 368kcal/1540kJ; Protein 56.8g; Carbohydrate 1.4g, of which sugars 0.9g; Fat 14g, of which saturates 3.2g; Cholesterol 0mg; Calcium 82mg; Fibre 1.1g; Sodium 454mg.

Pheasant and Mushroom Ragoût

Serves 4
oil, for frying
4 pheasant breast fillets, skinned, diced and seasoned
12 shallots, halved
2 garlic cloves, crushed
75g/3oz wild mushrooms, sliced
75ml/5 tbsp/⅓ cup port
150ml/¼ pint/⅔ cup stock
sprigs of fresh parsley and thyme
1 bay leaf
grated rind of 1 lemon
200ml/7fl oz/scant 1 cup cream
salt and ground black pepper

1 Heat a little oil in a wok and cook the meat for 5–6 minutes. Remove from the wok and set aside. Add the shallots, garlic and mushrooms. Reduce the heat and cook gently for 5 minutes.

2 Add the port, stock, herbs and lemon to the wok. Bring to the boil, then simmer until the sauce has reduced a little. When the shallots are cooked, add the cream, reduce to thicken, then add the meat to the pan and cook for a few minutes before serving.

Crispy Quail

Quail is not as popular as some other types of poultry, but when you can get them, these birds make delicious eating. They are usually sold in packs of two or four as each bird is very small.

Serves 2
4 quail
5ml/1 tsp salt
2.5ml/½ tsp five-spice powder
30ml/2 tbsp Chinese wine
vegetable oil for deep frying
lemon wedges, to serve

1 Rinse the quail inside and out and pat them dry thoroughly with kitchen paper. The drier the skin before cooking, the crispier it will be after cooking. Mix the salt, five-spice powder and wine in a small bowl. Rub the quail all over with the mixture. Set aside for 30 minutes.

2 Heat the vegetable oil in a wok. Add the quail and deep-fry for 4–6 minutes, turning once or twice, until crisp and golden brown. Drain on kitchen paper. Serve hot, with the lemon wedges for squeezing over the crispy skin.

Stir-fried Giblets with Garlic and Ginger

In Vietnam and Cambodia no food is wasted: almost every part of a chicken is used, and there are specific recipes to which each piece is assigned. Apart from being tossed into the stockpot, chicken giblets are often quickly stir-fried with a spicy seasoning of chilli garlic and ginger and served with rice. If you dislike the idea of eating chicken hearts and neck, this dish will work very well using just livers, which are available fresh or frozen from butchers and supermarkets.

Serves 2–4
30ml/2 tbsp groundnut (peanut) oil
2 shallots, halved and finely sliced
2 garlic cloves, finely chopped
1 Thai chilli, seeded and finely sliced
25g/1oz fresh root ginger, peeled and shredded
225g/8oz chicken livers, trimmed and finely sliced
115g/4oz mixed giblets, finely sliced
15–30ml/1–2 tbsp nuoc mam (Vietnamese fish sauce)
1 small bunch coriander (cilantro), finely chopped
ground black pepper
steamed rice, to serve

1 Heat the oil in a wok or heavy pan. Stir in the shallots, garlic, chilli and ginger, and stir fry for 2–3 minutes until golden but not browned. Add the chicken livers and mixed giblets and stir-fry for a few minutes more, until browned.

2 Stir in the nuoc mam, adjusting the quantity according to taste, and half the chopped coriander. Season with ground black pepper and garnish with the rest of the coriander. Serve hot, with steamed fragrant rice.

Cook's Tip
Nuoc mam is the Vietnamese version of fish sauce, a salty, pungent liquid made from fermented anchovies or other fish, which is an essential condiment in the cooking of the whole region of South-east Asia. It is used both as a seasoning and as a dipping sauce, normally mixed with other ingredients.

Pheasant Energy 530kcal/2200kJ; Protein 34.1g; Carbohydrate 7.4g, of which sugars 5.9g; Fat 33g, of which saturates 20.2g; Cholesterol 69mg; Calcium 91mg; Fibre 1.1g; Sodium 114mg.
Crispy Quail Energy 462kcal/1938kJ; Protein 77.1g; Carbohydrate 0.2g, of which sugars 0.2g; Fat 15.1g, of which saturates 3.9g; Cholesterol 0mg; Calcium 99mg; Fibre 0g; Sodium 212mg.
Stir-fried Giblets Energy 134kcal/556kJ; Protein 15g; Carbohydrate 1.5g, of which sugars 1.1g; Fat 7.4g, of which saturates 1.3g; Cholesterol 290mg; Calcium 12mg; Fibre 0.2g; Sodium 360mg.

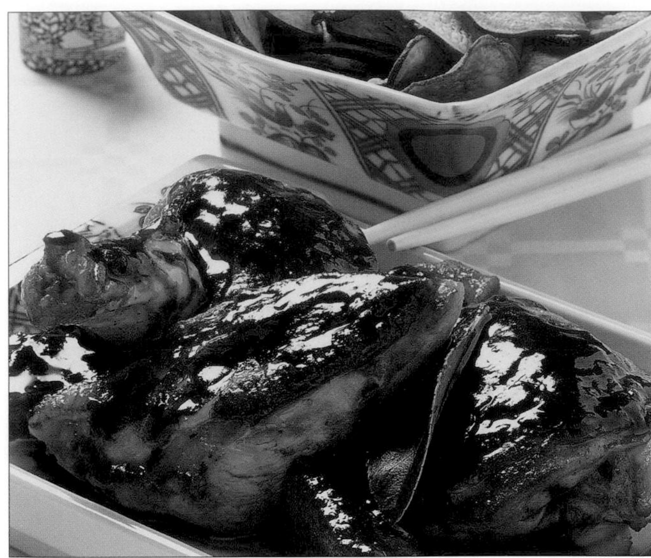

Adobo of Chicken and Pork

Four ingredients are essential in an adobo, one of the best-loved recipes in the Filipino repertoire. They are vinegar, garlic, peppercorns and bay leaves. Traditionally plantain chips accompany the dish, but sweet potato chips can be served instead.

Serves 4

1 chicken, about 1.3kg/3lb, or 4 chicken quarters
350g/12oz pork leg steaks (with fat)
10ml/2 tsp sugar
60ml/4 tbsp sunflower oil
75ml/5 tbsp wine or cider vinegar
4 plump garlic cloves, crushed
½ tsp black peppercorns, crushed lightly
15ml/1 tbsp light soy sauce
4 bay leaves
2.5ml/½ tsp annatto seeds, soaked in 30ml/2 tbsp boiling water, or 2.5ml/½ tsp ground turmeric
salt

For the plantain chips

vegetable oil, for deep-frying
1–2 large plantains and/or 1 sweet potato

1 Wipe the chicken with kitchen paper and cut it into eight even-size pieces, or halve the chicken quarters, if using. Cut the pork into neat pieces. Spread out all the meat on a board, sprinkle lightly with sugar and set aside.

2 Heat the oil in a wok and fry the chicken and pork pieces, in batches if necessary, until they are golden on both sides.

3 Add the vinegar, garlic, peppercorns, soy sauce and bay leaves and stir well. Strain the annatto seed liquid and stir it into the wok, and add the turmeric. Add salt to taste. Bring to the boil, cover, lower the heat and simmer the chicken for 30–35 minutes. When the chicken is cooked through, remove the lid and simmer for 10 minutes more to reduce the liquid a little.

4 Meanwhile, prepare the plantain chips. Heat the oil in a wok or deep-fryer to 195°C/390°F. Peel the plantains and slice them into rounds or chips. Deep-fry them, in batches if necessary, until cooked but not brown. Drain on kitchen paper. When ready to serve, reheat the oil and refry the plantains until crisp – it will take only seconds. Drain and serve with the adobo.

Chicken and Pork with Vinegar and Ginger

Originally from Mexico, adobo has become the national dish of the Philippines. It can be made with chicken (adobong manok), with pork (adobong baboy) or with both, as in this recipe. It can also be prepared with fish, shellfish and vegetables.

Serves 4-6

30ml/2 tbsp coconut or groundnut (peanut) oil
6–8 garlic cloves, crushed whole
50g/2oz fresh root ginger, sliced into matchsticks
6 spring onions (scallions), cut into 2.5cm/1in pieces
5–10ml/1–2 tsp black peppercorns, crushed
30ml/2 tbsp palm sugar (jaggery) or muscovado (molasses) sugar
8–10 chicken thighs, or a mixture of thighs and drumsticks
350g/12oz pork tenderloin, cut into chunks
150ml/¼ pint/⅔ cup suka (Filipino coconut vinegar) or white wine vinegar
150ml/¼ pint/⅔ cup dark soy sauce
300ml/½ pint/1¼ cups chicken stock
2–3 bay leaves
salt

To serve

stir-fried greens
cooked rice

1 Heat the oil in a wok with a lid or in a large, heavy pan. Stir in the garlic and ginger and fry until they become fragrant and begin to colour. Add the spring onions and black peppercorns and stir in the sugar.

2 Add the chicken and pork to the wok or pan, and fry for 3–4 minutes until they begin to colour.

3 Pour the vinegar, soy sauce and chicken stock to the pan and add the bay leaves. Bring to the boil, then reduce the heat, cover and simmer gently for about 1 hour, until the meat is tender and the liquid has reduced.

4 Season the stew with salt to taste and serve with stir-fried greens and rice, over which the cooking liquid is spooned.

Adobo of Chicken and Pork Energy 676Kcal/2825kJ; Protein 60.2g; Carbohydrate 28.8g, of which sugars 8.1g; Fat 36.2g, of which saturates 6g; Cholesterol 178mg; Calcium 38mg; Fibre 1.7g; Sodium 503mg.
Chicken and Pork Energy 270kcal/1135kJ; Protein 42.2g; Carbohydrate 9g, of which sugars 7.6g; Fat 7.4g, of which saturates 1.6g; Cholesterol 118mg; Calcium 24mg; Fibre 0.6g; Sodium 1892mg.

Duck and Sesame Stir-fry

For a special family meal that is a guaranteed success, this recipe is absolutely ideal. It tastes fantastic and cooks fast, so that you'll be eating in no time.

Serves 4

250g/9oz boneless duck meat
15ml/1 tbsp sesame oil
15ml/1 tbsp vegetable oil
4 garlic cloves, finely sliced
2.5ml/½ tsp dried chilli flakes
15ml/1 tbsp Thai fish sauce
15ml/1 tbsp light soy sauce
120ml/4fl oz/½ cup water
1 head broccoli, cut into small florets
coriander (cilantro) and 15ml/1 tbsp toasted sesame seeds, to garnish

1 Cut all the duck meat into bitesize pieces.

2 Heat the oils in a wok or large, heavy frying pan and stir-fry the garlic over a medium heat until it is golden brown.

3 Add the duck to the pan and stir-fry for a further 2–3 minutes, until the meat begins to brown.

4 Stir in the chilli flakes, fish sauce, soy sauce and water. Add the broccoli and continue to stir-fry for about 2 minutes, until the duck is just cooked through.

5 Serve the duck stir-fry on warmed individual plates, garnished with coriander and the toasted sesame seeds.

Cook's Tip

Broccoli has excited interest recently since it is claimed that eating this dark green vegetable regularly can help to reduce the risk of some cancers. Broccoli is a source of protein, calcium, iron and magnesium, as well as vitamins A and C.

Variation

Pak choi (bok choy) or Chinese flowering cabbage can be used instead of broccoli.

Soy-braised Duck with Star Anise and Cinnamon

This is a traditional Cantonese dish. It does take time to prepare but the end result is worth the effort. The star anise and cinnamon add a surprising depth of flavour. Soy-braised duck is usually served cold for festive occasions, washed down with brandy.

Serves 8

30ml/2 tbsp vegetable oil
30ml/2 tbsp sugar
1 oven-ready duck, about 2.5kg/5½lb
150ml/¼ pint/⅔ cup dark soy sauce
1 large knob galangal or fresh root ginger
6 garlic cloves, peeled and bruised
4 star anise
5cm/2in piece of cinnamon stick
2 litres/3½ pints/8 cups water
sliced cucumber, to garnish

1 Heat the oil in a wok large enough to hold the duck. Sprinkle in the sugar and cook over medium to high heat until the mixture froths and caramelizes. When it is pale brown in colour, add the duck and turn it several times to coat the skin.

2 Add the soy sauce to the wok. Using two spatulas or large forks, turn the duck several times to coat it thoroughly.

3 Add the galangal or ginger, with the garlic cloves, star anise and cinnamon. Pour in the water and bring to the boil. Lower the heat, cover the wok and simmer the duck for 1½ hours or until it is tender and the meat starts to come off the bones.

4 Lift the duck on to a board and set it aside to rest and absorb all the juices while you make the gravy.

5 Strain the cooking liquid into a clean pan, skim the surplus fat from the surface using a metal spoon and boil over high heat until reduced to the consistency of gravy.

6 Carve the duck and arrange on a platter. Garnish with cucumber slices and serve with the gravy.

Duck Stir-fry Energy 165kcal/686kJ; Protein 17.4g; Carbohydrate 2.3g, of which sugars 2g; Fat 10.6g, of which saturates 1.8g; Cholesterol 69mg; Calcium 72mg; Fibre 2.9g; Sodium 345mg.
Soy-braised Duck Energy 119kcal/498kJ; Protein 10.2g; Carbohydrate 4.6g, of which sugars 3.4g; Fat 6.9g, of which saturates 1.5g; Cholesterol 50mg; Calcium 35mg; Fibre 1.1g; Sodium 412mg.

Duck with Mushrooms and Ginger

This delicious duck dish is popular among the Chinese population of Indonesia.

Serves 4

2.5kg/5½lb duck
5ml/1 tsp sugar
50ml/2fl oz/¼ cup light soy sauce
2 garlic cloves, crushed
8 dried Chinese mushrooms, soaked in 350ml/12fl oz/1½ cups warm water for 15 minutes
1 onion, sliced
5cm/2in fresh root ginger, peeled and shredded
200g/7oz baby corn
½ bunch spring onions (scallions), white bulbs left whole, green tops sliced
15–30ml/1–2 tbsp cornflour (cornstarch), mixed to a paste with 60ml/4 tbsp water
salt and fresh black pepper
boiled rice, to serve

1 Cut the duck along the breast, open it up and cut along each side of the backbone. Use the backbone, wings and giblets to make stock and render any surplus fat in a wok, to use later in the recipe. Halve each leg and breast, rub with sugar and pour over the soy sauce and garlic.

2 Drain the mushrooms, reserving the liquid. Discard the stalks.

3 Fry the onion and ginger in the duck fat until they give off a good aroma. Push to one side of the wok. Lift the duck pieces out of the soy sauce and fry them until browned.

4 Add the mushrooms and their reserved liquid.600ml/1 pint/ 2½ cups of duck stock or water to the duck. Season, cover and cook over a gentle heat for about 1 hour, until the duck is tender.

5 Add the corn and the white part of the spring onions and cook for a further 10 minutes. Add the cornflour paste and bring to the boil, stirring. Cook for 1 minute until glossy. Serve, scattered with the spring onion tops, with boiled rice.

Variation
Replace the corn with chopped celery and slices of canned water chestnuts.

Duck with Plum Sauce

Sharp plums cut the rich flavour of duck wonderfully well in this updated version of an old English dish. In the past, duck was often considered to be a fatty meat, but nowadays leaner ducks are widely available. For an easy dinner party main course, serve the duck with creamy mashed potatoes and celeriac and steamed broccoli or other green vegetables.

Serves 4

4 duck quarters or duck breast fillets
1 large red onion, finely chopped
500g/1¼lb ripe plums, stoned (pitted) and quartered
30ml/2 tbsp redcurrant jelly

1 Prick the skin of the duck quarters or breast fillets all over with a fork to release the fat during cooking and help give a crisp finish to the skin, then place the duck in a large wok or heavy frying pan, skin side down.

2 Cook the duck pieces for 10 minutes on each side, or until they are golden brown and cooked right through. Remove the duck from the frying pan, using a slotted spoon, place on a warmed dish, and cover with foil to keep warm.

3 Pour off all but 30ml/2 tbsp of the duck fat, reserve and allow to cool, then keep in the refrigerator in an airtight container for future use.

4 Now stir-fry the onion in the remaining fat for 5 minutes, or until golden. Add the plums and cook for 5 minutes, stirring frequently. Then add the jelly and mix well.

5 Replace the duck portions and cook for a further 5 minutes, or until thoroughly reheated. Serve immediately.

Cook's Tip
It is important that the plums used in this dish are very ripe, otherwise the mixture will be too dry and the sauce will be extremely sharp and unpleasant to taste.

Duck with Mushrooms Energy 341kcal/1436kJ; Protein 52g; Carbohydrate 5.3g, of which sugars 1.5g; Fat 16.9g, of which saturates 3.4g; Cholesterol 275mg; Calcium 48mg; Fibre 1.6g; Sodium 835mg.
Duck with Plum Sauce: Energy 608kcal/2515kJ; Protein 15.1g; Carbohydrate 17.4g, of which sugars 17g; Fat 53.5g, of which saturates 14.5g; Cholesterol 0mg; Calcium 35mg; Fibre 2.2g; Sodium 102mg.

Stuffed Duck with Cabbage

An oven-ready duckling works best for this recipe, and a large, flat-bottomed wok is essential.

Serves 6

1 duck, about 2.25kg/5lb
5ml/1 tsp salt
1.5ml/¼ tsp ground black pepper
vegetable oil for deep-frying
1 chicken stock cube
2 litres/3½ pints/8 cups water
4 garlic cloves, crushed
3 bay leaves
75ml/5 tbsp orange liqueur
1 whole Chinese cabbage, quartered

For the stuffing
30ml/2 tbsp vegetable oil
10 shallots, chopped very finely
6 Chinese mushrooms, chopped
250g/9oz minced (ground) pork or chicken
2 eggs, lightly beaten
150g/5oz breadcrumbs

1 Prepare the stuffing. Heat the oil and fry the shallots gently for 3–4 minutes. Transfer to a bowl, allow to cool and add the mushrooms, pork, eggs and breadcrumbs. Mix well and set aside.

2 Wash the duck and pat dry with kitchen towel. Rub the skin with the salt and pepper and pack the cavity with the stuffing. Sew up with strong thread. Make leftover stuffing into small balls.

3 Heat enough oil for deep-frying in a large, flat-bottomed wok and deep-fry the duck, turning it over carefully until the skin is evenly browned. Transfer the duck to a deep roasting pan.

4 Dissolve the stock cube in a little boiling water, then add the measured water, garlic, bay leaves and liqueur. Pour this all over the duck. Cover with foil and bring to the boil, then reduce the heat and simmer for 45 minutes. Add the cabbage and any stuffing balls to the stock and cook for another 20 minutes.

5 Remove the cabbage and stuffing balls and keep warm. Braise the duck for another 20 minutes, opening the foil a little to let the steam out, until the sauce is thick and glossy.

6 Remove the duck and arrange it on a large plate with the cabbage and stuffing balls. Reduce the stock by fast boiling it in a pan for a couple of minutes, then strain and serve with the duck.

Duck Stuffed with Glutinous Rice

if you have a helpful butcher, ask him to debone the duck for you. Otherwise, stuff it on the bone. Start your preparations the day before you serve the dish.

Serves 6–8

75g/3oz/½ cup raw glutinous rice
6 dried black Chinese mushrooms
6 Medjool dates, pitted and chopped
20 canned ginkgo nuts, drained
2.5ml/½ tsp ground black pepper
45ml/3 tbsp oyster sauce
1 oven-ready duck, about 2.5kg/5½lb
60ml/4 tbsp dark soy sauce
150ml/¼ pint/⅔ cup oil
2 litres/3½ pints/8 cups water
30ml/2 tbsp sesame oil
2 spring onions (scallions)
6 garlic cloves, peeled and left whole
2.5ml/½ tsp ground black pepper

1 Rinse the glutinous rice in several changes of cold water, then leave it to soak overnight in a bowl of fresh cold water. Next day, drain the rice and spread it evenly in a steamer lined with cheesecloth. Cover and steam over simmering water in a wok for 25 minutes or until tender and fluffy.

2 Meanwhile, soak the mushrooms in boiling water for 20–30 minutes, until soft. Drain, remove the hard stalks and dice the caps finely. Put the mushrooms in a bowl and add the rice, dates, ginkgo nuts, pepper and oyster sauce. Mix well.

3 Remove the excess fat from the duck and enlarge the entrance to the cavity slightly. Stuff it with the rice mixture. Using a poultry needle and fairly strong thread, sew up the slit. Rub the duck all over with half the soy sauce.

4 Heat the oil in a large wok and add the duck. Fry, turning frequently, until the skin is well sealed and brown. Place the duck in a deep pan. Pour in the water and add the sesame oil, spring onions, garlic cloves, remaining soy sauce and black pepper. Bring to the boil. Cover, lower the heat and simmer for 2–2¼ hours, turning several times and topping up the water when necessary.

5 When the duck is cooked, lift it on to a platter. Carve it in the kitchen or serve it at the table, to be carved with a flourish.

Duck with Cabbage Energy 665kcal/2773kJ; Protein 41.4g; Carbohydrate 29.8g, of which sugars 10.3g; Fat 41.4g, of which saturates 11.5g; Cholesterol 271mg; Calcium 149mg; Fibre 4.6g; Sodium 723mg.
Duck with Rice Energy 504kcal/2092kJ; Protein 21.7g; Carbohydrate 14.1g, of which sugars 6.3g; Fat 40.3g, of which saturates 7.9g; Cholesterol 119mg; Calcium 28mg; Fibre 1.3g; Sodium 755mg.

Shredded Duck and Noodle Salad

This piquant marinated duck salad makes a lovely first course or a delicious light meal. If you like, toss the salad in a quick and easy dressing made by whisking together soy sauce, mirin, sugar, garlic and chilli oil.

Serves 4

4 skinless duck breast fillets, sliced
30ml/2 tbsp Chinese rice wine
10ml/2 tsp finely grated fresh root ginger
60ml/4 tbsp soy sauce
15ml/1 tbsp sesame oil
15ml/1 tbsp clear honey
10ml/2 tsp five-spice powder
15ml/1 tbsp sunflower oil
toasted sesame seeds, to sprinkle

For the noodles

150g/5oz cellophane noodles, cooked
large handful of fresh mint and coriander (cilantro) leaves
1 red (bell) pepper, seeded and finely sliced
4 spring onions (scallions), finely shredded and sliced
50g/2oz mixed salad leaves

1 Place the duck breast slices in a large non-metallic bowl. Mix together the rice wine, ginger, soy sauce, sesame oil, clear honey and five-spice powder. Toss to coat, cover and marinate the duck in the refrigerator for 3–4 hours.

2 Heat the sunflower oil in a wok or frying pan, add the slices of duck breast and stir-fry for 3-4 minutes until cooked. Set aside.

3 Double over a large sheet of heavy foil. Place the foil on a heatproof plate. Place the duck breast portions on it and spoon the marinade over. Fold the foil to enclose the duck and juices and scrunch the edges to seal.

4 Steam the duck packets on a rack over simmering water for 50–60 minutes, then leave to rest for 15 minutes.

5 Mix the noodles, herbs, red pepper, spring onions and salad leaves in a bowl. Remove the skin from the duck and discard it. Shred the flesh of the duck.

6 Divide the noodle salad among four plates and top with the duck. Sprinkle with the sesame seeds and serve immediately.

Chinese Five-spice Sweet and Sour Duck

Mango adds natural sweetness to this colourful stir-fry. Crispy deep-fried noodles make the perfect accompaniment.

Serves 4

225–350g/8–12oz duck breast fillet portions
45ml/3 tbsp dark soy sauce
15ml/1 tbsp Chinese rice wine
5ml/1 tsp sesame oil
5ml/1 tsp five-spice powder
15ml/1 tbsp soft brown sugar
10ml/2 tsp cornflour (cornstarch)
45ml/3 tbsp Chinese rice vinegar
15ml/1 tbsp tomato ketchup
1 mango, not too ripe
1 medium aubergine (eggplant)
1 red onion
1 carrot
60ml/4 tbsp groundnut (peanut) oil
1 garlic clove, sliced
2.5cm/1in piece fresh root ginger, cut into shreds
75g/3oz sugar snap peas

1 Thinly slice the duck breast portions and place in a bowl. Mix together 15ml/1 tbsp of the soy sauce with the rice wine, sesame oil and five-spice powder. Pour over the duck, cover and leave to marinate for 1–2 hours.

2 In a separate bowl, blend together the sugar, cornflour, rice vinegar, ketchup and remaining soy sauce. Set aside. Peel the mango, slice the flesh from the stone, then cut into thick strips. Slice the aubergine, onion and carrot into similar-sized pieces.

3 Heat a wok until hot, add 30ml/2 tbsp of the oil and swirl it around. Drain the duck, reserving the marinade. Stir-fry the duck slices over a high heat until the fat is crisp and golden. Remove and keep warm. Add 15ml/1 tbsp of the oil to the wok and stir-fry the aubergine for 3 minutes until golden.

4 Add the remaining oil to the wok and fry the onion, garlic, ginger and carrot for 2–3 minutes, then add the sugar snap peas and stir-fry for a further 2 minutes.

5 Add the mango and return the duck with the sweet-and-sour sauce and reserved marinade to the wok. Cook, stirring, until the sauce thickens slightly. Serve at once.

Shredded Duck Salad Energy 398kcal/1671kJ; Protein 32.8g; Carbohydrate 41.7g, of which sugars 10.8g; Fat 11.6g, of which saturates 2.2g; Cholesterol 165mg; Calcium 40mg; Fibre 1g; Sodium 1688mg.
Sweet and Sour Duck Energy 256kcal/1067kJ; Protein 14g; Carbohydrate 16.9g, of which sugars 12g; Fat 16.2g, of which saturates 2.3g; Cholesterol 62mg; Calcium 35mg; Fibre 4.2g; Sodium 668mg.

Chinese Duck Curry

The duck is best marinated for as long as possible, although it will taste good even if you only have time to marinate it briefly.

Serves 4

4 duck breast fillet portions, skin and bones removed
30ml/2 tbsp five-spice powder
30ml/2 tbsp sesame oil
grated rind and juice of 1 orange
1 medium butternut squash, peeled and cubed
10ml/2 tsp Thai red curry paste
30ml/2 tbsp Thai fish sauce
15ml/1 tbsp palm sugar or light muscovado (brown) sugar
300ml/½ pint/1¼ cups coconut milk
2 fresh red chillies, seeded
4 kaffir lime leaves, torn
small bunch coriander (cilantro), chopped, to garnish

1 Cut the duck meat into bitesize pieces and place in a bowl with the five-spice powder, sesame oil and orange rind and juice. Stir well to mix all the ingredients and coat the duck in the marinade. Cover and marinate for at least 10 minutes.

2 Meanwhile, cook the butternut squash in boiling water for 10 minutes, until just tender. Drain and set aside.

3 Pour the marinade from the duck into a wok or large heavy pan and heat until boiling. Stir in the curry paste and cook for 1 minute, until well blended and fragrant.

4 Add the duck to the pan and cook for 3 minutes, stirring constantly, until browned on all sides.

5 Add the fish sauce and palm sugar and cook for 1 minute more. Stir in the coconut milk until the mixture is smooth, then add the cooked squash, with the chillies and lime leaves. Simmer gently, stirring frequently, for 2 minutes, then spoon into a dish, sprinkle with the coriander and serve.

Cook's Tip
Save time by buying prepared butternut in bags from the supermarket. Small cubes are best, since they cook quickly.

Thai-style Red Duck Curry with Pea Aubergines

The rich flavour of duck is perfectly suited to this red hot curry with a spicy sauce enriched with coconut milk.

Serves 4

4 duck breast fillet portions
400ml/14fl oz can coconut milk
200ml/7fl oz/scant 1 cup chicken stock
30ml/2 tbsp red Thai curry paste
8 spring onions (scallions), finely sliced
10ml/2 tsp grated fresh root ginger
30ml/2 tbsp Chinese rice wine
15ml/1 tbsp nam pla (fish sauce)
15ml/1 tbsp dark soy sauce
2 lemon grass stalks, halved lengthways
3–4 kaffir lime leaves
300g/11oz pea aubergines (eggplants)
10ml/2 tsp caster (superfine) sugar
salt and ground black pepper
10–12 fresh basil and mint leaves, to garnish
steamed jasmine rice, to serve

1 Using a sharp knife or cleaver, cut the duck breast portions into even, bitesize pieces.

2 Place a wok over a low heat and add the coconut milk, stock, curry paste, spring onions, ginger, rice wine, nam pla, soy sauce, lemon grass and lime leaves. Slowly bring to the boil.

3 Add the duck, aubergines and sugar to the wok and gently simmer for 25–30 minutes, stirring occasionally.

4 Remove the wok from the heat and leave it to stand, covered, for about 15 minutes. Season to taste and serve ladled into warmed shallow bowls with steamed jasmine rice, garnished with fresh mint and basil leaves.

Cook's Tip
Tiny pea aubergines are available in specialist Asian stores, however if you have difficulty in finding them, then use larger aubergines cut into bitesize chunks.

Chinese Duck Curry Energy 295kcal/1241kJ; Protein 31.4g; Carbohydrate 13.3g, of which sugars 10g; Fat 10.5g, of which saturates 2.3g; Cholesterol 165mg; Calcium 65mg; Fibre 1.8g; Sodium 546mg.
Thai-style Red Duck Energy 241kcal/1017kJ; Protein 31.1g; Carbohydrate 10.2g, of which sugars 10g; Fat 10.5g, of which saturates 2.3g; Cholesterol 165mg; Calcium 65mg; Fibre 1.8g; Sodium 546mg.

Cabbage Leaves with Spicy Pork

In South-east Asia, spicy pork or shellfish mixtures are often wrapped in leaves and steamed, or stuffed into bamboo stems and smoked over open fires.

Serves 4–6

1 leafy green cabbage
15–30ml/1–2 tbsp palm or groundnut (peanut) oil
10ml/2 tsp coriander seeds
2 shallots, finely chopped
2 garlic cloves, finely chopped
2–3 red chillies, seeded and finely chopped
25g/1oz galangal or fresh root ginger, finely chopped
2–3 spring onions (scallions), finely chopped
10ml/2 tsp palm sugar (jaggery)
2–3 tomatoes, skinned, seeded and finely chopped
30ml/2 tbsp coconut cream
1 small bunch fresh coriander (cilantro) leaves, finely chopped
225g/8oz minced (ground) pork
50g/2oz pig's liver, finely chopped
50g/2oz pig's heart, finely chopped
salt and ground black pepper
kecap manis (sweet soy sauce), for dipping

1 Prepare the cabbage. Pull the cabbage apart so that you have about 20 leaves. Steam or blanch the leaves to soften, drain and refresh under cold water. Cut off any thick stems and set aside.

2 Heat the oil in a wok or heavy pan, stir in the coriander seeds and fry for 1 minute. Add the shallots, garlic, chillies, galangal, spring onions and sugar and stir-fry until they begin to colour.

3 Stir in the tomatoes, coconut cream and coriander leaves and cook for 5 minutes until the mixture resembles a thick sauce. Season with salt and pepper and transfer to a bowl to cool.

4 Add the minced pork and offal and, using your hand or a fork, mix them together well. Place a cabbage leaf, stem side down, on a flat surface in front of you and place a spoonful of the mixture in the centre. Fold in the sides of the leaf and roll it up into a log, making sure that all of the meat is enclosed. Repeat the process with the remaining leaves.

5 Place the stuffed cabbage leaves in a steamer, seam side down, and steam for 25–30 minutes, until the meat is cooked. Serve hot with kecap manis for dipping.

Pork Ribs in Pandanus Leaves

The Malays have a penchant for sweet tastes and pork is often married with sweet flavourings. The Dyaks love their pork coated in honey and grilled, stir-fried or roasted. In this Chinese-style Singapore dish, the pork is marinated in honey and Western flavourings, before being wrapped in the long, thin pandanus leaves and deep-fried. Serve the pork ribs as an appetizer or as a main course with stir-fried rice or noodles.

Serves 4–5

675g/1½lb meaty pork ribs
25 pandanus (screwpine) leaves
vegetable oil, for deep-frying
2 limes, cut into wedges, to serve

For the marinade

6 shallots, chopped
4 garlic cloves, chopped
25g/1oz fresh root ginger, peeled and chopped
30ml/2 tbsp clear honey
45ml/3 tbsp Worcestershire sauce
30ml/2 tbsp tomato ketchup
30ml/2 tbsp sour plum sauce
15ml/1 tbsp sesame oil

1 First make the marinade. Using a mortar and pestle or food processor, grind the shallots, garlic and ginger to a smooth paste. Beat in the honey, Worcestershire sauce, tomato ketchup, sour plum sauce and sesame oil.

2 Cut the pork ribs into bitesize pieces. Put them in a dish and smear the marinade all over them. Set aside for 2–3 hours.

3 Lay the pandanus leaves on a flat surface and place a marinated pork rib in the centre of each one. Tie a tight knot over each rib so that the ends poke out.

4 Heat enough oil in a wok or heavy pan for deep-frying and fry the wrapped ribs in batches for 4–5 minutes until cooked. Serve immediately with lime wedges, allowing each diner to untie the leaves and squeeze a splash of lime over the ribs.

Variation
Pandanus leaves emit a unique fragrance but you can instead use banana or bamboo leaves cut into strips.

Cabbage Leaves Energy 183kcal/764kJ; Protein 12.6g; Carbohydrate 7.3g, of which sugars 7g; Fat 11.8g, of which saturates 5g; Cholesterol 56mg; Calcium 55mg; Fibre 2.2g; Sodium 53mg.
Pork Ribs Energy 299Kcal/1250kJ; Protein 25.5g; Carbohydrate 4.1g, of which sugars 3.8g; Fat 20.3g, of which saturates 7.3g; Cholesterol 89mg; Calcium 24mg; Fibre 0.2g; Sodium 182mg.

Pork Rolls in Beancurd Skin

This classic dish of the Swatow people from Shantou is so sublime that it is often cooked as a festive offering during Taoist festivals. It is nothing like the ubiquitous spring roll and is unique in that it uses crinkly beancurd skins as wrappers.

Serves 4

400g/14oz/1¾ cups minced (ground) pork
1 small carrot, thinly shredded
10ml/2 tsp light soy sauce
5ml/1 tsp ground black pepper
50g/2oz/⅓ cup finely chopped drained canned water chestnuts
8 spring onions (scallions), finely chopped
1 egg
25g/1oz/1/4 cup cornflour (cornstarch)
1 package beancurd skins
vegetable oil for deep-frying
sliced cucumber and chilli dipping sauce, to serve

1 Put the pork in a bowl and add the shredded carrot. Stir in the soy sauce, black pepper, water chestnuts and spring onions.

2 Lightly beat the egg in a small bowl and add it to the mixture. Stir to combine, then stir in the cornflour and mix well.

3 Bring a small pan of water to the boil. Pinch off a small lump of the pork mixture, add it to the water and boil for 2 minutes. Scoop it out, cool slightly, then taste and adjust the seasoning..

4 Keeping the remaining beancurd sheets covered under a damp dish towel, place one sheet on a flat surface. Spread about 30ml/2 tbsp of the pork mixture along one edge. Roll the beancurd sheet over one and a half times, fold in the sides, then roll again to make a firm roll. Cut through the bean curd to separate the roll from the sheet.

5 Repeat the action to make more rolls, using more sheets when required, until all the filling has been used.

6 Heat the oil in a wok or deep-fryer to 190°C/375°F. Add the rolls and fry for 3–4 minutes until golden brown and crisp. Drain on kitchen paper and leave to cool. Slice diagonally and serve with sliced cucumber and a chilli dipping sauce.

Fresh Spring Rolls

All kinds of meat, seafood and vegetables are combined in this do-it-yourself dish.

Serves 4–6

45ml/3 tbsp vegetable oil
225g/8oz firm tofu, rinsed, drained and diced
4 garlic cloves, finely chopped
4 rashers (strips) streaky (fatty) bacon, finely sliced
45ml/3 tbsp fermented soya beans, mashed
450g/1lb fresh prawns (shrimp), peeled and deveined
225g/8oz jicama (sweet turnip), peeled and shredded
450g/1lb bamboo shoots, grated
15ml/1 tbsp dark soy sauce
10ml/2 tsp sugar
4–6 fresh red chillies, seeded and pounded
6–8 garlic cloves, crushed
kecap manis (sweet soy sauce)
12 cos or romaine lettuce leaves
1 small cucumber, peeled, seeded and finely shredded
225g/8oz/1 cup beansprouts
2 Chinese sausages, fried and sliced
225g/8oz cooked prawns (shrimp), peeled
225g/8oz cooked crab meat
1 omelette, sliced into thin ribbons
fresh coriander (cilantro) leaves, roughly chopped
12 popiah wraps or Mexican corn tortillas

1 Heat the oil in a wok or heavy pan. Fry the tofu until golden brown. Remove from the oil and pat dry on kitchen paper.

2 Fry the garlic and bacon in the oil until they begin to colour. Stir in the fermented soya beans and fresh prawns. Add the jicama, bamboo shoots, soy sauce and sugar. Fry over a high heat to reduce the liquid. Toss in the fried tofu and cook the mixture gently until almost dry. Transfer to a serving dish.

3 Put the remaining ingredients in separate bowls on the table. Place the wraps on a serving plate.

4 To serve, let everyone help themselves to a wrap. Smear the wrap with the chilli and garlic pastes, followed by the kecap manis, a lettuce leaf, a layer of cucumber and beansprouts, and a spoonful of the cooked filling. Add Chinese sausage, prawns and crab meat. Place a few strips of omelette on top with a sprinkling of coriander, then fold the edge of the wrap over the filling, tuck in the ends and roll it up.

Pork Rolls Energy 387kcal/1608kJ; Protein 23.8g; Carbohydrate 8.6g, of which sugars 2.4g; Fat 28.9g, of which saturates 6.1g; Cholesterol 114mg; Calcium 158mg; Fibre 0.9g; Sodium 361mg.
Fresh Spring Rolls Energy 457kcal/1916kJ; Protein 32.3g; Carbohydrate 39.3g, of which sugars 5.8g; Fat 20.1g, of which saturates 4.9g; Cholesterol 213mg; Calcium 396mg; Fibre 4.5g; Sodium 989mg.

Pork Belly with Five Spices

This recipe originated in China, but came to Thailand when colonists from south China settled in the country. Over the centuries, the dish has evolved and Thai cooks have produced their own variant. Pork belly is one of the cheaper cuts of meat but it has masses of succulent flavour.

Serves 4

1 large bunch fresh coriander (cilantro) with roots
30ml/2 tbsp vegetable or sunflower oil
1 garlic clove, crushed
30ml/2 tbsp five-spice powder
500g/1 ¼lb pork belly, cut into 2.5cm/1in pieces
400g/14oz can chopped tomatoes
150ml/¼ pint/⅔ cup hot water
30ml/2 tbsp dark soy sauce
45ml/3 tbsp fish sauce
30ml/2 tbsp sugar
1 lime, halved

1 Cut off the coriander roots. Chop five of them finely and freeze the remainder for another occasion. Chop the coriander stalks and leaves and set them aside. Keep the roots separate.

2 Heat the oil in a wok and cook the garlic until it is golden brown. Stirring constantly, add the coriander and five-spice powder.

3 Add the pork and stir-fry, stirring, until the meat is thoroughly coated in spices and has browned.

4 Stir in the tomatoes and hot water. Bring to the boil, then stir in the soy sauce, fish sauce and sugar.

5 Reduce the heat, cover the wok and simmer for 30 minutes. Stir in the chopped coriander stalks and leaves, squeeze over the lime juice and ladle into bowls. Serve.

Cook's Tip
Buy Chinese five-spice powder, which is made from equal parts of cinnamon, cloves, fennel seed, star anise and Szechuan peppercorns. The Indian variety is made from quite different spices.

Pork-stuffed Green Peppers

Small, thin-skinned peppers are best for this traditional Chinese dish.

Serves 4

225g/8oz minced (ground) pork
4–6 drained canned water chestnuts, finely chopped
2 spring onions (scallions), chopped
2.5ml/½ tsp finely chopped fresh root ginger
15ml/1 tbsp light soy sauce
15ml/1 tbsp Chinese rice wine
3–4 green (bell) peppers
15ml/1 tbsp cornflour (cornstarch)
oil for deep-frying

For the sauce

30ml/2 tbsp light soy sauce
5ml/1 tsp soft light brown sugar
1–2 fresh red chillies, chopped
75ml/5 tbsp ham stock or water

1 Mix the pork, water chestnuts, spring onions and ginger. Add the soy sauce and wine and work into the pork mixture.

2 Cut the peppers in half lengthways and remove the cores and seeds. If the peppers are large, halve again. Stuff the peppers with the pork mixture. Sprinkle a little cornflour over the peppers.

3 Heat the oil for deep-frying in a wok, or use a deep-fryer. Using a spider or a large slotted spoon, carefully add the stuffed peppers, meat-side down, and fry them for 2–3 minutes. If you have cut the peppers into quarters, you will probably need to do this in batches. Lift out and drain on kitchen paper.

4 Let the oil cool slightly, then pour most of it into a separate pan and set aside. Heat the oil remaining in the wok and add the peppers, this time placing them meat-side up. Add the sauce ingredients, shivering the wok so they do not stick to the bottom.

5 Braise the peppers over a gentle heat for 10–15 minutes until they are tender and cooked through. Lift them on to a serving dish, meat-side up, pour the sauce over and serve.

Cook's Tip
For a tasty variation, substitute yellow, orange or red (bell) peppers for the green peppers in this recipe.

Pork Belly Energy 581kcal/2405kJ; Protein 20.6g; Carbohydrate 11.6g, of which sugars 11.5g; Fat 50.5g, of which saturates 17.1g; Cholesterol 90mg; Calcium 71mg; Fibre 2.3g; Sodium 109mg.
Pork-stuffed Peppers Energy 198kcal/825kJ; Protein 12.5g; Carbohydrate 4.7g, of which sugars 4.3g; Fat 14.2g, of which saturates 3.1g; Cholesterol 37mg; Calcium 26mg; Fibre 2.3g; Sodium 942mg.

Five-spice Meatballs

In Vietnam a peanut dipping sauce is traditional with these meatballs. Serve with a green salad.

Serves 4

10ml/2 tsp sesame oil
4 shallots, chopped
2 garlic cloves, finely chopped
450g/1lb/2 cups minced (ground) pork
30ml/2 tbsp nuoc mam (Vietnamese fish sauce)
10ml/2 tsp five-spice powder
10ml/2 tsp sugar
115g/4oz/2 cups breadcrumbs or 30ml/2 tbsp potato starch
1 bunch fresh coriander (cilantro), stalks removed
salt and ground black pepper

For the sauce

10ml/2 tsp groundnut (peanut) oil
1 garlic clove, finely chopped
1 red chilli, seeded and chopped
30ml/2 tbsp roasted peanuts, finely chopped
15ml/1 tbsp nuoc mam
30ml/2 tbsp rice wine vinegar
30ml/2 tbsp hoisin sauce
60ml/4 tbsp coconut milk
100ml/3½fl oz/scant ½ cup water
5ml/1 tsp sugar

1 To make the sauce, heat the oil in a small wok or heavy pan, and stir in the garlic and chilli. When they begin to colour, add the peanuts. Stir-fry for a few minutes. Add the remaining ingredients, except the sugar, and boil for 1 minute. Adjust the sweetness and seasoning by adding sugar and salt, and set aside.

2 To make the meatballs, heat the oil in a wok or small pan and add the shallots and garlic. Stir-fry until golden, then leave to cool. Put the minced pork into a bowl, add the stir-fried shallots and garlic, and add the nuoc mam, five-spice powder and sugar. Season. Knead the mixture to combine, cover and chill for 2–3 hours or overnight.

3 Soak eight wooden skewers in water for 30 minutes. Add the breadcrumbs or potato starch to the mixture. Knead to bind. Divide the mixture into 20 and roll into balls. Thread on to the skewers. Cook either over the barbecue or under the grill (broiler), turning from time to time, until well browned.

4 Reheat the sauce. Arrange the meatballs on a serving dish with coriander leaves. Serve with the sauce.

Fragrant Thai Meatballs

These meatballs are especially delicious because of their spicy peanut sauce. Serve them with plain boiled rice or fresh noodles for a quick and easy weekday lunch or supper.

Serves 4–6

450g/1lb lean minced pork or beef
15ml/1 tbsp chopped garlic
1 stalk lemon grass, finely chopped
4 spring onions, finely chopped
15ml/1 tbsp chopped fresh coriander
30ml/2 tbsp red curry paste
15ml/1 tbsp lemon juice
15ml/1 tbsp fish sauce
1 egg
salt and freshly ground black pepper
rice flour for dusting
oil for frying
sprigs of coriander, to garnish

For the peanut sauce

15ml/1 tbsp vegetable or groundnut (peanut) oil
15ml/1 tbsp red curry paste
30ml/2 tbsp crunchy peanut butter
15ml/1 tbsp palm sugar
15ml/1 tbsp lemon juice
250ml/8fl oz/1 cup coconut milk

1 Make the peanut sauce. Heat the oil in a small saucepan, add the curry paste and fry for 1 minute.

2 Add the red curry paste, the crunchy peanut butter, palm sugar, lemon juice and the coconut milk to the pan and bring to the sauce to the boil, stirring all the time. Lower the heat and simmer for 5 minutes, stirring from time to time until the peanut sauce thickens.

3 Make the meatballs. Combine all the ingredients except for the rice flour, oil and coriander to garnish, and add some seasoning. Mix and blend everything together well.

4 Roll and shape the meat into small balls about the size of a walnut. Dust the meatballs with rice flour.

5 Heat the oil in a wok until hot and deep fry the meatballs in batches until nicely browned and cooked through. Drain on kitchen paper. Serve garnished with sprigs of coriander and accompanied with the peanut sauce.

Five-spice Meatballs Energy 339kcal/1414kJ; Protein 24.4g; Carbohydrate 12.6g, of which sugars 2.7g; Fat 21.6g, of which saturates 4.2g; Cholesterol 158mg; Calcium 343mg; Fibre 1.2g; Sodium 666mg.
Fragrant Thai Meatballs Energy 469kcal/1963kJ; Protein 34.8g; Carbohydrate 13.1g, of which sugars 6.7g; Fat 31.1g, of which saturates 17.8g; Cholesterol 129mg; Calcium 4mg; Fibre 2.3g; Sodium 723mg

Deep-fried Pork Fillet

This invigorating Japanese dish is so good that some restaurants serve nothing else. The pork is garnished with a heap of very finely shredded white cabbage.

Serves 4

1 white cabbage
4 pork loin chops or cutlets, boned
plain (all-purpose) flour, to dust
vegetable oil, for deep-frying
2 eggs, beaten
50g/2oz/1 cup dried white breadcrumbs
salt and ready-ground mixed pepper
prepared English (hot) mustard, to garnish
Japanese pickles, to serve

For the ton-katsu sauce

60ml/4 tbsp Worcestershire sauce
30ml/2 tbsp tomato ketchup
5ml/1 tsp shoyu

1 Quarter the cabbage and remove the central core. Slice the wedges very finely with a vegetable slicer or a sharp knife.

2 Using a sharp knife, make a few deep cuts horizontally across the fat of the meat. This prevents the meat curling up while cooking. Rub a little salt and pepper into the meat and dust with the flour, then shake off any excess.

3 Heat the oil in a wok or large pan to 180°C/350°F, or until a cube of bread browns in 45 seconds.

4 Dip the meat in the beaten eggs, then coat the meat with breadcrumbs. Deep-fry two pieces at a time for 8–10 minutes, or until golden brown. Drain on a wire rack or on kitchen paper. Repeat until all the pieces of pork are deep-fried.

5 Heap the cabbage on four warmed, individual serving plates. Cut the pork crossways into 2cm/¾in thick strips and arrange them to your liking on the cabbage.

6 To make the ton-katsu sauce, mix the Worcestershire sauce, ketchup and shoyu together in a jug (pitcher) or a gravy boat. Serve the pork and cabbage immediately, with the sauce, mustard and Japanese pickles. Japanese pickles can also be served in separate dishes, if you like.

Pork Chops with Field Mushrooms and Chilli Sauce

In Thailand, meat is frequently cooked over a brazier or open fire, so it isn't surprising that many tasty barbecue-style dishes come from there. These fabulous pork chops in a spicy sauce are a great favourite with everyone.

Serves 4

4 pork chops
4 large mushrooms
45ml/3 tbsp vegetable oil
4 fresh red chillies, seeded and thinly sliced
45ml/3 tbsp Thai fish sauce
90ml/6 tbsp fresh lime juice
4 shallots, chopped
5ml/1 tsp roasted ground rice
30ml/2 tbsp spring onions (scallions), chopped, plus shredded spring onions to garnish
tagliatelle, to serve

For the marinade

2 garlic cloves, chopped
15ml/1 tbsp granulated (white) sugar
15ml/1 tbsp Thai fish sauce
30ml/2 tbsp soy sauce
15ml/1 tbsp sesame oil
15ml/1 tbsp whisky or dry sherry
2 lemon grass stalks, finely chopped
2 spring onions (scallions), chopped

1 Make the marinade. Combine the chopped garlic, sugar, fish sauce, soy sauce, sesame oil and whisky or sherry in a large, shallow dish. Stir in the lemon grass and spring onions.

2 Add the pork chops, turning to coat them in the marinade. Cover and leave to marinate for 1–2 hours.

3 Lift the chops out of the marinade and place them on a barbecue grill over hot coals or on a grill (broiler) rack. Add the mushrooms and brush them with 15ml/1 tbsp of the oil. Cook the pork chops for 5–7 minutes on each side and the mushrooms for about 2 minutes. Brush both with the marinade while cooking.

4 Heat the remaining oil in a wok or small frying pan, then remove the pan from the heat and stir in the chillies, fish sauce, lime juice, shallots, ground rice and spring onions. Serve the pork chops and mushrooms and spoon over the sauce. Garnish with the shredded spring onion and serve with the tagliatelle.

Pork Fillet Energy 311Kcal/1304kJ; Protein 31.1g; Carbohydrate 21.7g, of which sugars 12g; Fat 11.6g, of which saturates 2.9g; Cholesterol 166mg; Calcium 141mg; Fibre 3.5g; Sodium 522mg.
Pork Chops Energy 339kcal/1418kJ; Protein 39.7g; Carbohydrate 2.3g, of which sugars 1g; Fat 19.1g, of which saturates 4.1g; Cholesterol 90mg; Calcium 26mg; Fibre 1g; Sodium 678mg.

Braised Pork Belly with Orange, Spices and Steamed Greens

Pork belly becomes meltingly tender in this slow-braised dish flavoured with orange, cinnamon, star anise and ginger. The flavours meld and mellow during cooking to produce a rich, complex, rounded taste. Serve simply with rice and steamed greens.

Serves 4

800g/1¾lb pork belly, trimmed and cut into 12 pieces
400ml/14fl oz/1⅔ cups beef stock
75ml/5 tbsp soy sauce
finely grated rind and juice of 1 large orange
15ml/1 tbsp finely shredded fresh root ginger
2 garlic cloves, sliced
15ml/1 tbsp hot chilli powder
15ml/1 tbsp muscovado (molasses) sugar
3 cinnamon sticks
3 cloves
10 black peppercorns
2–3 star anise
steamed greens and rice, to serve

1 Place the pork belly in a wok and pour over enough water to cover the pork. Bring the water to the boil. Cover the wok, reduce the heat and cook gently for 30 minutes.

2 Drain the pork and return it to the wok with the beef stock, soy sauce, grated orange rind and juice, shredded ginger, sliced garlic, chilli powder, muscovado sugar, cinnamon sticks, cloves, peppercorns and star anise.

3 Pour over water to just cover the pork belly pieces and cook on a high heat until the mixture comes to a boil.

4 Cover the wok tightly with a lid, then reduce the heat to low and cook gently for 1½ hours, stirring occasionally to prevent the pork from sticking to the base of the wok.

5 Taste the sauce and season to taste. It is unlikely that you will need to add pepper, since peppercorns are a prime ingredient in this dish, but you may wish to add a little salt to the sauce. Serve with the pork with steamed greens and rice.

Stir-fried Pork Ribs

Sweet-and-sour spare ribs is a Chinese classic that has been adopted by culinary cultures the world over and has given rise to interesting variations. This version includes basil leaves and fish sauce. This is finger food at its finest, requiring finger bowls and plenty of napkins, and is perfect served with sticky rice and a salad.

Serves 4–6

45ml/3 tbsp hoisin sauce
45ml/3 tbsp fish sauce
10ml/2 tsp five-spice powder
45ml/3 tbsp vegetable or sesame oil
900g/2lb pork ribs
3 garlic cloves, crushed
4cm/1½in fresh root ginger, peeled and grated
1 bunch fresh basil, stalks removed, leaves shredded

1 In a bowl, mix together the hoisin sauce, fish sauce and five-spice powder with 15ml/1 tbsp of the oil.

2 Bring a large wok to the boil, then add the pork ribs, bring back to the boil and blanch for 10 minutes. Lift the ribs out with a slotted spoon, drain well and set aside. Discard the liquid.

3 Heat the remaining oil in a clean wok or heavy pan. Add the crushed garlic and the grated ginger and cook, stirring, until fragrant, then add the blanched pork ribs.

4 Stir-fry for 5 minutes, or until the pork ribs are well browned, then add the hoisin sauce mixture, turning the ribs so that each is coated. Stir-fry for 10–15 minutes, or until there is almost no liquid in the wok and the ribs are caramelized and slightly blackened.

5 Stir in the basil leaves. Serve the ribs in individual warmed dishes. Offer guests finger bowls containing water and slices of lemon or lime, and plenty of napkins to wipe sticky fingers.

Variation

Five-spice powder that is popular in Chinese cooking. It has a pungent taste that is not to everyone's taste, so use it judiciously. As an alternative substitute 5ml/1 tsp ground coriander.

Pork Belly with Greens Energy 543kcal/2260kJ; Protein 38.9g; Carbohydrate 6.6g, of which sugars 6.4g; Fat 40.4g, of which saturates 14.6g; Cholesterol 142mg; Calcium 19mg; Fibre 0g; Sodium 1475mg.
Stir-fried Ribs Energy 633kcal/2638kJ; Protein 42.9g; Carbohydrate 11.5g, of which sugars 11.2g; Fat 45.2g, of which saturates 14.1g; Cholesterol 149mg; Calcium 43mg; Fibre 0.5g; Sodium 250mg.

Lemon Grass Pork

Chillies and lemon grass flavour this simple stir-fry, while peanuts add contrast in texture. Jars of chopped lemon grass are handy when fresh vegetables are unavailable.

Serves 4

675g/1½lb boneless pork loin
2 lemon grass stalks, finely chopped
4 spring onions (scallions), thinly sliced
5ml/1 tsp salt
12 black peppercorns, coarsely crushed
30ml/2 tbsp groundnut (peanut) oil
2 garlic cloves, chopped
2 fresh red chillies, seeded and chopped
5ml/1 tsp soft light brown sugar
30ml/2 tbsp fish sauce
25g/1oz/¼ cup roasted unsalted peanuts, chopped
ground black pepper
coarsely torn coriander (cilantro) leaves, to garnish
cooked rice noodles, to serve

1 Trim any excess fat from the pork. Cut the meat across into 5mm/¼in thick slices, then cut each slice into 5mm/¼in strips.

2 Put the pork into a bowl with the lemon grass, spring onions, salt and crushed peppercorns; mix well. Cover with clear film (plastic wrap) and marinate in a cool place for 30 minutes.

3 Preheat a wok and add the oil. Add the pork mixture and stir-fry over a medium heat for about 3 minutes.

4 Add the garlic and red chillies to the wok and stir-fry for a further 5–8 minutes over a medium heat, stirring gently, until the pork is cooked through and tender.

5 Add the sugar, fish sauce and chopped peanuts and toss to mix, then season to taste with black pepper. Serve immediately on a bed of rice noodles, garnished with the coriander leaves.

Cook's Tip
Lemon grass has long, thin, grey-green leaves and a scallion-like base. It is available fresh or dried and adds zest to any recipe.

Aromatic Pork with Basil

The combination of moist, juicy pork and mushrooms, crisp green mangetouts and fragrant basil in this ginger- and garlic-infused stir-fry is absolutely delicious.

Serves 4

40g/1½oz cornflour (cornstarch)
500g/1¼lb pork fillet (tenderloin), thinly sliced
15ml/1 tbsp sunflower oil
10ml/2 tsp sesame oil
15ml/1 tbsp very finely shredded fresh root ginger
3 garlic cloves, thinly sliced
200g/7oz/scant 2 cups mangetouts (snow peas), halved
300g/11oz/generous 4 cups mixed mushrooms, sliced if large
120ml/4fl oz/½ cup Chinese cooking wine
45ml/3 tbsp soy sauce
a small handful of sweet basil leaves
salt and ground black pepper
steamed jasmine rice, to serve

1 Place the cornflour in a strong plastic bag. Season well, seal the bag and add the sliced pork.

2 Shake the bag to coat the pork in flour and then remove the pork and shake off any excess flour. Set aside.

3 Preheat the wok over a high heat and add the sunflower and sesame oils. When very hot, stir in the ginger and garlic and cook for 30 seconds. Add the pork and cook over a high heat for about 5 minutes, stirring often, until sealed.

4 Add the mangetouts and mushrooms to the wok and stir-fry for 2–3 minutes. Add the Chinese cooking wine and soy sauce, stir-fry for 2–3 minutes and remove from the heat.

5 Just before serving, stir the sweet basil leaves into the pork. Serve with steamed jasmine rice.

Cook's Tip
For the mushroom medley, try to include fresh shiitake and oyster mushrooms as well as cultivated button (white) ones.

Lemon Grass Pork Energy 297kcal/1240kJ; Protein 37.9g; Carbohydrate 2.1g, of which sugars 1.7g; Fat 15.2g, of which saturates 3.6g; Cholesterol 106mg; Calcium 20mg; Fibre 0.6g; Sodium 119mg.
Aromatic Pork Energy 298kcal/1248kJ; Protein 30.4g; Carbohydrate 14.6g, of which sugars 4.8g; Fat 9.8g, of which saturates 2.4g; Cholesterol 79mg; Calcium 41mg; Fibre 2g; Sodium 903mg.

Stir-fried Pork with Ginger

Quick stir-fried pork marries extremely well with fresh root ginger, garlic and spring onions – the three classic ingredients of all good Chinese seasoning. This recipe is a good Cantonese stand-by for those occasions when you fancy a simple meal. Be lavish with the ginger as it is the hallmark of this dish.

Serves 4

250g/9oz pork rib-eye steak
30ml/2 tbsp sesame oil
30ml/2 tbsp vegetable oil
15ml/1 tbsp sliced garlic
40g/1½ oz fresh young root ginger, sliced into very fine strips
2 spring onions (scallions)
30ml/2 tbsp oyster sauce
5–10ml/1–2 tsp ground black pepper
30ml/2 tbsp Chinese rice wine
30ml/2 tbsp water

1 Using a sharp knife, cut the pork into thin strips. Place these strips on a board and tenderize them slightly, using a meat mallet or the blunt edge of a cleaver. Rub the strips with sesame oil and set them aside for 15 minutes.

2 Heat the vegetable oil in a wok. Add the sliced garlic and ginger and fry for 1 minute, until pale brown. Do not let the garlic burn or it will taste bitter.

3 Add the pork strips and spring onions. Stir-fry for 2 minutes, then add the oyster sauce and black pepper. Stir over the heat for 2 minutes, stirring from time to time, until the seasonings have been thoroughly absorbed by the pork.

4 Pour in the wine and water. Continue to cook, stirring, for 2 minutes, until the liquid bubbles and the pork is fully cooked. Spoon into a heated bowl and serve.

Cook's Tip
Pork rib-eye steak is a boneless cut from the rib section of a pig found at the blade of the loin section closest to the shoulder. It is extremely tender and responds well to stir-frying.

Pan-fried Pork with Ginger Sauce

Reputedly created by a canteen dinner lady at a Tokyo university during the 1970s, this dish, known as Buta-niku Shoga Yaki, is particularly popular with youngsters.

Serves 4

450g/1lb pork chops, boned and trimmed
1 small onion, thinly sliced lengthways
50g/2oz/¼ cup beansprouts
50g/2oz mangetouts (snow peas), trimmed
15ml/1 tbsp vegetable oil
salt

For the marinade

15ml/1 tbsp shoyu
15ml/1 tbsp sake
15ml/1 tbsp mirin (sweet rice wine)
4cm/1½in piece fresh root ginger, very finely grated, plus juice

1 Wrap the boned and trimmed pork chops in clear film (plastic wrap) and freeze them for 2–4 hours. Remove the package from the freezer and cut the chops into into 3mm/⅛in slices, and then into 4cm/1½in wide strips.

2 To make the marinade, mix all the ingredients in a plastic container. Add the pork and marinate for 15 minutes.

3 Heat the oil in a wok or heavy frying pan on a medium-high heat. Add the onion and fry for 3 minutes.

4 Take half of the pork slices out from the marinade and add to the pan. Transfer the meat to a plate when its colour changes; this will only take about 2–3 minutes. Repeat the process with the rest of the meat and reserve the marinade. Transfer all the cooked pork slices and onions to the plate.

5 Pour the reserved marinade into the pan and simmer until it has reduced by one-third. Add the beansprouts and mangetouts, then the pork and increase the heat to medium-high for 2 minutes.

6 Heap the beansprouts on individual, warmed serving plates and lean the pan-fried pork, onions and mangetouts against them. Serve immediately.

Stir-fried Pork Energy 179kcal/747kJ; Protein 25.3g; Carbohydrate 2.8g, of which sugars 2.1g; Fat 7.4g, of which saturates 1.9g; Cholesterol 71mg; Calcium 21mg; Fibre 0.7g; Sodium 614mg.
Pan-fried Pork Energy 179Kcal/747kJ; Protein 25.3g; Carbohydrate 2.8g, of which sugars 2.1g; Fat 7.4g, of which saturates 1.9g; Cholesterol 71mg; Calcium 21mg; Fibre 0.7g; Sodium 614mg.

Curried Pork with Pickled Garlic

This very rich curry is best accompanied by lots of plain rice and perhaps a light vegetable dish. It could serve four with a vegetable curry on the side, and perhaps some steamed greens, such as pak choi (bok choy) or curly kale.

Serves 2

130g/4½oz lean pork steaks
30ml/2 tbsp vegetable oil
1 garlic clove, crushed
15ml/1 tbsp red curry paste
130ml/4½fl oz/generous ½ cup coconut cream
2.5cm/1in piece fresh root ginger, finely chopped
30ml/2 tbsp vegetable or chicken stock
30ml/2 tbsp fish sauce
5ml/1 tsp sugar
2.5ml/½ tsp ground turmeric
10ml/2 tsp lemon juice
4 pickled garlic cloves, finely chopped
strips of lemon and lime rind, to garnish

1 Cover the pork steaks in clear film (plastic wrap). Place the steaks in the freezer for 30–40 minutes, until they are firm, then, using a sharp knife or cleaver, cut the meat into fine slivers, trimming off any excess fat.

2 Heat the oil in a wok or large, heavy frying pan and cook the garlic over a low to medium heat until golden brown. Do not let it burn. Add the curry paste and stir it in well.

3 Add the coconut cream to the pan and stir until the liquid begins to reduce and thicken. Stir in the pork. Cook for 2 minutes more until the pork is cooked through.

4 Add the ginger, stock, fish sauce, sugar and turmeric to the pan, stirring constantly, then add the lemon juice and pickled garlic and heat through. Serve in individual warmed bowls, garnished with strips of lemon and lime rind.

Cook's Tip
Asian stores sell pickled garlic. It is well worth purchasing, as the taste is sweet and delicious.

Braised Pork in Tomato Sauce

Unlike the Italian dish, which usually refers to an omelette, the Spanish frittata refers to dishes that are cooked with tomatoes, garlic and olive oil. The delicious and distinctive flavour of the Spanish frittata (meaning 'fried' in Spanish) comes from sautéed meat or chicken, simmered with tomatoes and bulked up with potatoes and onions. In some regions, jalapeño chillies are added. This tastes even better the day after cooking.

Serves 4

450g/1lb leg of pork, trimmed and cut into 2.5cm/1in cubes
2.5ml/½ tsp salt
2.5ml/½ tsp ground black pepper
30ml/2 tbsp olive oil
105ml/7 tbsp water
1 large Spanish onion, thinly sliced
3 garlic cloves, finely chopped
2 large beef tomatoes, sliced
105ml/7 tbsp tomato ketchup
300g/11oz potatoes, diced
2 jalapeño chillies (optional)
1 red (bell) pepper, seeded and sliced into strips
15ml/1 tbsp patis (fish sauce)
coriander (cilantro) leaves, to garnish

1 Sprinkle the cubed pork with salt and pepper. Place in a bowl, cover, and set aside at room temperature for 15 minutes.

2 Heat a wok or heavy frying pan. When hot, add the olive oil and swirl it round. Stir-fry the seasoned pork for 2–3 minutes until it is well sizzled and light brown all over.

3 Add the water, onion, garlic, tomatoes, tomato ketchup, potatoes and jalapeños, if using, and simmer for 30 minutes.

4 Add the pepper to the pan with the patis. Simmer for another 15 minutes and serve garnished with coriander.

Cook's Tip
For the best possible flavour, Spanish frittata should be prepared a day before eating. Leave the cooked dish to cool, cover it with clear film (plastic wrap) put in the refrigerator overnight, then reheat the next day. Serve hot or at room temperature.

Curried Pork with Garlic Energy 227kcal/947kJ; Protein 16.3g; Carbohydrate 9.8g, of which sugars 6.1g; Fat 14g, of which saturates 2.4g; Cholesterol 41mg; Calcium 30mg; Fibre 1g; Sodium 474mg.
Braised Pork Energy 328kcal/1376kJ; Protein 27.8g; Carbohydrate 31.8g, of which sugars 18g; Fat 10.8g, of which saturates 2.4g; Cholesterol 71mg; Calcium 48mg; Fibre 3.6g; Sodium 524mg.

Pork in Preserved Bean Curd

Cantonese chefs use two main types of preserved bean curd (tofu): the more common white variety, which is known as fu yee in Cantonese, and a red one that is known as lam yee. The latter variety not only has a more intense flavour, but you will find that it also gives the dish an attractive bright red colour.

Serves 4

450g/1lb pork rib-eye steak streaked with a little fat
15ml/1 tbsp cornflour (cornstarch)
½ large onion
2 garlic cloves
30ml/2 tbsp oil
30ml/2 tbsp preserved red bean curd
5ml/1 tsp sugar
120ml/4 fl oz/½ cup water
rice or noodles, to serve

1 With a sharp knife, cut the pork into thin slices.

2 Put the cornflour in a bowl or strong plastic bag, seal the top, and add the pork and toss lightly to coat.

3 Slice the onion and garlic finely. Heat the oil in a wok and fry the onion for 2 minutes. Add the garlic and fry for 1 minute.

4 Push the onion and garlic to the sides of the wok and add the pork slices to the centre. Stir-fry for 2–3 minutes, until the pork is well sealed. Bring the onion mixture back to the centre and mix it with the pork.

5 Add the preserved red bean curd and mash well with your ladle or a fork. Continue to stir-fry the mixture until the pork is thoroughly coated in the beancurd mixture.

6 Add the sugar and water and bring to a brisk boil. When the sauce has reduced to about half the volume, the pork should be done. Serve hot with rice or noodles.

Variation
Preserved red bean curd has a distinctive flavour. Try 30ml/2 tbsp ready-made yellow bean sauce or black bean paste for a change.

Singapore Spiced Pork

Traditionally made with offal, this curry represents a mix of Malay and Portuguese culinary traditions. Roasting the whole spices before grinding gives them a much fuller, richer flavour. If you are not a fan of offal, use a lean cut of pork from the hind leg.

Serves 4

1kg/2¼lb mixed pork offal (liver, lungs, intestines and heart), cleaned and trimmed
30ml/2 tbsp vegetable oil
50g/2oz fresh root ginger, peeled and shredded
15–30ml/1–2 tbsp white wine vinegar or rice vinegar
salt
bread or steamed rice, to serve

For the spice paste
8 shallots, chopped
4 garlic cloves, chopped
25g/1oz fresh root ginger, peeled and chopped
30ml/2 tbsp coriander seeds
10ml/2 tsp cumin seeds
10ml/2 tsp fennel seeds
10ml/2 tsp black peppercorns
5ml/1 tsp ground turmeric

1 First make the spice paste. Using a mortar and pestle or a food processor, grind the shallots, garlic and ginger to a paste. In a heavy pan, dry-roast the coriander, cumin and fennel seeds with the peppercorns until they emit a nutty aroma. Stir the spices so that they roast evenly. Grind the roasted spices to a powder and stir them into the spice paste with the ground turmeric.

2 Put all the offal, apart from the liver, into a pan and cover with water. Bring to the boil, reduce the heat and cook for 40 minutes. Add the liver and cook for a further 5 minutes, until all the offal is tender. Drain the offal but reserve the cooking broth. Cut the offal into bitesize pieces.

3 Heat the oil in a wok or earthenware pot. Stir in the ginger and fry until crisp. Lift the ginger out and set aside. Stir the spice paste into the oil and fry until fragrant.

4 Add the offal to the spice mix and toss it to brown lightly. Stir in the vinegar over a high heat and season. Stir in half the crispy, fried ginger and sprinkle the rest over the top. Serve hot with fresh, crusty bread or steamed rice.

Pork in Bean Curd Energy 215kcal/898kJ; Protein 24.9g; Carbohydrate 5.7g, of which sugars 1.9g; Fat 10.4g, of which saturates 2.3g; Cholesterol 71mg; Calcium 51mg; Fibre 0.2g; Sodium 82mg.
Singapore Pork Energy 444Kcal/1858kJ; Protein 53.6g; Carbohydrate 7.2g, of which sugars 1.4g; Fat 13.3g, of which saturates 5.9g; Cholesterol 650mg; Calcium 21mg; Fibre 0.4g; Sodium 218mg.

Seasoned Pork with Noodles and Mixed Vegetables

The Japanese name for this dish is gomoku yakisoba, meaning 'five different ingredients'; however, you can add as many different ingredients as you wish to make an exciting and tasty noodle stir-fry.

Serves 4

300g/11oz dried Chinese thin egg noodles or 500g/1¼lb fresh soba noodles
200g/7oz lean boneless pork, thinly sliced
22.5ml/4½ tsp sunflower oil
10g/¼oz grated fresh root ginger
1 garlic clove, crushed
200g/7oz green cabbage, roughly chopped
115g/4oz/2 cups beansprouts
1 green (bell) pepper, seeded and cut into fine strips
1 red (bell) pepper, seeded and cut into fine strips
salt and ground black pepper
20ml/4 tsp ao-nori seaweed, to garnish (optional)

For the seasoning mix

60ml/4 tbsp Worcestershire sauce
15ml/1 tbsp Japanese soy sauce
15ml/1 tbsp oyster sauce
15ml/1 tbsp sugar
2.5ml/½ tsp salt
ground white pepper

1 Cook the noodles according to the instructions on the packet. Drain well and set aside.

2 Cut the pork into 3–4cm/1¼–1½in strips and lay these on a board. Season with plenty of salt and pepper.

3 Heat 7.5ml/1½ tsp of the oil in a large wok or frying pan. Add the seasoned pork strips, stir-fry the pork until just cooked, then remove it from the wok or pan.

4 Wipe the wok or pan with kitchen paper, and heat the remaining oil in it. Add the ginger, garlic and cabbage and stir-fry for 1 minute. Add the beansprouts, stir until softened, then add the peppers and stir-fry for 1 minute more.

5 Return the pork to the pan and add the noodles. Stir in all the ingredients for the seasoning mix and stir-fry for 2–3 minutes. Serve immediately, sprinkled with ao-nori seaweed (if using).

Pork with Cellophane Noodles

Simple, speedy and very satisfying, this is an excellent way of using mung bean noodles. It scores high on presentation too, thanks to the contrast between the translucent, thread-like noodles and the vibrant colour of the vegetables.

Serves 2

200g/7oz cellophane noodles
30ml/2 tbsp vegetable oil
200g/7oz minced (ground) pork
1 fresh green or red chilli, seeded and finely chopped
300g/11oz/scant 1½ cups beansprouts
bunch spring onions (scallions), finely chopped
30ml/2 tbsp soy sauce
30ml/2 tbsp fish sauce
30ml/2 tbsp sweet chilli sauce
15ml/1 tbsp light brown sugar
30ml/2 tbsp rice vinegar
30ml/2 tbsp roasted peanuts, chopped, to garnish
small bunch fresh coriander (cilantro), chopped, to garnish

For the magic paste

5ml/1 tsp white peppercorns
2 cloves garlic, peeled
15ml/1 tbsp coriander roots, chopped
5ml/1 tsp salt

1 Place the noodles in a large bowl, cover with boiling water and soak for 10 minutes. Drain the noodles and set aside.

2 For the magic paste, grind the ingredients together using a pestle and mortar or a food processor.

3 Heat the oil in a wok or large frying pan. Add the magic paste and stir-fry for 2–3 seconds, then add the pork. Stir-fry the meat, breaking it up with a spatula, for 2–3 minutes, until browned.

4 Add the chopped chilli to the meat and stir-fry for 3–4 seconds, then add the beansprouts and chopped spring onions, stir-frying for a few seconds after each addition.

5 Snip the noodles into 5cm/2in lengths and add to the pan, with the soy sauce, fish sauce, sweet chilli sauce, sugar and rice vinegar.

6 Toss the ingredients together over the heat until the noodles have warmed through. Pile on to a platter or into a large bowl. Sprinkle the peanuts and coriander over the top and serve.

Seasoned Pork Energy 425kcal/1799kJ; Protein 28.2g; Carbohydrate 62.6g, of which sugars 9.4g; Fat 8.6g, of which saturates 2.6g; Cholesterol 67mg; Calcium 82mg; Fibre 4.4g; Sodium 844mg.
Cellophane Noodles Energy 593kcal/2504kJ; Protein 47.8g; Carbohydrate 72.1g, of which sugars 4.7g; Fat 14.6g, of which saturates 2.8g; Cholesterol 106mg; Calcium 53mg; Fibre 3.2g; Sodium 1461mg.

Savoury Pork Ribs with Snake Beans and Chilli

This is a rich and pungent dish. If snake beans are hard to find, you can substitute fine green or runner beans.

Serves 4–6

675g/1½lb pork spare ribs or belly of pork
30ml/2 tbsp vegetable oil
120ml/4fl oz/½ cup water
15ml/1 tbsp palm sugar
15ml/1 tbsp fish sauce
150g/5oz snake (yard-long) beans, cut into 5cm/2in lengths
2 kaffir lime leaves, finely sliced
2 red chillies, finely sliced, to garnish

For the chilli paste

3 dried red chillies, seeded and soaked
4 shallots, chopped
4 garlic cloves, chopped
5ml/1 tsp chopped galangal
1 stalk lemon grass, chopped
6 black peppercorns
5ml/1 tsp shrimp paste
30ml/2 tbsp dried shrimp, rinsed

1 Put all the ingredients for the chilli paste in a mortar and grind together with a pestle until it forms a thick paste.

2 Slice and chop the pork into 4cm/1½in lengths.

3 Heat the oil in a wok or frying pan. Add the pork and fry for about 5 minutes, until lightly browned.

4 Stir in the chilli paste and continue to cook for another 5 minutes, stirring constantly to stop the paste from sticking to the pan. Add the water, cover and simmer for 7–10 minutes or until the spare ribs are tender. Season with palm sugar and fish sauce.

5 Mix in the snake beans and kaffir lime leaves and fry until the beans are cooked. Serve garnished with sliced red chillies.

Cook's Tip

Known as belacan in Malay and ha cheong among the Cantonese, shrimp paste has a sharp pungency that is tempered and subtly muted when cooked.

Pork with Vegetables

This is a basic recipe for stir-frying any meat with any vegetables, according to seasonal availability. It works brilliantly well with chicken or beef fillet, and is delicious served with plain boiled rice or noodles.

Serves 4

225g/8oz pork fillet (tenderloin)
15ml/1 tbsp light soy sauce
5ml/1 tsp Chinese rice wine or dry sherry
5ml/1 tsp soft light brown sugar
10ml/2 tsp cornflour (cornstarch) mixed to a paste with a little water
115g/4oz/1⅔ cups mangetout (snow peas)
115g/4oz button (white) mushrooms
1 carrot
1 spring onion (scallion)
60ml/4 tbsp vegetable oil
5ml/1 tsp salt
stock (optional)
few drops sesame oil

1 Cut the pork into thin slices. Marinate with about 5ml/1 tsp of the soy sauce, rice wine or sherry, the sugar and cornflour paste.

2 Trim the mangetout. Thinly slice the mushrooms. Cut the carrot into pieces roughly the same size as the pork and cut the spring onion into short sections.

3 Heat the oil in a preheated wok or large, heavy pan, and stir-fry the pork for about 1 minute or until its colour changes. Remove with a slotted spoon and keep warm.

4 Add the vegetables to the wok and stir-fry for about 2 minutes. Add the salt and the partly cooked pork, and a little stock or water if necessary. Continue cooking and stirring for about 1 minute, then add the remaining soy sauce and blend well.

5 Spoon the pork and vegetables into warmed individual dishes, sprinkle with the sesame oil and serve.

Cook's Tip

When preparing vegetables for stir-frying, cut them to even sizes so that they will take the same amount of time to cook.

Savoury Pork Ribs Energy 513kcal/2154kJ; Protein 26.8g; Carbohydrate 8.8g, of which sugars 4.5g; Fat 41.6g, of which saturates 14.9g; Cholesterol 121mg; Calcium 0.2mg; Fibre 1.4g; Sodium 1557mg.
Pork with Vegetables Energy 291kcal/1222kJ; Protein 17.9g; Carbohydrate 7.4g, of which sugars 3.6g; Fat 21.2g, of which saturates 5.4g; Cholesterol 42mg; Calcium 0.3mg; Fibre 1.7g; Sodium 590mg.

Pork with Dried Shrimp

You might expect the dried shrimp to give this dish a fishy flavour, but instead it simply imparts a delicious savoury taste.

Serves 4

250g/9oz pork fillet (tenderloin), sliced
30ml/2 tbsp vegetable oil
2 garlic cloves, finely chopped
45ml/3 tbsp dried shrimp
10ml/2 tsp dried shrimp paste or 5mm/¼in piece from block of shrimp paste
30ml/2 tbsp soy sauce
juice of 1 lime
15ml/1 tbsp palm sugar (jaggery) or muscovado (brown) sugar
1 small fresh red or green chilli, seeded and finely chopped
4 pak choi (bok choy) or 450g/1lb spring greens (collards), shredded

1 Cover the pork steaks in clear film (plastic wrap). Place the pork in the freezer for about 30 minutes, until firm, to make slicing the meat easier. Using a sharp knife, cut it into thin slices.

2 Heat the vegetable oil in a wok or heavy, frying pan and cook the garlic until golden brown. Add the pork and stir-fry for about 4 minutes, until just cooked through.

3 Add the dried shrimp to the pan, then stir in the shrimp paste, with the soy sauce, lime juice and sugar. Add the chilli and the pak choi or spring greens and toss it all over the heat until the vegetables are just wilted.

4 Transfer the stir-fried pork and greens to warm individual bowls and serve immediately.

Cook's Tip
Shrimp paste has a strong fishy and salty flavour. It is used in a wide range of Asian dishes such as soups, sauces and rice dishes. The condiment is made from fermented ground shrimp, sun-dried and then cut into blocks. To many Westerners unfamiliar with this condiment, the pungent smell can be repellent; however, it does diminish a little after cooking and it is an essential ingredient in many curries and sauces.

Stir-fried Pork with Peanuts, Chillies and Lime

Pork or chicken stir-fried with nuts and herbs, with a splash of citrus flavour or fish sauce, is everyday home cooking in Vietnam. The combination of chilli, lime, basil and mint in this recipe makes it particularly refreshing and tasty. Serve with steamed or sticky rice, or with rice wrappers, salad and a dipping sauce.

Serves 4

45ml/3 tbsp vegetable or groundnut (peanut) oil
450g/1lb pork tenderloin, cut into fine strips
4 spring onions (scallions), chopped
4 garlic cloves, finely chopped
4cm/1½in fresh root ginger, finely chopped
2 green or red Thai chillies, seeded and finely chopped
100g/3½oz/generous ½ cup shelled, unsalted peanuts
grated rind and juice of 2 limes
30ml/2 tbsp nuoc mam (Vietnamese fish sauce)
30ml/2 tbsp grated fresh coconut
25g/1oz/½ cup chopped fresh mint leaves
25g/1oz/½ cup chopped fresh basil leaves
25g/1oz/½ cup chopped fresh coriander (cilantro) leaves

1 Heat a wok or heavy pan and pour in 30ml/2 tbsp of the oil. Add the pork and sear over a high heat, until browned. Transfer the meat and juices on to a plate and set aside.

2 Heat the remaining oil and add the spring onions, garlic, ginger and chillies. When the aromas begin to rise from the pan, add the peanuts and stir-fry for 1–2 minutes.

3 Add the meat back into the wok. Stir in the lime rind and juice, and the nuoc mam. Add the coconut and herbs, and serve.

Cook's Tip
Nuoc mam is a Vietnamese fish sauce, which is used in moderation because it is so intensely flavoured. It is traditionally made by fermenting anchovies with salt in wooden boxes. The fish are then slowly pressed, yielding the salty, fishy liquid.

Pork with Dried Shrimp Energy 202kcal/843kJ; Protein 32.1g; Carbohydrate 6.6g, of which sugars 6.2g; Fat 9.4g, of which saturates 1.7g; Cholesterol 96mg; Calcium 377mg; Fibre 3.8g; Sodium 554mg.
Stir-fried Pork Energy 401kcal/1668kJ; Protein 32g; Carbohydrate 7g, of which sugars 3g; Fat 27g, of which saturates 5g; Cholesterol 71mg; Calcium 42mg; Fibre 1.8g; Sodium 400mg.

Stir-fried Belly Pork with Aromatic Lychees

Crispy, succulent pieces of pork with aromatic, juicy lychees make an unusual and quickly cooked stir-fry that is ideal for a dinner party. Steamed, boiled rice is the usual accompaniment for this dish, although the northern Chinese have a version that is served with steamed breads.

Serves 4
450g/1lb fatty pork, such as belly pork
30ml/2 tbsp hoisin sauce
15ml/1 tbsp vegetable oil
4 spring onions (scallions), sliced
175g/6oz lychees, peeled, stoned (pitted) and cut into slivers
salt and ground black pepper
fresh lychees and fresh parsley sprigs, to garnish

1 Trim the pork, cut it into even, bite-sized pieces, and place the pork into a medium mixing bowl.

2 Pour the hoisin sauce over the prepared pork, cover the bowl with clear film (plastic wrap) and marinate it in the refrigerator for 30 minutes to an hour.

3 Heat the wok or a large, heavy pan, then add the vegetable oil and swirl it around the pan.

4 Add the pork and stir-fry for 5 minutes until crisp and golden. Add the spring onions and stir-fry for a further 2 minutes.

5 Scatter the lychee slivers over the pork, and season well with salt and pepper. Spoon into individual, warmed bowls. Garnish the pork with fresh lychees and parsley, and serve.

Cook's Tip
If you are unable to buy fresh lychees, then this recipe can be made using drained canned lychees in natural juice. When buying fresh lychees, look for fruit with brightly coloured red skins that are free of blemishes. To store, place the lychees in a plastic bag and refrigerate for up to a week.

Sweet and Sour Pork Thai-style

It was the Chinese who originally created sweet and sour cooking, but the Thais also do it very well. This version has a fresher and cleaner flavour than the Chinese version.

Serves 4
350g/12oz lean pork
30ml/2 tbsp vegetable oil
4 garlic cloves, thinly sliced
1 small red onion, sliced
30ml/2 tbsp Thai fish sauce
15ml/1 tbsp sugar
1 red (bell) pepper, seeded and diced
½ cucumber, seeded and very thinly sliced
2 plum tomatoes, cut into wedges
115g/4oz piece fresh pineapple, cut into small chunks
2 spring onions (scallions), cut into short lengths
ground black pepper

To garnish
coriander (cilantro) leaves
spring onions (scallions), shredded

1 Cut the pork into thin strips using a sharp knife or cleaver. This is easier to do if you freeze it for 30 minutes first.

2 Heat the vegetable oil in a wok or large frying pan. Add the thinly sliced garlic to the pan. Cook over a medium heat until golden, stirring from time to time, then add the pork and stir-fry for 4–5 minutes. Add the onion slices and toss to mix.

3 Add the fish sauce, sugar and ground black pepper to taste. Toss the mixture over the heat for 3–4 minutes more.

4 Add the red pepper, cucumber, tomatoes, pineapple and spring onions to the pan, stirring well to mix. Stir-fry for 3–4 minutes more, then spoon into a warmed serving bowl. Garnish with the coriander and spring onions and serve.

Cook's Tip
Also known as nam pla, Thai fish sauce is one of the most important ingredients in Thai cuisine. It is made from salted fish, usually anchovies, which are fermented to create the thin liquid that is the base of the sauce. The strong aroma and intense flavour becomes less pronounced with cooking.

Pork with Lychees Energy 465kcal/1926kJ; Protein 17.9g; Carbohydrate 8.7g, of which sugars 8.6g; Fat 40.1g, of which saturates 14.8g; Cholesterol 81mg; Calcium 17mg; Fibre 0.5g; Sodium 206mg.
Sweet and Sour Pork Energy 211kcal/885kJ; Protein 20g; Carbohydrate 12.4g, of which sugars 11.8g; Fat 9.4g, of which saturates 2g; Cholesterol 55mg; Calcium 29mg; Fibre 1.8g; Sodium 68mg.

Chinese Sweet and Sour Pork

The sweet and sour flavours of this iconic dish reflect the yin-yang principle of universal harmony that is at the heart of Chinese cooking. Although sweet and sour pork originated in Shanghai, every province has its own version. The sweetening agent used in the sauce is plum sauce and the sourness in the dish comes from vinegar or pineapple juice.

Serves 4
300g/11oz leg of pork
1 egg, beaten
75g/3oz/3⁄4 cup cornflour (cornstarch)
oil for deep-frying
1 small carrot, cubed
1 large onion, quartered
1 tomato, quartered
30ml/2 tbsp plum sauce
30ml/2 tbsp hoisin sauce
45ml/3 tbsp pineapple juice or 15ml/1 tbsp vinegar
200ml/7fl oz/scant 1 cup water

1 Cut the pork into 1cm/½in cubes. Have ready a shallow dish containing the beaten egg, and a clean, strong plastic bag, in which the cornflour has been placed. Dip the cubes in the egg, then add them to the bag. Shake well to coat them in the cornflour.

2 Heat the oil in a wok to 190°C/375°F. Fry the coated pork cubes, in batches if necessary, until cooked through and golden brown all over. Lift out and drain on kitchen paper.

3 Carefully drain off all but 15ml/1 tbsp of the oil from the wok. Add the carrot cubes to the oil in the wok and fry for 2 minutes. Add the onion and tomato and stir-fry for 1 minute.

4 In a bowl, mix the plum sauce, hoisin sauce and the pineapple juice or vinegar. Stir in the water. Add to the wok and cook, stirring, for 1 minute. Add the fried pork to the wok and stir until the ingredients are thoroughly mixed. Serve immediately.

Variation
Ring the changes in this dish further by adding a few drained canned lychees or half a dozen drained canned or fresh pineapple chunks to the sauce.

Chinese Pork

Serve this modern Chinese classic with plain boiled rice and steamed Asian greens.

Serves 4
45ml/3 tbsp light soy sauce
15ml/1 tbsp Chinese rice wine
15ml/1 tbsp sesame oil
5ml/1 tsp ground black pepper
500g/1¼lb pork loin, cut into 1cm/½in cubes
1 carrot
1 red (bell) pepper
4 spring onions (scallions)
65g/2½oz/9 tbsp cornflour (cornstarch)
65g/2½oz/9 tbsp plain (all-purpose) flour
5ml/1 tsp bicarbonate of soda (baking soda)
sunflower oil, for deep-frying
10ml/2 tsp finely grated garlic
5ml/1 tsp finely grated fresh root ginger
60ml/4 tbsp tomato ketchup
30ml/2 tbsp sugar
15ml/1 tbsp rice vinegar
15ml/1 tbsp cornflour (cornstarch) blended with 120ml/4fl oz/½ cup water

1 In a large mixing bowl, combine 15ml/1 tbsp of the soy sauce with the rice wine, sesame oil and pepper. Add the pork and toss to mix. Cover and chill for 3–4 hours. Meanwhile, cut the carrots, pepper and spring onions in shreds, and set aside.

2 Combine the cornflour, plain flour and bicarbonate of soda in a bowl. Add a pinch of salt and mix in 150ml/¼ pint/⅔ cup cold water to make a thick batter. Add the pork and mix well.

3 Separate the pork cubes and deep-fry in batches in hot oil in a wok , for 1–2 minutes, or until golden. Drain on kitchen paper.

4 Mix the garlic, ginger, tomato ketchup, sugar, the remaining soy sauce, rice vinegar and cornflour mixture together in a small pan. Stir the sauce over a medium heat for 2–3 minutes, until it is thickened. Add the carrot, red pepper and spring onions, stir and remove from the heat.

5 Reheat the deep-frying oil in the wok and then re-fry the pork pieces in batches for 1–2 minutes, until golden and crisp. Drain and add to the sauce and toss to mix well. Serve solo or with egg-fried rice or noodles.

Sweet and Sour Pork Energy 727kcal/3035kJ; Protein 32.7g; Carbohydrate 76.5g, of which sugars 39.4g; Fat 32.8g, of which saturates 5.8g; Cholesterol 272mg; Calcium 85mg; Fibre 2.7g; Sodium 1048mg.
Chinese Pork Energy 727kcal/3035kJ; Protein 32.7g; Carbohydrate 76.5g, of which sugars 39.4g; Fat 32.8g, of which saturates 5.8g; Cholesterol 272mg; Calcium 85mg; Fibre 2.7g; Sodium 1048mg.

Braised Pork in Soy Sauce

This recipe name describes a classic dish consisting of braised pork in soy sauce from Shantou, a 19th-century treaty port on the east coast of China.

Serves 6

30ml/2 tbsp vegetable or sunflower oil
15ml/1 tbsp sugar
900g/2lb belly pork, in one piece
60ml/4 tbsp dark soy sauce
15ml/1 tbsp five-spice powder
1 litre/1¾ pints/4 cups water
2 thumb-size knobs of fresh root ginger, bruised
sliced cucumber or pickled ginger, to serve

1 Heat the oil in a wok large enough to hold the piece of pork. Sprinkle in the sugar and cook over medium to high heat until the mixture froths and caramelizes. When it is golden brown in colour, add the pork and turn it on all sides so that it is coated all over with caramel.

2 Add the soy sauce, five-spice powder, water and ginger to the wok. Braise the pork over medium heat for 1 hour or until the pork is tender and the sauce is thick. If the liquid seems to be evaporating too rapidly, lower the heat and cover the wok, or add more water. Lift the pork on to a plate and set aside to cool.

3 Slice the pork and arrange on a platter, with the cucumber or pickled ginger. Remove the ginger from the sauce in the wok, reheat it, then transfer it to a bowl. Serve with the pork.

Flower Kidneys with Ginger

Kidneys are revered for their nutritional properties and symbolism in China. Sliced artfully, they open up like flowers when cooked.

Serves 4

1 pig's kidney
30ml/2 tbsp vegetable oil
15ml/1 tbsp chopped garlic
15ml/1 tbsp chopped fresh root ginger
8 spring onions (scallions), cut in short lengths
30ml/2 tbsp oyster sauce
10ml/2 tsp ground black pepper
30ml/2 tbsp Chinese rice wine
10ml/2 tsp cornflour (cornstarch) mixed with 120ml/4fl oz/½ cup cold water

1 Wash the kidney thoroughly and slice in half lengthways to reveal the white membrane. Remove this completely, then soak the kidney halves in plenty of cold water for 10 minutes.

2 Cut each kidney half into 5cm/2in squares. Using a sharp knife, score the squares deeply in a criss-cross pattern. Put them on a plate and set them aside.

3 Heat the oil in a wok and fry the garlic and ginger for 40 seconds, until light brown. Add the spring onions and stir-fry for 30 seconds. Add the kidney slices and stir-fry rapidly over high heat for 1 minute, until they curl up to resemble flowers.

4 Add the oyster sauce, pepper and wine and bring rapidly to the boil. Add the cornflour mixture and stir over the heat until the sauce thickens. Spoon into a heated dish and serve.

Okra and Pork Belly Stew

This classic Filipino dish is flavoured with the much-loved bagoong, a fermented anchovy sauce. If you can't find bagoong, you could replace it with a Filipino, Thai or Indonesian shrimp paste (terasi). The bagnet lends a rich meaty flavour to this stew, which complements the fermented fish, resulting in a tasty main course dish.

Serves 4–6

225g/8oz okra
juice of 1 lime
1 bitter melon
15ml/1 tbsp palm or corn oil
1–3 garlic cloves, crushed
25g/1oz fresh root ginger, peeled and grated
4 shallots, thickly sliced
350g/12oz bagnet (crispy fried pork belly)
15–30ml/1–2 tbsp bagoong (Filipino shrimp paste) or 15ml/1 tbsp of any shrimp paste
400g/14oz can plum tomatoes
250ml/8fl oz/1 cup pork stock
1 aubergine (eggplant), cut into bitesize wedges, or 2–3 Thai aubergines, quartered
salt and ground black pepper
cooked rice, to serve

1 Put the okra in a large bowl, add the lime juice, toss together and leave to marinate for 30 minutes.

2 Cut the melon in half lengthways, remove the core then cut the flesh into bitesize chunks. Put aside.

3 Meanwhile, heat the oil in a wok or a large, heavy pan, stir in the garlic and ginger and fry until fragrant.

4 Add the shallots and fry for about 5 minutes until they are golden brown. Stir in the bagnet and fry for 1 minute, then add the bagoong, tomatoes and stock.

5 Bring the stock mixture to the boil, reduce the heat and simmer the stew for about 10 minutes.

6 Drain the okra and add it to the pan with the aubergine and bitter melon. Cook for a further 10–15 minutes until the vegetables are tender but not too soft. Season the stew with salt and pepper to taste and serve in warmed bowls with rice.

Braised Pork Energy 551kcal/2276kJ; Protein 20.4g; Carbohydrate 2.6g, of which sugars 2.6g; Fat 51g, of which saturates 17.9g; Cholesterol 96mg; Calcium 12mg; Fibre 0g; Sodium 98mg.
Flower Kidneys with Ginger Energy 118kcal/491kJ; Protein 6.6g; Carbohydrate 6.4g, of which sugars 2.9g; Fat 6.6g, of which saturates 1g; Cholesterol 144mg; Calcium 15mg; Fibre 0.7g;
Okra and Pork Belly Stew Energy 323kcal/1340kJ; Protein 16.1g; Carbohydrate 9.4g, of which sugars 8.9g; Fat 24.8g, of which saturates 8.2g; Cholesterol 74mg; Calcium 118mg; Fibre 3.3g; Sodium 200mg.

Creamy Lamb Korma

A heritage of the talented cooks who served the Mughal emperors, this is a rich and luxurious dish. Mild in flavour, lamb korma is ideal for serving when you are unsure about how hot your guests like their curries to be.

Serves 4–6

15ml/1 tbsp white sesame seeds
15ml/1 tbsp white poppy seeds
50g/2oz/½ cup blanched almonds
2 fresh green chillies, seeded
6 garlic cloves, sliced
5cm/2in piece fresh root ginger, sliced
1 onion, finely chopped
45ml/3 tbsp ghee or vegetable oil
6 green cardamom pods
5cm/2in piece cinnamon stick
4 cloves
900g/2lb lean lamb, boned and cubed
5ml/1 tsp ground cumin
5ml/1 tsp ground coriander
300ml/½ pint/1¼ cups double (heavy) cream mixed with 2.5ml/½ tsp cornflour (cornstarch)
salt
roasted sesame seeds, to garnish

1 Preheat a karahi, wok or large pan over a medium heat without any fat, and add the first seven ingredients. Stir until they begin to change colour. They should go just a shade darker.

2 Leave the mixture to cool, then grind to a fine paste using a pestle and mortar or in a food processor. Heat the ghee or vegetable oil in the pan over a low heat.

3 Fry the cardamoms, cinnamon and cloves until the cloves swell. Add the lamb, ground cumin and coriander and the prepared paste, and season with salt to taste. Increase the heat to medium and stir well. Reduce the heat to low, then cover the pan and cook until the lamb is almost done.

4 Remove from the heat, leave to cool a little and gradually fold in the cream mixture, reserving 5ml/1 tsp to garnish.

5 When ready to serve, gently reheat the lamb, uncovered. Spoon into a warmed serving dish and garnish the lamb with the sesame seeds and the reserved cream. This korma is very good served with pilau rice.

Fragrant Spiced Lamb on Mini Poppadums

Crisp, melt-in-the-mouth mini poppadums make a great base for these divine little bites for a light lunch. Top them with a drizzle of yogurt and a spoonful of mango chutney, add a fresh green salad then serve immediately. To make an equally tasty variation, you can use chicken or pork in place of the lamb.

Makes 25

30ml/2 tbsp sunflower oil
4 shallots, finely chopped
30ml/2 tbsp medium curry paste
300g/11oz minced (ground) lamb
90ml/6 tbsp tomato purée (paste)
5ml/1 tsp caster (superfine) sugar
200ml/7fl oz/scant 1 cup coconut cream
juice of 1 lime
60ml/4 tbsp chopped fresh mint leaves
25 mini poppadums
vegetable oil, for frying
salt and ground black pepper
natural (plain) yogurt and mango chutney, to drizzle
red chilli slivers and mint leaves, to garnish

1 Heat the oil in a wok over a medium heat and add the shallots. Stir-fry for 4–5 minutes, until softened, then add the curry paste. Stir-fry for 1–2 minutes.

2 Add the lamb and stir-fry over a high heat for 4–5 minutes, then stir in the tomato purée, sugar and coconut cream.

3 Cook the lamb in the wok over a gentle heat for 25–30 minutes, or until the meat is tender and all the liquid has been absorbed. Season and stir in the lime juice and mint leaves. Remove from the heat and keep warm.

4 Fill a separate wok one-third full of oil and deep-fry the mini poppadums for 30–40 seconds, until puffed up and crisp. Drain them on kitchen paper.

5 Place the poppadums on a serving platter. Put a spoonful of spiced lamb on each one, then top with a little yogurt and mango chutney. Serve immediately, garnished with slivers of red chilli and mint leaves.

Creamy Lamb Korma Energy 220kcal/916kJ; Protein 14.2g; Carbohydrate 14.5g, of which sugars 11.1g; Fat 12.2g, of which saturates 3.8g; Cholesterol 42mg; Calcium 101mg; Fibre 2.1g; Sodium 90mg.
Fragrant Spiced Lamb Energy 63kcal/260kJ; Protein 2.7g; Carbohydrate 2.7g, of which sugars 1.3g; Fat 4.7g, of which saturates 1.4g; Cholesterol 9mg; Calcium 7mg; Fibre 0.3g; Sodium 45mg.

Spiced Lamb Fillet with Chillies and Onions

This is a fairly hot stir-fry dish, although you can reduce the amount of chilli you use.

Serves 4

225g/8oz lean lamb fillet
120ml/4fl oz/½ cup natural (plain) low-fat yogurt
1.5ml/¼ tsp ground cardamom
5ml/1 tsp crushed ginger
5ml/1 tsp crushed garlic
5ml/1 tsp chilli powder
5ml/1 tsp garam masala
5ml/1 tsp salt
15ml/1 tbsp corn oil
2 medium onions, chopped
1 bay leaf
300ml/½ pint/1¼ cups water
2 red chillies, seeded and sliced lengthways
2 green chillies, seeded and sliced lengthways
30ml/2 tbsp fresh coriander (cilantro) leaves

1 Using a sharp knife, cut the lamb into even strips. Mix together the yogurt, cardamom, ginger, garlic, chilli powder, garam masala and salt. Add the lamb, mix well, and leave for 1 hour to marinate.

2 Heat the oil in a non-stick wok or frying pan and fry the onions for 3–5 minutes, or until golden brown. Add the bay leaf, then add the lamb with the yogurt and spices and stir-fry for 2–3 minutes over a medium heat.

3 Pour over the water, cover and cook for 15–20 minutes over a low heat, checking occasionally. Once the water has evaporated, stir-fry the mixture for 1 minute more.

4 Add the red and green chillies and the fresh coriander to the pan, and stir well. Serve immediately.

Cook's Tip

Garam masala, meaning 'warm spice', is a blend of ground spices commonly used in Indian cuisine. Typically it will contain black pepper, black cumin, cinnamon, cloves, mace, cardamom, coriander seed, nutmeg, fennel and bay leaf, all dry-fried or roasted then dried and ground.

Spiced Lamb with Spinach

This recipe is based on the Indian dish sag gosht – meat cooked with spinach. It is flavoured with whole spices, which are not intended to be eaten.

Serves 3–4

45ml/3 tbsp vegetable oil
500g/1¼lb lean boneless lamb, cut into 2.5cm/1in cubes
1 onion, chopped
3 garlic cloves, finely chopped
1cm/½in piece fresh root ginger, finely chopped
6 black peppercorns
4 whole cloves
1 bay leaf
3 green cardamom pods, crushed
5ml/1 tsp ground cumin
5ml/1 tsp ground coriander
generous pinch of cayenne pepper
150ml/¼ pint/⅔ cup water
2 tomatoes, peeled, seeded and chopped
5ml/1 tsp salt
400g/14oz fresh spinach, trimmed, washed and finely chopped
5ml/1 tsp garam masala
crisp-fried onions and fresh coriander (cilantro) sprigs, to garnish
naan bread or spiced basmati rice, to serve

1 Heat a large pan or wok until hot. Add 30ml/2 tbsp of the oil and swirl it around. When hot, stir-fry the lamb in batches until evenly browned. Remove the lamb and set aside. Heat the remaining oil in the pan, add the onion, garlic and ginger and stir-fry for 2–3 minutes.

2 Add the peppercorns, cloves, bay leaf, cardamom pods, cumin, coriander and cayenne pepper. Stir-fry for 30–45 seconds.

3 Return the lamb to the pan, add the water, tomatoes and salt and bring to the boil. Simmer, covered, over a very low heat for about 1 hour, stirring occasionally, until the meat is tender.

4 Increase the heat, then gradually add the spinach to the lamb, stirring to mix. Keep stirring and cooking until the spinach wilts completely and most, but not all of the liquid has evaporated and you are left with a thick green sauce.

5 Stir in the garam masala. Garnish with crisp-fried onions and coriander sprigs. Serve with naan bread or spiced basmati rice.

Spiced Lamb Energy 183kcal/764kJ; Protein 15.5g; Carbohydrate 14.1g, of which sugars 9.1g; Fat 7.8g, of which saturates 3.2g; Cholesterol 43mg; Calcium 102mg; Fibre 1.8g; Sodium 77mg.
Lamb with Spinach Energy 359kcal/1494kJ; Protein 28.7g; Carbohydrate 7.1g, of which sugars 4.7g; Fat 24.1g, of which saturates 7.7g; Cholesterol 95mg; Calcium 237mg; Fibre 4.8g; Sodium 780mg.

Spicy Lamb and Potato Stew

Indian spices transform a simple lamb and potato stew into a mouthwatering dish fit for princes.

Serves 6

675g/1½lb lean lamb fillet (tenderloin)
15ml/1 tbsp sunflower oil
1 onion, finely chopped
2 bay leaves
1 fresh green chilli, seeded and finely chopped
2 garlic cloves, finely chopped
10ml/2 tsp ground coriander
5ml/1 tsp ground cumin
2.5ml/½ tsp ground turmeric
2.5ml/½ tsp chilli powder
2.5ml/½ tsp salt
2 tomatoes, peeled and chopped
600ml/1 pint/2½ cups chicken stock
2 large potatoes, cut in large chunks
chopped fresh coriander (cilantro), to garnish

1 Remove any visible fat from the lamb fillet and cut the meat into neat 2.5cm/1in cubes using a sharp knife or cleaver.

2 Heat the sunflower oil in a wok or large, heavy pan and fry the onion, bay leaves, chilli and garlic for 5 minutes.

3 Add the cubed meat to the pan and cook for about 6–8 minutes until lightly browned, stirring from time to time.

4 Add the ground coriander, ground cumin, ground turmeric, chilli powder and salt to the pan and cook the spices for 3–4 minutes, stirring all the time with a wooden spatula to prevent the spices from sticking to the bottom of the pan.

5 Add the tomatoes and stock and simmer for 5 minutes. Bring to the boil, cover and simmer for 1 hour.

6 Add the bitesize chunks of potato to the simmering mixture, stir in, and cook for a further 30–40 minutes, or until the meat is tender and much of the excess juices have been absorbed, leaving a thick but minimal sauce.

7 Transfer the lamb and potato stew to individual warmed bowls. Garnish the dish with scattered, chopped fresh coriander and serve the curry piping hot.

Stir-fried Lamb with Baby Onions and Mixed Peppers

The baby onions are stir-fried whole before being added to the lamb and pepper mixture in this recipe. Serve this dish with rice, lentils or naan bread.

Serves 4

15ml/1 tbsp oil
8 baby onions
225g/8oz boned lean lamb, cut into strips
5ml/1 tsp ground cumin
5ml/1 tsp ground coriander
15ml/1 tbsp tomato purée (paste)
5ml/1 tsp chilli powder
5ml/1 tsp salt
15ml/1 tbsp lemon juice
2.5ml/½ tsp onion seeds
4 curry leaves
300ml/½ pint/1¼ cups water
1 small red (bell) pepper, seeded and roughly sliced
1 small green (bell) pepper, seeded and roughly sliced
15ml/1 tbsp chopped fresh coriander (cilantro)
15ml/1 tbsp chopped fresh mint

1 Heat the oil in a karahi, wok or heavy pan and stir-fry the whole baby onions for about 3 minutes. Using a slotted spoon, remove the onions from the pan and set them aside to drain. Set the pan aside, with the oil remaining in it.

2 Mix together the lamb strips, cumin, ground coriander, tomato purée, chilli powder, salt and lemon juice in a bowl until the lamb is well coated. Set aside.

3 Reheat the oil and briskly stir-fry the onion seeds and curry leaves for 2–3 minutes.

4 Add the lamb and spice mixture, and stir-fry for about 5 minutes, then pour in the measured water. Lower the heat and cook the lamb mixture gently for about 10 minutes, stirring from time to time, until the lamb is cooked through.

5 Add the peppers and half the fresh coriander and mint to the pan. Stir-fry for a further 2 minutes.

6 Finally, add the baby onions and the remaining chopped fresh coriander and mint, and serve immediately.

Lamb and Potato Stew Energy 284kcal/1192kJ; Protein 24g; Carbohydrate 14.1g, of which sugars 3.1g; Fat 15.1g, of which saturates 6.3g; Cholesterol 86mg; Calcium 23mg; Fibre 1.3g; Sodium 109mg.
Stir-fried Lamb with Baby Onions Energy 155kcal/644kJ; Protein 16.0g; Carbohydrate 6.4g; Fat 9.4g, of which saturates 2.5g; Cholesterol 49mg; Calcium 2mg; Fibre 1.49g.

Balti Lamb Tikka

This is a traditional tikka recipe, in which the lamb is marinated in yogurt and spices. It is then stir-fried briefly with peppers and chillies and taken sizzling to the table.

Serves 4

450g/1lb lamb, cut into strips
175ml/6fl oz/¾ cup natural (plain) yogurt
5ml/1 tsp ground cumin
5ml/1 tsp ground coriander
5ml/1 tsp chilli powder
5ml/1 tsp garlic pulp
5ml/1 tsp salt
5ml/1 tsp garam masala
30ml/2 tbsp chopped fresh coriander (cilantro)
30ml/2 tbsp lemon juice
30ml/2 tbsp corn oil
15ml/1 tbsp tomato purée (paste)
1 large green (bell) pepper, sliced
3 large fresh red chillies

1 Put the lamb strips, yogurt, ground cumin, ground coriander, chilli powder, garlic, salt, garam masala, fresh coriander and lemon juice into a large mixing bowl and stir all the ingredients together thoroughly. Cover with clear film (plastic wrap) and set to one side for at least 1 hour to marinate.

2 Heat a deep round-bottomed pan or wok. Add the corn oil and swirl it round the wok. Lower the heat slightly and add the tomato purée, stirring it into the oil.

3 Add the lamb strips to the pan, a few at a time, leaving any excess marinade behind in the bowl.

4 Cook the lamb, stirring frequently with a wooden spatula, for 7–10 minutes or until it is well browned.

5 Finally, add the green pepper slices and the whole red chillies. to the pan Heat everything through, checking that the lamb is cooked, and serve.

Cook's Tip
The lamb for this dish is usually cut into cubes, but the cooking time can be halved by cutting it into thin strips.

Keema Lamb with Curry Leaves and Green Chillies

This delicious dry curry is made by cooking minced lamb in its own juices with a few spices and herbs, but no other liquid.

Serves 4

10ml/2 tsp corn oil
2 medium onions, chopped
10 curry leaves
6 green chillies
350g/12oz lean minced (ground) lamb
5ml/1 tsp crushed garlic
5ml/1 tsp crushed ginger
5ml/1 tsp chilli powder
1.5ml/¼ tsp ground turmeric
5ml/1 tsp salt
2 tomatoes, skinned and quartered
15ml/1 tbsp chopped fresh coriander (cilantro)

1 Heat the oil in a non-stick wok or frying pan. Stir-fry the onions together with the curry leaves and three of the whole green chillies for 3–4 minutes, until the onions begin to soften and turn translucent.

2 Put the lamb into a large mixing bowl and add the garlic and crushed ginger, chilli powder, turmeric and salt. Blend everything together thoroughly.

3 Add the lamb mixture to the pan with the translucent onions and stir-fry them together for about 7–10 minutes, lowering the heat to medium if necessary.

4 Add the tomatoes and coriander to the pan. Stir in the remaining whole green chillies. Continue to stir-fry for a further 2 minutes before serving.

Cook's Tip
• *This curry also makes a terrific brunch. Serve with fried eggs and light Indian breads such as pooris or chapatis.*
• *This curry would make an ideal filling for samosas, the spicy Indian snacks. Cook as above but ensure that all the ingredients are finely chopped before using.*

Balti Lamb Tikka Energy 438kcal/1827kJ; Protein 34.4g; Carbohydrate 7.8g, of which sugars 7.7g; Fat 30.3g, of which saturates 10.4g; Cholesterol 128mg; Calcium 74mg; Fibre 2.3g; Sodium 162mg.
Keema Lamb Energy 239kcal/998kJ; Protein 19.7g; Carbohydrate 13.5g, of which sugars 9.3g; Fat 12.3g, of which saturates 4.9g; Cholesterol 67mg; Calcium 50mg; Fibre 2.5g; Sodium 578mg.

Balti Lamb with Cauliflower

This tasty curry is given a final tarka, a dressing of oil, cumin seeds and curry leaves, to enhance the flavour.

Serves 4
10ml/2 tsp oil
2 medium onions, sliced
7.5ml/1½ tsp grated fresh root ginger
5ml/1 tsp chilli powder
5ml/1 tsp crushed garlic
1.5ml/¼ tsp ground turmeric
2.5ml/½ tsp ground coriander
30ml/2 tbsp fresh fenugreek leaves
275g/10oz boneless lean spring lamb, cut into strips
1 small cauliflower, cut into small florets
300ml/½ pint/1¼ cups water
30ml/2 tbsp fresh coriander (cilantro) leaves
½ red (bell) pepper, seeded and sliced
15ml/1 tbsp lemon juice

For the tarka
10ml/2 tsp oil
2.5ml/½ tsp cumin seeds
4–6 curry leaves

1 Heat the oil in a karahi, wok or heavy pan and gently fry the onions until they are golden brown. Lower the heat and then add the ginger, chilli powder, garlic, turmeric and ground coriander. Stir well, then add the fenugreek leaves and mix well.

2 Add the lamb strips to the pan and stir-fry until the lamb is completely coated with the spices.

3 Add half the cauliflower florets to the pan and stir well. Pour in the water, cover the wok, lower the heat and cook for 5–7 minutes until the cauliflower and lamb are almost cooked through.

4 Add the remaining cauliflower, half the fresh coriander, the red pepper and lemon juice and stir-fry for about 5 minutes, ensuring the sauce does not catch on the bottom of the pan. Check that the lamb is completely cooked, then remove the pan from the heat and set it aside.

5 To make the tarka, heat the oil and fry the seeds and curry leaves for about 30 seconds. While it is still hot, pour the seasoned oil over the cauliflower and lamb and serve garnished with the remaining fresh coriander leaves.

Balti Bhoona Lamb

Bhoona is a type of curry, in which the spices are cooked in oil with no water. Bhooning is a traditional way of stir-frying which simply involves semi-circular movements, scraping the bottom of the pan each time in the centre. Serve this dish with freshly made chapatis.

Serves 4
225–275g/8–10oz boneless lean spring lamb
3 medium onions
15ml/1 tbsp oil
15ml/1 tbsp tomato purée (paste)
5ml/1 tsp crushed garlic
7.5ml/1½ tsp finely grated fresh root ginger, plus 15ml/1 tbsp shredded
5ml/1 tsp salt
1.5ml/¼ tsp ground turmeric
600ml/1 pint/2½ cups water
15ml/1 tbsp lemon juice
15ml/1 tbsp chopped fresh coriander (cilantro)
15ml/1 tbsp chopped fresh mint
1 fresh red chilli, chopped

1 Using a sharp knife or cleaver, remove any excess fat from the lamb and cut the meat into small cubes.

2 Dice the onions finely. Heat the oil in a karahi, wok or heavy pan and fry the onions until soft.

3 Meanwhile, mix together the tomato purée, garlic and ginger, salt and turmeric. Pour the spice mixture on to the onions in the pan and stir-fry for a few seconds.

4 Add the lamb and continue to stir-fry for about 2–3 minutes. Stir in the water, lower the heat, cover the pan and cook for 15–20 minutes, stirring occasionally.

5 When the water has almost evaporated, start bhooning or stir-frying the lamb by stirring it, using semi-circular movements over a medium heat, making sure that the sauce does not catch on the bottom of the pan. Continue for 5–7 minutes.

6 Pour the lemon juice into the pan, followed by the shredded ginger, chopped fresh coriander, chopped fresh mint and red chilli. Stir to mix, then serve straight from the pan.

Balti Lamb Energy 277kcal/1154kJ; Protein 18.7g; Carbohydrate 14.4g, of which sugars 9g; Fat 16.7g, of which saturates 4.7g; Cholesterol 52mg; Calcium 62mg; Fibre 3.2g; Sodium 73mg.
Balti Bhoona Lamb Energy 188kcal/785kJ; Protein 13.7g; Carbohydrate 12.1g, of which sugars 7.8g; Fat 10g, of which saturates 3.3g; Cholesterol 43mg; Calcium 69mg; Fibre 2.5g; Sodium 67mg.

Lamb with Courgettes

In this recipe, lean lamb is cooked with yogurt and then the sliced courgettes (zucchini), which have already been browned, are added to the mixture.

Serves 4

15ml/1 tbsp vegetable or sunflower oil
2 medium onions, chopped
225g/8oz lean lamb steaks, cut into strips
120ml/4fl oz/½ cup natural (plain) yogurt
5ml/1 tsp garam masala
5ml/1 tsp chilli powder
5ml/1 tsp crushed garlic
5ml/1 tsp crushed fresh root ginger
2.5ml/½ tsp ground coriander
2 medium courgettes (zucchini), sliced
15ml/1 tbsp chopped fresh coriander (cilantro), to garnish

1 Heat the oil in a wok or heavy-based frying pan and fry the onions slowly and gently until golden brown.

2 Add the lamb strips and stir-fry for 1 minute to seal the meat.

3 Put the yogurt, garam masala, chilli powder, garlic, ginger and ground coriander into a bowl and mix together.

4 Pour the yogurt mixture over the lamb and stir-fry for 2 minutes. Cover and cook over a medium to low heat for 12–15 minutes, until the lamb is cooked.

5 Put the courgettes in a flameproof dish and cook under a preheated grill (broiler) for 3 minutes, turning once.

6 Check the lamb is cooked through and the sauce is thick, then add the courgettes and serve garnished with fresh coriander.

Cook's Tip
Ginger plays a big role in Asian and Indian cooking, particularly in the stir-fried dishes. Whenever possible, the juicier and more pungent young ginger is used. This is a simple and delicious way to cook chicken, pork or beef.

Glazed Lamb

Lemon and honey make a classic stir-fry combination in sweet dishes. The lemon cuts through the greasiness of lamb, and the honey provides added sweetness. This lamb recipe shows how well these two ingredients work together in savoury dishes. Serve with a fresh mixed salad to complete this delicious dish.

Serves 4

450g/1lb boneless lean lamb
15ml/1 tbsp grapeseed oil
175g/6oz mangetouts (snow peas), trimmed
3 spring onions (scallions), sliced
30ml/2 tbsp clear honey
juice of ½ lemon
30ml/2 tbsp chopped fresh coriander (cilantro)
15ml/1 tbsp sesame seeds
salt and ground black pepper

1 Using a cleaver or sharp knife, cut the lamb into thin strips.

2 Heat the wok or heavy frying pan, and then add the grapeseed oil. When the oil is hot, stir-fry the lamb for 3–4 minutes until browned all over and cooked through. Remove the lamb from the pan and keep warm.

3 Add the mangetouts and spring onions to the hot wok or pan and stir-fry for 30 seconds.

4 Return the lamb to the wok and add the honey, lemon juice, chopped coriander and sesame seeds and season well. Stir thoroughly to mix. Bring to the boil, then allow to bubble vigorously for 1 minute until the lamb is completely coated in the honey mixture. Serve immediately.

Cook's Tip
Use a tender cut of lamb such as leg for this recipe.

Variations
This recipe would work just as well made with pork or chicken instead of lamb. You could substitute chopped fresh basil for the coriander if using chicken.

Lamb with Courgettes Energy 197kcal /824kJ; protein 15.7g; carbohydrate 11.4g, of which sugars 8.2g; fat 10.3g, of which saturates 3.7g; cholesterol 43mg; calcium 120mg; fibre 1.7g; sodium 83mg.
Glazed Lamb Energy 223kcal/932kJ; Protein 19g; Carbohydrate 7.8g, of which sugars 7.4g; Fat 13.1g, of which saturates 4.9g; Cholesterol 67mg; Calcium 34mg; Fibre 1.2g; Sodium 78mg.

Javanese Goat Curry

This popular spicy goat dish is from Java but there are many variations all over the Indonesian archipelago.

Serves 4

30–60ml/2–4 tbsp palm, coconut or groundnut (peanut) oil
10ml/2 tsp shrimp paste
15ml/1 tbsp palm sugar (jaggery)
5ml/1 tsp coriander seeds
5ml/1 tsp cumin seeds
2.5ml/½ tsp grated nutmeg
2.5ml/½ tsp ground black pepper
2–3 lemon grass stalks, halved and bruised
700g/1lb 9oz boneless shoulder or leg of goat, or lamb, cut into bitesize pieces
400g/14oz can coconut milk
200ml/7fl oz/scant 1 cup water (if necessary)
12 snake (yard-long) beans
1 bunch fresh coriander (cilantro) leaves, roughly chopped
cooked rice and 2–3 chillies, seeded and finely chopped, to serve

For the spice paste

2–3 shallots, chopped
2–3 garlic cloves, chopped
3–4 chillies, seeded and chopped
25g/1oz galangal, chopped
40g/1½oz fresh turmeric, chopped, or 10ml/2 tsp ground turmeric
1 lemon grass stalk, chopped
2–3 candlenuts, finely ground

1 Using a mortar and pestle or food processor, grind all the spice paste ingredients together. Heat 15–30ml/1–2 tbsp of the oil in a wok or heavy pan. Fry the paste until fragrant. Add the shrimp paste and sugar and stir-fry for 2 minutes.

2 Heat the remaining oil in a wok or large pan. Stir in the coriander seeds, cumin seeds, nutmeg and black pepper, then add the paste and lemon grass. Stir-fry for 2–3 minutes, until dark and fragrant.

3 Stir the meat into the pan, making sure that it is well coated in the paste. Pour in the coconut milk and water, bring to the boil, then cover and simmer for about 3 hours, until the meat is tender.

4 Add the beans and cook for 10–15 minutes. Check the meat occasionally and add the water if the curry is too dry.

5 Toss a few coriander leaves into the curry and season to taste. Transfer the curry into a warmed serving dish and garnish with the remaining coriander. Serve with rice and chillies.

Spicy Meatballs with Red Rice

In this Moroccan dish, the nutty flavour of red rice is a perfect match for the spicy lamb meatballs.

Serves 4–6

225g/8oz/generous 1 cup Camargue red rice
675g/1½lb lamb leg steaks
2 onions
3–4 fresh parsley sprigs
3 fresh coriander (cilantro) sprigs, plus 30ml/2 tbsp chopped fresh coriander
1–2 fresh mint sprigs
2.5ml/½ tsp ground cumin
2.5ml/½ tsp ground cinnamon
2.5ml/½ tsp ground ginger
5ml/1 tsp paprika
30ml/2 tbsp sunflower oil
1 garlic clove, crushed
300ml/½ pint/1¼ cups tomato juice
450ml/¾ pint/scant 2 cups chicken or vegetable stock
salt and ground black pepper
flatbread and natural (plain) yogurt, to serve

1 Cook the rice in lightly salted water or stock for 20 minutes or according to the instructions on the packet. Drain.

2 Meanwhile, chop the lamb roughly, then place it in a food processor and process until finely chopped. Scrape the meat into a large bowl. Cut one onion into quarters and add it to the processor with the parsley, coriander and mint sprigs; process until finely chopped. Return the lamb to the processor, add the spices and seasoning and process again until smooth. Scrape the mixture into a bowl and chill for about 1 hour.

3 Shape the mixture into about 30 balls. Heat half the oil in a wok or frying pan, add the meatballs, in batches, and brown them evenly. Transfer to a plate.

4 Chop the remaining onion finely. Drain off the excess fat from the pan, leaving around 30ml/2 tbsp, and fry the chopped onion with the garlic for a few minutes until softened. Stir in the rice. Cook, stirring for 1–2 minutes, then add the tomato juice, stock and fresh coriander. Season to taste.

5 Arrange the meatballs over the rice, cover tightly with a lid or foil and simmer very gently for 15 minutes. Serve with flatbread and yogurt.

Javanese Goat Curry Energy 450kcal/1877kJ; Protein 37.9g; Carbohydrate 10.8g, of which sugars 9.1g; Fat 28.7g, of which saturates 10.3g; Cholesterol 146mg; Calcium 129mg; Fibre 2.4g; Sodium 375mg.
Meatballs Energy 405kcal/1694kJ; Protein 26.4g; Carbohydrate 36.1g, of which sugars 5.2g; Fat 17.3g, of which saturates 6.3g; Cholesterol 86mg; Calcium 42mg; Fibre 1.2g; Sodium 215mg.

Braised Mutton with Tamarind

Smoor, or semur, is the name for dishes that are cooked in dark soy sauce and flavoured with sugar and tamarind. It is believed that the dish originated in Java, where kecap manis (sweet soy sauce) is a primary ingredient. This is a dish that reflects both its Chinese and its indigenous Indonesian elements: combining soy sauce and the heady scent of nutmeg, cinnamon, cloves and star anise.

Serves 4

600g/1lb 6oz lean mutton or lamb
30ml/2 tbsp vegetable oil
1 large onion, sliced
pinch of ground nutmeg
6 cloves
1 cinnamon stick, about 4cm/1½in long
1 star anise
2.5ml/½ tsp black peppercorns
45ml/3 tbsp kecap manis (Indonesian sweet soy sauce)
15ml/1 tbsp tamarind concentrate
2.5ml/½ tsp salt

1 Boil the mutton or lamb in a large pot of water for 45 minutes or until tender. Strain, reserving the liquid. Cut the meat into thin slices or small chunks, as you prefer.

2 Heat the oil in a wok or frying pan and fry the onion for 2 minutes until soft. Add the meat and all other ingredients, and stir over a medium heat for 2 minutes.

3 Top up with about 400ml/14fl oz/1⅔ cups of the reserved stock, and cook, uncovered, over a high heat until the sauce is well reduced and thick, lowering the heat if the reduction is too rapid. This will take approximately 30 minutes, depending on your pan: the evaporation rate in a deep pan is less than in a wider wok or frying pan. Adjust the seasoning and serve in warmed, individual dishes.

Cook's Tip

For the very best results, use the very thick variety of dark soy sauce that is usually available in Chinese stores. This has a sweet edge to it that serves the dish well.

Stewed Mutton with Beancurd

Dry beancurd sticks are the perfect foil for rich meats like mutton and lamb.

Serves 4

100g/3¼oz beancurd sticks
350g/12oz lean mutton or lamb
15ml/1 tbsp oil
3 garlic cloves, sliced
5ml/1 tsp sugar
45ml/3 tbsp dark soy sauce
pinch of five-spice powder
600ml/1 pint/2½ cups water
2.5ml/½ tsp ground black pepper

1 Soak the beancurd sticks in a bowl of hot water for about 30 minutes, until soft.

2 Meanwhile, using a sharp knife, cut the mutton or lamb into bitesize chunks. Place them on a board and tenderize them slightly, using a meat mallet or the blunt edge of a cleaver.

3 Heat the oil in a wok and fry the garlic until golden brown. Add the meat and fry for 2 minutes to seal in the flavour until browned all over but not charred.

4 Sprinkle the sugar over the meat, then stir in the dark soy sauce, five-spice powder, water and pepper. Cover the wok with a tight-fitting lid and cook over medium heat for 30 minutes.

5 Drain the beancurd sticks and cut them into 5cm/2in lengths. Stir them into the stew, then replace the lid and simmer for 20 minutes more.

6 Remove the lid from the wok, then increase the heat to high and cook the stew for a further 10 minutes to drive off any excess liquid and reduce the sauce. Spoon the stew into a heated dish and serve immediately.

Cook's Tip

If the stew is too oily for your taste, cool it quickly, then put it in the refrigerator. On chilling, the fat will solidify on top and can easily be lifted off. Reheat the stew to serve.

Braised Mutton Energy 373kcal/1554kJ; Protein 31.7g; Carbohydrate 10.5g, of which sugars 6.3g; Fat 23.2g, of which saturates 8.5g; Cholesterol 114mg; Calcium 48mg; Fibre 1.4g; Sodium 846mg.
Stewed Mutton Energy 209kcal/870kJ; Protein 19.5g; Carbohydrate 2.2g, of which sugars 2g; Fat 13.6g, of which saturates 5g; Cholesterol 67mg; Calcium 137mg; Fibre 0g; Sodium 877mg.

Curried Mixed Meat Pastries

The European culinary heritage in the Philippines is most manifest in these savoury meat pies, often called Spanish meat pies. The Filipinos like to make the filling with a rich mixture of different meats but you can modify the recipe as you wish, and to save time use bought pastry. Traditionally, a small handful of sultanas and relish are added in the final stages, but here sweet bagoong and curry powder are used instead.

Makes about 20

15ml/1 tbsp vegetable oil
2 garlic cloves, very finely chopped
½ large onion, finely chopped
1 potato, about 150g/5oz, boiled and finely diced
1 carrot, finely chopped
100g/7oz minced (ground) beef
100g/7oz minced pork
15ml/1 tbsp sweet bagoong (Filipino shrimp sauce)
15ml/1 tbsp curry powder
5ml/1 tsp salt
2.5ml/½ tsp ground black pepper
300g/11oz pack puff pastry
vegetable oil, for deep-frying

1 Heat the vegetable oil in a karahi, wok or large, heavy frying pan and fry the garlic and onion for 2 minutes.

2 Add the potato and carrot to the pan and fry them for 3 minutes. Add the meats, bagoong, curry powder, salt and pepper and cook for 5 minutes. Remove the pan from the heat while you prepare the pastry.

3 Roll out the pastry to about 5mm/¼in thick and cut out rounds of about 10cm/4in in diameter.

4 Drain off and discard any excess oil from the meat mixture, then place 1 scant tablespoon of filling on each pastry round. Fold the pastry over the filling like a turnover and moisten and press the edges together firmly to seal.

5 Crimp the edges of each pastry with the prongs of a fork, then deep-fry the parcels in the oil in batches until golden brown. This may be done with care in a deep wok, or using a deep fat fryer. Drain the pies on kitchen towels to absorb any excess oil, then serve them warm.

Chargrilled Meat with Aubergine

Variations of this deliciously spiced dish crop up in different parts of South-east Asia. To attain its smoky flavour, the aubergines are charred over a flame, or charcoal grill, then skinned, chopped to a pulp and added to the dish – a method more associated with the cooking of India, the Middle East, and North Africa than Asia.

Serves 4

2 aubergines (eggplants)
15ml/1 tbsp vegetable oil
2 shallots, finely chopped
4 garlic cloves, peeled and finely chopped
1 red Thai chilli, finely chopped
350g/12oz minced (ground) lamb or beef
30ml/2 tbsp Thai fish sauce
sea salt and ground black pepper
crusty bread or rice and tossed green salad, to serve

1 Place the aubergines directly over an open flame or char them under a hot grill in a grill pan (broiling pan). Turn them over from time to time, until the skin is charred all over. Put the charred aubergines into a plastic bag and allow them to sweat for a few minutes.

2 Hold each aubergine by its stalk under cold running water, while you peel off the skin. Discard the skin and the stalks. Squeeze out any excess water from the aubergines and chop them roughly on a board.

3 Heat the oil in a wok or large, heavy pan. Stir in the finely chopped shallots, garlic and chilli and fry until golden. Add the minced beef and stir-fry for about 5 minutes.

4 Add the fish sauce and the aubergine to the pan, stir and cook gently for about 20 minutes, until the meat is tender. Season with salt and pepper and serve with crusty bread or boiled rice and a tossed green salad.

Variation

This dish can also be made with beef or pork – either way it is delicious served with chunks of fresh, crusty bread.

Curried Meat Pastries Energy 141kcal/588kJ; Protein 3.5g; Carbohydrate 7.5g, of which sugars 0.7g; Fat 11.2g, of which saturates 1.3g; Cholesterol 10mg; Calcium 25mg; Fibre 0.4g; Sodium 190mg.
Chargrilled Meat Energy 245kcal/1019kJ; Protein 19g; Carbohydrate 4g, of which sugars 3.4g; Fat 17g, of which saturates 6g; Cholesterol 53mg; Calcium 23mg; Fibre 2.2g; Sodium 607mg.

Seared Garlic Beef

Flavoured with lots of garlic, tender chunks of beef are wrapped in lettuce leaves and dipped in a piquant lime sauce. Beef is well suited to searing, and this can be done in a pan, but also chargrilled if you prefer.

Serves 4

15ml/1 tbsp sugar
juice of 3 limes
2 garlic cloves, crushed
7.5ml/1½ tsp ground black pepper
30ml/2 tbsp unsalted roasted peanuts, finely chopped
350g/12oz beef fillet (tenderloin) or sirloin, cut into bitesize chunks
12 lettuce leaves

For the marinade

15ml/1 tbsp groundnut (peanut) oil
45ml/3 tbsp mushroom soy sauce
10ml/2 tsp soy sauce
15ml/1 tbsp sugar
2 garlic cloves, crushed
7.5ml/1½ tsp ground black pepper

1 To make the marinade, beat together the oil, the two soy sauces and the sugar in a bowl, until the sugar has dissolved. Add the garlic and pepper and mix well. Add the beef and coat in the marinade. Leave for 1–2 hours.

2 In a small bowl, stir the sugar into the lime juice, until it has dissolved. Add the garlic and black pepper and beat well. Stir in the peanuts and put aside.

3 Heat a wok or large, heavy frying pan and sear the meat on all sides. Serve immediately with lettuce leaves for wrapping and the lime and peanut sauce for dipping.

Balti Beef

There's no marinating with this simple recipe, which can be prepared and cooked in under an hour.

Serves 4

1 red (bell) pepper
1 green (bell) pepper
15ml/1 tbsp oil
5ml/1 tsp cumin seeds
2.5ml/½ tsp fennel seeds
1 onion, cut into thick wedges
1 garlic clove, crushed
2.5cm/1in piece fresh root ginger, finely chopped
1 fresh red chilli, finely chopped
15ml/1 tbsp curry paste
2.5ml/½ tsp salt
675g/1½lb lean rump (round) or fillet steak (beef tenderloin), cut into thick strips
naan bread, to serve

1 Cut the red and green peppers into 2.5cm/1in chunks.

2 Heat the oil in a karahi, wok or heavy frying pan and fry the cumin and fennel seeds for 2 minutes or until they begin to splutter. Add the onion, garlic, ginger and chilli and fry them for a further 5 minutes.

3 Stir in the curry paste and salt and fry for a 3–4 minutes.

4 Add the peppers to the pan and toss over the heat for about 5 minutes. Stir in the beef strips and continue to fry for 10–12 minutes or until the meat is tender. Serve from the pan, with warm naan bread.

Sizzling Beef with Celeriac Straws

The crisp celeriac matchsticks look like fine pieces of straw when stir-fried, and they have a mild celery-like flavour that is quite delicious.

Serves 4

450g/1lb celeriac
150ml/¼ pint/⅔ cup oil
1 red (bell) pepper
6 spring onions (scallions)
450g/1lb rump steak (round steak)
60ml/4 tbsp beef stock
30ml/2 tbsp sherry vinegar
10ml/2 tsp Worcestershire sauce
10ml/2 tsp tomato purée (paste)
salt and ground black pepper

1 Peel and slice the celeriac and then cut into fine slivers the size of matchsticks, using a cleaver.

2 Heat a wok, then add two-thirds of the oil. When the oil is hot, fry the celeriac matchsticks in batches until golden brown and crispy. Drain well on kitchen paper and keep warm.

3 Halve, core and seed the red pepper, then slice thinly diagonally into 2.5cm/1in lengths. Slice the spring onions into 2.5cm/1in lengths diagonally so that they match the pepper slices.

4 Using a cleaver or sharp knife, cut the steak into thin strips, cutting across the grain of the meat.

5 Heat the wok again and add the remaining oil. When the oil is hot, stir-fry the red pepper and spring onion for 2–3 minutes.

6 Add the beef strips and stir-fry for a further 3–4 minutes until browned. Add the stock, vinegar, Worcestershire sauce and tomato purée. Season to taste and serve with the celeriac matchsticks.

Cook's Tip

Avoid buying very large celeriac roots, as they tend to be woody in texture. They need to be peeled thickly to obtain a neat edge. Then cut the slices into thin strips. The flesh discolours quickly, so keep the slices in water acidulated with lemon juice.

Seared Garlic Beef Energy 237kcal/986kJ; Protein 21.9g; Carbohydrate 5.2g, of which sugars 4.7g; Fat 14.3g, of which saturates 4.3g; Cholesterol 51mg; Calcium 12mg; Fibre 0.5g; Sodium 324mg.
Balti Beef Energy 374kcal/1556kJ; Protein 39.7g; Carbohydrate 7.8g, of which sugars 6.2g; Fat 20.5g, of which saturates 7g; Cholesterol 98mg; Calcium 43mg; Fibre 2.5g; Sodium 129mg.
Sizzling Beef Energy 237kcal/994kJ; Protein 26.7g; Carbohydrate 9.3g, of which sugars 8.9g; Fat 10.7g, of which saturates 2.6g; Cholesterol 66mg; Calcium 74mg; Fibre 3.7g; Sodium 123mg.

Chilli Beef with Butternut

Stir-fried beef and sweet, orange-fleshed squash flavoured with warm spices, oyster sauce and fresh herbs makes a robust main course when served with rice or egg noodles.

Serves 4

30ml/2 tbsp sunflower oil
2 onions, cut into thick slices
500g/1¼lb butternut squash, peeled, seeded and cut into thin strips
675g/1½lb fillet steak (beef tenderloin)
60ml/4 tbsp soy sauce
90g/3½oz/½ cup golden caster (superfine) sugar
1 fresh bird's eye chilli or a milder red chilli, seeded and chopped
15ml/1 tbsp finely shredded fresh root ginger
30ml/2 tbsp fish sauce
5ml/1 tsp ground star anise
5ml/1 tsp five-spice powder
15ml/1 tbsp oyster sauce
4 spring onions (scallions), shredded
a small handful of sweet basil leaves
a small handful of mint leaves

1 Heat a wok over a medium heat and add the oil. Stir in the onions and squash. Stir-fry for 2–3 minutes, then reduce the heat, cover and cook for 5–6 minutes, or until the vegetables are just tender.

2 Place the beef between two sheets of clear film (plastic wrap) and beat, with a mallet or rolling pin, until thin. Using a sharp knife, cut into thin strips.

3 In a separate wok, mix the soy sauce, sugar, chilli, ginger, fish sauce, star anise, five-spice powder and oyster sauce. Cook for 3–4 minutes, stirring frequently.

4 Add the beef to the wok and cook over a high heat for 3–4 minutes. Remove from the heat. Add the onion and squash beef and toss well with the spring onions and herbs. Serve immediately.

Variations
- *This recipe would also work well with chicken breast fillet.*
- *You could add mangetouts (snow peas), trimmed and left whole, to the dish for added crunch. As they need only minimum cooking, add them for the last 5 minutes of cooking only.*

Beef and Chorizo Stew with Plantain

This stew is rich and very flavoursome from the Philippines, with a distinctive Spanish tang.

Serves 4–6

30ml/2 tbsp groundnut (peanut) or corn oil
1 onion, chopped
2 garlic cloves, chopped
40g/1½oz fresh root ginger, chopped
2 x 175g/6oz chorizo sausages, cut diagonally into bitesize pieces
700g/1lb 9oz lean rump (round) beef, cut into bitesize pieces
4 tomatoes, skinned, seeded and quartered
900ml/1½ pints/3¾ cups beef or chicken stock
2 plantains, sliced diagonally
2 x 400g/14oz cans chickpeas, rinsed and drained
salt and ground black pepper
1 small bunch fresh coriander (cilantro) leaves, roughly chopped, to garnish

To serve
corn oil, for deep-frying
1–2 firm bananas or 1 plantain, sliced diagonally
stir-fried greens

1 Heat the oil in a large, heavy pan or wok with a lid, stir in the onion, garlic and ginger and fry until they begin to brown. Add the chorizo and beef and fry until they begin to brown. Add the tomatoes and pour in the stock. Bring to the boil, then reduce the heat, cover and simmer gently for about 45 minutes.

2 Add the plantains and chickpeas to the stew and cook for a further 20–25 minutes, adding a little extra water if the cooking liquid reduces too much.

3 Meanwhile, heat enough corn oil for deep-frying in a wok or large pan. Deep-fry the bananas or plantain, in batches, for about 3 minutes, until crisp and golden brown. Remove the bananas or plantain from the pan using a slotted spoon, drain on kitchen paper then arrange in a serving dish.

4 Season the stew with salt and pepper to taste and sprinkle with chopped coriander leaves to garnish. Serve with the deep-fried bananas or plantain and stir-fried greens.

Chilli Beef Energy 500kcal/2093kJ; Protein 41.3g; Carbohydrate 36.9g, of which sugars 33.8g; Fat 21.7g, of which saturates 7.2g; Cholesterol 98mg; Calcium 91mg; Fibre 2.9g; Sodium 1243mg.
Beef and Chorizo Energy 583kcal/2441kJ; Protein 40.5g; Carbohydrate 35.8g, of which sugars 6.2g; Fat 31.9g, of which saturates 11.1g; Cholesterol 91mg; Calcium 104mg; Fibre 6.1g; Sodium 778mg.

Green Beef Curry

Use good-quality meat for this quick-cook curry. Sirloin steak is recommended, but tender rump steak could be used instead. If you buy the curry paste, there's very little additional preparation.

Serves 4–6

450g/1lb sirloin steak or rump (round) steak
15ml/1 tbsp vegetable or sunflower oil
45ml/3 tbsp green curry paste
600ml/1 pint/2½ cups coconut milk
4 kaffir lime leaves, torn
15–30ml/1–2 tbsp fish sauce
5ml/1 tsp palm sugar (jaggery) or light muscovado (brown) sugar
150g/5oz small Thai aubergines (eggplants), halved
small handful of fresh Thai basil leaves
2 fresh green chillies, finely shredded, to garnish

1 Trim off any excess fat from the beef. Using a sharp knife, cut it into long, thin strips. Set the beef strips aside on a plate.

2 Heat the oil in a wok or large, heavy pan. Add the curry paste to the pan and then cook for 1–2 minutes, until you can smell the fragrances and aroma.

3 Stir in half the coconut milk, a little at a time. Cook, stirring frequently, for about 5–6 minutes, until an oily sheen appears on the surface of the liquid.

4 Add the beef to the pan with the lime leaves, fish sauce, sugar and aubergine halves. Cook for 2–3 minutes, stirring so that the beef and aubergine are evenly coated with the coconut milk, then stir in the remaining coconut milk.

5 Bring back to a simmer and cook until the meat and aubergines are tender. Stir in the Thai basil just before serving. Garnish with the shredded green chillies.

Cook's Tip
It's easiest to slice the beef if you place it in the freezer for about 20 minutes to firm up first.

Beef Rendang with Coconut, Tamarind and Spices

Marinating beef cubes in an aromatic spice paste gives this dish a great flavour.

Serves 6

1kg/2¼lb beef topside (pot roast) or rump (round) steak, cubed
115g/4oz fresh coconut, grated, or desiccated (dry unsweetened)
15ml/1 tbsp tamarind pulp, soaked in 90ml/6 tbsp water until soft
45ml/3 tbsp vegetable or groundnut (peanut) oil
2 onions, halved and sliced
3 lemon grass stalks, trimmed, halved and bruised
2 cinnamon sticks
1.2 litres/2 pints/5 cups coconut milk
15ml/1 tbsp sugar
salt and ground black pepper
bread and salad, to serve

For the spice paste

8–10 dried red chillies, soaked in warm water until soft, seeded and squeezed dry
8 shallots, chopped
4–6 garlic cloves, chopped
50g/2oz fresh galangal, chopped
25g/1oz fresh turmeric, chopped
15ml/1 tbsp coriander seeds
10ml/2 tsp cumin seeds
5ml/1 tsp black peppercorns

1 For the spice paste, grind the soaked chillies, shallots, garlic, galangal and turmeric until smooth. In a small pan, dry-roast the seeds with the peppercorns, then grind to a powder and stir into the spice paste. Use to coat the beef. Marinate for 1 hour.

2 Next, dry-roast the grated coconut in a heavy pan. Tip into a food processor, grind until it resembles brown sugar and set aside. Squeeze the tamarind, then strain it to extract the juice.

3 Heat the oil in a wok and fry the onions, lemon grass and cinnamon sticks for 3–4 minutes. Add the beef with all the spice paste and stir-fry until lightly browned. Pour in the coconut milk and tamarind juice. Bring to the boil, stirring, then simmer until the sauce begins to thicken.

4 Stir in the sugar and the ground coconut, and simmer, stirring occasionally, until the meat is tender (this may take 2–4 hours, depending on the cut). Season and serve with bread and salad.

Green Beef Curry Energy 176kcal/738kJ; Protein 17.6g; Carbohydrate 6.2g, of which sugars 6.1g; Fat 9.2g, of which saturates 3.3g; Cholesterol 44mg; Calcium 36mg; Fibre 0.5g; Sodium 159mg.
Beef Rendang Energy 289kcal/1210kJ; Protein 30.2g; Carbohydrate 15.4g, of which sugars 8.6g; Fat 12.2g, of which saturates 5g; Cholesterol 73mg; Calcium 63mg; Fibre 1.4g; Sodium 465mg.

Szechuan Beef with Tofu

China's western province is famous for its spicy cuisine, full of strong flavours. The Szechuan peppercorns in this meat dish are not, in fact, peppercorns, but the dried berries of a type of ash tree. But, they do have a very peppery flavour.

Serves 4

200g/7oz/1 cup fragrant jasmine or basmati rice
30ml/2 tbsp groundnut (peanut) or soya oil
4 garlic cloves, finely chopped
600g/1lb 6oz beef rump (round) steak or fillet (tenderloin), cut into thin strips
500g/1¼lb firm tofu, drained and diced
1 head broccoli, coarsely chopped
90ml/6 tbsp soy sauce
pinch of sugar
juice of 1 lime
ground Szechuan peppercorns
sweet chilli sauce or another dipping sauce, to serve

1 Cook the rice in a large pan of salted boiling water until tender, following the instructions on the packet, then put the rice into a bowl and keep it hot.

2 Heat the oil in a large non-stick wok or frying pan, then add the garlic and stir-fry it for a few seconds until golden. Increase the heat to high, add the strips of steak and stir-fry them for 1–2 minutes to seal.

3 Add the tofu cubes and broccoli and stir-fry for a few seconds. Stir in the soy sauce, sugar, lime juice and ground Szechuan peppercorns, then stir-fry for about 2 minutes. Transfer to warm serving plates or bowls and serve immediately with the rice and chilli sauce or other sauce.

Cook's Tip

Tofu, also known as bean curd, is a form of vegetable protein based on soya beans. There are two basic types: soft or silken tofu, which has a very light texture, and firm tofu, which is the type used in the recipe above.

Simmered Beef and Vegetables

This one-pot dish is a family favourite in Japan. It is a good example of how a small amount of meat can be stretched with vegetables to make a tasty and nutritious low-fat meal.

Serves 4

250g/9oz lean fillet (beef tenderloin) or rump (round) steak, trimmed of fat and very thinly sliced
1 large onion
15ml/1 tbsp vegetable oil
450g/1lb small potatoes, halved then soaked in water
1 carrot, cut into 5mm/¼in rounds
45ml/3 tbsp frozen peas, thawed and blanched for 1 minute

For the seasonings
30ml/2 tbsp caster (superfine) sugar
75ml/5 tbsp shoyu
15ml/1 tbsp mirin (sweet rice wine)
15ml/1 tbsp sake or dry sherry

1 Cut the thinly sliced beef slices into 2cm/¾in wide strips, and slice the onion lengthways into 5mm/¼n pieces.

2 Heat the vegetable oil in a wok or pan and lightly fry the beef and onion slices. When the colour of the meat changes, drain the potatoes and add to the pan.

3 Once the potatoes are coated with the oil in the pan, add the carrot. Pour in just enough water to cover, then bring to the boil, skimming them a few times.

4 Boil the mixture in the pan vigorously for 2 minutes, then rearrange the ingredients so that the potatoes are placed underneath the beef and vegetables.

5 Reduce the heat to medium-low and add all the seasonings. Simmer for 20 minutes, partially covered, or until most of the liquid has evaporated.

6 Check if the potatoes are cooked through by piercing them with a knife. Add the peas and cook to heat through, then remove the pan from the heat. Serve the beef and vegetables immediately in four individual, warmed serving bowls.

Szechuan Beef Energy 646kcal/2694kJ; Protein 55g; Carbohydrate 46.9g, of which sugars 4.1g; Fat 26.2g, of which saturates 7.6g; Cholesterol 87mg; Calcium 731mg; Fibre 3.8g; Sodium 1714mg.
Simmered Beef Energy 276kcal/1160kJ; Protein 17.8g; Carbohydrate 31.5g, of which sugars 13.2g; Fat 9.2g, of which saturates 2.9g; Cholesterol 36mg; Calcium 28mg; Fibre 2.3g; Sodium 1394mg.

Chilli Beef with Basil

This is a dish for chilli lovers! It is very easy to prepare – all you need is a karahi or a wok.

Serves 2

about 90ml/6 tbsp vegetable oil
16–20 large fresh basil leaves
275g/10oz rump steak
30ml/2 tbsp Worcestershire sauce
5ml/1 tsp soft dark brown sugar
1 or 2 fresh red chillies, sliced into rings
3 garlic cloves, chopped
5ml/1 tsp chopped fresh root ginger
1 shallot, thinly sliced
30ml/2 tbsp finely chopped fresh basil leaves, plus extra to garnish
squeeze of lemon juice
salt and ground black pepper
rice, to serve

1 Heat the oil in a karahi or wok. Add the whole basil leaves to the pan and fry for about 1 minute until crisp and golden. Drain on kitchen paper. Remove the pan from the heat and pour off all but 30ml/2 tbsp of the oil.

2 Cut the steak across the grain into thin strips. Mix the Worcestershire sauce and sugar in a bowl. Add the beef, mix well, then cover and leave to marinate for about 30 minutes.

3 Reheat the oil until hot, add the chilli, garlic, ginger and shallot and stir-fry for 30 seconds. Add the beef and chopped basil, then stir-fry for about 3 minutes. Flavour with lemon juice, and add salt and pepper to taste.

4 Transfer the chilli beef to a warmed serving plate, sprinkle over the basil leaves to garnish and serve immediately with rice.

Cook's Tip

Although Worcestershire sauce is often thought of as archetypally English, it is actually based on an Indian recipe. Ingredients include molasses, anchovies, tamarind extract, garlic, lime and soy sauce. It was first bottled in Worcester, England.

Spicy Shredded Beef

The key to making this recipe is that the beef must be cut into very fine, evenly sized strips. This is easier to achieve if the piece of beef is placed in the freezer for 30 minutes until it is very firm before being sliced with a sharp knife.

Serves 2

225g/8oz rump (round) or fillet (tenderloin) beef steak
15ml/1 tbsp each light and dark soy sauce
15ml/1 tbsp medium-dry sherry or Chinese rice wine
5ml/1 tsp soft dark brown sugar or golden sugar
90ml/6 tbsp vegetable oil
1 large onion, thinly sliced
2.5cm/1in piece fresh root ginger, peeled and grated
1–2 carrots, cut into matchsticks
2–3 fresh or dried chillies, halved, seeded (optional) and chopped
salt and ground black pepper
fresh chives, to garnish

1 With a sharp knife or cleaver, slice the beef very thinly, then cut each slice into fine strips or shreds.

2 Mix together the light and dark soy sauces with the sherry and sugar in a bowl. Add the strips of beef and stir well to ensure they are evenly coated with the marinade.

3 Heat a wok and add half the oil. When it is hot, stir-fry the onion and ginger for 3–4 minutes, then transfer to a plate. Add the carrots, stir-fry for 3–4 minutes until slightly softened, then transfer to a plate and keep warm.

4 Heat the remaining oil in the wok, then quickly add the beef, with the marinade, followed by the chillies. Cook the beef over high heat for 2 minutes, stirring all the time.

5 Return the fried onion and ginger to the wok and stir-fry for 1 minute more. Season with salt and pepper to taste, cover and cook for 30 seconds.

6 Spoon the meat into two warmed bowls and add strips of the carrot. Garnish with fresh chives and serve immediately.

Chilli Beef with Basil Energy 494kcal/2049kJ; Protein 31.1g; Carbohydrate 5.7g, of which sugars 4.9g; Fat 38.7g, of which saturates 6.2g; Cholesterol 81mg; Calcium 17mg; Fibre 0.4g; Sodium 1152mg.
Spicy Shredded Beef Energy 532kcal/2207kJ; Protein 27.3g; Carbohydrate 19.3g, of which sugars 15.4g; Fat 38.1g, of which saturates 5.8g; Cholesterol 66mg; Calcium 59mg; Fibre 3.3g; Sodium 1154mg.

Stir-fried Beef with Sesame Sauce

Similar to stir-fried beef with saté, an Indonesian favourite, the spicy peanut sauce, this recipe has a deliciously rich, spicy and nutty flavour.

Serves 4

450g/1lb beef sirloin or fillet (tenderloin), cut into thin strips
15ml/1 tbsp groundnut (peanut) or sesame oil
2 garlic cloves, finely chopped
2 fresh red chillies, seeded and finely chopped
7.5ml/1½ tsp sugar
30ml/2 tbsp sesame paste
30–45ml/2–3 tbsp beef stock or water
sea salt and ground black pepper
red chilli strips, to garnish
1 lemon, cut into quarters, to serve

For the marinade

15ml/1 tbsp groundnut (peanut) oil
30ml/2 tbsp fish sauce
30ml/2 tbsp soy sauce

1 To prepare the marinade, mix the oil, fish sauce and soy sauce together in a small bowl. Toss in the beef, making sure it is well coated. Leave to marinate for 30 minutes.

2 Heat the groundnut or sesame oil in a wok. Add the garlic and chillies and cook until golden and fragrant for 1–2 minutes.

3 Stir in the sugar. Add the beef, tossing it in the wok to sear it.

4 Stir in the sesame paste and add enough stock or water to thin it down. Cook for 1–2 minutes, making sure that the beef is coated with the sauce.

5 Season the sauce with salt and pepper. Spoon into warmed bowls, garnish with chilli strips and serve with lemon wedges.

Variations
Chicken breast fillet or pork fillet can be used instead of beef, but extend the cooking time to ensure that the poultry or pork is fully cooked through. Serve chicken or pork with orange wedges instead of lemon.

Stir-fried Beef with Mushrooms

In Thailand this spicy dish is often made with just straw mushrooms, which are readily available fresh, but oyster mushrooms or shiitake mushrooms will make a good substitute and if you use a mixture, then the dish will be more interesting to eat.

Serves 4 to 6

450g/1lb rump (round) steak
30ml/2 tbsp soy sauce
15ml/1 tbsp cornflour (cornstarch)
45ml/3 tbsp vegetable or sunflower oil
15ml/1 tbsp chopped garlic
15ml/1 tbsp chopped fresh root ginger
225g/8oz/3¼ cups mixed mushrooms such as shiitake, oyster and straw
30ml/2 tbsp oyster sauce
5ml/1 tsp sugar
4 spring onions (scallions), cut into short lengths
ground black pepper
2 fresh red chillies, seeded and cut into strips, to garnish

1 Place the steak in the freezer for 30 minutes, until firm, then slice diagonally into long thin strips. Mix the soy sauce and cornflour in a bowl. Add the steak, turning to coat well, cover with clear film (plastic wrap) and leave to marinate for 1–2 hours.

2 Heat half the oil in a wok or large, heavy frying pan. Add the garlic and ginger and cook for 1–2 minutes, until fragrant. Drain the steak, add it to the wok or pan and stir well. Cook, stirring frequently, for 1–2 minutes, until the steak is browned all over and tender. Remove from the wok or pan and set aside.

3 Heat the remaining oil in the wok or pan. Add the shiitake, oyster and straw mushrooms. Stir-fry them over a medium heat until they are golden brown.

4 Return the steak to the wok and mix it with the mushrooms. Spoon in the oyster sauce and sugar, stir well, then add ground black pepper to taste. Toss over the heat until all the ingredients are thoroughly combined.

5 Stir in the spring onions. Tip the mixture on to a serving platter, garnish with the strips of red chilli and serve.

Beef with Sesame Energy 269kcal/1119kJ; Protein 26.2g; Carbohydrate 0g, of which sugars 0g; Fat 18.2g, of which saturates 5.2g; Cholesterol 65mg; Calcium 31mg; Fibre 0.3g; Sodium 73mg.
Beef with Mushrooms Energy 282kcal/1177kJ; Protein 25.4g; Carbohydrate 10.7g, of which sugars 3.4g; Fat 15.5g, of which saturates 4.2g; Cholesterol 69mg; Calcium 16mg; Fibre 0.8g; Sodium 697mg.

Tangerine Peel Beef

The tangerine, like the orange, is a fruit with auspicious meaning. Tangerine is one of the most widely used flavourings and is popular in Cantonese and Szechuan cooking.

Serves 4

350g/12oz sirloin or rump (round) steak
5ml/1 tsp bicarbonate of soda (baking soda)
10g/¼oz dried tangerine peel
15ml/1 tbsp vegetable oil
2 garlic cloves, crushed
30ml/2 tbsp sesame oil
5ml/1 tsp sugar
8 spring onions (scallions), cut in 5cm/2in pieces
30ml/2 tbsp water

1 Slice the steak into thin strips. Put the bicarbonate of soda into a shallow dish, moisten it with a little water, then add the beef strips. Using clean hands, rub the bicarbonate of soda into the meat. Cover and set aside for 10 minutes.

2 Meanwhile, soak the tangerine peel in a bowl of water. When it is soft, drain it and slice it into thin strips.

3 Heat the oil in a wok and fry the garlic for 40 seconds, until light brown. Do not let it burn. Add the beef. Stir-fry over high heat for 1 minute, then stir in the tangerine peel.

4 Add the sesame oil, sugar, spring onions and water. Stir-fry for 2 minutes or until the beef is cooked the way you like it. Spoon into a dish or individual bowls and serve.

Cantonese Beefsteak

This is a typical Hong Kong restaurant dish, which echoes western-style steak but which is cooked by the traditional Cantonese stir-fried method. The unusual ingredient here is Worcestershire sauce, very likely a British colonial touch. This imparts a subtle vinegar and pepper flavour to the dish.

Serves 4

600g/1lb 6oz sirloin or rump (round) steak
15ml/1 tbsp cornflour (cornstarch)
30ml/2 tbsp Chinese Mui Kwai Lo wine or sweet sherry
15ml/1 tbsp Worcestershire sauce
30ml/2 tbsp oyster sauce
45ml/3 tbsp oil
15ml/1 tbsp grated root ginger
2.5ml/½ tsp sugar
lettuce leaves, to serve

1 Slice the sirloin or rump steak thinly into medallions. Put the cornflour in a bowl. Add the steak and toss to coat.

2 In a small bowl, mix the wine or sherry, Worcestershire sauce and oyster sauce. Stir, then set aside.

3 Heat the oil in a wok or frying pan. Add the grated ginger and fry for 30 seconds. Add the beef. Stir-fry over high heat for 1 minute, then pour in the wine and sauce mixture. Stir-fry for 1 minute more, then sprinkle over the sugar.

4 Continue to stir for 2 minutes more for medium-rare, or 3 minutes for well-done beef. Serve on a bed of lettuce leaves.

Dry Beef Curry with Peanut and Lime

This spicy dry curry can be served with a moist dish such as a vegetable curry.

Serves 4 to 6

400g/14oz can coconut milk
900g/2lb stewing steak, cubed
300ml/½ pint/1¼ cups beef stock
30ml/2 tbsp crunchy peanut butter
juice of 2 limes, plus lime slices, chopped coriander (cilantro) and chilli slices, to garnish
boiled rice, to serve

For the red curry paste

30ml/2 tbsp coriander seeds
5ml/1 tsp cumin seeds
seeds from 6 cardamom pods
2.5ml/½ tsp grated nutmeg
1.5ml/¼ tsp ground cloves
2.5ml/½ tsp ground cinnamon
20ml/4 tsp paprika
pared rind of 1 mandarin orange, finely chopped
4–5 small fresh red chillies, seeded and finely chopped
25ml/5 tsp sugar
2.5ml/½ tsp salt
1 piece lemon grass, shredded
3 garlic cloves, crushed
2cm/¾in piece fresh galangal, peeled and finely chopped
4 red shallots, finely chopped
2cm/¾in piece shrimp paste
50g/2oz coriander (cilantro) root or stem, chopped
juice of ½ lime
30ml/2 tbsp vegetable oil

1 Strain the coconut milk into a bowl, retaining the thicker coconut milk in the sieve (strainer). Pour the thin milk into a wok or large pan, then scrape in half the residue from the sieve. Reserve the remaining thick milk. Add the steak and the stock and bring to the boil, then simmer, covered, for 50 minutes.

2 Make the paste. Dry-fry all the seeds for 1–2 minutes. Transfer into a bowl and add the nutmeg, cloves, cinnamon, paprika and orange rind. Pound the chillies with the sugar and salt. Add the spice mixture, lemon grass, garlic, galangal, shallots and shrimp paste and pound. Mix in the coriander, lime juice and oil.

3 Strain the beef, and place a cupful of the cooking liquid in a wok. Stir in 30–45ml/2–3 tbsp of the paste. Boil until the liquid has evaporated. Stir in the reserved thick coconut milk, the peanut butter and beef. Simmer, uncovered, for 15–20 minutes.

4 Before serving, stir in the lime juice. Serve in bowls over rice, garnished with the lime slices, coriander and sliced red chillies.

Tangerine Peel Beef Energy 242kcal/1005kJ; Protein 20.3g; Carbohydrate 3.1g, of which sugars 3.1g; Fat 16.5g, of which saturates 4.5g; Cholesterol 51mg; Calcium 17mg; Fibre 0.4g; Sodium 65mg.
Cantonese Beefsteak Energy 365kcal/1518kJ; Protein 34.2g; Carbohydrate 5g, of which sugars 1.5g; Fat 22.2g, of which saturates 6.7g; Cholesterol 87mg; Calcium 17mg; Fibre 0g; Sodium 322mg.
Dry Beef Curry Energy 406kcal/1703kJ; Protein 55.4g; Carbohydrate 6.4g, of which sugars 5.9g; Fat 18g, of which saturates 5.1g; Cholesterol 170mg; Calcium 92mg; Fibre 0.6g; Sodium 812mg.

Madras Beef Curry

Madras, now known as Chennai, on the Coromandel Coast off the Bay of Bengal, is renowned for the best vegetarian food in India. However, meat-based recipes such as this classic beef curry are also extremely popular there.

Serves 4–6

60ml/4 tbsp vegetable oil
1 large onion, finely sliced
3 or 4 cloves
4 green cardamom pods
2 whole star anise
4 fresh green chillies, chopped
2 fresh or dried red chillies, chopped
45ml/3 tbsp Madras masala paste
5ml/1 tsp ground turmeric
450g/1lb lean beef, cubed
60ml/4 tbsp tamarind juice
granulated sugar, to taste
salt
a few fresh coriander (cilantro) leaves, chopped, to garnish
pilau rice and tomato and onion salad, to serve

1 Heat a karahi, wok or large pan over a medium heat. Add the vegetable oil and swirl it round the pan. Fry the onion slices for about 8 minutes until they turn golden brown.

2 Lower the heat, add all the spice ingredients to the pan, and fry for a further 2–3 minutes.

3 Add the cubed beef and mix well with the spices. Cover and cook over a low heat for 3–4 minutes until the beef is tender and fully cooked. Cook uncovered on a higher heat for the last few minutes to reduce any excess liquid.

4 Fold in the tamarind juice, sugar and salt.

5 Reheat the dish and garnish with the chopped coriander leaves. Serve the curry with pilau rice and a tomato and onion salad.

Cook's Tip

To tenderize the meat, add 60ml/4 tbsp white wine vinegar in step 2 along with the meat, and omit the tamarind juice.

Beef Stew with Star Anise and Chilli Spices

The Vietnamese eat this dish for breakfast, and on chilly mornings people queue up for a steaming bowl of this spicy stew on their way to work. In southern Vietnam, it is often served with chunks of baguette, but in other regions it is served with noodles. For the midday or evening meal, it is served with steamed or sticky rice. Traditionally, it has an orange hue from the oil in which annatto seeds have been fried, but in this recipe the colour comes from the turmeric.

Serves 4 to 6

500g/1¼lb lean beef, cut into bitesize cubes
10–15ml/2–3 tsp ground turmeric
30ml/2 tbsp sesame or vegetable oil
3 shallots, chopped
3 garlic cloves, chopped
2 red chillies, seeded and chopped
2 lemon grass stalks, cut into several pieces and bruised
15ml/1 tbsp curry powder
4 star anise, roasted and ground to a powder
700ml/scant 1¼ pints hot beef or chicken stock, or boiling water
45ml/3 tbsp Thai fish sauce
30ml/2 tbsp soy sauce
15ml/1 tbsp raw cane sugar
1 bunch of fresh basil, stalks removed
salt and ground black pepper
1 onion, halved and finely sliced, and chopped fresh coriander (cilantro) or leaves, to garnish

1 Toss the beef in the ground turmeric and set aside. Heat a wok or heavy pan and add the oil. Stir in the shallots, garlic, chillies and lemon grass, and cook until they become fragrant.

2 Add the curry powder and all but 10ml/2 tsp of the roasted star anise, followed by the beef. Brown the beef a little, then pour in the stock or water, the fish sauce, soy sauce and sugar. Stir well and bring to the boil. Reduce the heat and simmer for 40 minutes, or until the meat is tender and the liquid has reduced.

3 Season to taste with salt and pepper, stir in the reserved roasted star anise, and add the basil. Transfer the stew to a serving dish and garnish with the onion and coriander leaves.

Madras Beef Curry Energy 524kcal/2180kJ; Protein 37.6g; Carbohydrate 13.8g, of which sugars 7.4g; Fat 36g, of which saturates 13.8g; Cholesterol 133mg; Calcium 65mg; Fibre 2.6g; Sodium 160mg.
Beef Stew Energy 314kcal/1312kJ; Protein 33g; Carbohydrate 17g, of which sugars 11g; Fat 14g, of which saturates 4g; Cholesterol 64mg; Calcium 64mg; Fibre 1.7g; Sodium 1500mg

Pickled Beef with Tamarind and Galangal

In many parts of Indonesia, beef has traditionally come from water buffalo. Today, with imported meat from Australia and New Zealand, Indonesians use the kind of beef you would find in any supermarket. Cheaper beef cuts and buffalo meat, which is often tough, become deliciously tender using the long-cooking styles of Indonesian dishes.

Serves 4

450g/1lb stewing steak
500ml/17fl oz/2 cups water
25g/1oz galangal
45ml/3 tbsp vegetable oil
5ml/1 tsp salt
5ml/1 tsp sugar
5ml/1 tsp ground black pepper
30ml/2 tbsp tamarind concentrate
prawn crackers, to serve

1 Cut the beef into finger-length pieces, about 1.5cm/½in thick. Put it in a wok or pan with the water and bring to the boil. Cook until almost dry. This should take about 20–25 minutes.

2 Grind the galangal with a pestle and mortar until fine.

3 Heat a wok or heavy pan. Add the vegetable oil to the pan and fry the galangal for 1 minute. Add the boiled beef, salt, sugar and pepper, and stir-fry over a medium heat until the flavours are well incorporated, for about 1 minute.

4 Add the tamarind concentrate to the pan and continue to fry the ingredients until the tamarind is nearly dry and the beef is fork tender. Serve the pickled beef as part of a main meal, or as finger food with some prawn crackers.

Cook's Tip

Galangal is a rhizome, like ginger. There are two types: greater galangal, which comes from Indonesia, while lesser galangal is a native of southern China. The latter, used here, has a pungent flavour, like a cross between ginger and black pepper.

Venison with Lentils and Tomatoes

Venison curries well and tastes good in this simple dish. Serve it with pilau rice, naan bread or bhaturas.

Serves 4

60ml/4 tbsp corn oil
1 bay leaf
2 cloves
4 black peppercorns
1 medium onion, sliced
450g/1lb diced venison
2.5ml/½ tsp ground turmeric
7.5ml/1½ tsp chilli powder
5ml/1 tsp garam masala
5ml/1 tsp crushed coriander seeds
2.5cm/1in cinnamon stick
5ml/1 tsp crushed garlic
5ml/1 tsp grated fresh root ginger
7.5ml/1½ tsp salt
1.5 litres/2½ pints/6 cups water
50g/2oz/⅓ cup split red lentils
2 medium tomatoes, quartered
2 fresh green chillies, chopped
15ml/1 tbsp chopped fresh coriander (cilantro)

1 Heat the oil in a karahi, wok or deep pan. Lower the heat slightly and add the bay leaf, cloves, peppercorns and onion slices. Fry for about 5 minutes, or until the onions are golden brown, stirring occasionally.

2 Add the diced venison, turmeric, chilli powder, garam masala, coriander seeds, cinnamon stick, garlic, ginger and most of the salt, and stir-fry for about 5 minutes over a medium heat.

3 Pour 900ml/1½ pints/3¾ cups of the water into the pan and cover the pan with a lid. Simmer the venison over a low heat for about 35–40 minutes, or until the water has evaporated and the meat is tender.

4 Put the lentils into a pan with the remaining 600ml/1 pint/2½ cups water and boil for about 12–15 minutes, or until the water has almost evaporated and the lentils are soft enough to mash. If the lentils are too thick, add up to 150ml/¼ pint/⅔ cup more water to loosen the mixture.

5 When the meat is tender, stir-fry the mixture using a wooden spoon, until some free oil begins to appear on the sides of the pan. Add the cooked lentils to the venison and mix together well. Add the tomatoes, chillies and fresh coriander and serve.

Tamarind Pickled Beef Energy 279kcal/1158kJ; Protein 25.6g; Carbohydrate 1.9g, of which sugars 1.9g; Fat 18.7g, of which saturates 5.3g; Cholesterol 65mg; Calcium 8mg; Fibre 0g; Sodium 564mg.
Venison with Lentils and Tomato Energy 321kcal/1348kJ; Protein 29g; Carbohydrate 14.6g, of which sugars 3g; Fat 15.5g, of which saturates 1.9g; Cholesterol 0mg; Calcium 0.3mg; Fibre 1.6g.

Spiced Scallops and Sugar Snap Peas

Scallops are always popular, and this is a quick and easy dish that is certain to impress your guests for a very special party.

Serves 4

45ml/3 tbsp oyster sauce
10ml/2 tsp soy sauce
5ml/1 tsp sesame oil
5ml/1 tsp golden caster (superfine) sugar
30ml/2 tbsp sunflower oil
2 fresh red chillies, finely sliced
4 garlic cloves, finely chopped
10ml/2 tsp finely chopped fresh root ginger
250g/9oz sugar snap peas, trimmed
500g/1¼lb king scallops, cleaned and halved, roes discarded
3 spring onions (scallions), finely shredded

For the noodle cakes

250g/9oz fresh thin egg noodles
10ml/2 tsp sesame oil
120ml/4fl oz/½ cup sunflower oil

1 Prepare the noodle cakes. Cook the fresh egg noodles in boiling water until tender. Drain, toss them with the sesame oil and 15ml/1 tbsp of the sunflower oil and spread out on a large baking sheet. Leave to dry in a warm place for 1 hour.

2 Heat 15ml/1 tbsp of the oil in a wok. Add a quarter of the noodle mixture, flatten it and shape it into a cake.

3 Cook the cake for about 5 minutes on each side until crisp and golden. Drain on kitchen paper and keep hot while you make the remaining three noodle cakes in the same way.

4 Mix the oyster sauce, soy sauce, sesame oil and sugar, stirring until the sugar has dissolved completely.

5 Heat a wok, add the sunflower oil, then stir-fry the chillies, garlic, ginger and sugar snaps for 1–2 minutes. Add the scallops and spring onions and stir-fry for 1 minute, then add the sauce mixture and cook for 1 minute.

6 Place a noodle cake on each plate, top with the scallop mixture from the wok and serve immediately.

Herb and Chilli-seared Scallops

Tender, succulent scallops taste simply divine when marinated in fresh chilli, fragrant mint and aromatic basil, then quickly seared in a piping hot wok. If you can't find king scallops for this recipe, use twice the quantity of smaller queen scallops or use a mixture of prawns and scallops.

Serves 4

20–24 king scallops
120ml/4fl oz/¾ cup olive oil
finely grated rind and juice of 1 lemon
30ml/2 tbsp finely chopped mixed fresh mint and basil
1 fresh red chilli, seeded and finely chopped
salt and ground black pepper
500g/1¼lb pak choi (bok choy)

1 Rinse the king scallops thoroughly in cold water. Place them in a shallow, non-metallic bowl in a single layer.

2 In a clean bowl, mix together half the olive oil, the lemon rind and juice, chopped herbs and chilli, and spoon over the scallops. Season well with salt and black pepper, cover and set aside.

3 Using a sharp knife, cut each pak choi lengthways into four pieces. Place on a plate and set aside.

4 Heat a wok over a high heat. When hot, drain the scallops (reserving the marinade) and add to the wok. Cook for 1 minute on each side, or until cooked to your liking. Don't overcook the scallops or they will toughen.

5 Pour the marinade over the scallops and remove the wok from the heat. Transfer the scallops and juices to a platter and keep warm. Wipe out the wok with a piece of kitchen paper.

6 Place the wok over a high heat. When all traces of moisture have evaporated, add the remaining olive oil. When the oil is hot, add the pak choi to the wok and stir-fry over a high heat for 2–3 minutes, until the leaves wilt.

7 Divide the greens among four warmed serving plates, then top with the reserved scallops. Spoon the lemon, herb and chilli pan juices over the scallops and serve immediately.

Spiced Scallops Energy 689kcal/2888kJ; Protein 41.4g; Carbohydrate 59.9g, of which sugars 6.2g; Fat 33.3g, of which saturates 5.4g; Cholesterol 78mg; Calcium 73mg; Fibre 5g; Sodium 700mg.
Chilli-seared Scallops Energy 410Kcal/1714kJ; Protein 44.5g; Carbohydrate 8.3g, of which sugars 2.1g; Fat 22.3g, of which saturates 3.5g; Cholesterol 82mg; Calcium 286mg; Fibre 3.2g; Sodium 494mg.

Scallops with Cucumber and Ginger Relish

Buy scallops in their shells to ensure their freshness; your fishmonger will open them for you if you find this difficult. The shells make excellent serving dishes.

Serves 4

8 king or queen scallops
4 whole star anise
30ml/2 tbsp vegetable oil
salt and ground white pepper
fresh coriander (cilantro) sprigs and whole star anise, to garnish

For the relish
½ cucumber, peeled
salt, for sprinkling
5cm/2in piece fresh root ginger, peeled and sliced into thin strips
10ml/2 tsp caster (superfine) sugar
45ml/3 tbsp rice wine vinegar or sherry
10ml/2 tsp syrup from a jar of preserved stem ginger
5ml/1 tsp sesame seeds, for sprinkling

1 To make the relish, halve the cucumber lengthways, remove the seeds, then slice the cucumber into a colander and sprinkle liberally with salt. Set aside to drain for 30 minutes.

2 To prepare the scallops, rinse them well in cold water, separate the corals and then cut each scallop into 2–3 slices and place with the corals in a bowl. Grind the star anise coarsely using a mortar and pestle and add to the scallops with the seasoning. Cover the bowl and marinate in the refrigerator for about 1 hour.

3 Rinse the cucumber under cold water, then drain and pat dry with kitchen paper. Place in a bowl with the ginger, sugar, rice wine vinegar and syrup. Mix well, then cover with clear film (plastic wrap) and chill until the relish is needed.

4 Heat a wok and add the oil. When the oil is very hot, add the scallop slices and corals and stir-fry for 2–3 minutes. Place the cooked scallops on kitchen paper to drain off any excess oil.

5 Garnish the cooked scallops with sprigs of fresh coriander and whole star anise, and serve them with the cucumber relish, sprinkled lightly with sesame seeds.

Steamed Scallops with Ginger

It helps to have two woks when making this dish. Borrow an extra one from a friend, or use a large, heavy pan with a trivet for steaming the second plate of scallops. Take care not to overcook the tender seafood.

Serves 4

24 king scallops in their shells, cleaned
15ml/1 tbsp very finely shredded fresh root ginger
5ml/1 tsp very finely chopped garlic or garlic purée
1 large fresh red chilli, seeded and very finely chopped
15ml/1 tbsp light soy sauce
15ml/1 tbsp Chinese rice wine or sherry
a few drops of sesame oil
2–3 spring onions (scallions), very finely shredded
15ml/1 tbsp very finely chopped fresh chives
steamed rice or freshly cooked noodles, to serve

1 Remove the scallops from their shells, then remove the membrane and hard white muscle from each one. Arrange the scallops on two plates. Rinse the shells, dry and set aside.

2 Fill two woks with 5cm/2in water and place a trivet in the base of each one. Bring to the boil.

3 Meanwhile, mix together the ginger, garlic, chilli, soy sauce, rice wine, sesame oil, spring onions and chives.

4 Spoon the flavourings over the scallops and allow to marinade for 10 minutes. Lower a plate into each of the woks. Turn the heat to low, cover and steam for 10–12 minutes.

5 Divide the scallops among four, or eight, of the reserved shells and serve immediately with noodles or rice.

Cook's Tip
Use the freshest scallops you can find. If you ask your fishmonger to shuck them, remember to ask for the shells so that you can use them as serving dishes.

Scallops with Cucumber Energy 130kcal/542kJ; Protein 12.1g; Carbohydrate 4.9g, of which sugars 3.2g; Fat 7g, of which saturates 1g; Cholesterol 24mg; Calcium 31mg; Fibre 0.3g; Sodium 92mg.
Scallops with Ginger Energy 392kcal/1621kJ; Protein 13.6g; Carbohydrate 4.5g, of which sugars 2.5g; Fat 34.1g, of which saturates 22.4g; Cholesterol 115mg; Calcium 63mg; Fibre 0.4g; Sodium 168mg.

Stir-fried Prawns with Broccoli

This is a very colourful dish, highly nutritious and at the same time extremely delicious; furthermore, it is not time-consuming or difficult to prepare.

Serves 4

175–225g/6–8oz prawns (shrimp), shelled and deveined
5ml/1 tsp cornflour (cornstarch)
5ml/1 tsp salt
15ml/1 tbsp Chinese rice wine
½ egg white
225g/8oz broccoli head
about 300ml/½ pint/1¼ cups oil
1 spring onion (scallion), cut into short sections
5ml/1 tsp soft light brown sugar
about 30ml/2 tbsp stock or water
5ml/1 tsp light soy sauce
few drops sesame oil

1 Cut each prawn in half lengthways. Mix the cornflour to a paste with 10ml/2 tsp cold water and stir into the prawns with a pinch of salt, about 5ml/1 tsp of the rice wine and the egg white.

2 Cut the stalk off the broccoli head with a sharp knife. Make sure that you cut high enough so that large individual florets fall away as you cut. Divide the broccoli head into florets; remove the rough skin from the stalks, then slice the florets diagonally into diamond-shaped chunks.

3 Heat the oil in a wok and stir-fry the prawns for about 30 seconds. Remove with a slotted spoon and drain thoroughly.

4 Pour off the excess oil, leaving 30ml/2 tbsp in the wok. Add the broccoli and spring onion, stir-fry for about 2 minutes, then add the remaining salt and the sugar, followed by the prawns and stock or water. Add the soy sauce and remaining rice wine or sherry. Blend well, then finally add the sesame oil and serve.

Cook's Tip

When buying shell-on prawns (shrimp), buy twice the weight you would if you were buying shelled prawns. To prepare the prawns, grip the body in one hand and twist off the head with the other. Turn the prawn over and pull the shell open, working from the head downwards to pull the prawn free. Discard the head and shell.

Quick-fried Prawns with Spices

These spicy prawns are stir-fried in moments to make a wonderful appetizer. This is fabulous finger food, so be sure to provide your guests with finger bowls of warm water.

Serves 4

450g/1lb large raw prawns (shrimp), unshelled
5ml/1 tsp hot chilli powder
2.5cm/1in fresh root ginger, peeled and grated
2 garlic cloves, peeled and crushed
5ml/1 tsp ground turmeric
10ml/2 tsp black mustard seeds
seeds from 4 green cardamom pods, crushed
50g/2oz/¼ cup ghee or butter
120ml/4fl oz/½ cup coconut milk
salt and ground black pepper
30–45ml/2–3 tbsp chopped fresh coriander (cilantro), to garnish
naan bread, to serve

1 Peel the raw prawns carefully, leaving the tails attached. Twist off the prawns' heads, and pull the shells open, then discard the head and the shell.

2 Using a small, sharp knife, make a slit along the back of each prawn and remove the dark vein. Rinse the prawn under cold running water, drain and pat dry on kitchen paper.

3 Put the chilli powder, ginger, garlic, turmeric, mustard seeds and cardamom seeds in a bowl. Add the prawns and toss to coat them completely in the spice mixture.

4 Heat a karahi, wok or large frying pan until it is hot. Add the ghee or butter and swirl it around until foaming.

5 Add the spiced prawns to the pan and stir-fry them for 1–1½ minutes until they are just turning pink.

6 Add the coconut milk to the pan, stir well, and simmer the mixture for 3–4 minutes until the prawns are just cooked through. Season to taste with salt and black pepper.

7 Sprinkle the prawns with the chopped fresh coriander and serve immediately, in a large dish, with naan bread.

Stir-fried Prawns Energy 160kcal/673kJ; Protein 22.8g; Carbohydrate 5.9g, of which sugars 3.6g; Fat 4.7g, of which saturates 0.6g; Cholesterol 189mg; Calcium 97mg; Fibre 1.3g; Sodium 454mg.
Quick-fried Prawns Energy 388kcal/1618kJ; Protein 40.7g; Carbohydrate 5.1g, of which sugars 3.1g; Fat 22.9g, of which saturates 13.4g; Cholesterol 492mg; Calcium 248mg; Fibre 1.7g; Sodium 679mg

Fragrant Tiger Prawns with Dill

This elegant dish has a fresh, light flavour and is equally good served as a simple supper or for a dinner party. It takes only minutes to make, so you can spend more time with your guests. The delicate texture of fresh prawns goes really well with mild cucumber and fragrant dill, and all you need is some rice or noodles to serve.

Serves 4–6

500g/1¼lb raw tiger prawns (jumbo shrimp), heads and shells removed but tails left on
500g/1¼lb cucumber
30ml/2 tbsp butter
15ml/1 tbsp olive oil
15ml/1 tbsp finely chopped garlic
45ml/3 tbsp chopped fresh dill
juice of 1 lemon
salt and ground black pepper
steamed rice or noodles, to serve

1 Using a small, sharp knife, carefully make a shallow slit along the back of each prawn and use the point of the knife to remove the black vein. Set the prawns aside.

2 Peel the cucumber and slice in half lengthways. Using a small teaspoon, gently scoop out all the seeds and discard. Cut the cucumber into 4 x 1cm/1½ x ½in sticks.

3 Heat a wok over a high heat, then add the butter and oil. When the butter has melted, add the cucumber and garlic and fry over a high heat for 2–3 minutes, stirring continuously.

4 Add the prepared prawns to the wok and continue to stir-fry over a high heat for 3–4 minutes, or until the prawns turn pink and are just cooked through, then remove from the heat.

5 Add the fresh dill and lemon juice to the wok and toss to combine. Season well with salt and ground black pepper and serve immediately with steamed rice or noodles.

Cook's Tip

The best rice to use is jasmine rice, which is also known as Thai fragrant rice. Jasmine rice is long-grained and has a nutty flavour. It is less sticky than some other rices.

Prawns with Tamarind

The sour, tangy flavour that is characteristic of many Asian dishes comes from tamarind. Fresh tamarind pods can sometimes be bought, but preparing them is a laborious process. It is much easier to use ready-made tamarind paste, which is available in many Asian supermarkets.

Serves 4–6

6 dried red chillies
30ml/2 tbsp vegetable oil
30ml/2 tbsp chopped onion
30ml/2 tbsp palm sugar (jaggery) or light muscovado (brown) sugar
30ml/2 tbsp chicken or fish stock
15ml/1 tbsp fish sauce
90ml/6 tbsp tamarind juice, made by mixing tamarind paste with warm water
450g/1lb raw prawns (shrimp), peeled
15ml/1 tbsp fried chopped garlic
30ml/2 tbsp fried sliced shallots
2 spring onions (scallions), chopped, to garnish (optional)

1 Heat a karahi, wok or a large frying pan, but do not add any oil at this stage. Add the dried chillies to the pan and dry-fry them by pressing them against the surface of the pan with a spatula, turning them occasionally. Remove the chillies.

2 Add the oil to the wok or pan and reheat. Cook the chopped onion over a medium heat, stirring occasionally, for 2–3 minutes, until softened and golden brown.

3 Add the sugar, stock, fish sauce, dry-fried red chillies and the tamarind juice, stirring constantly until the sugar has dissolved. Bring to the boil, then lower the heat slightly.

4 Add the prawns, garlic and shallots to the pan. Toss over the heat for 3–4 minutes until the prawns are cooked through. Garnish with the spring onions, if liked, and serve.

Cook's Tip

The thickness and strength of tamarind paste varies widely depending on which brand you use. If it is a runny paste, you will need to add more in order to achieve the right flavour.

Fragrant Prawns Energy 192Kcal/798kJ; Protein 23.2g; Carbohydrate 2.5g, of which sugars 1.9g; Fat 9.8g, of which saturates 4.4g; Cholesterol 260mg; Calcium 123mg; Fibre 0.9g; Sodium 287mg.
Prawns with Tamarind Energy 112kcal/469kJ; Protein 13.4g; Carbohydrate 5.5g, of which sugars 5.2g; Fat 4.1g, of which saturates 0.5g; Cholesterol 146mg; Calcium 65mg; Fibre 0.2g; Sodium 321mg.

Yellow Prawn Curry

Colour is an important part of Indonesian food and the word *udang*, meaning 'yellow', is used to describe this delicious and attractive prawn dish. Big, juicy prawns are particularly favoured in Bali and Java, but you can easily substitute them with scallops, squid or mussels, or a combination of all three, depending on what you have available.

Serves 4

30ml/2 tbsp coconut or palm oil
2 shallots, finely chopped
2 garlic cloves, finely chopped
2 red chillies, seeded and finely chopped
25g/1oz fresh turmeric, finely chopped, or 10ml/2 tsp ground turmeric
25g/1oz fresh root ginger, finely chopped
2 lemon grass stalks, finely sliced
10ml/2 tsp coriander seeds
10ml/2 tsp shrimp paste
1 red (bell) pepper, seeded and finely sliced
4 kaffir lime leaves
about 500g/1¼lb fresh prawns (shrimp), shelled and deveined
400g/14oz can coconut milk
salt and ground black pepper
1 green chilli, seeded and sliced, to garnish

To serve

cooked rice
4 fried shallots or fresh chillies, seeded and sliced lengthways

1 Preheat the wok or a large, heavy frying pan, and then add the oil. Stir in the shallots, garlic, chillies, turmeric, ginger, lemon grass and coriander seeds and fry until fragrant.

2 Add the shrimp paste to the pan, stir well, and then cook the mixture for about 2–3 minutes. Add the red pepper and lime leaves and stir-fry for a further minute.

3 Add the prawns to the pan. Pour in the coconut milk, stirring to combine, and bring to the boil. Cook for 5–6 minutes until the prawns are cooked. Season with salt and pepper to taste.

4 Spoon the prawns on to a warmed serving dish and sprinkle with the sliced green chillies to garnish. Serve with rice and fried shallots or the fresh chillies on the side.

Prawn and Cauliflower Curry with Fenugreek and Star Anise

This is a basic fisherman's curry from the southern coast of Vietnam. Simple to make, it would usually be eaten with noodles, rice or chunks of baguette to mop up the deliciously fragrant, creamy sauce. Fenugreek seeds, which are much used in Indian cookery, have a distinctive curry aroma, brought out by dry frying.

Serves 4

450g/1lb raw tiger prawns (jumbo shrimp), shelled and deveined
juice of 1 lime
15ml/1 tbsp sesame or vegetable oil
1 red onion, roughly chopped
2 garlic cloves, roughly chopped
2 Thai chillies, seeded and chopped
1 cauliflower, broken into florets
5ml/1 tsp sugar
2 star anise, dry fried and ground
10ml/2 tsp fenugreek, dry fried and ground
450ml/¾ pint/scant 2 cups coconut milk
salt and ground black pepper
1 bunch fresh coriander (cilantro), stalks removed, leaves chopped, to garnish

1 In a large glass bowl, toss the prawns in the lime juice and set them aside. Heat a large wok or heavy pan and add the oil. When the oil is hot, stir in the onion, garlic and chillies. As they brown, add the cauliflower. Stir-fry for 2–3 minutes.

2 Toss in the sugar and spices. Add the coconut milk to the pan, stirring to make sure it is thoroughly combined. Reduce the heat and simmer for 10–15 minutes, or until the liquid has reduced and thickened a little.

3 Add the prawns and lime juice to the pan and cook for about 1–2 minutes, or until the prawns turn opaque. Season the dish to taste, and sprinkle with coriander. Serve immediately.

Variations
Other popular combinations you may like to try include prawns (shrimp) with butternut squash or pumpkin.

Yellow Prawn Curry Energy 230kcal/965kJ; Protein 26.4g; Carbohydrate 16g, of which sugars 13.5g; Fat 7.2g, of which saturates 1g; Cholesterol 263mg; Calcium 226mg; Fibre 2.7g; Sodium 519mg.
Prawn and Cauliflower Energy 232Kcal/971kJ; Protein 25g; Carbohydrate 13g, of which sugars 12g; Fat 10g, of which saturates 2g; Cholesterol 219mg; Calcium 167mg; Fibre 2.2g; Sodium 500mg

Chilli and Coconut Prawns

Supply plenty of bread or rice when serving these superb prawns. The sauce is so tasty that diners will want to savour every last drop. Be warned, though, the chilli makes these fiery, even though tamarind has a taming influence.

Serves 4

8 shallots, chopped
4 garlic cloves, chopped
8–10 dried red chillies, soaked in warm water until soft, squeezed dry, seeded and chopped
5ml/1 tsp shrimp paste
30ml/2 tbsp vegetable or groundnut (peanut) oil
250ml/8fl oz/1 cup coconut cream
500g/1¼lb fresh prawns (shrimp), peeled and deveined
10ml/2 tsp tamarind paste
15ml/1 tbsp palm sugar (jaggery)
salt and ground black pepper
2 fresh red chillies, seeded and finely chopped, and fresh coriander (cilantro) leaves, finely chopped, to garnish
crusty bread or steamed rice and pickles, to serve

1 Using a mortar and pestle or food processor, grind the chopped shallots and garlic and the dried red chillies to a coarse paste. Beat in the shrimp paste.

2 Heat the oil in a wok and stir in the paste until fragrant. Add the coconut cream and let it bubble up until it separates. Toss in the prawns, reduce the heat and simmer for 3 minutes.

3 Stir in the tamarind paste and the sugar and cook for a further 2 minutes until the sauce is very thick.

4 Season the prawn mixture with salt and pepper and then scatter the chopped chillies and coriander over the top. Serve immediately with chunks of fresh, crusty bread to mop up the sauce, or with steamed rice and pickles.

Cook's Tip

Tamarind used to be an exotic ingredient, available only as pods which needed to be processed before use. Fortunately the paste is now an item stocked in many supermarkets.

Goan Prawn Curry with Mango and Coconut Milk

This sweet and spicy hot-and-sour curry comes from the shores of Western India. It is simple to make, and the addition of mango and tamarind produces a very full, rich flavour. If you have time, make this dish the day before to give the flavours time to develop. Simply reheat to serve.

Serves 4

5ml/1 tsp hot chilli powder
15ml/1 tbsp paprika
2.5ml/½ tsp turmeric
4 garlic cloves, crushed
10ml/2 tsp finely grated fresh root ginger
30ml/2 tbsp ground coriander
10ml/2 tsp ground cumin
15ml/1 tbsp palm sugar (jaggery)
1 green mango, sliced and stoned
400g/14oz can coconut milk
10ml/2 tsp salt
15ml/1 tbsp tamarind paste
1kg/2¼lb large prawns (shrimp), heads and tails on
chopped coriander (cilantro), to garnish
steamed white rice, to serve
chopped tomato, cucumber and onion salad, to serve

1 In a large bowl, combine the chilli powder, paprika, turmeric, garlic, ginger, ground coriander, ground cumin and palm sugar. Add 400ml/14fl oz/1⅔ cups cold water to the bowl and stir well with a metal spoon or spatula to combine.

2 Pour the spice mixture into a wok or large heavy pan. Place the pan over a high heat and bring the mixture to the boil. Cover the pan with a lid, reduce the heat to low and leave to simmer gently for 8–10 minutes.

3 Add the mango, coconut milk, salt and tamarind paste to the pan and stir to combine. Bring to a simmer and then add the prawns. Cover the pan and cook gently for 10–12 minutes, or until the prawns have turned pink and are cooked through and the sauce is reduced.

4 Serve the prawn curry garnished with chopped coriander leaves, accompanied by steamed white rice and a mixed tomato, cucumber and onion salad.

Chilli Prawns Energy 211kcal/886kJ; Protein 23.6g; Carbohydrate 14.8g, of which sugars 13.1g; Fat 6.8g, of which saturates 1g; Cholesterol 244mg; Calcium 152mg; Fibre 1.1g; Sodium 351mg.
Prawn with Mango Energy 151kcal/648kJ; Protein 22.1g; Carbohydrate 14.1g, of which sugars 14g; Fat 1.1g, of which saturates 0.5g; Cholesterol 263mg; Calcium 143mg; Fibre 1g; Sodium 2102mg.

Prawn Fu-yung

Serves 4
3 eggs, reserving 5ml/1 tsp egg white
pinch of salt
15ml/1 tbsp finely chopped spring onions (scallions)
45–60ml/3–4 tbsp vegetable oil
225g/8oz raw prawns (shrimp), peeled
5ml/1 tsp cornflour (cornstarch), mixed with 10ml/2 tsp cold water
175g/6oz green peas
15ml/1 tbsp Chinese rice wine

1 Beat the eggs with a little salt and a few spring onions. Heat a little oil in a wok, add the egg and scramble. Remove and reserve.

2 Mix the prawns with salt, 5ml/1 tsp egg white and the cornflour paste. Stir-fry the peas in hot oil for 30 seconds Add the prawns and spring onions. Stir-fry for 1 minute, then stir into the egg with the wine or sherry and serve.

Red Cooked Prawns on the Shell

Known as ha loke in Cantonese, this delicious dish has become a staple in Chinese restaurants throughout South-east Asia. For aesthetic reasons, and to maximize the flavour, the prawns are not shelled, although you can improve the appearance of the dish by removing the heads without compromising the intrinsic flavour too much.

Serves 4
450g/1lb tiger prawns (jumbo shrimp)
30ml/2 tbsp vegetable oil
30ml/2 tbsp chopped root ginger
30ml/2 tbsp chopped garlic
1 large onion, sliced
30ml/2 tbsp tomato sauce (ketchup)
30ml/2 tbsp oyster sauce
100 ml/3½fl oz/scant ½ cup water
whole lettuce leaves, to serve

1 Clean the prawns and cut off 1cm/½in from the head end of each. Remove the black vein with a sharp knife. Slice each prawn in half down its length, leaving the shells on.

2 Heat a wok. Dribble the vegetable oil around the rim so that it flows down to coat the surface. When the oil is hot, add the ginger and garlic. Stir-fry for 30 seconds.

3 Add the onion slices to the wok and stir-fry for 2 minutes. Toss the prawns into the wok and stir-fry over high heat for 2–3 minutes or until they have turned pink. Using a slotted spoon, transfer the prawns to a bowl.

4 Pour the tomato sauce and oyster sauce into the wok, add the water and quickly bring to the boil, stirring all the time.

5 Arrange the lettuce on individual plates. Divide the prawns among them and spoon the sauce over. Serve immediately.

Cook's Tips
• *When shopping for prawns, buy the very largest prawns you can find, with fat bodies and large heads.*
• *Do not let the garlic burn or it will taste bitter.*

Green Prawn Curry

This fragrant, creamy curry can also be made with thin strips of chicken breast.

Serves 4_6
30ml/2 tbsp vegetable oil
30ml/2 tbsp green curry paste
450g/1lb large raw prawns (shrimp), shelled and deveined
4 kaffir lime leaves, torn
1 stalk lemon grass, bruised and chopped
250ml/8fl oz/1 cup coconut milk
30ml/2 tbsp Thai fish sauce
½ cucumber, seeded and cut into thin batons
10–15 basil leaves
4 green chillies, sliced, to garnish

1 Heat a wok and add the oil. Add the green curry paste and fry until bubbling and fragrant. Add the prawns, lime leaves and lemon grass. Fry for 1–2 minutes, until the prawns are pink.

2 Stir in the coconut milk and heat, stirring, until it starts to bubble. Simmer very gently, stirring occasionally, for about 5 minutes or until the prawns are tender.

3 Stir in the fish sauce, cucumber batons, and basil. Serve at once, topped with the sliced green chillies.

Red Cooked Prawns Energy 154kcal/643kJ; Protein 11.3g; Carbohydrate 13.4g, of which sugars 10.6g; Fat 6.5g, of which saturates 0.9g; Cholesterol 35mg; Calcium 93mg; Fibre 1.8g; Sodium 934mg.
Prawn Fu-yung Energy 228kcal/948kJ; Protein 18.6g; Carbohydrate 6.2g, of which sugars 1.1g; Fat 14.3g, of which saturates 2.6g; Cholesterol 281mg; Calcium 80mg; Fibre 2.1g; Sodium 171mg.
Green Prawn Curry Energy 115kcal/481kJ; Protein 14.1g; Carbohydrate 4g, of which sugars 2.6g; Fat 4.8g, of which saturates 0.6g; Cholesterol 146mg; Calcium 107mg; Fibre 1.3g; Sodium 567mg.

Paneer Balti with Prawns

Paneer is a protein food and makes an excellent substitute for red meat. Here it is combined with king prawns to make a dish with unforgettable flavour.

Serves 4

12 cooked king prawns (jumbo shrimp)
175g/6oz paneer
30ml/2 tbsp tomato purée (paste)
60ml/4 tbsp Greek (US strained plain) yogurt
7.5ml/1½ tsp garam masala
5ml/1 tsp chilli powder
5ml/1 tsp crushed garlic
5ml/1 tsp salt
10ml/2 tsp mango powder (amchur)
5ml/1 tsp ground coriander
115g/4oz/½ cup butter
15ml/1 tbsp vegetable or sunflower oil
3 fresh green chillies, chopped
45ml/3 tbsp chopped fresh coriander (cilantro)
150ml/¼ pint/⅔ cup single (light) cream

1 Peel and remove the black intestinal vein from the king prawns. Using a small, sharp knife, make a shallow cut along the length of the black line, then lift it out using the tip of the knife and discard. Cut the paneer into small cubes.

2 Put the tomato purée, yogurt, garam masala, chilli powder, garlic, salt, mango powder and ground coriander in a small mixing bowl. Mix to a paste and set aside.

3 Melt the butter with the oil in a karahi, wok or deep pan. Lower the heat slightly and quickly fry the paneer and prawns for about 2 minutes until the prawns are cooked. Remove with a slotted spoon and drain on kitchen paper.

4 Pour the spice paste into the fat left in the pan and cook for about 1 minute, stirring constantly.

5 Add the paneer and prawns to the pan, and cook for 7–10 minutes, stirring occasionally, until the prawns are heated through.

6 Add the fresh chillies and most of the coriander to the pan, and pour in the cream. Heat through for about 2 minutes, garnish with the remaining coriander and serve.

Salt and Pepper Prawns

These succulent shellfish beg to be eaten with the fingers, so provide finger bowls or hot cloths for all your guests. Peeling them after cooking makes for a juicier, more flavourful dish.

Serves 3–4

15–18 large raw prawns (shrimp), in the shell, about 450g/1lb
vegetable oil, for deep-frying
3 shallots or 1 small onion, very finely chopped
2 garlic cloves, crushed
1cm/½in piece fresh root ginger, peeled and very finely grated
1–2 fresh red chillies, seeded and finely sliced
2.5ml/½ tsp caster (superfine) sugar or to taste
3–4 spring onions (scallions), shredded, to garnish

For the fried salt
10ml/2 tsp salt
5ml/1 tsp Szechuan peppercorns

1 Make the fried salt by dry-frying the salt and peppercorns in a heavy frying pan over medium heat until the peppercorns begin to release their aroma. Cool the mixture, then tip into a mortar and crush with a pestle.

2 Carefully remove the heads and legs from the raw prawns and discard. Leave the body shells and the tails in place. Pat the prepared prawns dry with sheets of kitchen paper.

3 Heat the oil in a karahi, wok or large, heavy pan for deep frying to 190°C/375°F. Fry the prawns for 1 minute, then lift them out and drain them thoroughly on kitchen paper. Spoon 30ml/2 tbsp of the hot oil into a large wok or frying pan, leaving the rest of the oil to one side to cool.

4 Heat the oil in the wok or frying pan. Add the fried salt, with the shallots or onion, garlic, ginger, chillies and sugar. Toss together for 1 minute.

5 Add the prawns and toss them over the heat for about 1 minute more until they are coated and the shells are pleasantly impregnated with the seasonings. Spoon the shellfish mixture into heated serving bowls and garnish the dish with the shredded spring onions.

Paneer Balti Energy 414kcal/1712kJ; Protein 15.2g; Carbohydrate 4g, of which sugars 3g; Fat 37.6g, of which saturates 21.7g; Cholesterol 162mg; Calcium 195mg; Fibre 1.5g; Sodium 419mg.
Salt and Pepper Prawns Energy 122kcal/514kJ; Protein 20.1g; Carbohydrate 2.7g, of which sugars 2.4g; Fat 3.5g, of which saturates 0.5g; Cholesterol 219mg; Calcium 97mg; Fibre 0.3g; Sodium 1197mg.

Fried Jasmine Rice with Prawns and Green Peas

When you only have a short time for lunch, this simple stir-fry will fill the gap.

Serves 4–6

45ml/3 tbsp vegetable oil
1 egg, beaten
1 onion, chopped
15ml/1 tbsp chopped garlic
15ml/1 tbsp blachan or shrimp paste
1kg/2¼lb/4 cups cooked jasmine rice
350g/12oz cooked peeled prawns (shrimp)
50g/2oz thawed frozen peas
oyster sauce, to taste
2 spring onions (scallions), chopped
15–20 Thai basil leaves, roughly snipped, plus an extra sprig, to garnish

1 Heat 15ml/1 tbsp of the oil in a wok or frying pan. Add the beaten egg and swirl it around to set like a thin pancake.

2 Cook the egg pancake (on one side only) over a gentle heat until it is golden. Slide the pancake on to a board, roll up and cut into thin strips. Set aside.

3 Heat the remaining oil in the wok or pan, add the chopped onion and garlic and stir-fry for 2–3 minutes. Stir in the shrimp paste and mix well until thoroughly combined.

4 Add the rice, prawns and peas to the pan and toss and stir together, until everything is heated through.

5 Season with oyster sauce to taste, taking great care as the shrimp paste is salty. Mix in the spring onions and basil leaves. Transfer to a serving dish and top with the strips of egg pancake. Serve, garnished with a sprig of basil.

Cook's Tip
Thai basil, also known as holy basil, is a type of sweet basil native to south-east Asia. It has a unique, pungent flavour that is both spicy and sharp. It can be found in most Asian food stores.

Langoustines with Lemon Grass Risotto

The wok is wonderful for making risotto. For this version, the traditional Italian risotto is given a subtle Asian twist with the addition of fragrant lemon grass, Asian fish sauce and Chinese chives: the perfect accompaniment to simply steamed langoustines.

Serves 4

8 fresh langoustines
30ml/2 tbsp olive oil
15ml/1 tbsp butter
1 onion, finely chopped
1 carrot, finely diced
1 celery stick, finely diced
30ml/2 tbsp very finely chopped lemon grass
300g/11oz/1½ cups arborio or other risotto rice
200ml/7fl oz/scant 1 cup dry white wine
1.5 litres/2½ pints/6¼ cups boiling vegetable stock
50ml/2fl oz/¼ cup Thai fish sauce
30ml/2 tbsp finely chopped Chinese chives
salt and ground black pepper

1 Place the langoustines in a baking parchment-lined bamboo steamer, cover and place over a wok of simmering water. Steam for 6–8 minutes, remove from the heat and keep warm.

2 Heat the oil and butter in a wok and add the vegetables. Cook over a high heat for 2–3 minutes. Add the lemon grass and rice and stir-fry for 2 minutes.

3 Add the wine to the wok, reduce the heat and slowly stir until the wine is absorbed. Add about two-thirds of the stock and cook gently, stirring until absorbed. Continue adding the stock, stirring until absorbed before adding more. When the rice is tender, stir in the fish sauce and Chinese chives. Check the seasoning and serve immediately, topped with langoustines.

Cook's Tip
Langoustines, also known as scampi and Dublin Bay prawns, are a succulent, white shellfish, closely related to the lobster.

Jasmine Rice Energy 354kcal/1494kJ; Protein 17.8g; Carbohydrate 53.4g, of which sugars 0.9g; Fat 9.2g, of which saturates 1.5g; Cholesterol 158mg; Calcium 117mg; Fibre 0.8g; Sodium 233mg.
Langoustines Energy 467Kcal/1949kJ; Protein 23.8g; Carbohydrate 64.2g, of which sugars 3.4g; Fat 8.9g, of which saturates 2.3g; Cholesterol 201mg; Calcium 114mg; Fibre 0.9g; Sodium 218mg.

Chinese-style Stir-fried Squid with Broccoli and Garlic

The slightly chewy squid contrasts beautifully with the crisp crunch of the broccoli to give this dish the perfect combination of textures so beloved by the Chinese.

Serves 4

300ml/½ pint/1¼ cups fish stock
350g/12oz prepared squid, cut into large pieces
225g/8oz broccoli
15ml/1 tbsp vegetable oil
2 garlic cloves, finely chopped
15ml/1 tbsp Chinese rice wine or dry sherry
10ml/2 tsp cornflour (cornstarch)
2.5ml/½ tsp caster (superfine) sugar
45ml/3 tbsp cold water
15ml/1 tbsp oyster sauce
2.5ml/½ tsp sesame oil
noodles, to serve

1 Bring the fish stock to the boil in a wok or pan.

2 Add the squid pieces and cook for 2 minutes over medium heat until they are tender and have curled. Drain the squid pieces and set aside until required.

3 Trim the broccoli and cut it into small florets. Bring a pan of lightly salted water to the boil, add the broccoli and cook for 2 minutes until crisp-tender. Drain thoroughly.

4 Heat the vegetable oil in a wok or non-stick frying pan. When the oil is hot, add the garlic, stir-fry for a few seconds, then add the squid, broccoli and rice wine or sherry. Stir-fry the mixture over medium heat for about 2 minutes.

5 Mix the cornflour and sugar to a paste with the water. Stir the mixture into the wok or pan, with the oyster sauce. Cook, stirring, until the sauce thickens slightly. Just before serving, stir in the sesame oil. Serve with noodles.

Variation
Use pak choi (bok choy) instead of broccoli when it is available.

Stir-fried Squid and Tomatoes in a Tamarind Dressing

This is a lovely Vietnamese dish – sweet squid served in a tangy dressing made with tamarind, lime and nuoc mam. It is best made with baby squid because they are tender and sweet. The tomatoes and herbs add wonderful fresh flavours.

Serves 4

vegetable oil, for greasing
2 large tomatoes, skinned, halved and seeded
500g/1¼lb fresh baby squid
1 bunch each fresh basil, coriander (cilantro) and mint, stalks removed, leaves chopped

For the dressing
15ml/1 tbsp tamarind paste
juice of half a lime
30ml/2 tbsp nuoc mam (fish sauce)
15ml/1 tbsp raw cane sugar
1 garlic clove, crushed
2 shallots, halved and finely sliced
2 Serrano chillies, seeded and sliced

1 Put the ingredients for the dressing into a small bowl and stir until they are well mixed. Set aside.

2 Heat a wok, drizzle in a little oil, and stir-fry the tomatoes until lightly charred on both sides. Transfer them to a board, chop into bitesize chunks, and place in a bowl.

3 Clean the wok, then heat it up again and wipe with a little more oil. Stir-fry the baby squid for 2–3 minutes each side, pressing them down with a spatula, until they are nicely browned. Transfer to the bowl with the tomatoes, add the herbs and the dressing and toss well. Serve immediately.

Cook's Tip
To prepare squid yourself, get a firm hold of the head and pull it from the body. Reach down inside the body sac and then pull out the transparent backbone, as well as any stringy parts. Rinse the body sac inside and out and pat dry. Cut the tentacles off above the eyes and add to the pile of squid you are going to cook. Discard everything else.

Squid with Broccoli Energy 127kcal/536kJ; Protein 16g; Carbohydrate 4.4g, of which sugars 0.9g; Fat 4.8g, of which saturates 0.8g; Cholesterol 197mg; Calcium 44mg; Fibre 1.5g; Sodium 103mg.
Stir-fried Squid Energy 165Kcal/701kJ; Protein 22g; Carbohydrate 15g, of which sugars 10g; Fat 3g, of which saturates 1g; Cholesterol 281mg; Calcium 105mg; Fibre 1g; Sodium 500mg.

Squid Stuffed with Garlic Pork

This Vietnamese recipe calls for tender baby squid to be stuffed with a dill-flavoured pork mixture. The squid can be grilled or fried.

Serves 4

3 dried cloud ear (wood ear) mushrooms
10 dried tiger lily buds
25g/1oz bean thread (cellophane) noodles
8 baby squid, cleaned
350g/12oz minced (ground) pork
3–4 shallots, finely chopped
4 garlic cloves, finely chopped
1 bunch dill fronds, finely chopped
30ml/2 tbsp nuoc mam (Vietnamese fish sauce)
5ml/1 tsp palm sugar (jaggery)
ground black pepper
vegetable oil, for frying
coriander (cilantro) leaves, to garnish
nuoc cham (chilli sauce), for drizzling

1 Soak the mushrooms, tiger lily buds and bean thread noodles in lukewarm water for about 15 minutes, until softened. Rinse the squid and pat dry with kitchen paper. Chop the tentacles.

2 Drain the mushrooms, tiger lily buds and bean thread noodles. Squeeze them in kitchen paper to get rid of any excess water, then chop them finely and put them in a bowl. Add the chopped tentacles, minced pork, shallots, garlic and three-quarters of the dill. In a small bowl, stir the nuoc mam with the sugar, until it dissolves completely. Add it to the mixture in the bowl and mix well. Season with ground black pepper.

3 Using your fingers, stuff the pork mixture into each squid, packing it in firmly. Leave a little gap at the end to sew together with a needle and cotton thread or to skewer with a cocktail stick (toothpick) so that the filling doesn't spill out on cooking.

4 Heat some oil in a large wok or heavy pan, and fry the squid for about 5 minutes, turning them from time to time. Pierce each one several times to release any excess water – this will cause the oil to spit, so take care when doing this; you may wish to use a spatterproof lid. Continue cooking for a further 10 minutes, until the squid are nicely browned.

5 Serve whole or thinly sliced, garnished with the remaining dill and coriander, and drizzled with nuoc cham.

Squid in Hot Yellow Sauce with Lime and Lemon Grass

This recipe from Sabah, the northernmost state in Malaysian Borneo, includes enough chillies to set your tongue on fire. To temper the heat, the dish is often served with finely shredded green mango tossed in lime juice.

Serves 4

500g/1¼lb fresh squid
juice of 2 limes
5ml/1 tsp salt
4 shallots, chopped
4 garlic cloves, chopped
25g/1oz galangal, chopped
25g/1oz fresh turmeric, chopped
6–8 red chillies, seeded and chopped
30ml/2 tbsp vegetable or groundnut (peanut) oil
7.5ml/1½ tsp palm sugar (jaggery)
2 lemon grass stalks, crushed
4 lime leaves
400ml/14fl oz/1⅔ cups coconut milk
salt and ground black pepper
crusty bread or steamed rice, to serve

1 First prepare the squid. Hold the body sac in one hand and pull off the head with the other. Sever the tentacles just above the eyes, and discard the rest of the head and innards. Clean the body sac inside and out and remove the skin. Pat the squid dry, cut it into thick slices and put them in a bowl, along with the tentacles. Mix the lime juice with the salt and rub it into the squid. Set aside for 30 minutes.

2 Using a mortar and pestle or food processor, grind the shallots, garlic, galangal, turmeric and chillies to a coarse paste.

3 Heat the oil in a wok or heavy pan, and stir in the coarse paste. Cook the paste until fragrant, then add the palm sugar, lemon grass and lime leaves. Drain the squid of any juice and toss it around the wok, coating it in the flavourings. Pour in the coconut milk and bring it to the boil. Reduce the heat and simmer for 5–10 minutes, until the squid is tender.

4 Season the squid with salt and pepper and serve in warmed bowls with chunks of fresh, crusty bread or steamed rice.

Squid Stuffed with Pork Energy 315kcal/1311kJ; Protein 25g; Carbohydrate 7.9g, of which sugars 1.9g; Fat 20.4g, of which saturates 4.6g; Cholesterol 170mg; Calcium 18mg; Fibre 0.2g; Sodium 110mg.
Squid in Yellow Sauce Energy 185kcal/780kJ; Protein 19.8g; Carbohydrate 9.4g, of which sugars 7.6g; Fat 8g, of which saturates 1.4g; Cholesterol 281mg; Calcium 50mg; Fibre 0.2g; Sodium 739mg.

Thai Stir-fried Squid with Ginger and Garlic

The abundance of fish around the Gulf of Thailand in South-east Asia sustains lively, thriving markets for the restaurant and hotel trade, and every market naturally features food stalls where delicious, freshly caught seafood and shellfish is cooked in front of you and served. This quick and very tasty recipe is popular among street traders and their customers.

Serves 2
4 ready-prepared and cleaned baby squid, total weight about 250g/9oz
15ml/1 tbsp vegetable oil
2 garlic cloves, peeled and finely chopped
30ml/2 tbsp soy sauce
2.5cm/1in piece fresh root ginger, peeled and finely chopped
juice of ½ lemon
5ml/1 tsp granulated sugar
2 spring onions (scallions), chopped

1 Rinse the squid well in cold water and pat it dry with kitchen paper. With a sharp knife, slice the bodies into rings and halve the tentacles lengthways, if necessary.

2 Heat the oil in a wok or frying pan and cook the garlic, stirring, until golden brown – be careful not to let it burn. Add the squid and stir-fry for 30 seconds over a high heat.

3 Add the soy sauce, ginger, lemon juice, sugar and spring onions. Stir-fry for a further 30 seconds, then serve.

Variations
This dish is often prepared with fresh galangal rather than fresh root ginger, and it works well with most kinds of seafood, including prawns (shrimp) and scallops.

Cook's Tip
Squid has an undeserved reputation for being rubbery in texture. This is always a result of overcooking it.

Spicy Seafood and Tofu Laksa

This is the ultimate serve-yourself soup.

Serves 6
675g/1½lb small clams, scrubbed
50g/2oz ikan bilis (dried anchovies)
2–3 aubergines (eggplants)
675g/1½lb raw peeled prawns (shrimp)
10ml/2 tsp sugar
1 head Chinese leaves, thinly sliced
115g/4oz/2 cups beansprouts
2 spring onions (scallions), finely chopped
50g/2oz crispy fried onions
2 x 400ml/14fl oz cans coconut milk
115g/4oz shallots, finely chopped
4 garlic cloves, chopped
6 macadamia nuts, chopped
3 lemon grass stalks
90ml/6 tbsp sunflower oil
1cm/½in cube shrimp paste
25g/1oz/¼ cup curry powder
a few curry leaves
115g/4oz fried tofu
675g/1½lb noodles (laksa, mee or behoon, or mixed), cooked
prawn crackers

1 Put the clams in a large wok with 1cm/½in water. Bring to the boil, cover and steam for 3–4 minutes until opened. Drain.

2 Simmer the ikan bilis in 900ml/1½ pints/3¾ cups water for 20 minutes, then strain into a wok. Cook the aubergines in this for 10 minutes. Lift out, peel and cut into strips. Arrange on a platter.

3 Sprinkle the prawns with sugar. Cook in the stock for 2–4 minutes. Remove. Add to the aubergines with the Chinese leaves, beansprouts, spring onions, fried onions and clams.

4 Make up the coconut milk to 1.2 litres/2 pints/5 cups with water. Purée the shallots, garlic and nuts with the lower 5cm/2in of two lemon grass stalks. Fry the purée in the oil in a pan. Add the remaining lemon grass, shrimp paste, curry powder and a little coconut milk. Stir for 1 minute over low heat. Add the remaining coconut milk and curry leaves and simmer.

5 Stir the remaining stock into the soup and boil. Rinse the tofu in boiling water, cool and squeeze, then cut up and add to the soup. Simmer. Remove the curry leaves and lemon grass. Serve the soup with the noodles, seafood and vegetables, and prawn crackers. Provide big bowls for self-service soup.

Stir-fried Squid Energy 169kcal/709kJ; Protein 20g; Carbohydrate 5.3g, of which sugars 3.6g; Fat 7.7g, of which saturates 1.2g; Cholesterol 281mg; Calcium 26mg; Fibre 0.2g; Sodium 1207mg.
Seafood and Tofu Energy 524kcal/2200kJ; Protein 43.1g; Carbohydrate 65.1g, of which sugars 6.3g; Fat 10.1g, of which saturates 2g; Cholesterol 233mg; Calcium 162mg; Fibre 1.9g; Sodium 356mg.

Stuffed Squid with Shiitake Mushrooms

The smaller the squid, the sweeter the dish will taste. Be very careful not to overcook the flesh as it toughens very quickly. Squid should have a firm, chewy texture and a mild taste.

Serves 4

8 small squid
50g/2oz cellophane noodles
30ml/2 tbsp groundnut (peanut) oil
2 spring onions (scallions), finely chopped
8 shiitake mushrooms, halved if large
250g/9oz minced (ground) pork
1 garlic clove, chopped
30ml/2 tbsp fish sauce
5ml/1 tsp caster (superfine) sugar
15ml/1 tbsp finely chopped fresh coriander (cilantro)
5ml/1 tsp lemon juice
salt and ground black pepper

1 Cut off the tentacles of the squid just below the eye. Remove the transparent 'quill' from inside the body and rub off the skin on the outside. Wash the squid thoroughly in cold water and set aside on a plate.

2 Bring a pan of water to the boil and add the noodles. Remove from the heat and set aside to soak for 20 minutes.

3 Preheat the oven to 200°C/400°F/Gas 6.

4 Heat 15ml/1 tbsp of the oil in a preheated wok and stir-fry the spring onions, shiitake mushrooms, pork and garlic for 4 minutes until the meat is golden and cooked through and the spring onions and mushrooms have softened.

5 Drain the soaked cellophane noodles and add them to the wok, together with the fish sauce, sugar, coriander, lemon juice and salt and pepper to taste. Stir well.

6 Stuff the squid with the mixture and secure with cocktail sticks (toothpicks). Arrange the squid in an ovenproof dish, drizzle over the remaining oil and prick each squid twice. Bake in the preheated oven for 10 minutes. Serve hot.

Five-spice Squid

Squid is perfect for stir-frying as it should be cooked quickly. The spicy sauce makes the ideal accompaniment.

Serves 6

450g/1lb small squid, cleaned
45ml/3 tbsp vegetable oil
2.5cm/1in fresh root ginger, grated
1 garlic clove, crushed
8 spring onions (scallions), cut into 2.5cm/1in lengths
1 red (bell) pepper, seeded and cut into strips
1 fresh green chilli, seeded and thinly sliced
6 mushrooms, sliced
5ml/1 tsp Chinese five-spice powder
30ml/2 tbsp black bean sauce
30ml/2 tbsp soy sauce
5ml/1 tsp sugar
15ml/1 tbsp Chinese rice wine or dry sherry

1 Rinse the squid and pull away the outer skin. Dry on kitchen paper. Slit the squid open and score the inside into diamonds with a sharp knife. Cut the squid into strips.

2 Preheat the wok, add the vegetable oil and swirl round. Stir-fry the squid quickly. Remove the squid strips from the wok with a slotted spoon and set aside.

3 Add the grated ginger, crushed garlic, spring onions, red pepper, chilli and mushrooms to the oil remaining in the wok and stir-fry for 2 minutes, stirring frequently.

4 Return the squid to the wok and stir in the five-spice powder.

5 Add the black bean sauce, soy sauce, sugar and rice wine or dry sherry to the pan and stir well. Bring to the boil and cook, stirring, for 1 minute. Serve immediately.

Variation
Use button (white) mushrooms for this recipe, or try a mixture of cultivated and wild mushrooms. Dried shiitake mushrooms are also good but must first be soaked in water.

Stuffed Squid Energy 356kcal/1486kJ; Protein 21.8g; Carbohydrate 15.2g, of which sugars 3.6g; Fat 23.6g, of which saturates 11.1g; Cholesterol 321mg; Calcium 55mg; Fibre 1.9g; Sodium 352mg.
Five-spice Squid Energy 134kcal/562kJ; Protein 15.1g; Carbohydrate 4.8g, of which sugars 3.5g; Fat 6.2g, of which saturates 0.9g; Cholesterol 203mg; Calcium 23mg; Fibre 0.9g; Sodium 956mg.

Fiery Octopus in Chilli Sauce

Here octopus is stir-fried to give it a rich, meaty texture, then smothered in a fiery chilli sauce. This dish combines the deliciously charred octopus flavour with the spiciness from the gochujang – the Korean chilli paste – and the zing of jalapeño chillies. Serve with steamed rice and a bowl of soup.

Serves 2

2 small octopuses, cleaned and gutted
15ml/1 tbsp vegetable oil
½ onion, sliced 5mm/¼in thick
¼ carrot, thinly sliced
½ leek, thinly sliced
75g/3oz jalapeño chillies, trimmed
2 garlic cloves, crushed
10ml/2 tsp Korean chilli powder
5ml/1 tsp dark soy sauce
45ml/3 tbsp gochujang chilli paste
30ml/2 tbsp mirin or rice wine
15ml/1 tbsp maple syrup
sesame oil and sesame seeds, to garnish

1 First blanch the octopuses in boiling water to soften slightly. Drain well, and cut into pieces approximately 5cm/2in long.

2 Preheat a wok or large frying pan over a medium-high heat. Add the oil and swirl round the pan. Add the onion, carrot, leek and jalapeño chillies. Stir-fry for 3 minutes.

3 Add the octopus and garlic, and sprinkle over the chilli powder. Stir-fry for 3–4 minutes, or until the octopus is tender. Add the soy sauce, gochujang paste, mirin or rice wine, and maple syrup. Mix well and stir-fry for 1 minute more.

4 Transfer to a serving platter, and garnish with a drizzle of sesame oil and a sprinkling of sesame seeds.

Cook's Tips

• *If the taste is too fiery, mix some softened vermicelli noodles in with the stir-fry to dilute the chilli paste.*
• *To make the octopus more tender, knead it with a handful of plain (all-purpose) flour and rinse in salted water.*

Lobster and Crab Steamed in Beer and Hot Spices

Depending on the size and availability of the lobsters and crabs, you can make this delicious spicy dish for as many people as you like, because the quantities are simple to adjust.

Serves 4

4 uncooked lobsters, about 450g/1lb each, cleaned
4–8 uncooked crabs, about 225g/8oz each, cleaned
about 600ml/1 pint/2½ cups beer
4 spring onions (scallions), trimmed and chopped into long pieces
4cm/1½in fresh root ginger, peeled and finely sliced
2 green or red Thai chillies, seeded and finely sliced
3 lemon grass stalks, finely sliced
1 bunch of fresh dill, fronds chopped
1 bunch each of fresh basil and coriander (cilantro), stalks removed, leaves chopped
about 30ml/2 tbsp Thai fish sauce, plus extra for serving
juice of 1 lemon
salt and ground black pepper

1 Rub the lobsters and crabs with salt and pepper. Place half in a large steamer over a wok and pour the beer into the base. Sprinkle half the spring onions, ginger, chillies, lemon grass and herbs over the lobsters and crabs, and steam for 10 minutes, or until the lobsters turn red. Lift them on to a serving dish.

2 Cook the remaining half in the same way.

3 Add the lemon grass, herbs, fish sauce and lemon juice to the beer, then pour into a dipping bowl. Serve hot, dipping the lobster and crab into the broth and adding extra fish sauce, if you like.

Cook's Tip

Whether you cook the lobsters and crabs at the same time depends on the number of people you are cooking for and the size of your steamer. However, they don't take long to cook so it is easy to steam them in batches.

Fiery Octopus Energy 235kcal/988kJ; Protein 28.6g; Carbohydrate 13.2g, of which sugars 11.9g; Fat 8g, of which saturates 1.2g; Cholesterol 72mg; Calcium 76mg; Fibre 2.4g; Sodium 204mg.
Lobster and Crab Energy 264kcal/1112kJ; Protein 48g; Carbohydrate 4g, of which sugars 1g; Fat 7g, of which saturates 1g; Cholesterol 210mg; Calcium 185mg; Fibre 0.5g; Sodium 1.3mg.

Chilli Crab and Tofu Stir-fry

For a light, healthy meal, this speedy stir-fry is the ideal choice. The silken tofu has a fairly bland taste on its own but is excellent for absorbing all the delicious flavours of this dish – the crab meat, garlic, chillies, spring onions and soy sauce.

Serves 2

250g/9oz silken tofu
60ml/4 tbsp vegetable oil
2 garlic cloves, finely chopped
115g/4oz white crab meat
130g/4½oz/generous 1 cup baby corn, halved lengthways
2 spring onions (scallions), chopped
1 fresh red chilli, seeded and finely chopped
30ml/2 tbsp soy sauce
15ml/1 tbsp Thai fish sauce
5ml/1 tsp palm sugar (jaggery) or light muscovado (brown) sugar
juice of 1 lime
small bunch fresh coriander (cilantro), chopped, to garnish

1 Using a sharp knife, cut the silken tofu into 1cm/½in cubes.

2 Heat the oil in a wok or large, heavy frying pan. Add the tofu cubes to the pan and stir-fry them until they are golden all over, taking care not to break them up while cooking. Remove from the pan with a slotted spoon and set aside.

3 Add the chopped garlic to the wok or pan and stir-fry for 1–2 minutes until it is just golden. Ensure that it does not burn, otherwise it will have a slightly bitter taste.

4 Add the crab meat, tofu, corn, spring onions, red chilli, soy sauce, fish sauce and sugar to the pan. Cook, stirring constantly, until the vegetables are just tender.

5 Stir in the lime juice, transfer to warmed bowls, sprinkle with the coriander and serve immediately.

Cook's Tip

This is a very economical dish to prepare as you only need a small amount of crab meat. The canned variety could also be used in this recipe, which would make it even cheaper.

Crisp-fried Crab Claws

Crab claws are popular in Chinese restaurants all over the world. They are readily available from the freezer cabinet of many Asian stores and supermarkets. Thaw them thoroughly and dry on kitchen paper before coating them.

Serves 4

50g/2oz/⅓ cup rice flour
15ml/1 tbsp cornflour (cornstarch)
2.5ml/½ tsp sugar
1 egg
60ml/4 tbsp cold water
1 lemon grass stalk
2 garlic cloves, finely chopped
15ml/1 tbsp chopped fresh coriander (cilantro)
1–2 fresh red chillies, seeded and finely chopped
5ml/1 tsp fish sauce
vegetable oil, for deep-frying
12 half-shelled crab claws, thawed if frozen
ground black pepper

For the chilli vinegar dip
45ml/3 tbsp sugar
120ml/4fl oz/½ cup water
120ml/4fl oz/½ cup red wine vinegar
15ml/1 tbsp fish sauce
2–4 fresh red chillies, seeded and chopped

1 First make the chilli vinegar dip. Mix the sugar and water in a pan. Heat gently, stirring until the sugar has dissolved, then bring to the boil. Lower the heat and simmer for 5–7 minutes.

2 Stir in the red wine vinegar, fish sauce and chopped chillies, pour into a serving bowl and set aside.

3 Combine the rice flour, cornflour and sugar in a bowl. Beat the egg with the cold water, then stir the egg and water mixture into the flour mixture and beat well until it forms a light batter without any lumps.

4 Cut off the lower 5cm/2in of the lemon grass stalk and chop it finely. Add the lemon grass to the batter, with the garlic, coriander, red chillies and fish sauce. Stir in pepper to taste.

5 Heat the oil in a wok or deep-fryer to 190°C/375°F or until a cube of bread browns in 40 seconds. Dip the crab claws into the batter, then fry, in batches, until golden. Serve with the dip.

Crab Stir-fry Energy 370kcal/1532kJ; Protein 23.3g; Carbohydrate 6.2g, of which sugars 5.1g; Fat 28.1g, of which saturates 1g; Cholesterol 210mg; Calcium 185mg; Fibre 1.2g; Sodium 2487mg.
Crisp-fried Crab Claws Energy 224kcal/933kJ; Protein 10.1g; Carbohydrate 16.9g, of which sugars 0g; Fat 12.9g, of which saturates 1.7g; Cholesterol 78mg; Calcium 62mg; Fibre 0.3g; Sodium 256mg.

Singapore Chilli Crab

One of Singapore's signature dishes is chilli crab. An all-time favourite at street stalls and coffee shops, steaming woks of crab deep-frying are a common sight.

Serves 4

vegetable oil, for deep-frying
4 fresh crabs, about 250g/9oz each, cleaned
30ml/2 tbsp sesame oil
30–45ml/2–3 tbsp chilli sauce
45ml/3 tbsp tomato ketchup
15ml/1 tbsp soy sauce
15ml/1 tbsp sugar
250ml/8fl oz/1 cup chicken stock
2 eggs, beaten
salt and ground black pepper
finely sliced spring onions (scallions), and chopped coriander (cilantro) leaves, to garnish

For the spice paste

4 garlic cloves, chopped
25g/1oz fresh root ginger, chopped
4 fresh red chillies, seeded and chopped

1 Using a mortar and pestle or food processor, grind the ingredients for the spice paste and set aside.

2 Deep-fry the crabs in hot oil until the shells turn bright red. Remove from the oil and drain.

3 Heat the sesame oil in a wok and stir in the spice paste. Fry until fragrant and stir in the chilli sauce, ketchup, soy sauce and sugar. Toss in the fried crab and coat well. Pour in the chicken stock, bring to the boil, then simmer for 5 minutes. Season.

4 Pour in the eggs, stirring gently, to let them set in the sauce. Serve immediately, garnished with spring onions and coriander.

Stir-fried Mussels in Ginger Sauce

Mussels have a great affinity with aromatics like ginger and garlic and, when steeped in a wine sauce, echo the French Moules Marinière.

Serves 4

450g/1lb live green-lipped or standard mussels, scrubbed and bearded
30ml/2 tbsp vegetable oil
15ml/1 tbsp chopped fresh root ginger
3 garlic cloves, peeled and chopped
30ml/2 tbsp Chinese rice wine or sherry
150ml/¼ pint/⅔ cup water
2.5ml/½ tsp salt
2.5ml/½ tsp ground black pepper

1 Carefully check over the mussels, discarding any that have cracked shells, as well as any that are open and that do not snap shut when tapped on a firm surface.

2 Heat the oil in a wok and fry the ginger and garlic for 40 seconds, until light brown. Add the mussels and stir rapidly over high heat for 2 minutes, shaking the pan to move the mussels around.

3 Pour in the Chinese wine or sherry, and the water. Season with the salt and pepper and toss the mussels over the heat for a further 2–3 minutes, until all of them have opened. Discard any mussels that remain closed. Pile the mussels into a warm serving bowl and serve immediately.

Steamed Mussels in Coconut Milk

Any kind of edible bivalve can be used, but green-lipped mussels are ideal for this dish. Mussels have a great affinity with aromatics like ginger and garlic. This is an ideal dish for informal entertaining, mussels steamed in coconut milk and fresh aromatic herbs are quick and easy to prepare and great for a relaxed dinner with friends.

Serves 4

1.6kg/3½lb mussels
15ml/1 tbsp vegetable or sunflower oil
6 garlic cloves, peeled and roughly chopped
15ml/1 tbsp finely chopped fresh root ginger
2 large red chillies, seeded and finely sliced
6 spring onions (scallions), finely chopped
2 limes
400ml/14fl oz/1⅔ cups coconut milk
45ml/3 tbsp light soy sauce
5ml/1 tsp caster (superfine) sugar
a large handful of chopped coriander (cilantro)
salt and ground black pepper

1 Scrub the mussels in cold water. Scrape off any barnacles with a knife, then pull out and discard the fibrous beard visible between the hinge on any of the shells. Discard any mussels that are not tightly closed, or that fail to close when tapped sharply.

2 Heat a wok over a high heat and then add the oil. Stir in the garlic, ginger, chillies and spring onions and stir-fry over medium to high heat for 30 seconds.

3 Grate the rind of the limes into the ginger mixture, then squeeze both fruit and add the juice to the wok with the coconut milk, soy sauce and sugar. Stir to mix.

4 Bring the mixture to the boil, then add the mussels. Return to the boil, cover and cook briskly for 5–6 minutes, or until all the mussels have opened. Discard any unopened mussels.

5 Remove the wok from the heat and stir in the chopped coriander. Season the mussels well with salt and pepper. Ladle into warmed bowls and serve immediately.

Singapore Chilli Crab Energy 276kcal/1144kJ; Protein 12.1g; Carbohydrate 8.6g, of which sugars 8.1g; Fat 21.7g, of which saturates 3.1g; Cholesterol 126mg; Calcium 23mg; Fibre 0.3g; Sodium 674mg
Stir-fried Mussels Energy 97kcal/404kJ; Protein 5.7g; Carbohydrate 2.4g, of which sugars 0.2g; Fat 6.3g, of which saturates 0.8g; Cholesterol 18mg; Calcium 18mg; Fibre 0.3g; Sodium 355mg.
Steamed Mussels Energy 160kcal/679kJ; Protein 21.5g; Carbohydrate 6.7g, of which sugars 6.7g; Fat 5.5g, of which saturates 1g; Cholesterol 48mg; Calcium 272mg; Fibre 0.2g; Sodium 630mg.

Steamed Mussels with Chilli and Lemon Grass

This dish, called so hap xa, is Vietnam's version of the French classic, moules marinière. Here the mussels are steamed open in a herby stock with lemon grass and chilli instead of wine and parsley. Both versions are delicious, and this one can be served with chunks of baguette to mop up the cooking liquid, just like the French do with theirs. This is also a popular Vietnamese method of steaming clams and snails. Beer is sometimes used instead of stock and it makes a rich, fragrant sauce.

Serves 4

1kg/2¼lb fresh mussels
600ml/1 pint/2½ cups chicken stock or beer, or a mixture
1 green or red Thai chilli, seeded and finely chopped
2 shallots, finely chopped
2–3 lemon grass stalks, finely chopped
1 bunch of ginger leaves
salt and ground black pepper
baguette, to serve (optional)

1 Scrub the mussels in cold water, removing any barnacles and pull away any 'beards'. Discard any mussels that do not close when tapped sharply. Place the prepared mussels in a bowl in the refrigerator until ready to use.

2 Pour the stock into a deep wok or pan. Add the chilli, shallots, lemon grass and ginger leaves and bring it to the boil. Cover and simmer for 10–15 minutes to let the flavours mingle, then season to taste with salt and pepper.

3 Tip the mussels into the stock. Give the pan a good shake, cover it tightly with a lid and cook for about 2 minutes, simmering, or until the mussels have opened.

4 Discard any mussels that have remained closed. Ladle the remaining mussels into individual bowls, making sure that everyone gets some of the cooking liquid.

5 Serve the mussels decorated with ginger leaves and with a chunk of baguette, if using, so each diner can mop up the juices.

Clams with Chilli and Yellow Bean Sauce

Seafood is abundant in Thailand, especially at all of the beach holiday resorts. This delicious dish, which is simple to prepare, is a Thai favourite.

Serves 4–6

1kg/2¼lb fresh clams
30ml/2 tbsp vegetable or sunflower oil
4 garlic cloves, peeled and finely chopped
15ml/1 tbsp grated root ginger
4 shallots, finely chopped
30ml/2 tbsp yellow bean sauce
6 red chillies, seeded and chopped
15ml/1 tbsp Thai fish sauce
pinch of granulated sugar
handful of basil leaves, plus extra to garnish

1 Scrub the clams and discard any that fail to open when tapped. Heat the oil in a wok. Add the garlic and ginger and fry for 30 seconds, add the shallots and fry for a further minute.

2 Add the clams. Using a fish slice or spatula, turn them to coat with the oil. Discard any that remain open when tapped.

3 Add the yellow bean sauce and half the red chillies.

4 Continue to cook, stirring often, until all the clams open, about 5–7 minutes. You may need to add a splash of water .Discard any that fail to open. Season with fish sauce and sugar.

5 Finally add the basil to the wok and transfer to individual warmed bowls or a large warmed serving platter.

6 Garnish with the remaining red chillies and basil leaves.

Cook's Tip

- *Dried ground ginger should not be substituted for fresh root ginger since it has a completely different taste.*
- *When buying fresh root ginger, look out for firm ginger with smooth skin (if the skin is wrinkled then it means that the root is dry and will have less flavour).*

Steamed Mussels Energy 73kcal/311kJ; Protein 11g; Carbohydrate 3g, of which sugars 1g; Fat 2g, of which saturates 0g; Cholesterol 36mg; Calcium 37mg; Fibre 0.7g; Sodium 0.7mg.
Clams with Chilli Energy 94kcal/393kJ; Protein 11.6g; Carbohydrate 2.4g, of which sugars 0.6g; Fat 4.3g, of which saturates 0.6g; Cholesterol 45mg; Calcium 75mg; Fibre 0.7g; Sodium 998mg.

Seafood Balti with Vegetables

In this dish, the spicy seafood is cooked separately and combined with the melange of vegetables at the last minute to give a truly delicious combination of flavours.

Serves 4

225g/8oz cod, or any other firm white fish
225g/8oz cooked prawns (shrimp)
6 seafood sticks, halved lengthways, or 115g/4oz white crab meat
150ml/¼ pint/⅔ cup corn oil
lime slices, to garnish

For the marinade

15ml/1 tbsp lemon juice
5ml/1 tsp ground coriander
5ml/1 tsp chilli powder
5ml/1 tsp salt
5ml/1 tsp ground cumin
60ml/4 tbsp cornflour (cornstarch)

For the vegetables

150ml/¼ pint/⅔ cup corn oil
2 medium onions, chopped
5ml/1 tsp onion seeds
½ medium cauliflower, cut into florets
115g/4oz green beans, cut into 2.5cm/1in lengths
175g/6oz/1 cup corn
5ml/1 tsp shredded fresh root ginger
5ml/1 tsp chilli powder
5ml/1 tsp salt
4 fresh green chillies, sliced
30ml/2 tbsp chopped fresh coriander (cilantro)
plain rice and raita, to serve

1 Skin the fish and cut into small cubes. Put into a medium mixing bowl with the prawns and seafood sticks or crab meat.

2 Make the marinade. In a separate bowl, mix together the lemon juice, coriander, chilli powder, salt and cumin. Pour this over the seafood and mix together thoroughly, using your hands.

3 Sprinkle on the cornflour and mix again until the seafood is well coated. Cover with clear film (plastic wrap) and place in the refrigerator for about 1 hour to allow the flavours to develop.

4 To make the vegetable mixture, heat the corn oil in a karahi, wok or deep pan. Add the onions and the onion seeds, and stir-fry for 2–3 minutes until lightly browned.

5 Add the cauliflower, green beans, corn, ginger, chilli powder, salt, green chillies and fresh coriander to the pan. Stir-fry for about 7–10 minutes over a medium heat, making sure that the pieces of cauliflower retain their shape.

6 When cooked through, spoon the fried vegetables around the edge of a warmed and shallow serving dish, leaving a space in the middle for the seafood, and keep hot.

7 Wash and dry the pan, preheat the pan, then heat the oil to fry the seafood pieces. Fry the seafood pieces in 2 or 3 batches, until they turn a golden brown. Remove with a slotted spoon and drain on kitchen paper.

8 Arrange the seafood in the middle of the dish of vegetables and keep hot while you fry the remaining seafood.

9 Garnish with lime slices and serve. Plain boiled rice and raita make ideal accompaniments for this dish.

Clams with Miso and Mustard Sauce

Sweet and juicy, clams are excellent with this sweet-and-sour dressing.

Serves 4

900g/2lb carpet shell clams
15ml/1 tbsp sake
10g/¼oz dried wakame
8 spring onions (scallions)

For the dressing

60ml/4 tbsp shiro miso
20ml/4 tsp sugar
30ml/2 tbsp sake
15ml/1 tbsp rice vinegar
about 1.5ml/¼ tsp salt
7.5ml/1½ tsp English (hot) mustard

1 Wash the clams. Discard any that remain open when tapped. Pour 1cm/½in water into a wok. Add the clams and 15ml/1tbsp sake, cover, then bring to the boil. Cook for 5 minutes, then remove from the heat and leave to stand for 2 minutes.

2 Drain the clams, discarding any which have failed to open, and keep the liquid in a small bowl. When they have cooled slightly, remove the meat from most of the clam shells.

3 Soak the wakame in a bowl of water for about 10 minutes. Drain and squeeze out excess moisture.

4 Separate the green and white parts of the spring onions and chop in half. Cook the white part in a pan of boiling water for 2 minutes, then add the remaining green parts and cook them for 2 minutes more. Drain them well.

5 Mix the shiro miso, sugar, sake, rice vinegar and salt for the dressing in a pan. Stir in 45ml/3 tbsp of the reserved clam liquid, and heat gently, stirring until the sugar dissolves. Add the mustard, check the seasoning, remove from the heat and leave to cool.

6 Mix together the clams, onions, wakame and dressing in a bowl. Divide among four small bowls and serve cold.

Cook's Tip
When purchasing clams, ensure that they are all closed.

Seafood Balti Energy 454kcal/1894kJ; Protein 24.5g; Carbohydrate 31g, of which sugars 9.1g; Fat 26.7g, of which saturates 3.2g; Cholesterol 141mg; Calcium 84mg; Fibre 2.3g; Sodium 373mg.
Clams with Miso Energy 114kcal/482kJ; Protein 12.8g; Carbohydrate 13.2g, of which sugars 11.6g; Fat 0.6g, of which saturates 0.2g; Cholesterol 50mg; Calcium 71mg; Fibre 0.3g; Sodium 1764mg.

Thai Fish Stir-fry

This is a substantial dish, best served with a mound of plain rice, or crusty bread for mopping up the juices.

Serves 4

675g/1½lb mixed seafood, such as red snapper and cod, filleted and skinned, and raw prawns (shrimp)
300ml/½ pint/1¼ cups coconut milk
15ml/1 tbsp vegetable oil
salt and ground black pepper
crusty bread, to serve

For the sauce
2 large red fresh chillies
1 onion, roughly chopped
5cm/2in fresh root ginger, peeled and sliced
5cm/2in lemon grass stalk, outer leaf discarded, roughly sliced
5cm/2in piece galangal, peeled and sliced
6 blanched almonds, chopped
2.5ml/½ tsp turmeric
2.5ml/½ tsp salt

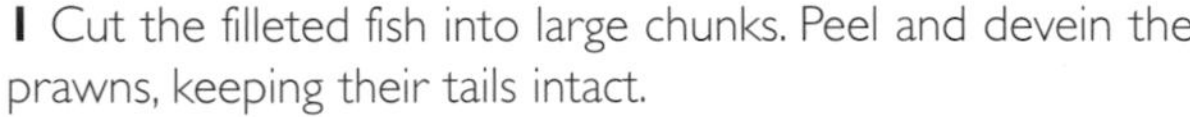

1 Cut the filleted fish into large chunks. Peel and devein the prawns, keeping their tails intact.

2 To make the sauce, remove the seeds from the chillies and chop the flesh roughly. Put the chillies and the other sauce ingredients in a food processor or blender with 45ml/3 tbsp of the coconut milk. Process until smooth.

3 Heat a wok, then add the oil. When the oil is hot, stir-fry the seafood for 2–3 minutes, then remove.

4 Add the sauce and the remaining coconut milk to the wok, then return the seafood and toss in the sauce. Bring to the boil, season well and serve with crusty bread.

Cook's Tip
Galangal is an important spice in South-east Asian cooking. In appearance, it looks rather like a knobbly Jerusalem artichoke. Galangal is peeled and sliced, chopped or grated in the same way as root ginger. It belongs to the same family as ginger, and has a similar but milder flavour.

Saigon Shellfish Curry

There are many variations of this tasty curry all over the south of Vietnam. This recipe is made with prawns, squid and scallops but you could use any combination of shellfish, or even add chunks of filleted fish.

Serves 4

4cm/1½in fresh root ginger, peeled and roughly chopped
2–3 garlic cloves, roughly chopped
45ml/3 tbsp groundnut (peanut) oil
1 onion, finely sliced
2 lemon grass stalks, finely sliced
2 green or red Thai chillies, seeded and finely sliced
15ml/1 tbsp raw cane sugar
10ml/2 tsp shrimp paste
15ml/1 tbsp Thai fish sauce
30ml/2 tbsp curry powder or garam masala
550ml/18fl oz can coconut milk
juice and rind of 1 lime
4 medium squid, cleaned and cut diagonally into 3 or 4 pieces
12 king or queen scallops, shelled
20 raw prawns (shrimp), shelled and deveined
1 small bunch of fresh basil, stalks removed
1 small bunch of fresh coriander (cilantro), stalks removed, leaves finely chopped, to garnish
salt

1 Using a mortar and pestle, grind the ginger with the garlic until it almost resembles a paste. Heat the oil in a traditional clay pot, wok or heavy pan and stir in the onion. Cook until it begins to turn brown, then stir in the garlic and ginger paste.

2 Once the aromas begin to lift from the pot, add the lemon grass, chillies and sugar. Cook for 2 minutes before adding the shrimp paste, fish sauce and curry powder or garam masala. Stir the mixture well and allow the flavours to mingle and combine over the heat for 1–2 minutes.

3 Add the coconut milk, lime juice and rind to the pan. Mix together well and bring the liquid to the boil. Simmer for 2–3 minutes. Season to taste with salt.

4 Gently stir in the squid, scallops and prawns. Bring the liquid to the boil once more. Reduce the heat and cook gently for 2–3 minutes or until the shellfish turns opaque. Add the basil leaves and sprinkle the coriander over the top. Serve immediately from the pot into warmed individual bowls.

Thai Fish Stir-fry Energy 207kcal/869kJ; Protein 32.3g; Carbohydrate 5.4g, of which sugars 5g; Fat 6.3g, of which saturates 0.8g; Cholesterol 78mg; Calcium 54mg; Fibre 0.6g; Sodium 186mg.
Saigon Shellfish Curry Energy 528kcal/2225kJ; Protein 68g; Carbohydrate 24g, of which sugars 14g; Fat 18g, of which saturates 4g; Cholesterol 699mg; Calcium 250mg; Fibre 2.5g; Sodium 1.3mg.

Fried Fish with Dill

The spicy, crispy coating on this fried fish goes beautifully with the large quantity of lovely, pungent fresh herbs, and the peanuts add texture and extra crunch. Serve the herby fish with plain boiled rice, lime wedges and nuoc cham or soy sauce.

Serves 4

500g/1¼lb white fish fillets
75g/3oz/⅔ cup rice flour
7.5ml/1½ tsp ground turmeric
vegetable oil, for deep-frying
1 large bunch fresh dill
15ml/1 tbsp groundnut (peanut) oil
30ml/2 tbsp roasted peanuts
4 spring onions (scallions), cut into bitesize pieces
1 small bunch fresh basil, stalks removed, leaves chopped
1 small bunch fresh coriander (cilantro), stalks removed
cooked rice, 1 lime, cut into wedges, and nuoc cham (Vietnamese chilli sauce), to serve

1 Skin the fish and cut it into chunks. Mix the flour with the turmeric and toss the chunks of fish in it until they are well coated. Heat the oil in a wok or a large heavy pan and cook the fish in batches until crisp and golden. Use a perforated ladle to remove the fish from the oil, and drain on kitchen paper.

2 Scatter some of the dill fronds on a serving dish, arrange the fish on top and keep warm. Chop some of the remaining dill fronds and set aside for the garnish.

3 Heat the groundnut oil in a small wok or frying pan. Stir in the peanuts and cook for 1 minute, then add the spring onions, the remaining dill fronds, basil and coriander. Stir-fry for no more than 30 seconds, then spoon the herbs and peanuts over the fish. Garnish with the chopped dill and serve with lime wedges and nuoc cham to drizzle over the top.

Variation
Any kind of white fish can be used in this dish, for example cod, haddock, coley, pollack or sea bass. They are all naturally low in fat and have light, white, flaky flesh.

Skate Wings with Wasabi

Whole skate wings dipped in a tempura batter and deep-fried until crisp and golden look stunning.

Serves 4

4 x 250g/9oz skate wings
15ml/1 tbsp lemon juice
500ml/17fl oz 2 cups water
65g/2½oz/9 tbsp cornflour (cornstarch)
65g/2½oz/9 tbsp plain (all-purpose) flour
5ml/1 tsp salt
5ml/1 tsp Chinese five-spice powder
15ml/1 tbsp sesame seeds
200ml/7fl oz/scant 1 cup ice-cold soda water (club soda)
sunflower oil, for frying

For the mayonnaise

200ml/7fl oz/scant 1 cup mayonnaise
15ml/1 tbsp light soy sauce
grated rind and juice of 1 lime
5ml/1 tsp wasabi
15ml/1 tbsp finely chopped spring onion (scallion)

1 Using kitchen scissors, trim away the frill from the edges of the skate wings and discard.

2 Rinse the skate in cold water. Mix together the lemon juice and water, and then soak the skate in it for 10 minutes. Drain.

3 In a large mixing bowl combine the cornflour, plain flour, salt, five-spice powder and sesame seeds. Gradually pour in the soda water and stir to mix. (It will be quite lumpy.)

4 Heat the oil for deep-frying in a large wok. One at a time, dip each skate wing in the batter, then lower it carefully into the hot oil and deep-fry for 4–5 minutes, until it is fully cooked and crispy. Drain on kitchen paper. Set the skate aside and keep warm.

5 Meanwhile, mix together all the mayonnaise ingredients and divide among four bowls. Serve immediately with the skate.

Cook's Tip
Look for packets of tempura batter mix at health food shops and Asian markets. It doesn't take long to make your own batter, but sometimes seconds count.

Fried Fish with Dill Energy 350Kcal/1458kJ; Protein 27g; Carbohydrate 17g, of which sugars 1g; Fat 19g, of which saturates 3g; Cholesterol 85mg; Calcium 112mg; Fibre 1.2g; Sodium 200mg.
Skate Wings Energy 705kcal/2921kJ; Protein 31.9g; Carbohydrate 11.7g, of which sugars 1.2g; Fat 59.3g, of which saturates 11g; Cholesterol 38mg; Calcium 112mg; Fibre 0.5g; Sodium 792mg.

Braised Fish Fillet with Mushrooms

This is the Chinese stir-fried version of the French filets de sole bonne femme (sole cooked with mushrooms and wine sauce).

Serves 4

450g/1lb lemon sole or plaice fillets
5ml/1 tsp salt
½ egg white
10ml/2 tsp cornflour (cornstarch)
about 600ml/1 pint/2½ cups vegetable oil
15ml/1 tbsp finely chopped spring onions (scallions)
2.5ml/½ tsp finely chopped fresh root ginger
115g/4oz white mushrooms, thinly sliced
5ml/1 tsp light brown sugar
15ml/1 tbsp light soy sauce
30ml/2 tbsp Chinese rice wine or dry sherry
15ml/1 tbsp brandy
about 120ml/4fl oz/½ cup fish or light chicken stock
few drops sesame oil

1 Trim off the soft bones along the edge of the fish, but leave the skin on the fillets. Cut each fillet into bitesize pieces. Blend the cornflour with 30ml/2tbsp cold water to make a paste. Mix the fish with a little salt, the egg white and about half of the cornflour paste.

2 Heat the oil to medium-hot in a wok or heavy pan and deep-fry the fish for about 1 minute, stirring gently. Remove the fish and drain. Pour off all but about 30ml/2 tbsp oil.

3 Stir-fry the spring onions, ginger and mushrooms in the wok for 1 minute. Add the sugar, soy sauce, rice wine or sherry, brandy and stock. Bring the mixture in the wok to the boil.

4 Return the deep-fried fish to the pan and braise for 1 minute, turning gently. Stir in the remaining cornflour paste to thicken the sauce and sprinkle with sesame oil.

Cook's Tip

You could substitute straw mushrooms, which are so called because they are grown on beds of rice straw. They have a wonderfully subtle flavour and a slightly slippery texture.

Chilli-spiced Fried Plaice

In this beautiful Japanese dish, you will be amazed to find that not only the flesh but also the skeleton of the fish is deep-fried to such crispness you can eat it all.

Serves 4

4 small plaice or flounder, about 500–675g/1¼–1½lb total weight, gutted
salt, for sprinkling
60ml/4 tbsp cornflour (cornstarch)
vegetable oil, for deep-frying

For the condiment

130g/4½oz mooli (daikon), peeled
4 dried chillies, seeded
1 bunch of chives, finely chopped (to make 50ml/2fl oz/½ cup)

For the sauce

20ml/4 tsp rice vinegar
20ml/4 tsp shoyu

1 Use a very sharp knife to make deep cuts around the gills and across the tail of the fish. Cut through the skin from the head down to the tail along the centre. Slide the tip of the knife under the flesh near the head and gently cut the fillet from the bone. Fold the fillet with your hand as you cut, as if peeling it from the bone. Keep the knife horizontal.

2 Repeat for the other half, then turn the fish over and do the same to get four fillets from each fish. Place in a dish and sprinkle with a little salt on both sides. Keep the bony skeletons.

3 To make the condiment, pierce the mooli with a skewer or chopstick in four places to make holes, then insert the chillies. Leave for 15 minutes then grate finely. Squeeze out the moisture. Press a quarter of the grated mooli and chilli into an egg cup, then turn out on to a plate. Make three more mounds.

4 Cut the fish fillets into four slices crossways and coat in cornflour. Heat the oil in a wok or pan to 175°C/345°F. Deep-fry the fillets, two to three at a time, until light golden brown. Raise the temperature to 180°C/350°F. Dust the skeletons with cornflour and cook until crisp. Drain and sprinkle with salt.

5 Mix the rice vinegar and shoyu in a bowl. Arrange the fish on the plates. with the mooli moulds and chives. To eat, mix the condiment and fish with the sauce.

Braised Fish Fillet Energy 241kcal/1003kJ; Protein 19.8g; Carbohydrate 1.7g, of which sugars 1.6g; Fat 15.5g, of which saturates 1.9g; Cholesterol 47mg; Calcium 55mg; Fibre 0.4g; Sodium 145mg.
Chilli-spiced Fried Plaice Energy 219kcal/911kJ; Protein 13.8g; Carbohydrate 13.3g, of which sugars 1.7g; Fat 12.6g, of which saturates 1.6g; Cholesterol 34mg; Calcium 60mg; Fibre 1g; Sodium 808mg.

Chunky Fish Balti with Peppers

Purchase peppers in several colours to make this dish as colourful as possible.

Serves 2–4

450g/1lb cod, or any other firm white fish, such as haddock
7.5ml/1½ tsp ground cumin
10ml/2 tsp mango powder (amchur)
5ml/1 tsp ground coriander
2.5ml/½ tsp chilli powder
5ml/1 tsp salt
5ml/1 tsp grated fresh root ginger
45ml/3 tbsp cornflour (cornstarch)
150ml/¼ pint/⅔ cup corn oil
1 each green, orange and red (bell) peppers, seeded and chopped
8–10 cherry tomatoes

1 Skin the fish and cut it into small cubes, removing any bones.

2 Put the cubes in a large mixing bowl and add the ground cumin, mango powder, ground coriander, chilli powder, salt, grated ginger and cornflour. Mix together thoroughly until the fish is well coated with the spice mix.

3 Heat the corn oil in a karahi, wok or a large, deep pan. Lower the heat slightly and add the fish pieces, 3 or 4 at a time. Fry the fish for about 3 minutes, turning constantly.

4 Drain the cooked fish pieces on kitchen paper and transfer to a serving dish. Keep hot while you fry the remaining fish pieces.

5 Fry the chopped peppers in the oil remaining in the pan for about 2 minutes, stirring from time to time. They should still be slightly crisp. Drain on kitchen paper.

6 Add the cooked peppers to the fish and garnish with the cherry tomatoes. Serve immediately.

Cook's Tip

Amchur powder is made from unripe mangoes and is often used to add sourness. If you cannot find mango powder substitute 10ml/2 tsp tamarind paste or fresh lemon juice.

Hoki Stir-fry

Any firm white fish, such as monkfish, hake, coley or cod, can be used for this attractive stir-fry. Vary the vegetables according to what is in season, but try to include at least three different colours. Red (bell) peppers, green beans and thinly sliced butternut squash would work well.

Serves 4–6

675g/1½lb hoki fillet, skinned
pinch of five-spice powder
2 carrots
115g/4oz/1 cup small mangetouts (snow peas)
115g/4oz asparagus spears
4 spring onions (scallions)
45ml/3 tbsp groundnut (peanut) oil
2.5cm/1in piece fresh root ginger, peeled and cut into thin slivers
2 garlic cloves, finely chopped
300g/11oz/scant 1½ cups beansprouts
8–12 small baby corn cobs
15–30ml/1–2 tbsp light soy sauce
salt and ground black pepper

1 Cut the hoki into finger-size strips and season with salt, pepper and five-spice powder. Cut the carrots diagonally into slices as thin as the mangetouts.

2 Trim the mangetouts. Trim the asparagus spears and cut them in half crossways. Trim the spring onions and cut them diagonally into 2cm/¾ in pieces, keeping the white and green parts separate. Set them all aside.

3 Heat a wok, then pour in the oil. As soon as it is hot, add the ginger and garlic. Stir-fry for 1 minute, then add the white parts of the spring onions and cook for 1 minute more.

4 Add the hoki strips to the wok and stir-fry for 2–3 minutes, until all the pieces of fish are opaque.

5 Add the beansprouts and toss them around to coat them in the oil, then put in the carrots, mangetouts, asparagus and corn.

6 Continue to stir-fry for 3–4 minutes, by which time the fish should be cooked, but all the vegetables will still be crunchy. Add soy sauce to taste, toss everything quickly together, then stir in the green parts of the spring onions. Serve immediately.

Chunky Fish Balti Energy 296kcal/1236kJ; Protein 22.9g; Carbohydrate 22.9g, of which sugars 11.1g; Fat 13g, of which saturates 1.6g; Cholesterol 52mg; Calcium 51mg; Fibre 3.8g; Sodium 98mg.
Hoki Stir-fry Energy 183kcal/764kJ; Protein 22.4g; Carbohydrate 5g, of which sugars 3.8g; Fat 8.2g, of which saturates 1.1g; Cholesterol 0mg; Calcium 49mg; Fibre 2.3g; Sodium 295mg.

Spiced Halibut Fillet in a Rich Tomato Curry

The chunky cubes of white fish contrast beautifully with the rich red spicy tomato sauce and taste just as good as they look.

Serves 4

60ml/4 tbsp lemon juice
60ml/4 tbsp rice wine vinegar
30ml/2 tbsp cumin seeds
5ml/1 tsp turmeric
5ml/1 tsp chilli powder
5ml/1 tsp salt
750g/1lb 10oz thick halibut fillets, skinned and cubed
60ml/4 tbsp sunflower oil
1 onion, finely chopped
3 garlic cloves, finely chopped
30ml/2 tbsp finely grated fresh root ginger
10ml/2 tsp black mustard seeds
2 x 400g/14oz cans chopped tomatoes
5ml/1 tsp sugar
chopped coriander (cilantro) leaves and sliced green chilli, to garnish
basmati rice, pickles and poppadums, to serve
natural (plain) yogurt, to drizzle (optional)

1 Mix together the lemon juice, vinegar, cumin, turmeric, chilli powder and salt in a shallow non-metallic bowl. Add the cubed fish and turn to coat evenly. Cover and put in the refrigerator to marinate for 25–30 minutes.

2 Meanwhile, heat a wok over a high heat and add the sunflower oil. When hot, add the onion, garlic, ginger and mustard seeds. Reduce the heat to low and cook very gently for about 10 minutes, stirring occasionally.

3 Add the tomatoes and sugar to the wok, bring to the boil, reduce the heat, cover and cook gently for 15–20 minutes.

4 Add the fish and its marinade to the wok, stir gently to mix, then cover and simmer gently for 15–20 minutes, or until the fish is cooked through and the flesh flakes easily with a fork.

5 Serve the curry ladled into shallow bowls with basmati rice, pickles and poppadums. Garnish with fresh coriander and green chillies, and drizzle over some natural yogurt, if liked.

Red-hot Fish Curry

The island of Bali has wonderful fish, surrounded as it is by sparkling blue sea. This simple fish curry is packed with many of the characteristic flavours of Indonesia.

Serves 4–6

675g/1½lb cod or haddock fillet
1cm/½in cube shrimp paste
2 red or white onions, chopped
2.5cm/1in fresh root ginger, peeled and sliced
1cm/½in fresh galangal, peeled and sliced
2 garlic cloves, chopped
1–2 fresh red chillies, seeded, or 10ml/2 tsp chilli sambal, or 5–10ml/1–2 tsp chilli powder
90ml/6 tbsp sunflower oil
15ml/1 tbsp dark soy sauce
5ml/1 tsp tamarind pulp, soaked in 30ml/2 tbsp warm water
250ml/8fl oz/1 cup water
celery leaves or chopped fresh chilli, to garnish
boiled rice, to serve

1 Skin the fish fillets using a very sharp knife, remove any bones and then cut the flesh into bitesize pieces. Pat the fish dry with kitchen paper and set aside until needed.

2 Grind the shrimp paste, chopped onions, fresh root ginger, galangal, garlic and fresh chillies, if using, to a coarse paste in a food processor or with a mortar and pestle. Stir in the chilli sambal or chilli powder, if using.

3 Heat 30ml/2 tbsp of the oil in a wok and fry the spice mixture, stirring, until it gives off a rich aroma.

4 Add the dark soy sauce to the pan. Strain the soaked tamarind pulp and add the juice and water, mixing well. Cook gently for 2–3 minutes, stirring from time to time.

5 In a separate pan or wok, fry the fish fillets in the remaining oil for 2–3 minutes. Turn the fish once only so that the pieces stay whole and don't break apart. Lift out with a slotted spoon and place them in the pan with the sauce.

6 Simmer the fish in the sauce for a further 3 minutes and serve with boiled rice. Garnish with feathery celery leaves or a little chopped fresh chilli, if you like.

Halibut and Tomato Curry Energy 335kcal/1409kJ; Protein 41.9g; Carbohydrate 8.4g, of which sugars 8.1g; Fat 15.2g, of which saturates 2.1g; Cholesterol 66mg; Calcium 73mg; Fibre 2.2g; Sodium 622mg.
Red-hot Curry Energy 322kcal/1342kJ; Protein 33g; Carbohydrate 8g, of which sugars 5g; Fat 18g, of which saturates 2g; Cholesterol 84mg; Calcium 53mg; Fibre 1.1g; Sodium 200mg.

Balti Fish Fillets in Spicy Coconut Sauce

Although coconut milk is a familiar ingredient in Indian fish dishes, it is quite unusual to find desiccated coconut in a starring role. It makes for a delicious and most unusual dish.

Serves 4

30ml/2 tbsp corn oil
5ml/1 tsp onion seeds
4 dried red chillies
3 garlic cloves, sliced
1 medium onion, sliced
2 medium tomatoes, sliced
30ml/2 tbsp desiccated (dry unsweetened shredded) coconut
5ml/1 tsp salt
5ml/1 tsp ground coriander
4 flat-fish fillets, such as plaice, sole or flounder, about 75g/3oz each
150ml/¼ pint/⅔ cup water
15ml/1 tbsp lime juice
15ml/1 tbsp chopped fresh coriander (cilantro)
plain rice, to serve

1 Heat the oil in a karahi, wok or deep pan. Lower the heat slightly and add the onion seeds, dried red chillies, garlic slices and onion. Cook for 3–4 minutes, stirring once or twice.

2 Add the sliced tomatoes, coconut, salt and ground coriander to the pan and stir it all thoroughly.

3 Cut each fish fillet into 3 pieces. Drop the fish pieces into the mixture and turn them over gently until they are well coated.

4 Cook for 5–7 minutes, lowering the heat if necessary.

5 Add the water, lime juice and fresh coriander and cook for a further 3–5 minutes until most of the water has evaporated. Serve immediately, with rice, if you like.

Cook's Tip
Use fresh fish fillets to make this dish if you can, as the flavour and texture will be superior. If you must use frozen fillets, ensure that they are completely thawed before cooking.

Fish Skewers on Rice Noodles

Fresh trout is perfect for summer entertaining. In this recipe, succulent fillets are marinated in a tangy citrus spice blend, then skewered and steamed in the wok before serving on a bed of fragrant herb noodles.

Serves 4

4 trout fillets, skinned
2.5ml/½ tsp turmeric
15ml/1 tbsp mild curry paste
juice of 2 lemons
15ml/1 tbsp sunflower oil
salt and ground black pepper
45ml/3 tbsp chilli-roasted peanuts, roughly chopped
chopped fresh mint, to garnish

For the noodles
300g/11oz rice noodles
15ml/1 tbsp sunflower oil
1 red chilli, seeded and finely sliced
4 spring onions (scallions), cut into slivers
60ml/4 tbsp roughly chopped fresh mint
60ml/4 tbsp roughly chopped fresh sweet basil

1 Trim each fillet and place in a large bowl. Mix together the turmeric, curry paste, lemon juice and oil and pour over the fish. Season with salt and black pepper and toss to mix well.

2 Place the rice noodles in a bowl and pour over enough boiling water to cover. Leave to soak for 3–4 minutes and then drain. Refresh in cold water, drain and set aside.

3 Thread 2 bamboo skewers through each trout fillet and arrange in two tiers of a bamboo steamer lined with baking parchment.

4 Cover the steamer and place over a wok of simmering water (making sure the water doesn't touch the steamer). Steam the fish skewers for 5–6 minutes, or until the fish is cooked through.

5 Meanwhile, in a clean wok heat the oil. Add the chilli, spring onions and drained noodles and stir-fry for about 2 minutes and then stir in the chopped herbs. Season with salt and ground black pepper and divide among four bowls or plates.

6 Top each bowl of spicy rice noodles with a steamed fish skewer and scatter over the chilli-roasted peanuts. Garnish with chopped mint and serve immediately.

Balti Fish Fillets Energy 177kcal/737kJ; Protein 14g; Carbohydrate 4.3g, of which sugars 3.9g; Fat 11.6g, of which saturates 5g; Cholesterol 32mg; Calcium 70mg; Fibre 2.6g; Sodium 595mg.
Fish Skewers Energy 555Kcal/2317kJ; Protein 36g; Carbohydrate 62.8g, of which sugars 1g; Fat 16.6g, of which saturates 1.6g; Cholesterol 0mg; Calcium 52mg; Fibre 1.3g; Sodium 97mg.

Steamed Fish with Spices and Chilli Sauce

Steaming is one of the best methods of cooking fish. By leaving the fish whole and on the bone, more flavour is retained and the flesh remains moist.

Serves 4

1 large or 2 medium firm fish such as sea bass or grouper, scaled and cleaned
30ml/2 tbsp rice wine
3 fresh red chillies, seeded and thinly sliced
2 garlic cloves, finely chopped
2cm/¾in piece fresh root ginger, peeled and finely shredded
2 lemon grass stalks, chopped
2 spring onions (scallions), chopped
30ml/2 tbsp Thai fish sauce
juice of 1 lime
1 fresh banana leaf

For the chilli sauce

10 fresh red chillies, seeded and chopped
4 garlic cloves, chopped
60ml/4 tbsp Thai fish sauce
15ml/1 tbsp sugar
75ml/5 tbsp fresh lime juice

1 Thoroughly rinse the fish under cold running water. Pat it dry with kitchen paper. With a sharp knife, slash the skin of the fish a few times on both sides being careful not to go too deep.

2 Mix together the rice wine, chillies, garlic, shredded ginger, lemon grass and spring onions in a non-metallic bowl. Add the fish sauce and lime juice and mix to a paste. Place the fish on the banana leaf and spread the spice paste evenly over it, rubbing it in well where the skin has been slashed.

3 Put a rack or a small upturned plate in the base of a wok. Pour in boiling water to a depth of 5cm/2in. Lift the banana leaf, together with the fish, and place it on the rack or plate. Cover with a lid and steam for 10–15 minutes, or until the fish is cooked.

4 Meanwhile, make the sauce. Place all the ingredients in a food processor and blend until smooth. If the mixture seems to be too thick, add a little cold water. Scrape into a serving bowl.

5 Serve the steamed fish hot, on the banana leaf if you like, with the sweet chilli sauce to spoon over the top.

Barbecued Red Snapper

The grilled fish is perfect for dipping into the chilli sauce.

Serves 4

2 red snapper, each 900g/2lb, cleaned and scaled
15ml/1 tbsp olive oil
5cm/2in piece of fresh root ginger, thinly sliced
4 banana shallots, total weight about 150g/5oz, thinly sliced
3 garlic cloves, thinly sliced
30ml/2 tbsp sugar
3 lemon grass stalks, 1 thinly sliced
grated rind and juice of 1 lime
5ml/1 tsp salt
4 small fresh green chillies, sliced
2 whole banana leaves
30ml/2 tbsp chopped fresh coriander (cilantro)

For the dipping sauce

1 large fresh red chilli, seeded and finely chopped
juice of 2 limes
30ml/2 tbsp fish sauce
5ml/1 tsp sugar
60ml/4 tbsp water

1 To make the dipping sauce, mix together the ingredients in a bowl. Cover and chill until needed. Make four slashes in either side of each fish and rub the skin with oil.

2 Place half the ginger, shallots and the garlic in a mortar. Add half the sugar, the sliced lemon grass, a little lime juice, the salt and chillies and pound. Mix in the remaining sugar and lime juice, with the rind. Rub into the slashes and cavity of each fish.

3 Trim the hard edge from each banana leaf and discard. Soak in a wok in hot water for 10 minutes, then drain. Rinse, then pour over boiling water to soften. Drain again.

4 Lay a fish on each leaf and sprinkle over the remaining ginger and shallots. Split the lemon grass stalks lengthways and lay over each fish. Bring the sides of the leaves up over the fish and secure each with three wooden skewers. Wrap in clear film (plastic wrap), and chill for 30 minutes.

5 Prepare the barbecue. Remove the clear film. Enclose each leaf in foil. When the coals are medium-hot, or have a coating of ash, lay the parcels on the grill rack and cook for 15 minutes. Turn over and cook for 10 minutes. Place on a serving dish, open and sprinkle with the coriander. Serve with the sauce.

Fish with Spices Energy 123kcal/519kJ; Protein 23.3g; Carbohydrate 0.8g, of which sugars 0.7g; Fat 3g, of which saturates 0.5g; Cholesterol 95mg; Calcium 158mg; Fibre 0.1g; Sodium 616mg.
Red Snapper Energy 382kcal/1591kJ; Protein 30.7g; Carbohydrate 8.6g, of which sugars 8.3g; Fat 25.2g, of which saturates 3.9g; Cholesterol 56mg; Calcium 97mg; Fibre 2.4g; Sodium 970mg.

Sea Bass Steamed in Coconut Milk with Ginger and Red Chilli

This is a delicious spicy recipe for any whole white fish, such as sea bass or cod, or for large chunks of trout or salmon.

Serves 4

200ml/7fl oz coconut milk
10ml/2 tsp raw cane or muscovado (molasses) sugar
about 15ml/1 tbsp sesame or vegetable oil
2 garlic cloves, finely chopped
1 red Thai chilli, seeded and finely chopped
4cm/1½in fresh root ginger, peeled and grated
750g/1⅔lb sea bass, gutted and skinned on one side
1 star anise, ground
1 bunch of fresh basil, stalks removed
30ml/2 tbsp cashew nuts
sea salt and ground black pepper

1 Heat the coconut milk with the sugar in a small pan, stirring until the sugar dissolves, then remove from the heat. Add the oil to a small frying pan and stir in the garlic, chilli and ginger. Cook until they begin to brown, then add the mixture to the coconut milk and mix well to combine.

2 Place the fish, skin side down, on a wide piece of foil and tuck up the sides to form a boat-shaped container. Using a sharp knife, cut several diagonal slashes into the flesh on the top and rub with the ground star anise. Season with salt and pepper and spoon the coconut milk over the top.

3 Sprinkle about half the basil leaves over the top of the fish and pull the sides of the foil over the top, so that it is almost enclosed. Gently lay the foil packet in a steamer over a wok. Cover the steamer, bring the water to the boil, then reduce the heat and simmer for 20–25 minutes, or until just cooked.

4 Meanwhile, roast the cashew nuts in the small frying pan, adding a little extra oil if necessary. Drain the nuts on kitchen paper, then grind them to crumbs. When cooked, lift the fish out of the foil and transfer it to a serving dish. Spoon the cooking juices over, sprinkle with the cashew nut crumbs and garnish with the remaining basil leaves. Serve immediately.

Braised Carp in Ginger Sauce

Braising fish in water and aromatics is a cooking method that is typical of the Fujian and Guangzhou provinces of China. The recipe is very easy to make – the fish is simply braised in a tasty stock – but the combination of flavours works extremely well.

Serves 4

1 large carp, about 1kg/2¼lb, cleaned and scaled
400ml/14fl oz/1⅔ cups water
15ml/1 tbsp grated fresh root ginger
45ml/3 tbsp dark soy sauce
30ml/2 tbsp sesame oil
5ml/1 tsp sugar
pinch of salt and ground black pepper
4 cloves
15ml/1 tbsp cornflour (cornstarch) mixed with 30ml/2 tbsp water
spring onions (scallions), to garnish (optional)

1 Rinse the carp inside and out. Pat dry with kitchen paper. Make deep cuts diagonally across both sides of the fish. If the fish is too large for your wok, cut it into two pieces.

2 Pour the measured water into the wok and stir in the grated fresh root ginger, dark soy sauce, sesame oil, sugar, a pinch of salt, pepper and cloves. Bring to the boil.

3 Carefully lower the fish into the liquid. Reduce the heat and braise the fish for 15 minutes or until it is cooked through. Lift the fish out and put it on a serving dish. Keep hot.

4 Stir the cornflour mixture into the liquid remaining in the wok. Bring to the boil and cook, stirring constantly, for 2 minutes or until the sauce thickens. Spoon the sauce over the fish, garnish with spring onions, if using, and serve immediately.

Variation

Carp is popular in China because of its abundance. Tilapia, a dark-skinned fish, is a good substitute, but any firm-fleshed fish like salmon and halibut will do as well. Monkfish is another option, although expensive for any but very special occasions.

Sea Bass Energy 235kcal/983kJ; Protein 26g; Carbohydrate 8g, of which sugars 6g; Fat 11g, of which saturates 2g; Cholesterol 100mg; Calcium 217mg; Fibre 0.3g; Sodium 300mg
Braised Carp Energy 211kcal/883kJ; Protein 22.2g; Carbohydrate 5.4g, of which sugars 1.9g; Fat 11.4g, of which saturates 1.9g; Cholesterol 84mg; Calcium 62mg; Fibre 0g; Sodium 590mg.

Sweet and Sour Fish

When fish such as red mullet or snapper is cooked in this way the skin becomes crisp, while the flesh stays moist and juicy.

Serves 4–6

1 large or 2 medium fish, such as snapper or mullet, heads removed
20ml/4 tsp cornflour (cornstarch)
120ml/4fl oz/½ cup vegetable oil
15ml/1 tbsp chopped garlic
15ml/1 tbsp chopped fresh root ginger
30ml/2 tbsp chopped shallots
225g/8oz cherry tomatoes
30ml/2 tbsp red wine vinegar
30ml/2 tbsp sugar
30ml/2 tbsp tomato ketchup
15ml/1 tbsp fish sauce
45ml/3 tbsp water
salt and ground black pepper
coriander (cilantro) leaves and shredded spring onions (scallions), to garnish

1 Rinse and dry the fish. Score the skin diagonally on both sides, then coat the fish lightly all over with 15ml/3 tsp of the cornflour. Shake off any excess.

2 Heat the oil in a wok or large frying pan. Add the fish and cook over a medium heat for 6–7 minutes. Turn the fish over and cook for 6–7 minutes more, until it is crisp and brown.

3 Remove the fish and place on a large platter. Pour off all but 30ml/2 tbsp of the oil from the wok or pan and reheat.

4 Add the garlic, ginger and shallots to the wok or pan and cook them over a medium heat, stirring the pan occasionally, for about 3–4 minutes, until golden but not brown.

5 Add the cherry tomatoes to the wok or pan and cook until they burst open. Stir in the vinegar, sugar, tomato ketchup and fish sauce. Lower the heat and simmer gently for 1–2 minutes, then taste and adjust the seasoning.

6 In a cup, mix the remaining 5ml/1 tsp cornflour to a paste with the water. Stir into the sauce. Heat, stirring, until it thickens.

7 Pour the sauce over the fish, garnish with coriander leaves and shredded spring onions and serve.

Red Snapper with Fresh Coriander and Almonds

Fried almonds are a standard accompaniment for trout but are equally good with red snapper.

Serves 4

75g/3oz/¾ cup plain (all-purpose) flour
4 red snapper fillets
salt and ground black pepper
75g/3oz/6 tbsp butter
15ml/1 tbsp vegetable oil
75g/3oz/¾ cup flaked (sliced) almonds
grated rind and juice of 1 lime
small bunch of fresh coriander (cilantro), finely chopped
boiled rice and warm wheat flour tortillas, to serve

1 Preheat the oven to 140°C/275°F/Gas 1. Spread out the flour in a shallow dish and add seasoning. Dry the fish fillets with kitchen paper, then coat each fillet in the seasoned flour.

2 Heat the butter and oil in a wok or frying pan. Add the snapper fillets, in batches if necessary, and cook for 2 minutes.

3 Turn the snapper fillets over carefully using a fish slice and cook the other side until golden.

4 Using a metal spatula, carefully transfer the fillets to a shallow dish and keep them warm in the oven. Add the almonds to the fat remaining and fry them for 3–4 minutes, until golden.

5 Add the lime rind, juice and coriander to the almonds in the wok or frying pan and stir well. Heat through for 1–2 minutes, then pour the mixture over the fish. Serve with a bowl of rice or with warm wheat flour tortillas.

Cook's Tip
Warm the tortillas by wrapping them in foil and steaming them on a plate over boiling water for a few minutes. Alternatively, wrap them in microwave-safe film and heat them in a microwave on full power for about 1 minute.

Sweet and Sour Fish Energy 233kcal/969kJ; Protein 21.9g; Carbohydrate 6.3g, of which sugars 3g; Fat 13.5g, of which saturates 1.6g; Cholesterol 54mg; Calcium 16mg; Fibre 0.5g; Sodium 335mg.
Red Snapper Energy 433kcal/1803kJ; Protein 25.4g; Carbohydrate 16g, of which sugars 1.2g; Fat 30.2g, of which saturates 11.3g; Cholesterol 77mg; Calcium 115mg; Fibre 2g; Sodium 194mg.

Braised Whole Fish in Chilli and Garlic Sauce

In India there are an increasing number of unusual dishes that borrow from other cultures. The vinegar in the sauce for this fish dish is typical of Goa, but the rice wine and bean sauce reveal a distinct Szechuan influence.

Serves 4–6

1 carp, bream, sea bass, trout, grouper or grey mullet, about 675g/1½lb, gutted
15ml/1 tbsp light soy sauce
15ml/1 tbsp rice wine or dry sherry
vegetable oil, for deep-frying

For the sauce
2 garlic cloves, finely chopped
2 or 3 spring onions (scallions), finely chopped, the white and green parts separated
5ml/1 tsp finely chopped fresh root ginger
30ml/2 tbsp chilli bean sauce
15ml/1 tbsp tomato purée (paste)
10ml/2 tsp light brown sugar
15ml/1 tbsp rice vinegar
120ml/4fl oz/½ cup chicken stock
15ml/1 tbsp cornflour (cornstarch), mixed to a paste with 10ml/2 tsp water
a few drops of sesame oil

1 Rinse and dry the fish well. Using a sharp knife, score both sides of the fish down to the bone with diagonal cuts about 2.5cm/1in apart. Rub both sides of the fish with the soy sauce and rice wine or sherry. Set aside for 10–15 minutes to marinate.

2 Heat sufficient oil for deep-frying in a wok or deep frying pan. When it is hot, carefully add the fish and fry for 3–4 minutes on both sides, until golden brown.

3 To make the chilli and garlic sauce, pour away all but about 15ml/1 tbsp of the oil. Push the fish to one side of the wok or pan and add the garlic, the white part of the spring onions, the ginger, chilli bean sauce, tomato purée, sugar, vinegar and chicken stock. Bring to the boil and braise the fish in the sauce for 4–5 minutes, turning it over once.

4 Add the green of the spring onions. Stir in the cornflour paste to thicken the sauce. Sprinkle over a little sesame oil and serve.

Sour Carp Wraps

Carp is popular in China and South-east Asia. For a slightly simpler version of this dish, toss the cooked fish in the coriander and basil and serve the fish with noodles or rice and a simple, green salad.

Serves 4

500g/1¼lb carp fillets, each cut into 3 or 4 pieces
30ml/2 tbsp sesame oil
10ml/2 tsp ground turmeric
1 small bunch each fresh coriander (cilantro) and basil, stalks removed
20 lettuce leaves or rice wrappers
noodles or rice and green salad, to serve
fish sauce or other dipping sauce, for dipping

For the marinade
30ml/2 tbsp tamarind paste
15ml/1 tbsp soy sauce
juice of 1 lime
1 fresh green or red chilli, finely chopped
2.5cm/1in galangal root, peeled and grated
a few sprigs of fresh coriander (cilantro) leaves, finely chopped

1 Prepare the marinade by mixing together all the marinade ingredients in a large glass bowl. Toss the fish pieces in the marinade, cover with clear film (plastic wrap) and chill in the refrigerator for at least 6 hours, or overnight.

2 Lift the pieces of fish out of the marinade and lay them on a plate. Reserve the marinade for use later. Heat a wok or heavy pan, add the oil and stir in the turmeric. Working quickly, so that the turmeric doesn't burn, add the fish pieces, gently moving them around the wok for 2–3 minutes.

3 Add any remaining marinade to the pan and cook for a further 2–3 minutes, or until the pieces of fish are cooked.

4 To serve, divide the carp among four plates, sprinkle with the coriander and basil, and add some of the lettuce leaves or rice wrappers and a small bowl of dipping sauce to each serving.

5 To eat, tear off a bitesize piece of the fish, place it on a lettuce leaf or rice wrapper with a few herb leaves, fold it up into a roll, then dip it into the sauce.

Braised Whole Fish Energy 171kcal/715kJ; Protein 16.2g; Carbohydrate 3g, of which sugars 2g; Fat 10.7g, of which saturates 1.8g; Cholesterol 27mg; Calcium 26mg; Fibre 0.2g; Sodium 61mg.
Sour Carp Wraps Energy 205kcal/1277kJ; Protein 39.3g; Carbohydrate 7.2g, of which sugars 3.8g; Fat 12.3g, of which saturates 2.4g; Cholesterol 142mg; Calcium 10mg; Fibre 0g; Sodium 466mg.

Fragrant Swordfish with Lemon Grass

Swordfish is a firm-textured, meaty fish that cooks well in a wok if it has been marinated as steaks rather than cut in strips. If you cannot get swordfish, use fresh tuna.

Serves 4

1 kaffir lime leaf
45ml/3 tbsp rock salt
75ml/5 tbsp brown sugar
4 swordfish steaks, about 225g/8oz each
1 lemon grass stalk, sliced
2.5cm/1in fresh root ginger, cut into matchsticks
1 lime
15ml/1 tbsp grapeseed oil
1 large ripe avocado, peeled and stoned
salt and ground black pepper

1 Bruise the lime leaf by crushing slightly, to release the flavour.

2 Process the salt, sugar and lime leaf in a food processor.

3 Place the swordfish steaks in a bowl. Sprinkle the sugar mixture over them and add the lemon grass and ginger. Leave the steaks for 3–4 hours to marinate.

4 Rinse off the marinade and pat the fish dry with kitchen paper.

5 Peel the lime. Remove any excess pith from the peel. Cut the peel into very thin strips. Squeeze the juice from the fruit.

6 Heat a wok, then add the oil. When the oil is hot, add the lime rind and then the swordfish steaks. Stir-fry for 3–4 minutes. Add the lime juice. Turn off the heat, slice the avocado and add to the fish. Season to taste and serve.

Cook's Tip

Kaffir lime leaves are intensely aromatic with a distinctive figure-of-eight shape. They are used extensively in Indonesian and Thai cooking, and Thai cuisine also makes use of the rind of the lime fruit from this particular type of tree.

Catfish with a Chilli Coconut Sauce

In this popular Indonesian dish, fish is fried and served with a fragrant and spicy sauce. Serve with rice and pickled vegetables or a green mango or papaya salad.

Serves 4

200ml/7fl oz/scant 1 cup coconut milk
30–45ml/2–3 tbsp coconut cream
30–45ml/2–3 tbsp rice flour, tapioca flour or cornflour (cornstarch)
5–10ml/1–2 tsp ground coriander
8 fresh catfish fillets
30–45ml/2–3 tbsp coconut, palm groundnut (peanut) or corn oil
salt and ground black pepper
1 lime, quartered, to serve

For the spice paste

2 shallots, chopped
2 garlic cloves, chopped
2–3 red chillies, seeded and chopped
25g/1oz galangal, chopped
15g/½ oz fresh turmeric, chopped, or 2.5ml/½ tsp ground turmeric
2–3 lemon grass stalks, chopped
15–30ml/1–2 tbsp palm or groundnut (peanut) oil
5ml/1 tsp shrimp paste
15ml/1 tbsp tamarind paste
5ml/1 tsp palm sugar (jaggery)

1 Make the paste. Using a mortar and pestle, pound the shallots, garlic, chillies, galangal, turmeric and lemon grass to a paste.

2 Heat the oil in a wok or heavy pan, stir in the paste and fry until it is fragrant and begins to colour. Add the shrimp and tamarind pastes and sugar and stir until the mixture darkens.

3 Stir the coconut milk and cream into the paste and boil for 10 minutes, until the milk and cream separate, leaving behind an oily paste. Season the sauce with salt and pepper to taste.

4 Meanwhile, mix the flour with the coriander on a plate and season. Toss the catfish fillets in the flour until lightly coated.

5 Heat the oil in a heavy frying pan and quickly fry the fillets for about 2 minutes on each side, until golden brown.

6 Transfer the catfish fillets to a warmed serving platter and serve them with the spicy coconut sauce and with wedges of lime to squeeze over the fish.

Fragrant Swordfish Energy 342kcal/1429kJ; Protein 41.2g; Carbohydrate 0.8g, of which sugars 0.3g; Fat 19.2g, of which saturates 3.9g; Cholesterol 92mg; Calcium 14mg; Fibre 1.3g; Sodium 295mg.
Catfish Energy 338kcal/1412kJ; Protein 38.1g; Carbohydrate 11.9g, of which sugars 4.9g; Fat 15.3g, of which saturates 5.7g; Cholesterol 92mg; Calcium 56mg; Fibre 0.9g; Sodium 190mg.

Cod in a Tomato Sauce

Dusting cod with spices before cooking gives it a delectable coating.

Serves 4

30ml/2 tbsp cornflour (cornstarch)
5ml/1 tsp salt
5ml/1 tsp garlic powder
5ml/1 tsp chilli powder
5ml/1 tsp ground ginger
5ml/1 tsp ground fennel seeds
5ml/1 tsp ground coriander
2 medium cod fillets, each cut into 2 pieces
15ml/1 tbsp sunflower oil
mashed potatoes, to serve

For the sauce

30ml/2 tbsp tomato purée (paste)
5ml/1 tsp garam masala
5ml/1 tsp chilli powder
5ml/1 tsp crushed garlic
5ml/1 tsp grated fresh root ginger
2.5ml/½ tsp salt
175ml/6fl oz/¾ cup water
15ml/1 tbsp sunflower oil
1 bay leaf
3 or 4 black peppercorns
1cm/½in piece cinnamon stick
15ml/1 tbsp chopped fresh coriander (cilantro)
15ml/1 tbsp chopped fresh mint
mashed potatoes, to serve

1 Mix together the cornflour, salt, garlic powder, chilli powder, ground ginger, ground fennel seeds and ground coriander. Use the mixture to coat the four cod pieces.

2 Preheat the grill (broiler) to very hot, then reduce the heat slightly and place the cod under the heat. After about 5 minutes spoon the sunflower oil over the cod. Turn the cod over and repeat the process. Cook for a further 5 minutes, check that the fish is cooked through and set aside.

3 Make the sauce by mixing together the tomato purée, garam masala, chilli powder, garlic, ginger, salt and water. Set aside.

4 Heat the oil in a karahi or wok and add the bay leaf, peppercorns and cinnamon. Pour the sauce into the pan and reduce the heat to low. Bring slowly to the boil, stirring occasionally, then simmer for about 5 minutes.

5 Gently slide the pieces of fish into this mixture and cook for a further 2 minutes. Add the chopped fresh coriander and mint and serve the dish with mashed potatoes.

Sour Fish Stew with Star Fruit and Chilli

Somewhere between a stew and a soup, this refreshing dish is just one of many variations on the theme of sour fish stew found throughout South-east Asia. The star fruit are added towards the end of cooking so that they retain a bite.

Serves 4–6

30ml/2 tbsp coconut or palm oil
900ml/1½ pints/3¾ cups water
2 lemon grass stalks, bruised
25g/1oz fresh root ginger, finely sliced
about 675g/1½lb freshwater or saltwater fish, such as trout or sea bream, cut into thin steaks
2 firm star fruit (carambola), sliced
juice of 1–2 limes

For the spice paste

4 shallots, chopped
4 red chillies, seeded and chopped
2 garlic cloves, chopped
25g/1oz galangal, chopped
25g/1oz fresh turmeric, chopped
3–4 candlenuts, chopped

To serve

1 bunch fresh basil leaves
1 lime, cut into wedges
steamed rice

1 Using a mortar and pestle or food processor, grind all the spice paste ingredients together to form a coarse paste.

2 Heat the oil in a wok, stir in the spice paste and fry until fragrant. Add the water, lemon grass and ginger. Bring to the boil, stirring, then reduce the heat and simmer for 10 minutes.

3 Slip the fish into the wok, making sure there is enough cooking liquid to cover the fish and adding more water as required. Simmer gently for 3–4 minutes, then add the star fruit and lime juice. Simmer for a further 2–3 minutes, until the fish is cooked.

4 Divide the fish and star fruit between four to six warmed serving bowls and add a little of the cooking liquid. Garnish with basil leaves and a wedge of lime to squeeze over it. Serve the stew with bowls of steamed rice, which is moistened by spoonfuls of the remaining cooking liquid.

Cod in a Tomato Sauce Energy 294kcal/1229kJ; Protein 41.8g; Carbohydrate 2.7g, of which sugars 2.7g; Fat 12.8g, of which saturates 1.9g; Cholesterol 104mg; Calcium 26mg; Fibre 0.9g; Sodium 143mg.
Sour Fish Stew Energy 240kcal/1001kJ; Protein 25.9g; Carbohydrate 7.3g, of which sugars 4.7g; Fat 12.1g, of which saturates 1.2g; Cholesterol 0mg; Calcium 27mg; Fibre 1.7g; Sodium 67mg.

Fish Moolie

Choose a firm-textured fish like snapper so that the pieces stay intact during the brief cooking process.

Serves 4

500g/1¼lb firm-textured fish fillets, skinned and cut into 2.5cm/1in cubes
2.5ml/½ tsp salt
50g/2oz/⅔ cup desiccated (dry unsweetened shredded) coconut
6 shallots, roughly chopped
6 blanched almonds
2–3 garlic cloves, roughly chopped
2.5cm/1in piece fresh root ginger, peeled and sliced
2 lemon grass stalks, trimmed
10ml/2 tsp ground turmeric
45ml/3 tbsp vegetable oil
2 x 400ml/14fl oz cans coconut milk
1–3 fresh red or green chillies, seeded and sliced
salt and ground black pepper
fresh chives, to garnish

1 Spread out the pieces of fish in a shallow dish and sprinkle them with the salt. Dry-fry the coconut in a wok over medium to low heat, tip it into a food processor and process to an oily paste. Scrape into a bowl and reserve.

2 Add the shallots, almonds, garlic and ginger to the food processor. Cut off the lower 5cm/2in of the lemon grass stalks, chop roughly and add them to the mixture. Process to a paste.

3 Bruise the remaining lemon grass and set the stalks aside.

4 Add the ground turmeric to the mixture in the processor and process briefly to mix.

5 Heat the oil in the clean wok. Add the onion mixture and cook for a few minutes without browning. Stir in the coconut milk and bring to the boil, stirring constantly.

6 Add the cubes of fish, most of the sliced chillies and the bruised lemon grass stalks. Cook for 3–4 minutes. Stir in the coconut paste and cook for 2 minutes. Season.

7 Remove the lemon grass stalks. Spoon the moolie on to a hot serving dish and sprinkle with the remaining slices of chilli. Garnish with chives and serve.

Curried Monkfish with Okra and Tomatoes

An interesting combination of textures is used in this delicious fish dish.

Serves 4

450g/1lb monkfish
5ml/1 tsp ground turmeric
2.5ml/½ tsp chilli powder
2.5ml/½ tsp salt
5ml/1 tsp cumin seeds
2.5ml/½ tsp fennel seeds
2 dried red chillies
45ml/3 tbsp vegetable oil
1 onion, finely chopped
2 garlic cloves, crushed
4 tomatoes, skinned and finely chopped
150ml/¼ pint/⅔ cup water
225g/8oz okra, trimmed and cut into 2.5cm/1in lengths
5ml/1 tsp garam masala
tomato rice, to serve

1 Remove the membrane and bones from the monkfish, cut into 2.5cm/1in cubes and place in a dish. Mix together the turmeric, chilli powder and 1.5ml/¼ tsp of the salt and rub the mixture all over the fish. Marinate for 15 minutes.

2 Put the cumin seeds, fennel seeds and chillies in a wok or a large frying pan and dry-roast for about 3–4 minutes until a fragrant aroma is released. Put the spices into a blender, or use a mortar and pestle, and grind to a coarse powder.

3 Heat 30ml/2 tbsp of the oil in the frying pan and and fry the fish for about 4–5 minutes, turning occasionally. Remove with a slotted spoon and drain on kitchen paper.

4 Add the remaining oil to the pan and gently fry the onion and garlic for about 5 minutes, until soft and translucent. Add the spice powder and the remaining salt to the pan and fry for a further 2–3 minutes.

5 Stir the chopped tomatoes and the water into the pan. Simmer the mixture gently for 5 minutes, stirring occasionally.

6 Add the prepared okra and cook for about 5–7 minutes. Return the fish to the pan with the garam masala. Cover and simmer for 5–6 minutes or until tender. Serve with tomato rice.

Fish Moolie Energy 287kcal/1204kJ; Protein 21.3g; Carbohydrate 13g, of which sugars 12.3g; Fat 17.2g, of which saturates 8.2g; Cholesterol 18mg; Calcium 79mg; Fibre 2.1g; Sodium 493mg.
Curried Monkfish Energy 203kcal/851kJ; Protein 20.9g; Carbohydrate 7.7g, of which sugars 5.4g; Fat 10.2g, of which saturates 1.5g; Cholesterol 16mg; Calcium 119mg; Fibre 3.5g; Sodium 36mg.

Malaysian Fish Curry with Dried Red Chillies

The fish curries of Malaysia differ slightly from region to region, but most of them include Indian spices and coconut milk. The Malay food stalls often feature a fish, chicken or beef curry, which is usually served with bread or rice, pickles and extra chillies.

Serves 4

30ml/2 tbsp vegetable oil
7.5ml/1½ tsp tamarind paste
8 thick fish cutlets, each about 90g/3½oz, such as grouper, red snapper, trout or mackerel
900ml/1½ pints coconut milk
salt
fresh coriander (cilantro) leaves, roughly chopped, to garnish
rice or crusty bread, to serve

For the curry paste

4 shallots, chopped
4 garlic cloves, chopped
50g/2oz fresh root ginger, peeled and chopped
25g/1oz fresh turmeric, chopped
4–6 dried red chillies, softened in warm water, seeded and chopped
15ml/1 tbsp coriander seeds, roasted
15ml/1 tbsp cumin seeds, roasted
10ml/2 tsp fish curry powder
5ml/1 tsp fennel seeds
2.5ml/½ tsp black peppercorns

1 First make the paste. Using a mortar and pestle or food processor, grind the shallots, garlic, ginger, turmeric and chillies to a paste and transfer to a bowl.

2 Again, using the mortar and pestle or food processor, grind the roasted coriander and cumin seeds, fish curry powder, fennel seeds and peppercorns to a powder and add to the paste. Bind with 15ml/1 tbsp water and mix together.

3 Heat the oil in a wok or heavy pan. Stir in the paste and fry until fragrant. Add the tamarind paste and mix well. Add the fish cutlets and cook for 1 minute on each side. Pour in the coconut milk. Bring to the boil, then simmer for 10–15 minutes.

4 Season to taste with salt. Sprinkle the coriander over the top and serve with rice for a substantial meal, or with chunks of crusty bread for an appetizer.

Salmon Teriyaki

Japanese dishes are very popular in Korea, and the taste of this traditional teriyaki sauce echoes the flavour of bulgogi, one of the signature dishes of Korean cuisine. For bulgogi, high quality meat, usually beef, is sliced paper-thin and marinated in soy sauce, sesame seeds, spring onions and ginger. This marinade is rich and complex, combining the sweetness of maple syrup with the saltiness of soy sauce. which combine to make a truly delicious sticky glaze when cooked.

Serves 4

1 garlic clove, crushed
5ml/1 tsp grated fresh root ginger
30ml/2 tbsp dark soy sauce
15ml/1 tbsp rice vinegar
400g/14oz salmon fillet, cut into 4 portions
10ml/2 tsp sugar
15ml/1 tbsp sake or mirin (sweet rice wine)
5ml/1 tsp maple syrup
30ml/2 tbsp light soy sauce
60ml/4 tbsp olive oil

For the garnish

5ml/1 tsp sesame seeds
whole chives

1 Combine the garlic, ginger, dark soy sauce and rice vinegar in a shallow dish large enough to hold the salmon. Mix well, then add the salmon portions and coat them with the marinade. Cover and leave to marinate for 1 hour.

2 Mix the sugar, sake or mirin, maple syrup and light soy sauce in a small jug (pitcher) until thoroughly combined.

3 Heat a large, heavy frying pan or wok over a medium heat. Add the oil and when hot swirl the oil around the pan. Add the salmon to the pan, reserving the marinade. Cook the salmon, turning as necessary, until it is lightly browned on both sides.

4 Reduce the heat and pour any reserved marinade and the sake mixture over the salmon. Turn the salmon to ensure that the pieces are evenly coated. Cook gently for a few minutes, until the juices form a sticky glaze on the fish.

5 Transfer the salmon to warmed individual plates, garnish them with sesame seeds and whole chives and serve.

Malaysian Fish Curry Energy 264kcal/1109kJ; Protein 36.6g; Carbohydrate 12.7g, of which sugars 12.1g; Fat 7.7g, of which saturates 1.3g; Cholesterol 89mg; Calcium 110mg; Fibre 1g; Sodium 354mg.
Salmon Teriyaki Energy 239kcal/995kJ; Protein 24.8g; Carbohydrate 2.1g, of which sugars 1.7g; Fat 13.3g, of which saturates 2.3g; Cholesterol 58mg; Calcium 93mg; Fibre 0.3g; Sodium 323mg.

Eel and Butternut Squash in a Spicy Caramel Sauce

The flesh of an eel is very rich and firm and it has a wonderful flavour. It is a fish that has become more popular in recent years. This Vietnamese dish comes from the northern highlands, where eels are caught in the rivers.

Serves 4

45ml/3 tbsp raw cane sugar
30ml/2 tbsp soy sauce
45ml/3 tbsp nuoc mam (Vietnamese fish sauce)
2 garlic cloves, crushed
2 dried chillies
2–3 star anise
4–5 black peppercorns
350g/12oz eel on the bone, skinned, cut into 2.5cm/1in chunks
200g/7oz butternut squash, cut into bitesize chunks
4 spring onions (scallions), cut into bitesize pieces
30ml/2 tbsp sesame oil
5cm/2in fresh root ginger, peeled and cut into matchsticks
salt
cooked rice or noodles, to serve

1 Put the sugar in a wok or heavy pan with 30ml/2 tbsp water, and gently heat until it turns golden. Remove from the heat. Add the soy sauce and nuoc mam with 120ml/4fl oz/½ cup water. Add the garlic, chillies, star anise and peppercorns.

2 Return to the heat, add the eel chunks, squash and spring onions, coating the fish in the sauce, and season with salt. Reduce the heat, cover the pan and simmer gently for about 20 minutes, until the eel and vegetables are tender.

3 Meanwhile, heat a small wok or frying pan, pour in the oil and stir-fry the ginger until crisp and golden. Remove and drain on kitchen paper. Serve the eel with rice or noodles, with the crispy ginger sprinkled on top.

Cook's Tip

The fat rendered from the fish melts into the caramel sauce, making it deliciously velvety. The dish is often served with chopped fresh coriander (cilantro) on top.

Spiced Salmon Stir-fry with Clear Honey

Marinating salmon allows all the flavours to develop.

Serves 4

4 salmon steaks, 225g/8oz each
2 lemon grass stalks, trimmed and finely sliced
4 whole star anise, crushed
juice and finely grated rind of 3 limes
30ml/2 tbsp clear honey
30ml/2 tbsp grapeseed oil
salt and ground black pepper
lime wedges, to garnish

1 Remove the middle bone from each steak, using a very sharp filleting knife, and divide the fish to make two strips from each steak. Remove the skin by inserting the knife at the thin end of each piece of salmon (sprinkle a little salt on the board to prevent the fish slipping). Cut into diagonal slices.

2 Place the salmon in a non-metallic dish and add the star anise, lemon grass, lime juice and rind and honey. Season well with salt and pepper. Turn the salmon strips to coat. Cover with plastic wrap, and leave in the refrigerator to marinate overnight.

3 Carefully drain the salmon from the marinade, pat dry on kitchen paper and reserve the marinade.

4 Heat the oil in a wok. When hot, add the salmon and stir-fry, stirring constantly until cooked. Increase the heat, pour over the marinade and bring to the boil. Garnish with lime and serve.

Fried Anchovies and Peanuts

The Malays love fried dried anchovies, which they call ikan bilis goreng.

Serves 4

4 dried red chillies, soaked in warm water until soft, then seeded and chopped
4 shallots, chopped
2 garlic cloves, chopped
30ml/2 tbsp tamarind paste
vegetable oil, for deep-frying
200g/7oz dried anchovies, heads removed, washed and drained
115g/4oz/1 cup peanuts
30ml/2 tbsp sugar
bread or coconut rice, to serve

1 Using a food processor, grind the chillies, shallots and garlic to a coarse paste. Mix the tamarind paste with 120ml/4fl oz/½ cup of water.

2 Heat enough oil for deep-frying in a wok. Add the anchovies and deep-fry until brown and crisp. Drain on kitchen paper.

3 Lower the heat and deep-fry the peanuts in a wire basket, until they colour. Drain them on kitchen paper.

4 Pour out most of the oil from the wok, reserving 30ml/2 tbsp. Stir in the spice paste and fry until fragrant. Add the sugar, anchovies and peanuts. Gradually stir in the tamarind water, allowing it to evaporate so the mixture remains dry.

5 Serve the dish hot or cold with bread or coconut rice.

Eel in a Spicy Caramel Sauce Energy 204Kcal/857kJ; Protein 11g; Carbohydrate 20g, of which sugars 14g; Fat 10g, of which saturates 1g; Cholesterol 0mg; Calcium 76mg; Fibre 1g; Sodium 110mg.
Spiced Salmon Stir-fry Energy 508kcal/2115kJ; Protein 45.5g; Carbohydrate 7.7g, of which sugars 7.7g; Fat 33g, of which saturates 5.3g; Cholesterol 113mg; Calcium 48mg; Fibre 0g; Sodium 102mg.
Anchovies and Peanuts Energy 338Kcal/1400kJ; Protein 17g; Carbohydrate 4.8g, of which sugars 2.6g; Fat 28g, of which saturates 4.4g; Cholesterol 24mg; Calcium 134mg; Fibre 2g; Sodium

Mackerel with Black Beans

Shiitake mushrooms, ginger and black beans are perfect served with robust mackerel.

Serves 4

20 dried shiitake mushrooms
15ml/1 tbsp finely julienned fresh root ginger
3 star anise
8 x 115g/4oz mackerel fillets
45ml/3 tbsp dark soy sauce
15ml/1 tbsp Chinese rice wine
15ml/1 tbsp salted black beans
6 spring onions (scallions), finely shredded
30ml/2 tbsp sunflower oil
5ml/1 tsp sesame oil
4 garlic cloves, very thinly sliced
sliced cucumber and steamed basmati rice, to serve

1 Place the dried mushrooms in a large bowl and cover with boiling water. Soak for 20 minutes. Drain, reserving the soaking liquid, discard the stems and slice the caps thinly.

2 Place a trivet rack in a large wok and pour in 5cm/2in of the mushroom liquid. Add half the ginger and the star anise.

3 Divide the mackerel between two lightly oiled heatproof plates, skin side up. Cut three diagonal slits in each one. Insert the remaining ginger strips and sprinkle over the mushrooms. Bring the liquid to the boil and put one of the plates on the trivet.

4 Cover the wok, reduce the heat and steam for about 10–12 minutes, or until the mackerel is cooked. Repeat with the second plate of fish. Put all the fish on a platter and keep warm.

5 Ladle 105ml/7 tbsp of the steaming liquid from the wok into a pan with the soy sauce, wine and black beans. Place over a gentle heat and bring to a simmer. Spoon over the fish and sprinkle over the spring onions.

6 Heat the oils and stir-fry the garlic until lightly golden. Pour over the fish and serve with the cucumber and rice.

Cook's Tip
Use two woks and trivets to cook the mackerel in half the time.

Spicy Pan-seared Tuna with Cucumber, Garlic and Ginger

This popular Vietnamese dish is made with many types of thick-fleshed fish. Tuna is particularly suitable for pan-searing, because it is delicious served a little rare.

Serves 4

1 small cucumber
10ml/2 tsp sesame oil
2 garlic cloves, crushed
4 tuna steaks

For the dressing

4cm/1½in fresh root ginger, peeled and roughly chopped
1 garlic clove, peeled and roughly chopped
2 green Thai chillies, seeded and roughly chopped
45ml/3 tbsp raw cane sugar
45ml/3 tbsp nuoc mam (Vietnamese fish sauce)
juice of 1 lime
60ml/4 tbsp water

1 To make the dressing, grind the root ginger, and the chopped garlic and chillies to a pulp with the sugar, using a mortar and pestle. Stir in the nuoc mam, lime juice and water, and mix well. Leave the dressing to stand for 15 minutes.

2 Cut the cucumber in half lengthways and remove the seeds. Cut the flesh into long, thin strips. Toss the cucumber in the dressing and leave to soak for at least 15 minutes.

3 Wipe a heavy wok or pan with the oil and rub the garlic around it. Heat the pan and add the tuna steaks. Sear for a few minutes on both sides, so that the outside is slightly charred but the inside is still rare. Lift the steaks on to a warm serving dish.

4 Using tongs or chopsticks, lift the cucumber strips out of the dressing and arrange them around the steaks. Drizzle the dressing over the tuna, and serve immediately.

Cook's Tip
Tuna is easy to overcook and dries out quickly. Use a heavy pan and make sure it is really hot before you add the fish so that the outside seals and browns quickly.

Mackerel with Beans Energy 693kcal/2872kJ; Protein 45.5g; Carbohydrate 1.9g, of which sugars 0.5g; Fat 55.9g, of which saturates 10.4g; Cholesterol 128mg; Calcium 35mg; Fibre 0.6g; Sodium 152mg.
Spicy Pan-seared Tuna Energy 262Kcal/1103kJ; Protein 31g; Carbohydrate 16g, of which sugars 13g; Fat 8g, of which saturates 2g; Cholesterol 35mg; Calcium 44mg; Fibre 0.5g; Sodium 150mg

Tuna Curry

This is the perfect fish curry for any cook with a well-stocked store cupboard since it can be made in a matter of minutes.

Serves 4

1 onion
1 red (bell) pepper
1 green (bell) pepper
30ml/2 tbsp oil
1.5ml/¼ tsp cumin seeds
2.5ml/½ tsp ground cumin
2.5ml/½ tsp ground coriander
2.5ml/½ tsp chilli powder
1.5ml/¼ tsp salt
2 garlic cloves, crushed
400g/14oz can tuna in brine, drained and flaked
1 fresh green chilli, finely chopped
2.5cm/1in piece fresh root ginger, grated
1.5ml/¼ tsp garam masala
5ml/1 tsp lemon juice
30ml/2 tbsp chopped fresh coriander (cilantro)
fresh coriander sprig, to garnish
pitta bread and cucumber raita, to serve

1 Thinly slice the onion and the red and green peppers, discarding the seeds from the peppers.

2 Heat the oil in a karahi, wok or heavy pan and stir-fry the cumin seeds for 2–3 minutes until they begin to spit and splutter.

3 Add the ground cumin, coriander, chilli powder and salt to the pan and cook for 2–3 minutes until fragrant. Then add the garlic, onion and peppers to the pan and stir in.

4 Fry the vegetables, stirring from time to time, for 5–7 minutes until the onion has browned. Stir in the tuna, chopped green chilli and grated ginger and cook for 5 minutes.

5 Add the garam masala, lemon juice and chopped fresh coriander to the pan, stir well to mix, and continue to cook the curry for a further 3–4 minutes.

6 Meanwhile, place the pitta breads on a grill (broiler) rack and grill (broil) until they just puff up. Split with a sharp knife.

7 Serve the curry in the pitta breads with the cucumber raita, garnished with a coriander sprig.

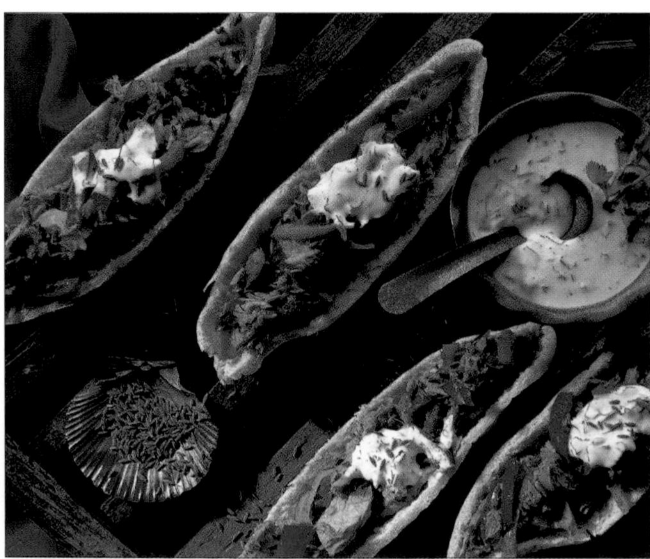

Vinegar Fish

Fish cooked in a spicy mixture that includes chillies, ginger and vinegar is delicious. The method lends itself particularly well to strong-flavoured oily fish, such as the mackerel that are regularly caught off the coast of Goa.

Serves 2–3

2 or 3 mackerel, filleted
2 or 3 fresh red chillies, seeded
4 macadamia nuts or 8 almonds
1 red onion, quartered
2 garlic cloves, crushed
1cm/½in piece fresh root ginger, sliced
5ml/1 tsp ground turmeric
45ml/3 tbsp coconut oil or vegetable oil
45ml/3 tbsp wine vinegar
150ml/¼ pint/⅔ cup water
salt
deep-fried onions and finely chopped fresh chilli, to garnish
steamed rice, to serve (optional)

1 Rinse the mackerel fillets in cold water and dry them well on kitchen paper. Set aside.

2 Put the chillies, macadamia nuts or almonds, onion, garlic, ginger, turmeric and 15ml/1 tbsp of the oil in a food processor and process to form a paste. Alternatively, pound them together in a mortar with a pestle.

3 Heat the remaining oil in a karahi, wok or pan. Add the spice and nut paste to the pan and cook for 1–2 minutes without browning. Stir in the wine vinegar and water, and season with salt to taste. Bring the sauce to the boil, then lower the heat.

4 Add the mackerel fillets to the sauce and simmer for 6–8 minutes, or until the fish is tender and cooked.

5 Transfer the mackerel to a large, warm serving platter. Bring the spicy sauce to the boil and cook for 1 minute, or until it has reduced slightly.

6 Pour the spicy sauce over the cooked mackerel, garnish the platter with the deep-fried onions and chopped chilli and serve with steamed rice, if you like.

Tuna Curry Energy 1209kcal/5077kJ; Protein 27.5g; Carbohydrate 8.2g, of which sugars 2.8g; Fat 120.1g, of which saturates 10.8g; Cholesterol 31mg; Calcium 1mg; 1.7g.
Vinegar Fish Energy 624kcal/2589kJ; Protein 40.4g; Carbohydrate 1.4g, of which sugars 0.6g; Fat 50.8g, of which saturates 8.5g; Cholesterol 108mg; Calcium 65mg; Fibre 1.4g; Sodium 135mg.

Singapore Fish Head Curry

The origins of this popular Singaporean dish have become a little blurred with time. Some say it came with immigrants from south India; others claim an Indian chef in Singapore created it as a way of using a part of the fish that was usually thrown away. It is now made in numerous versions in Singapore and Malaysia. There is a surprising amount of delicate flesh to be found on a large fish head: the succulent cheeks are particularly prized.

Serves 2

30ml/2 tbsp ghee or vegetable oil
10ml/2 tsp brown mustard seeds
5ml/1 tsp fenugreek seeds
5ml/1 tsp cumin seeds
a handful of curry leaves
15ml/1 tbsp palm sugar (jaggery)
30ml/2 tbsp tamarind pulp, soaked in 150ml/¼ pint/⅔ cup water and strained for juice
600ml/1 pint/2½ cups coconut milk
1 large fresh fish head, such as red snapper (about 900g/2lb), cleaned
5 okra, halved diagonally
2 large tomatoes, skinned, seeded and quartered
salt and ground black pepper
steamed rice and pickles, to serve

For the spice paste
8 shallots, chopped
6 garlic cloves, chopped
4 red chillies, seeded and chopped
50g/2oz fresh root ginger, peeled and chopped
25g/1oz fresh turmeric, chopped
1 lemon grass stalk, trimmed and chopped
30ml/2 tbsp fish curry powder

1 To make the spice paste, grind all the ingredients together using a mortar and pestle or food processor.

2 Heat the ghee or oil in a wok or heavy pan. Stir in the mustard seeds, fenugreek and cumin seeds along with the curry leaves. Fry until the mustard seeds begin to pop and then stir in the spice paste. Fry until fragrant, then stir in the sugar, followed by the tamarind juice and coconut milk.

3 Bring to the boil, reduce the heat and add the fish head. Simmer gently for 10 minutes, then add the okra and tomatoes to the pan. Simmer for another 10 minutes or until the fish head is cooked. Season the sauce and serve with steamed rice and pickles.

Sardines in Spicy Coconut Milk

This deliciously spiced fish dish is based on coconut milk. The dish is particularly fiery but its heat is tempered by the use of herbs.

Serves 4

6–8 red chillies, according to taste, seeded and chopped
4 shallots, chopped
4 garlic cloves, chopped
1 lemon grass stalk, chopped
25g/1oz galangal, chopped
30ml/2 tbsp coconut or palm oil
10ml/2 tsp coriander seeds
5ml/1 tsp cumin seeds
5ml/1 tsp fennel seeds
1 small bunch fresh mint leaves, finely chopped
1 small bunch fresh flat leaf parsley, finely chopped
15ml/1 tbsp palm sugar (jaggery)
15ml/1 tbsp tamarind paste
4 sardines or small mackerel, gutted, but kept whole
300ml/½ pint/1¼ cups coconut milk
salt and ground black pepper
steamed rice or sago, 1 large bunch fresh flat leaf parsley and fresh basil leaves, to serve

1 Using a mortar and pestle, pound the chillies, shallots, garlic, lemon grass and galangal to a paste.

2 Heat the oil in a wok or wide, heavy pan, stir in the coriander, cumin and fennel seeds and fry until they give off a fragrant aroma. Add the spicy paste and stir until it becomes golden in colour. Add the chopped mint and parsley and stir for about 1 minute, then add the sugar and tamarind paste.

3 Carefully place the fish in the pan and toss gently to coat it thoroughly in the paste. Pour in the coconut milk and stir gently.

4 Bring the fish to the boil in the pan, then reduce the heat and simmer the mixture for 10–15 minutes, until the fish is tender when flaked using a fork. Season the sauce with salt and ground black pepper to taste.

5 Cover the bottom of a warmed serving dish with sprigs of parsley, place the fish on top, then spoon the sauce over.

6 Serve with a bowl of steamed rice or sago and extra stalks of fresh parsley and basil leaves to cut the spice.

Singapore Curry Energy 417kcal/1760kJ; Protein 42.2g; Carbohydrate 30.4g, of which sugars 29.1g; Fat 15.2g, of which saturates 2.7g; Cholesterol 74mg; Calcium 231mg; Fibre 2.7g; Sodium 497mg.
Sardines in Coconut Milk Energy 287kcal/1199kJ; Protein 22.8g; Carbohydrate 11g, of which sugars 10.2g; Fat 17.2g, of which saturates 3.7g; Cholesterol 0mg; Calcium 167mg; Fibre 2.1g; Sodium 213mg.

Fresh Spring Rolls with Palm Heart

This delicious recipe from the Philippines uses palm hearts.

Serves 3–4
6 spring onions (scallions)
30ml/2 tbsp coconut oil
225g/8oz tofu, rinsed, cut into 3
2 garlic cloves, finely chopped
2 carrots, cut into 5cm/2in strips
12 fresh prawns (shrimp), shelled and deveined
400g/14oz can coconut palm hearts, cut into 5cm/2in strips
30–45ml/2–3 tbsp light soy sauce
10ml/2 tsp sugar
soft lettuce leaves
suka (coconut vinegar), to serve
salt and ground black pepper

For the wrappers
115g/4oz/1 cup plain (all-purpose) white flour
15ml/1 tbsp cornflour (cornstarch)
pinch of salt
400ml/14fl oz/1⅔ cups water
corn oil, for frying

1 For the wrappers, sift the flour, cornflour and salt into a bowl, add the water and whisk to a batter. Rest for 30 minutes.

2 Heat a crêpe pan and wipe with a little oil. Ladle one-twelfth of the batter into the pan, tilting it to spread the batter evenly. Cook over a medium-low heat, on one side only, until the batter sets, is pale in colour and loosens at the edges. Transfer to a plate. Repeat. Put the wrappers aside.

3 To prepare the filling, cut off the green stems of the spring onions and halve lengthways. Cut the white stems into 5cm/2in lengths and then quarter each piece lengthways. Set aside.

4 Heat the oil in a wok, add the tofu and fry until golden. Drain on kitchen paper, cut each piece into thin strips and set aside.

5 Add the garlic and carrots to the wok and stir-fry for 2–3 minutes. Add the white parts of the spring onions and the prawns to the wok and fry for 2–3 minutes of until they turn opaque. Add the palm hearts, tofu, soy sauce and sugar, and heat through. Season to taste and tip on to a plate to cool.

6 Place a lettuce leaf on each wrapper. Spoon on some mixture and roll up. Use green spring onions to tie the bundles and place on a serving dish. Serve with suka for dipping.

Crispy Rolls with Pumpkin, Tofu, Peanuts and Chillies

This is one of the best Vietnamese 'do-it-yourself' dishes. You place all the ingredients on the table with the rice wrappers for everyone to assemble their own rolls.

Serves 4 to 5
about 30ml/2 tbsp groundnut (peanut) or sesame oil
175g/6oz tofu, rinsed and patted dry
4 shallots, halved and sliced
2 garlic cloves, finely chopped
350g/12oz pumpkin flesh, cut into strips
1 carrot, cut into strips
15ml/1 tbsp soy sauce
3–4 green Thai chillies, seeded and finely sliced
1 crispy lettuce, torn into strips
1 bunch fresh basil, stalks removed
115g/4oz/⅔ cup roasted peanuts, chopped
100ml/3½fl oz/scant ½ cup hoisin sauce
20 dried rice wrappers
salt
chilli sauce (optional), to serve

1 Heat a wok and smear with oil. Place the tofu in the wok and sear on both sides. Transfer to a plate and cut into thin strips.

2 Heat 30ml/2 tbsp oil in the wok and stir in the shallots and garlic. Add the pumpkin and carrot, then pour in the soy sauce and 120ml/4fl oz/½ cup water. Add a little salt and cook gently until the vegetables have softened but still have a bite to them.

3 Meanwhile, arrange the tofu, chillies, lettuce, basil, peanuts and hoisin sauce in separate dishes and put them on the table. Fill a bowl with hot water and place it on the table or fill a bowl for each person, and place the wrappers beside it. Transfer the vegetable mixture to a dish and place on the table.

4 To eat, dip a wrapper in the water for a few seconds to soften. Lay it flat on the table or on a plate and, just off-centre, spread a few strips of lettuce, then the pumpkin mixture, some tofu, a sprinkling of chillies, some hoisin sauce, some basil leaves and peanuts, to layer the ingredients. Pull the shorter edge (the side with filling on it) over the stack, tuck in the sides and roll into a cylinder. Dip the roll into chilli sauce, if you like.

Spring Rolls Energy 307kcal/1289kJ; Protein 19.5g; Carbohydrate 32.8g, of which sugars 7g; Fat 11.7g, of which saturates 1.4g; Cholesterol 122mg; Calcium 433mg; Fibre 2.8g; Sodium 797mg.
Crispy Rolls Energy 402kcal/1669kJ; Protein 14g; Carbohydrate 29g, of which sugars 13g; Fat 26g, of which saturates 5g; Cholesterol 0mg; Calcium 321mg; Fibre 4.1g; Sodium 0.4g.

Deep-fried Bean Curd Rolls Stuffed with Spiced Vegetables

Bean curd sheets are available in Asian supermarkets and need to be dunked briefly in water before they can be used.

Serves 4

30ml/2 tbsp groundnut (peanut) oil
50g/2oz fresh enokitake mushrooms, finely chopped
1 garlic clove, crushed
5ml/1 tsp grated fresh root ginger
4 spring onions (scallions), finely shredded
1 small carrot, cut into thin matchsticks
115g/4oz bamboo shoots, cut into thin matchsticks
15ml/1 tbsp light soy sauce
5ml/1 tsp chilli sauce
5ml/1 tsp sugar
15ml/1 tbsp cornflour (cornstarch)
8 bean curd sheets (approximately 18 x 23cm/7 x 9in each)
sunflower oil, for deep-frying
crisp salad leaves, to serve

1 Heat the oil in a wok and add the mushrooms, garlic, ginger, spring onions, carrot and bamboo shoots. Stir-fry for 2–3 minutes, add the soy sauce, chilli sauce and sugar, and mix thoroughly. Remove the vegetables from the heat and place in a sieve (strainer) to drain the juices. Set aside to cool.

2 In a small bowl, mix the cornflour with 60ml/4 tbsp of cold water to form a smooth paste. Soak the bean curd sheets in a bowl of warm water for 10–15 seconds and then lay them out on a clean work surface and pat dry with kitchen paper.

3 Brush the edges of one bean curd sheets with the cornflour paste and place 30ml/2 tbsp of the vegetable mixture at one end of the sheet. Fold the edges towards the centre and roll up to form a roll. Repeat with the remaining sheets and filling.

4 Place the filled rolls on a baking parchment-lined baking sheet or tray, cover and chill for 3–4 hours.

5 Fill a wok one-third full with oil and heat to 180°C/350°F. Working in batches, deep-fry the rolls for 2–3 minutes until golden. Drain on kitchen paper and serve with salad leaves.

Pancakes with Stir-fried Vegetables

To eat, each person spreads a little hoisin sauce over a pancake, adds some vegetables and rolls up the pancake.

Serves 4

3 eggs
30ml/2 tbsp water
60ml/4 tbsp groundnut oil
25g/1oz dried Chinese black mushrooms
25g/1oz dried cloud ear (wood ear) mushrooms
10ml/2 tsp cornflour (cornstarch)
30ml/2 tbsp light soy sauce
30ml/2 tbsp Chinese rice wine
10ml/2 tsp sesame oil
2 garlic cloves, finely chopped
1cm/½ in fresh root ginger, shredded
75g/3oz canned sliced bamboo shoots, drained and rinsed
175g/6oz beansprouts
4 spring onions (scallions), finely shredded
salt and ground black pepper
Chinese pancakes and hoisin sauce, to serve

1 Whisk the eggs, water and seasoning together. Heat 15ml/1 tbsp of the groundnut oil in a wok. Add the eggs and tilt the wok so they spread evenly. Cook for about 2 minutes until set. Turn on to a board, roll up and cut into thin strips. Wipe the wok clean.

2 Put the black mushrooms and the cloud ears into separate bowls. Pour over warm water to cover the mushrooms, and then leave to soak for 20–30 minutes until soft. Drain the mushrooms, squeezing out the excess liquid. Strain 20ml/4fl oz/ 1½ cup of the excess mushroom soaking liquid into a bowl.

3 Remove the stalks and thinly slice the black mushrooms. Finely shred the cloud ears. Set aside. Blend the cornflour with the reserved liquid, soy sauce, rice wine and sesame oil.

4 Heat the wok over a medium heat, add the remaining oil and swirl it around. Add the cloud ears and black mushrooms and stir-fry for about 2 minutes. Add the garlic, ginger, bamboo shoots and beansprouts and stir-fry for 1–2 minutes.

5 Pour in the cornflour mixture and cook, stirring, for 1 minute until thickened. Add the spring onions and omelette strips and toss gently. Adjust the seasoning, adding more soy sauce, if needed. Serve at once with Chinese pancakes and hoisin sauce.

Deep-fried Beancurd Energy 184kcal/773kJ; Protein 4g; Carbohydrate 25.3g, of which sugars 3.2g; Fat 7.1g, of which saturates 1.2g; Cholesterol 0mg; Calcium 4mg; Fibre 1.7g; Sodium 260mg.
Pancakes with Vegetables Energy 219kcal/910kJ; Protein 8g; Carbohydrate 6.6g, of which sugars 2.6g; Fat 17.3g, of which saturates 2.8g; Cholesterol 143mg; Calcium 46mg; Fibre 1.8g; Sodium 328mg.

Sweet Yellow Peppers Stuffed with Mushrooms and Garlic

This is an unusual recipe in that the stuffed peppers are steamed rather than baked. The technique is speedy and the result is beautifully light and tender.

Serves 4

3 garlic cloves, finely chopped
2 coriander (cilantro) roots, finely chopped
400g/14oz/3 cups button (white) or field (portabello) mushrooms, quartered
5ml/1 tsp Thai red curry paste
1 egg, lightly beaten
15–30ml/1–2 tbsp light soy sauce
2.5ml/½ tsp sugar
3 kaffir lime leaves, finely chopped
4 yellow (bell) peppers, halved lengthways and seeded

1 In a mortar or spice grinder pound or blend the finely chopped garlic and the coriander roots. Scrape into a bowl.

2 Put the mushrooms in a food processor and pulse briefly until they are finely chopped. Add to the garlic mixture in the bowl, then stir in the curry paste, beaten egg, soy sauce, sugar and lime leaves until thoroughly mixed.

3 Place the pepper halves in a single layer in a steamer basket over a wok. Spoon the mixture loosely into the pepper halves.

4 Bring the water in the steamer to the boil, then lower the heat to a simmer. Steam the peppers for 15 minutes, or until the flesh feels tender when tested with a knife tip.

5 Lift out the pepper halves out of the steamer, taking care not to disturb the filling, and place them on a serving platter. They can be eaten hot, at room temperature or cold.

Variation
For a colourful change, use red, orange or green (bell) peppers, or try a combination. This recipe can easily be doubled or trebled to serve more guests.

Spicy Bitter Gourds

Bitter gourds are widely used in Indian cooking, both on their own as a side dish and combined with other vegetables in a curry.

Serves 4

675g/1½lb bitter gourds
60ml/4 tbsp vegetable oil
2.5ml/½ tsp cumin seeds
6 spring onions (scallions), chopped
5 tomatoes, finely chopped
2.5cm/1in piece root ginger, finely chopped
2 garlic cloves, crushed
2 fresh green chillies, seeded and finely chopped
2.5ml/½ tsp salt, plus extra to taste
2.5ml/½ tsp chilli powder
5ml/1 tsp ground coriander
5ml/1 tsp ground cumin
45ml/3 tbsp peanuts, crushed
45ml/3 tbsp soft dark brown sugar
15ml/1 tbsp gram flour
fresh coriander (cilantro) sprigs, to garnish

1 Bring a large pan of lightly salted water to the boil. Peel the gourds using a sharp knife and halve them. Discard the seeds. Cut into 2cm/¾in pieces, then cook in the water for 10–15 minutes, or until they are tender. Drain well and set aside.

2 Heat the oil in a large wok and fry the cumin seeds for about 2 minutes until they begin to splutter. Add the spring onions and fry for 3–4 minutes. Add the tomatoes, ginger, garlic and chillies and cook for 5 minutes.

3 Add the salt, remaining spices, the peanuts and sugar and cook for about 2–3 minutes, stirring constantly.

4 Add the bitter gourds and mix well. Sprinkle over the gram flour. Cover and simmer over a low heat for 5–8 minutes, or until all of the flour has been absorbed into the sauce. Serve garnished with fresh coriander sprigs.

Cook's Tip
For a quick and easy way to crush peanuts, put them into a food processor or blender and process them for about 20–30 seconds.

Sweet Yellow Peppers Energy 89kcal/374kJ; Protein 5.1g; Carbohydrate 10.6g, of which sugars 9.9g; Fat 3.2g, of which saturates 0.8g; Cholesterol 48mg; Calcium 27mg; Fibre 3.5g; Sodium 563mg.
Spicy Bitter Gourds Energy 304kcal/1268kJ; Protein 8.9g; Carbohydrate 27g, of which sugars 19.6g; Fat 18.6g, of which saturates 2.8g; Cholesterol 0mg; Calcium 89mg; Fibre 3.8g; Sodium 19mg.

Pan-fried Chilli Parsnip and Shiitake Mushrooms

This dish has its roots in the temples of Korea, although this contemporary version adds more spices and seasoning than the originals.

Serves 4

150g/5oz parsnips, finely sliced
a little sesame oil, for coating
a little vegetable oil, for stir-frying
115g/4oz fresh shiitake mushrooms
salt
15ml/1 tbsp pine nuts, ground, to garnish
sesame oil, to season

For the sauce

45ml/3 tbsp gochujang chilli paste
5ml/1 tsp Korean chilli powder
15ml/1 tbsp maple syrup
5ml/1 tsp sugar
5ml/1 tsp soy sauce
5ml/1 tsp sesame oil

1 Place the parsnips in a bowl and add a little sesame oil and salt. Coat the slices evenly. Set aside for 10 minutes.

2 For the sauce, mix the chilli paste and powder, maple syrup, sugar, soy sauce and sesame oil with a little water.

3 Heat a wok or frying pan and add a little vegetable oil. Sauté the finely sliced parsnips until they are softened and lightly browned. Then transfer the parsnips to a bowl and then add enough of the chilli sauce to coat them well.

4 Discard the stalks from the shiitake mushrooms and spoon the remaining chilli sauce into the caps.

5 Return the sautéed parsnips to the pan, with their sauce, and then add the mushrooms with their sauce.

6 Cook the parsnip and mushroom mixture over low heat, allowing the chilli mixture to infuse the vegetables and form a sticky glaze. Then add more of the chilli sauce if necessary.

7 When the vegetables are cooked and the liquid has reduced, transfer them to a warmed serving dish, season with sesame oil and sprinkle with ground pine nuts.

Yard-long Bean Stew with Chillies

The southern Luzon peninsula in the Philippines is renowned for its fiery food, laced with hot chillies and coconut milk. In typical style, this rich, pungent dish is hot and, believe it or not, it is served with extra chillies to chew on.

Serves 3 to 4

30–45ml/2–3 tbsp coconut or groundnut (peanut) oil
1 onion, finely chopped
2–3 garlic cloves, finely chopped
40g/1½oz fresh root ginger, finely chopped
1 lemon grass stalk, bruised and finely chopped
4–5 red chillies, seeded and finely chopped
15ml/1 tbsp shrimp paste
15–30ml/1–2 tbsp tamarind paste
15–30ml/1–2 tbsp palm sugar (jaggery)
2 x 400g/14oz cans unsweetened coconut milk
4 kaffir lime leaves
500g/1¼lb yard-long (snake) beans
sea salt and freshly ground black pepper
1 bunch of fresh coriander (cilantro) leaves, roughly chopped, to garnish
cooked rice and raw chillies, to serve

1 Heat the oil in a wok or large, heavy frying pan that has a lid. Swirl the oil round the pan, then stir in the onion, garlic, ginger, lemon grass and chillies and fry until fragrant and beginning to colour. Add the shrimp paste, tamarind paste and sugar and mix well. Stir in the coconut milk and the lime leaves.

2 Bring the mixture to the boil, reduce the heat and toss in the whole yard-long beans. Partially cover the pan and cook the beans gently for 6–8 minutes until tender.

3 Season the stew with salt and pepper and garnish with chopped coriander. Serve with rice and extra chillies, if you like.

Cook's Tip

If you prefer, then you can reduce the quantity of chillies used in the recipe to suit your taste buds, and omit the extra chillies served with the stew.

Pan-fried Chilli Parsnip Energy 86kcal/362kJ; Protein 2.3g; Carbohydrate 10.4g, of which sugars 6.4g; Fat 4.4g, of which saturates 0.5g; Cholesterol 0mg; Calcium 26mg; Fibre 2.1g; Sodium 106mg.
Yard-long Bean Stew Energy 200kcal/840kJ; Protein 5.5g; Carbohydrate 24.4g, of which sugars 22.9g; Fat 9.7g, of which saturates 1.5g; Cholesterol 19mg; Calcium 158mg; Fibre 3.4g; Sodium 384mg.

Mixed Stir-fry with Peanut Sauce

Wherever you go in Asia, stir-fried vegetables will be on the menu.

Serves 4–6

6 Chinese black mushrooms (dried shiitake), soaked in lukewarm water for 20 minutes
20 tiger lily buds, soaked in lukewarm water for 20 minutes
60ml/4 tbsp sesame oil
225g/8oz tofu, sliced
1 large onion, finely sliced
1 large carrot, finely sliced
300g/11oz pak choi (bok choy), leaves separated from stems
225g/8oz can bamboo shoots, drained and rinsed
50ml/2fl oz/¼ cup soy sauce
10ml/2 tsp sugar

For the peanut sauce

15ml/1 tbsp sesame oil
2 garlic cloves, finely chopped
2 fresh red chillies, seeded and finely chopped
90g/3½oz/scant 1 cup unsalted roasted peanuts, finely chopped
150ml/5fl oz/⅔ cup coconut milk
30ml/2 tbsp hoisin sauce
15ml/1 tbsp soy sauce
15ml/1 tbsp sugar

1 To make the sauce, heat the oil in a wok and stir-fry the garlic and chillies until they begin to colour, then add almost all of the peanuts. Stir-fry for 2–3 minutes, then add the remaining ingredients. Boil, then simmer until thickened. Keep warm.

2 Drain the mushrooms and lily buds and squeeze out any excess water. Cut the mushroom caps into strips using a sharp knife, and discard the stalks. Trim off the hard ends of the lily buds and discard. Tie a knot in the centre of each lily bud.

3 Heat 30ml/2 tbsp of the oil in a wok and brown the tofu on both sides. Drain and cut it into strips.

4 Heat the remaining oil in the wok and stir-fry the onion, carrot and pak choi stems for 2 minutes.

5 Add the mushrooms, lily buds, tofu and bamboo shoots and stir-fry for 1 minute more. Toss in the pak choi leaves, soy sauce and sugar. Stir-fry until heated through.

6 Transfer to a large warmed serving dish, garnish with the remaining peanuts and serve with the peanut sauce.

Black Bean and Vegetable Stir-fry

This is a great supper dish for vegetarians. When stir-frying a mixture of vegetables, the ingredients need to be added to the wok in the right order so that larger pieces have a longer cooking time than the smaller ones. This dish can be eaten at room temperature, but it is also delicious hot. Serve with flat breads to mop up the juices from the black bean sauce.

Serves 4

8 spring onions (scallions)
225g/8oz button (white) mushrooms
1 red (bell) pepper
1 green (bell) pepper
2 large carrots
60ml/4 tbsp sesame oil
2 garlic cloves, crushed
60ml/4 tbsp black bean sauce
90ml/6 tbsp warm water
225g/8oz beansprouts
salt and ground black pepper

1 Thinly slice the spring onions and button mushrooms.

2 Cut the peppers and carrots into fine strips of equal size.

3 Heat the oil in a large preheated wok until very hot. Add the spring onions and garlic and stir-fry for 30 seconds.

4 Add the sliced mushrooms and the strips of pepper and carrots. Stir-fry for 5–6 minutes over a high heat until the vegetables are just beginning to soften.

5 Mix the black bean sauce with the water. Add the mixture to the wok and cook for 3–4 minutes.

6 Add the beansprouts to the wok and stir them in. Cook for 1 minute more, until all the vegetables are coated in the sauce. Season to taste, then serve immediately.

Cook's Tip

Black bean sauce is quite a thick paste and readily available in jars, bottles and cans from large supermarkets and Asian food stores. Store the sauce in the refrigerator after opening.

Mixed Stir-fry Energy 157kcal/656kJ; Protein 5.5g; Carbohydrate 13g, of which sugars 11.4g; Fat 9.6g, of which saturates 2.1g; Cholesterol 0mg; Calcium 110mg; Fibre 5.5g; Sodium 65mg.
Black Bean Stir-fry Energy 196kcal/817kJ; Protein 6.5g; Carbohydrate 16.1g, of which sugars 9.4g; Fat 12.2g, of which saturates 1.9g; Cholesterol 0mg; Calcium 45mg; Fibre 4.6g; Sodium 19mg.

Stir-fried Vegetables with Omelette

The glaze in this dish gives the vegetables an appealing shine and does not constitute a sauce.

Serves 3–4

For the omelette

2 eggs
30ml/2 tbsp water
45ml/3 tbsp chopped fresh coriander (cilantro)
salt and ground black pepper
15ml/1 tbsp groundnut oil

For the glazed vegetables

15ml/1 tbsp cornflour (cornstarch)
30ml/2 tbsp dry sherry
15ml/1 tbsp sweet chilli sauce
120ml/4 fl oz/½ cup vegetable stock
30ml/2 tbsp groundnut oil
5ml/1 tsp grated fresh root ginger
6–8 spring onions (scallions), sliced
115g/4oz mangetouts (snow peas)
1 yellow (bell) pepper, sliced
115g/4oz fresh shiitake or button mushrooms
115g/4oz canned water chestnuts, drained and rinsed
115g/4oz beansprouts
½ small Chinese cabbage, roughly shredded

1 To make the omelette, whisk the eggs, water, coriander and seasoning together. Heat the oil in a wok. Pour in the eggs, then tilt the wok so that the mixture spreads in an even layer.

2 Cook the omelette over a high heat until the edges are slightly crisp. Flip the omelette over with a spatula and cook the other side for about 30 seconds until lightly browned. Turn the omelette on to a board and leave to cool, then roll up loosely and cut into thin slices. Wipe the wok clean.

3 In a small bowl, blend together the cornflour, sherry, chilli sauce and stock to make the glaze. Set aside.

4 Heat the wok, add the oil and swirl it around. Add the ginger and spring onions and stir-fry for a few seconds to flavour the oil. Add the mangetouts, sliced pepper, mushrooms and water chestnuts and stir-fry for 3 minutes. Add the beansprouts and Chinese cabbage and stir-fry for 2 minutes.

5 Pour in the glaze and cook, stirring, until it thickens. Top with the omelette shreds and serve at once.

Mushroom and Choi Sum Stir-fry

The mushrooms that are recommended for this dish – wild oyster and shiitake mushrooms – have particularly distinctive, delicate flavours that work well when stir-fried.

Serves 4

4 dried black Chinese mushrooms
150ml/¼ pint/⅔ cup hot water
450g/1lb pak choi (bok choy) or choi sum
50g/2oz/¾ cup oyster mushrooms, preferably wild
50g/2oz/¾ cup fresh shiitake mushrooms
15ml/1 tbsp vegetable or sunflower oil
1 garlic clove, crushed
30ml/2 tbsp oyster sauce

1 Place the dried Chinese mushrooms in a small bowl and pour over the hot water. Leave for 15 minutes to soften.

2 Tear the pak choi or the choi sum into bitesize pieces with your fingers. Place in a bowl and set aside.

3 If any of the oyster or shiitake mushrooms are particularly large, use a sharp knife to halve them.

4 Strain the Chinese mushrooms, cut off the stems and discard them. Heat a wok, then add the oil. When the oil is hot, stir-fry the garlic until it has softened but not coloured.

5 Add the torn greens to the wok and stir-fry for 1 minute. Toss in the oyster and shiitake mushrooms with the Chinese mushroom caps, and stir-fry for 1 minute.

6 Add the oyster sauce, toss well and serve immediately.

Cook's Tip

Pak choi, also called bok choy, and its cousin, choi sum, are both attractive members of the cabbage family, with long, smooth white stems and dark green leaves. Choi sum is also known as flowering cabbage and is distinguished by its yellow flowers.

Stir-fried Vegetables Energy 220kcal/916kJ; Protein 9.6g; Carbohydrate 16.7g, of which sugars 11.2g; Fat 12.3g, of which saturates 1.9g; Cholesterol 95mg; Calcium 127mg; Fibre 5.8g; Sodium 57mg.
Mushroom and Choi Sum Energy 57kcal/237kJ; Protein 3.7g; Carbohydrate 2.1g, of which sugars 1.8g; Fat 3.8g, of which saturates 0.5g; Cholesterol 0mg; Calcium 193mg; Fibre 2.7g; Sodium 159mg.

Okra and Coconut Stir-fry

Stir-fried okra spiced with mustard, cumin and red chillies and sprinkled with freshly grated coconut makes a great quick supper or lunch dish. It is the perfect way to enjoy these succulent pods, with the sweetness of the coconut complementing the warmth of the mustard, cumin, chilli and turmeric.

Serves 4
600g/1lb 6oz okra
60ml/4 tbsp sunflower oil
1 onion, finely chopped
15ml/1 tbsp mustard seeds
15ml/1 tbsp cumin seeds
2–3 dried red chillies
10–12 curry leaves
2.5ml/½ tsp ground turmeric
90g/3½oz freshly grated coconut
salt and ground black pepper
poppadums, rice or naan, to serve

1 With a sharp knife, cut each of the okra pods diagonally into 1cm/½in lengths. Set them aside. Heat a wok or large heavy pan and add the sunflower oil.

2 When the oil is hot add the chopped onion and stir-fry over a medium heat for about 5 minutes until softened.

3 Add the mustard seeds, cumin seeds, chillies and curry leaves to the onions and stir-fry over a high heat for about 2 minutes.

4 Add the okra and turmeric to the pan and continue to stir-fry over a high heat for 3–4 minutes.

5 Remove the pan from the heat, sprinkle over the coconut and season well with salt and ground black pepper. Serve the okra and coconut stir-fry immediately with poppadums, steamed rice or naan bread.

Cook's Tip
Fresh okra is widely available from many supermarkets and Asian stores. The okra pods have a ridged skin and a tapered, oblong shape. Look out for fresh, firm, green specimens and avoid any pods that are limp or turning brown.

Stir-fried Seeds and Vegetables

The contrast between the crunchy seeds and vegetables and the rich, savoury sauce is what makes this dish so delicious. Serve it on its own, or with rice or noodles.

Serves 4
30ml/2 tbsp vegetable oil
30ml/2 tbsp sesame seeds
30ml/2 tbsp sunflower seeds
30ml/2 tbsp pumpkin seeds
2 garlic cloves, finely chopped
2.5cm/1in piece fresh root ginger, peeled and finely chopped
2 large carrots, cut into batons
2 large courgettes (zucchini), cut into batons
90g/3½oz/1½ cups oyster mushrooms, torn in pieces
150g/5oz watercress or spinach leaves, coarsely chopped
small bunch fresh mint or coriander (cilantro), leaves and stems chopped
60ml/4 tbsp black bean sauce
30ml/2 tbsp light soy sauce
15ml/1 tbsp palm sugar (jaggery) or light muscovado (brown) sugar
30ml/2 tbsp rice vinegar

1 Preheat the wok, add the oil and swirl it around the wok when hot. Add the seeds and toss over a medium heat for 1 minute, stirring continuously so that the seeds do not burn.

2 Add the garlic and ginger to the wok and stir-fry until the ginger is aromatic and the garlic is golden but not burnt.

3 Add the carrot and courgette batons and the sliced oyster mushrooms to the wok and stir-fry over a medium heat for a further 5 minutes, or until all the vegetables are crisp-tender and are golden at the edges.

4 Add the watercress or spinach to the wok with the fresh herbs. Toss over the heat for 1 minute, then stir in the black bean sauce, soy sauce, sugar and vinegar. Stir-fry for 1–2 minutes, until combined and hot. Serve immediately.

Cook's Tip
Oyster mushrooms are delicate, so it is better to tear them into pieces along the lines of the gills, rather than slice them.

Okra Stir-fry Energy 191kcal/790kJ; Protein 5.1g; Carbohydrate 6.2g, of which sugars 5.1g; Fat 16.5g, of which saturates 5.1g; Cholesterol 0mg; Calcium 249mg; Fibre 7.1g; Sodium 15mg.
Stir-fried Seeds Energy 205kcal/849kJ; Protein 6.9g; Carbohydrate 9.7g, of which sugars 7.7g; Fat 15.6g, of which saturates 2g; Cholesterol 0mg; Calcium 159mg; Fibre 3.4g; Sodium 294mg.

Stir-fried Tofu and Asparagus

Vegetarian guests often draw the short straw at dinners where meat eaters are in the majority. However, serve this and there'll be envious looks at the table.

Serves 1–2

250g/9oz deep-fried tofu cubes
30ml/2 tbsp groundnut (peanut) oil
15ml/1 tbsp Thai green curry paste
30ml/2 tbsp light soy sauce
2 kaffir lime leaves, sliced
30ml/2 tbsp sugar
150ml/¼ pint/⅔ cup vegetable stock
250g/9oz asparagus, trimmed and sliced into 5cm/2in lengths
30ml/2 tbsp roasted peanuts, finely chopped

1 Preheat the grill (broiler) to medium. Place the tofu cubes in a grill (broiling) pan and grill (broil) for 2–3 minutes, then turn them over and cook until they are crisp and golden brown all over.

2 Heat the oil in a wok . Add the curry paste and cook over a medium heat, stirring , for 1–2 minutes, until it gives off its aroma.

3 Stir the soy sauce, lime leaves, sugar and vegetable stock into the wok and mix well. Bring to the boil, then reduce the heat to low so that the curried stock is just simmering. Add the asparagus and simmer for 5 minutes. Chop each piece of tofu into four, then add to the pan with the peanuts.

4 Toss to coat all the ingredients in the sauce, then spoon into a warmed dish and serve immediately.

Cook's Tip
When buying asparagus spears, look for firm bright green or pale ivory stalks with tight tips and aim to cook them the same day.

Variation
Substitute slim carrot batons, baby leeks or small broccoli florets for the asparagus, if you like.

Tofu Cabbage Stir-fry

The use of tofu in this recipe creates a pleasant creamy texture, which contrasts delightfully with the crunchy stir-fried vegetables.

Serves 2–4

115g/4oz hard white cabbage
2 green chillies
225g/8oz firm tofu
45ml/3 tbsp vegetable oil
2 garlic cloves, crushed
3 spring onions (scallions), chopped
175g/6oz green beans, topped and tailed
175g/6oz baby corn, halved
115g/4oz beansprouts
45ml/3 tbsp smooth peanut butter
25ml/1½ tbsp dark soy sauce
300ml/½ pint/1¼ cups coconut milk

1 Shred the white cabbage using a sharp knife. Carefully remove the seeds from the chillies and chop them finely. Wear rubber gloves to protect your hands, if necessary.

2 Using a sharp knife, cut the tofu into 5cm/2in strips.

3 Heat the wok, then add 30ml/2 tbsp of the oil. When the oil is hot, add the tofu, stir-fry for 3 minutes, then remove it and set it aside. Wipe out the wok with kitchen paper.

4 Add the remaining oil to the wok. When it is hot, add the garlic, spring onions and chillies and stir-fry for 1 minute. Add the green beans, corn and beansprouts and stir-fry for a further 2 minutes until cooked through.

5 Add the peanut butter and soy sauce to the wok. Stir well to coat the vegetables. Add the tofu to the vegetables in the wok.

6 Pour the coconut milk over the vegetables, simmer for 3 minutes and serve immediately in warmed bowls.

Variation
For a non-vegetarian option, replace the tofu with 225g/8oz thinly sliced chicken breast fillets and stir-fry until cooked.

Stir-fried Tofu Energy 551kcal/2287kJ; Protein 37.3g; Carbohydrate 7.8g, of which sugars 5.2g; Fat 41.4g, of which saturates 2.8g; Cholesterol 0mg; Calcium 1894mg; Fibre 3.1g; Sodium 1203mg.
Tofu Cabbage Stir-fry Energy 242kcal/1004kJ; Protein 11g; Carbohydrate 11.2g, of which sugars 8.9g; Fat 17.3g, of which saturates 2.9g; Cholesterol 0mg; Calcium 356mg; Fibre 3.4g; Sodium 1072mg.

Yellow Vegetable Curry with Coconut Milk

This hot and spicy curry made with coconut milk has a creamy richness that contrasts wonderfully with the heat of chilli and the bite of lightly cooked vegetables.

Serves 4

30ml/2 tbsp sunflower oil
30–45ml/2–3 tbsp yellow curry paste (see Cook's Tip)
200ml/7fl oz/scant 1 cup coconut cream
300ml/½ pint/1¼ cups coconut milk
150ml/¼ pint/⅔ cup vegetable stock
200g/7oz yard-long (snake) beans, cut into 2cm/¾in lengths
200g/7oz baby corn
4 baby courgettes (zucchini), sliced
1 small aubergine (eggplant), cubed or sliced
10ml/2 tsp palm sugar (jaggery)
fresh coriander (cilantro) leaves, to garnish
noodles or rice, to serve

1 Heat a large wok over a medium heat and add the oil. When hot add the curry paste and stir-fry for 1–2 minutes.

2 Add the coconut cream and cook gently for 8–10 minutes, or until the mixture starts to separate.

3 Add the coconut milk, stock and vegetables and cook gently for 8–10 minutes, until the vegetables are just tender.

4 Stir in the palm sugar, garnish with coriander leaves and serve in four individual warmed bowls with noodles or rice.

Cook's Tip

To make the curry paste, mix 10ml/2 tsp each hot chilli powder, ground coriander and ground cumin in a sturdy food processor. Add 5ml/1 tsp ground turmeric, 15ml/1 tbsp chopped fresh galangal, 10ml/2 tsp crushed garlic, 30ml/2 tbsp finely chopped lemon grass, 4 finely chopped red shallots and 5ml/1 tsp chopped lime rind. Add 30ml/2 tbsp cold water and blend to a smooth paste. Add a little more water if necessary.

Tofu and Green Bean Red Curry

This Thai curry is one of those versatile recipes that should be in every cook's repertoire. This version uses green beans, but other types of vegetable work equally well. The tofu takes on the flavour of the spice paste and also boosts the nutritional value of the dish.

Serves 4–6

600ml/1 pint/2½ cups canned coconut milk
15ml/1 tbsp Thai red curry paste
45ml/3 tbsp mushroom ketchup
10ml/2 tsp palm sugar (jaggery) or light muscovado (brown) sugar
225g/8oz/3¼ cups button (white) mushrooms
115g/4oz/scant 1 cup green beans, trimmed
175g/6oz firm tofu, rinsed, drained and cut into 2cm/¾in cubes
4 kaffir lime leaves, torn
2 fresh red chillies, seeded and sliced
fresh coriander (cilantro) leaves, to garnish

1 Pour about one-third of the coconut milk into a wok or large heavy pan and cook over a gentle heat until it starts to separate and an oily sheen appears on the surface.

2 Add the red curry paste, mushroom ketchup and sugar to the coconut milk in the pan. Mix thoroughly, then add the mushrooms. Increase the heat, stir and cook for 1 minute.

3 Add the remaining coconut milk to the pan. Bring the mixture back to the boil, then add the green beans and tofu cubes. Simmer gently for 4–5 minutes more.

4 Stir in the lime leaves and sliced red chillies into the pan. Spoon the curry into a serving dish, garnish with the coriander leaves and serve immediately.

Cook's Tip

The kaffir lime is a native of Indonesia but is grown in many other parts of the world. The leaves are a popular flavouring in the cooking of Thailand, Cambodia and Laos, and are widely available fresh, frozen or dried.

Yellow Vegetable Curry Energy 126kcal/528kJ; Protein 4.7g; Carbohydrate 12.7g, of which sugars 11.9g; Fat 6.7g, of which saturates 1.1g; Cholesterol 5mg; Calcium 90mg; Fibre 2.5g; Sodium 752mg.
Tofu and Green Bean Curry Energy 79kcal/333kJ; Protein 3.9g; Carbohydrate 8.2g, of which sugars 7.8g; Fat 3.6g, of which saturates 0.6g; Cholesterol 0mg; Calcium 189mg; Fibre 0.8g; Sodium 647mg.

Aromatic Corn and Nut Curry

A substantial curry, this dish combines all the essential flavours of southern Thailand. It is deliciously aromatic, but the flavour is fairly mild.

Serves 4

30ml/2 tbsp vegetable oil
4 shallots, chopped
90g/3½oz/scant 1 cup cashew nuts
5ml/1 tsp Thai red curry paste
400g/14oz potatoes, peeled and cut into chunks
1 lemon grass stalk, finely chopped
200g/7oz can chopped tomatoes
600ml/1 pint/2½ cups boiling water
200g/7oz/generous 1 cup drained canned whole kernel corn
4 celery sticks, sliced
2 kaffir lime leaves, rolled into cylinders and thinly sliced into ribbons
15ml/1 tbsp tomato ketchup
15ml/1 tbsp light soy sauce
5ml/1 tsp palm sugar or light muscovado (brown) sugar
5ml/1 tsp mushroom ketchup
4 spring onions (scallions), thinly sliced
small bunch fresh basil, chopped

1 Heat the oil in a large, heavy pan or wok. Add the shallots and stir-fry over a medium heat for 2–3 minutes, until softened. Add the cashew nuts and stir-fry for a few minutes until golden.

2 Stir in the red curry paste. Stir-fry for 1 minute, then add the potatoes, lemon grass, tomatoes and boiling water. Bring back to the boil, then reduce the heat to low, cover and simmer gently for 15–20 minutes, or until the potatoes are tender.

3 Stir the corn, celery, lime leaves, tomato ketchup, soy sauce, sugar and mushroom ketchup into the pan or wok. Stir to mix and simmer for a further 5 minutes, until heated through, then spoon into warmed serving bowls. Sprinkle with the sliced spring onions and basil and serve.

Cook's Tip
Rolling the lime leaves into cylinders before slicing produces very fine strips – a technique known as cutting en chiffonnade. *Remove the central rib from the leaves before cutting them.*

Thai Noodles with Chinese Chives and Chilli

This is a filling and tasty vegetarian dish, ideal for a weekend lunch.

Serves 4

350g/12oz dried rice noodles
1cm/½in piece fresh root ginger, peeled and grated
30ml/2 tbsp light soy sauce
45ml/3 tbsp vegetable oil
225g/8oz Quorn (mycoprotein), cut into small cubes
2 garlic cloves, crushed
1 large onion, cut into thin wedges
115g/4oz fried tofu, thinly sliced
1 fresh green chilli, seeded and thinly sliced
175g/6oz/2 cups beansprouts
2 large bunches garlic chives, total weight about 115g/4oz, cut into 5cm/2in lengths
50g/2oz/½ cup roasted peanuts, ground
30ml/2 tbsp dark soy sauce
30ml/2 tbsp chopped fresh coriander (cilantro), and 1 lemon, cut into wedges, to garnish

1 Place the noodles in a bowl, cover with warm water and leave to soak for 30 minutes. Drain and set aside.

2 Mix the ginger, light soy sauce and 15ml/1 tbsp of the oil in a bowl. Add the Quorn to the bowl, then set aside for 10 minutes. Drain, reserving the marinade.

3 Heat 15ml/1 tbsp of the remaining oil in a wok or frying pan and cook the garlic for a few seconds. Add the Quorn and stir-fry for 3–4 minutes. Transfer to a plate and set aside.

4 Heat the remaining oil in the pan and stir-fry the onion for 3–4 minutes, until softened and tinged brown. Add the tofu and chilli to the pan, stir-fry briefly and then add the noodles. Stir-fry over a medium heat for 4–5 minutes.

5 Stir in the beansprouts, garlic chives and most of the peanuts, reserving a little for the garnish. Stir well, then add the Quorn, the dark soy sauce and the reserved marinade.

6 When hot, spoon on to serving plates and garnish with the remaining ground peanuts, the coriander and lemon.

Corn and Nut Curry Energy 298kcal/1245kJ; Protein 8.8g; Carbohydrate 27.6g, of which sugars 8.9g; Fat 17.7g, of which saturates 3.1g; Cholesterol 0mg; Calcium 33mg; Fibre 3.5g; Sodium 981mg.
Thai Noodles Energy 444kcal/1857kJ; Protein 16g; Carbohydrate 77.6g, of which sugars 4.3g; Fat 6.5g, of which saturates 0.9g; Cholesterol 0mg; Calcium 230mg; Fibre 5g; Sodium 1227mg.

Noodles and Vegetables in Coconut Sauce with Fresh Red Chillies

When everyday vegetables are given the Thai treatment, the result is a delectable dish which everyone is certain to enjoy.

Serves 4 to 6

30ml/2 tbsp sunflower oil
1 lemon grass stalk, finely chopped
15ml/1 tbsp Thai red curry paste
1 onion, thickly sliced
3 courgettes (zucchini), thickly sliced
115g/4oz Savoy cabbage, thickly sliced
2 carrots, thickly sliced
150g/5oz broccoli, stem sliced and head separated into florets
2 x 400ml/14fl oz cans coconut milk
475ml/16fl oz vegetable stock
150g/5oz dried egg noodles
15ml/1 tbsp Thai fish sauce
30ml/2 tbsp soy sauce
60ml/4 tbsp chopped fresh coriander (cilantro)

For the garnish

2 lemon grass stalks
1 bunch fresh coriander (cilantro)
8–10 small fresh red chillies

1 Heat the oil in a large pan or wok. Add the lemon grass and red curry paste and stir-fry for 2–3 seconds. Add the onion and cook over a medium heat, stirring occasionally, for about 5–10 minutes, until the onion has softened but not browned.

2 Add the courgettes, cabbage, carrots and slices of broccoli stem. Toss the vegetables with the onion mixture. Reduce the heat and cook gently, stirring occasionally, for 5 minutes.

3 Increase the heat to medium, stir in the coconut milk and vegetable stock and bring to the boil. Add the broccoli florets and the noodles, then simmer gently for 20 minutes.

4 Meanwhile, make the garnish. Split the lemon grass stalks lengthways. Gather the coriander into a small bouquet and lay it on a platter, following the curve of the rim. Tuck the lemon grass halves into the bouquet and add chillies to resemble flowers.

5 Stir the fish sauce, soy sauce and chopped coriander into the noodle mixture. Spoon on to the platter, taking care not to disturb the herb bouquet, and serve immediately.

Hot Pineapple and Coconut Curry

Serves 4

1 small, firm pineapple
15–30ml/1–2 tbsp palm or coconut oil
4–6 shallots, finely chopped
2 garlic cloves, finely chopped
1 red chilli, seeded and chopped
15ml/1 tbsp palm sugar (jaggery)
400ml/14fl oz/1⅔ cups coconut milk
salt and ground black pepper
1 small bunch fresh coriander (cilantro) leaves, finely chopped, to garnish

For the spice paste

4 cloves
4 cardamom pods
1 small cinnamon stick
5ml/1 tsp coriander seeds
2.5ml/½ tsp cumin seeds
5–10ml/1–2 tsp water

1 First make the spice paste. Using a mortar and pestle, grind all the spices together to a powder. In a small bowl, mix the spice powder with the water to make a paste. Put aside.

2 Remove the skin from the pineapple, then cut the flesh lengthways into quarters and remove the core. Cut each quarter widthways into chunky slices and put aside.

3 Heat the oil in a wok or large, heavy frying pan, stir in the shallots, garlic and chilli and stir-fry until fragrant and beginning to colour. Stir in the spice paste and fry for 1 minute. Toss in the pineapple, making sure the slices are coated in the spicy mixture.

4 Stir the sugar into the coconut milk and pour into the wok. Stir and bring to the boil. Reduce the heat and simmer for 3–4 minutes to thicken the sauce, but do not allow the pineapple to become too soft. Season with salt and pepper to taste.

5 Transfer the curry to a serving dish and sprinkle with the coriander to garnish. Serve hot or at room temperature.

Sweet Pumpkin and Peanut Curry

Serves 4

30ml/2 tbsp vegetable oil
4 garlic cloves, crushed
4 shallots, finely chopped
30ml/2 tbsp yellow curry paste
600ml/1 pint/2½ cups stock
2 kaffir lime leaves, torn
15ml/1 tbsp chopped fresh galangal
450g/1lb pumpkin, peeled, seeded and diced
225g/8oz sweet potatoes, diced
90g/3½oz/scant 1 cup unsalted, roasted peanuts, chopped
300ml/½ pint/1¼ cups coconut milk
90g/3½oz/1½ cups chestnut mushrooms, sliced
30ml/2 tbsp soy sauce
50g/2oz/⅓ cup pumpkin seeds, toasted

1 Heat the oil in a wok. Add the garlic and shallots and cook over a medium heat for 10 minutes, until softened and golden.

2 Add the curry paste and stir-fry for 30 seconds, until fragrant, then add the stock, lime leaves, galangal, pumpkin and sweet potatoes. Bring to the boil, stirring , then simmer for 15 minutes.

3 Add the peanuts, coconut milk and mushrooms. Stir in the soy sauce and simmer for 5 minutes more. Spoon into bowls, garnish with the pumpkin seeds and serve.

Noodles with Chillies Energy 293kcal/1235kJ; Protein 8.9g; Carbohydrate 44.7g, of which sugars 17.3g; Fat 10g, of which saturates 2.1g; Cholesterol 11mg; Calcium 131mg; Fibre 4.2g; Sodium 1007m
Hot Pineapple Curry Energy 135kcal/573kJ; Protein 1.6g; Carbohydrate 25.4g, of which sugars 23.6g; Fat 3.8g, of which saturates 0.5g; Cholesterol 0mg; Calcium 87mg; Fibre 2.9g; Sodium 131mg.
Pumpkin and Peanut Energy 306kcal/1279kJ; Protein 9.6g; Carbohydrate 24.5g, of which sugars 11.4g; Fat 19.6g, of which saturates 3.3g; Cholesterol 0mg; Calcium 160mg; Fibre 6.4g; Sodium 409mg.

Sweet and Sour Vegetables with Spicy Tofu

Big, bold and beautiful, this is a hearty stir-fry that will satisfy the hungriest guests. Stir-fries are always a good choice when entertaining as you can prepare the ingredients ahead of time and then they take a short time to cook.

Serves 4
4 shallots
3 garlic cloves
30ml/2 tbsp groundnut (peanut) oil
250g/9oz Chinese leaves (Chinese cabbage), shredded
8 baby corn cobs, sliced on the diagonal
2 red (bell) peppers, seeded and thinly sliced
200g/7oz/1 3/4 cups mangetouts (snow peas), trimmed and sliced
250g/9oz tofu, rinsed, drained and cut in 1cm/1/2in cubes
60ml/4 tbsp vegetable stock
30ml/2 tbsp light soy sauce
15ml/1 tbsp sugar
30ml/2 tbsp rice vinegar
2.5ml/1/2 tsp dried chilli flakes
small bunch coriander (cilantro), chopped

1 Peel the shallots and slice them thinly using a sharp knife and then peel and finely chop the garlic.

2 Heat the oil in a wok or large frying pan and cook the shallots and garlic for 2–3 minutes over a medium heat, until golden. Do not let the garlic burn or it will taste bitter.

3 Add the shredded cabbage to the pan, toss over the heat for 30 seconds, then add the corn cobs and repeat the process.

4 Add the red peppers, mangetouts and tofu in the same way, each time adding a single ingredient then tossing it over the heat for about 30 seconds before adding the next ingredient.

5 Pour the stock and soy sauce into the pan. Mix together the sugar and vinegar in a small bowl, stirring until the sugar has completely dissolved, then add the mixture to the wok or pan. Sprinkle over the chilli flakes and chopped coriander, toss to mix well and serve immediately.

Chilli-stuffed Pan-fried Tofu

An easy accompaniment for a main course, or a great lunch. Squares of fried tofu stuffed with a blend of chilli and chestnut give a piquant jolt to the delicate flavour.

Serves 2
2 blocks firm tofu
30ml/2 tbsp Thai fish sauce
5ml/1 tsp sesame oil
2 eggs
7.5ml/1 1/2 tsp cornflour (cornstarch)
vegetable oil, for shallow-frying

For the filling
2 green chillies, finely chopped
2 chestnuts, finely chopped
6 garlic cloves, crushed
10ml/2 tsp sesame seeds

1 Drain the blocks of tofu. Cut each block into 2cm/3/4in slices, and then cut each slice in half. Place the tofu slices on a piece of kitchen paper to absorb any excess water.

2 Mix together the Thai fish sauce and sesame oil.

3 Transfer the tofu slices to a plate and coat them evenly with the fish sauce mixture. Leave to marinate for 20 minutes. Meanwhile, put all the filling ingredients into a bowl and combine them thoroughly. Set aside until needed.

4 Beat the eggs in a shallow dish. Add the cornflour and whisk until the mixture is well combined. Take the slices of tofu and dip them into the beaten egg mixture, coating evenly on all sides.

5 Place a wok or frying pan over medium heat and add the vegetable oil. Swirl the oil round the pan, then add the tofu slices and fry, turning over once, until golden brown.

6 Once cooked, make a slit down the middle of each slice with a sharp knife, without cutting all the way through. Gently push a large pinch of the filling into each slice, and serve.

Variation
Alternatively, you could serve the tofu with a light soy dip with a little chopped root ginger instead of the spicy filling.

Sweet Sour Vegetables Energy 177kcal/736kJ; Protein 10.5g; Carbohydrate 13.7g, of which sugars 12.5g; Fat 9.2g, of which saturates 1.5g; Cholesterol 0mg; Calcium 461mg; Fibre 4.3g; Sodium 844mg.
Chilli-stuffed Tofu Energy 291kcal/1213kJ; Protein 23g; Carbohydrate 7.8g, of which sugars 1.3g; Fat 19.1g, of which saturates 3.4g; Cholesterol 209mg; Calcium 1014mg; Fibre 0.8g; Sodium 88mg.

Tofu and Broccoli with Shallots

This meltingly tender tofu is flavoured with spices and served with broccoli.

Serves 4

500g/1¼lb tofu, drained
45ml/3 tbsp kecap manis (sweet soy sauce)
30ml/2 tbsp sweet chilli sauce
45ml/3 tbsp soy sauce
5ml/1 tsp sesame oil
5ml/1 tsp finely grated fresh root ginger
400g/14oz tenderstem broccoli, halved lengthways
45ml/3 tbsp chopped coriander (cilantro), and 30ml/2 tbsp toasted sesame seeds, to garnish
30ml/2 tbsp crispy fried shallots
white rice or noodles, to serve

1 Make the crispy shallots. Add the shallot rings to a wok one-third full of hot oil, then lower the heat and stir constantly until crisp. Lift out and spread on kitchen paper to drain.

2 Cut the tofu into 4 triangular pieces: slice the block in half widthways, then diagonally. Place in a heatproof dish.

3 In a small bowl, combine the kecap manis, chilli sauce, soy sauce, sesame oil and ginger, then pour over the tofu. Leave the tofu to marinate for at least 30 minutes, turning occasionally.

4 Place the broccoli on a heatproof plate and place on a trivet or steamer rack in the wok. Cover and steam for 4–5 minutes, until just tender. Remove and keep warm. Place the dish of tofu on the trivet or steamer rack in the wok, cover and steam for 4–5 minutes. Divide the broccoli among four warmed serving plates and top each one with a triangle of tofu.

5 Spoon the remaining juices over the tofu and broccoli, then sprinkle with the coriander, sesame seeds and crispy shallots. Serve immediately with steamed white rice or noodles.

Cook's Tip

Kecap manis is a sweet Indonesian soy sauce to be found in many supermarkets. If you cannot obtain it, then it can be replaced with an equal quantity of mirin and soy sauce.

Chinese Red-cooked Tofu and Mushroom Stir-fry

'Red-cooked' is a term applied to Chinese dishes that are cooked with dark soy sauce.

Serves 2–4

225g/8oz firm tofu
45ml/3 tbsp dark soy sauce
30ml/2 tbsp Chinese rice wine
10ml/2 tsp soft dark brown sugar
1 garlic clove, crushed
15ml/1 tbsp grated fresh root ginger
2.5ml/½ tsp Chinese five-spice powder
pinch of ground roasted Szechuan peppercorns
6 dried Chinese black mushrooms
5ml/1 tsp cornflour (cornstarch)
30ml/2 tbsp groundnut (peanut) oil
5–6 spring onions (scallions), sliced into 2.5cm/1in lengths
small basil leaves, to garnish
rice noodles, to serve

1 Drain the tofu, pat dry with kitchen paper and cut into 2.5cm/1in cubes. Place the tofu in a shallow dish.

2 In a small bowl, mix together the soy sauce, rice wine, sugar, garlic, ginger, five-spice powder and peppercorns. Pour the marinade over the tofu, toss well and leave to marinate for about 30 minutes. Drain, reserving the marinade.

3 Meanwhile, just cover the dried black mushrooms in warm water and soak for 20–30 minutes until softened. Drain, reserving 90ml/6 tbsp of the soaking liquid. Squeeze the mushrooms, discard the tough stalks and slice the caps.

4 In a small bowl, blend the cornflour with the reserved marinade and the mushroom liquid.

5 Heat the oil in a wok. Add the tofu and fry for 2–3 minutes until golden. Remove and set aside. Add the mushrooms and white parts of the spring onions to the wok and stir-fry for 2 minutes.

6 Pour the marinade mixture into the wok and stir for 1 minute until thickened. Return the tofu to the wok with the green parts of the onions. Simmer for 1–2 minutes. Garnish with basil leaves and serve with noodles.

Tofu and Broccoli Energy 202kcal/840kJ; Protein 16.5g; Carbohydrate 6.9g, of which sugars 5.6g; Fat 12.1g, of which saturates 1.7g; Cholesterol 0mg; Calcium 750mg; Fibre 3.5g; Sodium 938mg.
Tofu and Mushroom Energy 118kcal/491kJ; Protein 9.3g; Carbohydrate 2.9g, of which sugars 1.1g; Fat 7.4g, of which saturates 0.9g; Cholesterol 0mg; Calcium 456mg; Fibre 1.2g; Sodium 455mg.

Mixed Vegetable Curry

You can use any combination of vegetables that are in season for this basic recipe.

Serves 4

15ml/1 tbsp oil
2.5ml/½ tsp black mustard seeds
2.5ml/½ tsp cumin seeds
1 onion, thinly sliced
2 curry leaves
1 fresh green chilli, finely chopped
2.5cm/1in piece fresh root ginger, finely chopped
30ml/2 tbsp curry paste
1 small cauliflower, broken into florets
1 large carrot, thickly sliced
115g/4oz green beans, cut into 2.5cm/1in lengths
1.5ml/¼ tsp ground turmeric
1.5ml/¼ tsp chilli powder
2.5ml/½ tsp salt
2 tomatoes, finely chopped
50g/2oz/½ cup frozen peas, thawed
150ml/¼ pint/⅔ cup vegetable stock
fresh curry leaves, to garnish

1 Heat the oil in a large, heavy wok or pan and fry the mustard seeds and cumin seeds for 2 minutes until they begin to splutter. If they are very lively, put a lid on the pan.

2 Add the onion and the curry leaves and fry for 5 minutes.

3 Add the chopped chilli and fresh ginger and fry for 2 minutes. Stir in the curry paste, mix well and fry for 3–4 minutes.

4 Add the cauliflower florets, sliced carrot and beans, and cook for 4–5 minutes. Add the turmeric, chilli powder, salt and tomatoes and cook for 2–3 minutes.

5 Finally add the thawed peas and cook for a further 2–3 minutes. Pour in the stock. Cover and simmer over a low heat for 10–15 minutes until all the vegetables are tender. Serve garnished with curry leaves.

Variation
You might like to turn this dish into a non-vegetarian main course, by adding some prawns (shrimp) or cubes of cooked chicken breast fillet together with the stock.

Indian Mee Goreng with Tofu, Potato and Omelette Slices

Mee Goreng is a truly international noodle dish combining Indian, Chinese and Western ingredients. It is a delicious treat for lunch or supper, or any time of day.

Serves 4

450g/1lb fresh yellow egg noodles
60–90ml/4–6 tbsp vegetable oil
115g/4oz fried tofu or 150g/5oz firm tofu
2 eggs
30ml/2 tbsp water
salt and ground black pepper
1 onion, sliced
1 garlic clove, crushed
15ml/1 tbsp light soy sauce
30–45ml/2–3 tbsp tomato ketchup
15ml/1 tbsp chilli sauce
1 large cooked potato, diced
4 spring onions (scallions), shredded
1–2 fresh green chillies, seeded and thinly sliced (optional)

1 Bring a large pan of water to the boil, add the fresh egg noodles and cook for just 2 minutes. Drain the noodles, rinse under cold water, drain again and set aside.

2 If using fried tofu, cut each cube in half, refresh it in a pan of boiling water, then drain well and set aside. Heat 30ml/2 tbsp of the oil in a large wok or frying pan. If using plain tofu, cube it, fry until brown, then set aside.

3 Beat the eggs with 30ml/2 tbsp water and seasoning. Add to the pan and cook, without stirring, until set. Flip over, cook the other side, then slide it out of the pan, roll up and slice thinly.

4 Heat the remaining oil in a wok or large heavy pan and fry the onion and garlic for 2–3 minutes. Add the drained noodles, soy sauce, ketchup and chilli sauce. Toss well over medium heat for 2 minutes, then add the diced potato.

5 Reserve a few spring onion shreds for garnish and stir the rest into the noodles with the chilli, if using, and the tofu.

6 When hot, stir in the omelette slices. Serve on a hot platter, garnished with the remaining spring onion.

Mixed Vegetable Curry Energy 167kcal/701kJ; Protein 6.1g; Carbohydrate 21.7g, of which sugars 8.5g; Fat 7.7g, of which saturates 0.6g; Cholesterol 0mg; Calcium 0.9mg; Fibre 7.5g; Sodium 233mg.
Mee Goreng Energy 478kcal/2010kJ; Protein 16.8g; Carbohydrate 64.2g, of which sugars 5.1g; Fat 18.9g, of which saturates 3.2g; Cholesterol 86mg; Calcium 323mg; Fibre 2.9g; Sodium 466mg.

Steamed Rice

Rice is such a staple food in China, that "have you had rice?" is a synonym for "have you eaten?" Stick to the amounts given in this recipe for fail-safe results.

Serves 4
225g/8oz/generous 1 cup long grain rice, rinsed and drained
a pinch of salt

1 Put the rice into a heavy pan or clay pot.

2 Add 600ml/1 pint/ 2½ cups water to cover the rice by 2.5cm/1in. Add the salt, and then bring the water to the boil.

3 Reduce the heat, cover the pan and cook gently for about 20 minutes, or until all the water has been absorbed.

4 Remove the pan from the heat and leave to steam, covered, for a further 5–10 minutes. Fluff up with a fork, and serve.

Fragrant Coconut Rice

Originally from India and Thailand, coconut rice is popular throughout Asia. It is often served with a tangy fruit and vegetable salad, and complements some of the spicier curries from the continent. The pandanus provides the fragrance.

Serves 4
1 litre/1¾ pints/4 cups coconut milk
450g/1lb/2¼ cups short grain rice, washed and drained
1 pandanus (screwpine) leaf, tied in a loose knot
salt

1 Heat the coconut milk in a heavy pan and, using a wooden spoon, stir in the short grain rice with a little salt.

2 Add the pandanus leaf and bring the liquid to the boil. Simmer until the liquid has been absorbed.

3 Turn off the heat and cover with a clean dish towel and the lid. Steam for a further 15–20 minutes. Fluff it up and serve.

Steamed Sticky Rice

Sticky rice is popular throughout South-east Asia, especially in Thailand and Laos. It requires a long soak in water before being cooked in a bamboo steamer. Sticky rice is used for savoury and sweet dishes, especially rice cakes, and is available in Chinese and Asian stores, as well as some supermarkets.

Serves 4
350g/12oz/1¾ cups sticky rice

1 Put the rice into a large bowl and fill the bowl with cold water. Leave the rice to soak for at least 6 hours, then drain using a sieve (strainer), rinse thoroughly, and drain again.

2 Fill a wok or a large heavy pan one-third full with water. Place a bamboo steamer, with the lid on, over the wok or pan and bring the water to the boil.

3 Uncover the steamer and place a dampened piece of muslin (cheesecloth) over the rack. Tip the rice into the middle and spread it out.

4 Fold the muslin over the rice, cover and steam for 25 minutes until the rice is tender but firm. The measured quantity of rice grains doubles when cooked.

Cook's Tip
Because the grains clump together when cooked, this type of rice is ideal for moulding. It is fairly bulky, so is often served with a dipping sauce.

Variation
Sticky rice can be enjoyed as a sweet, filling snack with sugar and coconut milk or with a healthy and exotic fruit salad.

Steamed Rice Energy 202kcal/845kJ; Protein 4.2g; Carbohydrate 44.9g, of which sugars 0g; Fat 0.3g, of which saturates 0g; Cholesterol 0mg; Calcium 11mg; Fibre 0g; Sodium 0mg.
Fragrant Coconut Rice Energy 459kcal/1927kJ; Protein 9.1g; Carbohydrate 102g, of which sugars 12.3g; Fat 1.3g, of which saturates 0.5g; Cholesterol 0mg; Calcium 94mg; Fibre 0g; Sodium 275mg.
Steamed Sticky Rice Energy 314kcal/1314kJ; Protein 6.5g; Carbohydrate 69.8g, of which sugars 0g; Fat 0.5g, of which saturates 0g; Cholesterol 0mg; Calcium 17mg; Fibre 0g; Sodium 0mg.

Rice with Seeds and Spices

Serves 4
5ml/1 tsp sunflower oil
2.5ml/½ tsp ground turmeric
6 cardamom pods, lightly crushed
5ml/1 tsp coriander seeds, lightly crushed
1 garlic clove, crushed
200g/7oz/1 cup basmati rice
400ml/14fl oz/1⅔ cups stock
115g/4oz/½ cup yogurt
15ml/1 tbsp toasted sunflower seeds
15ml/1 tbsp toasted sesame seeds
salt and ground black pepper
coriander (cilantro) leaves, to garnish

1 Heat the oil in a wok and fry the turmeric, cardamom pods, coriander seeds and garlic for about 1 minute, stirring constantly.

2 Add the rice and stock, bring to the boil, then cover and simmer for 15 minutes, or until just tender.

3 Stir in the yogurt and the sunflower and sesame seeds. Season to taste and serve hot, garnished with coriander leaves.

Red Fried Rice

Serves 2
130g/4½oz/¾ cup basmati rice
30ml/2 tbsp groundnut (peanut) oil
1 red (bell) pepper, seeded and chopped
1 small red onion, chopped
225g/8oz cherry tomatoes, halved
2 eggs, beaten
salt and ground black pepper

1 Boil the rice in a pan of water for 10–12 minutes.

2 Meanwhile, heat the oil in a wok until very hot. Add the red pepper and onion and stir-fry for 2–3 minutes. Add the cherry tomatoes and continue stir-frying for 2 minutes more.

3 Add the egg, cook for 30 seconds then stir to break up the egg.

4 Drain the cooked rice thoroughly. Add to the wok and toss it over the heat with the vegetables and egg mixture for 3 minutes. Season with salt and pepper, and serve immediately.

Festive Rice

This pretty rice dish is traditionally shaped into a cone and surrounded by a variety of accompaniments before being served.

Serves 8
450g/1lb/2⅔ cups jasmine rice
60ml/4 tbsp oil
2 garlic cloves, crushed
2 onions, thinly sliced
2.5ml/½ tsp ground turmeric
750ml/1¼ pints/3 cups water
400ml/14fl oz can coconut milk
1–2 lemon grass stalks, bruised

For the accompaniments
omelette strips
2 fresh red chillies, seeded and shredded
cucumber chunks
tomato wedges
deep-fried onions
prawn (shrimp) crackers

1 Put the jasmine rice in a large strainer and rinse it thoroughly under cold water. Drain it well over a bowl.

2 Heat the oil in a wok or frying pan with a lid.

3 Add the garlic, onions and turmeric to the pan and cook over a low heat for 2–3 minutes, or until the onions have softened. Add the rice and stir well to coat in oil.

4 Pour in the water and coconut milk and add the lemon grass. Bring to the boil, stirring. Cover the pan and cook gently for 12 minutes, or until all the liquid has been absorbed by the rice.

5 Remove the pan from the heat and remove the lid. Cover the pan with a clean dish towel, replace the lid and leave to stand in a warm place for 15 minutes.

6 Remove the lemon grass, mound the rice mixture in a cone on a platter and garnish with the accompaniments, then serve.

Cook's Tip
Jasmine rice is widely available in most supermarkets and Asian stores. It has a delicately scented, almost milky, aroma.

Rice with Seeds Energy 310kcal/1294kJ; Protein 8.3g; Carbohydrate 53.5g, of which sugars 2.8g; Fat 6.7g, of which saturates 0.9g; Cholesterol 0mg; Calcium 117mg; Fibre 0.7g; Sodium 31mg.
Red Fried Rice Energy 437kcal/1821kJ; Protein 12.6g; Carbohydrate 57.4g, of which sugars 10.5g; Fat 17.6g, of which saturates 3.1g; Cholesterol 190mg; Calcium 62mg; Fibre 3g; Sodium 85mg.
Festive Rice Energy 303kcal/1263kJ; Protein 6.4g; Carbohydrate 49.5g, of which sugars 4.2g; Fat 8.6g, of which saturates 2g; Cholesterol 53mg; Calcium 41mg; Fibre 0.5g; Sodium 212mg.

Basmati and Nut Pilau

Versions of this rice dish are cooked throughout Asia, always with the best-quality long grain rice. In India, basmati rice is the natural choice. In this particular interpretation of the recipe, walnuts and cashew nuts are added. Serve the pilau with a raita or yogurt.

Serves 4

15–30ml/1–2 tbsp vegetable oil
1 onion, chopped
1 garlic clove, crushed
1 large carrot, coarsely grated
225g/8oz/generous 1 cup basmati rice, soaked for20–30 minutes
5ml/1 tsp cumin seeds
10ml/2 tsp ground coriander
10ml/2 tsp black mustard seeds
4 green cardamom pods
450ml/ ¾ pint/scant 2 cups vegetable stock
1 bay leaf
75g/3oz/ ¾ cup unsalted walnuts and cashew nuts
salt and ground black pepper
fresh coriander (cilantro) sprigs, to garnish

1 Heat the oil in a karahi, wok or large pan. Add the onion, garlic and carrot to the pan and stir-fry them for 3–4 minutes.

2 Drain the rice and add to the pan with the spices. Cook for 2 minutes, stirring to coat the grains in oil.

3 Pour in the stock, stirring. Add the bay leaf and season well. Bring to the boil, lower the heat, cover and simmer very gently for 10–12 minutes without stirring.

4 Remove the pan from the heat without lifting the lid. Leave to stand for 5 minutes, then check the rice. If it is cooked, there will be small steam holes on the surface of the rice. Discard the bay leaf and the cardamom pods.

5 Stir in the nuts and check the seasoning. Spoon on to a warmed platter, garnish with the fresh coriander and serve.

Variation
Match the sweetness of the grated carrot in this recipe by adding 50g/2oz/scant ½ cup when you add the bay leaf.

Stir-fried Vegetables and Rice with Fresh Ginger

The ginger gives this mixed rice and vegetable dish a wonderful flavour.

Serves 2–4

115g/4oz/generous ½ cup brown basmati rice, rinsed and drained
350ml/12fl oz/1½ cups vegetable stock
2.5cm/1in piece fresh root ginger
1 garlic clove, halved
5cm/2in piece pared lemon rind
115g/4oz/1½ cups shiitake mushrooms
15ml/1 tbsp vegetable oil
175g/6oz baby carrots, trimmed
225g/8oz baby courgettes (zucchini), halved
175–225g/6–8oz/about 1½ cups broccoli, broken into florets
6 spring onions (scallions), diagonally sliced
15ml/1 tbsp light soy sauce
10ml/2 tsp toasted sesame oil

1 Put the rice in a pan and pour in the vegetable stock. Thinly slice the ginger and add it to the pan with the garlic and lemon rind. Slowly bring to the boil, then cover and simmer together for 20–25 minutes until the rice is tender. Discard the flavourings and keep the rice hot.

2 Slice the mushrooms, discarding the stems. Heat the oil in a wok and stir-fry the carrots for 4–5 minutes, the add the mushrooms and courgettes and stir-fry for 2–3 minutes.

3 Add the broccoli and spring onions to the wok and cook for 3 minutes more, by which time all the vegetables should be tender but should still retain a bit of "bite".

4 Add the cooked rice to the vegetables, and toss briefly over the heat to mix and heat through. Toss with the soy sauce and sesame oil. Spoon into a bowl and serve immediately.

Cook's Tip
Fresh root ginger keeps well in the freezer. It can be sliced or grated when required and thaws very quickly.

Basmati and Nut Pilau Energy 376kcal/1562kJ; Protein 7.5g; Carbohydrate 50g, of which sugars 4g; Fat 16g, of which saturates 1.4g; Cholesterol 0mg; Calcium 42mg; Fibre 1.6g; Sodium 7mg..
Vegetables and Rice Energy 430kcal/1788kJ; Protein 12.5g; Carbohydrate 58.2g, of which sugars 11.2g; Fat 16.2g, of which saturates 2.2g; Cholesterol 0mg; Calcium 127mg; Fibre 6.5g; Sodium 569mg.

Mixed Vegetable Rice

The quick cucumber relish makes this dish sparkle.

Serves 4
200g/7oz/1 cup jasmine rice
5 green beans
¼ cucumber
2 hard-boiled eggs
3 fresh red chillies
4 lime leaves, finely shredded
5ml/1 tsp salt
1.5ml/¼ tsp ground black pepper
30ml/2 tbsp fresh lime juice
2 tomatoes, chopped

For the relish
⅓ cucumber, peeled and seeded
pinch of salt
15ml/1 tbsp terasi (Indonesian shrimp paste)
2 fresh red chillies
¼ sweet pineapple, peeled, eyes and thick core removed
15g/½oz dried shrimps, soaked in hot water until soft
juice of 1 lime
salt and sugar to taste

1 Rinse the rice, then put it in a pan and cover with water up to 4cm/1½in above the rice. Cook for 12–15 minutes until tender.

2 Blanch the beans in boiling water for 2 minutes. Drain, cool and dice finely. Peel the cucumber and remove the seeds. Cut into fine dice. Chop the eggs. Seed the chillies and chop finely.

3 For the relish, slice the cucumber flesh into diamond shapes, each 1cm/½in wide. Sprinkle with a pinch of salt, toss well and set aside for 20 minutes.

4 Toast the terasi for the relish in a frying pan over a live flame for 2 minutes, then grind the terasi with the chillies using a pestle and mortar until fine.

5 Squeeze the moisture from the cucumber, handfuls at a time, into the mix. Discard the cucumber flesh.

6 Cut the pineapple for the relish into small chunks. Grind the shrimps until coarse with a pestle and mortar. Mix all the relish ingredients in a large bowl and adjust the seasoning.

7 Just before serving, toss all the vegetable rice ingredients together and season. Serve the cucumber relish on the side.

Savoury Fried Rice with Chilli and Cashew Nuts

This is typical Thai street food, eaten at all times of the day. The recipe can be adapted to use whatever vegetables you have available and you could also add meat or shellfish.

Serves 2
30ml/2 tbsp vegetable oil
2 garlic cloves, finely chopped
1 small fresh red chilli, seeded and finely chopped
50g/2oz/½ cup cashew nuts, toasted
50g/2oz/⅔ cup desiccated (dry unsweetened shredded) coconut, toasted
2.5ml/½ tsp palm sugar (jaggery) or light muscovado (brown) sugar
30ml/2 tbsp light soy sauce
15ml/1 tbsp rice vinegar
1 egg
115g/4oz/1 cup green beans, sliced
½ spring cabbage or 115g/4oz spring greens (collards) or pak choi (bok choy), shredded
90g/3½oz jasmine rice, cooked
lime wedges, to serve

1 Heat the oil in a wok or large, heavy frying pan. Add the garlic and cook over a medium to high heat until golden. Do not let it burn or it will taste bitter.

2 Add the red chilli, cashew nuts and toasted coconut to the wok or the pan and stir fry briefly for about 1 minute, taking care to prevent the coconut from scorching.

3 Stir the sugar, soy sauce and rice vinegar into the pan. Cook, stirring, over the heat for 1–2 minutes.

4 Push the stir-fry to one side of the wok or pan and break the egg into the empty space. When the egg is almost set stir it into the garlic and chilli mixture.

5 Add the green beans, greens and cooked rice to the pan. Stir over the heat until the greens have just wilted.

6 Spoon the rice mixture into a warmed serving dish. Offer the lime wedges separately, for squeezing over the rice, and serve immediately in individual bowls.

Mixed Vegetable Rice Energy 199kcal/834kJ; Protein 4.6g; Carbohydrate 43.4g, of which sugars 6.6g; Fat 0.7g, of which saturates 0.1g; Cholesterol 105mg; Calcium 23mg; Fibre 1.6g; Sodium 232mg.
Savoury Fried Rice Energy 548kcal/2271kJ; Protein 14.6g; Carbohydrate 25.1g, of which sugars 7g; Fat 43.9g, of which saturates 18.2g; Cholesterol 110mg; Calcium 183mg; Fibre 7.5g; Sodium 1200mg.

Savoury Rice with Greens and Pork

A Cantonese staple, this originally called for ten different greens to be cooked with the rice. The tradition doesn't have to be followed to the letter, but it is a good idea to use several vegetables, plus a little meat for extra flavour.

Serves 4

4 dried Chinese black mushrooms
150ml/¼ pint/⅔ cup boiling water
30ml/2 tbsp vegetable oil
2 garlic cloves, chopped
150g/5oz lean pork, finely sliced
150g/5oz pak choi (bok choy), finely sliced
30ml/2 tbsp peas, thawed if frozen
30ml/2 tbsp light soy sauce
5ml/1 tsp ground black pepper
5ml/1 tsp cornflour (cornstarch) mixed to a paste with 15ml/1 tbsp cold water
800g/1¾lb/7 cups cooked rice

1 Put the mushrooms in a heatproof bowl and pour over the boiling water. Leave to soak for 20–30 minutes, until soft. Using a slotted spoon, transfer the mushrooms to a board. Cut off and discard the stems. Chop the caps finely. Strain the soaking liquid into a measuring jug (cup) and set aside.

2 Heat the oil in a wok, add the garlic and fry over medium heat for 40 seconds, until light brown. Do not let it burn or it will become bitter. Add the pork and fry for 2 minutes.

3 Add the pak choi, peas and mushrooms. Stir to mix, then add the soy sauce, black pepper and the mushroom soaking liquid. Cook, stirring frequently, for 4 minutes.

4 Add the cornflour paste and stir until the mixture thickens slightly. Finally stir in the cooked rice. As soon as it is piping hot, spoon the mixture into a heated bowl and serve.

Cook's Tip

When you cook the rice, crumble in a vegetarian stock cube. This will give the finished dish a well-rounded flavour.

Jewelled Rice with Fried Eggs

This vibrant stir-fry makes a tasty light meal if you are entertaining vegetarians, or you can serve it with grilled meat or fish.

Serves 4

2 fresh corn on the cob
60ml/4 tbsp sunflower oil
2 garlic cloves, finely chopped
4 red Asian shallots, thinly sliced
1 small fresh red chilli, finely sliced
90g/3½oz carrots, cut into thin matchsticks
90g/3½oz fine green beans, cut into 2cm/¾in lengths
1 red (bell) pepper, seeded and cut into 1cm/½in dice
90g/3½oz/1¼ cups baby button (white) mushrooms
500g/1¼lb/5 cups cooked long grain rice, completely cooled
45ml/3 tbsp light soy sauce
10ml/2 tsp green curry paste
4 eggs
crisp green salad leaves and lime wedges, to serve

1 First shuck the corn cobs. Remove all the papery leaves, and the silky threads, then with a sharp knife cut at the base of the kernels right down the length of the cob.

2 Heat 30ml/2 tbsp of the sunflower oil in a wok or large heavy pan over a high heat. When the oil is hot, add the garlic, shallots and chilli. Stir-fry for about 2 minutes.

3 Add the carrots, green beans, corn, red pepper and mushrooms to the pan and stir-fry for 3–4 minutes.

4 Add the cooked, cooled rice to the pan, stir to mix, and stir-fry for a further 4–5 minutes until the rice is heated through.

5 Mix together the light soy sauce and curry paste and add to the pan. Toss to mix well and stir-fry for 2–3 minutes.

6 Meanwhile, fry the eggs one at a time in the remaining oil in a frying pan. As each egg is cooked, remove it from the pan and place on a plate. Keep the cooked eggs hot.

7 Ladle the rice into four individual warmed bowls or plates and top each portion with a fried egg. Serve with crisp green salad leaves and wedges of lime to squeeze over.

Savoury Rice Energy 199kcal/834kJ; Protein 4.6g; Carbohydrate 43.4g, of which sugars 6.6g; Fat 0.7g, of which saturates 0.1g; Cholesterol 0mg; Calcium 23mg; Fibre 1.6g; Sodium 232mg.
Jewelled Rice Energy 392kcal/1648kJ; Protein 13.6g; Carbohydrate 51.4g, of which sugars 8.2g; Fat 16.1g, of which saturates 3.6g; Cholesterol 261mg; Calcium 79mg; Fibre 2.2g; Sodium 968mg.

Californian Citrus Fried Rice with Asparagus and Mushrooms

For the best results serve the cooked rice cold.

Serves 4–6

4 eggs
10ml/2 tsp Japanese rice vinegar
30ml/2 tbsp light soy sauce
about 45ml/3 tbsp groundnut (peanut) oil
50g/2oz/½ cup cashew nuts
2 garlic cloves, crushed
6 spring onions, diagonally sliced
2 carrots, cut into julienne strips
225g/8oz asparagus, each spear cut diagonally into 4 pieces
175g/6oz/2¼ cups button (white) mushrooms, halved
30ml/2 tbsp rice wine
30ml/2 tbsp water
450g/1lb/4 cups cooked white long grain rice
about 10ml/2 tsp sesame oil
1 orange, segmented
thin strips of orange rind, to garnish

For the hot dressing

5ml/1 tsp grated orange rind
30ml/2 tbsp Japanese rice wine or sherry
45ml/3 tbsp oyster sauce
30ml/2 tbsp freshly squeezed orange juice
5ml/1 tsp medium chilli sauce

1 Beat the eggs with the vinegar and 10ml/2 tsp of the soy sauce. Heat 15ml/1 tbsp of the oil in a wok and cook the eggs until lightly scrambled. Transfer to a plate and set aside.

2 Add the nuts to the wok and stir-fry for 1 minute. Set aside.

3 Heat the remaining oil and add the garlic and spring onions. Cook over a medium heat for 1–2 minutes until the onions begin to soften, then add the carrots and stir-fry for 4 minutes.

4 Add the asparagus and cook for 2–3 minutes, then stir in the mushrooms and stir-fry for a further 1 minute. Stir in the rice wine or sherry, the remaining soy sauce and the water. Simmer for a few minutes until the vegetables are just tender.

5 Mix the dressing, add to the wok and bring to the boil. Add the rice, eggs and nuts. Toss over a low heat for 3–4 minutes, until the rice is heated through. Stir in the sesame oil and orange segments. Garnish with strips of orange rind and serve at once.

Pumpkin and Pistachio Risotto

The wok is the perfect piece of equipment for cooking this unusual risotto. Vegetarians will love this elegant combination of creamy, golden saffron rice and orange pumpkin. It would look impressive served in the hollowed-out pumpkin shell.

Serves 4

1.2 litres/2 pints/5 cups vegetable stock or water
generous pinch of saffron strands
30ml/2 tbsp olive oil
1 onion, chopped
2 garlic cloves, crushed
900g/2lb pumpkin, peeled, seeded and cut into 2cm/¾in cubes (about 7 cups)
400g/14oz/2 cups risotto rice
200ml/7fl oz/scant 1 cup dry white wine
30ml/2 tbsp freshly grated Parmesan cheese
50g/2oz/½ cup pistachios, coarsely chopped
45ml/3 tbsp chopped fresh marjoram or oregano, plus leaves to garnish
salt, freshly grated nutmeg and ground black pepper

1 Bring the vegetable stock or water to the boil and reduce to a low simmer. Ladle a little of it into a small bowl. Add the saffron strands and leave to infuse.

2 Heat the olive oil in a large, heavy wok. Add the onion and garlic and cook gently for 5 minutes until softened. Add the pumpkin cubes and the rice and stir to coat everything in oil. Cook for a few more minutes until the rice looks transparent.

3 Pour in the dry white wine and allow it to bubble hard. When it has been absorbed, add a quarter of the hot stock or water and the saffron liquid. Stir until all the liquid has been absorbed. Then gradually add the remaining stock or water, a little at a time, allowing the rice to absorb the liquid before adding more, and stirring constantly.

4 After 20–30 minutes the rice should be golden yellow, creamy and *al dente*. Stir in the Parmesan cheese, cover the wok and leave it to stand for 5 minutes. To finish the risotto, stir in the pistachios and marjoram or oregano. Season the dish to taste with a little salt, nutmeg and pepper, sprinkle over a few marjoram or oregano leaves and serve.

Citrus Fried Rice Energy 264kcal/1107kJ; Protein 6.5g; Carbohydrate 32.3g, of which sugars 7.7g; Fat 12.6g, of which saturates 2.1g; Cholesterol 13mg; Calcium 48mg; Fibre 2.3g; Sodium 517mg.
Pumpkin Risotto: Energy 585kcal/2441kJ; Protein 14.4g; Carbohydrate 87.3g, of which sugars 5.7g; Fat 15.9g, of which saturates 3.5g; Cholesterol 8mg; Calcium 196mg; Fibre 3.2g; Sodium 151mg.

Spicy Fried Rice Sticks with Prawns

This well-known recipe is based on the classic Thai noodle dish called pad Thai. Popular all over Thailand, it is enjoyed morning, noon and night.

Serves 4

15g/½oz dried shrimps
15ml/1 tbsp tamarind pulp
45ml/3 tbsp Thai fish sauce (nam pla)
15ml/1 tbsp sugar
2 garlic cloves, chopped
2 fresh red chillies, seeded and chopped
45ml/3 tbsp groundnut (peanut) oil
2 eggs, beaten
225g/8oz dried rice sticks, soaked in warm water for 30 minutes, refreshed under cold running water and drained
225g/8oz cooked, peeled king prawns
3 spring onions cut into 2.5cm/1in lengths
75g/3oz beansprouts
30ml/2 tbsp roughly chopped roasted unsalted peanuts
30ml/2 tbsp chopped fresh coriander (cilantro)
lime slices, to garnish

1 Put the dried shrimps in a small bowl and pour over enough warm water to cover. Leave the dried shrimps to soak for 30 minutes until soft, then drain using a sieve (strainer).

2 Put the tamarind pulp in a bowl with 60ml/4 tbsp hot water. Blend them together, then press through a sieve to extract 30ml/2 tbsp thick tamarind water. Mix the tamarind water with the fish sauce and sugar.

3 Using a mortar and pestle or a food processor, pound the garlic and chillies to form a paste. Heat a wok over a medium heat, add 15ml/1 tbsp of the oil, then add the beaten eggs and stir for 1–2 minutes until the eggs are scrambled. Remove and set aside. Wipe the wok clean.

4 Reheat the wok until hot, add the remaining oil, then the chilli paste and dried shrimps and stir-fry for 1 minute. Add the rice sticks and tamarind mixture and stir-fry for 3–4 minutes.

5 Add the scrambled eggs, prawns, spring onions, beansprouts, peanuts and coriander, then stir-fry for 2 minutes until well mixed. Serve at once, garnishing each portion with lime slices.

Shellfish Risotto with Mixed Mushrooms

This is a quick and easy risotto, in which all the liquid is added in one go. The method is well-suited to this shellfish dish, as it means everything cooks together undisturbed.

Serves 6

225g/8oz mussels
225g/8oz Venus or carpet shell clams
45ml/3 tbsp olive oil
1 onion, chopped
450g/1lb/2⅓ cups risotto rice
1.75 litres/3 pints/7½ cups simmering chicken or vegetable stock
150ml/¼ pint/⅔ cup white wine
225g/8oz/2–3 cups assorted wild and cultivated mushrooms, trimmed and sliced
115g/4oz raw peeled prawns (shrimp), deveined
1 medium or 2 small squid, cleaned, trimmed and sliced
3 drops truffle oil (optional)
75ml/5 tbsp chopped mixed fresh parsley and chervil
celery salt and cayenne pepper

1 Scrub and debeard the mussels and clean the clams under cold running water. Discard any broken shellfish and any that are open and do not close when tapped sharply. Set aside.

2 Heat the oil in a wok or large frying pan and fry the onion for 6–8 minutes until soft but not browned.

3 Add the rice, stirring to coat the grains in oil, then pour in the stock and wine and cook for 5 minutes. Add the mushrooms and cook for 5 minutes more, stirring occasionally.

4 Add the prawns, squid, mussels and clams and stir into the rice. Cover the pan and simmer over a low heat for 15 minutes until the prawns have turned pink and the mussels and clams have opened. Discard any shellfish that remain closed.

5 Switch off the heat. Add the truffle oil, if using, and stir in the chopped mixed parsley and chervil. Cover the pan tightly and leave to stand for 5–10 minutes to allow all the flavours to blend. Season to taste with celery salt and a pinch of cayenne, pile into a warmed dish, and serve immediately.

Spicy Rice Sticks Energy 436kcal/1819kJ; Protein 21.1g; Carbohydrate 52.1g, of which sugars 5.4g; Fat 15.3g, of which saturates 2.5g; Cholesterol 224mg; Calcium 151mg; Fibre 1.5g; Sodium 318mg.
Shellfish Risotto Energy 423kcal/1768kJ; Protein 21.4g; Carbohydrate 62.5g, of which sugars 0.8g; Fat 7.5g, of which saturates 1.2g; Cholesterol 136mg; Calcium 64mg; Fibre 0.6g; Sodium 335mg.

Seafood Fried Rice

Serves 4
30ml/2 tbsp vegetable oil
2 garlic cloves, crushed
2 eggs, lightly beaten
100g/3¾oz raw or cooked prawns (shrimps), peeled
800g/1¾lb/7 cups cold cooked rice
30ml/2 tbsp light soy sauce
2.5ml/½ tsp ground black pepper
2 spring onions (scallions), chopped
spring onion curls, to garnish

1 Heat the oil in a wok and fry the garlic until golden brown. Do not let it burn or it will become bitter. Push the garlic aside to leave a clear space in the centre of the wok. Add the eggs and cook until they set to form an omelette.

2 Cut the omelette up roughly in the wok, and push it aside. Add the prawns and rice and stir rapidly for 5 minutes or until the shrimps are cooked and the rice is piping hot.

3 Sprinkle over the soy sauce. Add the black pepper and chopped spring onions. Toss to mix, then spoon into a bowl and serve garnished with the spring onion curls.

Celebration Rice

Serves 6–8
450g/1lb fresh mussels, scrubbed
90ml/6 tbsp white wine
6 small skinless, boneless chicken breast fillets, cut into pieces
30ml/2 tbsp seasoned flour
about 90ml/6 tbsp olive oil
12 raw prawns (shrimp), peeled
150g/5oz pork fillet (tenderloin), diced
2 onions, chopped
2–3 garlic cloves, crushed
1 red (bell) pepper, seeded and sliced
2 ripe tomatoes, chopped
900ml/1½ pints/3¾ cups stock
good pinch of saffron, dissolved in 30ml/2 tbsp hot water
350g/12oz/1¾ cups risotto rice
150g/5oz green beans, chopped
115g/4oz/1 cup frozen broad beans
225g/8oz chorizo sausage, sliced
115g/4oz/1 cup frozen peas
6–8 stuffed green olives, sliced

1 Place the mussels in a large pan with the wine, bring to the boil, then cover tightly and cook for 3–4 minutes. Drain, reserving the liquid and discard any mussels that have not opened.

2 Dust the chicken with the flour. Heat half the oil in a wok or paella pan and brown the chicken. Transfer to a plate. Fry the prawns briefly, then transfer to a plate. Heat 30ml/2 tbsp of the oil in the pan, brown the pork and transfer to a separate plate.

3 Heat the remaining oil and fry the onions and garlic for 3–4 minutes. Add the red pepper, cook for 2–3 minutes, then add the chopped tomatoes and cook until the mixture is fairly thick.

4 Add the stock, the mussel liquid and the saffron liquid. Season well, bring to the boil and add the rice. Stir, then add the chicken, pork, prawns, beans, chorizo and peas. Cook for 12 minutes, then lower the heat and simmer until the liquid is absorbed.

5 Add the mussels and olives and cook for a further 3–4 minutes. Remove the pan from the heat, cover with a clean damp dish towel and leave to stand for 10 minutes before serving.

Classic Spanish Paella with Chicken, Pork and Shellfish

Valencia's paella is Spain's best-known dish abroad.

Serves 6–8
90ml/6 tbsp white wine
450g/1lb mussels, scrubbed
115g/4oz/scant 1 cup small shelled broad (fava) beans
150g/5oz green beans, chopped
90ml/6 tbsp olive oil
6 small skinless, boneless chicken breast fillets, cut into pieces
150g/5oz pork fillet, cubed
6–8 large raw prawns (shrimp) tails, deveined
2 onions, chopped
2–3 garlic cloves, finely chopped
1 red (bell) pepper, sliced
2 ripe tomatoes, peeled, seeded and chopped
60ml/4 tbsp chopped fresh parsley
900ml/1½ pints/3¾ cups chicken stock
pinch of saffron threads, soaked in 30ml/2 tbsp hot water
350g/12oz/1¾ cups paella rice, washed and drained
225g/8oz frying chorizo, sliced
115g/4oz/1 cup peas
6–8 stuffed green olives, sliced
salt, paprika and ground black pepper

1 Heat the wine, add the mussels and steam until opened. Reserve the liquid and mussels separately. Blanch the beans in boiling water, then drain. Pop the broad beans out of their skins.

2 Heat 45ml/3 tbsp olive oil in a large wok or frying pan. Season the chicken pieces with salt and paprika, brown them on all sides and reserve. Do the same with the pork. Fry the prawns briefly and reserve separately.

3 Heat the remaining oil and fry the onions and garlic for 3–4 minutes. Add the pepper, cook for 2–3 minutes, then stir in the tomatoes and parsley and cook until thick. Stir in the stock, reserved mussel liquid and saffron liquid. Season well and bring to the boil. When it is bubbling, add the rice. Stir once, then add the chicken pieces, pork, shellfish, beans, chorizo and peas.

4 Cook over medium-high heat for 10 minutes. Then lower the heat and cook until the rice is done – another 10–12 minutes. Arrange the mussels and olives on top. Cover and leave to stand for 10 minutes, until all the liquid is absorbed.

Seafood Fried Rice Energy 386kcal/1629kJ; Protein 13.1g; Carbohydrate 62.6g, of which sugars 0.7g; Fat 11.1g, of which saturates 2.1g; Cholesterol 144mg; Calcium 73mg; Fibre 0.3g; Sodium 619mg.
Celebration Rice Energy 378kcal/1581kJ; Protein 27.4g; Carbohydrate 35.8g, of which sugars 4.6g; Fat 13.4g, of which saturates 3.5g; Cholesterol 80mg; Calcium 77mg; Fibre 2.6g; Sodium 264mg.
Spanish Paella Energy 504kcal/2108kJ; Protein 36.5g; Carbohydrate 47.7g, of which sugars 6.1g; Fat 17.9g, of which saturates 4.7g; Cholesterol 107mg; Calcium 103mg; Fibre 3.4g; Sodium 352mg.

Fragrant Harbour Fried Rice

This tasty rice dish celebrates the Chinese name for Hong Kong, which is Fragrant Harbour.

Serves 4

about 90ml/6 tbsp vegetable oil
2 eggs, beaten
8 shallots, sliced
115g/4oz peeled cooked prawns (shrimp)
3 garlic cloves, crushed
115g/4oz cooked pork, cut into thin strips
4 Chinese dried mushrooms, soaked, stems removed and sliced
115g/4oz Chinese sausage, cooked and sliced at an angle
225g/8oz/generous 1 cup long grain rice, cooked, cooled quickly and chilled
30ml/2 tbsp light soy sauce
115g/4oz/1 cup frozen peas, thawed
2 spring onions (scallions), shredded
salt and ground black pepper
coriander (cilantro) leaves, to garnish

1 Heat 15ml/1 tbsp oil in a frying pan, add the eggs and make an omelette. Slide it out out, roll it up and cut into strips. Set aside.

2 Heat a wok, add 15ml/1 tbsp oil and stir-fry the shallots until golden. Remove and set aside. Add the prawns and garlic, with a little more oil if needed, fry for 1 minute, then remove.

3 Heat 15ml/1 tbsp more oil in the wok and stir-fry the pork and mushrooms for 2 minutes; add the cooked Chinese sausage slices and heat for a further 2 minutes until everything is hot. Lift the ingredients out of the wok and keep warm.

4 Reheat the wok with the remaining oil and stir-fry the rice until it glistens. Stir in the soy sauce, salt and pepper, plus half the cooked ingredients. Add the peas and half the spring onions and toss over the heat until the peas are cooked. Pile the fried rice on a heated platter, top with the remaining cooked ingredients and garnish with the coriander leaves.

Cook's Tip
You don't have to wait until the day after you've served a roast to try this. Most delicatessens sell sliced roast pork.

Trout and Prosciutto Risotto Rolls

Risotto is a fine match for the robust flavour of these trout rolls.

Serves 4

4 trout fillets, skinned
4 slices prosciutto
caper berries, to garnish

For the risotto
30ml/2 tbsp olive oil
8 large raw prawns (shrimp), peeled and deveined
1 onion, chopped
225g/8oz/generous 1 cup risotto rice
about 105ml/7 tbsp white wine
about 750ml/1¼ pints/3 cups simmering fish or chicken stock
15g/½oz/¼ cup dried porcini or chanterelle mushrooms, soaked for 10 minutes in warm water to cover
salt and ground black pepper

1 To make the risotto, heat the oil in a wok or heavy pan and cook the prawns very briefly until flecked with pink. Lift out using a slotted spoon and transfer to a plate. Keep warm. Add the chopped onion to the pan and cook gently for 3–4 minutes, or until soft. Add the rice and stir for 3–4 minutes to coat in the oil. Add 75ml/5 tbsp of the wine and then the stock, a little at a time, stirring over a gentle heat and allowing the rice to absorb the liquid before adding more.

2 Drain the mushrooms, reserving the liquid, and cut the larger ones in half. Towards the end of cooking, stir the mushrooms into the risotto with 15ml/1 tbsp of the reserved liquid. Season to taste with salt and pepper. When the rice is *al dente*, remove from the heat and stir in the prawns. Preheat the oven to 190°C/375°F/Gas 5. Grease an ovenproof dish and set aside.

3 Take a trout fillet, place a spoonful of risotto at one end and roll up. Wrap each fillet in a slice of prosciutto and place in the prepared dish. Spoon any remaining risotto around the fish rolls and sprinkle over the remaining wine. Cover loosely with foil and bake for 15–20 minutes, or until the fish is cooked.

4 Spoon the risotto on to a large, warmed serving platter, arrange the trout and prosciutto rolls on top and garnish the dish with caper berries. Serve immediately.

Fragrant Fried Rice Energy 450kcal/1872kJ; Protein 14.5g; Carbohydrate 51g, of which sugars 4.4g; Fat 20.9g, of which saturates 3.1g; Cholesterol 113mg; Calcium 48mg; Fibre 1.1g; Sodium 58mg.
Trout Risotto Rolls Energy 501kcal/2094kJ; Protein 46g; Carbohydrate 27.8g, of which sugars 5g; Fat 22.8g, of which saturates 3.3g; Cholesterol 160mg; Calcium 144mg; Fibre 3.2g; Sodium 161mg.

Chicken and Seafood Paella

This Filipino version of the popular classic is flavoured with ginger and bay leaves to give it a distinctive aroma that sets it apart from the Mediterranean dish.

Serves 6

45ml/3 tbsp palm oil
12 chicken drumsticks and wings
2 onions, finely chopped
4 garlic cloves, finely chopped
40g/1½ oz fresh root ginger, chopped
30–45ml/2–3 tbsp tomato purée (paste)
5ml/1 tsp paprika
2–3 bay leaves
500g/1¼lb/2½ cups long grain rice
1.2 litres/2 pints/5 cups chicken or vegetable stock
15–30ml/1–2 tbsp patis (Filipino fish sauce)
400g/14oz can petits pois (baby peas), drained
12 prawns (shrimp) in their shells, cleaned and rinsed
12 medium clams, cleaned and rinsed
salt and ground black pepper

1 Heat the oil in a wok with a lid. Add the chicken and fry for 5 minutes, until browned. Remove from the pan and set aside.

2 Add the onions, garlic and ginger to the pan and fry until they are fragrant and beginning to colour.

3 Add the tomato purée, paprika, bay leaves, rice and chicken. Pour in the stock and bring to the boil. Add the patis and season to taste. Cover the pan and simmer gently for 15–20 minutes, until the rice and chicken are almost cooked.

4 Toss in the peas and add the prawns and clams, sitting them on top of the rice. Cover the pan again and cook for a further 10 minutes or until all the liquid has evaporated.

Malacca Fried Rice

The many versions of this Asian dish are all based on leftover cooked rice.

Serves 4–6

45ml/3 tbsp vegetable oil
2 eggs, beaten
4 shallots or 1 onion, finely chopped
5ml/1 tsp chopped fresh root ginger
1 garlic clove, crushed
225g/8oz raw prawns, peeled
5ml/1 tsp chilli sauce
3 spring onions, green part only, roughly chopped
225g/8oz/2 cups frozen peas
225g/8oz thickly sliced roast pork, diced
45ml/3 tbsp light soy sauce
350g/12oz/3 cups cooked white long grain rice, cooled
salt and black pepper

1 Heat 15ml/1 tbsp oil in a frying pan, add the eggs and make an omelette. Slide it out out, roll it up and cut into strips. Set aside.

2 Heat the remaining vegetable oil in a preheated wok, add the shallots or onion, ginger, garlic and prawns, and cook for 1–2 minutes, taking care that the garlic does not burn.

3 Stir in the remaining ingredients and season to taste. Fry over a medium heat for 6–8 minutes, stirring to heat through. Spoon into a dish, decorate with the omelette strips and serve.

Indonesian Spicy Rice

This version of fried rice is an Indonesian national dish. Generally made with leftover cooked grains, the fried rice is served with crispy shallots and chillies or it is tossed with shrimp or crabmeat, and chopped vegetables.

Serves 4

½ cucumber
30–45ml/2–3 tbsp vegetable oil, plus extra for shallow frying
4 shallots, finely chopped
4 garlic cloves, finely chopped
3–4 fresh red chillies, seeded and chopped
45ml/3 tbsp kecap manis (Indonesian sweet soy sauce)
15ml/1 tbsp tomato purée (paste)
350g/12oz/1¾ cups cooked long grain rice
4 eggs

1 Peel the cucumber, cut it in half lengthways and scoop out the seeds. Discard the skin and the seeds. Cut the flesh into thin sticks. Put aside until it is required.

2 Heat the vegetable oil in a wok or large frying pan. Add the shallots, garlic and chillies to the pan and fry, stirring constantly, until they begin to colour.

3 Add the kecap manis and tomato purée and stir for about 2 minutes until thick, to form a sauce.

4 Add the cooked rice to the pan and continue to cook, stirring occasionally, for about 5 minutes until the rice is well coated with the sauce and heated through.

5 Meanwhile, in a large frying pan, heat a thin layer of oil for frying and crack the eggs into it. Fry for 1–2 minutes until the whites are cooked but the yolks remain runny.

6 Spoon the rice into four deep bowls. Alternatively, use one bowl as a mould to invert each portion of rice on to each plate, then lift off the bowl to reveal the mound of rice beneath.

7 Place the fried eggs on top of the spicy Indonesian rice and garnish each bowl with the cucumber strips.

Chicken Paella Energy 637kcal/2666kJ; Protein 54.4g; Carbohydrate 78.3g, of which sugars 4.6g; Fat 11.6g, of which saturates 2.1g; Cholesterol 266mg; Calcium 104mg; Fibre 3.8g; Sodium 628mg.
Malacca Fried Rice Energy 433kcal/1808kJ; Protein 23.5g; Carbohydrate 70.6g, of which sugars 5.8g; Fat 6.1g, of which saturates 3g; Cholesterol 158mg; Calcium 123mg; Fibre 3.2g; Sodium 189mg.
Indonesian Spicy Rice Energy 273kcal/1146kJ; Protein 9.9g; Carbohydrate 33g, of which sugars 4.7g; Fat 12.3g, of which saturates 2.5g; Cholesterol 190mg; Calcium 67mg; Fibre 1.1g; Sodium 884mg.

Classic Pork and Prawn Fried Rice

One of the most widely travelled Chinese dishes, this is a Cantonese invention, deriving from the pragmatic need to recycle leftovers. Some luxurious versions are packed with premium ingredients like crab meat and lobster. Others are really simple. What follows is a basic recipe, which can easily be adapted to suit the ingredients available.

Serves 4

2 spring onions (scallions), chopped
30ml/2 tbsp vegetable oil
3 eggs, lightly beaten
800g/1¾lb/7 cups cold cooked rice
150g/5oz roast pork or cooked ham, in 1cm/½in cubes
100g/3¾oz raw tiger prawns (jumbo shrimp), peeled
30ml/2 tbsp frozen green peas
30ml/2 tbsp light soy sauce
5ml/1 tsp ground black pepper
1 chicken stock cube

1 Set aside about one-fifth of the spring onions for the garnish.

2 Heat the vegetable oil in a wok or large, heavy pan and fry the remaining spring onions for 30 seconds. Push them aside to leave a clear space in the centre of the pan. Add the eggs and cook until they set to form an omelette.

3 Cut the omelette up roughly in the pan, then add the rice, pork or ham, and prawns. Stir vigorously for 3 minutes, then add the peas. Stir in the soy sauce and black pepper, and crumble the stock cube over the surface.

4 Toss over the heat for 3 minutes more, or until the rice is piping hot all the way through. Spoon into a bowl and garnish with the reserved spring onions. Serve immediately.

Cook's Tip

Spring onion (scallion) curls make a dramatic garnish. Trim 4 spring onions, removing the roots and bulbs. Using a sharp knife, finely shred the spring onions to within 2.5cm/1in of the root end. Place the shredded spring onions in a bowl of iced water and chill for at least 30 minutes or until the shredded ends have curled. Drain on kitchen paper.

Chinese Fried Rice

This dish is more elaborate than the more familiar egg fried rice, and you will find it makes a meal in itself. You can spice it up with a bowl of chillies on the side, or add crabs, clams and any kind of shellfish to make it a more substantial dish.

Serves 4

50g/2oz cold cooked smoked or cured ham
50g/2oz cooked prawns (shrimp), peeled
3 eggs
5ml/1 tsp salt
2 spring onions (scallions), finely chopped
60ml/4 tbsp vegetable oil
115g/4oz/1 cup green peas, thawed if frozen
15ml/1 tbsp light soy sauce
15ml/1 tbsp Chinese rice wine
450g/1lb/4 cups cooked white long grain rice

1 Dice the cooked ham finely using a sharp knife. Pat the cooked prawns dry on kitchen paper.

2 In a small bowl, beat the eggs lightly with a pinch of the salt and a few pieces of the spring onions.

3 Heat about half the vegetable oil in a wok, stir-fry the peas, prawns and ham for 1 minute, then add the soy sauce and the rice wine. Transfer to a bowl and keep hot.

4 Heat the remaining oil in the wok and scramble the eggs lightly, stirring to break them up.

5 Add the rice and stir to make sure the grains are separate. Add the remaining salt, the remaining spring onions and the prawn mixture. Toss over the heat to mix. Serve hot or cold.

Variations

- *This is a versatile recipe and is ideal for using up leftovers. Use cooked chicken or turkey instead of the ham, doubling the quantity if you omit the prawns.*
- *To add even more colour to this bright dish, you could add a red or orange (bell) pepper when you stir-fry the peas.*

Classic Pork and Prawn Energy 473kcal/1997kJ; Protein 25.3g; Carbohydrate 65.3g, of which sugars 2.5g; Fat 14.3g, of which saturates 2.9g; Cholesterol 238mg; Calcium 114mg; Fibre 1.3g; Sodium 1317mg.
Chinese Fried Rice Energy 86kcal/360kJ; Protein 9.8g; Carbohydrate 3.8g, of which sugars 1.2g; Fat 3.7g, of which saturates 1g; Cholesterol 127mg; Calcium 34mg; Fibre 1.4g; Sodium 477mg.

Spiced Chicken Biryani

Biryanis originated in Persia and are traditionally made with meat and rice.

Serves 4

275g/10oz/1½ cups basmati rice
30ml/2 tbsp vegetable oil
1 onion, thinly sliced
2 garlic cloves, crushed
1 green chilli, finely chopped
2.5cm/1in fresh root ginger, finely chopped
675g/1½lb skinless chicken breast fillets, cut into 2.5cm/1in cubes
45ml/3 tbsp curry paste
1.5ml/¼ tsp salt
1.5ml/¼ tsp garam masala
3 tomatoes, cut into thin wedges
1.5ml/¼ tsp ground turmeric
2 bay leaves
4 green cardamom pods
4 cloves
1.5ml/¼ tsp saffron strands
fresh coriander (cilantro), to garnish

1 Place the rice in a large sieve (strainer) and rinse it in several changes of cold water. Put the rice into a large bowl, cover with plenty of water and leave to soak for 30 minutes.

2 Meanwhile, heat the oil in a wok or large frying pan and fry the onion for about 5–7 minutes until lightly browned, then add the garlic, chilli and ginger and fry for about 2 minutes.

3 Add the cubed chicken to the pan and fry for about 5 minutes, stirring occasionally to coat the chicken on all sides.

4 Add the curry paste, salt and garam masala and cook for 5 minutes. Add the tomatoes and continue to cook for a further 3–4 minutes. Remove from the heat and set aside.

5 Preheat the oven to 190°C/375°F/Gas 5.

6 Bring a large pan of water to the boil. Drain the rice and add it to the pan with the turmeric. Cook for about 10 minutes, or until the rice is almost tender. Drain the rice and toss together with the bay leaves, cardamoms, cloves and saffron.

7 Layer the rice and chicken in a shallow, ovenproof dish until all the mixture has been used, finishing off with a layer of rice. Cover and bake in the oven for 15–20 minutes, or until the chicken is tender. Serve immediately, garnished with coriander.

Chicken Piri-Piri

This dish came from Portugal, and is based on a hot sauce made from Angolan chillies. It has become widely popular.

Serves 4

4 chicken breast portions
30–45ml/2–3 tbsp olive oil
1 large onion, finely sliced
2 carrots, cut into thin strips
1 large parsnip or 2 small parsnips, cut into thin strips
1 red (bell) pepper, sliced
1 yellow (bell) pepper, sliced
1 litre/1¾ pints/4 cups chicken stock
3 tomatoes, peeled, seeded and chopped
generous dash of piri-piri sauce
15ml/1 tbsp tomato purée (paste)
½ cinnamon stick
1 fresh thyme sprig, plus extra fresh thyme, to garnish
1 bay leaf
275g/10oz/1½ cups white long grain rice
15ml/1 tbsp lime or lemon juice
salt and ground black pepper

1 Preheat the oven to 180°C/350°F/Gas 4 and season the chicken with salt and pepper. Heat 30ml/2 tbsp of the oil in a wok and brown the chicken on all sides. Transfer to a plate.

2 Add some more oil if necessary and fry the onion for 2–3 minutes. Add the carrots, parsnip and peppers, fry for a few minutes then cover and sweat for 4–5 minutes until soft.

3 Pour in the stock, then add the tomatoes, piri-piri sauce, tomato purée and cinnamon stick. Stir in the thyme and bay leaf. Season to taste and bring to the boil. Spoon off 300ml/½ pint/1¼ cups of the liquid and set aside in a small pan.

4 Put the rice in a casserole. Using a slotted spoon, scoop the vegetables out of the pan and spread them over the rice. Arrange the chicken on top. Pour over the spicy stock from the pan, cover tightly and bake for about 45 minutes, until both the rice and chicken are completely tender.

5 Meanwhile, heat the reserved stock, adding a few more drops of piri-piri sauce and the lime or lemon juice. Spoon the piri-piri chicken and rice on to warmed serving plates. Serve the remaining sauce separately or poured over the chicken.

Chicken Biryani Energy 377kcal/1579kJ; Protein 30.3g; Carbohydrate 47.2g, of which sugars 8.3g; Fat 7.5g, of which saturates 1.2g; Cholesterol 71mg; Calcium 86mg; Fibre 1.8g; Sodium 255mg.
Chicken Piri-piri Energy 557kcal/2337kJ; Protein 44.3g; Carbohydrate 75.4g, of which sugars 15.5g; Fat 8.8g, of which saturates 1.5g; Cholesterol 105mg; Calcium 73mg; Fibre 5.8g; Sodium 122mg.

Spicy Chicken Jambalaya

This classic dish is great for a family supper, and perfect for making in a slow cooker.

Serves 6

225g/8oz skinless chicken breast fillets
175g/6oz piece raw smoked gammon (smoked or cured ham) or bacon
30ml/2 tbsp olive oil
1 large onion, peeled and chopped
2 garlic cloves, crushed
2 sticks celery, diced
5ml/1 tsp chopped fresh thyme or 2.5ml/½ tsp dried thyme
5ml/1 tsp mild chilli powder
2.5ml/½ tsp ground ginger
10ml/2 tsp tomato purée (paste)
2 dashes of Tabasco sauce
750ml/1¼ pints/3 cups boiling chicken stock
300g/11oz/1½ cups easy-cook (converted) rice
115g/4oz chorizo sausage, sliced
30ml/2 tbsp chopped fresh flat leaf parsley, plus extra, to garnish
salt and ground black pepper

1 Cut the chicken into 2.5cm/1in cubes and season. Trim any fat off the gammon or bacon, then cut the meat into 1cm/½in cubes.

2 Heat 15ml/1 tbsp of the olive oil in a wok, add the onion and fry gently for 5 minutes, until beginning to colour. Add the garlic, celery, thyme, chilli powder and ginger and cook for 1 minute. Transfer to the ceramic cooking pot and set to high.

3 Heat the remaining 15ml/1 tbsp olive oil in the wok, add the chicken pieces and fry briefly until lightly browned. Add to the ceramic cooking pot with the gammon or bacon cubes.

4 Add the tomato purée and Tabasco sauce to the stock and stir well. Pour into the pot, cover and cook on high for 1½ hours.

5 Sprinkle the rice into the pot and stir to mix. Cover and cook on high for 45 minutes to 1 hour, or until the rice is almost tender and most of the stock has been absorbed. Add a little extra hot stock or water if the mixture is dry.

6 Stir in the chorizo and cook on high for a further 15 minutes, or until heated through. Stir in the parsley, then taste and adjust the seasoning. Turn off the slow cooker and leave to stand for 10 minutes. Serve garnished with chopped fresh parsley.

Chicken and Mushroom Rice

'Donburi' means a one-dish meal, and its name comes from the eponymous Japanese porcelain food bowl. This recipe is ideal for using the mushrooms that are abundant in autumn.

Serves 4

225–275g/8–10oz/generous 1–1½ cups Thai fragrant rice
10ml/2 tsp groundnut (peanut) oil
50g/2oz/4 tbsp butter
2 garlic cloves, crushed
2.5cm/1in fresh root ginger, grated
5 spring onions (scallions), diagonally sliced
1 green chilli, seeded and sliced
3 skinless chicken breast fillets, cut into thin strips
150g/5oz tofu, cut into small cubes
115g/4oz/1¾ shiitake mushrooms, stalks discarded and cups sliced
15ml/1 tbsp Japanese rice wine
30ml/2 tbsp light soy sauce
10ml/2 tsp sugar
400ml/14fl oz/1⅔ cups hot chicken stock

1 Cook the Thai fragrant rice by the absorption method or by following the instructions on the packet.

2 While the rice is cooking, heat the oil and half the butter in a wok. Stir-fry the garlic, ginger, spring onions and chilli for 1–2 minutes until slightly softened. Add the strips of chicken and fry, in batches if necessary, until all the pieces are browned.

3 Transfer the chicken mixture to a plate using a slotted spoon, and add the tofu to the wok. Stir-fry for a few minutes, then add the mushrooms. Stir-fry for 2–3 minutes over a medium heat until the mushrooms are tender.

4 Add the rice wine, soy sauce and sugar to the wok and cook briskly for 1–2 minutes, stirring all the time. Return the chicken to the wok, toss over the heat for about 2 minutes, then pour in the stock. Stir well and cook over low heat for about 5–6 minutes until the stock is bubbling.

5 Spoon the rice into individual, warmed serving bowls and pile the chicken mixture on top, making sure that each portion gets a generous amount of chicken sauce.

Spicy Jambalaya Energy 384kcal/1617kJ; Protein 21.2g; Carbohydrate 48.6g, of which sugars 2.9g; Fat 13g, of which saturates 3.6g; Cholesterol 43mg; Calcium 57mg; Fibre 1.1g; Sodium 630mg.
Chicken and Mushroom Rice Energy 408kcal/1709kJ; Protein 35.2g; Carbohydrate 46.3g, of which sugars 1.1g; Fat 8.8g, of which saturates 1.2g; Cholesterol 79mg; Calcium 216mg; Fibre 0.5g; Sodium 605mg.

Curried Chicken and Rice

This simple meal is made in a single pot, so it is perfect for casual entertaining. It can be made using virtually any meat or vegetables that you have to hand, but chicken is quick and easy to cook and combines extremely well with Indian spices.

Serves 4

60ml/4 tbsp vegetable oil
4 garlic cloves, finely chopped
1 medium-sized chicken or 1.3kg/3lb chicken portions, skin and bones removed and meat cut into bitesize pieces
5ml/1 tsp garam masala
450g/1lb/2⅔ cups jasmine rice, rinsed and drained
10ml/2 tsp salt
1 litre/1¾ pints/4 cups chicken stock
small bunch fresh coriander (cilantro), chopped, to garnish

1 Heat the vegetable oil in a wok or flameproof casserole that has a lid. Add the garlic and cook over a low to medium heat until golden brown. Add the chicken, increase the heat and brown the pieces on all sides.

2 Add the garam masala to the wok or casserole, stir well to coat the chicken pieces all over in the spice, then tip in the drained rice. Add the salt and stir to mix.

3 Pour in the stock, stir well, then cover the wok or casserole and bring to the boil. Reduce the heat to low and simmer gently for 10 minutes, until the rice is tender.

4 Lift the wok or casserole off the heat, leaving the lid on, and leave for 10 minutes for the flavours to mingle. Fluff up the rice grains with a fork and spoon on to a platter. Sprinkle the dish with the coriander and serve.

Cook's Tip
You will probably need to brown the chicken pieces in batches. Don't be tempted to add too much chicken to the pan at once, as this will lower the temperature of the oil and the chicken will stew rather than fry.

Paprika Chicken with Rice

This Spanish rice dish with chicken is a casserole, designed to be more liquid than a paella. You can vary the recipe by adding seasonal vegetables, and peas and corn can also be included if you wish. The paprika and the slices of chorizo give the rice a warm, spicy flavour.

Serves 4

60ml/4 tbsp olive oil
6 chicken thighs, halved along the bone
5ml/1 tsp paprika
1 large Spanish onion, roughly chopped
2 garlic cloves, finely chopped
1 chorizo sausage, sliced
115g/4oz Serrano or cooked ham or gammon, diced
1 red (bell) pepper, roughly chopped
1 yellow (bell) pepper, roughly chopped
225g/8oz/1 generous cup paella rice, washed and drained
2 large tomatoes, chopped or 200g/7oz can chopped tomatoes
120ml/4fl oz/½ cup amontillado sherry
750ml/1¼ pints/3 cups chicken stock
5ml/1 tsp dried oregano or thyme
1 bay leaf
salt and ground black pepper
15 green olives and chopped fresh flat leaf parsley, to garnish

1 Heat the oil in a wok or wide flameproof casserole. Season the chicken pieces with salt and paprika. Fry for 3–4 minutes until nicely brown all over, then reserve on a plate.

2 Add the onion and garlic to the pan and fry gently until they are beginning to soften. Add the sliced chorizo and ham or gammon and stir-fry. Add the chopped peppers to the pan and cook until they begin to soften.

3 Sprinkle in the drained rice and cook, stirring, for 1–2 minutes. Add the tomatoes, sherry, chicken stock and dried herbs and season well. Arrange the chicken pieces deep in the mixture, and tuck in the bay leaf.

4 Cover and cook over a very low heat for 30–40 minutes, until the chicken and rice are done. Stir, then garnish with olives and chopped parsley and serve.

Curried Chicken Energy 715kcal/2994kJ; Protein 56.3g; Carbohydrate 89.8g, of which sugars 0g; Fat 13.8g, of which saturates 1.9g; Cholesterol 140mg; Calcium 32mg; Fibre 0g; Sodium 120mg.
Paprika Chicken Energy 194kcal/813kJ; Protein 26g; Carbohydrate 2.1g, of which sugars 1.6g; Fat 9.1g, of which saturates 1.4g; Cholesterol 74mg; Calcium 42mg; Fibre 1.1g; Sodium 69mg.

Fried Rice with Turkey

Turkey is great for a stir-fry as it cooks so quickly. Use fillets from the breast for this dish, or you can use chicken if you prefer. Complete the finished dish just before serving with fine strips of omelette as an attractive and tasty garnish.

Serves 4–6

45ml/3 tbsp vegetable or sunflower oil
1 onion or 3 shallots, peeled and chopped
15ml/1 tbsp chopped garlic
115g/4oz turkey breast fillet, cut into small cubes
2 eggs, beaten
1kg/2¼lb/4 cups cooked long-grain rice, cooled
30ml/2 tbsp Thai fish sauce
15ml/1 tbsp dark soy sauce
2.5 ml/½ tsp caster (superfine) sugar
4 spring onions (scallions), finely sliced, to garnish
2 red chillies, sliced, to garnish
1 lime, cut into wedges, to garnish
strips of omelette, to garnish (optional)

1 Heat the oil in a wok or large frying pan. Add the onion and garlic and cook for about 2 minutes until softened.

2 Add the turkey to the softened onion and garlic. Stir-fry until the meat is cooked and evenly browned. Add the eggs and cook until scrambled into small lumps.

3 Add the rice to the pan and continue to stir and toss, to coat it with the oil and prevent it from sticking.

4 Add the fish sauce, soy sauce and sugar and mix well. Continue to fry until the rice is thoroughly heated.

5 Garnish with sliced spring onion, red chillies and lime wedges. Top with a few strips of omelette, if you like.

Cook's Tip
As with all fried rice dishes, the important thing is to make sure the rice is cold. Add the rice after cooking the other ingredients, and stir to heat it through completely.

Peruvian Duck with Rice

This is a very rich dish, brightly coloured with tomatoes and fresh herbs.

Serves 4–6

4 duck breast fillets
1 Spanish (Bermuda) onion, chopped
2 garlic cloves, crushed
10ml/2 tsp grated fresh root ginger
4 tomatoes, peeled and chopped
225g/8oz Kabocha or onion squash, cut into 1cm/½in cubes
275g/10oz/1½ cups long grain rice
750ml/1¼ pints/3 cups chicken stock
15ml/1 tbsp finely chopped fresh coriander (cilantro)
15ml/1 tbsp finely chopped fresh mint
salt and ground black pepper

1 Heat a wok, heavy frying pan or flameproof casserole. Using a sharp knife, score the fatty side of the duck breast fillets in a criss-cross pattern, rub the fat with a little salt, then dry-fry the duck, skin side down, for about 6–8 minutes to render some of the fat.

2 Pour all but 15ml/1 tbsp of the fat into a jar or cup, then fry the duck fillets, meat side down, in the fat remaining in the pan for 3–4 minutes until brown all over. Transfer to a board, slice thickly and set aside in a shallow dish. Deglaze the pan with a little water and pour this liquid over the duck.

3 Fry the onion and garlic in the same pan for 4–5 minutes until the onion is fairly soft, adding a little extra duck fat if necessary. Stir in the ginger, cook for 1–2 minutes more, then add the tomatoes and cook, stirring, for another 2 minutes.

4 Add the squash, stir-fry for a few minutes, then cover and allow to steam for about 4 minutes.

5 Stir in the rice and cook, stirring, until the rice is coated in the tomato and onion mixture. Pour in the stock, return the slices of duck to the pan and season with salt and pepper.

6 Bring to the boil, then lower the heat, cover and simmer gently for 30–35 minutes until the rice is tender. Stir in the coriander and mint and serve.

Fried Rice with Turkey Energy 343kcal/1448kJ; Protein 11.3g; Carbohydrate 54.3g, of which sugars 2.2g; Fat 10.6g, of which saturates 2g; Cholesterol 82mg; Calcium 51mg; Fibre 0.6g; Sodium 220mg.
Peruvian Duck Energy 754kcal/3130kJ; Protein 22.5g; Carbohydrate 58.6g, of which sugars 3.3g; Fat 45.1g, of which saturates 13.5g; Cholesterol 90mg; Calcium 53mg; Fibre 1.3g; Sodium 99mg.

Chinese Jewelled Rice

This special fried rice is so tasty and substantial that it can be served as a meal in itself. In China, fried rice is usually served at the end of a meal, not as an accompaniment, and is often cooked in order to use up left over boiled rice from the day before. The "jewels" in this lovely rice dish are of course the added ingredients – the pink ham, bright green peas and dark Chinese mushrooms.

Serves 4

350g/12oz/1¾ cups long grain rice
45ml/3 tbsp vegetable oil
1 onion, roughly chopped
4 dried black Chinese mushrooms, soaked, drained and diced
115g/4oz cooked ham, diced
175g/6oz/½ cup drained canned white crabmeat
75g/3oz canned water chestnuts, drained and cut into cubes
115g/4oz/1 cup frozen peas, thawed
30ml/2 tbsp oyster sauce
5ml/1 tsp sugar
salt

1 Rinse the rice in cold water, drain well, then add to a pan of lightly salted boiling water. Cook for 10–12 minutes. Drain, refresh under cold water, drain again and cool quickly.

2 Heat half the oil in a preheated wok, then stir-fry the rice for 3 minutes. Remove and set aside.

3 Add the remaining oil to the wok. When the oil is hot, cook the onion until softened but not coloured.

4 Add all the remaining ingredients and stir-fry for 2 minutes until everything is hot and coated in the sauce.

5 Return the rice to the wok and stir-fry for 3 minutes, until everything is heated through. Remove from the wok and serve immediately, in four individual warmed dishes.

Variations

This dish can be made with various ingredients. Try using chicken or pork instead of ham, or make a vegetarian version using mushrooms and peppers or tofu.

Thai Fried Rice

This hot and spicy dish is easy to prepare and makes a complete meal in itself as it includes chunks of chicken and stir-fried eggs.

Serves 4

225g/8oz Thai fragrant rice
45ml/3 tbsp vegetable oil
1 small red (bell) pepper, cut into 2cm/¾in cubes
1 onion, chopped
350g/12oz skinless, chicken breast fillets, cut into 2cm/¾in cubes
1 garlic clove, crushed
15ml/1 tbsp mild curry paste
2.5ml/½ tsp paprika
2.5ml/½ tsp ground turmeric
30ml/2 tbsp Thai fish sauce
2 eggs, beaten
salt and ground black pepper
fried basil leaves, to garnish

1 Put the rice in a pan with 1.5 litres/2½ pints/6¼ cups boiling water. Return to the boil, then simmer, uncovered, for 8–10 minutes; drain well. Spread the grains on a tray and leave to cool.

2 Heat a wok and add 30ml/2 tbsp of the oil. Stir-fry the red pepper and onion for 1 minute.

3 Add the chicken, garlic, curry paste and spices to the wok and stir-fry for 2–3 minutes, so that the chicken is coated in the spices.

4 Reduce the heat to medium, add the cooled rice, fish sauce and seasoning. Stir-fry for 2–3 minutes until the rice is very hot.

5 Make a well in the centre and add the remaining oil. When hot, add the beaten eggs, leave to cook for about 2 minutes until lightly set, then stir into the rice.

6 Scatter the fried basil leaves over the rice and serve at once.

Cook's Tip

The curry should be fairly dry, but take care that it does not catch on the bottom of the pan. If you want to leave it unattended, cook it in a heavy-based pan or flameproof casserole, either on the hob or in an oven preheated to 180°C/350°F/Gas 4.

Chinese Jewelled Rice Energy 474kcal/1979kJ; Protein 22.5g; Carbohydrate 77.5g, of which sugars 4.3g; Fat 7.8g, of which saturates 1.1g; Cholesterol 48mg; Calcium 86mg; Fibre 1.9g; Sodium 710mg.
Thai Fried Rice Energy 508kcal/2127kJ; Protein 24.7g; Carbohydrate 83.9g, of which sugars 8.7g; Fat 8g, of which saturates 1.6g; Cholesterol 135mg; Calcium 57mg; Fibre 1.3g; Sodium 204mg.

Chilli Rice with Chinese Sausage

Traditional Vietnamese stir-fried rice includes cured Chinese pork sausage, or thin strips of pork combined with prawns or crab meat. Prepared this way, the dish can be eaten as a snack, or as part of the meal with grilled and roasted meats accompanied by a vegetable dish or salad.

Serves 4

25g/1oz dried cloud ear (wood ear) mushrooms, soaked for 20 minutes
15ml/1 tbsp vegetable or sesame oil
1 onion, sliced
2 green or red Thai chillies, seeded and finely chopped
2 Chinese sausages (15cm/6in long), each sliced into 10 pieces
175g/6oz prawns (shrimp), shelled and deveined
30ml/2 tbsp Thai fish sauce, plus extra for drizzling
10ml/2 tsp five-spice powder
1 bunch of fresh coriander (cilantro), stalks removed, leaves finely chopped
450g/1lb/4 cups cold steamed rice
ground black pepper

1 Drain the soaked cloud ear mushrooms then cut into thin strips. Heat a wok or large, heavy pan and add the oil. Add the onion and chillies and fry until they begin to colour, then stir in the cloud ear mushrooms.

2 Add the Chinese sausage slices, moving them around the wok or pan until they begin to brown.

3 Add the prawns to the pan and move them around until they turn opaque. Stir in the fish sauce, the five-spice powder and 30ml/2 tbsp of the coriander.

4 Season the mixture in the pan to taste with freshly ground black pepper. Add the rice, and cook, stirring constantly, to make sure that it does not stick to the pan.

5 As soon as the rice is heated through, sprinkle with the remainder of the chopped fresh coriander and serve with Thai fish sauce to drizzle over it.

Nasi Goreng

This recipe name means 'fried rice' in Indonesian, and it is one of the best-known dishes from Indonesia. It is a great way to use up left-over rice and meats.

Serves 4–6

350g/12oz/1¾ cups basmati rice (dry weight), cooked and cooled
2 eggs
30ml/2 tbsp water
105ml/7 tbsp sunflower oil
10ml/2 tsp shrimp paste
2–3 fresh red chillies, shredded, keeping some aside to garnish
2 garlic cloves, crushed
1 onion, sliced
225g/8oz fillet (tenderloin) of pork or beef, cut into strips
115g/4oz cooked, peeled prawns (shrimp)
225g/8oz cooked chicken, chopped
30ml/2 tbsp dark soy sauce
salt and ground black pepper
deep-fried onions, to serve

1 Separate the grains of the cooked rice with a fork. Cover and set aside. Beat the eggs with the water and seasoning.

2 Heat 15ml/1 tbsp of the oil in a frying pan or wok, pour in about half the egg mixture and cook until set, without stirring. Roll up the omelette, slide it on to a plate, cut into strips and set aside. Make another omelette in the same way.

3 Put the shrimp paste and half the shredded chillies into a food processor. Add the garlic and onion. Process to a paste.

4 Heat the remaining oil in a wok. Fry the paste, without browning, until it gives off a spicy aroma. Add the strips of pork or beef and toss the meat over the heat, to seal in the juices. Cook in the wok for about 2 minutes, stirring constantly.

5 Add the prawns, cook for 2 minutes, then add the chicken, rice and soy sauce, with salt and pepper to taste, stirring constantly. Serve in individual bowls, garnished with omelette strips, shredded chilli and deep-fried onions.

Variation
To make bahmi goreng, substitute noodles for the rice.

Chilli Rice Energy 398kcal/1673kJ; Protein 19g; Carbohydrate 44g, of which sugars 4g; Fat 18g, of which saturates 5g; Cholesterol 116mg; Calcium 158mg; Fibre 2g; Sodium 800mg.
Nasi Goreng Energy 463kcal/1929kJ; Protein 27.3g; Carbohydrate 49.4g, of which sugars 2.1g; Fat 17.1g, of which saturates 2.7g; Cholesterol 151mg; Calcium 49mg; Fibre 0.5g; Sodium 288mg.

Fried Rice with Pork and Chillies

This classic rice dish looks particularly pretty garnished with strips of omelette.

Serves 4–6

45ml/3 tbsp vegetable or sunflower oil
1 onion, chopped
15ml/1 tbsp chopped garlic
115g/4oz pork, cut into small cubes
2 eggs, beaten
1kg/2¼lb/4 cups cooked rice
30ml/2 tbsp Thai fish sauce
15ml/1 tbsp dark soy sauce
2.5ml/½ tsp caster (superfine) sugar

For the garnish

4 spring onions (scallions), finely sliced
2 fresh red chillies, seeded and finely sliced
1 lime, cut into wedges

1 Heat the oil in a wok or large frying pan. Add the onion and garlic and cook for about 2–3 minutes until the onion is beginning to turn soft and translucent.

2 Add the pork to the softened onion and garlic. Fry, stirring constantly, until the pork changes colour and is cooked through.

3 Add the beaten eggs to the pan and cook, stirring, for 1–2 minutes until they are scrambled into small lumps.

4 Add the cooked rice to the pan and continue to stir and toss for 2–3 minutes, to coat it with the oil and prevent it from sticking to the base of the pan.

5 Add the fish sauce, soy sauce and sugar and mix well. Continue to fry until the rice is thoroughly heated.

6 Spoon the rice into warmed individual bowls and serve immediately, garnished with finely sliced spring onions, seeded and sliced chillies and the lime wedges.

Cook's Tip

To make 1kg/2¼lb/4 cups cooked rice, you will need approximately 400g/14oz/2 cups uncooked rice.

Dirty Rice

Contrary to popular belief, this dish doesn't get its name from its appearance, but from its association with New Orleans, the home of jazz, which has often been referred to as "dirty music".

Serves 4

60ml/4 tbsp vegetable or sunflower oil
25g/1oz/¼ cup flour
50g/2oz/4 tbsp butter
1 large onion, chopped
2 garlic cloves, crushed
200g/7oz minced (ground) pork
225g/8oz chicken livers, trimmed and finely chopped
dash of Tabasco sauce
1 green (bell) pepper, seeded and sliced
2 celery sticks, sliced
300ml/½ pint/1¼ cups chicken stock
225g/8oz/generous 1 cup cooked white long grain rice
4 spring onions, chopped
45ml/3 tbsp chopped fresh parsley
salt and freshly ground black pepper
celery leaves, to garnish

1 Heat half the oil in a heavy-based saucepan. Stir in the flour and cook over a low heat, stirring constantly, until the roux is smooth and the colour is a rich chestnut-brown. Immediately remove the pan from the heat and place it on a cold surface such as the draining board of a sink.

2 Heat the remaining oil with the butter in a wok or large frying pan and stir-fry the onion for 5 minutes.

3 Add the garlic and pork. Cook for 5 minutes, breaking up the pork and stirring until it is evenly browned, then stir in the chicken livers and fry for 2–3 minutes until they have changed colour all over. Season with salt, pepper and Tabasco sauce. Stir in the green pepper and celery.

4 Stir the roux into the stir-fried mixture, then gradually add in the stock. When the mixture begins to bubble, cover and cook for 30 minutes, stirring occasionally.

5 Stir in the rice, spring onions and parsley. Toss over the heat until the rice has heated through. Serve in four individual warmed bowls, garnished with the celery leaves.

Rice with Pork Energy 513kcal/2165kJ; Protein 17.1g; Carbohydrate 80g, of which sugars 2.1g; Fat 16.1g, of which saturates 2.3g; Cholesterol 132mg; Calcium 75mg; Fibre 0.7g; Sodium 511mg.
Dirty Rice Energy 581kcal/2417kJ; Protein 25.7g; Carbohydrate 56.1g, of which sugars 5g; Fat 28.1g, of which saturates 10.1g; Cholesterol 273mg; Calcium 58mg; Fibre 2.1g; Sodium 165mg.

Savoury Rice with Madras Curry

Bitesize beef is simmered with spices until it is so tender it melts in the mouth.

Serves 4

15ml/1 tbsp sunflower oil
30ml/2 tbsp ghee
1 onion, finely chopped
1 garlic clove, crushed
5ml/1 tsp ground cumin
2.5ml/½ tsp ground coriander
4 green cardamom pods
1 cinnamon stick
1 small red (bell) pepper and 1 small green (bell) pepper, seeded and diced
225g/8oz/generous 1 cup basmati rice
300ml/½ pint/1¼ cups beef stock

For the curry

30ml/2 tbsp vegetable or sunflower oil
30ml/2 tbsp ghee
675g/1½lb stewing beef, cut into bitesize cubes
1 onion, chopped
3 green cardamom pods
2 fresh green chillies, seeded and finely chopped
2.5cm/1in piece of fresh root ginger, grated
2 garlic cloves, crushed
15ml/1 tbsp Madras curry paste
5ml/1 tsp ground cumin
5ml/1 tsp ground coriander
150ml/¼ pint/⅔ cup beef stock
salt

1 Make the curry. Heat half the oil and ghee in a wok and fry the meat, until browned all over. Transfer to a plate. Heat the remaining oil and ghee in the wok and fry the onion for 4 minutes. Add the cardamom pods, chillies, ginger and garlic and fry for 2 minutes. Add the remaining curry ingredients, season with salt, bring to the boil, then lower the heat and simmer very gently for 1–1½ hours, until the meat is tender.

2 When the curry is almost ready, heat the oil and ghee in a flameproof casserole and fry the onion and garlic gently for 3–4 minutes until softened and lightly browned. Stir in the cumin and ground coriander, cardamom pods and cinnamon stick. Fry for 1 minute, then add the diced peppers.

3 Add the rice, stirring to coat the grains in the spice mixture, and pour in the stock. Bring to the boil, then lower the heat, cover the pan tightly and simmer for about 8–10 minutes, or until the rice is tender and the stock has been absorbed. Spoon into a bowl and serve with the curry.

Filipino Risotto with Stir-fried Liver

This type of rice dish is served in the Philippines as a snack and is often enjoyed at Christmas and Easter.

Serves 3–4

900ml/1½ pints/scant 4 cups pork or chicken stock
45ml/3 tbsp vegetable oil
3–4 shallots, finely chopped
3 garlic cloves, finely chopped
25g/1oz fresh root ginger, chopped
25g/1oz fresh turmeric, chopped
175g/6oz/¾ cup small raisins
225g/8oz pork fillet (tenderloin), cut into thin bitesize strips
225g/8oz/generous 1 cup sticky rice
450g/1lb pig's or lamb's liver, cut into bitesize strips
30ml/2 tbsp rice flour or plain (all-purpose) white flour
salt and ground black pepper

To serve

45–60ml/3–4 tbsp roasted, unsalted peanuts, crushed
2 hard-boiled eggs, quartered
2–3 spring onions (scallions), white parts only, sliced
2 fresh red or green chillies, seeded and finely shredded
suka (Filipino coconut vinegar)

1 Pour the stock into a pan and bring it to the boil. Make sure it is well seasoned, and then reduce the heat and leave to simmer.

2 Meanwhile, heat 30ml/2 tbsp of the oil in a wok or heavy pan, stir in the shallots, garlic, ginger and turmeric and fry until fragrant and beginning to colour. Add the raisins and toss in the pork. Stir-fry for 2–3 minutes, until the pork is well browned.

3 Stir the rice into the pork mixture. Gradually add ladlefuls of the hot stock to the rice and cook over a medium heat until the liquid has been absorbed, stirring from time to time. When all the stock has been added, cover the pan and leave to cook gently, until almost all the liquid has been absorbed.

4 Meanwhile, toss the liver in the flour. Just before the rice is cooked, heat the remaining oil in a frying pan or wok. Add the liver and stir-fry for 2–3 minutes. Season the liver to taste.

5 Tip the risotto into warmed individual dishes. Spoon the liver on top and scatter over the crushed peanuts. Arrange the eggs, spring onions and chillies over the dish and serve immediately, with suka as a condiment for diners to add as they wish.

Savoury Rice Energy 738kcal/3070kJ; Protein 44.3g; Carbohydrate 56.5g, of which sugars 9.6g; Fat 37.1g, of which saturates 15.3g; Cholesterol 130mg; Calcium 48mg; Fibre 2.5g; Sodium 205mg
Filipino Risotto Energy 756kcal/3167kJ; Protein 49.2g; Carbohydrate 87.7g, of which sugars 33.3g; Fat 23.3g, of which saturates 4.6g; Cholesterol 423mg; Calcium 74mg; Fibre 2.3g; Sodium 197mg.

Filipino Risotto with Chorizo

This rice dish is a classic Filipino breakfast. To make a substantial meal to start the day, it is served at street stalls and cafés with fried dried fish, such as the crispy danggit from Cebu, fried eggs, pork jerky or the spicy sausage longaniza, which can be substituted for the similar-tasting Spanish chorizo. This delicious recipe is a great way of using up leftover rice.

Serves 4

45ml/3 tbsp palm, groundnut (peanut) or vegetable oil
2–3 garlic cloves, crushed
450g/1lb cooked long grain rice
15–30ml/1–2 tbsp patis (Filipino fish sauce)
2 small, thin chorizo sausages, about 175g/6oz each, sliced diagonally
4 eggs
salt and ground black pepper
suka (Filipino coconut vinegar), to serve

1 Heat 15ml/1 tbsp of the oil in a wok or heavy pan, stir in the garlic and fry until fragrant and golden brown. Toss in the rice, breaking up any lumps, and add the patis. Season the rice with salt to taste, if needed, and black pepper. Turn off the heat and cover the wok or pan to keep the rice warm.

2 In another wok or heavy pan, heat 15ml/1 tbsp of the oil, add the sliced chorizo and fry until crispy on both sides. Drain the chorizo on crumpled kitchen paper.

3 Heat the remaining 15ml/1 tbsp oil in a separate frying pan and fry the eggs for 1–2 minutes.

4 Spoon the rice into individual bowls. Place the fried eggs on top of the rice and arrange the chorizo around the edge. Alternatively, pack the rice into a cup or bowl and invert each portion on to a plate. Serve warm with the suka.

Variation
If you prefer, carefully turn the eggs over once cooked on one side, then fry for no more than 30 seconds until a film is set over the yolk without browning.

Fried Rice with Beef

One of the joys of cooking Chinese food is the ease and speed with which a really good meal can be prepared. This delectable beef and rice stir-fry can be on the table in 15 minutes.

Serves 4

200g/7oz beef steak, chilled
15ml/1 tbsp vegetable oil
2 garlic cloves, finely chopped
1 egg
250g/9oz/2¼ cups cooked jasmine rice
½ medium head broccoli, coarsely chopped
30ml/2 tbsp dark soy sauce
15ml/1 tbsp light soy sauce
5ml/1 tsp light muscovado (brown) sugar
15ml/1 tbsp fish sauce
ground black pepper
chilli sauce, to serve

1 Trim the steak and cut into very thin strips with a sharp knife.

2 Heat the oil in a wok or frying pan and cook the garlic over a low to medium heat until golden. Do not let it burn. Increase the heat to high, add the steak and stir-fry for 2 minutes.

3 Move the pieces of beef to the edges of the wok or pan and break the egg into the centre. When the egg starts to set, break it up with chopsticks and then stir-fry it with the meat.

4 Add the rice and toss all the contents of the wok together, scraping up any residue on the base, then add the broccoli, soy sauces, sugar and fish sauce and stir-fry for 2 minutes more. Season to taste with pepper, spoon into heated bowls and serve immediately with chilli sauce.

Cook's Tips
- *Soy sauce is made from fermented soya beans. The first extraction is sold as light soy sauce and has a delicate, "beany" fragrance. Dark soy sauce is more intensely flavoured and has been allowed to mature for longer. The darker kind is also traditionally used to intensify the colour of a dish.*
- *If you don't have any leftover cooked rice, cook 225g/8oz/ generous 1 cup rice, allow to cool and then use.*

Filipino Rice Energy 567kcal/2367kJ; Protein 17.7g; Carbohydrate 45.4g, of which sugars 2g; Fat 36.4g, of which saturates 11.6g; Cholesterol 225mg; Calcium 92mg; Fibre 0.6g; Sodium 1136mg.
Fried Rice with Beef Energy 385kcal/1606kJ; Protein 20.7g; Carbohydrate 52.7g, of which sugars 2.5g; Fat 9.8g, of which saturates 2.8g; Cholesterol 81mg; Calcium 59mg; Fibre 1.6g; Sodium 590mg.

Fresh Rice Noodles

Dried rice noodles are generally available in Asian supermarkets, but fresh ones are quite different and not that difficult to make. The freshly made noodle sheets can be served as a snack, drenched in sugar or honey, or dipped into a savoury sauce.

Serves 4

225g/8oz/2 cups rice flour
600ml/1 pint/2½ cups water
a pinch of salt
15ml/1 tbsp vegetable or sunflower oil, plus extra for brushing
slivers of fresh red chilli and fresh ginger, and coriander (cilantro) leaves, to garnish (optional)

1 Place the flour in a bowl and stir in some of the water to form a paste. Pour in the rest of the water using a whisk and beating it to make a lump-free batter. Add the salt and oil and leave to stand for 15 minutes.

2 Meanwhile, fill a wide round and heatproof pan with water. Cut a piece of smooth cotton cloth a little larger than the diameter of the pan. Stretch it over the top of the pan, pulling the edges tautly down over the sides, then wind a piece of string around the edge, to secure.

3 Using a sharp knife or a pair of scissors, make three small slits, about 2.5cm/1in from the edge of the cloth, at regular intervals. Bring the water to the boil.

4 Stir the batter and ladle 30–45ml/2–3 tbsp on to the cloth, swirling it to form a 13–15cm/5–6in wide circle. Cover with a domed lid, such as a wok lid, and steam for 1 minute, or until the noodle sheet is translucent.

5 Carefully insert a metal spatula or knife under the noodle sheet and prise it off the cloth. (If it doesn't peel off easily, you may need to steam it a little longer.) Transfer the noodle sheet to a lightly oiled baking tray, brush lightly with oil, and cook the remaining batter in the same way.

6 Transfer to a large warmed serving platter, garnish with slivers of fresh chillies and the coriander leaves, if you like, and serve.

Plain Noodles with Four Flavours

A wonderfully simple way of serving noodles, this dish allows each individual diners to season their own. Flavourings are always put out in little bowls whenever noodles are served.

Serves 4

4 small fresh red or green chillies
60ml/4 tbsp fish sauce
60ml/4 tbsp rice vinegar
sugar
mild or hot chilli powder
350g/12oz fresh or dried noodles

1 Finely chop the chillies, and mix half of them with the fish sauce in a bowl. Mix the remaining chillies with the rice vinegar in another small bowl. Put the sugar and chilli powder in separate small bowls.

2 Cook the noodles until tender, following the instructions on the packet. Drain well, tip into a large bowl, and serve with the four flavours handed separately.

Soft Fried Noodles

This is a great dish for times when you are feeling a little peckish and fancy something simple but satisfying. Drain the cooked noodles and ladle them into the wok a few at a time, swirling them with the onions, so they don't all clump together on contact with the hot oil.

Serves 4–6

30ml/2 tbsp vegetable or sunflower oil
30ml/2 tbsp finely chopped spring onions (scallions)
350g/12oz dried egg noodles, cooked and drained
soy sauce, to taste
salt and ground black pepper

1 Heat a wok, add the oil and swirl it around. Then add the spring onions and stir-fry them for about 30 seconds.

2 Add the egg noodles and separate the strands. Fry the noodles until they are heated through, lightly browned and crisp on the outside, but still soft inside. Season with soy sauce, salt and pepper. Serve immediately.

Fresh Rice Noodles Energy 217kcal/908kJ; Protein 6.4g; Carbohydrate 46.1g, of which sugars 1.5g; Fat 0.6g, of which saturates 0.1g; Cholesterol 0mg; Calcium 51mg; Fibre 1.3g; Sodium 11mg.
Plain Noodles Energy 321kcal/1341kJ; Protein 4.5g; Carbohydrate 72.4g, of which sugars 1g; Fat 0.2g, of which saturates 0g; Cholesterol 0mg; Calcium 12mg; Fibre 0.2g; Sodium 278mg.
Soft Fried Noodles Energy 262kcal/1107kJ; Protein 7.2g; Carbohydrate 42g, of which sugars 1.3g; Fat 8.5g, of which saturates 1.8g; Cholesterol 18mg; Calcium 18mg; Fibre 1.8g; Sodium 105mg.

Egg Noodles with Asparagus

This dish is simplicity itself with a wonderful contrast of textures and flavours. Use young asparagus, which is beautifully tender and cooks in minutes. If you have a large wok, then you can easily double the quantities of noodles and vegetables to serve four. Don't double the amount of the soy sauce, though – just add enough to taste.

Serves 2

115g/4oz dried egg noodles
15ml/1 tbsp vegetable oil
1 small onion, chopped
2.5/1in piece fresh root ginger, grated
2 garlic cloves, crushed
175g/6oz young asparagus spears, trimmed
115g/4oz/½ cup beansprouts
4 spring onions (scallions), sliced
45ml/3 tbsp light soy sauce
salt and ground black pepper

1 Bring a large pan of salted water to the boil. Add the noodles and cook according to the instructions of the packet or until they are just tender. Drain the noodles, rinse them under cold running water, drain again and set aside.

2 Heat a wok and add the oil. When the oil is very hot, stir-fry the onion, ginger and garlic for 2–3 minutes.

3 Add the asparagus and stir-fry for a further 2-3 minutes, then add the noodles and beansprouts and toss over fairly high heat for 2 minutes, until the noodles are hot.

4 Add the spring onions and soy sauce to the noodle and vegetable mixture in the wok and mix well to combine.

5 Season to taste, adding salt sparingly as the sauce will add quite a salty flavour. Stir-fry for 1 minute more before serving in a large bowl or in individual bowls.

Variation
For a contrast in textures, stir-fry half the asparagus spears and cook the rest under a hot grill (broiler) or on a hot griddle pan until lightly charred.

Fried Noodles with Ginger

Here is a simple noodle dish that is low in saturated fat and goes with most Oriental dishes. It can also be served as a light meal for 2 or 3 people. The combination of fresh root ginger, spring onions and light soy sauce is a popular classic throughout south-east Asia. It is also good served cold the next day as the basis of a salad.

Serves 4

handful of fresh coriander (cilantro)
225g/8oz dried egg noodles
10ml/2 tsp sesame oil
15ml/1 tbsp groundnut (peanut) oil or vegetable oil
5cm/2in piece fresh root ginger, cut into fine shreds
6–8 spring onions (scallions), cut into shreds
30ml/2 tbsp light soy sauce
salt and ground black pepper

1 Strip the leaves from the coriander stalks. Discard the stalks. Pile the leaves on to a chopping board and coarsely chop them using a cleaver or large, sharp knife.

2 Bring a large pan of lightly salted water to the boil and cook the noodles according to the instructions on the packet.

3 Drain the noodles, rinse under cold water, drain again and tip into a bowl. Add the sesame oil and toss to coat.

4 Heat a wok until hot, add the groundnut or vegetable oil and swirl it around. Add the ginger and stir-fry for a few seconds, then add the noodles and spring onions. Stir-fry for 3–4 minutes, until the noodles are hot.

5 Drizzle the soy sauce over the dish, then sprinkle the chopped coriander on top of the noodles.

6 Add salt and ground black pepper to taste. Toss and serve in four individual heated bowls.

Variation
If you don't like the flavour of coriander (cilantro), use flat leaf parsley or even some chopped rocket (arugula).

Noodles with Asparagus Energy 339kcal/1427kJ; Protein 12.6g; Carbohydrate 50.1g, of which sugars 7.9g; Fat 11.2g, of which saturates 2.2g; Cholesterol 17mg; Calcium 71mg; Fibre 4.8g; Sodium 1712mg.
Fried Noodles with Ginger Energy 253kcal/1067kJ; Protein 7.4g; Carbohydrate 41.6g, of which sugars 2.2g; Fat 7.5g, of which saturates 1.6g; Cholesterol 17mg; Calcium 25mg; Fibre 1.9g; Sodium 637mg.

Crispy Noodles with Mixed Vegetables

In this dish, the noodles are deep fried, then tossed into colourful vegetables. Fry the noodles in small batches and drain on kitchen paper to keep them crisp.

Serves 4

2 large carrots
2 courgettes (zucchini)
4 spring onions (scallions)
115g/4oz green beans
115g/4oz dried vermicelli rice noodles
groundnut (peanut) oil, for deep frying
2.5cm/1in fresh root ginger, shredded
1 fresh red chilli, sliced
115g/4oz fresh shiitake or button mushrooms, thickly sliced
few Chinese cabbage leaves, roughly shredded
75g/3oz beansprouts
30ml/2 tbsp light soy sauce
30ml/2 tbsp Chinese rice wine
5ml/1 tsp sugar
30ml/2 tbsp roughly torn fresh coriander (cilantro) leaves

1 Cut the carrots and courgettes into fine sticks. Shred the spring onions into similar-sized pieces. Trim the green beans and cut them into short lengths.

2 Break the noodles into pieces about 7.5cm/3in long. Half-fill a wok with oil and heat it to 180°C/350°F.

3 Deep-fry the raw noodles, a handful at a time, for 1–2 minutes until puffed and crispy. Drain them on kitchen paper. Pour off all but 30ml/2 tbsp of the oil.

4 Reheat the oil in the wok. When it is hot, add the green beans and stir-fry them for 2–3 minutes.

5 Add the ginger, red chilli, mushrooms, carrots and courgettes to the wok and stir-fry them for 1–2 minutes. Add the Chinese cabbage, beansprouts and spring onions. Stir-fry for 1 minute, then add the soy sauce, rice wine and sugar. Cook, stirring, for about 30 seconds.

6 Add the noodles and coriander and toss, taking care not to crush the noodles too much. Serve at once.

Sweet and Hot Vegetable Noodles

This noodle dish has the colour of fire, but only the mildest suggestion of heat. The ginger and plum sauce give it a fruity flavour.

Serves 4

130g/4½oz dried rice noodles
30ml/2 tbsp groundnut (peanut) oil
2.5cm/1in piece fresh root ginger, sliced into thin batons
1 garlic clove, crushed
130g/4½oz drained canned bamboo shoots, sliced in batons
2 medium carrots, sliced in batons
130g/4½oz/1½ cups beansprouts
1 small white cabbage, shredded
30ml/2 tbsp nam pla
30ml/2 tbsp soy sauce
30ml/2 tbsp plum sauce
10ml/2 tsp sesame oil
15ml/1 tbsp palm sugar (jaggery) or light muscovado (brown) sugar
juice of ½ lime
90g/3½oz mooli (daikon), sliced into thin batons
small bunch fresh coriander (cilantro), chopped
60ml/4 tbsp sesame seeds, toasted

1 Cook the noodles in a large pan of boiling water, following the instructions on the packet. Meanwhile, heat the oil in a wok or large frying pan and stir-fry the ginger and garlic together for 2–3 minutes over a medium heat, until golden.

2 Drain the noodles and keep warm. Add the bamboo shoots to the wok, increase the heat to high and stir-fry for 5 minutes. Add the carrots, beansprouts and cabbage and stir-fry for a further 5 minutes, until they are beginning to char at the edges.

3 Stir in the sauces, sesame oil, sugar and lime juice. Add the mooli and coriander, toss to mix, and serve with the noodles in warmed bowls, sprinkled with toasted sesame seeds.

Cook's Tip

Use a large, sharp knife for shredding cabbage. Remove any tough outer leaves, if necessary, and any brown or shrivelled leaves, then cut the cabbage into quarters. Cut off and discard the hard core from each quarter, place the cabbage flat side down, then slice it very thinly to make fine shreds.

Crispy Noodles Energy 230kcal/964kJ; Protein 7.9g; Carbohydrate 44.6g, of which sugars 5.4g; Fat 2.4g, of which saturates 0.3g; Cholesterol 0mg; Calcium 52mg; Fibre 2.8g; Sodium 623mg.
Sweet and Hot Noodles: Energy 368kcal/1530kJ; Protein 8.8g; Carbohydrate 45.8g, of which sugars 17.6g; Fat 16.5g, of which saturates 2.3g; Cholesterol 0mg; Calcium 200mg; Fibre 6.2g; Sodium 650mg.

Spiced Stir-fried Noodles

Originally from China, spicy stir-fried noodles are also a common sight at street stalls throughout Indonesia, and there are as many delicious variations.

Serves 4

450g/1lb fresh egg noodles
15–30ml/1–2 tbsp palm, groundnut (peanut) or corn oil, plus extra for shallow frying
2 shallots, finely chopped
2–3 spring onions (scallions), finely chopped
2–3 garlic cloves, crushed
3–4 Thai chillies, seeded and finely chopped
15ml/1 tbsp shrimp paste
15ml/1 tbsp tomato purée (paste)
15–30ml/1–2 tbsp kecap manis (Indonesian sweet soy sauce)
4 eggs
salt

For the garnish
15ml/1 tbsp palm or corn oil
3–4 shallots, finely sliced

1 First prepare the garnish. Heat the oil in a wok or heavy pan, stir in the shallots and fry until they are a deep golden brown. Drain them on kitchen paper and put aside.

2 Fill a deep pan with water and bring it to the boil. Drop in the egg noodles, untangling them with chopsticks, and cook for about 3 minutes until tender but still firm to the bite. Drain and refresh under running cold water.

3 Heat the oil in a wok or large, heavy frying pan and fry the shallots, spring onions, garlic and chillies until fragrant. Add the shrimp paste and cook until the mixture darkens.

4 Toss the noodles into the pan, making sure that they are thoroughly coated in the mixture. Add the tomato purée and kecap manis, toss thoroughly, and cook for 2–3 minutes. Season the noodles with salt to taste. Divide the noodles between four warmed bowls and keep warm.

5 Heat a thin layer of oil in a large, heavy frying pan, and crack the eggs into it. Fry for 1–2 minutes until the whites are cooked but the yolks remain runny. Place on the noodles and serve immediately with the fried shallots sprinkled over the top.

Mixed Rice Noodles with Avocado and Spinach

A delicious noodle dish made extra special by the addition of avocado and a garnish of prawns. Tahini and peanut butter enrich the simple sauce.

Serves 4

15ml/1 tbsp sunflower oil
2.5cm/1in fresh root ginger, peeled and grated
2 cloves garlic, crushed
45ml/3 tbsp dark soy sauce
225g/8oz peas, thawed if frozen
450g/1lb fresh rice noodles
450g/1lb spinach, stalks removed
30ml/2 tbsp smooth peanut butter
30ml/2 tbsp tahini
150ml/¼ pint/⅔ cup milk
1 ripe avocado, peeled and stoned (pitted)
roasted peanuts and peeled, cooked prawns (shrimp), to garnish

1 Heat the wok, then add the oil. When the oil is hot, stir-fry the ginger and garlic for 30 seconds. Add 15ml/1 tbsp of the soy sauce and 150ml/¼ pint/⅔ cup boiling water.

2 Add the peas and noodles to the wok, then cook for 3 minutes. Stir in the spinach. Remove the vegetables and noodles, drain and keep warm.

3 Stir the peanut butter, remaining soy sauce, tahini and milk together in the wok, and simmer for 1 minute.

4 Add the vegetables and noodles, slice in the avocado and toss together gently to avoid breaking the avocado slices.

5 Serve the rice noodles and vegetables piled on four warmed, individual plates. Spoon some sauce over each portion and garnish with roasted peanuts and prawns.

Cook's Tip
Rice noodles are extremely thin noodles made from rice flour. They resemble long, translucent, white hairs. They need practically no cooking, just immerse them briefly in boiling water.

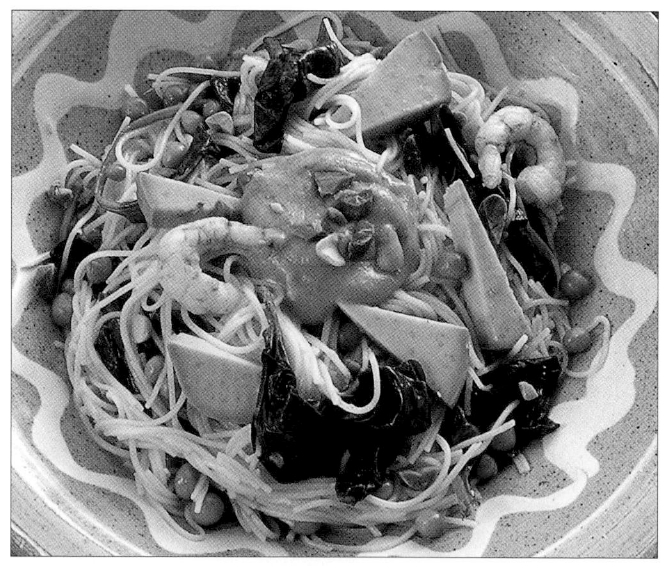

Spiced Noodles Energy 549kcal/2317kJ; Protein 20.5g; Carbohydrate 82.9g, of which sugars 3.9g; Fat 17.6g, of which saturates 4.5g; Cholesterol 224mg; Calcium 68mg; Fibre 3.7g; Sodium 549mg.
Mixed Rice Noodles Energy 648kcal/2698kJ; Protein 16.5g; Carbohydrate 102.3g, of which sugars 4.5g; Fat 17.7g, of which saturates 3.2g; Cholesterol 0mg; Calcium 275mg; Fibre 6.9g; Sodium 1002mg.

Mee Krob Crispy Chilli Noodles

This Thai dish is a stunning combination of sweet and hot, salty and sour, while the texture contrives to be both crisp and chewy.

Serves 1

vegetable oil, for deep-frying
130g/4½oz rice vermicelli noodles

For the sauce

30ml/2 tbsp vegetable oil
130g/4½oz fried tofu, cut into thin strips
2 garlic cloves, finely chopped
2 small shallots, finely chopped
15ml/1 tbsp light soy sauce
30ml/2 tbsp palm sugar (jaggery) or light muscovado (brown) sugar
60ml/4 tbsp vegetable stock
juice of 1 lime
2.5ml/½ tsp dried chilli flakes

For the garnish

15ml/1 tbsp vegetable oil
1 egg, lightly beaten with 15ml/1 tbsp cold water
25g/1oz/⅓ cup beansprouts
1 spring onion (scallion), thinly shredded
1 fresh red chilli, seeded and finely chopped
1 whole head pickled garlic, sliced across to resemble a flower

1 Heat the oil for deep-frying in a wok or large pan to 190°C/375°F, or until a cube of bread added to the oil browns in about 45 seconds. Add the noodles and deep-fry until golden and crisp. Drain on kitchen paper and set aside.

2 Make the spicy tofu sauce. Heat the oil in a wok, add the fried tofu and cook over a medium heat until crisp. Using a slotted spoon, transfer it to a plate.

3 Add the garlic and shallots to the pan and cook until golden brown. Stir in the soy sauce, sugar, stock, lime juice and chilli flakes. Cook, stirring, until the mixture caramelizes. Add the reserved tofu and stir. Remove the wok from the heat and set aside.

4 Prepare the egg garnish. Heat the oil in a wok or frying pan. Pour in the egg in a thin stream to form trails. As soon as it sets, lift it out with a metal spatula and place on a plate.

5 Crumble the noodles into the tofu sauce, mix well, then spoon into serving bowls. Sprinkle with the beansprouts, spring onion, fried egg strips, chilli and pickled garlic and serve.

Tomato Noodles with Fried Egg and Mushrooms

This is a great emergency dish to put together quickly when you have hungry people to feed. The soft yolk of the fried egg mingles deliciously with the sauced noodles.

Serves 4

350g/12oz medium dried noodles
60ml/4 tbsp vegetable oil
2 garlic cloves, very finely chopped
4 shallots, chopped
2.5ml/½ tsp chilli powder
5ml/1 tsp paprika
2 carrots, finely diced
115g/4oz button (white) mushrooms,quartered
50g/2oz peas
15ml/1 tbsp tomato ketchup
10ml/2 tsp tomato purée (paste)
salt and freshly ground black pepper
butter, for frying
4 eggs

1 Cook the noodles in boiling water until just tender. Drain, rinse under cold running water and drain well.

2 Heat the oil in a wok or large frying pan. Add the garlic, shallots, chilli powder and paprika. Stir-fry for about 1 minute, then add the carrots, mushrooms and peas.

3 Continue to stir-fry until the vegetables are cooked. Stir the tomato ketchup and purée into the mixture.

4 Add the noodles and cook, stirring, over a medium heat until the noodles are heated through.

5 Meanwhile melt the butter in a frying pan and fry the eggs. Season the noodle mixture, divide it among four serving plates and top each portion with a fried egg.

Cook's Tip

For a perfect fried egg, melt the butter in a frying pan over a moderate heat. Then break each egg into a saucer and slide it gently into the pan. When the egg is done to your liking, remove it from the pan using a fish slice (metal spatula).

Mee Krob Energy 1293kcal/5362kJ; Protein 28.8g; Carbohydrate 109.1g, of which sugars 5.2g; Fat 80.5g, of which saturates 10.6g; Cholesterol 509mg; Calcium 733mg; Fibre 0.4g; Sodium 1180mg.
Tomato Noodles Energy 566kcal/2377kJ; Protein 18.8g; Carbohydrate 75.5g, of which sugars 8.5g; Fat 23.2g, of which saturates 3g; Cholesterol 190mg; Calcium 73mg; Fibre 4.9g; Sodium 148mg.

Noodles with Yellow Bean Sauce

Served solo, steamed leeks, courgettes and peas might be bland, but add a punchy bean sauce and they acquire an attitude that even the addition of noodles can't assuage.

Serves 4

150g/5oz thin egg noodles
200g/7oz baby leeks, sliced lengthways
200g/7oz baby courgettes (zucchini), halved lengthways
200g/7oz sugar snap peas, trimmed
200g/7oz/1¾ cups fresh or frozen peas
15ml/1 tbsp vegetable or sunflower oil
5 garlic cloves, sliced
45ml/3 tbsp yellow bean sauce
45ml/3 tbsp sweet chilli sauce
30ml/2 tbsp sweet soy sauce
50g/2oz/½ cup cashew nuts, to garnish

1 Cook the noodles according to the packet instructions, drain using a sieve (strainer) and set aside.

2 Line a large bamboo steamer with some perforated baking parchment and add the leeks, courgettes, sugar snaps and peas. Cover and stand over a wok of simmering water.

3 Steam the vegetables for about 5 minutes, then remove the steamer from the wok and set aside. Drain and dry the wok.

4 Heat the oil in the wok and stir-fry the garlic for 1–2 minutes.

5 In a separate bowl, mix together the yellow bean, sweet chilli and soy sauces using a small whisk.

6 Pour the mixed sauces into the wok. Stir to mix them thoroughly with the garlic, then add the steamed vegetables and the noodles and toss together to combine.

7 Cook the vegetables and noodles for 2–3 minutes, stirring frequently, until heated through.

8 Divide the vegetable noodles among four warmed serving bowls and sprinkle over the cashew nuts to garnish.

Stir-fried Noodles with Wild Mushrooms

The greater the variety of wild mushrooms you have available, the more interesting this dish will be. Of course, a mixture of cultivated mushrooms can be used instead.

Serves 6

350g/12oz broad flat egg noodles
45ml/3 tbsp vegetable oil
115g/4oz rindless back (lean) or streaky (fatty) bacon, cut into small pieces
225g/8oz wild mushrooms, trimmed and cut in half
115g/4oz garlic chives, snipped
225g/8oz beansprouts
15ml/1 tbsp oyster sauce
15ml/1 tbsp soy sauce
salt and freshly ground black pepper

1 Cook the egg noodles in a large pan of boiling water for about 3–4 minutes or until just tender. Drain using a sieve (strainer), rinse under cold water and drain them well.

2 Heat 15ml/1 tbsp of the vegetable oil in a wok or large frying pan. Add the bacon and fry until browned and crisp.

3 Using a slotted spoon, transfer the cooked bacon to a small bowl and set it aside until needed. Add the rest of the vegetable oil to the wok or pan. When the oil is hot, add the mushrooms and stir-fry for 3 minutes.

4 Add the garlic chives and beansprouts to the wok and fry for another 3 minutes, then add the drained noodles.

5 Season with salt, pepper, oyster sauce and soy sauce. Continue to stir-fry until the noodles are thoroughly heated through. Sprinkle the crispy bits of bacon on top and serve.

Variation
For a quick lunch or supper dish, replace the bacon with cooked ham or gammon (cooked, smoked or cured ham). Or add cold cooked chicken, sliced thinly.

Noodles with Yellow Bean Energy 296kcal/1241kJ; Protein 14.2g; Carbohydrate 44.9g, of which sugars 7.4g; Fat 7.8g, of which saturates 1.6g; Cholesterol 11mg; Calcium 61mg; Fibre 8.2g; Sodium 209mg.
Stir-fried Noodles Energy 310kcal/1307kJ; Protein 10.1g; Carbohydrate 47.9g, of which sugars 6.6g; Fat 10g, of which saturates 2.1g; Cholesterol 8mg; Calcium 26mg; Fibre 3.2g; Sodium 173mg.

Chow Mein

This is a hugely popular way of dealing with leftovers.

Serves 2–3

225g/8oz lean beef steak
225g/8oz can bamboo shoots, drained
1 leek, trimmed
25g/1oz dried shiitake mushrooms, soaked until soft
150g/5oz Chinese leaves (Chinese cabbage)
450g/1lb cooked egg noodles, drained
90ml/6 tbsp vegetable oil
30ml/2 tbsp dark soy sauce
15ml/1 tbsp cornflour (cornstarch)
15ml/1 tbsp dry sherry
5ml/1 tsp sesame oil
5ml/1 tsp caster (superfine) sugar
salt and ground black pepper

1 Slice the beef, bamboo shoots and leek into matchsticks. Drain the mushrooms, reserving 90ml/6 tbsp of the soaking water. Cut off and discard the stems, then slice the caps. Chop the Chinese leaves and sprinkle with salt. Pat the noodles dry.

2 Heat a third of the vegetable oil in a large wok or frying pan and sauté the noodles. After turning them over once, use a wooden spatula to press against the bottom of the pan until they form a flat, even cake. Cook for about 4 minutes or until crisp at the bottom. Turn over, cook for 3 minutes more, then slide on to a heated plate and keep warm.

3 Heat 30ml/2 tbsp of the remaining oil in a wok. Add the leek and meat strips and stir-fry for 10–15 seconds. Sprinkle over half the soy sauce and then add the bamboo shoots and mushrooms. Toss for 1 minute, then push to one side.

4 Heat the remaining oil in the centre of the wok and sauté the Chinese leaves for 1 minute. Mix with the meat and vegetables and toss together for 30 seconds.

5 Mix the cornflour with the reserved mushroom water. Stir into the wok with the sherry, sesame oil, sugar and remaining soy sauce.

6 Cook the meat and vegetable sauce in the wok for 15 seconds to thicken, then serve with the noodle cake.

Stir-fried Tofu with Noodles

Toasting the cashew nuts gives them a richer flavour as well as adding texture to this tasty, easy dish.

Serves 4

225g/8oz firm tofu, cut into 2.5cm/1in cubes
groundnut (peanut) oil, for deep-frying
175g/6oz medium dried egg noodles
15ml/1 tbsp sesame oil
5ml/1 tsp cornflour (cornstarch)
10ml/2 tsp dark soy sauce
30ml/2 tbsp Chinese rice wine or dry sherry
5ml/1 tsp sugar
6–8 spring onions (scallions), cut diagonally into 2.5cm/1in lengths
3 garlic cloves, sliced
1 fresh green chilli, seeded and sliced
115g/4oz Chinese leaves (Chinese cabbage), roughly shredded
50g/2oz beansprouts
50g/2oz toasted cashew nuts, to garnish

1 Using a sharp knife cut the tofu into 2.5cm/1in cubes.

2 Half-fill a wok with oil and heat to 180°C/350°F. Deep-fry the tofu in batches for 1–2 minutes until golden and crisp. Drain on kitchen paper. Pour all but 30ml/2 tbsp of the oil from the wok.

3 Cook the noodles in boiling water for about 4 minutes, until tender. Rinse them thoroughly under cold water and drain well. Toss them in 10ml/2 tsp of the sesame oil and set aside.

4 In a bowl, blend together the cornflour, soy sauce, rice wine or sherry, sugar and remaining sesame oil.

5 Reheat the 30ml/2 tbsp of oil and add the spring onions, garlic, chilli, Chinese cabbage and beansprouts. Stir-fry for 1–2 minutes.

6 Add the tofu with the noodles and sauce. Cook, stirring, for about 1 minute. Sprinkle over the cashew nuts. Serve at once.

Cook's Tip
Toast cashew nuts by dry-frying in a wok or heavy frying pan, tossing constantly so that they brown evenly on all sides.

Chow Mein Energy 604kcal/2541kJ; Protein 41.1g; Carbohydrate 71.5g, of which sugars 15.1g; Fat 18.9g, of which saturates 4.5g; Cholesterol 100mg; Calcium 115mg; Fibre 7.4g; Sodium 1194mg.
Stir-fried Tofu Energy 460kcal/1921kJ; Protein 13.5g; Carbohydrate 38.7g, of which sugars 4.9g; Fat 29g, of which saturates 4.6g; Cholesterol 13mg; Calcium 327mg; Fibre 2.7g; Sodium 122mg.

Curry Fried Noodles

On its own, tofu has a fairly bland flavour, but it also absorbs the flavours of the other ingredients it is cooked with. This satisfying curry takes full advantage of the tofu by cooking it with a traditional spice paste.

Serves 4

60ml/4 tbsp vegetable oil
30–45ml/2–3 tbsp curry paste
225g/8oz smoked tofu, cut into 2.5cm/1in cubes
225g/8oz green beans, cut into 2.5cm/1in lengths
1 red (bell) pepper, seeded and cut into fine strips
350g/12oz rice vermicelli, soaked in warm water until soft
15ml/1 tbsp soy sauce
salt and ground black pepper
2 spring onions (scallions), finely sliced, 2 red chillies, seeded and cut into thin slices, and 1 lime, cut into wedges, to garnish

1 Heat half the vegetable oil in a wok or large frying pan. Add the curry paste to the pan and stir-fry for a few minutes until it releases all the fragrant aromas.

2 Add the tofu to the pan and fry until it is golden brown all over. Using a slotted spoon remove the tofu cubes from the pan and set aside until required.

3 Add the remaining oil to the wok or pan. When the oil is hot, add the green beans and red pepper strips. Stir-fry for about 4–5 minutes until the vegetables are cooked. You may need to moisten them with a little water.

4 Drain the soaked rice vermicelli thoroughly, and then add them to the wok or frying pan.

5 Continue to stir-fry until the noodles are heated through, then return the curried tofu to the wok or pan. Season with soy sauce, salt and black pepper.

6 Transfer the mixture to a warmed serving dish. Sprinkle with the sliced spring onions and chillies and serve immediately with the lime wedges on the side.

Vegetarian Fried Noodles

The combination of omelette strips, potatoes and noodles in this typically South-east Asian dish results in a very substantial meal.

Serves 4

2 eggs
5ml/1 tsp unsalted butter
5ml/1 tsp chilli powder
5ml/1 tsp ground turmeric
60ml/4 tbsp vegetable or sunflower oil
1 large onion, finely sliced
2 fresh red chillies, seeded and finely sliced
15ml/1 tbsp soy sauce
2 large cooked potatoes, cut into small cubes
6 pieces fried tofu, sliced
225g/8oz/4 cups beansprouts
115g/4oz green beans, blanched in boiling water for 2 minutes
350g/12oz fresh thick egg noodles
salt and ground black pepper
sliced spring onions (scallions), to garnish

1 Beat the eggs lightly, then strain them into a bowl.

2 Use the butter to grease an omelette pan very lightly, and place over the heat. Pour in half of the egg to cover the bottom of the pan thinly. When the egg is just set, turn the omelette over and fry the other side briefly. Slide the omelette on to a plate, blot with kitchen paper, roll up and cut into narrow strips. Make and slice a second omelette. Set aside.

3 In a small bowl, mix together the chilli powder and turmeric. Form a paste by stirring in a little water.

4 Heat the oil in a wok or large frying pan. Fry the onion until soft. Reduce the heat and add the chilli paste, sliced chillies and soy sauce. Fry for 2–3 minutes.

5 Add the potatoes to the pan and fry for about 2 minutes, mixing well with the chillies. Add the tofu, then the beansprouts, green beans and noodles.

6 Gently stir-fry until the noodles are evenly coated and heated through. Take care not to break up the potatoes or the tofu. Season with salt and pepper. Serve hot, garnished with the reserved omelette strips and spring onion slices.

Curry Fried Noodles Energy 479kcal/1996kJ; Protein 13.8g; Carbohydrate 73.7g, of which sugars 4.3g; Fat 14.2g, of which saturates 1.7g; Cholesterol 0mg; Calcium 332mg; Fibre 2g; Sodium 11mg.
Vegetarian Noodles Energy 696kcal/2923kJ; Protein 28.3g; Carbohydrate 83g, of which sugars 8.2g; Fat 30.3g, of which saturates 4.2g; Cholesterol 121mg; Calcium 813mg; Fibre 5g; Sodium 476mg.

Fiery Prawn Rice Vermicelli with Red-hot Chillies

Malaysia and Singapore have an extensive variety of stir-fried noodle dishes. Some of these are classic Chinese recipes, others have a Chinese influence but are adapted to suit the tastes of the local communities. The rice vermicelli in this favourite snack are stir-fried with prawns and lots of chilli.

Serves 4

30ml/2 tbsp vegetable oil
1 carrot, cut into matchsticks
225g/8oz fresh prawns (shrimp), peeled
120ml/4fl oz/½ cup chicken stock or water
30ml/2 tbsp light soy sauce
15ml/1 tbsp dark soy sauce
175g/6oz beansprouts
115g/4oz mustard greens or pak choi (bok choy), shredded
225g/8oz dried rice vermicelli, soaked in water and drained
1–2 fresh red chillies, seeded and finely sliced, and fresh coriander (cilantro) leaves, to garnish

For the spice paste

4 dried red chillies, soaked until soft and seeded
4 garlic cloves, chopped
4 shallots, chopped
25g/1oz fresh root ginger, peeled and chopped
5ml/1 tsp ground turmeric

1 Place all the ingredients for the spice paste in a mortar and pestle or food processor and grind to a smooth paste.

2 Heat the oil in a wok or heavy pan and stir in the spice paste until it begins to colour and become fragrant.

3 Add the carrots to the pan and cook, stirring constantly, for a minute. Then add the prawns to the pan and mix well.

4 Pour the stock or water and soy sauces into the pan and mix well until it is all combined. Cook for about 1–2 minutes. Add the beansprouts and mustard greens to the pan, followed by the noodles. Toss well to make sure the vegetable noodles are well coated and heated through.

5 Transfer the noodles to a warmed serving plate. Garnish with the sliced chillies and coriander.

Noodles with Fresh Crab and Dried Mushrooms

This is a dish of contrasting flavours, textures and colours, and requires some skill and dexterity from the cook. While one hand gently turns the noodles in the pan, the other takes chunks of fresh crab meat and drops them into the steaming wok. Here the crab meat is cooked separately to make it easier.

Serves 4

25g/1oz dried cloud ear (wood ear) mushrooms, soaked in warm water for 20 minutes
115g/4oz dried cellophane noodles, soaked in warm water for 20 minutes
30ml/2 tbsp vegetable or sesame oil
3 shallots, halved and thinly sliced
2 garlic cloves, crushed
2 fresh green or red chillies, seeded and sliced
1 carrot, peeled and cut into thin diagonal rounds
5ml/1 tsp sugar
45ml/3 tbsp oyster sauce
15ml/1 tbsp soy sauce
225g/8oz fresh, raw crab meat, cut into bitesize chunks
ground black pepper
fresh coriander (cilantro) leaves, to garnish

1 Remove the centres from the soaked cloud ear mushrooms and cut the mushrooms in half. Discard the stalks.

2 Drain the soaked cellophane noodles, then cut them into 30cm/12in pieces and put aside.

3 Heat a wok and add 15ml/1 tbsp oil. Stir in the shallots, garlic and chillies, and cook until fragrant. Add the carrots and cook for 1 minute, then add the mushrooms and cook for 1 minute more. Stir in the sugar with the oyster and soy sauce, followed by the noodles. Pour in 400ml/14fl oz/1⅔ cups water or chicken stock, cover the wok and cook for about 5 minutes, or until the noodles are soft and have absorbed most of the sauce.

4 Meanwhile, heat the remaining oil in a heavy pan. Add the crab meat and cook until it is nicely pink and tender. Season well with black pepper. Arrange the noodles and crab meat on a serving dish and garnish with coriander.

Fiery Prawn Vermicelli Energy 330kcal/1377kJ; Protein 17.5g; Carbohydrate 49.9g, of which sugars 4.5g; Fat 6.6g, of which saturates 0.8g; Cholesterol 110mg; Calcium 125mg; Fibre 1.9g; Sodium 960mg.
Noodles with Crab Energy 252kcal/1051kJ; Protein 12.9g; Carbohydrate 35.7g, of which sugars 10.3g; Fat 6.3g, of which saturates 0.7g; Cholesterol 41mg; Calcium 97mg; Fibre 1.6g; Sodium 770mg.

Egg Noodles with Tuna and Tomato Sauce

Raid the store cupboard and add a few fresh ingredients, and you can produce a scrumptious main meal in just moments.

Serves 4

45ml/3 tbsp olive oil
2 garlic cloves, finely chopped
2 dried red chillies, seeded and chopped
1 large red onion, finely sliced
175g/6oz canned tuna, drained
115g/4oz pitted black olives
400g/14oz can chopped tomatoes
30ml/2 tbsp chopped parsley
350g/12oz medium egg noodles
salt and freshly ground black pepper

1 Heat the olive oil in a wok and fry the garlic and chillies for a few seconds before adding the sliced onion. Fry, stirring, for about 5 minutes until the onion softens.

2 Add the tuna and black olives to the pan and stir well.

3 Stir in the tomatoes and any juices. Bring to the boil, season with salt and pepper, add the parsley, then lower the heat and simmer gently for about 15 minutes, stirring occasionally.

4 Meanwhile, bring a pan of salted water to the boil and cook the noodles for about 4 minutes, until just tender, following the directions on the packet. Drain them well using a sieve (strainer).

5 Adjust the seasoning of the sauce, if necessary, toss the noodles with the sauce and serve at once.

Cook's Tip
This is a perfect store-cupboard meal, since almost all the ingredients are likely to be there already. For a quality meal, look for solid or fancy canned tuna, which comes in large pieces, rather than tuna chunks or flaked or grated tuna. Choose no-drain tuna for a low-fat meal.

Buckwheat Noodles with Smoked Trout and Pak Choi

The light, crisp texture of the pak choi balances the earthy flavours of the mushrooms, the buckwheat noodles and the smokiness of the trout

Serves 4

350g/12oz buckwheat noodles
30ml/2 tbsp vegetable oil
115g/4oz fresh shiitake mushrooms, quartered
2 garlic cloves, finely chopped
15ml/1 tbsp grated fresh root ginger
225g/8oz pak choi (bok choy)
1 spring onion (scallion), finely sliced diagonally
15ml/1 tbsp dark sesame oil
30ml/2 tbsp mirin (sweet rice wine)
30ml/2 tbsp soy sauce
2 smoked trout, skinned and boned, flaked into bitesize pieces
salt and freshly ground black pepper
30ml/2 tbsp coriander (cilantro) leaves, to garnish
10ml/2 tsp sesame seeds, toasted, to garnish

1 Bring a large pan of water to the boil and cook the buckwheat noodles for about 7–10 minutes or until just tender.

2 Meanwhile heat the oil in a wok or a frying pan. Add the mushrooms and stir-fry over a medium heat for 3 minutes.

3 Add the garlic, ginger and pak choi to the pan, and continue to stir-fry the mixture for about 2 minutes.

4 Drain the buckwheat noodles and add them to the mushroom mixture with the spring onion, sesame oil, mirin and soy sauce. Toss and season with salt and pepper.

5 Arrange the noodles on four warmed, individual serving plates and place the smoked trout on top. Garnish with coriander and sesame seeds and serve at once.

Variation
Replace the smoked trout with cooked fresh salmon.

Egg Noodles Energy 518kcal/2182kJ; Protein 22.8g; Carbohydrate 67.4g, of which sugars 5.9g; Fat 19.4g, of which saturates 3.9g; Cholesterol 49mg; Calcium 77mg; Fibre 5g; Sodium 958mg.
Buckwheat Noodles Energy 343kcal/1443kJ; Protein 16.3g; Carbohydrate 47.9g, of which sugars 3.8g; Fat 10.9g, of which saturates 1.2g; Cholesterol 10mg; Calcium 29mg; Fibre 3.5g; Sodium 814mg.

Shanghai Noodles with Chinese Sausage

Lap cheong are firm, cured waxy pork sausages, available from Chinese food markets. Sweet and savoury, they can be steamed with rice, chicken or pork, added to an omelette or stir-fried with vegetables.

Serves 4

30ml/2 tbsp vegetable oil
115g/4oz rindless back (lean) bacon, cut into bitesize pieces
2 lap cheong, rinsed in warm water, drained and finely sliced
2 garlic cloves, finely chopped
2 spring onions (scallions), roughly chopped
225g/8oz Chinese greens or fresh spinach leaves, cut into 5cm/2in pieces
450g/1lb fresh Shanghai noodles
30ml/2 tbsp oyster sauce
30ml/2 tbsp soy sauce
ground black pepper

1 Heat half the oil in a wok or large frying pan. Add the bacon and lap cheong with the garlic and spring onions. Stir-fry for a few minutes until golden. Using a slotted spoon, remove the mixture from the wok or pan and keep warm.

2 Add the remaining oil to the wok or pan. When hot, stir-fry the Chinese greens or spinach over a high heat for about 3 minutes until it just starts to wilt.

3 Add the noodles and return the lap cheong mixture to the wok or pan. Season with oyster sauce, soy sauce and pepper. Stir-fry until the noodles are heated through.

Variation
Use chipolata sausages instead of the lap cheong.

Cook's Tip
You can buy rindless bacon already cut into bitesize pieces. To remove the rind from bacon rashers (strips) cut it off with sharp kitchen scissors, occasionally dipping them in hot water.

Crispy Thai Noodles

Rice noodles become light and crispy when deep-fried and make a lovely base for this tangy, fragrant salad.

Serves 4

sunflower oil, for deep-frying
115g/4oz rice vermicelli
45ml/3 tbsp groundnut (peanut) oil
2 eggs, lightly beaten with 15ml/1 tbsp water
30ml/2 tbsp palm sugar (jaggery)
30ml/2 tbsp Thai fish sauce (nam pla)
15ml/1 tbsp rice wine vinegar
30ml/2 tbsp tomato ketchup
1 fresh red chilli, thinly sliced
3 garlic cloves, crushed
5ml/1 tsp grated fresh root ginger
200g/7oz minced (ground) pork
400g/14oz cooked peeled tiger prawns (shrimp)
4 spring onions (scallions), shredded
60ml/4 tbsp chopped coriander (cilantro) leaves

1 Fill a wok one-third full of sunflower oil and heat to 180°C/350°F. Working in batches, deep-fry the vermicelli, for 15 seconds, or until puffed up. Remove with a slotted spoon and drain on kitchen paper.

2 Carefully discard the oil and wipe out the wok. Heat 15ml/1 tbsp of groundnut oil in the wok. Add half the egg mixture and swirl the wok to make a thin omelette. Cook gently for 2–3 minutes, until the egg has just set and then carefully transfer to a board.

3 Repeat with a further 15ml/1 tbsp of groundnut oil and the remaining egg mixture to make a second omelette. Place the second omelette on top of the first and roll up into a cylinder. Cut the cylinder crossways to make thin strips, then set aside.

4 Mix together the palm sugar, fish sauce, rice wine vinegar, tomato ketchup, chilli, garlic and ginger. Mix half into the pork.

5 Heat the remaining groundnut oil in the wok. When hot, add the pork mixture and stir-fry for 4–5 minutes until cooked through. Add the prawns and stir-fry for 1–2 minutes.

6 Remove the wok from the heat and mix in the remaining palm sugar mixture, fried vermicelli, spring onions and coriander.

7 Divide the mixture among four warmed plates and top with the shredded omelette. Serve immediately.

Shanghai Noodles Energy 485kcal/2043kJ; Protein 30.5g; Carbohydrate 60.7g, of which sugars 5.3g; Fat 14.9g, of which saturates 2.8g; Cholesterol 63mg; Calcium 47mg; Fibre 3.2g; Sodium 440mg.
Crispy Thai Noodles Energy 508Kcal/2118kJ; Protein 35.1g; Carbohydrate 33.1g, of which sugars 10.5g; Fat 26.4g, of which saturates 5g; Cholesterol 371mg; Calcium 142mg; Fibre 0.8g; Sodium 405mg.

Fried Cellophane Noodles

This is a very versatile dish. Vary the vegetables if you wish and substitute ham, chorizo or salami for the lap cheong (Chinese dried pork sausage).

Serves 4

175g/6oz cellophane (bean thread) noodles
45ml/3 tbsp vegetable oil
3 garlic cloves, finely chopped
115g/4oz cooked prawns (shrimp)
2 lap cheong, rinsed, drained and finely diced
2 eggs
2 celery sticks, including leaves, diced
115g/4oz beansprouts
115g/4oz spinach leaves
2 spring onions (scallions), chopped
15–30ml/1–2 tbsp Thai fish sauce
5ml/1 tsp sesame oil
15ml/1 tbsp sesame seeds, toasted, to garnish

1 Soak the noodles in hot water for about 10 minutes or until soft. Drain and cut into 10cm/4in lengths.

2 Heat the vegetable oil in a wok or large, heavy pan, add the garlic and fry until it is golden brown. Add the prawns and the lap cheong; stir-fry for 2–3 minutes.

3 Stir in the noodles and fry for 2 minutes. Make a well in the centre of the mixture, then break in the eggs and slowly stir them until they are creamy and just set.

4 Add the diced celery, beansprouts, spinach leaves and spring onions to the pan and toss to mix. Season with fish sauce and stir in the sesame oil. Continue to stir-fry the mixture until all the ingredients are cooked, mixing well.

5 Transfer the noodles and vegetables to a large, warmed serving dish. Sprinkle with sesame seeds to garnish.

Cook's Tip

Cellophane or bean thread noodles, which are very fine and translucent, are made from mung beans.

Stir-fried Rice Noodles with Chicken and Prawns

This Thai-style recipe combines chicken with prawns and has a characteristic sweet, sour and salty flavour.

Serves 4

225g/8oz dried flat rice noodles
120ml/4fl oz/½ cup water
60ml/4 tbsp Thai fish sauce
15ml/1 tbsp sugar
15ml/1 tbsp fresh lime juice
5ml/1 tsp paprika
pinch of cayenne pepper
45ml/3 tbsp oil
2 garlic cloves, finely chopped
1 skinless, boneless chicken breast fillet, finely sliced
8 raw prawns (shrimp), peeled, deveined and cut in half
1 egg
50g/2oz roasted peanuts, coarsely crushed
3 spring onions (scallions), cut into short lengths
175g/6oz beansprouts
coriander (cilantro) leaves and 1 lime, cut into wedges, to garnish

1 Place the rice noodles in a large bowl, cover with warm water and soak for 30 minutes until soft. Drain.

2 Combine the water, fish sauce, sugar, lime juice, paprika and cayenne in a small bowl. Set aside until required. Heat the oil in a wok. Add the garlic and stir-fry for 30 seconds until brown.

3 Add the chicken and prawns to the wok and stir-fry for 3–4 minutes. Push the chicken and prawn mixture in the wok out to the sides. Break the egg into the centre, stir to break up the yolk and cook over a medium heat until lightly scrambled.

4 Add the noodles and fish sauce mixture to the wok. Mix well. Add half the crushed peanuts and cook, stirring frequently, until the noodles are soft and most of the liquid has been absorbed.

5 Add the spring onions and half of the beansprouts. Cook, stirring, for 1 minute more, to heat through.

6 Spoon the chicken and prawn mixture on to a serving dish. Sprinkle with the remaining peanuts and beansprouts. Garnish with the coriander and lime wedges and serve.

Cellophane Noodles Energy 593kcal/2504kJ; Protein 47.7g; Carbohydrate 72g, of which sugars 4.7g; Fat 14.6g, of which saturates 2.8g; Cholesterol 106mg; Calcium 53mg; Fibre 3.2g; Sodium 1461mg.
Stir-fried Rice Noodles Energy 388kcal/1625kJ; Protein 22.5g; Carbohydrate 54.3g, of which sugars 5.9g; Fat 8.4g, of which saturates 1.7g; Cholesterol 113mg; Calcium 76mg; Fibre 2.4g; Sodium 105mg.

Chinese Stir-fried Noodles with Red Chillies

This Chinese dish of stir-fried rice noodles and seafood is an essential component of the Chinese hawker stalls – you will find this dish anywhere and at any time of day. Variations include red snapper, clams and pork. Use the broad, fresh rice noodles available in Chinese markets.

Serves 3 to 4

45ml/3 tbsp vegetable oil
2 garlic cloves, finely chopped
2 red chillies, seeded and finely sliced
1 Chinese sausage, finely sliced
12 fresh prawns (shrimp), peeled
2 small squid, trimmed, cleaned, skinned and sliced
500g/1¼lb fresh rice noodles
30ml/2 tbsp light soy sauce
45ml/3 tbsp kecap manis (Indonesian sweet soy sauce)
2–3 mustard green leaves, chopped
a handful of beansprouts
2 eggs, lightly beaten
ground black pepper
fresh coriander (cilantro) leaves, finely chopped, to serve

1 Heat a wok or large frying pan and add the oil. Stir in the garlic and chillies and fry until fragrant.

2 Add the Chinese sausage, followed by the prawns and squid, tossing them to mix thoroughly.

3 Toss in the noodles and mix well. Add the soy sauce and kecap manis, and toss in the mustard leaves and beansprouts.

4 Stir in the eggs for a few seconds until set. Season with black pepper, garnish with coriander and serve immediately.

Cook's Tip
Kecap manis is an Indonesian soya bean condiment similar to soy sauce but sweeter and with a more complex flavour. If it is not available you can replace it with the same quantity of dark soy sauce mixed with a little sugar.

Chicken Chow Mein

Chow Mein is arguably the best-known Chinese noodle dish in the West. The noodles are quickly stir-fried with whatever meat, seafood or vegetables are available for a swift meal.

Serves 4

350g/12oz fresh medium egg noodles
225g/8oz skinless, boneless chicken breast fillets
45ml/3 tbsp soy sauce
15ml/1 tbsp Chinese rice wine or dry sherry
15ml/1 tbsp dark sesame oil
60ml/4 tbsp vegetable oil
2 garlic cloves, finely chopped
50g/2oz mangetouts (snow peas), topped and tailed
115g/4oz beansprouts
50g/2oz ham, finely shredded
4 spring onions (scallions), finely chopped
salt and freshly ground black pepper

1 Cook the noodles in a saucepan of boiling water until tender. Drain, rinse under cold water and drain well.

2 Slice the chicken into fine shreds about 5cm/2in in length.

3 Place in a bowl with 10ml/2 tsp of the soy sauce, the rice wine or sherry and sesame oil.

4 Heat half the vegetable oil in a wok or large frying pan over a high heat. When it starts smoking, add the chicken mixture. Stir-fry for 2 minutes until the chicken is cooked through, then transfer to a plate and keep hot.

5 Wipe the wok clean and heat the remaining oil. Stir in the garlic, mangetouts, beansprouts and ham, stir-fry for another minute or so, then add the cooked noodles.

6 Continue to stir-fry for 2–3 minutes until the egg noodles are heated through. Add the remaining soy sauce to taste and season with salt and pepper.

7 Return the chicken and any juices to the noodle mixture, then add the chopped spring onions and give the mixture a final stir. Serve at once in warmed, individual bowls.

Chinese Noodles Energy 618kcal/2582kJ; Protein 24.8g; Carbohydrate 100g, of which sugars 1.1g; Fat 12.9g, of which saturates 2.1g; Cholesterol 217mg; Calcium 96mg; Fibre 0.5g; Sodium 717mg.
Chicken Chow Mein Energy 593kcal/2494kJ; Protein 31.1g; Carbohydrate 69.7g, of which sugars 4.4g; Fat 22.6g, of which saturates 2.7g; Cholesterol 44mg; Calcium 44mg; Fibre 3.4g; Sodium 995mg.

Special Chow Mein with Chinese Sausage and Prawns

Slices of lap cheong add piquancy to this delectable mixture, setting off the sweet, succulent large prawns. You can substitute another spicy cured sausage such as chorizo or salami.

Serves 4–6

450g/1lb egg noodles
45ml/3 tbsp vegetable oil
2 garlic cloves, peeled and sliced thinly
5ml/1 tsp finely chopped fresh root ginger
2 red chillies, chopped
2 lap cheong, about 75g/3oz, rinsed and sliced
1 boneless chicken breast fillet, thinly sliced
16 uncooked tiger prawns (jumbo shrimp), peeled, tails left intact, and deveined
115g/4oz green beans
225g/8oz beansprouts
50g/2oz garlic chives
30ml/2 tbsp soy sauce
15ml/1 tbsp oyster sauce
salt and freshly ground black pepper
15ml/1 tbsp sesame oil
2 spring onions (scallions), shredded, to garnish
15ml/1 tbsp coriander (cilantro) leaves, to garnish

1 Bring a pan of salted water to the boil and cook the noodles for about 4 minutes, until just tender. Drain well.

2 Heat 15ml/1 tbsp of the oil in a wok or large frying pan and fry the garlic, ginger and chillies. Add the lap cheong, chicken, prawns and beans. Stir-fry for about 2 minutes over a high heat or until the chicken and prawns are cooked. Transfer the mixture to a bowl and set aside.

3 Heat the rest of the oil in the same wok. Add the beansprouts and garlic chives. Stir fry for 1–2 minutes.

4 Add the noodles and toss and stir to mix. Season with soy sauce, oyster sauce, salt and pepper.

5 Return the prawn mixture to the wok. Reheat and mix well with the noodles. Stir in the sesame oil. Serve garnished with spring onions and coriander leaves.

Chiang Mai Noodles

An interesting noodle dish from Thailand that combines soft, boiled noodles with crisp, deep-fried ones.

Serves 4

250ml/8fl oz/1 cup coconut cream
15ml/1 tbsp magic paste
5ml/1 tsp Thai red curry paste
450g/1lb chicken thigh meat, chopped into small pieces
30ml/2 tbsp dark soy sauce
2 red (bell) peppers, seeded and finely diced
600ml/1 pint/2½ cups chicken or vegetable stock
90g/3½oz dried rice noodles

For the garnishes

vegetable oil, for deep-frying
90g/3½oz fine dried rice noodles
2 pickled garlic cloves, chopped
small bunch fresh coriander (cilantro), chopped
2 limes, cut into wedges

1 Pour the coconut cream into a wok and bring to the boil over a medium heat. Boil, stirring frequently, for 8–10 minutes, until the milk separates and an oily sheen appears on the surface.

2 Add the magic paste and red curry paste to the wok and cook, stirring constantly, for 3–5 seconds, until fragrant.

3 Add the chicken and seal it on all sides. Stir in the soy sauce and the diced peppers and stir-fry for 3–4 minutes. Pour in the stock. Bring to the boil, then lower the heat and simmer for 10–15 minutes, until the chicken is fully cooked.

4 Meanwhile, make the noodle garnish. Heat the oil in a wok to 190°C/375°F or until a cube of bread added to the oil browns in 40 seconds. Break the rice noodles in half, then divide them into four portions. Add one portion at a time to the hot oil. They will puff up on contact. As soon as they are crisp, lift the noodles out with a slotted spoon and drain on kitchen paper.

5 Bring a large pan of water to the boil and cook the noodles until tender, following the instructions on the packet. Drain well, divide among four warmed individual dishes, then spoon the curry sauce over. Top each portion with a cluster of fried noodles. Sprinkle the chopped pickled garlic and coriander over the top and serve immediately, offering lime wedges for squeezing.

Special Chow Mein Energy 359kcal/1516kJ; Protein 19.6g; Carbohydrate 47.6g, of which sugars 2.9g; Fat 11.4g, of which saturates 2.3g; Cholesterol 106mg; Calcium 53mg; Fibre 2.3g; Sodium 1102mg.
Chiang Mai Noodles Energy 245Kcal/1034kJ; Protein 29.4g; Carbohydrate 27.6g, of which sugars 9g; Fat 1.8g, of which saturates 0.6g; Cholesterol 79mg; Calcium 35mg; Fibre 1.4g; Sodium 677mg.

Curried Noodles with Stir-fried Chicken or Pork

Chicken or pork can be used in this tasty dish.

Serves 2

30ml/2 tbsp vegetable oil
10ml/2 tsp magic paste
1 lemon grass stalk, finely chopped
5ml/1 tsp red curry paste
90g/3½oz skinless chicken breast fillets or pork fillet (tenderloin), sliced into thin strips
30ml/2 tbsp light soy sauce
400ml/14fl oz/1⅔ cups coconut milk
2 kaffir lime leaves, rolled into cylinders and thinly sliced
250g/9oz dried medium egg noodles
90g/3½oz Chinese leaves (Chinese cabbage), shredded
90g/3½oz watercress, shredded
juice of 1 lime
small bunch fresh coriander (cilantro), chopped

1 Heat the oil in a wok. Add the magic paste and lemon grass and stir-fry over a low to medium heat for 4–5 seconds.

2 Stir in the curry paste, then add the chicken or pork to the wok. Stir-fry over a medium to high heat for 2 minutes, until the chicken or pork is coated in the paste and seared on all sides.

3 Add the soy sauce, coconut milk and lime leaves. Bring to a simmer, then add the noodles. Simmer for about 4 minutes, tossing the mixture occasionally to make sure that the noodles cook evenly and do not clump together.

4 Add the Chinese leaves and shredded watercress. Stir well. Add the lime juice. Spoon into a serving bowl or two individual bowls, sprinkle with the chopped fresh coriander, and serve.

Cook's Tip
Magic paste is a commercial product that is sold in jars in Asian stores and supermarkets. It is a blend of garlic, coriander (cilantro) root and white pepper. This combination of flavours is widely used in Thai home cooking. When mixed with red curry paste, magic paste gives a great flavour to this combination of chicken, red (bell) peppers and noodles.

Fried Pork and Prawn Noodles with Thai Fish Cakes

Thai fish cakes add a wonderful spiciness to this stir-fry. Make them yourself or buy them from an Asian supermarket. They vary considerably in size and spiciness. This dish is quick and easy to prepare and cooks in next to no time, making it the perfect snack for busy people.

Serves 4

175g/6oz fresh or dried rice noodles
60ml/4 tbsp vegetable or sunflower oil
2.5ml/½ tsp salt
75g/3oz cooked prawns (shrimp), shelled and heads and tails removed
175g/6oz cooked pork, cut into matchsticks
1 green (bell) pepper, chopped into matchsticks
2.5ml/½ tsp sugar
10ml/2 tsp curry powder
75g/3oz Thai fish cakes
10ml/2 tsp dark soy sauce

1 Soak the rice noodles in water for about 10 minutes, drain them well using a sieve (strainer), and then pat them dry with kitchen paper. Set aside.

2 Heat the wok, then add half the oil. When the oil is hot, add the noodles and half the salt and stir-fry for 2 minutes. Transfer to a heated serving dish and keep warm.

3 Heat the remaining oil in the wok, and then add the prawns, pork, pepper, sugar, curry powder and the remaining salt. Stir-fry the mixture for 1 minute, tossing frequently.

4 Return the noodles to the wok and stir-fry with the Thai fish cakes for 2 minutes. Stir in the soy sauce and serve at once.

Cook's Tip
Rice noodles are made from ground rice and water. They range in thickness from very thin to wide ribbons and sheets. Dried ribbon rice noodles are usually sold tied together in bundles.

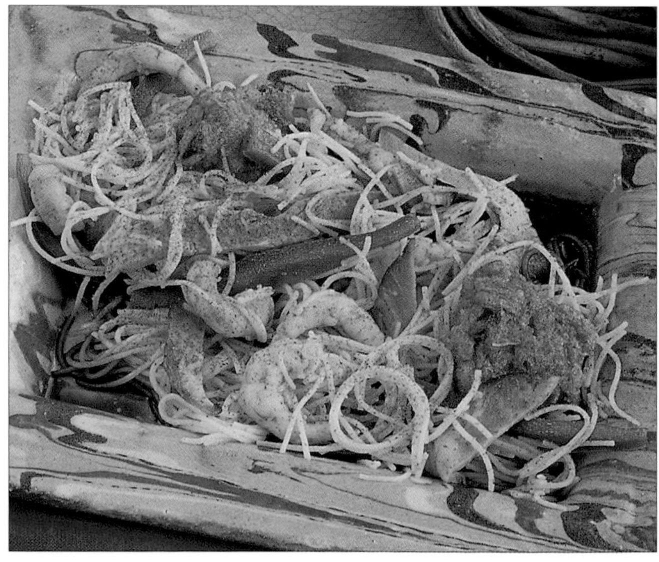

Curried Noodles Energy 702kcal/2965kJ; Protein 28.7g; Carbohydrate 101.6g, of which sugars 14.2g; Fat 23g, of which saturates 4.9g; Cholesterol 69mg; Calcium 187mg; Fibre 4.7g; Sodium 1564mg.
Fried Pork Noodles Energy 664kcal /2798kJ; protein 21.4g; carbohydrate 94.9g, of which sugars 6.5g; fat 22.5g, of which saturates 4.9g; cholesterol 129mg; calcium 250mg; fibre 4.3g; sodium 636mg.

Singapore Noodles with Shiitake Mushrooms and Chinese Leaves

Dried Chinese mushrooms add an intense flavour to this lightly curried dish.

Serves 4

20g/¾oz dried shiitake mushrooms
225g/8oz fine egg noodles
10ml/2 tsp sesame oil
45ml/3 tbsp groundnut (peanut) oil
2 garlic cloves, crushed
1 small onion, chopped
1 fresh green chilli, seeded and thinly sliced
10ml/2 tsp curry powder
115g/4oz green beans, halved
115g/4oz Chinese leaves (Chinese cabbage), thinly shredded
4 spring onions (scallions), sliced
30ml/2 tbsp soy sauce
115g/4oz cooked prawns (shrimp), peeled and deveined
salt

1 Soak the mushrooms for 30 minutes. Drain, reserving 30ml/2 tbsp of the water. Discard the stems and slice the caps.

2 Bring a pan of lightly salted water to the boil and cook the noodles according to the directions on the packet. Drain, tip into a bowl and toss with the sesame oil.

3 Heat the groundnut oil in a preheated wok and stir-fry the garlic, onion and chilli for 3 minutes. Stir in the curry powder and cook for 1 minute. Add the mushrooms, green beans, Chinese leaves and spring onions. Stir-fry for 3–4 minutes until the vegetables are tender, but still crisp.

4 Add the noodles, soy sauce, reserved mushroom soaking water and prawns. Toss over the heat for 2–3 minutes until the noodles and prawns are heated through.

Cook's Tip

Ring the changes with the vegetables used in this dish. Try mangetouts (snow peas), broccoli, sweet peppers or baby corn cobs. The prawns (shrimp) can be omitted.

Thick Egg Noodles with Pork and Seafood

Otherwise known as Hokkein mee, this is a classic stir-fried dish in Singapore, where the majority of the Chinese population is Hokkein. The dish takes its name from the people, as well as from the thick egg noodles, commonly called Hokkein noodles, which are also used in Malay and Indian hawker dishes. Filled with squid, prawns, fish and pork, this is a deliciously satisfying meal in itself.

Serves 4

30ml/2 tbsp vegetable or sunflower oil
3 garlic cloves, finely chopped
115g/4oz pork fillet (tenderloin), cut into thin strips
115g/4oz fresh fish fillets (such as red snapper, grouper or trout), cut into bitesize pieces
115g/4oz fresh prawns (shrimp), shelled and deveined
2 small squid, with innards and backbone removed, cleaned and sliced (reserve tentacles)
300ml/½ pint/1¼ cups chicken stock
450g/1lb fresh egg noodles
1 carrot, shredded
6 long white Chinese cabbage leaves, shredded
30ml/2 tbsp dark soy sauce
30ml/2 tbsp light soy sauce
ground black pepper
a small bunch of fresh coriander (cilantro), roughly chopped

1 Heat a wok or large, heavy pan and add the oil. Swirl the oil round the pan and when hot stir in the garlic. Stir-fry for 1–2 minutes until it becomes fragrant but does not brown.

2 Add the pork, fish, prawns and squid to the pan, tossing them around for 1 minute. Ensure that they are cooked through, and then pour in the stock and bubble it up to reduce it.

3 Add the noodles and toss them around the pan for 1 minute.

4 Add the shredded carrot and cabbage to the pan and toss to mix well. When they are tender, after 3–4 minutes, add the soy sauces and cook until most of the liquid has evaporated. Season with pepper, sprinkle with coriander, divide the noodles among four bowls and eat while steaming hot.

Singapore Noodles Energy 314kcal/1316kJ; Protein 19.2g; Carbohydrate 50.3g, of which sugars 5.9g; Fat 4g, of which saturates 0.6g; Cholesterol 70mg; Calcium 74mg; Fibre 1.6g; Sodium 81mg.
Thick Egg Noodles Energy 609Kcal/2571kJ; Protein 35.2g; Carbohydrate 84.4g, of which sugars 5.3g; Fat 16.9g, of which saturates 3.8g; Cholesterol 186mg; Calcium 81mg; Fibre 4.2g; Sodium 867mg.

Celebration Noodles

Reserved for special occasions and celebrations such as birthdays and weddings, this is one of the national dishes of the Philippines.

Serves 4

30ml/2 tbsp palm or coconut oil
1 large onion, finely chopped
2–3 garlic cloves, finely chopped
250g/9oz pork loin, cut into thin strips
250g/9oz fresh shelled prawns (shrimp)
2 carrots, cut into matchsticks
½ small green cabbage, finely shredded
about 250ml/8fl oz/1 cup pork or chicken stock
50ml/2fl oz/¼ cup soy sauce
15ml/1 tbsp palm sugar (jaggery)
450g/1lb fresh egg noodles
2 hard-boiled eggs, finely chopped
1 lime, quartered

1 Heat 15ml/1 tbsp of the oil in a wok or a large, heavy frying pan over a medium–high heat, stir in the onion and garlic and fry until fragrant and beginning to colour.

2 Toss in the pork and prawns and stir-fry for 2 minutes, then transfer the mixture to a plate and set aside.

3 Return the wok to the heat, add the remaining oil, then stir in the carrots and cabbage and stir-fry for 2–3 minutes. Add the vegetables to the plate with the pork and prawns.

4 Pour the stock, soy sauce and sugar into the wok and stir until the sugar has dissolved. Add the noodles and cook for about 3 minutes, until tender but still firm to the bite.

5 Mix in the pork, prawns, cabbage and carrots.

6 Transfer the noodles on to a warmed serving dish and sprinkle the chopped eggs over the top. Serve the dish while piping hot, with the lime wedges to squeeze over.

Cook's Tips
If you cannot buy palm sugar (jaggery), then you can substitute demerara (raw) sugar instead.

Chilli Noodles

Street stalls and tea houses all over Hong Kong almost always have this on their menus, each establishment having a slightly different version from the next, depending on the class of diner. Humble places offer basic noodles tossed in chilli sauce with slices of roast pork. More upmarket eateries add lavish accents like oyster sauce and sesame oil and even offer wonton soup on the side. This recipe is one of the more luxurious versions.

Serves 4

400g/14oz dry wheat flour noodles
200g/7oz choi sum or pak choi (bok choy)
250g/9oz cold roast pork, thinly sliced
60ml/4 tbsp chilli and garlic sauce
30ml/2 tbsp vegetable or sesame oil
30ml/2 tbsp light soy sauce
30ml/2 tbsp tomato ketchup

1 Cook the noodles in boiling water until tender, following the package directions for timing. Drain the noodles using a sieve (strainer) and put them in a bowl.

2 Cut the choi sum or pak choi into bitesize pieces. Bring a large pan of water to the boil, add the greens and blanch for 1 minute. Drain and mix with the noodles.

3 Halve the roast pork slices if necessary; the aim is to have about 32 pieces of pork in all. Set aside.

4 In a bowl, mix the chilli and garlic sauce with the oil, soy sauce and tomato ketchup. Add to the noodles and greens and toss lightly to coat. Top with the pork. Serve at once.

Variations
- *Spinach, cos or romaine lettuce can be used instead of choi sum, or use beansprouts.*
- *Serve with prawn wonton soup for a satisfying meal.*

Celebration Noodles Energy 728kcal/3069kJ; Protein 43.6g; Carbohydrate 98g, of which sugars 16.9g; Fat 20.8g, of which saturates 5g; Cholesterol 290mg; Calcium 159mg; Fibre 6.3g; Sodium 1303mg.
Chilli Noodles Energy 208kcal/879kJ; Protein 18.9g; Carbohydrate 26.6g, of which sugars 7.1g; Fat 3.5g, of which saturates 0.9g; Cholesterol 39mg; Calcium 101mg; Fibre 2.3g; Sodium 975mg.

Warm Lamb and Noodle Salad

Here, thin slices of wok-fried lamb, fresh vegetables and rice noodles are tossed in an aromatic dressing.

Serves 4

30ml/2 tbsp red curry paste
60ml/4 tbsp sunflower oil
750g/1lb 11oz lamb neck (US shoulder or breast) fillets, thinly sliced
250g/9oz sugar snap peas
500g/1¼lb fresh rice noodles
1 red (bell) pepper, seeded and very thinly sliced
1 cucumber, sliced paper thin
6–7 spring onions (scallions), sliced diagonally
a large handful of fresh mint leaves

For the dressing

15ml/1 tbsp vegetable or sunflower oil
juice of 2 limes
1 garlic clove, crushed
15ml/1 tbsp sugar
15ml/1 tbsp fish sauce
30ml/2 tbsp soy sauce

1 In a shallow dish, mix together the red curry paste and half of the oil. Add the lamb slices and toss to coat. Cover with clear film (plastic wrap) and leave the lamb to marinate in the refrigerator for up to 24 hours.

2 Blanch the sugar snap peas in a pan of lightly salted boiling water for 1–2 minutes. Drain, refresh under cold water, drain again thoroughly and transfer to a large bowl.

3 Put the noodles in a separate bowl and pour over boiling water to cover. Leave to soak for 5–10 minutes, until tender, then drain well and separate into strands with your fingers.

4 Add the noodles to the sugar snap peas, then add the sliced red pepper, cucumber and spring onions. Toss lightly to mix.

5 Heat a wok over a high heat and add the remaining sunflower oil. Stir-fry the lamb, in two batches, for 3–4 minutes, or until cooked through, then add to the bowl of salad.

6 Place all the dressing ingredients in a jar, screw on the lid and shake well. Pour the dressing over the warm salad, sprinkle over the mint leaves and toss well to combine. Serve immediately.

Crispy Noodles with Beef

Rice vermicelli is deep-fried before being added to this multi-textured dish.

Serves 4

450g/1lb rump (round) steak
teriyaki sauce, for brushing
175g/6oz rice vermicelli
groundnut (peanut) oil, for deep-frying and stir-frying
8 spring onions (scallions), diagonally sliced
2 garlic cloves, crushed
4–5 carrots, cut into julienne strips
1–2 fresh red chillies, seeded and finely sliced
2 small courgettes (zucchini), diagonally sliced
5ml/1 tsp grated fresh root ginger
60ml/4 tbsp rice vinegar
90ml/6 tbsp light soy sauce
about 475ml/16fl oz/2 cups spicy stock

1 Beat the steak to about 2.5cm/1in thick. Place in a shallow dish, brush with teriyaki sauce and marinate for 2–4 hours.

2 Separate the rice vermicelli into manageable loops. Pour oil into a large wok to a depth of about 5cm/2in, and heat until a strand of vermicelli cooks as soon as it is lowered into the oil.

3 Carefully add a loop of vermicelli to the oil. Almost immediately, turn to cook on the other side, then remove and drain on kitchen paper. Repeat with the remaining loops. Transfer the cooked noodles to a bowl and keep them warm.

4 Clean out the wok and heat 15ml/1 tbsp groundnut oil. When the oil is hot, fry the steak for about 30 seconds on each side, then remove and cut into thick slices.

5 Add a little extra oil to the wok, and stir-fry the spring onions, garlic and carrots for 5–6 minutes. Add the chillies, courgettes and ginger and stir fry for 1–2 minutes.

6 Stir in the rice vinegar, soy sauce and stock. Cook for 4 minutes until the sauce has thickened slightly.

7 Return the steak slices to the wok and cook for a further 1–2 minutes. Spoon the steak, vegetables and sauce over the crispy noodles in a large, warmed bowl and toss lightly.

Lamb and Noodle Salad Energy 820kcal/3418kJ; Protein 46g; Carbohydrate 76.4g, of which sugars 9.4g; Fat 36g, of which saturates 11.7g; Cholesterol 143mg; Calcium 55mg; Fibre 4.1g; Sodium 709mg.
Crispy Noodles with Beef Energy 410kcal/1712kJ; Protein 30.7g; Carbohydrate 41.4g, of which sugars 6.6g; Fat 13.5g, of which saturates 3g; Cholesterol 66mg; Calcium 49mg; Fibre 1.9g; Sodium 1687mg.

Spicy Fried Noodles with Chicken

This is a wonderfully versatile dish as you can adjust it to include your favourite ingredients.

Serves 4

225g/8oz egg thread noodles
60ml/4 tbsp vegetable oil
2 garlic cloves, finely chopped
175g/6oz pork fillet (tenderloin), sliced into thin strips
1 skinless chicken breast fillet, sliced into thin strips
115g/4oz/1 cup peeled cooked prawns (shrimp)
45ml/3 tbsp fresh lemon juice
45ml/3 tbsp Thai fish sauce (nam pla)
30ml/2 tbsp soft light brown sugar
2 eggs, beaten
½ fresh red chilli, seeded and finely chopped
50g/2oz/⅔ cup beansprouts
60ml/4 tbsp roasted peanuts, chopped
3 spring onions (scallions), cut into 5cm/2in lengths and shredded
45ml/3 tbsp chopped fresh coriander (cilantro)

1 Bring a large pan of lightly salted water to the boil, add the noodles and cook, then leave for 5 minutes.

2 Meanwhile, heat 45ml/3 tbsp of the oil in a wok or large frying pan, add the garlic and cook for 30 seconds.

3 Add the pork and chicken and stir-fry until lightly browned, then add the prawns and stir-fry for 2 minutes. Stir in the lemon juice, then add the fish sauce and sugar. Stir-fry in the pan until the sugar has dissolved.

4 Drain the noodles and add to the wok or pan with the remaining 15ml/1 tbsp oil. Toss all the ingredients together. Pour the beaten eggs over the noodles and stir-fry until the eggs are almost set, then add the chilli and beansprouts.

5 Divide the roasted peanuts, spring onions and coriander leaves into two equal portions, add one portion to the pan and stir-fry for about 2 minutes.

6 Transfer the noodles to a serving platter. Sprinkle on the remaining roasted peanuts, spring onions and chopped coriander and serve immediately.

Wheat Noodles with Stir-fried Pork

Dried wheat noodles, sold in straight bundles like sticks, are versatile and robust. They keep well, so are handy items to have in the store cupboard, ready for quick and easy recipes like this one.

Serves 4

225g/8oz pork loin, cut into thin strips
225g/8oz dried wheat noodles, soaked in lukewarm water for 20 minutes
15ml/1 tbsp groundnut (peanut) oil
2 garlic cloves, finely chopped
2–3 spring onions (scallions), trimmed and chopped
45ml/3 tbsp kroeung or magic paste
15ml/1 tbsp fish sauce
30ml/2 tbsp unsalted roasted peanuts, finely chopped
chilli oil, for drizzling

For the marinade

30ml/2 tbsp fish sauce
30ml/2 tbsp soy sauce
15ml/1 tbsp groundnut (peanut) oil
10ml/2 tsp sugar

1 In a bowl, combine the ingredients for the marinade, stirring constantly until the all the sugar dissolves. Toss in the strips of pork, making sure that they are well coated in the marinade. Put aside for 30 minutes, so that the pork absorbs the flavours.

2 Drain the wheat noodles. Bring a large pan of water to the boil. Drop in the noodles, untangling them with chopsticks, if necessary. Cook for 4–5 minutes, until tender.

3 Drain the wheat noodles thoroughly, and then divide them among four individual, warmed serving bowls. Keep the noodles warm until the dish is ready to serve.

4 Meanwhile, heat a wok or large heavy pan. Add the oil and stir-fry the garlic and spring onions, until fragrant. Add the pork, tossing it around the wok for 2 minutes.

5 Stir in the kroeung or magic paste and fish sauce for 2 minutes – add a splash of water if the wok gets too dry – and tip the pork on top of the noodles. Sprinkle the peanuts over the top and drizzle with chilli oil to serve.

Spicy Fried Noodles Energy 605kcal/2537kJ; Protein 39.8g; Carbohydrate 52.1g, of which sugars 11.5g; Fat 27.9g, of which saturates 5.5g; Cholesterol 226mg; Calcium 83mg; Fibre 3.1g; Sodium 1052mg.
Wheat Noodles Energy 340kcal/1435kJ; Protein 19.6g; Carbohydrate 46g, of which sugars 4.4g; Fat 9.9g, of which saturates 1.4g; Cholesterol 35mg; Calcium 23mg; Fibre 1.9g; Sodium 41mg.

Stir-fried Udon Noodles

Udon noodles originated in Japan but quickly became popular in Korea. This is an ideal lunch dish.

Serves 4

200g/7oz squid, cleaned and skinned
350g/12oz udon noodles
8 tiger prawns (shrimp), shelled
4 mussels, shucked
30ml/2 tbsp vegetable oil
115g/4oz beef sirloin, cut into strips
½ onion, finely sliced
1 green (bell) pepper, seeded and finely sliced
1 carrot, finely sliced
50g/2oz oyster mushrooms, sliced
½ lettuce, shredded
15ml/1 tbsp chilli oil
salt and ground black pepper

For the sauce
15ml/1 tbsp oyster sauce
10ml/2 tsp sugar
30ml/2 tbsp sake
45ml/3 tbsp dark soy sauce

1 Score diagonal cuts across the squid flesh with a sharp knife, taking great care not to cut right through, and then cut the sacs into strips of about 2cm/¾in.

2 Bring a pan of water to the boil and add the udon noodles. Boil them for 3 minutes and then drain the noodles. Rinse the cooked noodles under cold water and set aside.

3 Bring 1 litre/1¾ pints/4 cups water to the boil in a pan and add a pinch of salt. Add the squid, prawns and mussels to the pan, bring the water back to the boil, and then drain and set aside.

4 For the sauce, mix the oyster sauce, sugar, sake and soy sauce in a bowl. Set the sauce aside, to allow the flavours to mingle.

5 Heat the vegetable oil in a wok or large heavy pan over a high heat and add the beef, then stir-fry for 3 minutes. Continue stir-frying, add the onion, pepper, carrot, mushrooms and lettuce, and stir-fry for 2 more minutes.

6 Add the blanched seafood to the pan. Add the noodles and sauce, and toss to mix. Stir-fry until the seafood is reheated and cooked and all the ingredients are coated. Season to taste with chilli oil and black pepper, and serve.

Beef and Black Bean Noodles

This is an excellent combination – tender strips of beef in a chilli sauce are tossed with silky smooth rice noodles.

Serves 4

450g/1lb fresh rice noodles
60ml/4 tbsp vegetable oil
1 onion, finely sliced
2 garlic cloves, finely chopped
2 slices fresh root ginger, finely chopped
225g/8oz mixed (bell) peppers, seeded and cut into strips
350g/12oz rump (round) steak, finely sliced across the grain
45ml/3 tbsp fermented black beans, rinsed in warm water, drained and chopped
30ml/2 tbsp soy sauce
30ml/2 tbsp oyster sauce
15ml/1 tbsp chilli black bean sauce
15ml/1 tbsp cornflour (cornstarch)
120ml/4fl oz/½ cup stock
2 spring onions (scallions), finely chopped, and 2 red chillies, seeded and sliced, to garnish

1 Rinse the rice noodles under hot water; drain well. Heat half the oil in a wok or large frying pan, swirling it around.

2 Add the sliced onion, chopped garlic, chopped ginger and mixed pepper strips to the pan. Stir-fry for 3–5 minutes, then remove with a slotted spoon and keep hot.

3 Add the remaining oil to the pan. When hot, add the sliced beef and fermented black beans and stir-fry over a high heat for 5 minutes or until the beef is cooked.

4 In a small bowl, blend the soy sauce, oyster sauce and chilli black bean sauce with the cornflour and stock until smooth.

5 Add the mixture to the pan, then return the onion mixture to the wok and cook, stirring, for 1 minute.

6 Add the rice noodles to the pan and mix them in lightly. Stir over a medium heat until the noodles are heated through. Adjust the seasoning if necessary.

7 Serve at once in individual warmed dishes, garnished with the chopped spring onions and chillies.

Udon Noodles Energy 594kcal/2502kJ; Protein 36g; Carbohydrate 76g, of which sugars 10.1g; Fat 18.1g, of which saturates 2.4g; Cholesterol 232mg; Calcium 85mg; Fibre 3.8g; Sodium 1072mg.
Beef and Black Bean Energy 567kcal/2376kJ; Protein 25.8g; Carbohydrate 100.4g, of which sugars 4.7g; Fat 5.5g, of which saturates 1.7g; Cholesterol 52mg; Calcium 29mg; Fibre 1.2g; Sodium 338mg.

Fried Noodles with Spicy Peanut Sauce, Beef and Fragrant Herbs

If you like chillies and peanuts, this delicious dish is the perfect choice. The stringy rice sticks can be fiddly to stir-fry as they have a tendency to cling together, so it is advisable to work quickly. In Vietnam this dish is usually served with a salad or pickled vegetables.

Serves 4

300g/11oz beef sirloin
15–30ml/1–2 tbsp vegetable oil
225g/8oz dried rice sticks (vermicelli), soaked in warm water for 20 minutes
225g/8oz/1 cup beansprouts
5–10ml/1–2 tsp nuoc mam (Vietnamese fish sauce)
1 small bunch each of fresh basil and mint, stalks removed, leaves shredded, to garnish
Vietnamese pickles, to serve

For the peanut sauce

4 dried Serrano chillies, seeded
60ml/4 tbsp groundnut (peanut) oil
4–5 garlic cloves, crushed
5–10ml/1–2 tsp medium curry powder
40g/1½oz/⅓ cup roasted peanuts, finely ground

1 To make the peanut sauce, grind the chillies in a mortar with a pestle. Heat the oil in a heavy pan and stir in the garlic until it begins to colour. Add the chillies, curry powder and ground peanuts and stir over a low heat, until the mixture forms a paste. Remove the pan from the heat and leave to cool.

2 Slice the beef thinly, cutting across the grain. Heat a wok or heavy pan, and pour in 15ml/1 tbsp of the oil. Add the sliced beef and cook for 1–2 minutes, then stir in 7.5ml/1½ tsp of the spicy peanut sauce. Tip the beef on to a clean plate and set aside. Drain the rice sticks.

3 Add 7.5ml/1½ tsp oil to the wok and add the rice sticks and 15ml/1 tbsp peanut sauce. Toss the noodles until coated in the sauce and cook for 4–5 minutes, or until tender. Toss in the beef for 1 minute, then add the beansprouts with the nuoc mam.

4 Tip the noodles on to a serving dish and sprinkle with the basil and mint. Serve with pickles.

Stir-fried Noodles with Beef and Mixed Vegetables

This is a Korean stir-fry of beef, mixed vegetables and noodles.

Serves 4

225g/8oz rump (round) steak
marinade (see Cook's Tip)
115g/4oz cellophane noodles, soaked for 20 minutes in hot water to cover, then drained
4 Chinese dried mushrooms, soaked, stems removed, caps sliced
oil, for stir-frying
2 eggs, separated
1 carrot, cut into matchsticks
1 onion, sliced
2 courgettes (zucchini) and ½ red (bell) pepper, cut into strips
4 button mushrooms, sliced
75g/3oz/⅓ cup beansprouts
15ml/1 tbsp light soy sauce
salt and ground black pepper
sliced spring onions (scallions) and sesame seeds, to garnish

1 Put the steak in the freezer until it is firm enough to cut into 5cm/2in strips, and mix with the marinade in a shallow dish. Cook the noodles in boiling water for 5 minutes. Drain the noodles and snip them into short lengths.

2 For the garnish, first fry the beaten egg yolks and then the whites in oil in a small frying pan. When set, remove, cut into diamond shapes and set aside.

3 Heat the oil in a wok. Drain the beef and stir-fry it until it changes colour. Add the vegetables; cook until crisp and tender.

4 Add the noodles and season with soy sauce, salt and pepper. Cook for 1 minute. Spoon into a serving dish and garnish with egg diamonds, spring onions and sesame seeds.

Cook's Tip

To make the marinade, blend together 15ml/1 tbsp sugar, 30ml/2 tbsp light soy sauce, 45ml/3 tbsp sesame oil, 4 finely chopped spring onions (scallions), 1 crushed garlic clove and 10ml/2 tsp crushed toasted sesame seeds.

Fried Noodles and Herbs: Energy 603Kcal/2507kJ; Protein 26g; Carbohydrate 52g, of which sugars 2g; Fat 32g, of which saturates 6g; Cholesterol 38mg; Calcium 73mg; Fibre 2.2g; Sodium 200mg.
Stir-fried Noodles with Beef Energy 321kcal/1337kJ; Protein 19.6g; Carbohydrate 28.5g, of which sugars 4.2g; Fat 14g, of which saturates 3.7g; Cholesterol 128mg; Calcium 52mg; Fibre 1.6g; Sodium 348mg.

Beef with Glass Noodles

Quick and easy to prepare, the delicate texture of the glass noodles combines well with the crunchy vegetables and the rich sesame beef.

Serves 4

250g/9oz glass noodles
5 dried shiitake mushrooms, soaked in warm water
275g/10oz beef, sliced thinly
90g/3½oz spinach
15ml/1 tbsp sesame oil, plus extra for drizzling
2 eggs, beaten
25ml/1½ tbsp vegetable oil
1 carrot, cut into thin strips
1 spring onion (scallion), sliced
salt
sesame seeds, to garnish

For the marinade

2 garlic cloves, crushed
30ml/2 tbsp soy sauce
15ml/1 tbsp sesame oil
5ml/1 tsp sugar
10ml/2 tsp mirin or rice wine

For the seasoning

30ml/2 tbsp soy sauce
15ml/1 tbsp sugar
1 garlic clove, crushed

1 Soak the glass noodles in warm water for 30 minutes. Drain and slice the mushrooms, discarding the stems.

2 Combine the marinade ingredients. Add the beef and mushrooms to the marinade. Coat and marinate for 20 minutes.

3 Blanch the spinach for 1 minute then rinse. Squeeze out any liquid and season with salt and 15ml/1 tbsp sesame oil.

4 Add a pinch of salt to the eggs. Coat a frying pan with 10ml/2 tsp vegetable oil and heat over a medium heat. Add the egg and make a thin omelette, cut into thin strips, then set aside.

5 Heat the remaining vegetable oil in a wok. Add the beef and mushrooms, and stir-fry for 3–4 minutes. Remove and set aside.

6 Add the carrot, spinach, spring onion and the seasoning ingredients to the pan and coat well. Reduce the heat, stir in the beef and mushrooms, and mix all the ingredients well.

7 Drizzle with a little sesame oil and transfer to a serving dish. Garnish with the omelette strips and a sprinkling of sesame seeds.

Bamie Goreng

The medley of seafood, meat and vegetables in this stir-fry is deliciously enhanced by the sweet, salty flavours in the sauce. This fried noodle dish is wonderfully accommodating. You can add other vegetables, such as mushrooms, tiny pieces of chayote, broccoli, leeks or beansprouts. Use whatever is to hand, balancing textures, colours and flavours.

Serves 6–8

450g/1lb dried egg noodles
2 eggs
25g/1oz/2 tbsp butter
90ml/6 tbsp vegetable oil
1 chicken breast fillet, sliced
115g/4oz pork fillet (tenderloin), sliced
115g/4oz calf's liver, sliced (optional)
2 garlic cloves, crushed
115g/4oz peeled cooked prawns (shrimp)
115g/4oz pak choi (bok choy)
2 celery sticks, finely sliced
4 spring onions (scallions), shredded
about 60ml/4 tbsp chicken stock
dark soy sauce and light soy sauce
salt and ground black pepper
deep-fried onions and shredded spring onions (scallions), to garnish

1 Cook the noodles in a pan of lightly salted water for about 3–4 minutes. Drain, rinse and drain again. Set aside.

2 Put the eggs in a bowl, beat and season to taste. Heat the butter with 5ml/1 tsp oil in a small pan, add the eggs and stir over a low heat until scrambled but still moist. Set aside.

3 Heat the remaining oil in a wok and fry the chicken, pork and liver, if using, with the garlic for 2–3 minutes, until the meat has changed colour. Add the prawns, pak choi, sliced celery and shredded spring onions and toss to mix.

4 Add the noodles and toss over the heat until the prawns and noodles are heated through and the greens are lightly cooked. Add enough stock to moisten, and season with dark and light soy sauce to taste. Add the scrambled eggs and toss to mix.

5 Spoon on to a serving platter and serve, garnished with onions.

Beef with Glass Noodles Energy 458kcal/1911kJ; Protein 22.8g; Carbohydrate 54.5g, of which sugars 3.4g; Fat 15.8g, of which saturates 4.2g; Cholesterol 135mg; Calcium 71mg; Fibre 1g; Sodium 390mg.
Bamie Goreng Energy 478kcal/2010kJ; Protein 16.8g; Carbohydrate 64.2g, of which sugars 5.1g; Fat 18.9g, of which saturates 3.2g; Cholesterol 86mg; Calcium 323mg; Fibre 2.9g; Sodium 466mg.

Sweet-and-sour Cucumber with Chillies, Coriander and Mint

For this delicious side salad, cucumbers are sliced and dressed Thai-style with fresh lime juice and roughly chopped herbs to make a delightful accompaniment to meat, poultry and seafood dishes. This salad is also a great addition to a summer barbecue or salad table.

Serves 4–6
2 cucumbers
salt
30ml/2 tbsp sugar
100ml/3½fl oz/scant ½ cup rice wine vinegar
juice of half a lime
1–2 green Thai chillies, seeded and finely sliced
2 shallots, halved and finely sliced
1 small bunch fresh coriander (cilantro), stalks removed, leaves roughly chopped
1 small bunch mint, stalks removed, leaves roughly chopped

1 Use a vegetable peeler to remove strips of the cucumber peel. Halve the cucumber lengthwise and cut into slices.

2 Place the cucumber slices on a plate and sprinkle them with a little salt. Leave to stand for 15 minutes, then rinse and drain.

3 In a small glass bowl, mix the sugar with the vinegar until it has dissolved, then stir in the lime juice and a little salt to taste.

4 Add the chillies, shallots, herbs and cucumber to the dressing and leave to stand for 15–20 minutes before serving.

Variations

- *To make a tasty tuna and cucumber salad, drain a 200g/7oz can tuna, flake the flesh and stir into the bean salad. Add some lightly cooked, halved green beans, hard-boiled egg and tomato quarters.*
- *For extra flavour and colour, stir in a handful of pitted black olives and a handful of chopped fresh dill.*

Mustard Greens with Oyster Sauce

Also known as mustard cabbage (or gai choy in Cantonese) mustard greens have thick, curved, ribbed stalks and ruffled bright green leaves. Shantou people are inordinately fond of this vegetable and usually serve it with congee for breakfast or lunch. In China, the bulk of the crop is salted and preserved.

Serves 4
500g/1¼lb mustard greens
30ml/2 tbsp vegetable oil
30ml/2 tbsp crushed garlic
30ml/2 tbsp oyster sauce
200ml/7fl oz/scant 1 cup water
cooked rice or congee, to serve

1 Cut off any fibrous bits from the stalks of the mustard greens, then cut both the stalks and the leaves into bitesize pieces. Rinse thoroughly in cold water, then drain.

2 Bring a large pan of water to the boil. Add the mustard greens and blanch them for 2 minutes, then drain and pat dry with kitchen paper or a clean dish towel.

3 Heat the oil in a wok. Add the garlic and fry until golden brown. Do not let the garlic burn or it will become bitter.

4 Add the blanched greens to the wok. Sprinkle over the oyster sauce, then add the water.

5 Cook the blanched greens over high heat for 2–3 minutes, tossing constantly with two spoons, so that they cook evenly. Spoon into a heated dish and serve immediately with rice.

Cook's Tip

Mustard greens are widely grown and are especially popular with home gardeners and allotment holders. Look for them at farmers' markets or Chinese food stores. Mustard greens have wonderfully peppery leaves and belong to the same family as broccoli, Brussels sprouts, kohlrabi and kale.

Sweet-and-sour Cucumber Energy 59Kcal/248kJ; Protein 2g; Carbohydrate 12g, of which sugars 11g Fat 0g, of which saturates 0g; Cholesterol 0mg; Calcium 63mg; Fibre 0.8g; Sodium 0.2g
Mustard Greens Energy 89kcal/369kJ; Protein 3.6g; Carbohydrate 4.2g, of which sugars 4g; Fat 6.5g, of which saturates 0.8g; Cholesterol 0mg; Calcium 214mg; Fibre 2.7g; Sodium 297mg.

Gado Gado with Chilli Peanut Sauce

Served at room temperature with a bowl of rice, this spicy Indonesian dish makes a tasty vegetarian meal.

Serves 4–6
500g/1¼lb tofu block
corn oil, for deep frying
4 shallots, finely sliced
3 carrots, sliced diagonally
about 12 snake (yard-long) beans, cut into bitesize pieces
225g/8oz kangkung (water spinach), washed and thinly sliced
1 firm mango, cut into bitesize chunks
½ pineapple, cut into bitesize chunks
225g/8oz mung bean sprouts
2–3 hard-boiled eggs, quartered
salt
1 small bunch fresh coriander (cilantro) leaves, roughly chopped, to garnish

For the peanut sauce
30ml/2 tbsp coconut or groundnut (peanut) oil
3 shallots, finely chopped
3 garlic cloves, finely chopped
3–4 red chillies, seeded and finely chopped
175g/6oz/1 cup unsalted roasted peanuts, finely ground
15g/½oz galangal or fresh root ginger, finely chopped
5–10ml/1–2 tsp shrimp paste
15ml/1 tbsp palm sugar (jaggery)
600ml/1 pint/2½ cups coconut milk
juice of 1 lime
30ml/2 tbsp kecap manis (Indonesian sweet soy sauce)

1 First make the peanut sauce. Heat the oil in a wok or heavy pan, stir in the shallots, garlic and chillies and fry until beginning to colour. Add the peanuts, galangal, shrimp paste and palm sugar and fry for about 4 minutes, until the peanuts begin to darken and ooze a little oil.

2 Pour the coconut milk, lime juice and kecap manis into the pan and bring to the boil. Reduce the heat and simmer gently for 15–20 minutes, until the sauce has reduced a little and thickened. Leave to cool.

3 Cut the tofu into four rectangular pieces. Heat enough oil in a wok for deep-frying, add the tofu pieces and fry until golden brown. Using a slotted spoon, remove from the pan and drain on kitchen paper. Cut the tofu into slices and put aside.

4 Heat 15–30ml/1–2 tbsp of the oil in a small, heavy pan, add the shallots and fry until deep golden in colour. Drain on kitchen paper and put aside.

5 Fill a large pan a third of the way up with water and place a steaming basket over it. Bring the water to the boil and put the carrots and snake beans in the steaming basket. Put the lid on, reduce the heat, and steam for 3–4 minutes. Add the kangkung for a minute, then drain the vegetables and refresh under cold running water.

6 Put the vegetables in a large bowl. Add the mango, pineapple and bean sprouts and pour in half the peanut sauce. Toss well then transfer to a serving dish.

7 Arrange the egg quarters and tofu slices around the edge of the dish and drizzle the remaining peanut sauce over the top. Sprinkle with the reserved fried shallots and chopped coriander to garnish, and serve immediately.

Stir-fried Pineapple with Ginger and Chilli

Throughout South-east Asia, fruit is often treated like a vegetable and tossed in a salad, or stir-fried, to accompany spicy dishes. In this Cambodian dish, the pineapple is combined with the tangy flavours of ginger and chilli and served as a side dish.

Serves 4
30ml/2 tbsp groundnut (peanut) oil
2 garlic cloves, finely shredded
40g/1½oz fresh root ginger, peeled and finely shredded
2 red Thai chillies, seeded and finely shredded
1 pineapple, trimmed, peeled, cored and cut into bitesize chunks
15ml/1 tbsp fish sauce
30ml/2 tbsp soy sauce
15ml–30ml/1–2 tbsp sugar
30ml/2 tbsp roasted unsalted peanuts, finely chopped
1 lime, cut into quarters, to serve

1 Heat a large wok or large, heavy frying pan and add the groundnut oil. Stir in the garlic, ginger and chillies. Stir-fry for 2 minutes until the ingredients begin to colour. Ensure that the garlic does not burn, otherwise it will impart a bitter taste to the rest of the dish.

2 Add the pineapple to the pan and stir-fry for a further 1–2 minutes, until the edges turn golden.

3 Add the fish sauce and soy sauce to the pan and mix well. Add sugar to taste and continue to stir-fry until the pineapple begins to caramelize.

4 Transfer to a serving dish, sprinkle with the roasted peanuts and serve with lime wedges.

Cook's Tip
This dish is an excellent accompaniment to grilled (broiled) meats, and will be perfect on a summer's day to be eaten alongside spicy chicken or satays cooked on the barbecue.

Gado Gado Energy 449kcal/1873kJ; Protein 22.2g; Carbohydrate 24.5g, of which sugars 20.7g; Fat 30g, of which saturates 5.1g; Cholesterol 108mg; Calcium 611mg; Fibre 5.1g; Sodium 675mg.
Stir-fried Pineapple Energy 185kcal/780kJ; Protein 3g; Carbohydrate 24.1g, of which sugars 23.6g; Fat 9g, of which saturates 1g; Cholesterol 0mg; Calcium 43mg; Fibre 2.9g; Sodium 271mg.

Mixed Thai Vegetables in Coconut Milk

This is a most delicious way of cooking vegetables. If you don't like highly spiced food, use fewer red chilli peppers.

Serves 4–6

450g/1lb mixed vegetables, such as aubergines (eggplants), baby corn, carrots, snake (yard-long) beans and patty pan squash
8 red chillies, seeded
2 lemon grass stalks, chopped
4 kaffir lime leaves, torn
30ml/2 tbsp vegetable oil
250ml/8fl oz/1 cup coconut milk
30ml/2 tbsp fish sauce
salt
15–20 Thai basil leaves, to garnish

1 Cut the vegetables into similar-size shapes using a sharp knife.

2 Put the red chillies, lemon grass and lime leaves in a mortar and grind together with a pestle.

3 Heat the oil in a wok or large, deep frying pan. Add the chilli mixture and fry for 2–3 minutes.

4 Stir in the coconut milk and bring to the boil.

5 Add the mixed vegetables and cook them for about 5 minutes or until they are tender. Season with the fish sauce and salt, and garnish with basil leaves.

Variation
For Broccoli and Courgettes in Coconut, steam or lightly boil 350g/12oz broccoli florets and 350g/12oz thickly sliced courgettes (zucchini). Stir-fry 15ml/1 tbsp black mustard seeds and 6 curry leaves for 1 minute and then add 225g/8oz sliced onion and 2 chopped fresh green chillies. Cook for 10 minutes until softened. Add 250ml/8fl oz/1 cup coconut milk and salt. Add a pinch of saffron threads and 30ml/2 tbsp fresh coriander (cilantro). Serve.

Stir-fried Mixed Vegetables

The name Cap cai ca is a Sino-Indonesian stir-fry; the name is a phonetic spelling from the Fujian dialect, which literally means 'ten vegetables fry' but actually alludes to any multiple vegetable dish. This Chinese dish has been absorbed into the Indonesian culinary lexicon and is featured on many local restaurant menus. Try serving it with flat breads, steamed white rice or with steamed rice noodles for a truly satisfying lunch.

Serves 4

200g/7oz pak choi (bok choy)
16 mangetouts (snow peas)
200g/7oz canned bamboo shoot slices
30ml/2 tbsp vegetable oil
3 garlic cloves, crushed
16 water chestnuts
8 Chinese mushrooms, soaked until soft and sliced
15ml/1 tbsp light soy sauce
15ml/1 tbsp oyster sauce
15ml/1 tbsp sesame oil
2.5ml/½ tsp ground black pepper
105ml/7 tbsp water
10ml/2 tsp cornflour (cornstarch)

1 Rinse the vegetables in cold water. Cut the pak choi leaves into short lengths. Trim the tops and tails of the mangetouts.

2 Wash and drain the bamboo shoots to remove some of the canning liquid scent, which can be overpowering.

3 Heat the oil in a wok or frying pan and fry the garlic over a low heat until golden brown, then add the pak choi, mangetouts, bamboo shoots, water chestnuts and mushrooms. Stir-fry over a high heat for 3 minutes.

4 Add the soy sauce, oyster sauce, sesame oil and black pepper to the pan and continue to stir well, so that all the vegetables are coated in each flavouring.

5 Mix the water with the cornflour to form a smooth, thin blend and pour into the pan, stirring well.

6 Continue to stir over a medium-high heat until the sauce is fairly thick, then serve the dish immediately with noodles or rice, or as a vegetable side dish.

Mixed Thai Vegetables Energy 80kcal/335kJ; Protein 1.2g; Carbohydrate 5.5g, of which sugars 5.3g; Fat 6.1g, of which saturates 0.9g; Cholesterol 0mg; Calcium 29mg; Fibre 2.3g; Sodium 71mg.
Stir-fried Mixed Vegetables Energy 84kcal/352kJ; Protein 5.4g; Carbohydrate 7.9g, of which sugars 4.2g; Fat 3.6g, of which saturates 0.5g; Cholesterol 0mg; Calcium 121mg; Fibre 3.2g; Sodium 610mg.

Root Vegetables with Spiced Salt

All kinds of root vegetables can be finely sliced and deep fried to make 'crisps'. You can serve these as an accompaniment to an Asian-style meal or simply by themselves as much tastier nibbles than commercial snacks with pre-dinner drinks.

Serves 4–6

1 carrot
2 parsnips
2 raw beetroots (beets)
1 sweet potato
groundnut (peanut) oil, for deep-frying
1.5ml/1/4 tsp chilli powder
5ml/1 tsp sea salt flakes

1 Peel the carrot, parsnips, beetroots and sweet potato. Slice the carrot and parsnips into long, thin ribbons.

2 Cut the beetroots and sweet potato into thin rounds. Pat all the cut vegetables dry on kitchen paper.

3 Half-fill a wok with oil and heat to 180°C/350°F. Add the vegetable slices in batches and deep-fry for 2–3 minutes until golden and crisp. Remove and drain on kitchen paper.

4 Place the chilli powder and sea salt flakes in a mortar and grind them together with a pestle to form a coarse powder.

5 Pile up the vegetable 'crisps' on a serving plate and sprinkle over the spiced salt.

Variations

- *For a simple, speedy, Italian-style dip, stir 15ml/1 tbsp ready-made red or green pesto into a carton of soured cream. Serve with crisp crudités or wedges of oven-roasted Mediterranean vegetables, such as peppers, courgettes and onions, for a delicious starter.*
- *Make a quick and easy soft cheese and chive dip by mixing a tub of soft cheese with 30–45ml/2–3 tbsp snipped fresh chives and season to taste with salt and black pepper. If the dip is too thick, stir in a little milk to soften it.*

Fried Tofu Salad with a Tangy Tamarind Sauce

The sweet-sour sauce makes this traditional street snack the perfect foil to grilled meats and stir-fried noodles. If you cannot find kecap manis, simply use dark soy sauce with a little more tomato ketchup to achieve the same balance of flavour.

Serves 4

vegetable oil, for deep-frying
450g/1lb firm rectangular tofu, rinsed, patted dry and cut into blocks
1 small cucumber, partially peeled in strips, seeded and shredded
2 spring onions (scallions), trimmed, halved and shredded
2 handfuls of fresh beansprouts rinsed and drained
fresh coriander (cilantro) leaves, to garnish

For the sauce

30ml/2 tbsp tamarind pulp, soaked in water until soft
15ml/1 tbsp sesame or groundnut (peanut) oil
4 shallots, finely chopped
4 garlic cloves, finely chopped
2 fresh red chillies, seeded
2.5ml/½ tsp shrimp paste
115g/4oz/1 cup roasted peanuts, crushed
30–45ml/2–3 tbsp kecap manis (Indonesian sweet soy sauce)
15ml/1 tbsp tomato ketchup

1 First make the sauce. Squeeze the tamarind pulp to soften it in the water, and then strain through a sieve (strainer). Measure out 120ml/4fl oz/½ cup tamarind pulp.

2 Heat the oil in a wok or heavy pan, and stir in the shallots, garlic and chillies, until fragrant. Stir in the shrimp paste and the peanuts, until they emit a nutty aroma. Add the kecap manis, tomato ketchup and tamarind pulp and blend to form a thick sauce. Set aside and leave to cool.

3 Deep-fry the blocks of tofu in oil until golden brown all over. Pat dry on kitchen paper and cut each block into slices. Arrange the fried tofu slices on a plate with the cucumber, spring onions and beansprouts.

4 Drizzle a little of the sauce over the top and serve the remainder separately in a bowl, garnished with the coriander.

Root Vegetables Energy 244kcal/1010kJ; Protein 1.4g; Carbohydrate 13.5g, of which sugars 5.9g; Fat 20.8g, of which saturates 2.5g; Cholesterol 0mg; Calcium 28mg; Fibre 3g; Sodium 358mg.
Fried Tofu Salad Energy 423kcal/1749kJ; Protein 17.9g; Carbohydrate 7.8g, of which sugars 4.5g; Fat 35.8g, of which saturates 5.3g; Cholesterol 0mg; Calcium 607mg; Fibre 2.8g; Sodium 296mg.

Spicy Chickpeas with Spinach

This richly flavoured dish makes a great main meal for vegetarians, but it will be equally popular with meat-eaters. It is particularly good served drizzled with a little lightly beaten natural yogurt – the sharp, creamy flavour complements the complex spices perfectly.

Serves 4

200g/7oz dried chickpeas
30ml/2 tbsp sunflower oil
2 onions, halved and thinly sliced along the grain
10ml/2 tsp ground coriander
10ml/2 tsp ground cumin
5ml/1 tsp hot chilli powder
2.5ml/½ tsp turmeric
15ml/1 tbsp medium curry powder
400g/14oz can chopped tomatoes
5ml/1 tsp caster (superfine) sugar
30ml/2 tbsp chopped fresh mint leaves
115g/4oz baby leaf spinach
salt and ground black pepper
plain steamed rice or bread and natural (plain) yogurt, to serve

1 Soak the dried chickpeas in cold water overnight. Drain, rinse and place in a large pan. Cover with water and bring to the boil. Reduce the heat and simmer for 45 minutes, or until just tender. Drain and set aside.

2 Heat the oil in a wok or large frying pan, add the sliced onions and cook over a low heat for 15 minutes, stirring occasionally, until soft and lightly golden.

3 Add the ground coriander and cumin, chilli powder, turmeric and curry powder and stir-fry for 1–2 minutes.

4 Add the tomatoes, sugar and 105ml/7 tbsp water to the wok or pan and bring to the boil. Cover, reduce the heat and simmer gently for 15 minutes.

5 Add the chickpeas to the wok, season well and cook gently for 8–10 minutes. Stir in the chopped mint.

6 Divide the spinach leaves between warmed shallow bowls, top with the chickpea mixture and serve with some steamed rice or bread and natural yogurt.

Asian-style Courgette Fritters

This is an excellent cultural fusion: a twist on Japanese tempura using Indian spices and gram flour in the batter. Also known as besan, gram flour is more commonly used in Indian cooking and gives a wonderfully crisp texture, while the courgette baton inside becomes meltingly tender. If you're feeling adventurous, vary the vegetable content by dipping some thinly sliced squash or pumpkin batons with the courgettes. This is an ideal treat for kids.

Serves 4

90g/3½oz/¾ cup gram flour
5ml/1 tsp baking powder
2.5ml/½ tsp ground turmeric
10ml/2 tsp ground coriander
5ml/1 tsp ground cumin
5ml/1 tsp chilli powder
250ml/8fl oz/1 cup beer
600g/1lb 6oz courgettes (zucchini), cut into batons
sunflower oil, for deep-frying
salt
steamed basmati rice, natural (plain) yogurt and pickles, to serve

1 Using a sieve (strainer) sift the gram flour, baking powder, ground turmeric, ground coriander, ground cumin and chilli powder into a large bowl. Stir lightly to mix through.

2 Season the mixture with salt and make a hollow in the centre. Pour in a little of the beer, and gradually mix in the surrounding dry ingredients. Add more beer, continuing to mix gently, to make a thick batter. Be careful not to overmix.

3 Fill a large wok or heavy pan one-third full with sunflower oil and heat to 180°C/350°F or until a small cube of bread dropped into the oil browns in 45 seconds.

4 Working in batches, dip the courgette batons in the spiced batter and then deep-fry for 1–2 minutes, or until crisp and golden. Lift out of the wok using a slotted spoon. Drain on kitchen paper and keep warm.

5 Serve the courgette fritters on four individual heated plates, or on banana leaves if these are available, accompanied by steamed basmati rice, yogurt and pickles.

Chickpeas with Spinach Energy 267kcal/1122kJ; Protein 13.3g; Carbohydrate 35.5g, of which sugars 10.2g; Fat 9g, of which saturates 1.1g; Cholesterol 0mg; Calcium 170mg; Fibre 8.2g; Sodium 83mg.
Courgette Fritters Energy 241kcal/999kJ; Protein 7.3g; Carbohydrate 15.3g, of which sugars 4.6g; Fat 15.6g, of which saturates 1.9g; Cholesterol 0mg; Calcium 83mg; Fibre 3.8g; Sodium 15mg.

Deep-fried Garlic Aubergines

This dish is often served at the rice street stalls in Singapore as an accompaniment to a main rice dish. Many of the cooks will make up large batches of different sambals to be stored and used for making quick and simple dishes like this one. Generally, the aubergines will be cooked by deep-frying at the hawker stalls, but you could bake them in the oven at home. Serve this dish as a spicy snack to go with a chunk of fresh bread or as a side dish to accompany a more substantial rice dish or grilled meats.

Serves 2 to 4

6 shallots, chopped
4 garlic cloves, chopped
2 red chillies, seeded and chopped
1 lemon grass stalk, trimmed and chopped
5ml/1 tsp shrimp paste
15ml/1 tbsp sesame oil
15–30ml/1–2 tbsp soy sauce
7.5ml/1½ tsp sugar
vegetable oil, for deep-frying
2 slender, purple aubergines (eggplants), partially peeled in strips and halved lengthways

To garnish

1 green chilli, seeded and finely chopped
a small bunch each of fresh mint and coriander (cilantro), stalks removed, finely chopped

1 Using a mortar and pestle or food processor, grind the shallots, garlic, chillies and lemon grass to a paste.

2 Beat in the shrimp paste and mix well.

3 Heat the sesame oil in a small wok or heavy pan. Stir in the spice paste and cook until fragrant and brown. Stir in the soy sauce and sugar and cook until smooth. Remove from the heat.

4 Heat enough oil for deep-frying in a wok or heavy pan. Drop in the aubergine halves and fry until tender. Drain on kitchen paper, then press the centres to make a dip or shallow pouch.

5 Arrange the aubergine halves on a plate and smear with the spicy sauce. Garnish with the chopped green chilli, mint and coriander and serve at room temperature.

Aubergines with Sesame Sauce

Steaming is a wonderful way of cooking aubergines as it caters perfectly to their tendency to soak up oil.

Serves 4

2 large aubergines (eggplants)
400ml/14fl oz/1⅔ cups second dashi stock made using water and instant dashi powder
25ml/1½ tbsp sugar
15ml/1 tbsp shoyu
15ml/1 tbsp sesame seeds, ground
15ml/1 tbsp sake
15ml/1 tbsp cornflour (cornstarch)
salt

For the vegetables

130g/4½oz shimeji or shiitake mushrooms
115g/4oz/¾ cup fine green beans
100ml/3fl oz/scant ½ cup second dashi stock
25ml/1½ tbsp sugar
15ml/1 tbsp sake
1.5ml/¼ tsp salt
dash of shoyu

1 Peel the aubergines and cut them in quarters lengthways. Prick all over then soak in salted water for 30 minutes. Drain and steam in a covered bamboo basket over a wok of simmering water for 20 minutes.

2 Mix the stock, sugar, shoyu and 1.5ml/¼ tsp salt in a large wok or pan. Add the aubergines, cover and simmer for a further 15 minutes. Mix a few tablespoonfuls of stock from the pan with the ground sesame seeds. Add this mixture to the pan and stir well to combine.

3 Mix the sake and the cornflour, add to the pan with the aubergines and stock and shiver the pan over the heat until the sauce becomes quite thick. Remove the pan from the heat.

4 Prepare the vegetables. Cut off the hard base part of the mushrooms and separate the large block into smaller chunks. Trim the green beans and cut them in half.

5 Mix the remaining ingredients with the green beans and mushrooms in a pan and cook for 7 minutes until just tender. Serve the aubergines and their sauce in four warmed individual bowls with the vegetables on the top.

Deep-fried Garlic Aubergines Energy 158kcal/654kJ; Protein 1.6g; Carbohydrate 6.5g, of which sugars 5.1g; Fat 14.2g, of which saturates 1.8g; Cholesterol 0mg; Calcium 24mg; Fibre 2.7g; Sodium 271mg.
Aubergines with Sesame Sauce Energy 79kcal/333kJ; Protein 2.9g; Carbohydrate 10.2g, of which sugars 9.6g; Fat 2.9g, of which saturates 0.5g; Cholesterol 0mg; Calcium 52mg; Fibre 3.3g; Sodium 272mg.

Herb and Chilli Aubergines

Plump and juicy aubergines taste sensational when steamed until tender and tossed in a fragrant mint and coriander dressing with crunchy water chestnuts.

Serves 4

500g/1¼lb firm baby aubergines (eggplants)
30ml/2 tbsp vegetable oil
6 garlic cloves, very finely chopped
15ml/1 tbsp fresh root ginger, very finely chopped
8 spring onions (scallions), cut diagonally into 2.5cm/1in lengths
2 fresh red chillies, seeded and thinly sliced
45ml/3 tbsp light soy sauce
15ml/1 tbsp Chinese rice wine
15ml/1 tbsp golden caster (superfine) sugar
a large handful of mint leaves, stalks removed
30–45ml/2–3 tbsp roughly chopped coriander (cilantro) leaves
8 drained canned water chestnuts
50g/2oz/½ cup roasted peanuts, roughly chopped
steamed egg noodles or rice, to serve

1 Cut the aubergines in half lengthways and place them on a heatproof plate. Fit a steamer rack in a wok and add 5cm/2in of water. Bring the water to the boil, lower the plate on to the rack and reduce the heat to low.

2 Cover the plate and steam the aubergines for 25–30 minutes, until they are cooked through. Remove the plate from on top of the steamer and set the aubergines aside to cool.

3 Heat the oil in a clean, dry wok and place over medium heat.

4 When the oil is hot, add the garlic, ginger, spring onions and chillies and stir-fry for 2–3 minutes. Remove from the heat and stir in the soy sauce, rice wine and sugar.

5 Add the mint leaves, chopped coriander, water chestnuts and peanuts to the cooled aubergine and toss.

6 Pour the garlic-ginger mixture evenly over the vegetables, toss gently and serve with steamed egg noodles or rice.

Braised Aubergine and Courgettes

Black bean sauce is the key to this simple, spicy and sensational accompaniment. This is a cooking sauce made from fermented, salt-preserved soybeans. It is widely used in regional Chinese cuisine, and has a subtle, deeply savoury taste. The soybeans used in blackbean sauce may be black or yellow.

Serves 4

1 large aubergine (eggplant),
2 small courgettes (zucchini)
2 fresh red chillies
2 garlic cloves
15ml/1 tbsp vegetable oil
1 small onion, diced
15ml/1 tbsp black bean sauce
15ml/1 tbsp dark soy sauce
45ml/3 tbsp cold water
salt

1 Halve and slice the aubergines. Layer the slices of aubergine in a colander, sprinkling each layer with salt. Leave in the sink to stand for about 20 minutes. Cut the courgettes into wedges.

2 Remove the stalks from the chillies, cut in half lengthways and scrape out and discard the pith and seeds. Chop finely.

3 Cut the garlic cloves in half. Place them cut side down and chop finely by slicing first in one direction and then in the other.

4 Rinse the aubergine slices under cold running water to remove the salt. Drain and dry thoroughly on kitchen paper.

5 Heat the oil in a wok or non-stick frying pan. Quickly stir-fry the garlic, chillies and onion with the black bean sauce.

6 Add the aubergine and stir-fry for 2 minutes, sprinkling over a little water to prevent them from burning. Stir in the courgettes, soy sauce and water. Cook, stirring often, for 5 minutes. Spoon into a heated dish and serve.

Variation
For a fiery result, retain the chilli seeds and add to the mixture.

Herb and Chilli Aubergines Energy 177kcal/739kJ; Protein 6.2g; Carbohydrate 12.1g, of which sugars 9g; Fat 12g, of which saturates 1.9g; Cholesterol 0mg; Calcium 46mg; Fibre 4.4g; Sodium 823mg.
Braised Aubergine and Courgettes Energy 66kcal/276kJ; Protein 3g; Carbohydrate 6.1g, of which sugars 4.2g; Fat 3.5g, of which saturates 0.5g; Cholesterol 0mg; Calcium 34mg; Fibre 2.9g; Sodium 270mg.

Crispy Seven-spice Aubergines

Seven-spice powder is the key ingredient that gives these aubergines a lovely warm flavour, perfect for a summer garden party – or enjoy them cold on a picnic.

Serves 4

2 egg whites
90ml/6 tbsp cornflour (cornstarch)
5ml/1 tsp salt
15ml/1 tbsp Thai or Chinese seven-spice powder
15ml/1 tbsp mild chilli powder
sunflower oil, for deep-frying
500g/1¼lb aubergines (eggplants), thinly sliced
fresh mint leaves, to garnish
steamed rice or noodles and hot chilli sauce, to serve

1 Put the egg whites in a large grease-free bowl and beat them with an electric whisk until light and foamy, but not dry.

2 In a separate bowl, combine the cornflour, salt, seven-spice powder and chilli powder using a fork. Spread this spice mixture evenly on to a large plate.

3 Fill a wok one-third full of sunflower oil and heat to 180°C/350°F or until a cube of day-old bread, dropped into the oil, browns in about 40 seconds.

4 Dip the aubergine slices in the egg white and then into the spiced flour mixture to coat. Deep-fry, in batches, for 3–4 minutes, or until crisp and golden.

5 Drain the slices on kitchen paper and transfer to a platter to keep hot, while you cook the remaining slices.

6 Serve the aubergines on a large, warmed serving platter, garnished with mint leaves and with hot chilli sauce for dipping.

Cook's Tip
Seven-spice powder is a commercial blend of spices, widely available in Asian markets. It usually comprises coriander, cumin, cinnamon, star anise, chilli, cloves and lemon peel.

Spring Vegetable Stir-fry

Fast, fresh and packed with healthy vegetables, this stir-fry is delicious served with marinated tofu and rice or noodles. This recipe contains very little saturated fat, so scores highly with slimmers, but has sufficient bulk to ward off hunger. Ideal as a quick supper on the go.

Serves 4

2 spring onions (scallions)
175g/6oz spring greens or collard greens
15ml/1 tbsp vegetable oil
5ml/1 tsp toasted sesame oil
1 garlic clove, chopped
2.5cm/1in piece fresh root ginger, finely chopped
225g/8oz baby carrots
350g/12oz broccoli florets
175g/6oz asparagus tips
30ml/2 tbsp light soy sauce
15ml/1 tbsp apple juice
15ml/1 tbsp sesame seeds, toasted

1 Trim the spring onions top and bottom, and cut them diagonally into thin slices, using a sharp knife.

2 Wash the spring greens or collard greens and drain in a colander, then blot with kitchen paper and shred finely.

3 Heat a large wok or frying pan over high heat. Add the vegetable oil and the sesame oil, and reduce the heat to medium. Add the garlic and sauté for 2 minutes. Do not let the garlic burn or it will gain a bitter taste.

4 Add the chopped ginger, carrots, broccoli and asparagus tips to the pan and stir-fry for 4 minutes.

5 Add the spring onions and spring greens or collard greens and stir-fry for a further 2 minutes.

6 Add the soy sauce and apple juice and cook for 1–2 minutes until the vegetables are tender. If they appear too dry, simply add a little water to soften them up.

7 Tip the mixture into warmed serving bowls or four individual dishes, sprinkle the sesame seeds on top and serve.

Crispy Seven-spice Aubergines Energy 203Kcal/850kJ; Protein 2.7g; Carbohydrate 23.5g, of which sugars 2.5g; Fat 11.7g, of which saturates 1.4g; Cholesterol 0mg; Calcium 17mg; Fibre 2.5g; Sodium 45mg.
Spring Vegetable Stir-fry Energy 134kcal/554kJ; Protein 7.8g; Carbohydrate 9.4g, of which sugars 8.6g; Fat 7.4g, of which saturates 1.1g; Cholesterol 0mg; Calcium 195mg; Fibre 6.2g; Sodium 566mg.

Bamboo Shoot Salad

This hot, sharp-flavoured salad is the perfect foil for rich roast duck or pork.

Serves 4

400g/14oz canned bamboo shoots, in large pieces
25g/1oz/about 3 tbsp glutinous rice
30ml/2 tbsp shallots, chopped
15ml/1 tbsp garlic, chopped
45ml/3 tbsp spring onions (scallions), chopped
30ml/2 tbsp fish sauce
30ml/2 tbsp fresh lime juice
5ml/1 tsp sugar
2.5ml/½ tsp dried chilli flakes
20–25 small fresh mint leaves
15ml/1 tbsp toasted sesame seeds

1 Drain the canned bamboo shoots using a sieve (strainer), rinse them under cold running water, then drain again and pat thoroughly dry with kitchen paper. Set aside.

2 Dry-roast the rice in a wok or frying pan until it is golden brown. Leave to cool slightly, then tip into a mortar and grind them to fine crumbs with a pestle.

3 Transfer the rice to a bowl and add the shallots, garlic, spring onions, fish sauce, lime juice, sugar, chillies and half the mint leaves.

4 Add the bamboo shoots to the serving bowl and toss with the other ingredients to mix. Serve sprinkled with the toasted sesame seeds and the remaining mint leaves.

Variation
Use canned whole bamboo shoots, if you can get hold of them – they have more flavour than sliced ones. Even better are fresh bamboo shoots, which are sometimes available in Asian supermarkets or in the specialist section of gourmet stores.

Cook's Tip
Despite the name, glutinous rice does not, in fact, contain any gluten – it's just sticky.

Dry-cooked Green Beans

A particular style of Szechuan cooking is 'dry cooking', which means that no stock or water is involved. The slim green beans, available all year round from supermarkets, are ideal for use in this quick and tasty recipe, but, as with all of these versatile vegetable dishes, there are worthy substitutes.

Serves 6

175ml/6fl oz/¾ cup vegetable or sunflower oil
450/1lb fresh green beans, topped, tailed and cut in half
5 x 1cm/2 x ½in piece fresh root ginger, peeled and cut into matchsticks
5ml/1 tsp sugar
10ml/2 tsp light soy sauce
salt and ground black pepper

1 Heat the oil in a wok. When the oil is just beginning to smoke, carefully add the beans and stir-fry them for 1–2 minutes until just tender.

2 Using a slotted spoon, lift the green beans out of the oil and on to a plate lined with kitchen paper.

3 Using a ladle, carefully remove all but 30ml/2 tbsp oil from the wok. The excess oil will play no further part in this recipe, so it should be allowed to cool completely before it is strained and bottled for future use.

4 Reheat the remaining 30ml/2 tbsp oil in the wok, add the ginger and stir-fry for a minute or two to flavour the oil.

5 Return the green beans to the wok, stir in the sugar, soy sauce and salt and pepper, and toss all together quickly to ensure the beans are well coated. Tip the beans into a large heated bowl and serve immediately.

Variation
Fresh green beans are available for most of the year now, but this simple recipe works just as well with other more seasonal vegetables such as baby asparagus spears or okra.

Bamboo Shoot Salad Energy 72kcal/305kJ; Protein 3.9g; Carbohydrate 13g, of which sugars 6.2g; Fat 0.7g, of which saturates 0.1g; Cholesterol 0mg; Calcium 31mg; Fibre 1.9g; Sodium 185mg.
Dry-cooked Beans Energy 223kcal/917kJ; Protein 1.4g; Carbohydrate 3.1g, of which sugars 2.4g; Fat 22.9g, of which saturates 2.8g; Cholesterol 0mg; Calcium 27mg; Fibre 1.7g; Sodium 0mg.

Green Beans with Ginger

This is a simple way of infusing interesting new flavours into green beans. The dish can be served hot or cold and, accompanied by an omelette and some crusty bread, makes a perfect light lunch or supper.

Serves 4
450g/1lb/3 cups green beans
15ml/1 tbsp olive oil
5ml/1 tsp sesame oil
2 garlic cloves, crushed
2.5cm/1in piece fresh root ginger, finely chopped
30ml/2 tbsp dark soy sauce

1 Steam the beans over a pan of boiling salted water, or in an electric steamer, for 4 minutes or until just tender.

2 Meanwhile, heat the olive oil and sesame oil in a wok or a heavy pan. Swirl the oil around the pan. Add the crushed garlic and sauté for 2 minutes.

3 Stir in the ginger and soy sauce and cook, stirring constantly, for a further 2–3 minutes until the liquid has reduced, then pour this mixture over the warm beans.

4 Leave the beans for a few minutes to allow all the flavours to absorb and mingle, then toss the beans several times before tipping into a bowl.

Variation
Substitute other green beans, if you wish. Runner beans and other flat varieties should be cut diagonally into thick slices before steaming. Try to use fresh green beans that are in season since they will always have an improved flavour.

Cook's Tip
Sesame oil has a delicious, nutty taste and is valued more for its flavour than as a cooking medium. It burns easily, so if you do use it for frying, mix it with other more durable oils such as the olive oil used in this recipe.

Sautéed Green Beans

The smoky flavour of the dried shrimps used in this recipe adds an extra dimension to green beans when cooked in this way.

Serves 4
450g/1lb green beans
15ml/1 tbsp vegetable oil
3 garlic cloves, finely chopped
5 spring onions (scallions), cut into 2.5cm/1in lengths
25g/1oz dried shrimps, soaked in warm water and drained
15ml/1 tbsp light soy sauce
salt

1 Trim the green beans. Cut each green bean in half.

2 Bring a pan of lightly salted water to the boil and cook the beans for 3–4 minutes until tender but still crisp. Drain, refresh under cold water and drain again.

3 Heat the oil in a non-stick frying pan or wok until very hot. Stir-fry the garlic and spring onions for 30 seconds, then add the shrimps. Mix lightly.

4 Add the green beans and soy sauce. Toss the mixture over the heat until the beans are hot. Serve immediately.

Variations
- *For more colour and textural contrasts, stir-fry sliced red, yellow or orange (bell) peppers in the wok and cook for a few minutes until just tender but still crunchy. Add the garlic and spring onions, and proceed as above.*
- *For a vegetarian dish, omit the dried shrimps and replace the king prawns with cubes of deep-fried tofu.*

Cook's Tip
Don't be tempted to use too many dried shrimps in this dish. Their flavour is very strong and could overwhelm the more delicate taste of the green beans.

Green Beans with Ginger Energy 64kcal/265kJ; Protein 2.6g; Carbohydrate 4.6g, of which sugars 3.2g; Fat 4.1g, of which saturates 0.6g; Cholesterol 0mg; Calcium 42mg; Fibre 2.6g; Sodium 534mg.
Sautéed Green Beans Energy 62kcal/254kJ; Protein 2.4g; Carbohydrate 4.2g, of which sugars 3.1g; Fat 4.1g, of which saturates 0.6g; Cholesterol 0mg; Calcium 42mg; Fibre 2.5g; Sodium 534mg.

Thai Asparagus with Ginger and Chilli

This recipe has an intriguingly different way of cooking asparagus. The crunchy texture is retained and the flavour is complemented by the use of galangal and chilli.

Serves 4

350g/12oz asparagus spears
30ml/2 tbsp vegetable oil
1 garlic clove, crushed
15ml/1 tbsp sesame seeds, toasted
2.5cm/1in piece fresh galangal, finely shredded
1 fresh red chilli, seeded and finely chopped
15ml/1 tbsp Thai fish sauce
15ml/1 tbsp light soy sauce
45ml/3 tbsp water
5ml/1 tsp palm sugar (jaggery) or light muscovado (brown) sugar

1 Snap the asparagus spears. They will break naturally at the junction between the woody base and the more tender upper portion of the stalk. Discard the woody parts of the stems.

2 Heat the oil in a wok and stir-fry the garlic, sesame seeds and galangal for 3–4 seconds. Do not allow to brown but cook until the garlic is just beginning to turn golden.

3 Add the asparagus spears and the finely chopped chilli to the pan. Cook for 1 minute, stirring constantly, then add the fish sauce, soy sauce, water and sugar.

4 Using two spoons or a couple of spatulas, toss over the heat for a further 2 minutes, or until the asparagus just begins to soften and the liquid is reduced by about half.

5 Carefully transfer the asparagus to a warmed serving dish and serve immediately with the ginger and chilli sauce.

Variation
This recipe is equally delicious if you use broccoli or pak choi (bok choy) in place of the asparagus. The sauce also works well with green beans.

Asparagus with Crispy Noodles

An easily prepared dish of tender asparagus spears tossed with sesame seeds and served on a bed of crispy, deep-fried noodles works for casual entertaining or for a light mid-week supper. The lightly cooked asparagus retains all its fresh flavour and bite and contrasts wonderfully with the noodles.

Serves 4

15ml/1 tbsp sunflower oil
350g/12oz thin asparagus spears
5ml/1 tsp salt
5ml/1 tsp freshly ground black pepper
5ml/1 tsp golden caster (superfine) sugar
30ml/2 tbsp Chinese cooking wine
45ml/3 tbsp light soy sauce
60ml/4 tbsp oyster sauce
10ml/2 tsp sesame oil
60ml/4 tbsp toasted sesame seeds, to garnish

For the noodles
50g/2oz dried cellophane noodles or thin rice vermicelli
sunflower oil, for deep-frying

1 First make the crispy noodles. Fill a wok or large, heavy pan one-third full of sunflower oil and heat the oil to 180°C/350°F or until a cube of bread dropped into the oil browns in 45 seconds. Using a slotted spoon, add a small bunch of noodles to the oil; they will crisp and puff up in seconds.

2 Using a slotted spoon, remove the first batch of crispy noodles from the wok and drain on kitchen paper. Set aside. Cook the remaining noodles in the same way.

3 Heat a clean wok or heavy pan over a high heat and add the sunflower oil. Add the asparagus and stir-fry for 3 minutes.

4 Add the salt, pepper, sugar, wine and both sauces to the wok or pan and stir-fry for 2–3 minutes.

5 Add the sesame oil, toss to combine and remove from the heat.

6 To serve, divide the crispy noodles between 4 warmed plates or bowls and top with the asparagus and juices. Scatter over the toasted sesame seeds and serve immediately.

Thai Asparagus Energy 120kcal/492kJ; Protein 4.1g; Carbohydrate 2.4g, of which sugars 2.3g; Fat 10.4g, of which saturates 1.4g; Cholesterol 0mg; Calcium 75mg; Fibre 2.1g; Sodium 537mg.
Asparagus with Crispy Noodles Energy 131kcal/547kJ; Protein 4.6g; Carbohydrate 16.5g, of which sugars 6.9g; Fat 5.6g, of which saturates 0.6g; Cholesterol 0mg; Calcium 31mg; Fibre 2g; Sodium 1047mg.

Tofu and Cucumber Salad

This refreshing salad with its hot, sweet-and-sour dressing is ideal for buffets.

Serves 4–6

1 small cucumber
115g/4oz square tofu
oil, for frying
115g/4oz/½ cup beansprouts
salt
celery leaves, to garnish

For the dressing

1 small onion, grated (shredded)
2 garlic cloves, crushed
5–7.5ml/1–1½ tsp chilli sauce
30–45ml/2–3 tbsp dark soy sauce
15–30ml/1–2 tbsp rice wine vinegar
10ml/2 tsp dark brown sugar

1 Cut the cucumber into neat cubes. Place the cucumber in a colander and sprinkle with salt to extract excess liquid. Put the colander over a bowl and leave to drain for 1 hour, while you prepare the remaining ingredients.

2 Cut the tofu into cubes. Heat a little oil in a wok and fry the tofu on both sides until golden brown. Drain on kitchen paper.

3 To make the dressing, place the onion, garlic and chilli sauce in a screw-top jar. Close the jar tightly, then shake vigorously to mix. Add the soy sauce, vinegar and sugar with salt to taste. Shake the jar again until the ingredients are well combined.

4 Just before serving, rinse the cucumber under cold running water. Drain and thoroughly pat dry with kitchen paper.

5 Toss the cucumber, tofu and beansprouts together in a serving bowl and pour over the dressing. Garnish with celery leaves and serve the salad immediately.

Cook's Tip

Tofu is made from soya beans and is a good source of protein for vegetarians. It is bland tasting so needs a flavourful dressing or the addition of dark soy sauce, chopped chilli or root ginger. Tofu has a creamy texture, yet it is firm enough to slice well.

Soya Beansprout Salad with a Sweet Sesame Dressing

High in protein and fat, soya beansprouts are nutritious and good to eat, and are classic ingredients in Cambodian meals. Unlike mung beansprouts, they are slightly poisonous when raw and need to be parboiled before use, though this only takes a minute. This salad is eaten with noodles and rice.

Serves 4

450g/1lb/2 cups fresh soya beansprouts
2 spring onions (scallions), finely sliced
1 small bunch fresh coriander (cilantro), stalks removed

For the dressing

30ml/2 tbsp tuk trey (fish sauce)
15ml/1 tbsp white rice vinegar
10ml/2 tsp palm sugar (jaggery) or soft dark brown sugar.
15ml/1 tbsp sesame oil
1 red chilli, seeded and finely sliced
15g/½oz fresh young root ginger, finely shredded

1 First make the sweet sesame dressing. In a bowl, beat the oil, tuk trey and rice vinegar with the sugar, until it dissolves. Stir in the chilli and ginger and leave to stand for 30 minutes to allow the flavours to develop.

2 Bring a large pan of salted water to the boil. Drop in the beansprouts and blanch for 1 minute only.

3 Tip the beansprouts into a colander, drain, then refresh them under running cold water until they are cool. Drain again and put them into a clean dish towel. Shake out the excess water.

4 Put the beansprouts and spring onions into a serving bowl.

5 Pour over the dressing, toss, garnish with coriander and serve.

Variation

Any other edible sprouted bean or pea, such as pea shoots or mung bean sprouts, can be used instead of the beansprouts.

Tofu and Cucumber Salad Energy 52kcal/215kJ; Protein 2.6g; Carbohydrate 4.3g, of which sugars 3.6g; Fat 2.8g, of which saturates 0.3g; Cholesterol 0mg; Calcium 109mg; Fibre 0.5g; Sodium 537mg
Soya Beansprout Salad Energy 95kcal/396kJ; Protein 4.5g; Carbohydrate 8.4g, of which sugars 5.6g; Fat 5.6g, of which saturates 0.5g; Cholesterol 3mg; Calcium 54mg; Fibre 2.4g; Sodium 79mg.

Noodle, Tofu and Beansprout Salad

Cellophane or bean thread noodles look like spun glass on this stunning salad, which owes its goodness to fresh beansprouts, diced tomato and cucumber in a sweet-sour dressing.

Serves 4

25g/1oz cellophane noodles
500g/1¼lb mixed sprouted beans and pulses (aduki, chickpea, mung, red lentil)
4 spring onions (scallions), finely shredded
115g/4oz firm tofu, diced
1 ripe plum tomato, seeded and diced
½ cucumber, peeled, seeded and diced
60ml/4 tbsp chopped fresh coriander (cilantro)
45ml/3 tbsp chopped fresh mint
60ml/4 tbsp rice vinegar
10ml/2 tsp caster sugar
10ml/2 tsp sesame oil
5ml/1 tsp chilli oil
salt and ground black pepper

1 Place the noodles in a bowl and pour over enough boiling water to immerse them. Cover and soak for 12–15 minutes.

2 Drain the noodles and then refresh them under cold running water and drain again. Using a pair of scissors, cut the noodles into roughly 7.5cm/3in lengths and transfer to a bowl.

3 Fill a wok or large, heavy pan one-third full of boiling water and place over high heat. Add the sprouted beans and pulses and blanch the mixture for 1 minute.

4 Drain, transfer to the noodle bowl and add the spring onions, tofu, tomato, cucumber and herbs.

5 Combine the rice vinegar, sugar, sesame oil and chilli oil in a small bowl and toss into the noodle mixture. Transfer to a serving dish and chill for 30 minutes before serving.

Cook's Tip
If you leave the salad to stand for half an hour to an hour, the flavours will improve as they develop, and fuse together.

Cabbage Salad

This is a simple and delicious way of serving a somewhat mundane vegetable. A wok comes in handy for stir-frying the aromatic vegetables.

Serves 4–6

30ml/2 tbsp vegetable oil
2 large fresh red chillies, seeded and cut into thin strips
6 garlic cloves, thinly sliced
6 shallots, thinly sliced
1 small cabbage, shredded
30ml/2 tbsp coarsely chopped roasted peanuts, to garnish

For the dressing
30ml/2 tbsp fish sauce
grated rind of 1 lime
30ml/2 tbsp fresh lime juice
120ml/4fl oz/½ cup coconut milk

1 Make the dressing by mixing the fish sauce, lime rind, lime juice and coconut milk in a bowl. Whisk until they are thoroughly combined, then set aside.

2 Heat the oil in a wok. Stir-fry the chillies, garlic and shallots over a medium heat for 3–4 minutes, until the shallots are brown and crisp. Remove with a slotted spoon and set aside.

3 Bring a large pan of lightly salted water to the boil. Add the shredded cabbage and blanch for 2–3 minutes. Tip it into a colander, drain well and put into a bowl.

4 Whisk the dressing again, add it to the warm cabbage and toss to combine. Transfer the salad to a serving dish.

5 Just before serving, sprinkle with the fried shallot mixture and garnish with the chopped peanuts.

Variations
- *Other vegetables, such as cauliflower, broccoli and Chinese leaves (Chinese cabbage), can be cooked in this way.*
- *As a healthier option, use low-fat or light coconut milk if you prefer. You can create your own lighter version by using equal parts full-cream coconut milk and distilled water.*

Noodle Salad Energy 126kcal/528kJ; Protein 7.2g; Carbohydrate 14.8g, of which sugars 7.2g; Fat 4.4g, of which saturates 0.6g; Cholesterol 0mg; Calcium 209mg; Fibre 3.1g; Sodium 17mg.
Cabbage Salad Energy 96kcal/400kJ; Protein 2.7g; Carbohydrate 7.7g, of which sugars 6.6g; Fat 6.2g, of which saturates 0.9g; Cholesterol 0mg; Calcium 50mg; Fibre 2.2g; Sodium 147mg.

Hot Lettuce with Conpoy Sauce

Chinese cooks rarely eat vegetables raw, even when using the most tender salad-type greens. Stir-frying them with aromatics like garlic and ginger is popular, and a liquid is often added toward the end of cooking to soften the ingredients slightly and provide a tasty sauce.

Serves 4

4 pieces conpoy (see Cook's Tip)
200ml/7fl oz/scant 1 cup warm water
2 heads cos or romaine lettuce
15ml/1 tbsp vegetable oil
15ml/1 tbsp chopped fresh root ginger
2 garlic cloves, chopped
30ml/2 tbsp Chinese wine

1 Put the pieces of conpoy in a small glass bowl and pour over the warm water. Soak for 2–3 hours until soft.

2 Meanwhile, shred the lettuce, discarding the core, put in a colander and rinse it under cold water. Drain well, then dry the lettuce thoroughly in a clean dish towel.

3 Drain the conpoy, reserving the soaking liquid. Use a sharp knife to shred the pieces finely.

4 Heat the vegetable oil in a wok and fry the ginger and garlic for 40 seconds, until light brown. Add the lettuce and stir-fry over high heat for 1 minute.

5 Add the conpoy, with the reserved soaking liquid, to the wok. Bring to a quick simmer, stirring constantly, for 2 minutes. Tip into a serving dish and serve immediately.

Cook's Tip

Conpoy is an expensive shellfish closely related to the sea scallop. It is produced by cooking raw scallops and then drying them. It is only available dried and is used as a master seasoning in a variety of dishes, including a version of the humble congee. If you do not have time to soak it as described in the recipe, soften it by heating it in the measured water in a microwave set to high for 1 minute.

Cabbage Curry

Called kobis lemak (lemak applies to all dishes cooked with coconut milk, and implies an intrinsic richness only this ingredient can give), this is a simple dish with peasant origins. It is cooked with blends of spices depending on the region: in Sumatra it is subtle, while in Bali it can be very fiery. Use the Balinese spice paste bese gade, or shallot and lemon grass sambal (sambal matah) depending on your taste.

Serves 4

1 whole cabbage
350ml/12fl oz/scant 1½ cups coconut milk
5ml/1 tsp salt
2.5ml/½ tsp sugar
3 salam leaves (Indonesian bay leaves)

For the sambal

2.5ml/½ tsp terasi
1 black peppercorn, crushed
5 shallots, thinly sliced
2 garlic cloves, sliced
2 lime leaves, shredded
3 fresh red chillies, thinly sliced
1 lemon grass stalk, 2cm/¾in of root end very finely sliced
2.5ml/½ tsp salt
15ml/1 tbsp lime juice
2.5ml/½ tsp sugar
25ml/1½ tbsp vegetable or sunflower oil

1 Begin by making the shallot and lemongrass sambal. Toast the terasi briefly over a live flame.

2 Combine all the ingredients except the oil in a mixing bowl and blend well. Heat the oil and fry the sambal over a low heat for 8–10 minutes until the oil seeps out again.

3 Cut the cabbage into small pieces, removing the tough core, then blanch in boiling water for 2 minutes.

4 Combine the remaining ingredients in a wok and bring to the boil. Add the cabbage and simmer for 15 minutes.

Cook's Tip

For added bulk, take a square of firm tofu cut into triangles and add the pieces in the last 5 minutes of cooking.

Hot Lettuce Energy 131kcal/549kJ; Protein 12.4g; Carbohydrate 3.5g, of which sugars 1.8g; Fat 6.7g, of which saturates 1g; Cholesterol 24mg; Calcium 43mg; Fibre 0.9g; Sodium 94mg.
Cabbage Curry Energy 97kcal/406kJ; Protein 3.9g; Carbohydrate 17.9g, of which sugars 17.5g; Fat 1.3g, of which saturates 0.3g; Cholesterol 1mg; Calcium 151mg; Fibre 5.3g; Sodium 629mg.

Cabbage in Coconut Milk

The idea of cooking cabbage in coconut milk comes from Melaka and Johor, where the culinary culture is influenced by the Chinese, Malay, and Peranakan Chinese. With good agricultural ground, there is an abundance of vegetables which, in this part of Malaysia, are often cooked in coconut milk. For this dish, you could use green beans, curly kale, or any type of cabbage, all of which are delicious served with steamed, braised or grilled fish dishes.

Serves 4

4 shallots, chopped
2 garlic cloves, chopped
1 lemon grass stalk, trimmed and chopped
25g/1oz fresh root ginger, peeled and chopped
2 red chillies, seeded and chopped
5ml/1 tsp shrimp paste
5ml/1 tsp turmeric powder
5ml/1 tsp palm sugar (jaggery)
15ml/1 tbsp sesame or groundnut (peanut) oil
400ml/14fl oz/1⅔ cups coconut milk
450g/1lb Chinese leaves (Chinese cabbage) or kale, cut into thick ribbons, or pak choi (bok choy), separated into leaves, or a mixture of the two
salt and ground black pepper

1 Using a mortar and pestle or food processor, grind the shallots, garlic, lemon grass, ginger and chillies to a paste.

2 Scrape into a bowl and add the shrimp paste, turmeric and sugar. Beat well to combine the ingredients.

3 Heat the oil in a wok or heavy pan, and stir in the spice paste. Cook until fragrant and beginning to colour.

4 Add the coconut milk to the pan, mix it well, and let it bubble it up to thicken.

5 Drop in the cabbage leaves, coating them in the coconut milk, and cook for a minute or two until wilted.

6 Season with salt and pepper to taste, spoon into a warmed serving dish and serve immediately.

Florets Polonaise

Spring vegetables become something very special with this pretty egg topping.

Serves 6

500g/1¼lb mixed vegetables, such as cauliflower, broccoli, romanesco and calabrese
50g/2oz/¼ cup butter
finely grated rind of ½ lemon
1 large garlic clove, crushed
25g/1oz/½ cup fresh breadcrumbs, lightly baked or grilled (broiled) until crisp
2 eggs, hard-boiled
sea salt and ground black pepper

1 Trim the vegetables and break into florets. Place in a steamer over a wok or pan of boiling water for 5–7 minutes, until just tender. Toss in butter or oil and transfer to a serving dish.

2 Meanwhile, combine the lemon rind, garlic, seasoning and breadcrumbs. Finely chop the eggs and mix with the remaining ingredients. Sprinkle the mixture over the vegetables and serve.

Stir-fried Spring Greens

Garlic enhances the slightly bitter flavour of spring greens, and they taste great with bacon and chillies.

Serves 6

450g/1lb spring greens (collards)
15ml/1 tbsp vegetable oil
150g/5oz smoked streaky (fatty) bacon, in one piece
2 garlic cloves, crushed
1.5ml/¼ tsp crushed dried chillies
salt

1 Cut off the stalks from the greens. Lay the leaves flat on top of each other and roll into a cigar shape and slice very thinly. Heat the oil in a wok or frying pan. Cut the bacon into small cubes and sauté gently in the oil for 5 minutes, or until golden brown. Lift out with a slotted spoon and drain on kitchen paper.

2 Increase the heat, add the crushed garlic and dried chillies to the oil remaining in the pan, and stir-fry for 30 seconds. Add the spring greens and toss until just tender. Season to taste with salt, stir in the bacon cubes and serve immediately.

Cabbage in Coconut Energy 112kcal/469kJ; Protein 2.1g; Carbohydrate 13g, of which sugars 12.6g; Fat 6.1g, of which saturates 1g; Cholesterol 0mg; Calcium 89mg; Fibre 2.6g; Sodium 119mg.
Florets Polonaise Energy 71kcal/297kJ; Protein 5.2g; Carbohydrate 4.7g, of which sugars 1.4g; Fat 3.6g, of which saturates 0.7g; Cholesterol 32mg; Calcium 57mg; Fibre 2.3g; Sodium 50mg.
Stir-fried Greens Energy 106kcal/438kJ; Protein 5g; Carbohydrate 3.8g, of which sugars 3.7g; Fat 7.9g, of which saturates 2.2g; Cholesterol 16mg; Calcium 38mg; Fibre 1.6g; Sodium 320mg.

Stir-fried Spinach with Pine Nuts

There are endless versions of spinach and yogurt meze dishes, ranging from plain spinach served with yogurt, to this sweet and tangy Anatolian creation tamed with garlic-flavoured yogurt. Serve while still warm, with flatbread or a crusty loaf.

Serves 3–4

350g/12oz fresh spinach leaves, thoroughly washed and drained
about 200g/7oz/scant 1 cup thick and natural (plain) yogurt
2 garlic cloves, crushed
30–45ml/2–3 tbsp olive oil
1 red onion, cut in half lengthways, in half again crossways, and sliced along the grain
5ml/1 tsp sugar
15–30ml/1–2 tbsp currants, soaked in warm water for 5–10 minutes and drained
30ml/2 tbsp pine nuts
5–10ml/1–2 tsp Turkish red pepper, or 1 fresh red chilli, seeded and finely chopped
juice of 1 lemon
salt and ground black pepper
a pinch of paprika, to garnish

1 Steam the spinach for 3–4 minutes, until wilted and soft. Drain off any excess water and chop the spinach.

2 In a bowl, beat the yogurt with the garlic. Season to taste.

3 Heat the oil in a wok and fry the onion and sugar, stirring, until the onion begins to colour. Add the currants, pine nuts and red pepper or chilli and fry until the nuts begin to darken slightly.

4 Add the spinach, tossing it around the wok until well mixed, then pour in the lemon juice and season with salt and pepper.

5 Serve the spinach straight from the wok with the yogurt spooned on top, or tip into a serving dish and spoon the yogurt into a well in the middle, drizzling some of it over the spinach. Serve hot, garnished with a sprinkling of paprika.

Cook's Tip
Pine nuts go rancid very quickly, so store them in an airtight container in the refrigerator and use them within three months.

Spinach with Mushrooms

A tasty vegetable that is often overlooked, spinach is highly nutritious. Cooked in this way it tastes wonderful. Serve with chapatis.

Serves 4

450g/1lb fresh or frozen spinach, thawed
30ml/2 tbsp oil
2 medium onions, diced
6–8 curry leaves
1.5ml/¼ tsp onion seeds
5ml/1 tsp crushed garlic
5ml/1 tsp grated fresh root ginger
5ml/1 tsp chilli powder
5ml/1 tsp salt
7.5ml/1½ tsp ground coriander
1 large red (bell) pepper, seeded and sliced
115g/4oz/1½ cups mushrooms, roughly chopped
225g/8oz/1 cup low-fat fromage frais or ricotta cheese
30ml/2 tbsp fresh coriander (cilantro) leaves

1 If using fresh spinach, blanch it briefly in boiling water and drain thoroughly. If using frozen spinach, drain well. Set aside.

2 Heat the oil in a karahi, wok or heavy pan and fry the onions with the curry leaves and the onion seeds for 1–2 minutes. Add the garlic, ginger, chilli powder, salt and ground coriander. Stir-fry for a further 2–3 minutes.

3 Add half the red pepper slices and all the mushrooms and continue to stir-fry for 2–3 minutes.

4 Add the spinach and stir-fry for 4–6 minutes, then add the fromage frais or ricotta and half the fresh coriander, followed by the remaining red pepper slices. Stir-fry for a further 2–3 minutes before serving straight from the pan or in a warmed serving dish, garnished with the remaining coriander.

Cook's Tip
Whether you use fresh or frozen spinach, make sure it is well drained, otherwise the stir-fried mixture will be too wet when you add the fromage frais or ricotta. Tip the spinach into a colander, and press it against the sides of the colander with a wooden spoon to extract as much liquid as possible.

Stir-fried Spinach Energy 145kcal/603kJ; Protein 5.8g; Carbohydrate 10.2g, of which sugars 9.8g; Fat 9.3g, of which saturates 1.3g; Cholesterol 1mg; Calcium 252mg; Fibre 2.2g; Sodium 165mg.
Spinach with Mushrooms Energy 225kcal/945kJ; Protein 7.1g; Carbohydrate 14.4g, of which sugars 7.3g; Fat 16.4g, of which saturates 2.4g; Cholesterol 3mg; Calcium 19mg; Fibre 3.2g; Sodium 1559mg.

Stir-fried Chinese Leaves

This simple way of cooking Chinese leaves preserves their delicate flavour and is very quick to prepare. Chinese leaves have pale, tightly wrapped, succulent leaves with crisp, broad, white ribs and a delicate, mild, sweet flavour. There are two basic types of Chinese leaves – firm-headed and loose-headed.

Serves 4

675g/1½lb Chinese leaves (Chinese cabbage)
15ml/1 tbsp vegetable oil
2 garlic cloves, finely chopped
2.5cm/1in piece of fresh root ginger, finely chopped
2.5ml/½ tsp salt
15ml/1 tbsp oyster sauce
4 spring onions (scallions), cut into 2.5cm/1in lengths

1 Stack the Chinese leaves together and cut them into 2.5cm/1in slices, discarding the ends.

2 Heat the oil in a wok or large deep pan. Stir-fry the garlic and ginger for 1 minute.

3 Add the Chinese leaves to the wok or pan and stir-fry for 2 minutes. Sprinkle the salt over and drizzle with the oyster sauce. Toss the leaves over the heat for 2 minutes more.

4 Stir in the spring onions. Toss the mixture well, transfer it to a heated serving plate and serve.

Variation

Use the same treatment for shredded cabbage and leeks. If you want to cut down on preparation time, you can often find this combination of vegetables ready-prepared at supermarkets.

Cook's Tip

For guests who are vegetarian, substitute 15 ml/1 tbsp light soy sauce and 5ml/1 tsp of caster (superfine) sugar for the oyster sauce. This rule can be applied to many dishes.

Braised Chinese Leaves

Chinese leaves, also known as Chinese cabbage, taste delicious in a salad or stir-fry and need little seasoning apart from soy sauce as they have a natural, sweet flavour. This dish is somewhat soupy, since the leaves contribute extra liquid. It is often served with rice porridge or congee, and keeps well.

Serves 4–6

1 head Chinese leaves (Chinese cabbage)
30ml/2 tbsp sesame oil
300ml/½ pint/1¼ cups water
5ml/1 tsp ground black pepper
30ml/2 tbsp light soy sauce

1 To prepare the Chinese leaves, cut off the base, rinse the leaves under cold running water and dry them thoroughly. Cut across the leaves and stalk or slice lengthways into strips, then cut in 2.5cm/1in slices and place in a colander. Rinse under cold water, then drain thoroughly.

2 Mix the oil, water, black pepper and soy sauce in a wok. Bring to simmering point, add the Chinese leaves and braise for 15 minutes. Spoon into a heated dish and serve immediately.

Variation

For an even fresher taste, steam the Chinese leaves and then toss the leaves with the other ingredients before serving.

Cook's Tips

- *Don't confuse Chinese leaves with bok choy, which has thick white stems topped by glossy green leaves.*
- *Chinese leaves are available all year round, look for fresh, firm heads that feel heavy for their size. Tiny black flecks on the leaves are harmless. Reject heads that look wilted or bruised.*
- *Chinese leaves will keep well for a few weeks. Store unwashed in a plastic bag in the salad drawer of the refrigerator.*

Stir-fried Chinese Leaves Energy 77kcal/321kJ; Protein 2.6g; Carbohydrate 9.8g, of which sugars 9.6g; Fat 3.2g, of which saturates 0.3g; Cholesterol 0mg; Calcium 87mg; Fibre 3.7g; Sodium 74mg.
Braised Chinese Leaves Energy 58kcal/239kJ; Protein 1.3g; Carbohydrate 4.6g, of which sugars 4.5g; Fat 3.8g, of which saturates 0.5g; Cholesterol 0mg; Calcium 42mg; Fibre 1.8g; Sodium 362mg.

Spiced Coconut Mushrooms

Here is a simple and delicious way to cook mushrooms. They can be served with almost any Indian meal as well as with traditional Western grilled or roasted meats and poultry.

Serves 4

30ml/2 tbsp groundnut (peanut) oil
2 garlic cloves, finely chopped
2 fresh red chillies, seeded and sliced into rings
3 shallots, finely chopped
225g/8oz/3 cups brown cap (cremini) mushrooms, thickly sliced
150ml/¼ pint/⅔ cup coconut milk
30ml/2 tbsp chopped fresh coriander (cilantro)
salt and ground black pepper

1 Heat a karahi, wok or shallow pan until hot, add the groundnut oil and swirl it around. Add the chopped garlic and sliced chillies, then stir-fry for a few seconds.

2 Add the shallots and stir-fry them for 2–3 minutes until softened. Add the mushrooms and stir-fry for 3 minutes.

3 Add in the coconut milk to the shallots and mushrooms in the pan and bring to the boil, stirring from time to time. Boil rapidly over a high heat until the coconut milk liquid has reduced by about half and coats the mushrooms all over. Season to taste with salt and pepper.

4 Sprinkle over the chopped coriander and toss the mushrooms gently to mix. Serve immediately.

Variations

- *Use chopped fresh chives instead of chopped fresh coriander (cilantro), if you wish.*
- *White (button) mushrooms or field (portobello) mushrooms would also work well instead of brown cap (cremini) mushrooms.*
- *Sprinkle some chopped toasted cashew nuts over the mushrooms before serving, if you like.*

Slow-cooked Shiitake with Shoyu

Shiitake mushrooms cooked slowly are so rich and filling, that some people call them 'vegetarian steak'. This is a useful side dish which also makes a flavoursome addition to other dishes.

Serves 4

20 dried shiitake mushrooms
30ml/2 tbsp vegetable oil
30ml/2 tbsp shoyu
5ml/1 tsp toasted sesame oil

1 Start by soaking the dried shiitake the day before you wish to serve this dish. Put them in a large bowl almost full of water. Cover the shiitake with a plate or lid to stop them floating to the surface of the water. Leave to soak overnight.

2 On the following day, remove the shiitake mushrooms from the soaking water. Gently squeeze out the mushroom water into a bowl with your fingers, reserving the liquid.

3 Measure 120ml/4fl oz/½ cup of the mushroom liquid into a small jug (pitcher), and set aside.

4 Heat the oil in a wok or a large frying pan. Stir-fry the shiitake mushrooms over a high heat for 5 minutes, stirring continuously.

5 Reduce the heat to the lowest setting, then stir in the reserved soaking liquid and the shoyu.

6 Cook the shiitake mushrooms until there is almost no moisture left, stirring frequently. Sprinkle with the toasted sesame oil and remove from the heat.

7 Leave to cool, then slice and arrange the shiitake mushrooms on a large serving platter and serve.

Variation

Cut the slow-cooked shiitake into thin strips. Mix with 600g/1lb 6oz/generous 5 cups cooked brown rice and 15ml/1 tbsp finely chopped chives. Sprinkle with toasted sesame seeds.

Spiced Coconut Mushrooms Energy 76kcal/313kJ; Protein 2g; Carbohydrate 3.4g, of which sugars 3g; Fat 6.1g, of which saturates 0.8g; Cholesterol 0mg; Calcium 26mg; Fibre 0.8g; Sodium 46mg.
Slow Cooked Shiitake Energy 16kcal/69kJ; Protein 2g; Carbohydrate 1g, of which sugars 0.8g; Fat 0.5g, of which saturates 0.1g; Cholesterol 0mg; Calcium 7mg; Fibre 1.1g; Sodium 539mg.

Fragrant Mushrooms in Lettuce Leaf Saucers

This quick and easy vegetable dish looks great served on lettuce leaves, and it means the mushrooms can be scooped up and eaten with the fingers. It's a lovely treat for children, and an attractive canape for parties.

Serves 2

30ml/2 tbsp vegetable oil
2 garlic cloves, finely chopped
2 baby cos or romaine lettuces, or 2 Little Gem (Bibb) lettuces
1 lemon grass stalk, chopped
2 kaffir lime leaves, rolled in cylinders and thinly sliced
200g/7oz/3 cups oyster or chestnut mushrooms, or a mixture of the two, sliced
1 small fresh red chilli, seeded and finely chopped
juice of ½ lemon
30ml/2 tbsp light soy sauce
5ml/1 tsp palm sugar (jaggery) or light muscovado (brown) sugar
small bunch fresh mint, leaves removed from the stalks

1 Heat the vegetable oil in a wok or frying pan. Add the finely chopped garlic to the pan and cook it over a medium heat, stirring occasionally, until golden. Do not let the garlic burn or become brown so this will make it taste bitter.

2 Meanwhile, separate the individual lettuce leaves, discarding the tough stalks. Rinse the leaves well, dry in a salad spinner or blot with kitchen paper, and set them aside.

3 Increase the heat under the wok or pan and add the chopped lemon grass, sliced lime leaves and sliced mushrooms. Stir-fry for about 2 minutes.

4 Add the chilli, lemon juice, soy sauce and sugar to the wok or pan. Toss the mixture over the heat to combine the ingredients together, then stir-fry for a further 2 minutes.

5 Arrange the lettuce leaves on one large or two individual salad plates. Spoon a small amount of the mushroom mixture on to each leaf, top with a mint leaf and serve.

Stir-fried Bamboo Shoots and Chinese Mushrooms

Another name for this dish is 'twin winter vegetables' because both bamboo shoots and mushrooms are at their best during the winter months.

Serves 4

50g/2oz dried Chinese mushrooms
275g/10oz can winter bamboo shoots
45ml/3 tbsp vegetable oil
1 spring onion (scallion), cut into short sections
30ml/2 tbsp light soy sauce or oyster sauce
15ml/1 tbsp Chinese rice wine or dry sherry
2.5ml/½ tsp light brown sugar
5ml/1 tsp cornflour (cornstarch), mixed to a paste with 15ml/1 tbsp cold water
few drops sesame oil

1 Soak the mushrooms in cold water for at least 3 hours, until softened. Drain and squeeze dry, reserving the water. Remove the tough stalks and cut the mushrooms in half or in quarters if they are large – keep them whole if small.

2 Rinse and drain the bamboo shoots. Cut into small, wedge-shaped pieces. Heat the vegetable oil in a wok.

3 Swirl the oil around the wok. Stir-fry the mushrooms and bamboo shoots for about 1 minute. Add the spring onion, soy or oyster sauce, rice wine or sherry and sugar, with about 3 tbsp of the reserved mushroom liquid.

4 Bring everything in the wok to the boil and braise for 1–2 minutes. Stir in the cornflour paste to thicken, add a few drops of sesame oil and serve at once.

Variations
Today dried Chinese mushrooms come in many varieties, and have an uplifting earthy taste and meaty texture. Look out for dried shiitake or oyster mushrooms in specialist delicatessens or Oriental food stores.

Fragrant Mushrooms Energy 145kcal/600kJ; Protein 3.6g; Carbohydrate 5.5g, of which sugars 4g; Fat 12.2g, of which saturates 1.5g; Cholesterol 0mg; Calcium 87mg; Fibre 2g; Sodium 12mg.
Bamboo and Mushrooms Energy 112kcal/465kJ; Protein 2.5g; Carbohydrate 5.4g, of which sugars 2.9g; Fat 8.7g, of which saturates 1.1g; Cholesterol 0mg; Calcium 18mg; Fibre 1.2g; Sodium 539mg.

Hot and Spicy Yam

The yam of the title isn't the vegetable that resembles sweet potato, but is rather a name given to a spicy sauce based on coconut milk and mushrooms. It is easy to make in the wok and tastes really good with steamed greens, beansprouts, beans and broccoli.

Serves 4

90g/3½oz Chinese leaves (Chinese cabbage), shredded
90g/3½oz/scant 2 cups beansprouts
90g/3½oz/scant 1 cup green beans, trimmed
90g/3½oz broccoli, preferably the purple sprouting variety, divided into florets
15ml/1 tbsp sesame seeds, toasted, to garnish

For the yam

60ml/4 tbsp coconut cream
5ml/1 tsp Thai red curry paste
90g/3½oz/1¼ cups oyster mushrooms or field (portabello) mushrooms, sliced
60ml/4 tbsp coconut milk
5ml/1 tsp ground turmeric
5ml/1 tsp thick tamarind juice, made by mixing tamarind paste with warm water
juice of ½ lemon
60ml/4 tbsp light soy sauce
5ml/1 tsp palm sugar or light muscovado (brown) sugar

1 Steam the shredded Chinese leaves, beansprouts, green beans and broccoli separately or blanch in boiling water for 1 minute per batch. Drain, place in a serving bowl and leave to cool.

2 Make the yam. Pour the coconut cream into a wok or frying pan and heat gently for 2–3 minutes, until it separates. Stir in the red curry paste. Cook over a low heat for 30 seconds.

3 Increase the heat to high and add the mushrooms to the wok or pan. Cook for a further 2–3 minutes.

4 Pour in the coconut milk and add the ground turmeric, tamarind juice, lemon juice, soy sauce and sugar to the wok or pan. Mix it altogether thoroughly.

5 Pour the yam mixture over the prepared in the serving bowl and toss well so they are all coated with the sauce. Sprinkle with the toasted sesame seeds and serve immediately.

Tender Karahi Potatoes with Whole Spices and Seeds

The potato is transformed into something quite exotic when it is cooked like this.

Serves 4

15ml/1 tbsp oil
5ml/1 tsp cumin seeds
3 curry leaves
5ml/1 tsp crushed dried red chillies
2.5ml/½ tsp mixed onion, mustard and fenugreek seeds
2.5ml/½ tsp fennel seeds
3 garlic cloves, sliced
2.5cm/1in piece fresh root ginger, grated
2 onions, sliced
6 new potatoes, thinly sliced
15ml/1 tbsp chopped fresh coriander (cilantro)
1 fresh red chilli, seeded and sliced
1 fresh green chilli, seeded and sliced

1 Heat the oil in a karahi, wok or heavy pan. Lower the heat slightly and add the cumin seeds, curry leaves, dried red chillies, mixed onion, mustard and fenugreek seeds, fennel seeds, garlic slices and ginger. Fry for 1 minute.

2 Add the onions and fry them for a further 5 minutes, or until the onions are golden brown.

3 Add the potatoes, fresh coriander and sliced fresh red and green chillies to the pan and mix well. Cover the pan tightly with a lid or foil; if using foil, make sure that it does not touch the food. Cook over a very low heat for about 7 minutes or until the potatoes are tender.

4 Remove the pan from the heat, and take off the lid or foil cover. Serve hot straight from the pan.

Cook's Tip

Choose a waxy variety of new potato for this fairly hot vegetable dish; if you use a very soft potato, it will not be possible to cut it into thin slices without it breaking up. Suitable varieties are often labelled 'salad potatoes' when sold at supermarkets. Leave the skin on for a tastier result.

Hot and Spicy Yam Energy 66Kcal/277kJ; Protein 3.9g; Carbohydrate 6.6g, of which sugars 5.8g; Fat 2.9g, of which saturates 0.5g; Cholesterol 0mg; Calcium 74mg; Fibre 2.4g; Sodium 752mg.
Karahi Potatoes Energy 152kcal/641kJ; Protein 3.8g; Carbohydrate 27.5g, of which sugars 6g; Fat 3.9g, of which saturates 0.5g; Cholesterol 0mg; Calcium 46mg; Fibre 2.6g; Sodium 19mg.

Cantonese Beansprouts with Salt Fish

This simple peasant dish has been elevated to gourmet status. Use the best salt fish available, ideally salted fillets of snapper or an expensive tropical fish called threadfin (ma yeow yu in Cantonese). If this is not obtainable, the closest substitute is salt cod.

Serves 4
100g/3¾oz salt fish fillet
60ml/4 tbsp vegetable oil
600g/1lb 6oz/2⅓ cups beansprouts
2 spring onions (scallions)
30ml/2 tbsp crushed garlic
15ml/1 tbsp light soy sauce

1 Cut the salt fish into small chunks. Heat the oil in a wok and fry the pieces of salt fish until fragrant and slightly brittle. With a slotted spoon, transfer them to a board. Let them cool slightly, then shred them roughly.

2 Wash the beansprouts, drain them thoroughly and remove any green husks. Cut the spring onions into 5cm/2in lengths.

3 Pour off all but 30ml/2 tbsp of the oil from the wok. Heat the remaining oil and fry the garlic until golden brown. Add the beansprouts and salt fish and stir rapidly for 2 minutes.

4 Add the spring onions and stir-fry for 1 minute. Drizzle over the soy sauce, stir for 1 minute more and serve immediately.

Variation
Soak the salt fish in cold water overnight and then drain. Dry the fish on kitchen paper and proceed as in step 1 above.

Cook's Tip
Sprout your own soya beans, if possible. If you do buy the sprouts, however, look for ones with large heads, as these are the healthiest option.

Thai Seafood Salad with Pomelo and Peanuts

A Thai meal will include a selection of dishes, one of which is often a refreshing and palate-cleansing salad that features tropical fruit, as with the pomelo here.

Serves 4–6
30ml/2 tbsp vegetable oil
4 shallots, finely sliced
2 garlic cloves, finely sliced
1 large pomelo, peeled
15ml/1 tbsp roasted peanuts
115g/4oz cooked peeled prawns (shrimp)
115g/4oz cooked crab meat
10–12 small fresh mint leaves

For the dressing
30ml/2 tbsp Thai fish sauce
15ml/1 tbsp palm sugar (jaggery) or light muscovado (brown) sugar
30ml/2 tbsp fresh lime juice

For the garnish
2 spring onions (scallions), thinly sliced
2 fresh red chillies, seeded and thinly sliced
fresh coriander (cilantro) leaves
grated fresh coconut (optional)

1 Make the dressing. Mix the fish sauce, sugar and lime juice in a bowl. Whisk well, then cover and set aside.

2 Heat the vegetable oil in a wok or frying pan, add the finely sliced shallots and garlic and cook until they are golden. Remove from the pan and set aside.

3 Break the pomelo flesh into small pieces, taking care to remove any membranes. Grind the peanuts and mix with the pomelo, prawns, crab, mint and shallots. Toss in the dressing and sprinkle with spring onions, chillies and coriander. Then add the coconut, if using. Serve immediately.

Cook's Tip
The pomelo is a large citrus fruit that looks like a grapefruit, although it is not, as is often thought, a hybrid. It is slightly pear-shaped with thick, yellow, dimpled skin and pinkish-yellow flesh that is drier than a grapefruit's. It also has a sharper taste.

Beansprouts with Salt Fish Energy 185kcal/772kJ; Protein 13.2g; Carbohydrate 6.5g, of which sugars 3.7g; Fat 12.1g, of which saturates 1.5g; Cholesterol 0mg; Calcium 68mg; Fibre 2.3g; Sodium 2157mg.
Thai Seafood Salad Energy 159kcal/665kJ; Protein 13.4g; Carbohydrate 8.4g; of which sugars 8.1g; Fat 4.9g; of which saturates 0.9g; Cholesterol 44mg; Calcium 107mg; Fibre 1.1g; Sodium 612mg.

Lime-marinated Beef Salad

This is a great Chinese favourite and versions of it are enjoyed in Vietnam, Thailand, Cambodia and Laos. It is also one of the traditional dishes that appear in the *bo bay mon* – beef seven ways feast – in which there are seven different beef dishes. For the most delicious result, buy an excellent-quality piece of tender fillet steak because the meat is only just seared before being dressed in the spicy, fragrant lime dressing and tossed in a crunchy salad of beansprouts and fresh, aromatic herbs.

Serves 4

about 7.5ml/1½ tsp vegetable oil
450g/1lb beef fillet, cut into steaks 2.5cm/1in thick
115g/4oz/½ cup beansprouts
1 bunch each fresh basil and mint, stalks removed, leaves shredded
1 lime, cut into quarters, to serve

For the marinade

juice (about 80ml/3fl oz/⅓ cup) and rind of 2 limes
30ml/2 tbsp Thai fish sauce
30ml/2 tbsp raw cane sugar
2 garlic cloves, crushed
2 lemon grass stalks, very finely sliced
2 green serrano chillies, seeded and finely sliced

1 To make the marinade, beat the lime juice, rind and Thai fish sauce in a bowl with the sugar, until the sugar dissolves. Stir in the garlic, lemon grass and chillies and set aside.

2 Pour the oil into a heavy wok or pan and rub it over the base with a piece of kitchen paper.

3 Heat the pan and sear the steaks for 1–2 minutes each side. Transfer them to a board and leave to cool a little.

4 Using a sharp knife, cut the seared steaks into thin slices. Toss the slices in the marinade, cover the bowl and leave them to marinate for about 1–2 hours.

5 Drain the meat of any excess juice from the marinade and transfer it to a wide serving bowl.

6 Add the beansprouts and herbs and toss them all together. Serve immediately with lime quarters to squeeze over.

Chilli Beef and Mushroom Salad

All the ingredients for this traditional, tasty Thai salad, known as yam nua yang, are widely available in most large supermarkets as well as in Asian food stores.

Serves 4

675g/1½lb beef fillet or rump (round) steak
30ml/2 tbsp olive oil
2 small mild red chillies, seeded and sliced
225g/8oz/3¼ cups fresh shiitake mushrooms, stems removed and caps sliced

For the dressing

3 spring onions (scallions), finely chopped
2 garlic cloves, finely chopped
juice of 1 lime
15–30ml/1–2 tbsp Thai fish sauce
5ml/1 tsp soft light brown sugar
30ml/2 tbsp chopped fresh coriander (cilantro)

To serve

1 cos or romaine lettuce, in strips
175g/6oz cherry tomatoes, halved
5cm/2in piece cucumber, peeled, halved and thinly sliced
45ml/3 tbsp toasted sesame seeds

1 Preheat the grill (broiler) to medium, then cook the steak for 2–4 minutes on each side, depending on how well done you like it. (In Thailand, the beef is traditionally served quite rare.) Leave the steak to cool for at least 15 minutes.

2 Slice the beef fillet or rump steak as thinly as possible (freezing it for 30 minutes before slicing will help make this easier). Place the slices in a bowl.

3 Heat the olive oil in a small, heavy wok or frying pan. Add the seeded and sliced red chillies and the sliced shiitake mushroom caps. Cook for 5 minutes, stirring occasionally.

4 Remove from the heat and add the steak slices to the pan. Stir well to coat the beef slices in the chilli and mushroom mixture.

5 Make the dressing by mixing all the ingredients in a bowl, then pour it over the meat mixture and toss gently.

6 Arrange the lettuce, tomatoes and cucumber on a serving plate. Spoon the steak mixture in the centre and sprinkle the sesame seeds over. Serve immediately.

Lime-marinated Beef Salad Energy 233kcal/979kJ; Protein 26g; Carbohydrate 12g, of which sugars 9g; Fat 9g, of which saturates 3g; Cholesterol 69mg; Calcium 74mg; Fibre 0.5g; Sodium 400mg.
Chilli Beef Salad Energy 381kcal/1588kJ; Protein 39.7g; Carbohydrate 4g, of which sugars 3.8g; Fat 23g, of which saturates 6.6g; Cholesterol 103mg; Calcium 105mg; Fibre 2.4g; Sodium 352mg.

Rich Spiced Carrot and Raisin Halwa

Halwa is a classic Indian sweet, and there are many variations on the basic recipe. In this version, which comes from the Udupi cuisine of south-west India, grated carrots are cooked in milk with ghee, sugar, spices and raisins until meltingly tender and sweet. You will only need a small bowl because it is very rich.

Serves 4

90g/3½oz ghee
300g/11oz carrots, coarsely grated
250ml/8fl oz/1 cup milk
150g/5oz/¾ cup golden caster (superfine) sugar
5–6 lightly crushed cardamom pods
1 clove
1 cinnamon stick
50g/2oz/scant ½ cup raisins

1 Place a wok or a large deep frying pan over a low heat and add half the ghee. When the ghee has melted, add the grated carrot to the pan and stir-fry for 6–8 minutes.

2 Pour the milk into the wok, stir into the carrots and raise the heat to bring the mixture to the boil. Once it is bubbling reduce the heat to low again and leave to simmer gently for 10–12 minutes, stirring from time to time.

3 Stir the remaining ghee into the carrot mixture in the pan, then add the caster sugar, crushed cardamom pods, clove, cinnamon stick and raisins, and stir well to mix.

4 Gently simmer the carrot and raisin halwa mixture for 6–7 minutes, stirring occasionally, until it is thickened and glossy. Fish out the whole spices if you wish, and serve scoops of the halwa immediately in small serving bowls.

Cook's Tip

Ghee is clarified butter, widely used in Indian cooking. It is an essential ingredient in halwa and is available in cans from Asian stores and many supermarkets.

Vanilla, Honey and Saffron Pears

These sweet juicy pears, poached in a honey syrup fragrant with vanilla, saffron and lime, make a truly elegant dessert. They are lovely eaten just as they are, but for a really luxurious, indulgent treat, serve them with thin pouring cream or ice cream.

Serves 4

150g/5oz/¾ cup caster (superfine) sugar
105ml/7 tbsp clear honey
5ml/1 tsp finely grated lime rind
a large pinch of saffron
2 vanilla pods (beans)
4 large, firm ripe dessert pears
single (light) cream or ice cream, to serve

1 Place the caster sugar and honey in a medium, non-stick wok or large pan, then add the lime rind and the saffron strands. Using a small, sharp knife, split the vanilla pods in half and scrape the seeds into the wok, then add the pods as well.

2 Pour 500ml/17fl oz/generous 2 cups water into the wok and bring the mixture to the boil. Reduce the heat to low and simmer, stirring occasionally, while you prepare the pears.

3 Peel the pears, then add them to the wok and gently turn the pears in the syrup to coat evenly. Cover the wok and simmer gently for 12–15 minutes, turning the pears halfway through cooking, until they are just tender.

4 Lift the pears from the syrup using a slotted spoon and transfer to four serving bowls. Set aside.

5 Bring the syrup back to the boil and cook gently for about 10 minutes, or until thickened. Spoon the syrup over the pears and serve warm or chilled with single cream or ice cream.

Variations

Try using different flavourings in the accompanying syrup: add 10ml/2 tsp chopped fresh root ginger and 1–2 star anise, or 1 cinnamon stick and 3 cloves. The honey can be replaced with the same quantity of maple syrup.

Carrot and Raisin Halwa Energy 439kcal/1838kJ; Protein 3g; Carbohydrate 56.7g, of which sugars 56.3g; Fat 23.8g, of which saturates 15.6g; Cholesterol 67mg; Calcium 119mg; Fibre 2.1g; Sodium 56mg.
Vanilla Pears Energy 283kcal/1207kJ; Protein 0.8g; Carbohydrate 74.3g, of which sugars 74.3g; Fat 0.2g, of which saturates 0g; Cholesterol 0mg; Calcium 38mg; Fibre 3.3g; Sodium 10mg.

Caramelized Pineapple with Lemon Grass

This stunning dessert, garnished with jewel-like pomegranate seeds,has lemon grass and mint to bring out the exquisite sweetness of the pineapple.

Serves 4

30ml/2 tbsp very finely chopped lemon grass, and 2 lemon grass stalks, halved lengthways
350g/12oz/1¾ cups caster (superfine) sugar
10ml/2 tsp chopped fresh mint leaves
2 small, ripe pineapples, about 600g/1lb 5oz each
15ml/1 tbsp sunflower oil
60ml/4 tbsp pomegranate seeds
crème fraîche, to serve

1 Place the chopped lemon grass, 250g/9oz of the sugar and the mint leaves in a non-stick wok. Pour over 150ml/¼ pint/⅔ cup of water and bring to the boil over medium heat.

2 Simmer for 10–15 minutes, until thickened. Strain into a bowl, reserving the lemon grass stalks, then set aside.

3 Peel and core the pineapples and cut into 1cm/½in-thick slices, then sprinkle the slices with the remaining sugar.

4 Brush a large non-stick wok with the oil and place over a medium heat. Working in batches, cook the sugared pineapple slices for 2–3 minutes until they are lightly caramelized, then turn over and cook the other side for another 2–3 minutes.

5 Transfer the pineapple to a serving dish and scatter over the pomegranate seeds. Pour over the lemon grass syrup and garnish with the reserved stalks. Serve hot with crème fraîche.

Cook's Tip
To remove pomegranate seeds easily, halve the fruit using a sharp knife and hold it over a bowl, cut side down. Tap all over with a wooden spoon and the seeds should drop out.

Fried Pineapple

This is a very simple and quick dessert to make. The slightly sharp flavour of the fruit makes this a very refreshing treat, ideal for serving at the end of a rich or spicy meal.

Serves 4

1 pineapple
40g/1½oz/3 tbsp butter
15ml/1 tbsp desiccated (dry unsweetened) coconut
60ml/4 tbsp soft light brown sugar
60ml/4 tbsp fresh lime juice
lime slices, to decorate
thick and creamy natural (plain) yogurt, to serve

1 Using a sharp knife, cut the top off the pineapple and peel off the skin, taking care to remove the eyes.

2 Cut the pineapple in half and remove and discard the woody core. Cut the flesh lengthways into 1cm/½in wedges.

3 Heat the butter in a large, heavy frying pan or wok. When it has melted, add the pineapple wedges and cook over a medium heat for 1–2 minutes on each side, or until they have turned pale golden in colour.

4 Meanwhile, dry-fry the coconut in a small frying pan until lightly browned. Remove from the heat and set aside.

5 Sprinkle the sugar into the pan with the pineapple, add the lime juice and cook, stirring constantly, until the sugar has dissolved to make a syrupy sauce.

6 Divide the warm pineapple wedges among four individual bowls, sprinkle them with the coconut, decorate with the lime slices and serve with the yogurt.

Variation
A generous splash of rum, added with the lime juice, turns this dessert into an adult treat, perfect with after-dinner drinks.

Caramelized Pineapple Energy 493Kcal/2101kJ; Protein 1.6g; Carbohydrate 121.7g, of which sugars 121.7g; Fat 3.4g, of which saturates 0.3g; Cholesterol 0mg; Calcium 101mg; Fibre 3.6g; Sodium 11mg.
Fried Pineapple Energy 238kcal/1004kJ; Protein 1.2g; Carbohydrate 36.2g, of which sugars 36.2g; Fat 11g, of which saturates 7.2g; Cholesterol 21mg; Calcium 47mg; Fibre 2.9g; Sodium 67mg.

Mango and Coconut Stir-fry

Choose a ripe mango for this recipe. If you buy one that is a little underripe, leave it in a warm place for a day or two before using.

Serves 4

¼ coconut
1 large, ripe mango
juice and finely grated rind of 2 limes
15ml/1 tbsp sunflower oil
15g/½oz/1 tbsp butter
30ml/2 tbsp clear honey
crème fraîche or ice cream, to serve

1 Prepare the coconut if necessary. Drain the milk and remove the flesh. Peel with a vegetable peeler so that it forms flakes.

2 Prepare the mango. Cut the stone (pit) out of the middle of the fruit. Cut each half of the mango into slices and peel off the skin. Place the mango slices in a small bowl and pour over the lime juice and rind. Set aside.

3 Meanwhile heat a karahi or wok, then add 10ml/2 tsp of the sunflower oil. When the oil is hot, add the butter. Once the butter has melted, stir in the coconut flakes and stir-fry for 1–2 minutes until the coconut is golden brown. Remove and drain on kitchen paper. Wipe out the pan. Strain the mango slices, reserving the juice.

4 Heat the pan again and add the remaining sunflower oil. When the oil is hot, add the mango and stir-fry for 1–2 minutes, then add the juice and leave to bubble and reduce for 1 minute.

5 Stir in the honey. When it has dissolved, spoon the mango and its juices into one large serving bowl or individual dishes.

6 Sprinkle the stir-fried coconut flakes over the prepared mango and serve with crème fraîche or ice cream.

Variation
Nectarine or peach slices can be used instead of the mango.

Steamed Ginger Custards

Delicate and warming, ginger custard is a favourite among the Chinese. These individual custards are often served warm, straight from the steamer, and enjoyed as a mid-afternoon snack. They work just as well served as a chilled dessert.

Serves 4

115g/4oz fresh root ginger, chopped
400ml/14fl oz/1⅔ cups coconut milk
60ml/4 tbsp sugar
2 egg whites

1 Using a mortar and pestle or food processor, grind the ginger to a fine paste. Press the ginger paste through a fine sieve (strainer) set over a bowl, or twist the ginger paste in a piece of muslin (cheesecloth), to extract the juice.

2 Fill a wok one-third of the way up with water. Place a bamboo steamer in the wok, bring the water to the boil and then reduce the heat to low.

3 In a large bowl, whisk together the coconut milk, sugar and the egg whites with the ginger juice until the mixture is smooth and the sugar has dissolved.

4 Carefully pour the mixture into four individual heatproof bowls and place them in the steamer. Cover and steam for 15–20 minutes, until the mixture sets.

5 Remove the bowls from the steamer and leave them to cool. Cover each bowl with clear film (plastic wrap) and place them in the refrigerator overnight. Serve the custards chilled or at room temperature.

Variation
Slice about 6 pieces of preserved (stem) ginger thinly using a sharp knife or cleaver and add them to the coconut mixture before pouring into bowls for steaming. This will intensify both the flavour and the aroma of this sweet custard dessert.

Mango and Coconut Stir-fry Energy 301kcal/1243kJ; Protein 2.4g; Carbohydrate 7.7g, of which sugars 7.6g; Fat 29.2g, of which saturates 22.4g; Cholesterol 8mg; Calcium 14mg; Fibre 6.1g; Sodium 34mg.
Steamed Ginger Custards Energy 89kcal/380kJ; Protein 2g; Carbohydrate 20.8g, of which sugars 20.8g; Fat 0.4g, of which saturates 0.2g; Cholesterol 0mg; Calcium 50mg; Fibre 0.3g; Sodium 159mg.

Coconut and Mandarin Custards

These scented custards with a fabulous melt-in-the-mouth texture are best served warm. However, they are also delicious served chilled, making them perfect for easy entertaining. If you prefer, make the praline the day before.

Serves 4

200ml/7fl oz/scant 1 cup coconut cream
200ml/7fl oz/scant 1 cup double (heavy) cream
2.5ml/½ tsp finely ground star anise
75ml/5 tbsp golden caster (superfine) sugar
15ml/1 tbsp very finely grated mandarin or orange rind
4 egg yolks

For the praline

175g/6oz/scant 1 cup caster (superfine) sugar
50g/2oz/½ cup roughly chopped mixed nuts, to serve

1 Make the praline. Place the sugar in a non-stick wok with 15–30ml/1–2 tbsp water. Cook over a medium heat until the sugar dissolves and turns light gold.

2 Remove the syrup from the heat and pour on to a baking sheet lined with baking parchment. Spread it out using the back of a spoon, then sprinkle the chopped nuts evenly over the top and leave the praline to harden.

3 Meanwhile place the coconut cream, double cream, star anise, sugar, mandarin or orange rind and egg yolks in a large bowl. Whisk to combine and pour the mixture into four lightly greased ramekins or small, heatproof bowls.

4 Place the ramekins or cups in a large steamer, cover and place in a wok and steam over gently simmering water for 12–15 minutes, or until the custards are just set.

5 Carefully lift the custards from the steamer and leave them to cool slightly, for about 10 minutes.

6 Meanwhile, break the hardened praline into rough pieces and serve it on top of the custards once the latter have cooled.

Steamed Custard in Nectarines

Steaming nectarines or peaches brings out their natural colour and sweetness, so this is a good way of making the most of underripe or less flavourful fruit from the market.

Serves 6

6 nectarines
1 large (US extra large) egg
45ml/3 tbsp light brown sugar or palm sugar (jaggery)
30ml/2 tbsp reduced-fat coconut milk

1 Cut the nectarines in half. Using a teaspoon, scoop out the stones (pits) and a little of the surrounding flesh.

2 Lightly beat the egg, then add the sugar and the coconut milk. Beat until the sugar has dissolved.

3 Line a large bamboo steamer with baking parchment. Transfer the nectarines to the steamer and carefully fill the cavities three-quarters full with the custard mixture.

4 Place the steamer over a wok of simmering water and steam for 5–10 minutes. Remove from the heat and leave to cool completely before transferring to plates and serving.

Variations

- *Instead of nectarines, use peaches, skinning them first by dunking them in boiling water until the skins peel back and they can easily be removed.*
- *An alternative method of preparation is to chop 3 nectarines and spoon the fruit into six ramekins. Divide the custard among them and steam until the custard is set.*
- *Use full-fat coconut milk if you prefer.*

Cook's Tip

Palm sugar, also known as jaggery, is made from the sap of certain Asian palm trees, such as coconut and palmyrah. It is available from Asian food stores. If you buy it as a cake or large lump, grate it before use, so it will dissolve easily.

Coconut and Mandarin Energy 643kcal/2688kJ; Protein 6.7g; Carbohydrate 71g, of which sugars 69.3g; Fat 38.9g, of which saturates 19.6g; Cholesterol 270mg; Calcium 100mg; Fibre 0.4g; Sodium 115mg.
Steamed Custard Energy 119kcal/507kJ; Protein 3.8g; Carbohydrate 25.2g, of which sugars 25.2g; Fat 1.1g, of which saturates 0.3g; Cholesterol 32mg; Calcium 24mg; Fibre 2.3g; Sodium 20mg.

Toffee Plums with Coconut Rice

Red, juicy plums seared in a wok with sugar acquire a rich caramel coating.

Serves 4
6 or 8 firm, ripe plums
90g/3½oz/½ cup caster (superfine) sugar

For the rice
115g/4oz sticky glutinous rice
150ml/¼ pint/⅔ cup coconut cream
45ml/3 tbsp caster (superfine) sugar
a pinch of salt

1 First prepare the rice. Rinse it in several changes of water, then leave to soak overnight in a bowl of cold water.

2 Line a large bamboo steamer that will fit in your wok with muslin (cheesecloth). Drain the rice and transfer to the steamer.

3 Cover the rice and steam over simmering water for 25–30 minutes, until tender. Transfer the rice to a wide bowl and set aside.

4 Heat the coconut cream with the sugar and salt in a clean wok. When it boils, pour it over the rice. Stir to mix well.

5 Using a sharp knife, cut the plums in half and remove their stones (pits). Sprinkle the sugar over the cut sides.

6 Heat a non-stick wok over a medium-high flame. Working in batches, place the plums in the wok, cut side down, and cook for 1–2 minutes, or until the sugar caramelizes. You may need to wipe out the wok with kitchen paper in between batches.

7 Mould the rice into rounds and place on warmed plates, then spoon over the caramelized plums. Alternatively, simply spoon the rice into four warmed bowls and top with the plums. Drizzle any syrup remaining in the wok over the fruit.

Variation
Try this recipe with bananas or pineapple pieces instead of the plums for an alternative fruit sweetness.

Mini Toffee Apples

Serves 4
115g/4oz/1 cup plain (all-purpose) flour
10ml/2 tsp baking powder
60ml/4 tbsp cornflour (cornstarch)
175ml/6fl oz/¾ cup water
4 firm apples, peeled and cored
sunflower oil, for deep-frying
200g/7oz/1 cup caster (superfine) sugar

1 Beat the flour, baking powder, cornflour and water to make a smooth batter. Cut each apple into 8 wedges.

2 Fill a wok one-third full of oil and heat to 180°C/350°F. Dip the apple in the batter, and fry for 2 minutes. Drain on kitchen paper. Reheat the oil to 180°C/350°F and fry the wedges for a second time, for about 2 minutes. Drain well on kitchen paper.

3 Pour off all but 30ml/2 tbsp of the oil and add the sugar. Heat until it caramelizes. Add the apple and toss to coat evenly. Plunge briefly into iced water to set the caramel, and serve immediately.

Caramelized Apple Fritters

Serves 4
115g/4oz/1 cup plain (all-purpose) flour, plus extra for dusting
about 120ml/4fl oz/½ cup water
1 egg, beaten
4 firm apples, peeled and cored
vegetable oil, for deep-frying, plus 30ml/2 tbsp for the toffee
115g/4oz/½ cup granulated sugar

1 Mix the flour, water and egg to make a smooth batter. Cut each apple into 8 wedges and dust with a little flour.

2 Heat the oil in a wok to 190°C/375°F. Dip the apple pieces in the batter and deep-fry for about 3 minutes or until golden. Remove and drain on kitchen paper. Drain the oil from the pan.

3 Heat the remaining oil in the pan, add the sugar and stir constantly until caramelized. Quickly add the apple pieces and blend well so that each piece is thoroughly coated with the toffee. Dip the pieces in cold water to harden before serving.

Toffee Plums Energy 271kcal/1148kJ; Protein 2.8g; Carbohydrate 66.3g, of which sugars 43.4g; Fat 0.4g, of which saturates 0.2g; Cholesterol 0mg; Calcium 52mg; Fibre 0.8g; Sodium 86mg.
Toffee Apples Energy 457kcal/1940kJ; Protein 3.4g; Carbohydrate 97.3g, of which sugars 61.6g; Fat 8.8g, of which saturates 1.1g; Cholesterol 0mg; Calcium 73mg; Fibre 2.5g; Sodium 14mg.
Apple Fritters Energy 424kcal/1780kJ; Protein 4.3g; Carbohydrate 73.2g, of which sugars 46.2g; Fat 13.9g, of which saturates 2.8g; Cholesterol 47mg; Calcium 1mg; Fibre 5.9g; Sodium 16mg.

Honeyed Apples

These scrumptious treats are best prepared for a select number as they require the cook's complete attention. The honey coating crispens when the fritters are dipped in iced water.

Serves 4–5

4 crisp eating apples
juice of ½ lemon
25g/1oz/¼ cup cornflour (cornstarch)
sunflower oil, for deep-frying
toasted sesame seeds, for sprinkling

For the fritter batter
115g/4oz/1 cup plain (all-purpose) flour
generous pinch of salt
120–150ml/4–5fl oz/½–⅔ cup water
30ml/2 tbsp sunflower oil
2 egg whites

For the sauce
250ml/8fl oz/1 cup clear honey
120ml/4fl oz/½ cup sunflower oil
5ml/1 tsp white wine vinegar

1 Peel, core and cut the apples into eighths, brush each piece lightly with lemon juice then dust with cornflour.

2 To make the sauce, heat the honey and sunflower oil in a pan, stirring continuously until blended. Remove from the heat and stir in the white wine vinegar.

3 For the batter, sift the flour and salt into a bowl, then stir in the water and oil. Whisk the egg whites in a separate bowl until stiff peaks form and then fold them into the batter.

4 Heat the sunflower oil in a karahi, wok or deep-fryer to a temperature of 190°C/375°F, or until a cube of bread dropped in the oil browns in about 45 seconds.

5 Spear each piece of apple in turn on a skewer, dip in the batter and fry in the hot oil until golden. Drain on kitchen paper. Place the fritters in a dish and pour the sauce over.

6 Transfer the honeyed apple fritters to a lightly oiled serving dish, and sprinkle them with the toasted sesame seeds. Serve the honeyed fritters at once, offering bowls of iced water for dipping to crispen the honey coating.

Sesame Fried Fruits

For this deep-fried dessert you can use any firm fruit that are in season. Bananas are fantastic, but the batter also works well with pineapple and apple. Serve them as soon as they are fried so that they retain their crispness.

Serves 4

115g/4oz/1 cup plain (all-purpose) flour
2.5ml/½ tsp bicarbonate of soda (baking soda)
30ml/2 tbsp sugar
1 egg
90ml/6 tbsp water
15ml/1 tbsp sesame seeds or 30ml/2 tbsp desiccated (dry unsweetened shredded) coconut
4 firm bananas
oil, for deep-frying
salt
30ml/2 tbsp clear honey, to serve
fresh mint sprigs and lychees, to decorate

1 Using a sieve (strainer) sift the flour, bicarbonate of soda and a pinch of salt into a bowl. Stir in the sugar.

2 Whisk in the egg and just enough water to make a thin batter. Then whisk in the sesame seeds or the desiccated coconut.

3 Peel the bananas. Cut them in half lengthways and crossways.

4 Heat the oil in a wok to a temperature of 190°C/375°F, or until a cube of bread dropped in the oil browns in about 45 seconds. Dip the bananas in the batter, then gently drop a few pieces at a time into the hot oil. Fry until golden brown.

5 Remove the bananas from the oil and drain on kitchen paper.

6 Serve the fritters immediately with clear honey, and decorate with mint sprigs and lychees.

Cook's Tip
Don't peel or slice the bananas until you are ready to cook them, since they will discolour very quickly.

Honeyed Apples Energy 779kcal/3271kJ; Protein 6.1g; Carbohydrate 100g, of which sugars 66g; Fat 43g, of which saturates 4.2g; Cholesterol 0mg; Calcium 3mg; Fibre 6g; Sodium 518mg.
Sesame Fried Fruits Energy 342kcal/1436kJ; Protein 6.3g; Carbohydrate 57.3g, of which sugars 22.1g; Fat 11.1g, of which saturates 1.7g; Cholesterol 47mg; Calcium 5mg; Fibre 4.3g; Sodium 398mg.

Vietnamese Fried Bananas

Serves 4
115g/4oz/1 plain (all-purpose) flour
2.5ml/½ tsp baking powder
45ml/3 tbsp caster (superfine) sugar, plus extra for sprinkling
150ml/¼ pint/⅔ cup water
150ml/¼ pint/⅔ cup beer
4 ripe but firm bananas
vegetable oil, for deep-frying

1 Sift the flour with the baking powder into a bowl. Add the sugar and beat in a little water to make a paste. Beat in the rest of the water and beer to form a thick batter. Leave to stand for 20 minutes.

2 Peel the bananas and cut them in half crossways, then in half again lengthways. Heat enough oil for deep-frying in a wok.

3 Cook the bananas in batches. Coat each one in the beer batter and slip it into the hot oil. Use tongs or chopsticks for turning and make sure each piece is crisp and golden all over.

4 Drain the fried bananas on kitchen paper and sprinkle them with sugar. Serve immediately and eat hot.

Banana Fritters

Serves 8
115g/4oz/1 cup self-raising (self-rising) flour
40g/1½ oz/¼ cup rice flour
2.5ml/½ tsp salt
200ml/7fl oz/scant 1 cup water
finely grated lime rind
8 baby bananas
vegetable oil, for deep frying
strips of lime rind, to garnish
sugar, for dredging
lime wedges, to serve

1 Sift the flour, rice flour and salt into a bowl. Mix in just enough water to make a smooth, coating batter. Add the lime rind.

2 Heat the oil in a wok to 190°C/375°F. Peel the bananas and dip them into the batter, then deep-fry until crisp and golden.

3 Drain on kitchen paper. Serve hot, dredged with sugar and garnished with strips of lime, and with lime wedges for squeezing.

Coconut Fried Bananas

These deliciously sweet treats are a favourite with children and adults alike. In Thailand, you will find them on sale from portable roadside stalls and markets at almost every hour of the day and night.

Serves 4
115g/4oz/1 cup plain (all-purpose) flour
2.5ml/½ tsp bicarbonate of soda (baking soda)
pinch of salt
30ml/2 tbsp granulated sugar
1 egg, beaten
90ml/6 tbsp water
30ml/2 tbsp desiccated (dry unsweetened shredded) coconut or 15ml/1 tbsp sesame seeds
4 firm bananas
vegetable oil, for deep-frying
fresh mint sprigs, to decorate
30ml/2 tbsp clear honey, to serve (optional)

1 Sift the flour, bicarbonate of soda and salt into a large bowl. Stir in the granulated sugar and the egg, and whisk in just enough of the water to make quite a thin batter.

2 Whisk the coconut or sesame seeds into the batter so that they are evenly distributed.

3 Peel the bananas. Carefully cut each one in half lengthways, then in half crossways to make 16 pieces of about the same size. Don't do this until you are ready to cook them because, once peeled, bananas will quickly discolour.

4 Heat the oil in a karahi, wok or deep-fryer to a temperature of 190°C/375°F or until a cube of bread, dropped in the oil, browns in about 45 seconds. Dip the banana pieces in the batter, then gently drop a few into the oil.

5 Deep-fry the bananas until they are crisp and golden brown, then lift out and drain well on kitchen paper.

6 Cook the remaining banana pieces in the same way. Serve immediately with honey, if using, and decorated with sprigs of fresh mint.

Vietnamese Fried Bananas Energy 290Kcal/1211kJ; Protein 3g; Carbohydrate 48g, of which sugars 22g; Fat 9g, of which saturates 1g; Cholesterol 0mg; Calcium 22mg; Fibre 1.7g; Sodium 600mg
Banana Fritters Energy 204kcal/855kJ; Protein 3.9g; Carbohydrate 26.6g, of which sugars 14.8g; Fat 9.8g, of which saturates 4.4g; Cholesterol 48mg; Calcium 47mg; Fibre 1.7g; Sodium 75mg.
Coconut Fried Bananas Energy 325kcal/1365kJ; Protein 5.9g; Carbohydrate 57.6g, of which sugars 22.6g; Fat 9.3g, of which saturates 3.7g; Cholesterol 47mg; Calcium 2mg; Fibre 4.5g; Sodium 845mg.

Mango Wontons with Raspberry Sauce

These crisp, golden parcels filled with meltingly sweet, hot mango are perfect for a summertime supper or a sophisticated dinner. The sweet raspberry sauce looks stunning drizzled over the wontons and adds a taste of summer to the dessert. Serve any extra raspberry sauce in a jug at the table so that your dinner guests can add more.

Serves 4

2 firm, ripe mangoes
24 fresh wonton wrappers (approximately 7.5cm/3in square)
oil, for frying
icing (confectioners') sugar, to dust

For the sauce

400g/14oz/3½ cups raspberries
45ml/3 tbsp icing (confectioners') sugar
a squeeze of lemon juice

1 First make the sauce. Place the raspberries and icing sugar in a food processor and blend until smooth. Press the raspberry purée through a sieve (strainer) to remove the seeds, then stir a squeeze of lemon juice into the sauce. Cover and place in the refrigerator until ready to serve.

2 Peel the mangoes, then carefully slice the flesh away from one side of the flat stone (pit). Repeat on the second side, then trim off any remaining flesh from around the stones. Cut the mango flesh into 1cm/½in dice.

3 Lay 12 wonton wrappers on a clean work surface and place 10ml/2 tsp of the chopped mango in the centre of each one. Brush the edges with water and top with the remaining wonton wrappers. Press the edges to seal.

4 Heat the oil in a wok to 180°C/350°F (or until a cube of bread dropped into the oil browns in 15 seconds). Deep-fry the wontons, 2 or 3 at a time, for about 2 minutes, or until crisp and golden. Remove from the oil using a slotted spoon and drain on kitchen paper.

5 Dust the wontons with icing sugar and serve on individual plates. Drizzle the raspberry sauce over each serving or pour it into small individual bowls on the side.

Fried Wontons and Ice Cream

Americans eat cookies with ice cream – here is the Chinese equivalent. Serve it with fresh or poached fruits or fruit sauces for an impressive treat.

Serves 4

oil for deep frying
12 wonton wrappers

For the ice cream

500ml/17fl oz/generous 2 cups double (heavy) cream
2.5ml/½ tsp vanilla extract
90g/3½ oz/½ cup caster (superfine) sugar
4 large (US extra large) egg yolks

1 To make the ice cream, heat the cream in a pan to just below boiling point, then remove from the heat, add the vanilla extract and leave to cool.

2 In another pan, dissolve the sugar in 150ml/¼ pint/⅔ cup water, stirring constantly. Bring to the boil for a few minutes to form a light syrup, then leave to cool for 1 minute.

3 Whisk the egg yolks in a bowl. Trickle in the hot syrup, whisking constantly, until the mixture becomes mousse-like. Pour in the infused cream through a sieve (strainer), and whisk until mixed.

4 Pour the mixture into a freezerproof container and freeze for 4 hours, beating twice with a fork or whisking with an electric mixer to break up the ice crystals.

5 Heat the oil in a deep wok, fryer or large pan to 190°C/375°F. Add a few wonton wrappers at a time so that they do not crowd the pan too much. Fry for 1–2 minutes on each side until the wrappers are crisp and light golden brown. Remove from the pan using a slotted spoon.

6 Leave the cooked wontons to drain on kitchen paper.

7 To serve, place one wonton on each plate. Place a scoop of ice cream on top of each wonton. Top with a second wonton, then add another ball of ice cream and finish with a final wonton. Serve at once.

Mango Wontons Energy 314kcal/1331kJ; Protein 5.5g; Carbohydrate 56.1g, of which sugars 27.3g; Fat 9.2g, of which saturates 1.2g; Cholesterol 0mg; Calcium 93mg; Fibre 5.6g; Sodium 6mg.
Fried Wontons Energy 370kcal/1541kJ; Protein 5.3g; Carbohydrate 32g, of which sugars 12.9g; Fat 25.4g, of which saturates 8.5g; Cholesterol 0mg; Calcium 110mg; Fibre 0.8g; Sodium 46mg.

Pancakes Filled with Sweet Coconut

Traditionally, the pale green colour used for the pancake batter was obtained from the juice squeezed from fresh pandanus leaves. Green food colouring can be used instead.

Makes 12–15

175g/6oz/¾ cup soft dark brown sugar
450ml/¾ pint/scant 2 cups water
1 pandanus (screwpine) leaf, stripped through with a fork and tied into a knot
175g/6oz/2 cups desiccated (dry unsweetened shredded) coconut
oil, for frying
salt

For the pancake batter
225g/8oz/2 cups plain (all-purpose) flour, sifted
2 eggs, beaten
2 drops of edible green food colouring
few drops of vanilla extract
450ml/¾ pint/scant 2 cups water
45ml/3 tbsp groundnut (peanut) oil

1 Dissolve the sugar in the water with the pandanus leaf in a pan over gentle heat, stirring all the time. Increase the heat and allow to boil gently for 3–4 minutes, until the mixture just becomes syrupy. Do not let it caramelize.

2 Put the coconut in a karahi or wok with a pinch of salt. Pour over the prepared sugar syrup and cook over a very gentle heat, stirring from time to time, until the mixture becomes almost dry; this will take 5–10 minutes. Set aside until required.

3 To make the batter, blend together the flour, eggs, food colouring, vanilla extract, water and oil either by hand or in a food processor.

4 Brush an 18cm/7in frying pan with oil and cook 12–15 pancakes.

5 Keep the pancakes warm. Fill each pancake with a generous spoonful of the sweet coconut mixture, roll up and serve immediately.

Spiced Spanish Leche Frita

The name of this dessert means 'fried milk'. It has a melting, creamy centre and crunchy, golden coating.

Serves 6–8

550ml/18fl oz/2½ cups milk
3 finely pared strips of lemon rind
½ cinnamon stick
90g/3½oz/½ cup caster (superfine) sugar
60ml/4 tbsp cornflour (cornstarch)
30ml/2 tbsp plain (all-purpose) flour
3 egg yolks and 2 whole eggs
90–120ml/6–8 tbsp breadcrumbs
sunflower oil, for frying
ground cinnamon, for dusting

For the sauce
450g/1lb blackberries or blackcurrants
90g/3½oz/½ cup caster (superfine) sugar

1 Put the milk, lemon rind, cinnamon stick and sugar in a pan and bring to the boil. Cover and leave to infuse for 20 minutes. Mix the cornflour and flour in a bowl and beat in the egg yolks. Add a little of the milk and beat to make a smooth batter.

2 Strain the remaining hot milk into the batter, then pour back into the pan. Cook over a low heat, stirring constantly until it thickens. Beat the mixture hard for a smooth consistency. Pour into an 18–20cm/7–8in, 1cm/½in deep rectangular dish, and smooth the top. Cool, then chill until firm.

3 To make the sauce, cook the fruit with the sugar and a little water for about 10 minutes until soft. Reserving 30–45ml/2–3 tbsp whole fruit, put the rest in a processor and blend to make a smooth purée. Return to the pan and keep warm.

4 Cut the chilled custard into eight or twelve squares. Beat the eggs in a shallow dish and spread the breadcrumbs on a plate. Coat each square in egg, then in crumbs.

5 Heat about 1cm/½in oil in a wok or frying pan until very hot. Fry the squares in batches for a couple of minutes, shaking or spooning the oil over the top, until golden. Drain on kitchen paper while frying the other batches. Arrange on plates and sprinkle with sugar and cinnamon. Pour a circle of warm sauce round the squares, distributing the whole berries evenly.

Pancakes with Coconut Energy 200kcal/836kJ; Protein 2.6g; Carbohydrate 21.9g, of which sugars 8.8g; Fat 11.7g, of which saturates 4.4g; Cholesterol 24mg; Calcium 33mg; Fibre 1.3g; Sodium 49mg.
Spanish Leche Frita Energy 257kcal/1089kJ; Protein 6.9g; Carbohydrate 45.9g, of which sugars 30.6g; Fat 6.4g, of which saturates 2.7g; Cholesterol 133mg; Calcium 159mg; Fibre 2.3g; Sodium 143mg.

Calas

These sweet rice fritters are an American/Creole speciality, sold by 'Calas' women on the streets of the French quarter of New Orleans to residents and office workers, for whom they make a popular and tasty breakfast.

Makes over 40

115g/4oz/generous ½ cup short grain pudding rice
900ml/1½ pints/3¾ cups mixed milk and water
30ml/2 tbsp caster (superfine) sugar
50g/2oz/½ cup plain (all purpose) flour
7.5ml/1½ tsp baking powder
5ml/1 tsp grated lemon rind
2.5ml/½ tsp ground cinnamon
1.5ml/¼ tsp ground ginger
generous pinch of grated nutmeg
2 eggs
sunflower oil, for deep frying
salt
icing sugar, for dusting
cherry or strawberry jam and thick cream, to serve

1 Put the rice in a pan and add the milk and water. Add a pinch of salt and bring to the boil. Cover and simmer over a gentle heat for 15–20 minutes until the rice is tender. Switch off the heat, then stir in the sugar. Cover and leave until completely cool.

2 Put the rice in a food processor or blender and add the flour, baking powder, lemon rind, spices and eggs. Process for about 20–30 seconds so that the mixture is like a thick batter.

3 Heat the oil in a wok to 160°C/325°F. Scoop up a generous teaspoon of batter and, using a second spoon, push into the hot oil. Add four or five more and fry for 3–4 minutes, turning them occasionally, until the calas are golden brown. Drain on kitchen paper and keep warm while cooking in batches.

4 Dust the calas generously with icing sugar and serve warm with fruit jam and thick cream.

Variation
For a slightly spicy variation mix the icing sugar with some cinnamon and grated nutmeg before dusting.

Coconut Rice Fritters

Makes 28

150g/5oz/⅔ cup long grain rice, cooked
30ml/2 tbsp coconut milk powder
45ml/3 tbsp sugar
2 egg yolks
juice of ½ lemon
75g/3oz desiccated (dry unsweetened shredded) coconut
oil, for deep-frying
icing sugar, for dusting

1 Process 75g/3oz of the cooked rice in a food processor until smooth and sticky. Put into a bowl and mix in the remaining rice, the coconut milk powder, sugar, egg yolks and lemon juice.

2 Spread out the coconut on a tray. With wet hands, divide the rice into thumb-sized pieces and roll in the coconut to make balls.

3 Heat the oil in a wok to 180°C/350°F. Fry the rice balls in batches for 1–2 minutes, until the fritters brown. When brown, lift each one out, drain on kitchen paper and transfer to a plate. Dust with icing sugar. Place a wooden skewer in each one and serve.

Sweet Fried Loops

Makes about 24

450ml/15fl oz/scant 2 cups water
15ml/1 tbsp olive oil
15ml/1 tbsp caster (superfine) sugar, plus extra for dredging
2.5ml/½ tsp salt
150g/5oz/1¼ cups plain (all-purpose) flour
1 large egg
sunflower oil, for deep-frying

1 Bring the water, oil, sugar and salt to the boil in a large pan. Remove from the heat, and beat in the flour until smooth. Beat in the egg to make a smooth, glossy mixture with a piping consistency. Spoon into a pastry bag fitted with a large star nozzle.

2 Heat the oil in a wok to 190°C/375°F. Pipe loops of the mixture, two at a time, into the hot oil. Cook the loops for 3–4 minutes until they are golden. Lift out the loops with a wire skimmer or slotted spoon and drain them on kitchen paper. Dredge them with caster sugar and serve warm.

Calas Energy 50Kcal/206kJ; Protein 0.9g; Carbohydrate 3.5g, of which sugars 1.3g; Fat 3.6g, of which saturates 0.6g; Cholesterol 10mg; Calcium 16mg; Fibre 0g; Sodium 8mg.
Coconut Rice Fritters Energy 61kcal/254kJ; Protein 0.5g; Carbohydrate 3.5g, of which sugars 1.9g; Fat 5.1g, of which saturates 2.1g; Cholesterol 14mg; Calcium 4mg; Fibre 0.4g; Sodium 2mg.
Sweet Fried Loops Energy 122kcal/517kJ; Protein 2.6g; Carbohydrate 21.4g, of which sugars 2.3g; Fat 3.5g, of which saturates 0.5g; Cholesterol 17mg; Calcium 38mg; Fibre 0.8g; Sodium 2mg.

Orange and Date Buttermilk Pancakes

Serve these sweet, sticky, golden pancakes for breakfast, brunch or dessert. They're bursting with the flavour of zesty orange and sweet juicy dates and are utterly moreish. Medjool dates have an intensely sweet flesh and will give the best results.

Serves 4

150g/5oz/1 1/4 cups self-raising (self-rising) flour
2.5ml/1/2 tsp baking powder
a pinch of salt
250ml/8fl oz/1 cup buttermilk
3 eggs
15ml/1 tbsp caster (superfine) sugar
200g/7oz/1 1/4 cup Medjool dates, stoned
finely grated rind and juice from 1 small orange
50g/2oz/1/4 cup unsalted (sweet) butter, melted
sunflower oil, for greasing
clear honey, to drizzle
natural (plain) yogurt, to serve

1 Sift the flour and baking powder into a large bowl with a pinch of salt. Whisk in the buttermilk, eggs, sugar, dates, orange rind and juice and melted butter. Leave to stand for 15 minutes.

2 Brush a wok with a little oil and heat over a medium heat. When hot, pour a small ladleful of the mixture into the wok. Cook for 2–3 minutes until just set.

3 Cook the second side for 35–45 seconds. Transfer to a plate and keep warm while you cook the remaining batter in the same way. (You should make about 16 pancakes in total.)

4 To serve, divide the pancakes among four warmed plates, piling them up in a stack. Drizzle honey over each stack and top with a dollop of yogurt.

Variation
Add 2.5ml/1/2 tsp ground cinnamon to the batter for sprinkling, if you like, to give the pancakes a warm, spicy flavour.

Sweet Rice Vermicelli

The combination of sweetened rice vermicelli, dried fruit, nuts and spices may sound a little unusual, but it makes a deliciously moist, aromatic dessert that tastes divine drizzled with cream or served with big scoops of ice cream.

Serves 4

65g/2 1/2oz/5 tbsp unsalted (sweet) butter
60ml/4 tbsp vegetable oil
185g/6 1/2oz thin rice vermicelli, broken into 3cm/1 1/4in lengths
1.5ml/1/4 tsp ground allspice
30ml/2 tbsp roasted unsalted cashew nuts
15ml/1 tbsp chopped almonds
30ml/2 tbsp sultanas (golden raisins)
50g/2oz/1/3 cup ready-to-eat dried apricots, roughly chopped
90g/3 1/2oz/1/2 cup caster (superfine) sugar
175ml/6fl oz/3/4 cup warm water
15ml/1 tbsp rose water
pistachio nuts, to garnish
single (light) cream or vanilla ice cream, to serve (optional)

1 Put the butter and oil in a wok or a large, deep frying pan and place over a low heat. When the butter has melted, add the rice vermicelli and stir-fry for 3–4 minutes, or until the vermicelli starts to turn a light golden brown.

2 Add the allspice, cashew nuts, almonds, sultanas and apricots to the wok and stir-fry for 1–2 minutes.

3 Sprinkle the sugar over the vermicelli mixture and stir to combine, then add the warm water. Cover the pan and bring to the boil. Reduce the heat and simmer gently for 8–10 minutes until the liquid has been absorbed and the vermicelli is tender.

4 Stir the rose water into the vermicelli mixture until well mixed, then ladle into individual warmed bowls, sprinkle the nuts over and serve with single cream or ice cream, if liked.

Cook's Tip
Also known as thin rice noodles or rice sticks, rice vermicelli is available in Asian stores and large supermarkets.

Orange Pancakes Energy 373Kcal/1569kJ; Protein 11.2g; Carbohydrate 51.5g, of which sugars 23g; Fat 15.2g, of which saturates 7.8g; Cholesterol 172mg; Calcium 166mg; Fibre 2.1g; Sodium 161mg.
Rice Vermicelli Energy 589kcal/2455kJ; Protein 8.6g; Carbohydrate 71.1g, of which sugars 29.4g; Fat 31.1g, of which saturates 10.3g; Cholesterol 32mg; Calcium 64mg; Fibre 0.7g; Sodium 124mg.

Classic Noodle Pudding

There are many versions of this traditional Jewish dish, known as kugel. Noodle pudding is a rich and comforting dessert, and quite delicious.

Serves 4–6

175g/6oz wide egg noodles
225g/8oz cottage cheese
115g/4oz cream cheese or curd (farmer's) cheese
75g/3oz caster (superfine) sugar
2 eggs
120ml/4fl oz/½ cup sour cream
5ml/1 tsp vanilla extract
pinch of ground cinnamon
pinch of grated nutmeg
2.5ml/½ tsp grated lemon rind
50g/2oz butter
25g/1oz nibbed almonds
25g/1oz fine dried white breadcrumbs
unsalted (sweet) butter, for greasing
icing (confectioners') sugar, to dust

1 Preheat the oven to 180°C/350°F/ Gas 4. Grease a shallow baking dish. Cook the noodles in a large pan of boiling water until just tender. Drain well.

2 Beat the cottage cheese, cream cheese and sugar together in a bowl. Add the eggs, one at a time, and then stir in the sour cream, followed by the vanilla extract, cinnamon, nutmeg and lemon rind.

3 Fold the noodles into the cheese mixture. Spoon into the prepared baking dish and level the surface.

4 Melt the butter in a wok or frying pan. Add the almonds and fry for about 1 minute until starting to brown. Remove from the heat. Stir in the breadcrumbs, mixing well.

5 Sprinkle the almond and breadcrumb mixture over the pudding. Bake for 30–40 minutes or until the custard is set. Serve hot, dusted with a little icing sugar.

Cook's Tip
You can cut down on fat by using the wok to dry-roast all kinds of ingredients including nuts, seeds and whole spices.

Lemon, Ginger and Pistachio Steamed Puddings

These moist little puddings, served with a luscious cardamom-spiced syrup, make a good winter dessert.

Serves 4

150g/5oz/10 tbsp butter
150g/5oz/¾ cup golden caster (superfine) sugar
10ml/2 tsp ground ginger
finely grated rind of 2 lemons
2 eggs
150g/5oz/1¼ cups self-raising (self-rising) flour
a pinch of salt
115g/4oz/1 cup finely chopped pistachio nuts
shredded lemon rind, pistachio nuts and chopped preserved stem ginger, to garnish

For the syrup

150g/5oz/¾ cup golden caster (superfine) sugar
1.5ml/¼ tsp crushed cardamom seeds
5ml/1 tsp ground ginger
10ml/2 tsp finely grated lemon rind and juice of 2 lemons
5ml/1 tsp arrowroot powder

1 To make the syrup, place the sugar, cardamom seeds and ginger in a non-stick pan and add 150ml/¼ pint/⅔ cup water. Heat gently until the sugar has dissolved, then add the lemon rind and juice. Bring to the boil and cook for 3–4 minutes.

2 Mix the arrowroot with 30ml/2 tbsp cold water and whisk into the syrup. Simmer gently for 2 minutes, or until the syrup has thickened slightly. Transfer to a bowl and set aside. Grease four 200ml/7fl oz/scant 1 cup heatproof bowls and set aside.

3 Whisk together the butter and sugar until pale and fluffy. Add the ginger and beat in the eggs, one at a time. Sift in the flour and salt and add the nuts and lemon rind, mixing to combine.

4 Spoon 20ml/4 tsp of the syrup into the base of each greased bowl and swirl to coat the sides. Spoon in the pudding mixture. Cover tightly with foil and secure with string. Place in a bamboo steamer over a wok and steam for 1¼ hours, until risen and firm to the touch. Reheat the remaining syrup, unmould the puddings on to individual plates and spoon over the syrup. Garnish with the lemon rind, pistachio nuts and ginger and serve.

Noodle Pudding Energy 412kcal/1724kJ; Protein 12.4g; Carbohydrate 38.7g, of which sugars 15.1g; Fat 24.1g, of which saturates 12.3g; Cholesterol 114mg; Calcium 108mg; Fibre 1.3g; Sodium 329mg.
Lemon Puddings Energy 868kcal/3630kJ; Protein 12.4g; Carbohydrate 98.4g, of which sugars 69.1g; Fat 50g, of which saturates 22.5g; Cholesterol 175mg; Calcium 139mg; Fibre 2.9g; Sodium 420mg.

Index